Good Pub Food

PINT

A guide to Britain's best 600 pubs for real food and real ale

Good Pub Food

Susan Nowak & Jill Adam

Foreword by Jean-Christophe Novelli

CAMPAIGN FOR REAL ALE

Published by Campaign for Real Ale
230 Hatfield Road
St Albans
Hertfordshire AL1 4LW

www.camra.org.uk/books

ISBN 10: 1-85249-214-7
ISBN 13: 978-1-85249-214-4

A CIP catalogue record for this book is available from the British Library

Printed and bound in Belgium by Proost BV

Head of Publications: Joanna Copestick
Publications Project Editor: Emma Lloyd
Publications Assistant: Debbie Williams
Copy Editor: Ione Brown
Designer: Alison Fenton
Cover Photography: Cephas/Stockfood
Front Cover Digital Image Manipulation: Debbie Williams
Picture Research: Nadine Bazar and Sarah Airey
Maps: Russell Bell

Susan Nowak would like to thank all CAMRA branches and members who care about real food as well as real ale for their nominations. Thanks also to pub licensees and chefs for finding the time to supply extra information and generously sharing their recipes

Jill Adam would like to thank her mum, Marjorie Harvey, for her help in checking details with publicans and her excellent telephone technique

Susan and Jill would also like to thank Emma Lloyd, Kim Adams and all staff at CAMRA HQ involved in the production of this book

CAMRA would like to thank the following for permission to reproduce photographs:
1 Swan, Inkpen; 14 Angel, Lavenham; 42 Black Horse, Ireland; 49 Ivy House, Chalfont St Giles; 90 Maltsters Arms, Tuckenhay; 101 Axe & Compasses, Arkesden; 107 Baker's Arms, Broad Campden; 115 Oak Inn, Bank; 126 Crown Inn, Woolhope; 138 Beacon, Rusthall; 171 Le Gothique, SW18; 195 Cock, Denford; 207 Chequers Inn, Chipping Norton; 213 Coalbrookdale Arms, Coalbrookdale; 235 Crown Inn, Wrinehill; 240 Angel, Lavenham; 250 Hatch Inn, Colemans Hatch; 270 Bunch of Grapes, Bradford-on-Avon; 272 Tollgate Inn, Holt; 294 Cubley Hall Hotel, Cubley; 296 Tunnel End Inn, Marsden; 310 Crown, Pantygelli; 328 Burts Hotel, Melrose; 367 Falcon's Nest Hotel, Port Erin

Additional photography: 2 Rex Features/Ilpo Musto; 9 Alamy/Gavan Goulder; 15 Jean Cazals; 17 Alamy/Justin Leighton; 18 Alamy/Gavan Goulder; 24 Jason Lowe; 130, 143 Fran Nowak; 319, 343 Jason Lowe; 348 Britain on View/Martin Brent; All other photographs from the CAMRA archive

CONTENTS

FOREWORD BY JEAN-CHRISTOPHE NOVELLI

Growing up in northern France where they brew fine beers, I learned to cook the sort of peasant dishes that go so well with beer. Then I came to the UK and met my great friend and mentor Keith Floyd, and became chef at the wonderful pub he owned in Devon. We used fantastic local produce such as fish from Brixham, game in winter, Devon lamb and superb cheeses made in the area. In the bar we served real ale from small local breweries – I even learned how to pull a pint!

I then went on to achieve four consecutive Michelin stars for my own restaurants in London, and to appear on TV programmes like Hell's Kitchen.

I have cooked haute cuisine in some of the world's greatest restaurants, for royalty and celebrities. But I still enjoy the sort of simple, delicious dishes made from fresh local ingredients you will find in pubs in this guide - pubs offering greater accessibility to good food, where you can eat well and get good value for money; equally I'm excited by the creative young chefs in the listed gastropubs.

Now I have turned full circle and come back to pubs for my new venture at the White Horse in Hatching Green, Harpenden – not far from my cookery school. I have enjoyed creating a new menu there, and hope it lives up to CAMRA's standards for good pub food!

Bon appetit

Jean Christophe Novelli

Michelin-star winning Jean-Christophe Novelli, who recently starred in Hell's Kitchen, is director of the internationally recognised Novelli Academy, with master classes by himself and other celebrity chefs. He created the beer menus for two CAMRA awards banquets, and has now opened his own Hertfordshire pub. (www.jeanchristophenovelli.com)

INTRODUCTION

When I began to compile the first edition of this guide, 15 years ago, a CAMRA member wrote to me saying: 'You'll be pushed to find even a hundred pubs serving good food.'

Although this was the late eighties – the era of chicken in a basket, microwaved lasagne and wilting ham rolls under plastic domes – it wasn't quite as bleak as that: the first guide boasted nearly 400 entries. But neither he nor I could have foretold the explosion in the pub food sector that was to burst upon us over the next few years.

At that time CAMRA was breaking new ground. Our brief – for the whole CAMRA branch network nominates the pubs for this guide – was to seek out pubs selling Real Ale and Real Food. I mentally added 'and real people', for care and love are necessary ingredients in a tasty meal.

This organisation was the first to produce a guide specifically for pub food. And this is still the only guide where the quality of the beer is as important as the food. Other guides commenting on pub food – and it's a sign of the times that Michelin, ultimate arbiter of the swankiest restaurants, two years ago launched its first guide to rather upmarket pub food – tend to concentrate on a pub's wine list rather than the handpumps on the bar.

In this guide beer comes first with a capital B. You'll find precious few references to wine, but many to real ale. Those served at each pub are listed in the entry, we also tell you which pubs encourage beer drinking with meals through tasting notes on blackboards, or a beer suggestion with a dish, and we even mention dishes cooked in beer.

One of the major advances since this guide last appeared is the huge interest in craft beers and a willingness to involve them in cuisine, especially as the range of styles and flavours (from fruit to seaweed) continues to grow. Chefs like to cook with beer and match beer to dishes, breweries are doing more to promote beer with food, celebrity chefs are into beer cuisine. There's a feature on them in this guide, and a section filled with beer and cider recipes sent by pub chefs.

More power to their elbow, for in my view linking beer to food is one of the best ways of encouraging people to drink and buy beer, and to demonstrate that it is just as complex and full of character as wine. CAMRA's new 'real ale in a bottle' campaign promoting bottle-conditioned beer is doing much to encourage people to put a bottle of beer, not wine, on the dining table.

Less encouraging is the quality of children's menus in pubs. Our kids are still, in the main, served basic pub grub offering little nutrition or inspiration for healthy eating. A cue for Jamie Oliver to campaign and, while he's at it, he can examine vegetarian food in pubs.

Throughout all the years I have been involved with this guide, pub food has remained an incredibly volatile and evolving sector. Even as I write, the Government's intentions on a smoking ban are still unclear. Will there be a blanket ban in all public places – or will ministers push their prior proposal to allow drinkers to continue to light up in pubs that don't serve food?

While the whole situation is becoming a bit of a farce, I would hate to see any measure that might discourage pubs from serving food. I cannot believe that any publicans in this guide, whose food clearly attracts custom to their pubs, and who rely on meals for a large part of their turnover, would put tobacco on the menu instead.

Already, unbidden, many licensees have introduced no smoking policies in dining rooms or areas where food is consumed at meal times. (I still smile over the landlord who told me recently: 'My entire pub is no smoking – well, apart from one table, I don't know why I keep that.' Nor do I, because I don't expect the smoke confines itself to that table…)

But I spend a lot of time dining in pubs and these days rarely find myself inconvenienced by smokers while eating. Only once in the past year was I next to a table where three people chain smoked so heavily throughout their meal that I had to abandon mine.

Will 24-hour licensing have any effect on the food side? Will it, for instance, make some city centre pubs more likely to serve bought-in ready meals or fast food snacks that can be produced quickly around the clock? I hope not.

We've all gone into a pub feeling ravenous at 2.03pm only to be told that lunches finished at 2pm, so perhaps extended hours will bring a bit more flexibility. Though I can't really see myself suddenly getting an urge for a steak and kidney pie and a pint at 3am, but you never know...

One of the very best changes since the last guide is the huge increase in pubs using local produce. Many take real interest and pleasure in finding nearby farmers raising beef, pork and lamb – sometimes organic too. And there are eggs from free range hens, fish landed at the harbour, sausages home made by the butcher, local craft cheesemakers, fruit from orchards and home-grown herbs. Game comes from nearby shoots, pickles and preserves from cottage industries, even publicans who find the time to grow some of their own vegetables or hunt for wild mushrooms.

What's more, this policy tends to be followed through with beer from local micros, real cider from local presses, perhaps English or fruit wine from nearby vineyards.

The best publicans really are beginning to think about food miles and the importance of becoming part of the local food chain and economy – acknowledging that the best dishes are made from the freshest, seasonal produce. A feature on some of them is in the guide.

I am slightly more ambivalent about the rise and rise of the gastropub. It is certainly the catering phenomenon of the past five years – a new one seems to open every week – with the added spice of all those celebrity or TV chefs who suddenly seem called to the bar!

To me, if it's an expensive establishment with an over-fussy menu and bar intended for diners only then it is not a pub, it is a restaurant. But if it is a genuine pub that wants to major in fine food offering good value for money, with well kept cask ales and a warm welcome to those who just want a drink, good luck to it.

At its best, a gastropub should attract the real food cooks of the future – the imaginative young chefs who prefer the flexibility and informality of a pub, bringing a new dimension to pub food.

But like any other concept, it is in danger of being corrupted by huge pub companies and groups who view this as simply another pub sector to be exploited. We are beginning to see some remarkably similar gastro menus, in places pushing wine and designer bottles of lager.

There are several gastropubs where I find the cooking and beer exciting – but I do love the many pubs in this guide producing the sort of simple, fresh, tasty dishes that go so well with a pint. Long live the ploughman's, the steak and ale pudding, the game pie, the cod in beer batter, the home cooked ham, free range egg and hand cut chips, the real pork sausages with real ale gravy – and the regional dishes from haggis, neeps and tatties to Cumbrian tattie ash or Cornish pasties.

May we long enjoy them alongside the supreme pleasure of a great British pint.

PUBS IN EVERY EDITION

CAMRA's Good Pub Food is now celebrating its sixth edition. The number of entries has grown from around 300 to over 600 pubs. Here is the Roll of Honour – the pubs whose dedication to real ale and real food has gained them entries in all six editions:

CAMBRIDGESHIRE
Bell Inn, Stilton

CORNWALL
Driftwood Spars, St Agnes

CUMBRIA
Bay Horse Inn, Cumbria

DEVON
Nobody Inn, Doddiscombsleigh
Rising Sun, Woodland
(landlady/chef formerly in every edition in Berks, now at Rising Sun)

HAMPSHIRE
Milbury's, Beauworth

LEICESTERSHIRE
Black Horse, Walcote

GREATER LONDON
White Horse, Parsons Green, SW6

GREATER MANCHESTER
Nursery, Heaton Norris

NOTTINGHAMSHIRE
Nelson & Railway, Kimberley

OXFORDSHIRE
Falkland Arms, Great Tew

SOMERSET
Ring O' Bells, Compton Martin

SUFFOLK
Star Inn, Lidgate

SCOTLAND
Craw Inn, Auchencrow (Borders)
Birds & Bees, Causewayhead (Central)

HOW TO USE THIS GUIDE

Pub listings are arranged alphabetically by county in England and Wales, and by region in Scotland. County names appear at the top of each page. Greater Manchester appears under M, Greater London appears under L, East and West Sussex under S and the four counties of Yorkshire under Y. West Midlands appears under W.

Locality ▸		INKPEN
Pub name ▸	☆	**Swan**
Address ▸		Craven Road, Lower Green, RG17 9DX
Directions ▸	▶	Follow signs to Inkpen from Hungerford Common
Opening hours ▸	☼	Mon-Sat 11am-2.30pm, 7-11.30pm, Sun 12-3, 7-10.30pm
Food serving times ▸	🍴	Daily 12-2.30pm, 7-9.30pm
Telephone ▸	T	(01488) 668326
Fax ▸	F	(01488) 668306
E mail ▸	E	enquiries@theswanninn-organics.co.uk
Website ▸	W	www.theswaninn-organics.co.uk
Real ales available ▸	🍺	Butts Jester, Traditional, seasonal; guests
Description of Food ▸	☺	Imaginative food using mainly organic produce with beef from their own herd
Description of pub ▸	◙	Part 17th-century inn with beams, open fires and farm shop
Facilities ▸		★ ♨ Q ❀ 🛏 S V 🍺 ♿ ♣ ● Ⓟ 🚭 👪 C

Key to symbols

☆	Outstanding pub for food	⛺	Camping
★	Rare and unspoilt pub interior	⇌	Near Rail Station
♨	Real fire	⊖	Near Underground, metro or tram station
Q	Quiet pub	♣	Traditional pub games played
❀	Outdoor drinking area	●	Real draught cider
🛏	Accommodation	Ⓟ	Pub car park
S	Snacks	🚭	No-smoking room or area
V	Vegetarian food available	🥛	Oversized lined pint glass
🍺	Public bar	👪	Children allowed
♿	Wheelchair access	C	Credit cards accepted

Every effort is made to ensure the accuracy of information contained in this Guide, but no responsibility can be accepted for errors and it is inevitable that some pubs will change their character during the currency of this Guide.

WHAT IS REAL ALE?

Real ale is a definition accepted by the Concise Oxford Dictionary. It is also known as traditional draught beer or cask-conditioned beer. Real ale is brewed from malted barley, using pure water and hops, and fermented by top-fermenting yeast. At the end of fermentation, the beer is allowed to condition for a few days and is then racked into casks, often with the addition of priming sugar and a handful of dry hops for aroma. The beer continues to 'work' or ferment in the cask while a clearing agent called finings drags the yeasty deposits to the floor of the cask. This secondary fermentation gives the real ale its natural carbonation. The beer is neither filtered nor pasteurised and must not be served by any method using applied gas pressure.

Real ale can be served straight from the cask and many country pubs still use this method, while some special winter brews in town pubs are often dispensed from a cask on the bar. But most real ale is drawn – hence the word 'draught' – by a suction pump from the pub cellar. The pump is operated either by a handpump, a tall lever on the bar, or by an electric pump. Electric pumps are rare in the south of England but are used widely in the Midlands and the North. In Scotland air pressure is sometimes used to serve real ale via tall fonts.

Real ale should be served at a temperature of 55-56 degrees F (12-13 degrees C). This is a cool temperature that brings out the best characteristics of a top-fermented beer. It is a higher temperature than that used for serving lagers, but it is pure bunkum that real ale is 'warm'.

PUB HOURS

Please note that as this book was being prepared, many pubs in England and Wales were being granted extending opening hours. We have not attempted to indicate this here but the times given were correct as of autumn 2005.

SMOKING IN PUBS

There has been great pressure to ban smoking in public places and it will be illegal in all pubs in Scotland from March 2006 and probably in Wales and Northern Ireland in 2007. In England the government has decided against public opinion to ban smoking from pubs that serve food but not from pubs that don't, although a firm date has not yet been set for this change and there may still be changes in what is finally decided. CAMRA has proposed a more sensible option, which would have supported the traditional multi-room pub – to set aside a separate room for smokers.

BEER & FOOD

Yes! It's been a bitter battle – literally a long, slow slog – but we're finally on our way. Where? To that happy day when diners recognise beer as a serious challenger to wine as a companion to food.

When this guide last appeared, precious few pubs and barely a restaurant were switched on to the culinary possibilities of real ale, the glorious partnership between sassy menus and beautiful beers.

Since then the beer label's now on the other pump. Top restaurateurs such as Gordon Ramsay have introduced a beer section on their wine lists, celebrity chef Jean-Christophe Novelli has created beer banquets, CAMRA has launched Beer and Food Year, breweries have gone all out to link their beers with different dishes…it's all happening!

If the only downside is that restaurants seem to be taking the lead rather than pubs, I tell myself that it's like Paris fashion week. The haute couture quickly filters down to the high street.

And on the plus side, pubs are certainly getting more enthusiastic. So many beer recipes were donated by publicans for this guide that we can't fit them all in – try them, you'll find them much more inventive than the standard steak and ale casserole.

In the past 12 months it's been all the rage for TV chefs to open pubs. Two of them are in this guide, Anthony Worrall Thompson's Angel Coaching Inn in Wiltshire and Phil Vickery's King of Prussia in Berkshire.

Happily, both have realised that real pubs need real ale as well as decent grub. I visited Phil at his pub in Royal Farnham soon after the opening and found him enthusiastic about teaming dishes with beer. He had already served onion, squash and honey beer stew on TV's Ready Steady Cook! and was also creating beer dishes for Shepherd Neame in Kent including lamb and mint cobbler with Spitfire.

At his pub he's found a way of encouraging diners to try beer with food by serving a shot glass of appropriate ale with the dish. One particularly happy match was raspberry beer with Rocky Road brownies and crème fraîche. 'Raspberry beer is fantastic with the chocolate in the brownies and the cream in the dip. We've also served it in champagne flutes without telling people what it is and they're amazed to discover they're drinking beer,' he says.

As well as giving a devilish performance in TV's Hell's Kitchen, Michelin-starred chef Jean-Christophe Novelli is a stylish advocate of beer in cooking. One of his first jobs in England was at Keith Floyd's The Maltsters Arms in Devon (still in this guide under its present owners) where he quickly appreciated the ales from local micros, and their affinity with local cheese and seafood. Growing up in northern France also exposed him to good beers. 'I like to use it in bread, in pancakes and in some superb soups,' he says.

He created the menus for two recent CAMRA awards lunches. Guests were impressed with the sophisticated dishes such as lamb confit flavoured with Pitfield 1824 mild, steamed lettuce and carrot gâteau with beer hollandaise or steamed wild mushrooms with O'Hanlon's Port Stout sauce in ale crepes lightened with Coniston Bluebird.

As this guide went to press, Jean-Christophe was about to become a partner in a new gastropub, The White Horse at Harpenden in Hertfordshire. I'm looking forward to a little hop cuisine there!

For CAMRA's 2005 awards, I designed a 'pub grub beer banquet' of more traditional dishes such as pheasant and venison pudding with Theakston Old Peculier stock and 'death by chocolate', a dark chocolate pyramid enriched with porter on a cherry beer coulis. The sort of dishes, in my view, that pubs could easily put on their menus.

And some pubs do. I have been bowled over by the passion that enlightened publicans in this Guide show for cooking with beer – still a minority, granted, but a growing one. At the well known Holly Bush in London's fashionable Hampstead the cooks use beer as others use wine – rabbit in pilsner and mustard sauce, pan-roast chicken paprika ale gravy, beef and Harvey's pie and Adnams rarebit plus unusual sausages such as duck and cherry beer.

At 500-year-old Tudor pub the White Hart in Great Yeldham, Essex, the Connaught-trained head chef is particularly inspired by beer, and the pub has hosted beer cuisine evenings. One held for CAMRA members featured starters such as game terrine with elderberry black ale chutney, twice baked cheese and Chimay soufflé and prawn cocktail with Dorothy Goodbody stout followed by honey stout braised shank of lamb, rib eye steak with Old Hooky sauce, ravioli of ricotta, spinach and wild mushrooms in Anchor Steam beer broth, and poached pear chantilly with Young's double chocolate stout sauce.

If only other pubs followed its example, it would do so much to promote the image of quality real ale as a serious accompaniment to serious food – and start to create the fabulous beer cuisine enjoyed in Belgium. Top restaurants in Brussels and Bruges have beer lists of over 100 and dedicated beer sommeliers to recommend just the one to drink with your dish.

Pioneering support for beer with food has come from the industry over the past few years. Brewers big and small have shown real commitment, even if it's simply making beer and food links on bottle labels.

Greene King in particular has put huge effort into boosting beer with food. As well as several events based around bottled Beer to Dine For, last year the brewery invited leading journalists to renowned chef Michael Moore's Blandford Street restaurant in Marylebone where he served its beers alongside his modern global menu.

Greene King IPA went with lightly-spiced coriander scallops, Old Speckled Hen was malty enough to enrich lamb in parma ham, but the real star was Abbot Ale with four cheese and poached pear soufflé – Abbot and blue cheese is a marriage made in heaven.

CAMRA has also played its part. The campaign has a beer and food section on its website and launched the first Beer and Food Year in 2004. At last year's Great British Beer Festival I held a beer and cheese tasting which left nobody in any doubt that beer is better than wine with cheese, be it a mature farmhouse cheddar with Worthington White Shield, or a creamy goats' cheese from the Dales with raspberry beer.

So take the plunge and use some of the recipes in this guide to hold your own beer supper. Whenever I do, at the end of an evening when fascinating beers accompany each course, friends who started out as sceptics always admit they didn't miss the wine at all.

GASTROPUB REVOLUTION

Somewhere in SW3 a chef is dribbling a few drops of truffle oil over his rocket salad, the barman giving a final polish to his wine glasses. Are we in the latest celebrity restaurant? No – it's a gastropub!

Gastropub is a new word that has entered the language since the last edition of this guide, and no one is entirely sure what it means. To some it's a pretentious, poncy pub posing as a restaurant. To others it's a restaurant posing as a pub. To many it's a term of derision, to more, a licence to print money.

What it does reflect is the mind-boggling revolution in pub food we have witnessed since the first edition of Good Pub Food 15 years ago. Pub food is by far the biggest, and still growing, sector of the catering industry – you can now eat anything in a pub from a banger to a blini. And up there at the top is the gastropub. Yes, folks, the rise and rise of the gastropub – but is it, like a soufflé, all hot air?

At its best, it is a place serving delicious, imaginative food created from fine, fresh ingredients by dedicated cooks, at reasonable prices. At its best, it is also a place with an equally dedicated cellarman proffering superbly kept cask ales – and welcoming people to enjoy them in the bar even if they don't want to eat. At its best it is the White Horse in south-west London.

The White Horse in Parsons Green, SW6, run by the redoubtable Mark Dorber, came top of the Morning Advertiser's top 20 pubs in the UK. Mr Dorber appreciates fine food and has an outstanding kitchen where an energetic team creates sassy, exciting dishes that leap off the menu. But Mr Dorber is also a pub devotee and a leading authority on beer and cellarmanship, who makes sure the White Horse is never just a restaurant with bolt-on bar.

Indeed, the separate restaurant is fairly recent, and people can also eat in the big, handsome bar of this genuine pub. The bar is still as popular for drinking and socialising as dining, with a wondrous changing range of ales on offer. And those who do dine find beer, as well as wine, recommendations to accompany their meal.

Not every gastropub can be a White Horse, but nor do they have to ape those pubs that put the ghastly into gastro. These are the bland places with stripped pine floors, carefully distressed furniture, modern British or Mediterranean menus at inflated prices, and a massive turnover in wine and designer lagers; in short, today's version of the theme pub.

Of course it is wonderful to feast on fine food and drink real ale under the same roof and I do want to encourage gastropubs – honest! But am I being perverse in wondering if some 'aspirational' food would be more comfortable on a restaurant menu?

I still find myself drawn to the pubs that feature the regional flavours of their area – and there are many in this guide. I'm perfectly happy for talented young chefs to give these ingredients a modern twist as long as the results are simple and honest dishes not drowned in culinary confusion. These, to me, are the rural pubs that come closest to small, provincial French eating places and I salute their custom of often offering just one good dish of the day!

And I do admit a nostalgia for those pubs offering the most basic, but high quality, pub grub alongside equally high quality ales. Take the Birch Hall Inn at Beck Hole near Whitby. It is little more than a pork pie and a pint establishment. But these meaty turkey and ham pies are specially made for the pub by the local butcher. It also serves big, wholemeal stotties made by an old-fashioned baker, filled with Cheddar, corned beef, farmhouse pâté or ham home roasted in the Rayburn. Landlady Glenys Crampton bakes the scones and, 'our famous beer cake made with whichever beer is on the pumps'. And that's it, no frills at the Birch Hall, just fresh, quality snacks that so well partner a pint.

I have a soft spot, too, for the Great Western in Wolverhampton, a grade II listed railway pub providing Black Country treats like 'grey payes' and bacon, double faggot and chips (£1.40 and £2.95 respectively) and, most popular, giant cobs filled with hot pork and crackling carved from huge joints supplied by the same butcher for 16 years. Nothing gastro about this former national CAMRA pub of the year but, alongside a pint of Batham's Best or Holden's Mild, might this be real pub food?

When TV chef Antony Worrall-Thompson and food show impresario Tim Etchells took over The Angel at Heytesbury near Stonehenge, Tim balked at the term gastropub. 'We are just a pub with good food,' he said. In my view a dish such as 'steamed mutton and foie gras suet pudding with red onion marmalade' could only be served in a gastropub, but as the food is delicious and there are four handpumps on the bar, why quibble?

Still determined to define gastropub, I put Nick Otley on the spot. Nick, co-director of 10-barrel Otley Brewing plant in Pontypridd, opened in the summer of 2005, is also landlord of the family's Bunch of Grapes and describes it as a 'gastropub with down-to-earth bar'.

So what does he mean by gastropub? 'A pub serving restaurant quality food at pub prices in an informal, relaxed atmosphere,' he says without hesitation. 'Great food without pretence alongside great ales, which is what a good pub should be. People can come here in jeans and t-shirt or jacket and tie and still get the same service, whether they just want a pint and a chat or a meal.' And as his hostelry was named best gastropub in Wales, and his beer has won a South Devon CAMRA award, I'll settle for that.

CAMRA is a broad church. Good food is the saviour of many pubs and there is room for every type as long as they stick to two fundamentals: real ale and real food.

LOCAL PRODUCE

'Throughout the autumn we make use of many local fruits and berries such as elderberries, rosehips, bullaces, damsons, blackberries and crab apples...' *George Inn, Chardstock*

'We attend the local auction market most weeks to source meat from local farmers. Usually we use meat from farms within a five mile radius of the pub – and our eggs are from Vera's hens next door...' *Greyhound, Shap*

'When available all our lamb and beef comes from Belsay Barns Farm, and every bit of the animal is put to use from pressing the tongue, making rich stocks from the bones, suet from the kidneys, soup from the tails and even our own corned beef...' *Magnesia Bank, Tyne & Wear*

Quotes from just three of the many pubs in the 2006 guide taking pride and pleasure in tracking down the tastiest ingredients on their own doorsteps, and music to my ears.

Yes, the very best news since Good Pub Food last appeared is the explosion of pubs now sourcing fine local produce – the publicans who go that extra mile to cut food miles. Whether it is beef from a herd the chef can see grazing in a field across the road, vegetables home grown or from the farmers' market, cheese made by small local producers from the milk of cows or goats chewing local cud, game caught by hunters who are regulars, pickles and chutneys from a neighbouring cottage industry, meaty sausages made by the village butcher, fish and shellfish landed at the harbour a few miles away – many, many more pubs are buying local. I like to think this is not just to benefit the environment but, damn it, because it tastes better!

Following through, lots of pubs are now buying their real ale from regional and micro breweries in their area, giving small brewers a huge boost. Those pubs who serve real cider often stock local farmhouse cider. This means that pubs are, uniquely, serving the beers and ciders of their region alongside products and dishes which are often traditional to their region, and partner each other so perfectly.

What could be better than a dark Midlands mild with black pudding or faggots and mushy peas, West Country cider with a pork and apple pasty, Irish stout with oysters from Galway Bay, a pint of Pendle Witches with Lancashire hotpot or a great Yorkshire ale with roast beef and Yorkshire pudding?

It is equally heartening that many talented young chefs cooking in pubs enthusiastically seek out local ingredients to put a new slant on regional dishes, part of the modern British cooking revolution that now ranks our food among the best in the world.

But even among pubs sourcing local produce, some are truly outstanding. I especially applaud all the pubs listing their suppliers on their menus. Take the Talbot at Knightwick, one of my favourite pubs, where cooking sisters Annie and Wiz Clift not only have the rich harvest of Worcestershire to call upon, but beers and cider from their own Teme Valley Brewery.

'We are firmly rooted in the traditions and seasonal produce of our own Teme Valley, and strongly believe that what we cannot produce ourselves should come from a known local source – hams, bacons, sausages and cheese,' they say on table cards listing their suppliers of cheese, eggs, game, rabbits, pigeons, meat, soft fruit and vegetables, not forgetting walnuts from Knightwick Manor.

They also grow as many vegetables as they can in their organic kitchen garden, including salad leaves and herbs such as the lovage used to make lovage soup. The Talbot kitchen makes many of its own preserves, as well as bread and black puddings, and I have been wild mushroom hunting with Wiz. A pub that is truly part of the local rural economy and food chain.

Apart from sourcing local products from named farms and suppliers, and making all its own chutneys, pickles, pasta, bread and ice cream, the Tollgate Inn near Holt in Wiltshire has a policy of supporting small breweries, many of them from the region, buying direct from Westbury Ales, Box Brewery, Bath Ales, Teignworthy, Exmoor Ales and Glastonbury Ales, to name a few. With at least four cask ales at any one time, the selection changes twice a week.

At the Spread Eagle in Stokesley, North Yorkshire, they don't have far to go for meat. The pub has its own butcher's shop, Adlingtons in the High Street, selling lamb from its own pedigree Madewell Herd of Tescel sheep, to make its most popular dish, a joint of lamb slow braised for several hours. The shop also sells pork from pigs raised by David Johnson at Hill End Farm, Chopgate, and beef from W Bambridge and Sons of Greystone Farm, Seamer.

Another pub with its own shop, though rather different, is Garth Mill near the Royal Welsh showground in Powys. Apart from a handsome pub, the renovated mill is also home to a farmers' market shop selling local Welsh and English produce as well as goodies made on the premises. These number 60 different flavoured sausages, including gluten free, dry cured bacon, cooked meats and home-made pies, all produced without additives or preservatives. Local free range pork, grass fed lambs, Dexter and Aberdeen Angus beef, Welsh goats' and cows' cheese, jam, honey, whole foods and locally grown vegetables as well as Welsh and English wines are both on sale and on the menu.

Not all local produce comes from the land. The ancient Driftwood Spars, St Agnes, overlooking Trevaunance Cove on the north Cornwall coast, has been in every edition of this guide. It is another pub that features a list of its local suppliers – game, chickens, sausages, eggs laid by the pub's free range hens, a Cornish cheeseboard, clotted cream from Roddas Creamery, wine from Camel Valley Vineyard and Cuckoo Ale brewed at the pub.

But in addition it gets fresh fish and shellfish landed in Newlyn and smoked from Atlantis Fish nearby, so landlady Jill Treleaven has a whole fish menu which may feature saffron-infused mussels, poached smoked haddock, grilled sardines with coriander, smoked mackerel mousse with horseradish coulis, and whole roast sea bass stuffed with apricots and hazelnuts.

Food that is not only mouth watering and wholesome but, springing from the local environment, brings a whole new meaning to the words 'community pub'.

STAR RATED PUBS

Look out for the pubs listed below, these pubs are star rated to pinpoint the best pub food and real ale in Britain.

ENGLAND

Tudor Oaks, Astwick, Bedfordshire
Swan, Inkpen, Berkshire
Swan, Ley Hill, Buckinghamshire
Hit or Miss, Penn Street, Buckinghamshire
Oliver Cromwell, St Ives, Cambridgeshire
Albion, Chester, Cheshire
Crown, Wrinehill, Cheshire
Trengilly Wartha, Nancenoy, Cornwall
Rashleigh Inn, Polkerris, Cornwall
Punch Bowl, Crosthwaite, Cumbria
Watermill Inn, Ings, Cumbria
Queen's Head, Troutbeck, Cumbria
Old Poet's Corner, Ashover, Derbyshire
Bentley Brook, Fenny Bentley, Derbyshire
Black Horse, Hulland Ward, Derbyshire
Culm Valley Inn, Culmstock, Devon
Old Inn, Kilmington, Devon
Maltsters Arms, Tuckenhay, Devon
Museum Inn, Farnham, Dorset
Mitre, Shaftesbury, Dorset
Smith's Arms, Carlton, Durham
Sun Inn, Feering, Essex
King's Head, Gosfield, Essex
King's Head, Bledington, Gloucestershire
Fox, Lower Oddington, Gloucestershire
Falcon, Poulton, Gloucestershire
Wheatsheaf, Brushfield, Hampshire
Wykeham Arms, Winchester, Hampshire
Riverside Inn, Aymestrey, Herefordshire
Bridge Inn, Kentchurch, Herefordshire
Portland Arms, St Albans, Hertfordshire
Plume of Feathers, Tewin, Hertfordshire
Coastguard, Margaret's Bay, Kent
Sankey's, Tunbridge Wells, Kent
Eagle & Child, Bispham Green, Lancashire
Cow & Plough, Oadby, Leicestershire
Masons Arms, Louth, Lincolnshire
Morgan Arms, London E3
Dove, London E8
Crown, London N1
Holly Bush, London NW3
White Horse, London SW6
Chelsea Ram, London SW10
Windmill, London W1
Teddington Arms, Teddington, Middlesex
White Hart, Lydgate, Greater Manchester
White Horse, Brancaster Staithe, Norfolk
Walpole Arms, Itteringham, Norfolk
Hare Arms, Stow Bardolph, Norfolk
Three Horseshoes, Warham All Saints, Norfolk
Dipton Mill Inn, Dipton Mill, Northumberland
Keans Head, Nottingham, Nottinghamshire
Chequers Inn, Chipping Norton, Oxfordshire
Odfellows, Shifnall, Shropshire
Fighting Cocks, Stottesden, Shropshire
Ring O'Bells, Ashcott, Somerset
Devonshire Arms, Long Sutton, Somerset

Fountain Inn, Wells, Somerset
Royal Oak, Kings Bromley, Staffordshire
Holly Bush, Salt, Staffordshire
Crown Inn, Wrinehill, Staffordshire
Station, Framlingham, Suffolk
Angel, Lavenham, Suffolk
Parrot, Forest Green, Surrey
Royal Oak, Staffhurst Wood, Surrey
Hatch Inn, Colemans Hatch, East Sussex
Coach & Horses, Danehill, East Sussex
Half Moon, Warninglid, West Sussex
Magnesia Bank, North Shields, Tyne & Wear
Vine, West Bromwich, West Midlands
Great Western, Wolverhampton, West Midlands
Tollgate Inn, Holt, Wiltshire
George & Dragon, Rowde, Wiltshire
Admiral Rodney, Berrow Green, Worcestershire
Talbot, Knightwick, Worcestershire
Seabirds, Flamborough, East Yorkshire
Old Star, Kilham, East Yorkshire
Nag's Head, Pickhill, North Yorkshire
Spread Eagle, Stokesley, North Yorkshire
Dog & Gun, Sutton In Craven, North Yorkshire
Wig & Pen, Sheffield, South Yorkshire
Commercial, Cleckheaton, West Yorkshire
Licensed Refreshment Rooms, Dewsbury, West Yorkshire

WALES

Bunch of Grapes, Pontypridd
Clytha Arms, Clytha
Crown, Pantygelli
Lion Inn, Trellech
Garth Mill, Garth
White Horse, Hendrerwydd
Groes Inn, Conwy
Queen's Head, Glanwydden
Tynllidiart Arms, Capel Bangor

SCOTLAND

Wheatsheaf, Swinton
Masonic Arms, Gatehouse of Fleet
Balgedie Toll Tavern, Wester Balgedie
Creel Inn, Catterline
Cawdor Tavern, Cawdor
Anderson, Fortrose
Plockton Inn, Plockton
Johnsburn House, Balerno
Halfway House, Edinburgh
Babbity Bowster, Glasgow
Fox and Hounds, Houston

NORTHERN IRELAND

Esplanade, Bangor
Hillside, Hillsborough

ISLE OF MAN

Sulby Glen Hotel, Sulby

CHILDREN'S FOOD

Jamie Oliver, where are you? The nation's youngest pub goers need you! It's time to get out of the classroom and into pubs the length and breadth of this land to launch a campaign for real food for children.

If you saw and tasted what far too many publicans are dishing up to our kids, you would be appalled. Far too many pubs seem to believe there is still a place in their hostelry for the nastiest and least nutritious pub grub – and it's on the plates of children.

What's more, if the average spend on a child's meal in the school canteen was somewhere below £1 before Jamie's TV shocker, and pubs are buying these products at the same sort of price, then they are making a handsome profit out of our kids.

On one of the worst menus I've seen, parents were being charged £3.50 for 'meals' including chicken nuggets and chips, dinosaur shapes, chips and cheese with gravy, golden tiddlers, chips and peas or tomato pasta shapes on toast – followed by ice cream at £1.50.

And this was in a pub otherwise spoiling adults with home-made dishes such as steak and ale pie, cod in home-made batter or a traditional roast with Yorkshire pudding at less than twice the price of a child's meal – and what's more offering one of the best vegetarian selections I've come across.

All too often in compiling this guide I have found pubs rightly boasting about their local produce and creating outstanding dishes for lucky grown ups – then putting out lamentable kids' menus. Among them I did actually find the dreaded turkey twizzlers. The norm is fish fingers, sausages, burgers, chicken nuggets and chips or one of those small, cheap cheese and tomato pizzas.

A publican actually told me quite cheerfully that I wouldn't want to eat anything on his children's menu. You're dead right I wouldn't.

Happily it's not all bad news. Just over a year ago CAMRA launched Beyond the Chicken Nugget, a competition to find the best children's food in pubs, with winners for the most imaginative children's menu and for best use of regional produce.

The first category was won by the Three Horseshoes at Scottow in Norfolk, with a spooky theme menu including a free gift where Eye of Toad and Wing of Bat was actually a plate of raw crunchy vegetables.

At the Three Fishes in Mitton, Lancs, the second category winner, delicious adults' dishes prepared from fresh seasonal produce were scaled down for their offspring, including fresh home-made bread.

I know children are picky and often demand junk food (my grown up son blushes to be reminded he once told Keith Floyd he didn't fancy anything on his menu and the splendid fellow then cooked him proper chips). But that doesn't mean pubs should use that as an excuse to serve the sausages and burgers meanest in meat, or ready-made products with high salt content.

So congrats to pubs in this guide such as the Cherry Tree Inn at Tintern where the cod bites are home made in fresh batter, pasta is topped with fresh tomato and basil sauce and grated cheddar, and there are both king prawn and ham salads on the children's menu, all £3.25 or less.

One pub offers a dual children's menu – turkey dinosaurs and chicken nuggets on one side, half portions of steak and ale pie or pork casserole on the other – putting the onus on parents.

And I take my hat off to the Dog and Gun at Sutton-in-Craven with a 12-item menu for under 12s catering for larger as well as smaller children. Okay, chicken nuggets are there, but so is fresh battered haddock, a 4oz locally farmed rump steak at £2.95, 4oz gammon ('introduced especially for Phoebe and Frankie'), home-made lasagne and eggs and chips ('for Will, his favourite'). These cost £2.25-£3.80 accompanied by crisp home-made chips or mash and peas or beans.

Until more pubs take more care with our children's nutrition, my advice is to steer your kids towards items such as jacket potatoes, pasta with vegetable sauces, good sandwiches with salad garnish and fries on the side as a treat – or request a mini portion of a main meal.

BEER & CIDER RECIPES

Beer cuisine is really catching on at last. And here you can try it for yourself, with some mouth-watering recipes featuring beer and cider created by pubs in this guide.

Of course, beer is the ideal accompaniment to many foods, and you can add beer to so many dishes, from soups and starters to hot puddings and cold desserts, not forgetting bread, batter, pastry, pickles and preserves. Ale is ideal for stir-fries, a tenderising marinade, slow casseroling, roasting, poaching, preserving and caramelising, as I describe in The Beer Cook Book.

Here are a few tips on pairing beer with food to get you started:

Dark milds: low in alcohol so good at the start of a meal – try with wild mushroom pâté, French onion soup, warm bacon and spinach salad, but also fabulous for making a long cooked oxtail casserole.
Light ales: wonderful for crisping up the batter for cod and haddock, not forgetting pancakes and Yorkshire puddings.
Pale lagers or pilsners and wheat beers: perfect with fish and in sauces to accompany, the citrus in wheat beer makes it ideal for poaching salmon and in moules marinière. Also try with cheese and asparagus flan. Both are good alongside spicy foods including curries.
Full bodied, hoppy bitters: not surprisingly, great with pub dishes such as pork pies, ploughman's, sausage and mash with beer gravy, liver and bacon, steak and kidney pudding or roast beef and Yorkies.
Malty ales: sweeter, full bodied beers, ideal for caramelising – delicious with red meats, game birds, farmhouse cheddar and sticky toffee pudding.
Porter: a dark, roast brew often with a distinctive chocolate note – try with roast gammon or pork with crackling, but also alongside raspberry, cherry or coffee desserts.
Stout: that creamy head and dark, sweetish body make the classic accompaniment to seafood, bringing oysters, crabs and lobsters out of their shells.
Fruit and flavoured beers: now a huge range – try cherry beer with roast duck or bitter chocolate torte, sparkling raspberry wheat beer as an aperitif or in gravy with spring lamb, ginger beer with Thai food or in stir fries, heather beer with grouse and honey beer in rabbit pie.
Trappist or Abbey-style beers: complex, vinous, strong – a match for full-flavoured meats such as roast venison or game pie, turkey at Christmas, and the big cheeses like Stilton, ripe Camembert or Gorgonzola.
Winter or Christmas ales: feisty, spicy and full of yuletide flavours such as nutmeg, cinnamon, chestnuts, raisins and candied peel. Pour into Christmas puddings and rich fruit cakes, to jug a hare or with festive pheasant.

Everyone knows that beer makes the lightest, crispest batter for fish 'n' chips. Here is a recipe using honey beer at a pub on the Cornish coast, where they know all about cooking fish. The Watering Hole at Perranporth uses locally caught fresh cod, and a touch of spice.

COD IN HONEY BEER BATTER

Serves 4

225g (8oz) self-raising flour
Pinch of Cajun spice
4 large, fresh cod fillets
600ml (1 pint) Skinner's Heligan Honey ale (or another honey beer, such as Waggledance)
Handful of chopped parsley
Salt and pepper

Mix the flour with the Cajun spice and season with salt and pepper, dust the cod in the flour mix and set aside. Add the ale to the flour and whisk until smooth, then stir in the chopped parsley. Dip the cod into the batter and deep fry in medium hot oil or dripping until the batter is crisp and golden brown and the fish cooked through – around 15-20 minutes. Serve with lemon wedges, real chips and mushy peas.

The Ivy House at Chalfont St Giles, Buckinghamshire, is a guide regular and renowned for delicious, imaginative food. This recipe combines scallops and cider.

PAN FRIED KING SCALLOPS IN CREAMY THYME AND DRY CIDER SAUCE

3 shallots, finely chopped
Olive oil for frying
150ml (¼ pint) good dry cider
1tsp vegetable stock
Handful fresh thyme leaves
Salt and pepper
Cornflour
150ml (¼ pint) double cream
King scallops
(3-4 scallops with coral per person for a main meal, 2 for a starter)

Fry shallots gently in a little olive oil until just starting to colour, add cider, stock and thyme leaves. Simmer gently for 5 minutes, season to taste and thicken with a little cornflour. Add the cream and keep warm while you cook the scallops. Slice the scallops in half, heat a little olive oil in a pan, then fry the scallops briefly (30 seconds-1 minute each side). Serve immediately with the sauce.

Here is an imaginative starter combining poppy seeds, smoked haddock and real ale from Sam Wydymus, landlady of the Coastguard on the coast at St Margaret's Bay in Kent.

POPPYSEED TARTS WITH SMOKED HADDOCK, ALE AND OLDE SUSSEX

Serves 6

PASTRY

125g (5oz) plain flour
Pinch of salt
50g (2oz) butter
1 tbsp poppy seeds
1 medium free range egg
A little cold water

FILLING

1 medium fillet undyed smoked haddock
2 medium onions, finely sliced
Olive oil for frying
2 tsps sugar
300ml (½ pint) real ale (Sam uses Hopdaemon's Leviathan)
1 medium free range egg
100ml (3 floz) double cream
2 tsps mustard
150g (6oz) Olde Sussex or mature Cheddar
Freshly ground black pepper

To make the pastry, sift flour and salt together, rub in butter, stir in poppy seeds, add egg and enough water to make a smooth dough. Wrap in cling film and rest in the fridge for 30 minutes. Grease and flour 6 tartlet tins, line with rolled out pastry and bake blind for 8-10 minutes until just cooked but not brown.

Pre-heat oven to 230C/450F/gas mark 8. To prepare the filling, poach the haddock in milk until just opaque. Fry the onion in a little olive oil until softened, add sugar, raise heat, and cook until slightly brown. Add a fruity, hoppy ale and reduce heat. Cook until onion is soft and syrupy and all the beer has been soaked up, then divide between tartlet cases. Skin and flake the smoked haddock and scatter over the onion. Whisk together the egg, cream, mustard and a grating of black pepper, then pour into the pastry cases. Sprinkle over the grated cheese and bake in a hot oven for around 15 minutes until golden brown and bubbling.

Here's a robust dish from the Highlands of Scotland. Christopher Bentley, chef of the Old Inn at Gairloch, chooses the ideal ale for 'jugging' his hare – Red Cuillin, brewed on the Isle of Skye.

HARE IN RED CUILLIN ALE WITH SAFFRON

Serves 6

1 large hare, cut into pieces
Dripping, oil or butter for frying
900ml (1½ pints) Red Cuillin
450g (1lb) onions, finely chopped
225g (8oz) celery, sliced
2 sprigs thyme
225g (8oz) fresh breadcrumbs
Half tsp saffron strands
Salt and pepper

Pre-heat oven to 190C/375F/gas mark 5. Lightly brown hare pieces in the fat in a deep casserole. Cover with the real ale, add the onion, celery and thyme, bring to the boil, put the lid on and transfer to the oven. Casserole for around three hours until tender. Take out of the oven, remove the hare pieces with a slotted spoon, and keep warm. Strain the cooking liquor into a saucepan, stir in the breadcrumbs and saffron, and bring slowly to simmering point. Season to taste. Serve the hare with the sauce on a bed of tagliatelle or couscous – or mashed neeps and tatties if you prefer.

Passionate pub cook Ben Ashworth at the Queen's Head in Troutbeck, Cumbria, really makes his menu sing. Here he combines traditional and contemporary ingredients in an exciting starter.

BRAISED OXTAIL AND REAL ALE RISOTTO WITH CRISPY SHALLOTS

Serves 4 as a starter

1 oxtail, trimmed and separated between the joints (the butcher will do it for you)
Oil for frying
450g (1lb) diced root vegetables
1 glass red wine
2 pints real ale (dark mild would be good)
1 pint veal stock (available in supermarkets)
1 bulb garlic, sliced through the middle
1 bay leaf
50g (2oz) soft butter
6 shallots
100g (4oz) Arborio risotto rice
1 tbsp finely chopped parsley
Milk
50g (2oz) soft seasoned flour
Salt and pepper

Pre-heat oven to 200C/400F/gas mark 6. Lightly brown oxtail pieces on all sides in a little oil, season. Drain in a colander, fry off the root vegetables, and drain again. Place meat and diced vegetables in a casserole with the red wine, ale, veal stock, garlic and bay leaf and bring to the boil. Cover and transfer to oven, braise for 1½-2 hours until the meat is tender. Remove oxtail from the stock and allow to cool slightly before removing meat from the bones. Simmer to reduce the braising liquor by half, and keep warm.

To make risotto, melt butter in a pan and add 2 of the shallots, finely diced, sauté for a few minutes until translucent. Add rice, then stock a ladleful at a time, stirring all the time. As the rice absorbs the stock add another ladleful, repeating for about 20 minutes until the rice is tender. Add the bits of oxtail and a little more stock if the risotto needs loosening up. Place in bowls and sprinkle with chopped parsley.

Peel remaining 4 shallots, separate into rings, cover with milk for about 10 minutes, drain and dust with flour. Deep fry until crisp. Scatter on top of the risotto and serve immediately.

Beer is a traditional ingredient in Welsh Rarebit. The Bell at Skenfrith goes one further and also puts the local Breconshire ale in the marrow chutney to accompany it.

WELSH RAREBIT WITH HOME-GROWN MARROW CHUTNEY

Serves 4

Welsh Rarebit

50g (2oz) butter
50g (2oz) plain flour
600ml (1 pint) Breconshire Golden Valley Bitter
2 tbsps coarse grain mustard
100g (4oz) strong Cheddar (or Caerphilly)
4 slices warm toast
Salt and pepper

Melt butter in a small pan, add flour. Cook for 3-4 minutes stirring constantly. Stir in beer a little at a time, while beating to a smooth paste. When all the beer is added, season to taste and add the mustard and grated cheese. Leave to chill slightly before spreading thickly on warm toast, finish under a hot grill until browned and bubbling.

Marrow Chutney

1 kg (2lb) marrows, slightly under-ripe
450g (1lb) shallots
3 cloves garlic
225g (8oz) sultanas
2 tsps cumin
1 stick cinnamon
2 bay leaves
50g (2oz) mustard powder
6 fresh chillies
2 tsps ground ginger
600ml (1 pint) malt vinegar
450g (1lb) brown sugar
600ml (1 pint) Breconshire Golden Valley Bitter
Salt and pepper to taste

Peel and finely chop marrows, shallots and garlic and place in a pan with all the other ingredients. Bring to the boil, reduce heat, cover and simmer very gently for 6 hours, adding a drop more beer if it gets too dry. Chill in Kilner jars or airtight containers and leave for as long as you can, at least 4-6 weeks, to let the flavour develop.

Tony Warburton, chef at the Crown Inn, Church Enstone in Oxfordshire, dishes up old English traditional pub dishes bursting with flavour.

ROAST HAM HOCK IN CIDER AND MUSTARD

Serves 4

4 ham hocks
1 onion
1 bay leaf
1 carrot
5 peppercorns
Clear English honey
1 tbsp brown sugar
600ml (1 pint) medium cider
1 dsp wholegrain mustard
300ml (½ pint) chicken stock
Salt and pepper

Cover hocks in cold water, add the onion, bay leaf, carrot and peppercorns. Bring to the boil, turn down to a gentle simmer, cover and cook for around 2 hours. Cool and remove outer skin, leaving a layer of fat.

Pre-heat the oven to 220C/425F/gas mark 7. Spread honey over the hocks, sprinkle with sugar, and roast until nicely glazed – around 15 minutes. Place cider in a pan and simmer briskly to reduce by two thirds. Add mustard, 1 tbsp honey and chicken stock, and reduce again to sauce consistency. Season to taste and serve with the ham hock.

They're always up to something interesting on the cooking front at The Maltsters Arms, Tuckenhay in Devon. Michelin starred Jean-Christophe Novelli, who wrote the foreword to this guide, cooked there when Keith Floyd was the owner, but this recipe comes from current landlady Denise Thwaites.

BARBECUED QUAILS IN REAL CIDER AND FIVE SPICES

Serves 2

4 quails
(ask your butcher to spatchcock
them on skewers)

Marinade

1-2 tbsps local honey
Good pinch each of 5-spice powder,
ginger, garlic and saffron
600ml (1 pint) real cider (they use Shag)
Sea salt and black pepper

Salsa

1 large pepper
2 plum tomatoes
1 red onion
2 cloves garlic
hot red chillies to taste
1 tbsp caster sugar
White wine

Veg

2 aubergines and 3 different
coloured peppers, thickly sliced

Spread some honey over each quail, skin side up, and sprinkle with 5-spice powder, saffron, ginger and garlic. Place in a deep dish, almost cover with cider, season and refrigerate overnight.

To make salsa, finely chop pepper, tomatoes, onion and chillies to taste. Add caster sugar and a generous slosh of white wine. Season to taste (add tomato purée to thicken if wished).

Barbecue the peppers and aubergines without oil until slightly blackened, then heat salsa in a pan and immerse peppers and aubergines in it for a few minutes. Barbecue the quails quite slowly to a golden brown colour – about 5 minutes each side.

To make sauce, pour a cupful of marinade into a pan, add a dollop each of honey and butter, and leave to bubble away until nice and gloopy.

Arrange peppers and aubergine on a plate, spoon salsa around, place 2 quails per portion on top and ladle over the sauce.

A different way to cook your Christmas goose, from Keith and Karen Horton of the Shetwynd Arms at Brocton in Staffordshire.

POT ROASTED GOOSE WITH SAGE AND CIDER

Serves 4

2 goose breasts
450g (1lb) good pork sausage meat
450g (1lb) cooking apples, chopped
1 dsp chopped fresh sage
1 litre (2 pints) dry cider
Salt and pepper

Pre-heat oven to 180C/350F/gas mark 4. Butterfly each goose breast – slice a sharp knife along an edge and opening up the breast so that there is a 'hinge' holding the two sides together. Mix together the sausage meat, chopped apple and sage, and season. Divide the mixture between the goose breasts, fold over the breast and tie with fine string. Place the stuffed goose in a roasting dish with the cider, cover with foil or tight fitting lid, and cook in a medium oven for around 90 minutes, until cooked through. When cooked, remove goose and leave somewhere warm to rest. Bring cooking liquor to simmering point and lightly thicken. Remove string from goose breasts, carve and serve with the cider gravy.

The Kintail Lodge Hotel at Glenshiel in the Highlands describes its menu as 'plain and simple modern Scottish cuisine with the occasional twist towards fine dining'. This chicken recipe has certainly got a Scottish twist.

CHICKEN BREAST STUFFED WITH SKIRLIE WITH CIDER AND THYME

Serves 4

2 onions, peeled and finely chopped
50g (1oz) butter
Freshly ground black pepper
225g (8oz) medium oatmeal
1 tbsp fresh chopped parsley
Vegetable stock
4 chicken breasts
8 rashers streaky bacon
150ml (¼ pint) good medium cider
150ml (¼ pint) chicken stock
Spring of fresh thyme

Pre-heat oven to 220C/425F/gas mark 7. Make the skirlie by gently frying the diced onion in the butter, season with black pepper. When soft, stir in the oatmeal and cook gently, stirring, until it has absorbed the butter. Stir in the parsley, and enough vegetable stock to make a thick porridge. Set aside to cool. While the skirlie is cooking, with a sharp knife make 5cm (2 in) slits in the undersides of the chicken breasts. Stuff with a heaped tablespoon of the skirlie, then wrap streaky bacon around the chicken to secure the stuffing. Carefully sauté each breast in a little oil until golden brown on both sides, transfer to an ovenproof dish and place above the middle of a hot oven for 20-25 minutes until cooked through. Remove from the oven and keep the chicken warm. Deglaze the sauté pan with the cider and chicken stock, add the thyme, and reduce to a syrupy jus. Discard the thyme.

Serve each chicken breast on a portion of crushed, hot new potatoes with the cider jus spooned around, accompanied by a green vegetable.

David Scott, chef and proprietor of the Swan, Great Easton in Essex, is an imaginative cook who gives traditional dishes extra glitz. Here is his take on pork in cider.

PORK TENDERLOIN WITH APRICOT STUFFING, CIDER AND DIJON MUSTARD CREAM SAUCE

Serves 8

4 x 450g (1lb) pork fillets

Stuffing

225g (8oz) sausagemeat
1 onion, finely diced
1 egg
175g (6oz) dried apricots, finely sliced
Salt and pepper

Sauce

Trimmings from the pork
1 onion, finely sliced
600ml (1 pint) dry cider
300ml (½ pint) good quality cloudy apple juice
2 tbsps Dijon mustard
1 litre (1 pint) double cream
Runny honey
Salt and pepper

Trim pork fillets of all sinews and fat, keep for sauce. Cut each fillet in half to give 8 portions, then make an incision along each and fold open the fillet, possibly beating it out a little.

Pre-heat oven to 200C/400F/gas mark 6. Make stuffing by mixing all the ingredients together, season to taste. Divide stuffing into 8 and place along centre of each fillet leaving about 1 cm (half inch) at each end; roll each fillet and tie with string to seal stuffing. Chill until ready to cook. Seal each fillet in a hot, lightly oiled pan, then roast in a hot oven for 20 to 30 minutes, depending on thickness, until cooked through.

To make the sauce, gently sauté the pork trimmings and onion in butter until the onions are soft and pork has released its fats and flavours. Add cider and apple juice, then increase heat and reduce by half. Strain into a clean pan, add mustard and cream, and reduce to the consistency of double cream. Add honey to taste (depending on dryness of the cider) and season.

To serve: carefully remove string and place each pork fillet on a bed of creamed potatoes, pour over sauce. Accompany with seasonal vegetables.

The Rising Sun at Woodland in Devon is a regular guide entrant and the landlady, Heather Humphreys, always donates one of her inspiring recipes – this time it was created by the pub's chef Paul Cheakley.

LOCAL PORK, HOG'S PUDDING AND SUMMER VEGETABLES IN DEVONSHIRE CIDER AND GRAIN MUSTARD SAUCE

Serves 8

450g (1lb) hog's pudding
450g (1lb) pork fillet, sliced into 5cm (2in) medallions
Olive oil
200g (7oz) courgettes, diced
200g (7oz) young broad beans
12 cherry tomatoes
250ml (9fl oz) Devon cider
4 tsps wholegrain mustard
250ml (9fl oz) double cream
Salt and pepper

Pre-heat oven to 200C/400F/gas mark 6. Sear the whole hog's pudding and pork medallions in a little olive oil, transfer to a hot oven for around 5 minutes to complete cooking. Roast the courgettes, broad beans and cherry tomatoes in a little olive oil in a hot oven for around 5 minutes. Drain any fat from the pan and deglaze with cider, add the mustard and cream, and reduce to a coating consistency. Slice the hog's pudding on the slant. Pile the roasted vegetables in the centre of a hot plate and top with the slices of pork and hog's pudding. Spoon the sauce around, and accompany with new potatoes.

The first licensed house in Wales, the Groes Inn, has been serving ale since 1573. Here is one of its real rural recipes.

SEARED WILD RABBIT, BACON AND CIDER CASSEROLE

Serves 8

1 rabbit, jointed
Olive oil
Black pepper
1 onion, chopped
4 rashers bacon, chopped
2 sticks celery, chopped
600ml (1 pint) dry cider
3 fresh sage leaves
Sprig of thyme
1 Bramley apple

Pre-heat oven to 190C/375F/gas mark 5. Sear the rabbit joints in a hot pan with a little olive oil, season with black pepper. When browned, add the onion, bacon and celery and fry for two more minutes. Slowly pour in the cider which will steam and sizzle in the pan, releasing the flavours. Add the chopped herbs and peeled, coarsely chopped Bramley. Cover the pan and casserole in a moderate oven for around two hours. When cooked, drain off the cooking liquor and keep the rabbit hot while simmering the liquor briskly to reduce by half. Pour the cider sauce over the rabbit and serve with new potatoes.

Here's an unashamedly indulgent dessert from Kim Scicluna of the Sun Inn, Feering, in Essex. The main ingredient is beer, proving that bitter can sometimes turn out sweet!

BEER TART

Serves 8

200g (7oz) plain flour
1 tbsp caster sugar
Pinch of salt
115g (4½ oz) butter
2-3 tbsps iced water
200g (7oz) soft brown sugar
2 large eggs
175ml (7fl oz) strong ale

Pre-heat oven to 220C/425F/gas mark 7. Sift the flour into a bowl with the sugar and salt and rub in three quarters of the butter. Mix with enough iced water to make a dough. Chill for 30 minutes. Roll out the pastry and use it to line a 22cm (9 in) tart tin. Sprinkle the brown sugar over the pastry base. Break the eggs into a bowl and beat in the beer, then pour through a sieve directly onto the sugar. Cut remaining butter into slivers and scatter over. Cook for 35 minutes towards the top of the oven until the filling is just firm to the touch, then leave to stand for at least 10 minutes. Serve hot or cold with cream.

A dark, delicious crème brûlée made with Guinness has been donated by the inventive cooks at the Esplanade at Bangor in Northern Ireland.

SWEET DUCK EGG AND GUINNESS CRÈME BRÛLÉE

Serves 8-9

400ml (¾ pint) double cream
300ml (½ pint) Guinness
4 duck eggs plus 3 yolks
250g (10oz) caster sugar

Pre-heat oven to 150C/300F/gas mark 2. Heat the cream and Guinness in separate pans. Whisk the eggs and egg yolks with the sugar until smooth. Pour the hot Guinness over the eggs, then add the boiled cream. Pour mixture into the cream pan and simmer until the mix coats the back of a spoon. Divide between brûlée ramekins or moulds and bake for 30 minutes. Allow to cool, top with caster sugar and flash under a very hot grill to caramelise the sugar (or use cook's blow torch).

ENGLAND

ASTWICK

☆ Tudor Oaks

1 Taylors Road, SG5 4AZ

▶ A1 northbournd 1 mile past jct 10
Mon-Sat 11am-11pm; Sun 12-3pm, 7-10.30pm
Daily 12-2pm, 6.30-10.30pm (9pm Sun)
T (01462) 831433
E tudoroakslodge@aol.com
W www.tudoroakslodge.co.uk
Beer range varies
Wonderful selection focusing on seafood and home-smoked meat and fish
Mock Tudor coaching inn with oak beams and B&B chalets around the courtyard

Innovative chef and landlord Eric Welek brought some of his home-smoked produce to the launch of the last issue of this guide and it went down a treat. In a small smoking oven in the kitchen of his hop-festooned pub he smokes Scotch beef, lamb, chicken and duck breast, trout, salmon, prawns, oysters and mussels over Jack Daniels whisky barrels, applewood and rosewood for a more delicate flavour, as well as the usual oak chips. The smoked meat is then served thinly sliced as starters, with salad or used in cooking.

Sample starters from Eric's ever-changing menu might be fresh rock oysters on crushed ice, Greek salad, sautéed wild mushrooms, king prawns in filo with hoisin sauce, angels on horseback – oysters wrapped in bacon in cheese sauce – priced £5.50-£7.50. Main dishes might be a whole lobster with prawns in tomato, onion and garlic sauce, pan-fried sirloin steak with all the trimmings, grilled tuna with parsley butter and vegetables, home-made steak pie, a proper Spanish paella Valenciana, deep-fried cod in beer batter, sirloin steak in port and Stilton sauce, baked whole seabass with a dusting of sea salt and seaweed, half a guinea fowl with port and redcurrant sauce or pan-fried Welsh lamb chops with fresh rosemary. Prices range from £9.95 to around £14. S V P C

GREAT BARFORD

Anchor Inn

High Street, MK44 3LF

▶ Off A421, next to the church
Mon-Fri 12-3pm, 6-11pm; Sat & Sun 12-11pm
Sun-Thu 12-2pm, 6-9pm; Fri & Sat 12-2pm, 6.30-9.30pm
T (01234) 870364
Wells Eagle; guests
Home-cooked food, particularly good for steaks, fish and chef's specials
Picturesque village pub by the River Ouse, popular with boaters in summer; meals are served in the bar or restaurant

Fresh fish delivered from Grimsby, steaks cut and cooked to order and an excellent specials board are all good reasons for visiting this attractive village pub. Prawns on draught are a popular choice here, £5.50 for half a pint, £7.50 a pint, and there are plenty of other seafood starters too: prawn and mackerel cocktail, whitebait with tartare sauce or seafood platter (prawns, herrings, squid and cockles served with Marie Rose sauce). There is also soup of the day, chef's pâté with Cumberland sauce, breaded Brie with cranberry sauce or vegetable samosas with apricot and ginger chutney, £3.75-£6.95.

A good choice of main courses includes the steaks (10, 12 or 14oz), thick grilled lamb chops marinated with garlic and rosemary, gammon steak topped with a fan of peach and sugar glaze, or you can combine all three with sausage, chips and salad in the mixed grill, £10.50. The menu offers three vegetarian dishes: creamy spinach and penne pasta ragout, spicy vegetable enchiladas topped with sour cream and chive sauce or three cheese and broccoli bake, all £9.50. Chicken dishes are garlic-grilled breast or chicken supreme with mushroom sauce and rice timbale. Good, fresh salads are served with farmhouse bread at £8.95.
★ Q S V P C

HOUGHTON CONQUEST
Knife & Cleaver
The Grove, MK45 3LA

- Off A6, five miles S of Bedford
- Mon-Sat 12-2.30pm, 7-11pm; Sun 12-2.30pm
- Mon-Sat 12-2.30pm, 7-9.30pm; Sun 12-2.30pm
- T (01234) 740387
- F (01234) 740900
- E info@knifeandcleaver.com
- W www.knifeandcleaver.com
- Bateman XB; Potton Village Bike
- Varied menus offering a wonderful fish and seafood selection
- 17th-century inn with an elegant dining room featuring Jacobean panelling from the ruined Houghton House nearby

The Knife and Cleaver offers a fantastic fish menu that changes according to market availability, so you might be tempted by seabass, halibut steak, Sri Lankan marlin or king scallops. Mussels and Loch Fyne oysters often feature and the chef is not afraid to offer offbeat dishes such as sage-smoked shark, apple and cheddar pâté with home made sweet pickle, £5.95 as a starter. Lobster is served plain, thermidor or as you like it, £25 for a half.

The main menu lists some equally inventive starters such as cassoulet terrine of duck confit, pork and Toulouse sausage with garlic mayonnaise bean salad, a warm venison tart with Cheddar crumb crust, shallot and mushroom marmalade or fried English Brie in ciabatta crumbs with tomato salad and basil oil, £5.95 as a starter or £11.95 as a veggie main course. To follow there may be rack of Welsh lamb and fresh mint risotto with bacon and redcurrant sauce, or pan-fried beef fillet on fried bread croûton with leek and onion confit. In the evenings a £22.50 set menu, with four or five choices for each of the three courses, is also available. The Sunday lunch menu at £15.95 for three courses is extensive.

Q S V C

IRELAND
Black Horse
SG17 5QL

- Off A600 between Shefford and Bedford, near Old Warden
- Mon-Sat 11am-3pm, 6-11pm; Sun 12-5pm
- Mon-Sat 12-2.30pm, 6.30-10.30pm; Sun 12-5pm
- T (01462) 811398
- F (01462) 817238
- E info@blackhorseireland.com
- W www.blackhorseireland.com
- Fuller's London Pride; Greene King IPA; Potton Village Bike
- English and continental menu, good for steaks and fish
- Lovely old country inn set in attractive gardens, handy for visitors to the Shuttleworth Collection of historic aircraft at Old Warden

Ideally, dining at the Black Horse should be a lingering, relaxed affair as the menu is too enticing to rush. However, if you do just want a quick meal you can opt for the light lunch menu – crab and avocado timbale with strips of smoked salon and lobster oil, ballotine of duck with celeriac and horseradish slaw and caramelised balsamic, shellfish risotto with lemon mascarpone or grilled tuna steak or chicken breast served with Caesar salad. Prices range from £5-£7. To follow there is a wide choice including chef's suet crusted pie of the day with market veg, braised shoulder of lamb with crushed new potatoes, roasted shallots and wild mushrooms, local farmed gammon and pork cassoulet with spiced apple mash and good fish dishes such as salmon poached in white wine with a sea salted crust or griddled barramundi fillet in crab velouté. Prices range from £8 to £13.95 for steak.

The à la carte menu offers starters from soup of the day to oven-baked gambas with lardoons of pancetta, £5-£8, followed by Scotch beef fillet with black pepper mash, baby veg and Madeira wine jus or vegetarian spicy roasted Mediterranean vegetables and saffron risotto with wild forest mushrooms. Make sure you leave room for dessert, £4.95, including vanilla, apricot and cardamom crème brûlée, ginger and dark chocolate fondant, or cinnamon spiced apple suet pudding.

★ S V P C

SALFORD

Red Lion Hotel

Wavendon Road, MK17 8AZ

▶ Between jct 13 and 14 of the M1, 5 miles from Milton Keynes

☼ Daily 11am-2.30pm, 6-11pm

Daily 12-2pm, 7-10pm

T (01908) 583117

Wells Eagle, Bombardier

☺ Mostly traditional British dishes, steaks are a speciality

Small, friendly, country inn with a secluded garden in a charming village convenient for the M1 and central Milton Keynes

The Red Lion is a good place to stay if you have business in Milton Keynes but want to get away from the centre. Just east of the motorway, it offers a pleasant environment, good food and an award-winning selection of wines. It won the Morning Advertiser's Wine Pub of the Year competition in 2005, and is a regular finalist in pub food awards. The management place an emphasis on consistency and quality, so they buy organic steak from a local farm butcher and their vegetables and salads are freshly delivered from Covent Garden. All the staff are trained to cook so that they understand the quality and standards the pub is aiming for.

The menu, served in the bar and the no-smoking dining room, concentrates mostly on traditional pub favourites, particularly steaks, but also steak and kidney pies, bangers and mash and all the usual suspects in generous portions. However, you will also usually find a fine selection of fish and seafood dishes, vegetarian options and some international cuisine. With a log fire adding to the atmosphere in the winter and a large garden with children's playground set in the orchard for enjoying the local ales in summer, the pub believes it offers a true taste of an English hostelry.

Q S V P C

SUTTON
John O'Gaunt

30 High Street, SG19 2NE

▶ Village centre, off Biggleswade to Potton road
☼ Daily 12-2.30pm, 7-11pm
🍴 Mon-Sat 12-1.45pm, 7-9pm; Sun 12-1.45pm
T (01767) 260377
🍺 Greene King IPA, Abbot; guests
☺ Good pub food supplemented by seasonal game dishes
◙ Three cottages converted into a pub in 1830; meals are served in the saloon bar where the Sutton village quilt hangs

Run by the Ivalls for almost 30 years, the John O'Gaunt is a longstanding entry in CAMRA's Good Beer Guide. A menu of wholesome fare is served here with the addition of seasonal game and excellent Balti dishes. Sauces and spices are made especially for the pub by an Indian chef to which they add their own meats or vegetables. You can choose from lamb, prawn, spinach or vegetable balti, hot chicken jalfrezi with ginger, Thai red chicken or chicken tikka masala, priced between £7-£9.

More traditional choices include steak and kidney pud, moussaka, chicken, spinach and mushroom lasagne, pork dijonnaise or chicken breast in a sun-dried tomato sauce with a pesto and cream cheese mousse. For fish fans there are grilled loin of cod, fisherman's pie or supreme of salmon in a cranberry and orange sauce, while vegetarians can choose from vegetable tagine with couscous or spinach and mushroom lasagne. Mains are £7-£9. Desserts, maybe treacle pudding, chocolate fudge cake or vanilla and honeycomb ice cream pot, are around £3. The pub also offers a range of good value snacks, such as various toasted sandwiches for under £3, filled baguettes or jacket spuds with salad.

★ 🏰 Q ❀ S V 🍺 ♣ P ⚟

THURLEIGH
Jackal

3 High Street, MK44 2DB

▶ Off B660 between Bedford and Kimbolton
☼ Tue-Sat 12-2.30pm, 6-11pm; Sun 12-2.30pm, 4-10.30pm
🍴 Tue-Sat 12-2pm, 7-9pm; Sun 12-2pm
T (01234) 771293
E info@thejackal.fsbusiness.co.uk
W www.thejackal.fsbusiness.co.uk
🍺 Wells Eagle, Bombardier; guest
☺ Award-winning home-cooked fare on seasonal menus
◙ Attractive, partly-thatched pub with a large garden backing on to rolling fields; the lounge is mostly devoted to diners while drinkers fill the bar

Specialist food evenings are a regular treat at this Charles Wells pub, focusing perhaps on Thai cuisine, fish or even bangers and mash when the local butcher Paul Langford produces a special sausage for the occasion. The high-quality fare includes some innovative dishes such as a starter of double-baked goats' cheese and hazelnut cheesecake with red onion marmalade. Other appetisers, mostly under £5, include warm smoked salmon with thyme and lemon risotto, slow-roasted Mediterranean vegetables with Parmesan shavings in a Parmesan pastry tart or baked vine tomatoes and red onion salad with crispy bacon and sweetened balsamic dressing.

To follow there is always a good choice of fish such as swordfish loin with chilli and lime dressing, as well as steaks, plus maybe roulade of chicken filled with crab meat and served with a light citrus sauce, fillet of beef glazed with Stilton with a rich green peppercorn and port sauce or pork and sage parcel wrapped in pancetta with honey and grain mustard. Vegetarians could be tempted by fragrant Thai red vegetable curry, hot and sweet stir fried vegetables, wild mushrooms and cashews with egg noodles, or a courgette, onion and sun dried tomato risotto. Salads and risottos are £8.50, other main courses £10-£16.

🏰 Q ❀ S V 🍺 ♿ P ⚟ 👪 C

ALDWORTH
Bell
Bell Lane, RG8 9SE

- ▶ Just off B4009 near village centre
- Mon-Sat 11am-3pm, 6-11pm; Sun 12-3pm, 7-10.30pm
- Throughout opening times
- T (01635) 578272
- Arkell's 3B, Kingsdown; West Berkshire Maggs Mild, seasonal
- Good home-made snacks from hearty soup to rolls
- 1340 manor hall and rural gem near the Ridgeway path; basic homely bars and central servery

You won't find a six-page menu at the Bell because this beautiful inn, run by the same hosts for many years, without piped music or games machines, simply offers excellent, freshly-made snacks to accompany the well-kept draught ales. Organic home-made soup accompanied by warm rolls at £2.95 could be parsnip, tomato, celery or broccoli and Stilton. Hot crusty rolls from the Aga have delightful old-fashioned fillings such as honey roast ham, turkey, salt beef cured at the local deli, ox tongue, corned beef, mature Cheddar and Stilton, Brie, Devon crab, smoked salmon with cream cheese, spiced prawns, chicken liver, wild mushroom and pork or turkey with brandy and herb pâté, priced £1.90-£2.30, or £5 if accompanied by salads of iceberg lettuce, red and white cabbage, carrots, celery, apple, cucumber, baby tomatoes, banana and pineapple. And what could be better than such heart-warming, filling fare after an appetite-sharpening walk along the Ridgeway Path?
★ Q S V P

BEEDON
Langley Hall
World's End, RG20 8SA

- ▶ 1 mile S of village, near A34/M4 jct
- Mon-Thu 11am-3pm, 5.30-11pm; Fri & Sat 11am-11pm; Sun 11am-7pm
- Mon-Sat 12-2.30pm, 7-10pm; Sun 12.30-4pm
- T (01635) 248332
- F (01635) 248571
- W www.langley-hall-inn.co.uk
- Caledonian Deuchars IPA; West Berkshire Good Old Boy; guests
- Quality, freshly prepared, imaginative meals cooked to order including fresh seafood
- Lively, family-run pub with traditional horseshoe bar and B&B

This friendly, welcoming pub has built up a good reputation for its food, beginning with starters such as home-made soup, warm salad of roasted shallots, tomato and feta, smoked chicken filo parcels, duck liver pâté with toasted brioche, Thai fishcakes with sweet chilli and coriander or home-cured salmon gravadlax, priced £4.75-£6.50. Specials include rib eye and fillet steaks, the tasty home-made Langley Hall burger, salmon fishcakes with spinach and parsley sauce or char-grilled gammon with egg and chips.

Main courses could be roast duck breast with ginger, soy sauce, spring onion and pak choi, char-grilled pork loin with apple, Madeira sauce and dauphinoise potatoes, the Langley Hall kedgeree of smoked haddock with soft boiled eggs and rice in mild, creamy curry sauce, grilled fish of the day with fresh vegetables or vegetarian leek and parmesan tart with rocket salad, priced £10.50-£14.20. The set menu includes Thai fishcakes, home-made soup and smoked chicken filo parcels followed by Thai chicken curry with jasmine rice, beef fillet medallions with brandy and peppercorn sauce, a vegetarian dish or salmon fishcakes with beurre blanc and fresh vegetables, priced £18 for two courses. ★ S V P C

FINCHAMPSTEAD

Queen's Oak

Church Lane, RG40 4LS

- ▶ Take A321 from Wokingham, then follow signs to Finchampstead church
- ☼ Mon-Sat 11am-11pm; Sun 12-10.30pm
- (🍴) Daily 12-2.30pm; Mon-Sat 6.30-9pm
- T (0118) 973 4855
- E angelabrockway@btinternet.com
- 🍺 Brakspear Bitter, Special, seasonal beers
- ☺ Traditional, home-cooked pub meals and a good snack menu
- ◙ Meals are served throughout this pleasant pub and children are welcome in the dining room until 9pm; the garden boasts an award-winning barbecue

This friendly pub gets its name from the (long gone) oak tree planted on the village green in 1887 to celebrate Victoria's golden jubilee. Nowadays a marquee can be erected in the pub garden to celebrate a special occasion, catered for by the chef and his team. Normally, though, they are busy producing wholesome meals from fresh produce, including their speciality, steak and ale pie using meat from a long-established local butcher.

Starters include roasted vegetable tartlet and pork Calvados with melba toast and plum and apple chutney, both £3.75, or there are platters to share – oriental with spring rolls, dim sums, prawn toast, or American with ribs, wings of fire, breaded mushrooms and satay chicken with barbecue sauce, £9.50. To follow there is a choice of stir fries, interesting salads such as Brie and smoked bacon, minute steak and Stilton or Thai chicken Caesar as well as the usual pub favourites: curry of the day, chilli con carne, bangers and mash, lasagne and a choice of steaks. Other dishes include braised lamb shank, poached chicken filled with mozzarella cheese and wrapped in parma ham, home-made quiche or mushroom ravioli as well as plaice filled with salmon, spinach and gruyere cheese, prices from £6.95.

★ ♔ Q ❀ S V ♣ P ⚡ 👪 C

INKPEN

Crown & Garter

Inkpen Common, RG17 9QR

- ▶ Follow signs for Inkpen Common from Kintbury
- ☼ Mon-Sat 12-3pm (not Mon & Tue), 5.30-11pm; Sun 12-3pm, 7-10.30pm
- (🍴) Mon-Sat 12-2pm, 6.30-9.30pm; Sun 12-2.30pm, 7-9.30pm
- T (01488) 668325
- E gill.hern@btopenworld.com
- W www.crownandgarter.com
- 🍺 Arkell's Moonlight; West Berkshire Mr Chubb's Lunchtime Bitter, Good Old Boy; guest
- ☺ Home-cooked food using local produce with plenty of specials
- ◙ Local CAMRA Pub of the Year 2002; 17th-century inn with lovely garden

Faced with closure only six years ago, this rural pub is now thriving – no doubt due to the excellent food as well as well-kept, fine local ales. Using local produce as much as possible, starters on the specials board could be cream of Jerusalem artichoke soup with shredded hare, warm salad of field mushrooms and pancetta, roast garlic and tiger prawn risotto, confit of duck and leek terrine, priced £4.95-£5.25.

Main dish specials include grilled monkfish with crayfish sauce, pheasant supreme with wild blueberry game jus, chicken with chorizo stuffing and roast carrots, Christmas Farm's 16oz pork chop with roast parsnip mash and cider apple gravy, pan-fried venison steak with spiced red cabbage and a veggie choice such as courgette and apple charlotte with barley and veg risotto, priced £8.95-£12.35 with seasonal vegetables. The bar menu, too, changes regularly and includes Cumberland sausages with champ and onion gravy, faggots with baked onion, venison and root vegetable pie, Chinese spiced pork collar plus a good selection of Thai curries. Tempting desserts, all £4.25, include lemon posset with vanilla shortbread.

♔ Q ❀ 🛏 V 🍺 ♿ P ⚡ 👪 C

INKPEN
☆ Swan
Craven Road, Lower Green, RG17 9DX

- ▶ Follow signs to Inkpen from Hungerford Common
- ☼ Mon-Sat 11am-2.30pm, 7-11.30pm, Sun 12-3pm, 7-10.30pm
- 🍴 Daily 12-2.30pm, 7-9.30pm
- T (01488) 668326
- F (01488) 668306
- E enquiries@theswanninn-organics.co.uk
- W www.theswaninn-organics.co.uk
- 🍺 Butts Jester, Traditional, seasonal; guests
- ☺ Imaginative food using mainly organic produce with beef from its own herd
- ◉ Part 17th-century inn with beams, open fires and farm shop

The Swan cooks up great food using its own local produce including beef from an organic herd on the family farm, meat, sausages and other products. All beef served is from the herd including, on the bar menu, home-made beef, leek and ale sausages with mash and onion gravy, rump steak, traditional cottage pie, steak and ale pie with fresh vegetables, beef curry or braised steak and vegetables in a jumbo Yorkshire pud. Other bar dishes, all £9.50, include Mediterranean pasta bake, cod in beer batter and home-made salmon, cod and smoked haddock fish cakes, plus organic ice creams.

The restaurant menu might start with warm bacon salad topped with a poached egg, cullen skink soup of smoked haddock and potato or home-cured beef bresaola, all £6.50. Restaurant main courses might be roast guinea fowl with burgundy sauce, steak, kidney and oyster pudding with real ale gravy, beef fillet medallions pan fried with wild mushrooms then flamed in Cognac, grilled sirloin steak with green peppercorn sauce, slow roasted half shoulder of lamb or ratatouille pancake with Gruyere sauce, £14.50-£21. Desserts, all £6.50, include rich chocolate cheesecake with local Guernsey cream and a selection of English cheese.

★ ♔ Q ❀ 🛏 S V 🍺 ♿ ♣ 🍎 P ⚡ 👪 C

KINTBURY
Dundas Arms
53 Station Road, RG17 9UT

- ▶ Between village and A4
- ☼ Mon-Sat 11am-2.30pm, 6-11pm; Sun 12-2.30pm
- 🍴 Daily 12-2pm, 7-9pm (not Sun eve)
- T (01488) 658263
- F (01488) 658568
- E info@dundasarms.co.uk
- W www.dundasarms.co.uk
- 🍺 Adnams Bitter; West Berkshire Good Old Boy, Mr Chubb's Lunchtime Bitter; guest
- ☺ Award-winning, home-made food
- ◉ Imposing, white washed 18th-century pub between Kennet river and canal

Using local ingredients as far as possible including game from a nearby dealer, sausages home made by the local butcher, bread from the village baker, only free-range eggs, plus ham and bacon from Dorset, fish and crab delivered twice a week from Looe in Cornwall, and smoked fish from Loch Fyne, the Dundas Arms cooks up all sorts of interesting dishes.

A changing menu could include starters such as grilled goats' cheese with sweet tomato purée on Italian bread, home potted shrimps, fresh dressed Dorset crab, home-made pâté with orange or Parma ham with melon and parmesan, priced £4.50-£6.95. Main dishes might be hot, spicy chicken breast with chilli and peanut sauce, avocado with hot smoked salmon salad, traditional steak and kidney pie with vegetables, Cumberland sausage with mash and onion gravy, Thai green chicken curry and rice, calves' liver fried with bacon on mash with onion gravy, roast duck breast with cider and apple sauce, prices £7-£13.50. The veggie dish of the day might be spinach and red pepper lasagne, while fish generally includes fresh cod, lemon sole, monkfish and seabream. And don't forget home-made puds such as chocolate pave with coffee bean sauce, apple crumble and brown sugar meringues, all £4.50.

Q ❀ 🛏 S V ⇌ (Kintbury) P ⚡ 👪 C

STANFORD DINGLEY
Old Boot
RG7 6LT

▶ Centre of village
☼ Mon-Sat 11am-3pm, 6-11pm;
Sun 12-3pm, 7-10.30pm
Ⓣ Daily 12-2.30pm, 7-9.30pm
T (01189) 744292
W www.theoldbootinn.co.uk
Beer range varies
☺ Home-made seasonal dishes using game, poultry and fresh fish; outstanding vegetarian menu
18th-century village free house with open fire and large garden

Food at the Boot can be eaten throughout the pub, either in the bar warmed by an open fire or the conservatory restaurant. Bar meals include fresh cod in beer batter with chips and mushy peas, chef's curry pot of the day, Cumberland sausage with mash and onion gravy, steak and kidney pudding, Cajun chicken breast, braised lamb shank with vegetables, lasagne or burger and chips, plus home-made veggie dishes such as tortellini Gorgonzola, baked, stuffed butternut squash or aubergine boat plus filled baguettes, salads and at least eight starters.

On the à la carte restaurant menu dishes include fresh fish every day such as salmon paprika, oven roast cod, Dover sole, seabream and fresh bass. Other main dishes might be honey roast partridge with juniper and thyme, pork medallions layered with English apples in prune and calvados sauce, char-grilled fillet steak topped with Stilton in Madeira gravy, chicken breast stuffed with apricot and Stilton in mushroom and port sauce, calfves' liver with bacon and onion gravy, rump of lamb cooked with honey and mint sauce, or half a roast duck flambéed with black cherry and kirsch or orange and Cointreau, all served with fresh vegetables and potato dish of the day. Desserts range from raspberry crème brûlée to hot chocolate cake. Beers include ales from West Berkshire Brewery as well as Young's. ★ Q V P C

WINKFIELD
Duke of Edinburgh
Woodside Road, Windsor Forest, SL4 2DF

▶ Off A332, near Ascot Racecourse
☼ Daily 11am-11pm
Ⓣ Daily 12-2pm, 6.30-9pm
T (01344) 882736
Arkell's 2B, 3B, Kingsdown, seasonal beers
☺ Home-cooked food served in the bar and restaurant
Friendly, family-run pub full of character with exposed beams

Arkell's most easterly tied house, the Duke of Edinburgh has only been a pub for the last 100 years, before that it was reputedly a post office. It is now a very sporty venue, not least because it is just a mile and a half from Ascot racecourse (and naturally gets terribly busy during Ascot Week). The landlord is a Chelsea fan and the saloon has two televisions showing live sport. He has also pulled the odd pint for local sportsmen Glen Hoddle and Nick Faldo.

On the food front, straightforward pub meals are served in the bar – fish and chips, ploughman's and the usual favourites. For the restaurant the chef mostly produces specials that are changed on a daily basis, so to start you might find home-made soup, pâté, pan-fried mushrooms, salads of mozzarella, tomato and basil or Greek style with feta cheese, or potato skins with dips. For the main courses, traditional dishes feature such as steak and kidney or other meat pies, but unusually haggis also often appears on the board, due to the chef hailing from Edinburgh. Puddings, too, are all home made: you could be offered coconut cheesecake, cherry pie or spotted dick and custard. ★ V (Ascot) ♣ P C

CHALFONT ST GILES

Ivy House

London Road, HP8 4RS

- ▶ On A413 2 miles S of Amersham
- ☼ Mon-Fri 12-3pm, 6-11pm; Sat 12-11pm; Sun 12-10.30pm
- (Ψ) Mon-Fri 12-2.30pm, 6.30-9.30pm; Sat 12-9.30pm; Sun 12-9pm
- T (01494) 872184
- F (01494) 872870
- E enquiries@theivyhouse-bucks.co.uk
- W www.theivyhouse-bucks.co.uk
- Fuller's London Pride; guests
- ☺ Updated traditional dishes – an eclectic mix at a free house that has won food awards
- Beautiful 18th-century brick and flint free house

Multi-award winning pub the Ivy House is splendid in the dining department under chef and proprietor Jane Mears. Much of the produce used in cooking is locally sourced, supporting small businesses such as the milkman with his farm across the road. Herbs and fruit are home grown. Specials are a joy, from soups such as roast sweet potato and apple to crayfish and tiger prawn cocktail with ginger, lemon and lime grass mayonnaise, followed by pan-fried marlin with chilli salsa, char-grilled Gressingham duck breast with orange and ginger marmalade, medallions of wild red deer with wild mushrooms, chicken breast stuffed with Boursin wrapped in Parma ham and veggie choices such as cheese and wild mushroom roulade.

Set menus are seasonal and include a mixed hors d'oeuvre platter of continental meats, home-made chutney, pickled quails' eggs and olives at £7.50, and starters from soup of the day to ragout of button mushrooms. Main courses include pan-fried lean ostrich fillet with mango and orange sauce, char-grilled fillet and sirloin steaks with a choice of sauces, Gressingham duck breast cooked pink with sauce of the day, and fish such as seabass, char-grilled swordfish or mixed seafood tagliatelle. Main meals are £10.95-£16.95. Veggie choices include roast vegetables with herbed Scotch pancakes with rice, sweet chilli sauce and roasted cashews. Healthy option dishes are marked, but desserts such as the Ivy House bread and butter pudding with extra fruit and spice served with custard are not among them. ★ S V C

CHALFONT ST GILES
White Hart

High Street, HP8 4LP

- Mon-Sat 11.30am-3pm, 5.30-11pm; Sun 12-3pm, 7pm-11pm
- Mon-Sat 12-2pm, 5.30-9.30pm; Sun 12-2pm, 7pm-9.30pm
- T (01494) 872441
- F (01494) 876375
- E enquiries@thewhitehartstgiles.co.uk
- Greene King IPA, Morland Original, Old Speckled Hen; guests
- Imaginative menu featuring international cuisine
- Smart, modern, cosmopolitan pub with real fire and B&B

In an area with plenty of competition for fine food, the White Hart rises to the challenge with a scintillating specials board that might feature roast Spanish sardines on wild mushroom sauce, baked baby quail on char-grilled vegetables and lobster and king prawn bisque as starters. Mains include baked chump of lamb on vegetable ratatouille with port and redcurrant sauce, Gressingham duck breast on honeyed vegetables or sole stuffed with crayfish mousse, prices around £16. A light lunch menu ranges from smoked salmon and asparagus quiche to the Bangkok wok of stir fry peppered chicken and vegetables in oyster plum sauce, moules marinière and smoked salmon and haddock fishcakes, £6.95-£7.95.

Main courses on the set menu are three sausages on creamy mash with caramelised onion gravy, loin of pork en croute with Madeira and truffle sauce, braised lamb shank on cheesy bubble and squeak, chicken supreme stuffed with sun-dried tomato and olive mousse, or cod in beer batter with thick chips and home-made mushy peas, prices £10.75-£15.95. Caramelised, peppered pineapple with vodka strawberry compote and mango crème brûlée with berries are among the desserts.

Q V C

CHALFONT ST PETER
Village Hall

Gold Hill West, SL9 9HH

- Top Gold Hill Common between Chalfont St Peter and Gerrards Cross
- Mon-Sat 11am-11pm; Sun 11am-10.30pm
- Daily 12-10pm (9.30pm Sun)
- T (01753) 887596
- F (01753) 893531
- W www.morethanjustapub.com
- Beer range varies
- Mainly traditional home-made English meat and fish dishes
- Comfortable and atmospheric family and community pub

Such a community pub that they call it the Village Hall, you do indeed find here the sort of wholesome comfort food the WI might serve up. In this case, though, it is a mainly Polish kitchen team led by head chef Andrzej Wica who loves doing hog roasts and will be found at the barbecue most Saturdays in summer. The pub also likes to highlight links between food and real ale, holding regular ale dinners, often hosted by brewers. So the menu always features haddock in beer batter with real chips and home-made tartare sauce. Other dishes include sausage of the day with onion gravy, vegetable kebabs, pork belly slowly braised then seared for crispy crackling with mash and chilli apple jam, grilled smoked chicken breast with pancetta, asparagus and Italian mushroom open pie, loin of lamb with rosemary and red wine, 8oz beef fillet pan seared then oven roasted with rosemary potato gratin or whole seabass stuffed with lemon and thyme on red pepper salsa, prices £7.50-£11.50. Starters range from home-made soup to continental meat platter. Side dishes include hand-cut chips, horseradish, mustard or garlic mash and rocket with Parmesan salad. The key food session is Sunday lunch when people from all walks of life come streaming in for hearty well cooked roasts, fresh vegetables and ale based gravy – a joy to watch. S V C

CHEDDINGTON
Old Swan
58 High Street, LU7 0RQ

- ▶ Off B488 between Leighton Buzzard and Tring
- ☼ Mon-Fri 12-3pm, 5-11pm; Sat 12-11pm; Sun 12-10.30pm
- Mon-Fri 12-2pm, 6-9pm (9.30pm Thu & Fri); Sat 12-9.30pm; Sun 12-9pm
- T (01296) 668226
- F (01296) 663811
- E geoffrsmith@btconnect.com
- Fuller's London Pride; Greene King IPA; guests
- ☺ Freshly-cooked, upmarket pub food with a good specials board
- Thatched 16th-century village pub with large garden and new patio for diners; the no-smoking restaurant is open in the evenings

Most of the dishes are freshly prepared and cooked in the pub kitchen, and most of the vegetables are home-grown here, too.The pub stages themed evenings: Indian, Thai, Chinese. At lunchtime there is a good range of sandwiches or baguettes served with chips, £4.25/£5.95, filled jacket spuds, salads or home-cooked main dishes such as tuna pasta bake, steak and ale pie or mushroom stroganoff.

The specials list changes every evening and might include starters such as prawn brochettes in garlic and parsley butter, peeled scampi tails in tomato and white wine sauce or a heart-warming broccoli and Stilton soup, all under £5.50. To follow there could be lamb leg steaks in a fresh mint sauce, pan-fried red snapper with mushroom and prawn butter, beef bourgignon or red Thai chicken curry, prices from £9-£13. The main menu majors on steaks and pub favourites such as lambs' liver, chilli and home-made lasagne, but also offers mixed grilled fish in lemon butter, crayfish and salmon pasta, plus some vegetarian options such as spinach and ricotta cannelloni, and Brie, basil and sun-dried tomato cheesecake.

V (Cheddington) P C

CHENIES
Red Lion
WD3 6ED

- ▶ Off A404 between Chorleywood and Little Chalfont
- ☼ Daily 11am-2.30pm; 5.30-11pm
- Daily 12-2pm, 7-10pm
- T (01923) 282722
- F (01923) 283791
- Wadworth 6X; guest
- ☺ Home-made food with a good selection of pies, plus snacks
- Popular rural free house in a picturesque village near the River Chess

A proper pub, it even has its own beer, Lions Pride, produced especially for the bar by local brewery Rebellion and the guest beers are chosen mostly from micro-breweries. Food is also taken seriously here by landlady and chief cook Heather Norris and all the meals are made on the premises. She is particularly proud of her pies: lamb, ham and parsley, mahi mahi chilli (white fish), and beef, mustard and cheese pie, all served with fresh veg for less than £10. Other British classic dishes include a huge ham hock on creamy mash with parsley sauce, steak and kidney hotpot with toasted croutons, wonderful, old-fashioned oxtail with root vegetables and mash, or bangers with bubble and squeak and a rich red wine gravy.

Heather produces more exotic stuff, too, including Moroccan chicken breast with couscous and Mediterranean vegetables, beef goulash topped with sour cream, and fresh tuna loin lightly seared on a bed of rocket with roasted Mediterranean veg. For vegetarians there is either balti potatoes with spinach and feta cheese or roasted aubergine stuffed with mushrooms and tomatoes, topped with a cheese crumb. Main courses are mostly priced between £9-£13. There's a good choice of snacks, although I was slightly troubled by the hot bacon and Milky Bar sandwich!

★ Q S V P C

FARNHAM ROYAL
King of Prussia
Blackpond Lane, SL2 3EG

- ▶ Off High Street, down winding lane
- ☼ Mon-Fri 12-3pm, 5.30-11pm; Sat 12-11pm; Sun 12-5pm
- 🍴 Mon-Fri 12-2.15pm; Sat 12-9.15pm; Sun 12-4pm
- T (01753) 643006
- W www.thekingofprussia.com
- Fuller's London Pride; Shepherd Neame Spitfire; guest
- ☺ Traditional dishes with modern touches freshly made from quality ingredients at a celeb chef's pub
- Refurbished 19th-century pub with two open fires, no smoking throughout

You would expect fine English fare in a pub owned by Michelin starred Ready Steady Cook chef Phil Vickery, who is rated as one of the top 20 exponents of traditional British food. Hand-cut chunky chips are cooked in beef dripping, and proper pub meals include creamy chicken, leek and pea pie, pot roast loin of pork, char-grilled Barnsley chop with mint gravy, naturally-smoked haddock fishcakes or the special home-made beef burger with cheese and tomato pickle, prices £10.95-£12.95.

Starters could be Stinking Bishop perry-washed cheese with spring onions and warm Jersey Royals, balsamic smoked mackerel with pickled cabbage and horseradish mayo or, in season, grilled marinated English asparagus with pink grapefruit. Other main courses, on a regularly changing seasonal menu, might be veal sausages with saffron risotto, swordfish loin with peach, olive and chilli salsa, or 18-day aged rump steak at £17.95. Phil is not the pub chef but he influences the menus and is renowned for his puds – all priced £5.95 including his signature Rocky Road marshmallow brownies, saffron blancmange with rose petal syrup or baked egg custard tart with green apple crumble ice cream.

S V P C

HADDENHAM
Green Dragon
8 Churchway, HP17 8AA

- ▶ Off A418 between Thame and Aylesbury, follow signs to Church End
- ☼ Mon-Sat 12-2pm, 6.30-11pm; Sun 12-2.30pm
- 🍴 Mon-Sat 12-2pm, 6.30-9.15pm; Sun 12-2.30pm
- T (01844) 291403
- F (01844) 299532
- W www.eatatthedragon.co.uk
- Beer range varies
- ☺ Traditional and modern British cooking at 2004-5 Bucks Dining Pub of the Year
- 17th-century inn in the village, no-smoking throughout

The Green Dragon has long been a byword for imaginative cooking and fine dining but visitors just wanting a drink are equally welcome to enjoy beers from Vale Brewery in the village. The main menu includes starters such as duck confit glazed with local honey, steamed mussels with white wine, home-made soup or salmon and crab fishcake, from £4.25-£5.95. Home-made steak and kidney pudding with Wychert Ale is a main course, also braised Bucks lamb shank, halibut fillet with wild mushrooms and pine nuts, chicken on sweet potato bubble and squeak, Cornish seabass on saffron potato cake, mildly spiced duck breast with parsnip purée tart, and open wild mushroom and leek ravioli with thyme veloute, prices from £9.50-£13.

Specials might be shepherd's pie with Welsh Cheddar and curly kale or guinea fowl with root vegetables and black pudding. Set suppers on Tuesday and Thursday evenings cost £11.95 for two courses, starting perhaps with duck confit or avocado and pancetta salad, followed by beef fillet with horseradish mash or poached salmon with champagne butter. Mouth-watering desserts range from banana toffee crumble with home-made honeycomb ice cream to caramelised ice cream with black cherries.

V P C

HAWRIDGE COMMON
Full Moon
HP5 2UH

- ▶ Off A416 near Chesham
- ☼ Mon-Fri 12-3pm, 5.30-11pm; Sat & Sun 12-11pm
- 🍴 Daily 12-2pm, 6.30-9pm (not Sun eve)
- T (01494) 758959
- F (01494) 758797
- E annie@alberto1142.freeserve.co.uk
- Adnams Bitter; Draught Bass; Brakspear Special; Fuller's London Pride; guest
- ☺ From plain and simple to more adventurous
- Traditional 16th-century Chilterns pub with a large garden and pergola covered patio

Recently voted local council Pub of the Year, the Full Moon illuminates good food using fresh local produce as far as possible including meat, poultry and game from Eastwoods, the Organic Butcher of the Year in nearby Berkhamsted. Fresh fish comes weekly direct from Salcombe in Devon. Dishes on a typical specials board include cod and pancetta fishcakes and sardines with pepper and coriander salsa, both £5.25, followed by main meals of salmon fricassee, beef braised in Guinness with mash, chicken supreme stuffed with avocado and pancetta and the day's veggie dish: potato, cheese and leek bake.

The main bar menu offers a smoked fish platter and ginger and lemongrass chicken kebabs as starters, followed by roast chicken and stuffing suet pudding, cod in beer batter, pork and apple sausages with roast shallot gravy on mash, both steak and cottage pie and home-cooked ham with fried egg and chips, all around £9. At lunchtime there is also an excellent variety of sandwiches and jacket potatoes. The evening menu features fine steaks, monkfish tail wrapped in Parma ham, cod pan fried with chorizo, venison sausages in red wine and a vegetarian dish such as gnocchi with wild mushroom and sage ragout, priced £9.25 up to £15.95 for fillet steak.

★ Q ❀ S V ♿ ▲ P C

KINGSWOOD
Plough & Anchor
Bicester Road, HP18 0RB

- ▶ A 41 between Bicester and Waddesdon
- ☼ Mon-Sat 11am-3pm, 6-12pm; Sun 12-5pm
- 🍴 Mon-Sat 12-2.30pm, 6.30-9.30pm; Sun 12-5pm
- T (01296) 770251
- F (01296) 770640
- Fuller's London Pride; guest
- ☺ Fine food on an à la carte menu featuring local produce
- 16th-century roadside pub with giant logs on a roaring open fire

This is a food-oriented pub catering mainly for diners but drinkers are always very welcome –London Pride and a weekly changing guest (from a regional or micro, usually under four per cent ABV) are served direct from the barrel by a custom-built dispense and cooling system. Since the present owner acquired the Plough and Anchor in 1999 it has undergone a total renovation and also gained Cask Marque accreditation.

Chef James Wilkie has travelled the world and amassed a collection of international recipes that now appear in the pub restaurant, made from local produce as far as possible. Meat comes from the local butcher, his beef is used in one of the pub's best selling dishes – rump steak marinated in London Pride with cinnamon, garlic, shallots and brown sugar for 24 hours before being char grilled to your liking then served with hand-cut chips, vegetables and salad garnish. There is a choice of fish dishes as well, and vegetarians are well catered for. A traditional Sunday lunch is served all afternoon with orders taken until around 5pm; the pub closes when people have finished eating.

★ ❀ S V ♿ P C

LEY HILL

☆ Swan

HP5 1UT

- Near Chesham
- Daily 12-11pm (10.30pm Sun)
- Daily 12-2.15pm, 7-9.15pm
- T (01494) 783075
- E swanleyhill@btconnect.com
- Adnams Bitter; Brakspear Bitter; Fuller's London Pride; Taylor Landlord; guests
- Varied bar and restaurant menus all freshly prepared
- Originally three timber-framed cottages, built in the 16th and 17th centuries, this is one of the county's oldest pubs

The Swan's chef Nelson Linhares has achieved recognition by reaching the finals in the Pub Chef awards. Just a glance at the bar menu will tell you that the food here is something special: plates of cold charcuterie or mixed fish vie with warm salads of goats' cheese or duck with raspberry vinaigrette, or smoked ham and Gruyère omelette, prices are £7-£10.

In the restaurant you can opt for the good value weekday set menu, £9.95 for two courses or £12.50 for three, or the enticing à la carte selection. Starters include grilled sardines with tomato and olive sauce and wild rocket, duck liver parfait, cherry and port compote with toasted brioche, king scallops with asparagus, pancetta, pine nuts and basil pesto, langoustine, avocado and apple cocktail or a plate of charcuterie. Next you could have char-grilled sirloin with tarragon confit potatoes, half a duck with pommes Anna, baby veg and a port and cherry sauce, roast rack of lamb on chorizo and shallot potatoes with crisp parsnips, or maybe a brochette of monkfish, salmon and king scallop. For vegetarians there is herb pancake stuffed with Mediterranean veg and mozzarella with garlic and tomato sauce. Mouth-watering desserts, £4-£5, include orange and lemon tart with meringue and lemon sorbet, and raspberry and white chocolate cheesecake with raspberry coulis. ★ Q ❀ S V C

PENN STREET

☆ Hit or Miss

HP7 0PX

- Penn Street signed off A404 between Amersham and High Wycombe
- Daily 11am (12pm Sun)-11pm
- Mon-Sat 12-2.30pm, 6.45-9.30pm; Sun 12-8pm
- T (01494) 713109
- F (01494) 718010
- E camra@hitormissinn.co.uk
- W www.hitormissinn.co.uk
- Badger K&B Sussex, Best; guest
- Eclectic menu of dishes with a difference on both main menu and specials board
- Warm and friendly traditional pub

A cooking team of five creates culinary excitement starting on the specials board with beetroot and spring onion stir fry, foie gras terrine or smoked trout with warm eggs. Main course specials might be fresh tuna salad niçoise, gammon with pineapple sauce, trout stuffed with lemon grass, poussin with tarragon sauce, beef bourguignon with mash, seabass with garlic and cream sauce or wild boar and apple sausages with sauerkraut and juniper. Interesting veggie choices include Moroccan couscous with plums and onions, potato rosti with grilled halloumi stack or fettuccine with mushroom and spinach.

But the mark of a good restaurant is a main menu as tempting as the specials, and here it is no Hit or Miss affair. Sandwiches and baked potatoes are filled with lemon and thyme chicken and bacon, home-cooked ham with Cheddar, or roast pepper and Greek feta. Starters include home-made soups, veggie mezze platter, trio of cured salmon with samphire or taleggio and caramelised onion on walnut bread, £4-£6. Main courses range from roast cod and mussels with vanilla and saffron sauce to glazed pork tenderloin with squash champ and cider sauce, both £11.95. Chips are home made and so are the children's chicken nuggets and ham. ★ Q ❀ S V ♿ P C

BROUGHTON

Crown

Bridge Road, PE28 3AY

- ▶ 2 miles off A141 between Huntingdon and Warboys
- ☼ Tue-Fri 12-3pm, 6-11pm; Sat & Sun 12-11pm (10.30pm Sun)
- Tue-Fri 12-2pm, 6.30-9pm; Sat 12-2pm, 6-9.30pm; Sun 12-3pm, 7-9pm
- T (01487) 824428
- E simon@thecrownbroughton.co.uk
- W www.thecrownbroughton.co.uk
- City of Cambridge Hobson's Choice; Greene King IPA; Potton Shambles; guests
- ☺ Modern British
- Open-plan pub with tiled floor, owned by village residents

The Crown was saved by village residents who raised the money to buy it in 2000 and carried out a major revamp and renovation project. Today chef/licensee Simon Cadge cooks with local, seasonal produce offering a two-course lunch menu for £10 from Wednesday to Saturday, plus an a la carte. Daily specials might be cod in beer batter with hand-cut chips and pease pudding, rare breed pork and Stilton sausages with mash and red onion gravy, slow-braised blade of beef with savoy cabbage and wild mushrooms, or Thai spiced fishcake with lemon butter sauce, £8.50-£11.50.

The regular menu changes monthly, perhaps starting with ham hock and parsley terrine or tempura tuna with nori seaweed, £6, followed by goats' cheese, red onion and spinach tart, Barnsley chop with boulangère potatoes, roast corn-fed chicken and sweet potato, honey-glazed pork belly with parsnip purée or smoked haddock topped with a poached egg on spring onion mash, priced from £8.50-£10.50. For Sunday lunch choose from roast rib of Scottish beef or apricot chicken among the main courses, preceded by home-made soup, or venison salad, and followed by desserts such as bramley apple and sultana crumble, £15 for two courses. **Q** ❀ **S V** ♿ P **C**

CAMBRIDGE

Kingston Arms

33 Kingston Street, CB1 2NU

- ▶ Off Mill Road
- ☼ Mon-Thu 12-2.30pm, 5-11pm; Fri-Sun 12-11pm (10.30pm Sun)
- Mon-Thu 12-2pm, 6-9pm; Fri-Sun 12-3pm, 6-9pm
- T (01223) 319414
- E director.kingston.arms@ntlworld.com
- W www.kingston-arms.co.uk
- Crouch Vale Brewers Gold; Elgood's Black Dog Mild; Hop Back Summer Lightning; Oakham JHB; Taylor Landlord; guests
- ☺ Gastropub serving modern British and European dishes
- Bustling pub serving 10 real ales and no keg beers stocked

Very much a food-oriented pub and so popular that booking is advisable, all meals are freshly made using local ingredients as much as possible. For example, sausages from the local butcher's with flavours such as Lincoln, Oxford, Cumberland, wild boar with Grand Marnier or pork with honey and ginger are served with gravy made from stock and Entire Stout, and local Maris Piper spuds are mashed with farmhouse butter – and the same applies across the board, with no bought-in ready meals.

Specials vary widely according to fresh fish, organic meat and vegetables available, but could include organic chicken roasted with garlic and tarragon, cod with a horseradish and rosemary crust, leek and potato pie with parsnip chips, or pork and ale pie with home made piccalilli. The ploughman's cheeseboard consists entirely of British farmhouse cheeses such as Lincolnshire Poacher, Stinking Bishop, Ragstone goats' cheese or Colton Bassett Stilton. A special lunchtime menu offers light meals and in summer diners enjoy the enclosed garden. The 10 handpumps serve six regular beers plus a changing range of guest ales. ❀ **V** ⇌ (Cambridge) **C**

ELLINGTON
Mermaid
High Street, PE28 0AB

▶ Three miles from Huntingdon, exit 20 from A14
☼ Daily 12-3pm, 6-11pm (10.30pm Sun)
🍴 Daily 12-2pm, 6-9pm
T (01480) 891450
F (01480) 891381
🍺 Adnams Bitter; Courage Directors; Fuller's London Pride; Taylor Landlord; guests
☺ Home-cooked meals made with fresh local produce on a regularly-changing menu
◉ Archetypal olde village inn, warmed by open fires

Using solely fresh produce from local suppliers, licensee Andrew Burton and his head chef Justin Brown conjure up a limited but tasty menu. Everything, including soups and sauces, is made in the pub kitchen and meals are all cooked to order. There is a daily specials board and dishes to suit vegetarians and fish lovers are always on offer. Hearty sandwiches, £4.50-£6, come with interesting fillings such as grilled Mediterranean vegetables, grilled bacon with goats' cheese, or a 5oz steak with fried mushrooms and onion.

Starters, £5.50 or under, might include soup of the day, potted shrimp cocktail, stuffed flatcap mushrooms, chicken liver, sage and brandy pâté or smoked salmon bruschetta. To follow you could choose king prawn curry, grilled duck breast with orange sauce, char-grilled vegetable and pasta al fredo, or pub favourites such as home-made steak and kidney pie, freshly battered cod and chips or pork and leek bangers and mash. All main courses cost less than a tenner except the fillet steak with peppercorn sauce, £15.95, with fries, veg or salad extra. There is usually cheese and three or four puddings to choose from (again all home made of course), such as crème brûlée, sticky chocolate pudding or Baileys and banana bread and butter pud, all around £4.

★ ♔ Q ❀ S V 🍺 ♿ C

EYNESBURY
Chequers Inn
St Mary's Street, PE19 2TA

☼ Mon-Sat 10.30am-2.30pm, 7-11pm; Sun 12-2pm (closed eve)
🍴 Mon-Sun 12-2pm, 7-9.30pm (not Sun)
T (01480) 472116
E ann@thechequers.co.uk
W www.thechequers.co.uk
🍺 Beer range varies
☺ Superior food from sandwiches and bar snacks to classy a la carte
◉ 16th-century inn with a wealth of beams and wood panelling

Tempting and imaginative food, albeit at restaurant prices, is served in a pub that regards itself as primarily a restaurant. On the sandwich menu the cheapest round is egg and cress at £4, rising to £7.25 for smoked salmon with cucumber or a toasted open sandwich of pancetta, asparagus and melted Brie, all with salad, red onion and potato crisps. In the bar you'll pay £10.95 for home-cooked ham with two fried eggs and hand cut chips, £8.95 for omelette, chips and salad (Stilton, potato and onion or cheese and asparagus), or £9.95 for bangers and mash – local Cambridgeshire sausage with onion gravy, creamed potato and cabbage. Or choose from poached naturally-smoked haddock with two poached eggs and minted peas, grilled lamb and mint burgers with new potatoes and vegetables, a cold meat platter with real chips and pickles, or grilled sirloin steak with all the trimmings. Salad bowls include ham with apple, warm potatoes and cider dressing.

In the restaurant delights such as pigeon breasts wrapped in bacon in peppercorn sauce, poached sea bass with lemon and basil beurre blanc, and grilled lamb cutlets glazed in honey with red wine and juniper berry jus are on a menu priced from £10.95-£21.50. A daily special two-course menu is £15. Coeliac and vegetarian dishes are a speciality.

★ ♔ Q ❀ V ♿ ⇌ (St Neots) P ✂ ▯ 👪 C

GODMANCHESTER
Exhibition
2-3 London Road, PE29 2HZ

- ▶ Just off A14 near Huntingdon
- ☼ Daily 11.30am (12 Sun)-3pm, 5 (7pm Sun)-11pm
- Daily 12-2.15pm, 6 (7pm Sun)-9.15pm
- T (01480) 459134
- F (01480) 431512
- Fuller's London Pride; Greene King IPA; guest
- ☺ Freshly-cooked European and modern British menu
- Combination of pub, restaurant and bar

Clearly a pub not afraid to make an exhibition of its food, there are some nice touches on a menu featuring sterling British food with Mediterranean touches. You could almost make a meal of the side orders – spinach with garlic oil, rosemary and rock salt roast potatoes, mixed salad with balsamic vinaigrette, marinated Italian olives, vegetables in herb butter, tomato and shallot salad and real home made chips.

To start, duck and chicken liver terrine with home made chutney or prawn and crab tian with gazpacho sauce are just two of the choices. Main meals come with vegetables and include rump of lamb on Mediterranean polenta bake with rosemary gravy, duck breast glazed with orange and soy sauce with pak choi and fondant potatoes, pasta of the day, baked cod with chorizo and Provençal vegetables, pan fried calf's liver flambéed in balsamic vinegar with mash and wilted spinach, baked corn-fed chicken wrapped in pancetta on linguine with wild mushroom sauce, halibut with spinach, tomato purée, Muscat grapes and cream sauce, or butterflied pork loin stuffed with Stilton on spinach and parsnip purée, or butternut squash with parsnip soufflé. Prices range from £8.95-£14.85.

S V P C

HEMINGFORD GREY
Cock
47 High Street, PE28 9BJ

- ▶ Off A14, follow signs for St Ives
- ☼ Daily 11.30am-3pm, 6-11pm; Sun 12-4pm, 6.30-10.30pm
- Mon-Sat 12-2.30pm, 7-9.30pm; Sun 12-3pm, 6.30-8.30pm
- T (01480) 463609
- F (01480) 461747
- E ot@cambscuisine.com
- W www.cambscuisine.com
- Elgood's Black Dog Mild; Wolf Golden Jackal; Woodforde's Wherry; guest
- ☺ Well presented English and European
- Stylish village restaurant and pub close to Hemingford Grey Manor

Voted CAMRA local real ale pub 2003, the Cock uses seasonal fresh produce with great flair – its home-made sausages are famous. Dishes change constantly, fresh fish is delivered daily, and there is a good selection of veggie dishes. A light lunch menu with two courses for a bargain £8.95 offers home-made soup, pear and Stilton tart with roasted almonds or potted beef with beetroot marmalade, main dishes such as thyme tagliatelle with pistachios and goats' cheese, seafood crumble or game pie followed by apricot and passion fruit bavarois. Sandwiches, around £5, include sausage and roast onion or char-grilled aubergine with mozzarella.

Starters on the main menu include baked duck parcel with sweet and sour cucumber or roast onion and fennel salad with sage and hazelnut pesto, followed by leek, spinach and mushroom timbale, chicken supreme with grain mustard potato cake, leek and cider sauce, duck breast with confit potatoes, calf's liver with savoy cabbage, pancetta and chestnuts, prices from £10.95-£13.95. A set Sunday menu, main course £10.95, two courses £14.95, offers plenty of choice including roast shorthorn beef, slow roast shoulder of lamb with port or roast cod with apple and thyme mash.

★ Q S V P C

HUNTINGDON
Old Bridge
High Street, PE29 3TQ

▶ Off inner ring road, by the river
☼ Daily 11am-11pm
🍴 Daily 12-2.30pm, 7-10pm
T (01480) 424300
F (01480) 411017
E oldbridge@huntsbridge.co.uk
W www.huntsbridge.com
🍺 Adnams Bitter; guests
☺ Exciting, award-winning menu bringing Mediterranean touches to English dishes in two no-smoking restaurants
◉ Smart hotel and restaurant with a lively real ale bar

The menus here are imaginative and extensive, with dishes created by a team of some 16 chefs who make everything themselves from bread to pasta and the black pudding for breakfast. The menu changes monthly but includes light dishes such as Caesar salad with char-grilled chicken, risotto of the day and Serrano ham with piquillo peppers. Traditional favourites are fish and chips with pease pudding of split peas and bacon and Cotswold pork sausages with onion and Dijon mustard sauce. Sandwiches are priced from £5 for Montgomery cheddar with home-made pickle to £8.50 for steak on hot ciabatta.

Typical first courses might be Asian salad of sweet roast potato with pickled ginger, soy and sesame, pumpkin agnolotti with marjoram and parmesan, Portland crab with potato gnocchi or warm salad of pheasant confit, priced from £5.75-£7.50. Main dishes include baked hake with sprouting broccoli and tapenade, daily changing fresh fish from Cornwall, shank of Aberdeen beef with carrots, cavolo nero, tarragon and polenta, roast corn-fed Goosnargh chicken with puy lentils and smoky bacon, and braised shoulder of Cornish lamb with cumin potatoes and red cabbage, priced from £9.95-£14.95. For pudding there is steamed ginger sponge with fresh egg custard.
S V (Huntingdon) P C

LONGSTOWE
Red House
134 Old North Road, CB3 7UT

▶ On A1198 between Arrington and Caxton
☼ Mon 5.30-11pm; Tue-Fri 12-3pm, 5.30-11pm; Sat & Sun 12-11pm (10.30pm Sun)
🍴 Mon 6-9pm; Tue-Fri 12-2pm, 6-9pm; Sat & Sun 12-9.30pm
T (01954) 718480
E willisrdhs@aol.com
W www.theredhousepub.co.uk
🍺 Greene King IPA, Morland Original; Wychwood Fiddler's Elbow; guest
☺ British cooking, both traditional and modern
◉ Delightful country pub, once part of a working farm, where drinkers and diners feel equally at home

A simple lunchtime menu in the bar offers a choice of freshly-cut sandwiches from home-cooked beef to cheese and onion on farmhouse or granary bread, as well as filled hot baguettes with salad and chips, ploughman's of Brie, Cheddar, Stilton and pâté, warm chicken and ginger salad, and pizza portions. Favourites from the evening menu such as four Cumberland sausages with mash and onion gravy and Cajun chicken with salsa sauce are also available, as well as curry, pie, pasta and vegetarian dishes of the day and grilled T-bone, sirloin and fillet steaks.

On the evening menu in the restaurant expect fish in beer batter, beef and ale pie, locally-made sausages of the week with bubble and squeak and fresh vegetables, baked salmon with herb crust and watercress Hollandaise, chicken supreme filled with spinach and sun dried tomato mousseline, pot roast corn fed chicken with mushrooms and parsnips in a thyme broth, braised lamb shank with potato dumplings, confited duck leg with cabbage and bacon, seared swordfish, pork in apple and cider sauce, whole Cajun roasted sea bass and chicken Caesar salad. Prices range from £10.95-£14.95. ★ S V P C

SPALDWICK

George

High Street, PE28 0TD

▶ Just off A14 near Huntingdon
☼ Daily 11am-11pm
Ⓨ Daily 12-2.30pm, 6-9.30pm
T (01480) 890293
F (01480) 896847
Adnams Broadside; Fuller's London Pride; Theakston Old Peculier
☺ Traditional British dishes with lovely touches and a Mediterranean twist
Original beams and fireplaces blend with contemporary decor

Freshly-made meals here are guaranteed to tempt carnivores and vegetarians alike. At lunchtime starters include home-made soup with artisan breads, and maybe caramelised onion and goats' cheese tart, timbale of fresh crab with guacamole, or crispy duck salad with plum dressing, priced from £3.95-£6.95. Main dishes might include pork and ale sausages with mash, buttered spinach and red onion gravy, battered cod with fat chips and pea purée, smoked haddock fish cakes topped with a soft poached egg, beef and ale stew with herb dumplings, home-made lamb and coriander burger with tomato relish, or wild mushroom and tarragon risotto with parmesan crackling. Prices range from £8.95-£9.95. The George ploughman's with Neal's Yard cheeses, home made pâté and breads is £7.95.

In the evening main courses include salmon en croute with cheese fondue and lobster sauce, roast pheasant breast with savoy cabbage, bread sauce and pancetta, corn-fed duck with home-made black pudding and Normandy red cabbage, char-grilled yellow fin tuna loin, haunch of venison with Montgomery's rarebit and char-grilled rib eye steak with home-made ketchup. Prices are from £9.95-£15.95. To finish, pear and almond tart or blackberry and apple crumble with unpasteurised Jersey cream are just two tempting choices.

Q V P C

STILTON

Bell Inn

Great North Road, PE7 3RA

▶ Half a mile S of jct16 A1(M)
☼ Daily 12-2.30pm, 6-11pm
Ⓨ Daily 12-2pm, 6.30-9.30pm
T (01733) 241066
F (01733) 245173
E reception@thebellstilton.co.uk
W www.thebellstilton.co.uk
Fuller's London Pride; Greene King IPA; Oakham JHB; guest
☺ Traditional British with modern touches
Stone-floored village bar with roaring log fire; beamed, award-winning restaurant

Stilton cheese was born at this historic inn on the old Great North Road, so naturally it appears on the tempting menu. For instance, you can start with Stilton and watercress soup or Stilton pâté with toasted hazelnuts followed by slow braised English lamb in Oakham JHB with Stilton dumplings, and end with glazed Stilton cheesecake with mulled wine figs, or simply a plate of famous Long Clawson Stilton with home-made plum bread. Otherwise the bar menu offers starters of game and smoked bacon terrine, parmesan and leek risotto, or the Bell Inn prawn cocktail, prices from £4.95-£6.95.

Main courses include coq au vin with spicy chorizo, rainbow trout filled with cod mousse, roast cod fillet with smoked bacon, peas and black pudding mash, or the massive Bell Inn mixed grill with sirloin and gammon steak, lamb chop, sausage, liver and kidney with roast vegetables. Dishes for vegetarians include tomato and goats' cheese penne or seared artichokes on crushed new potato cake, prices from £8.95-£15.50.

The three-course restaurant menu at £25.95 includes pan-fried sweetbread and calf's liver among the starters, followed by char-grilled fillet of English beef, roast guinea fowl, or pair of baked, stuffed quails. To finish choose from afters such as prune and Armagnac tart.

★ Q S V P C

ST IVES
☆ Oliver Cromwell
13 Wellington Street, PE27 5AZ

▶ Along the quay from the bridge
☼ Daily 11am-11pm
(🍴) Mon-Sat 12-3pm
T (01480) 465601
E olivercromwell@waitrose.com
🍺 Adnams Bitter; Oakham JHB; Woodforde's Wherry; guests
☺ Honest, traditional cooking with some ethnic details using local produce
◉ Congenial, wood-panelled pub popular with locals and diners

With meat and vegetables sourced locally, and fish delivered fresh by van twice a week, everything is cooked in house including desserts. A wide choice of at least nine specials daily might include delightful traditional dishes such as beef stew and dumplings, Lancashire hot pot, steak and kidney pudding or pie, fresh haddock in beer batter, chicken and mushroom pie or fish pie topped with mash. The ethnic touches could be butternut squash with chilli and tomato sauce on penne, prosciutto wrapped around mozzarella with rocket pesto, sea bass with toasted pine nuts and rosemary dressing or Thai green curry with rice. Prices are a modest £5.25-£6.50, with sea bass £9.50.

The lunch menu offers a smashing range of baguettes, tortilla wraps and sandwiches with two dozen fillings from cheese with black pudding or Stilton and bacon to tuna, sweetcorn and mayonnaise and sausage and fried onion. Hot meals include sizzling steak and chicken fajitas, freshly made omelettes, sausage and mash with onion gravy, home-made soup with a roll, ham, egg and chips or chilli con carne with rice. Cheese ploughman's and chicken and bacon ploughman's come with mango chutney. Prices range from £4.75-£7.25. Desserts might be tiramisu, sticky toffee pudding or blackberry and apple pie with ice cream or cream. ★ ❀ S V ♿ ♣ ♠ ⚟ 👪 C

ASTON
Bhurtpore Inn
Wrenbury Road, CW5 8DQ

▶ In village, 5 miles S of Nantwich via the A530
☼ Mon-Sat 12-2.30pm, 6.30-11pm; Sun 12-10.30pm
(🍴) Mon-Sat 12-2pm, 6.45-9.30pm; Sun 12-9pm
T (01270) 780917
E simonbhurtpore@yahoo.co.uk
🍺 Beer range varies
☺ Good variety of freshly-cooked dishes on an imaginative, changing menu
◉ Multi-roomed, village free house with a restaurant, family-run for many years

Despite its name, the Bhurtpore is definitely not a curry house, although the landlord's home-made curries do appear regularly on the menu. The pub offers an exciting variety of home-cooked dishes from carefully sourced produce. Sausages and game come from nearby Maynard's farm shop (one of Rick Stein's 'food heroes') or Cheerbrook's farm, while ice cream is supplied by the wonderfully named Snugbury's of Nantwich. There is no set menu; the dishes are simply chalked up on boards and may be rubbed off several times during a busy evening, usually to be replaced by a similar dish. So if the red mullet stuffed with sun dried tomato and pine nuts runs out, monkfish in red wine sauce with mushrooms and bacon might take its place.

Tempting starters might include king prawns in crème fraîche with tarragon under a cheese and crumb topping, sautéed field mushrooms in a herb pancake with Shropshire blue sauce, or honey and mustard glazed chicken salad with pine nuts, goats' cheese and balsamic dressing, all around a fiver. Mains, £9.50-£13.50, could be lamb fillet in pastry with port and cranberry sauce or char-grilled fillet of pork in green peppercorn sauce, while seasonal desserts include spiced raisin and ginger pudding and raspberry meringue roll.
♛ Q ❀ S V 🍺 ♿ ≈ (Wrenbury) ♣ ♠ Ⓟ ⚟ C

BURLEYDAM
Combermere Arms
Near Whitchurch, SY13 4AT

▶ Take Newcastle turn off A525 between Whitchurch and Nantwich
☼ Mon-Sat 11.30am-11pm; Sun 12-10.30pm
🍴 Daily 12-10.30pm (9.30pm Sun)
T (01948) 871223
F (01948) 661371
E combermere.arms@brunningandprice.co.uk
W www.combermerearms-burleydam.co.uk
🍺 Flowers Original; Hanby Drawwell; Hydes Mild; Robinson's Cumbria Way
☺ High quality, varied menu to suit all tastes
◙ Well preserved 16th-century pub with outside seating

The pub company Brunning and Price owns just 12 pubs in the north west of England and the Combermere Arms exemplifies its commitment to preserving the character of its inns and the promotion of real ale. The attention to detail extends to the kitchen which provides a menu that changes daily to appeal to all tastes, offering dishes with an adventurous twist. Not every pub would be brave enough to list grilled mackerel fillets with pickled cucumber as a starter, however if you prefer you can opt for the home-made soup or local black pudding served with spring onion mash and mustard sauce. All starters are priced under £6.

On the main menu you might find straightforward lamb hotpot with savoy cabbage, £9.95, or an unusual vegetarian choice of roasted fennel and pear quiche. The puddings are all somewhat individual, too – the lemon meringue pie comes served with mango sorbet. If you do not want a full meal, 'Lighter Things' covers pasta dishes and tasty snacks – at £6.95 the lamb's kidneys with wild mushrooms on granary toast sounds tempting. Sandwiches are less than £5, with interesting fillings such as toasted Welsh goats' cheese with pepper and basil, or rare roast beef with tomato and beer mustard.

★ V P C

CHESTER
☆ Albion
4 Park Street, CH1 1RN

▶ Beneath city walls between Newgate and river
☼ Mon-Thu 12-3pm, 5-11pm; Fri & Sat 12-11pm; Sun 12-3pm, 7-10.30pm
🍴 Daily 12-2pm, 5-8pm (6-8.30pm Sat)
T (01244) 340345
E mike@albioninn.freeserve.co.uk
W www.albioninnchester.co.uk
🍺 Banks's Original; Jennings Cumberland Bitter; Taylor Landlord; guests
☺ 'Mum's comfort food, no chips, no fry-ups'
◙ Victorian corner pub dedicated to the Great War, 1914-18, with three bars

Longstanding landlord Mike Mercer has created a time warp pub and much of the menu, entitled Trench Rations, is the sort of food the army might have dreamed of marching on. All produce is sourced from local and regional suppliers including Staffs oatcakes, Bury black puds, Cumberland sausage from Penrith, fish from Fleetwood and bread from a small baker's. The set menu offers boiled gammon with pease pudding and parsley sauce, savoury minced beef and tatties, Cumberland sausage and apple sauce with caramelised onions, lamb's liver, bacon and onions in cider gravy, cottage pie with cheese, leek and potato topping and pickled red cabbage or McConickie's corned beef hash. And finally haggis with tatties and fresh veg, all £6.95.

Snacks include Tunstall tortillas – Staffordshire oatcakes filled with haggis and melted cheese, black pudding with potato and bacon, mature cheddar with ham and leeks, all £3.90. At lunchtime there are Great British Butties of home cooked ham, turkey and stuffing or cheese and Branston. Desserts can include chocolate torte made with Green and Black's organic chocolate, rice pudding with lemongrass and cinnamon, or pannacotta with caramelised fresh oranges. Rich fruitcake is served traditionally with Cheshire cheese, and there is an all-English cheeseboard.

★ Q S V

FADDILEY
Thatch Inn
Wrexham Road, CW5 8JE

- ▶ On A534 Nantwich-Wrexham approx 1.5 miles from Llangollen Canal
- Mon-Sat 11am-11pm; Sun 12-10.30pm
- Mon-Sat 11am-9.30pm; Sun 12-9.30pm
- T (01270) 524223
- F (01270) 924674
- E thethatchinn@aol.com
- Marston's Pedigree; Taylor Landlord; guests
- Traditional pub food with bistro/à la carte influences
- Large country free house with thatched part dating from 15th century

The Thatch in Faddiley offers something for everyone, ranging from traditional pub food to exciting modern dishes, from a classic roast beef dinner to yellow fin tuna in Cajun spices, created from fresh ingredients by a team of three. Fresh fish delivered daily might be wild Scottish salmon, barramundi, grouper, marlin or shark, while seafood could include moules marinière, dressed crab, seared scallops with samphire and coriander. One day's specials included dim sum of Thai seafood spring rolls with fish balls and corn fritter and Irish mussels with white wine and dill, followed by yellow fin tuna on couscous with calamari in batter, grilled venison steak, duck breast with hoi sin and black bean vegetable stir fry, or pasta Milanaise.

The set menu opens with their special honeyed pork ribs, roast chicken liver and pork pâté and freshly made soup. Main courses range from the daily roast with vegetables such as braised red cabbage and tarragon carrots, pie of the day with home-made short crust pastry, braised liver and bacon and giant filled Yorkies, all £7.95. There are grilled steaks and 'tastes from afar' such as Thai red curry. An ice cream menu of Cheshire farm ice cream includes forest fruit fool, and there are home-made cheesecakes, rice pud and spotted dick.

★ Q S V P C

FARNDON
Farndon Arms
High Street, CH3 6PU

- ▶ Off A534 5 miles from Chester
- Daily 11am-3pm, 5-11pm
- Daily 11am-3pm, 5-10pm
- T (01829) 270570
- F (01829) 271428
- E info@farndonarms.com
- W www.farndonarms.com
- Worthington's Bitter; guests
- Award-winning traditional and modern cooking
- Black and white timbered building with Victorian style restaurant upstairs

A winner of awards from Chester Young Chef to the national Steak and Kidney Pie competition, the pub aims to feature locally sourced produce on its menu, from gourmet local bangers to Cholmondley Castle Gloucester Olde Spot black pudding. Dishes on the main menu include Welsh rarebit with home-made tomato sauce, potted Cheshire blue cheese with pear soup, twice baked local cheese soufflé with onion marmalade, its famous banana, bacon and blue cheese starter and – really cute this – mini Sunday lunch of roast beef rib in a little Yorkshire pud, all around £4.

A section on the menu wittily entitled 'stolen from other restaurants?' includes minted lamb with red wine gravy, chicken layered with pâté in Madeira sauce, seared Black country pork with black pudding and apple cake, bangers with mash, onion and red wine gravy, calf's liver with crushed potato and balsamic dressing, the Desperate Dan pie of beef in beer with mushrooms, bacon and potato, or honey roast duck with apple sauce and stuffing, priced £8.50-£10.50. Seafood includes spaghetti with lemon pepper tiger prawns and Parmesan, cod and seabass layered with wild mushroom ragout, halibut steak in garlic butter with white wine and prawns, and a proper paella of saffron rice, chicken and seafood, prices from £8.50-£10.25.

Q S V P C

OVER PEOVER
Dog Inn
Well Bank Lane, WA16 8UP

- Near Knutsford, leave A50 at Whipping Stocks Inn, continue for 2 miles
- Mon-Fri 11.30am-3pm, 4.30-11pm; Sat 11.30am-11pm; Sun 12-10.30pm
- Mon-Sat 12-2.30pm, 6-9pm; Sun 12-8.30pm
- T (01625) 861421
- F (01625) 864800
- E info@doginn-overpeover.co.uk
- W www.doginn-overpeover.co.uk
- Hydes Bitter; Moorhouses Black Cat; Weetwood Best Bitter
- Traditional menu of freshly-cooked dishes with a good selection of snacks
- Comfortable bar where games are played by the open fire and two dining rooms

A regular entry in CAMRA's Good Beer Guide, this free house hosts an annual beer festival. An extensive 'lite bites' menu will assuage many a drinker's appetite, with sandwiches, hot baguettes served with chips, filled jacket spuds, ploughman's, salads or simple dishes such as the daily curry or gourmet sausage with mash. For diners there is a good choice of starters, £3-£6, such as egg Benedict, black pudding stack (local pudding layered with bacon and a mustard dressing), sticky chilli prawns, smoked salmon salad or Manx kippers.

The 'Main Event' lists mostly traditional English dishes, £9-£16, such as lamb shank slowly braised in red wine sauce with root veg and mash, rib eye steak, liver and bacon or prime fillet steak. A more unusual option is the freshly-made pancakes, filled with either smoked salmon and prawns or leek, Stilton and mushroom. Vegetarians may also enjoy spaghetti primavera with garden veg and garlic bread. Fish dishes include haddock and prawn au gratin, salmon fillet and halibut steak on spinach. The chef sources meat and game locally, while herbs are grown in the pub garden.

S V C

WARMINGHAM
Bear's Paw
School Lane, CW11 3QN

- Village centre, 4 miles N of Crewe
- Mon-Fri 5-11pm; Sat 12-11pm; Sun 12-10.30pm
- Mon-Fri 6-9pm (9.30pm Fri); Sat 12-9.30pm; Sun 12-9pm
- T (01270) 526317
- F (01270) 526465
- E enquiries@thebearspaw.co.uk
- W www.thebearspaw.co.uk
- Tetley Bitter; guests
- Award-winning eclectic mix from snacks to à la carte
- Imposing hotel built in the 1870s by the Earl of Crewe with 12 en suite bedrooms

Hoegaarden beer batter coating the cod sounds tempting, and there are plenty more interesting options on a menu both trad and modern. Traditional pub meals include steak and real ale pie with a suet pastry topping, roast Mediterranean vegetables with pasta and fresh pesto, Cumberland sausage with mash and caramelised red onion gravy, tikka-style marinated chicken, roast of the day with all the trimmings, prices £7.95-£8.95.

On the 'gourmet' menu you might start with tempura battered prawns, wild mushrooms flamed in brandy, hot smoked duck breast on rice noodle cake with sweet chilli jam, bacon and black pudding salad, priced £4.95-£6.25. Main dishes include loin of wild boar on potato rosti with wild mushroom and brandy sauce, pork fillet stuffed with black pudding in port reduction, pheasant breast with celery and leek stuffing, red mullet on crab mash, barramundi fish on chive mash with chilli oil, prices from £11.95 rising to £15.95 for fillet steak stuffed with Stilton. Veggie choices include sweet peppers stuffed with wild mushrooms topped with Brie and stuffed pasta parcels on fresh tomato and mascarpone sauce. The snack menu includes filled baguettes and jacket potatoes.

S V C

WISTASTON
Rising Sun
Middlewich Road, CW2 8SB

▶ On A530, 2 miles from Crewe centre towards Chester
☼ Mon-Sat 10am-11pm; Sun 12-10.30pm
🍴 Daily 11am (12 Sun) – 10pm (opens for coffee and snacks at 10am)
T (01270) 213782
F (01270) 256710
🍺 Beer range varies
☺ Varied menu based on traditional home cooking
◉ Although close to Crewe centre, this is a proper country pub with log fires, polished brass and candles

Staff at the Rising Sun take a lot of care in providing menus to suit all their customers, in particular that often neglected group, vegetarians. The soups are freshly made and only use vegetarian ingredients. All vegetables served as side dishes are freshly prepared, changing every day with respect to the seasons, so in winter you will find delicious honey roast parsnips and swede on your plate. The traditional Sunday lunch is always accompanied by a nut roast alternative. All sections of the menu – snacks, starters and main courses – have a selection of vegetarian dishes but, having said that, one of the most popular dishes on the menu is duck breast with braised red cabbage, cooked with shallots, onions, mushrooms, green beans, bacon and potatoes. Game is also a seasonal feature here. The majority of meals are prepared freshly in house. Specials change on a two-weekly cycle and usually follow a theme, such as Italian, Best of British or Australian. Fresh fish from a local supplier is always available. The menus are wide ranging, with everything from crusty filled baguettes and jacket spuds through to full meals at reasonable prices. For a Chef & Brewer pub the beer range is surprisingly good, too!

★ Q ❀ S V ♿ P C

WRENBURY
Dusty Miller
CW5 8HG

▶ In the village, next to the canal
☼ Daily 12-3pm, 6.30-11pm
🍴 Daily 12-2pm, 6.30-9.30pm
T (01270) 780537
W www.dustymiller-wrenbury.co.uk
🍺 Robinson's Hatters Light Mild, Old Tom (winter), seasonal
☺ Meals cooked to order featuring plenty of produce from the North West
◉ Converted old mill situated next to the canal and river

Ingredients sourced in the North West, from Bury black pudding to Cumbrian lamb, fish from Fleetwood to wonderful cheese, are turned into something special by chef and landlord Mark Summer and his team. You might start with deep-fried Burland Green cheese with cranberry, Mr Ireland's Bury black pudding with smoked Cheshire bacon and apple relish, locally cured gravadlax or Morecambe Bay potted shrimps, from £3-£5.

More local flavours feature in main dishes such as dressed Manx crab, pasta with rocket in Cheshire cheese sauce and baked chicken stuffed with black pudding. And fresh seabass, cold home-cooked ham, Aberdeen Angus beef with salad and horseradish mayonnaise, or the braised beef cooked in Robinson's Old Tom, a superb cooking beer. Main meals are priced £7.50-£11.95. Light bites include soft rolls from the local craft baker with fillings such as char-grilled Cheshire smoked bacon, Bury black pudding, mushroom, caramelised onion and melted Cheddar or Lancashire pork sausage with egg. A cheese platter can be chosen from Cheshire, creamy Lancashire hand made by the Sandham family, Shropshire Blue, mature Cheddar and Blue Stilton by the Skailes brothers, £6.25 with warm bread, pickle and salad.

★ Q ❀ S V (Wrenbury) P C

BLISLAND
Blisland Inn
The Green, PL30 4JF

- ▶ 2 miles off A30 Launceston-Bodmin, well signed
- ☼ Mon-Sat 11.30am-11pm; Sun 12-10.30pm
- Ⓨ Mon-Sat 12-2.15pm, 6.30-9.30pm; Sun 12-2pm, 7-9pm
- T (01208) 850739
- Beer range varies
- ☺ Simple English country cooking using seasonal ingredients
- National CAMRA Pub of the Year 2000, a delightful rural community pub in a picturesque hamlet on the only village green in Cornwall

The Blisland Inn is best known for its amazing and daily changing selection of real ales, over 2,000 chalked up in ten years. But landlady and cook Margaret Marshall ensures blissful food, too, with delicious, home-cooked meals made to secret recipes - which won't stay secret for much longer because she is writing a little cookery book to sell for charity. Seasonal food made from local produce includes all sorts of pies – steak and ale, game, rabbit, turkey, chicken, lamb, pork with one of their real local ciders, and more, while soup is always home made. Sandwiches are freshly cut including the triple decker crab sarnie, in great demand when fresh crab is in season.

In the evening the menu changes, with steaks and more fresh fish, including the incredible mixed grill – apparently most men opt for the ladies' grill because there are 16 items on the gentlemen's and it requires a giant's appetite to finish it! Gluten-free sausages and burgers are made for the pub by the local butcher. Comfort puddings are home made, too, such as spotted dick and syrup sponge. Six ales are generally on handpump, at least two from Cornish breweries, with exclusives such as Blisland Special and Bulldog.

Q S V C

BOTALLACK
Queen's Arms
TR19 7QG

- ▶ Turn off B3061 at Botallack, pub 100 yards
- ☼ Mon-Fri winter 4-11pm, Sat & summer 12-11pm; Sun 12-10.30pm
- Ⓨ Daily 12-2pm, 6-9pm
- T (01736) 788318
- E petermbeech@btopenworld.com
- W www.queensarms.info
- Beer range varies, all Cornish
- ☺ Bar and a la carte meals using local produce
- Welcoming, 300-year-old Cornish granite pub in mining area

Local game is popular at the Queen's Arms, including pheasant shot by the landlord who is also the chef. With locally-made venison sausages and plenty of fish from Newlyn and St Ives on the specials board, as well as fresh lobster and crab in season, you will be spoilt for choice. This traditional English fare is occasionally enlivened with something more exotic such as kangaroo or ostrich steaks. Half a pint of prawns is among the starters, with home-made soup of the day, home-cured gravadlax, locally-smoked duck and goats' cheese tartlet.

Fish dishes include a plate of three Cornish fish – bass, John Dory and sole – with white wine, dill and cream sauce, moules marinière, large fillet of cod in batter, or fillets of seabass with white wine, fennel and cream, priced from £8.50-£14.95. Other main meals are breast of duck with red wine and cherry tomato sauce, lamb shank with red wine and mushroom gravy, venison with chestnut mushroom and shallot sauce, home-made lamb curry or chicken balti with rice and naan bread, or strips of chicken pan fried with shallots, mushrooms, garlic, tarragon and port, prices from £8.50-£14.95. The vegetarian menu offers home-made tomato, chive and mushroom pasta, nut and lentil roast, and over 30 types of bean in a spicy sauce.

★ Q V P C

EDMONTON
Quarryman Inn
Wadebridge, PL27 7JA

- ▶ A39 opposite Royal Cornwall showground
- ☼ Daily 12-11pm (10.30pm Sun)
- Daily 12-2.30pm, 6-9pm
- T (01208) 816444
- F (01208) 815674
- E quarrymaninn@hotmail.com
- W www.quarrymaninn.co.uk
- Sharp's and Skinner's full range; guests
- ☺ Specialising in steaks and fresh sea food using local produce
- Popular free house with beamed public and lounge bars, simple furnishings

Cornish haddock fillets in real ale batter as well as slow braised beef in ale and onion gravy are among the specials at the Quarryman, run by the same family for the past 14 years, where you can eat and drink al fresco in an unusual courtyard setting. Other specials with a beer connection include home-made steak, kidney and ale pie or rich onion and ale soup with Cornish Yarg cheese melt. A popular cider dish is west country loin of pork on the bone with cider, whole grain mustard and cream sauce. Examples of fish dishes might be local plaice fillets stuffed with Cornish oysters in Vermouth cream sauce, or baked wild seabass.

The regular menu features those popular steaks served char-grilled on a sizzling platter with mushrooms, tomatoes, onion rings and chips, fillet, sirloin, rib eye, rump and 16oz T-bone, priced from £12.50-£16.50. Other dishes include gammon steak with pineapple, chips and salad or wholetail scampi in batter. At lunchtime freshly made sandwiches range from roast local sirloin or home-baked gammon to Cornish crab or Davidstow mature Cheddar with salad and crisps, £3.50-£4.90, as well as baguettes and bagels stuffed with smoked bacon and melted Cornish blue cheese or smoked salmon with prawns and fresh crab. Guest beers are from breweries nationwide.

Q S V ♣ P C

GUNWALLOE
Halzephron Inn
TR12 7QB

- ▶ 4 miles S of Helston off A3083
- ☼ Daily 11am-2.30pm, 6.30-11pm
- Daily 12-2pm, 7-9pm
- T (01326) 240406
- F (01326) 241442
- E halzephroninn@gunwalloe1.fsnet.co.uk
- Halzephron Gold; St Austell Tribute; Sharp's Doom Bar, Own, Special
- ☺ Mainly traditional English
- Cliff-top free house built 500 years ago, once the haunt of smugglers

Just 300 yards from the South Cornwall footpath, the Halzephron is the only pub on the coastal route between Mullion and Porthleven, so walkers will be cheered to find such good food and ale. The former Cornwall Dining Pub of the Year offers different specials at lunchtime and evening as well as set menus. Specials may include starters such as seafood chowder with aioli, home-made mushroom soup, warm pigeon breast salad or smoked duck with wild mushroom risotto, priced £3.95-£6.50.

Main course specials include char-grilled beef fillet on bubble and squeak with Madeira sauce, pan-fried salmon and asparagus on fresh pasta, roast cod on potato purée with wild mushrooms and bacon, lamb ragout in port wine or chicken chasseur with vegetables, prices from £8.95 up to £15.50 for steak. Veggie specials are especially good – maybe Provençale risotto in puff pastry with tomato and basil sauce. Main menu starters include pâté of the day with home-made toasted brioche and trio of smoked, kiln and gravadlax salmon. Main meals range from the home-baked gammon ploughman's to fresh crab salad platter with home-made rolls, tempura battered hake, cod in beer batter with plaice, salmon and scampi and home-made tartare sauce, priced £7.40-£13.60.

★ Q S V P C

LOSTWITHIEL

Globe Inn

3 North Street, PL22 0EG

- ▶ Stone's throw from old medieval bridge
- ☼ Mon-Sat 12-2.30pm, 6 (Fri 5)-11pm; Sun 12-2.30pm, 7-10.30pm
- 🍴 Mon-Sat 12-2.30pm, 6.30-9pm; Sun 12-2.30pm, 7-10.30pm
- T (01208) 872501
- F (01208) 872559
- E will@globeinn.com
- W www.globeinn.com
- Sharp's Doom Bar; Skinner's Betty Stogs; guests
- ☺ Extensive, freshly-cooked menu with emphasis on 'real food'
- Cosy centuries-old free house with B&B

Globe landlord and co-chef Will Erwin says they concentrate on real food, not 'a tiny mound in the middle of a big white plate drizzled with artistic swirls'. Dishes are prepared from real ingredients and served in generous portions, including local game such as pheasant, quail, partridge and rabbit, fish from Fowey, perhaps wild seabass, John Dory or Cornish lobster.

The daily specials board is as long as a menu, and may include beef in real ale with horseradish dumplings, fisherman's pie of Cornish smoked haddock, prawns, fresh salmon and cod with home-made parsley sauce, chicken pie with short crust pastry, monkfish with salmon and scallops in white wine sauce, poacher's pie containing rabbit, pheasant, venison and pigeon. A vegetarian roast mixes puy and green lentils, split peas and spices with port and mushroom sauce, or aubergine and courgette lasagne. Prices range from £8.95-£11.95.

Always on the menu are smoked haddock and spinach fishcakes, Greek salad, wild boar sausages with mash and onion gravy, steak and Stilton pie, a choice of grilled steaks, with prices from £7.95 rising to £15.95 for fillet steak. Fourteen freshly-made desserts and a local cheeseboard complete the picture.

★ Q ❀ S V ♿ (Lostwithiel) ♣ ⅍ C

NANCENOY

☆ Trengilly Wartha

Constantine, TR11 5RP

- ▶ Off B3291, follow signs for Gweek from Constantine
- ☼ Mon-Sat 11am-3pm, 6.30-11pm; Sun 12-3pm, 7-10.30pm
- 🍴 Mon-Sat 12-2.15pm, 6.30-9.30pm; Sun 12-2pm, 7-9.30pm
- T (01326) 340332
- F (01326) 341121
- E reception@trengilly.co.uk
- W www.trengilly.co.uk
- Sharp's Cornish Coaster, Doom Bar; Skinner's Cornish Knocker; guest
- ☺ Award winning, inspirational food
- Hidden away free house overlooking lake

Chef/landlord Mike Maguire fled an advertising career in London 15 years ago to create a real ale free house with great food. He believes in 'sustainable and sympathetic food tourism', making virtually everything on the premises. Crab and fish arrive from the Lady Hamilton on Helford River, vegetables from an organic farm, his home-made marmalade and pickles are sold over the bar. You might get Provençal fish soup with fennel and orange for £4.80, ploughman's of home-made bread, pickles and chutneys with local cheeses from £6.70, tagliolini cipriani of pasta and local crab at £9.80, mixed squash gratin or local sausages with mustard mash and onion gravy at £7.50. In winter, Wednesday is pudding night – home made steak and kidney at £5.50.

In the evening, sample dishes include fish such as smoked haddock fillet with grain mustard mash and poached organic egg, line-caught seabass on Cornish blue cheese risotto, grilled John Dory with saffron corn pancake filled with creamed leeks and lentils, priced £13.80-£15.50. Other main courses might be Cornish fillet steak on a tortilla with Tallegio cheese or English lamb slow braised with haggis mash, £7.50-£15.20.

★ Q ❀ S V ♿ ♣ P ⅍ C

PERRANPORTH
Watering Hole
TR6 0BH

- On Perranporth beach, near car park
- Easter-Oct & Dec 9am-midnight; winter, weekends only
- Daily 9am-10pm
- T (01872) 572888
- F (01872) 571935
- E info@the-wateringhole.co.uk
- W www.the-wateringhole.co.uk
- Skinner's Spriggan, Heligan Honey; guests
- Extensive, wide-ranging menu from fresh fish to sandwiches
- Claimed to be England's only beach bar; modern-design, open-plan pub

Cooks at the Watering Hole are kept busy over the summer, starting with breakfast on the beach at 9am and carrying on right through until 10pm making soups, snacks, sandwiches, curries, Mexican and much else. On the specials board locally-caught fish is especially popular including cod cooked in a batter made with Heligan honey ale and a dash of Cajun spice. You could also find pan-fried fillets of locally-caught bass in a rich wine and seafood sauce, or home-made fish cakes with rich tomato and basil sauce, topped with crispy bacon and parmigiano. Vegetarian meals might be fresh peppers stuffed with broccoli and local Brie topped with rosemary and thyme crumble, or Mexican tart filled with spiced vegetables in a rich white sauce accompanied by coriander rice. Meat dishes could include wild boar with Heligan honey ale and sweet pepper sauce, served with roast potatoes and green beans, mint and coriander kebabs on turmeric rice with sweet chilli sauce and raita or local braised lamb shank in red wine with roast carrots and garlic mash. Apart from food, there are live music sessions at weekends, to which card-carrying CAMRA members gain free admission.

S V C

POLKERRIS
☆ Rashleigh Inn
PL24 2TL

- Signposted off A3082
- Daily 11am-11pm
- Main meals 12-2pm, 6-9pm; snacks 3-5pm
- T (01726) 813991
- F (01726) 815619
- E jonspode@aol.com
- W www.therashleighinnpolkerris.co.uk
- Sharp's Doom Bar; Taylor Landlord; guests
- Fine traditional English cuisine using fresh local produce, fish and game
- Wood and stone free house on an isolated beach with panoramic sea views

A former pilchard boathouse set on the beach in a village once famous for the fish. The pilchards are now returning and are served in summer straight out of the water, simply grilled with fresh herbs. Fish caught by boats in Polkerris Bay are featured on the menu as much as possible including mackerel, plaice, Dover sole, seabass, John Dory, lobster and crab (sometimes made into a fantastic bisque by landlord Jon Spode), and another summer favourite is diver-caught scallops from the Fal cooked in cider. Other specials could include quail stuffed with cranberry and orange, 'boozy' sausages in onion and ale gravy with mash, moules marinière or liver and bacon casserole. Cornish smoked fish and smoked meat, west country cheeses, Cornish ice cream and clotted cream, and ham honey roasted on the premises are all local favourites.

Food on the bar menu includes tempting open salad sandwiches such as home-roast beef with beetroot, horseradish and more at £6.50, three west country cheese ploughman's with crusty bread, apple and pickle at £5.50. Restaurant meals include Gressingham duck breast with Grand Marnier and orange, priced £14.50, plus steaks and at least four vegetarian dishes.

★ Q S V P C

POLPERRO
Blue Peter
Quay Road, PL13 2QZ

- ▶ On quayside, follow road down through village past harbour and fish quay
- Mon-Sat 10.30am-11pm; Sun 12-10.30pm
- Daily 12-2pm
- T (01503) 272743
- F (01503) 273254
- E sjsbluepeter@btinternet.com
- Sharp's Doom Bar, Special; guests
- ☺ Fantastic, locally caught fish and seafood, plus pub specials
- Quaint, friendly, quayside inn, known as the 'last pub before France'

If you are planning to eat at the Blue Peter, skip breakfast and arrive at the door on the dot of noon as lunch is only served until 2pm (this may be extended according to demand). Although some of the dishes may not sound substantial – many come with salad and crusty bread, rather than veg – you certainly get a generous plateful.

The pub specialises, unsurprisingly, in fish and seafood, most of which is landed locally, so the menu changes according to what is available. You may be tempted by Caribbean crab cakes with fresh or Mediterranean vegetables, 'catch of the day' from Polperro's fishermen with a Mediterranean salad, or locally landed sardines, mackerel or scallops, the latter served drizzled with Cornish butter and bacon with crusty bread as an alternative to the salad option. House specials include roast lamb in pitta pockets with mint sauce, Mediterranean salad and feta, red flannel hash (corned beef and char-grilled vegetables), or home made pub favourites such as lamb rogan josh.

For a light meal there are ploughman's (cheese, ham or beef), soups, salads, toasted sandwiches and wraps. The meals are freshly prepared to order by landlady Caroline Steadman and her daughter who purchase all the produce locally. ★ V

RUAN LANIHORNE
King's Head
Roseland Peninsula, TR2 5NX

- ▶ Off B3078, follow signs from bottom of Tregony Hill
- Mon-Sat 12-2pm, 6-11pm; Sun 12-2.30pm, 6-10pm (Nov-Easter, closed Mon)
- Daily 12.30-2pm, 6.30-9pm
- T (01872) 501263
- F (01872) 501263
- E Andrew@law1601.fsnet.co.uk
- Skinner's Betty Stogs, Cornish Knocker and a house beer; guests
- ☺ Wholesome meals made from local produce including fresh fish
- Quiet, traditional pub overlooking Fal estuary, reached by road or the King Harry ferry

Landlord/chef Andrew Law specialises in 'no fuss' cooking, using the best local produce available. All meat is Cornish, including beef hung for 21 days and sausages from award-winning producer Tywardreath. Butter and clotted cream come from a nearby organic Jersey herd, and cheeses from Cornwall and the south west. All fish is fresh, including lemon sole, monkfish, red mullet and scallops.

At lunchtime you might find baguettes with fillings such as smoked bacon topped with melted Cornish Brie, home-made chicken liver pâté with walnut bread, ploughman's with home-made chutney and piccalilli, trio of Tywardreath sausages with olive mash and red onion marmalade, Cornish rump steak and a choice of sandwiches including local crab. In the evening starters include Thai fishcakes of local white fish with lime and Thai fish sauce, or home-cured gravadlax and fresh soup, priced from £4.75-£6. Main courses could be fish pie, Cornish chicken breast filled with Cornish herb and garlic cheese, Zipperback prawns on oriental stir fry, sherried pork loin steak and creamed spinach and Parmesan risotto, priced from £9.75-£12.50. The Sunday roast platter, £11.50, is of Cornish sirloin with home-made Yorkies.
★ Q S V P C

ST AGNES
Driftwood Spars Hotel
Trevaunance Cove, TR5 0RT

- ▶ Off A30, through St Agnes, past church
- Daily 11am-11pm (midnight Fri & Sat)
- Daily 12-2.30pm, 6.30-9.30pm; all day in August
- T (01872) 552428
- F (01872) 553701
- E driftwoodspars@hotmail.com
- W www.driftwoodspars.com
- Driftwood Cuckoo Ale; St Austell HSD; Sharp's Doom Bar, Own; guests
- ☺ Eclectic mix of traditional and modern with plenty of local seafood
- Former mine warehouse with huge log fire and beams, overlooking cove, plus light and airy restaurant, bedrooms with sea views

In every edition of this guide with the hand of redoubtable landlady Jill Treleaven firmly on the tiller, the Driftwood Spars is home to a micro brewery and real food. The menu is created from local produce including eggs from the pub's free range chickens, fish and shellfish landed at Newlyn fish market, sausages from the local butcher, smoked fish from a nearby smokehouse and a Cornish cheeseboard.

Blackboard specials could include steak and Cuckoo Ale pie, char-grilled swordfish with Mediterranean king prawn salsa, crispy duck confit with sticky jasmine rice, pork and leek sausages with onion gravy, or baked flat mushrooms with a garlic crust. Bar food features locally smoked prawns, smoked fish platter, sirloin steak with red onion jam, or the cheeseboard, £4.45, with Cornish Brie, Cornish Blue, Old Smokey and Cornish Tiskey.

In the restaurant maybe start with seared scallops and black pudding or game terrine with cider apple chutney, followed by poached smoked haddock, saffron infused mussels, monkfish with Moroccan spices or pot roast local pheasant with haggis and port. All desserts are home made.

★ S V P C

TREBELLAN
Smugglers' Den Inn
TR8 5PY

- ▶ Off A3075, towards Cubert
- Summer Mon-Sat 11am-11pm; Sun 12-10.30pm; winter 11.30am-2.30pm (not Mon-Wed), 6-11pm; Sun 12-3pm, 6-10.30pm
- Daily 12-2.30pm, 6-9.30pm
- T (01637) 830209
- F (01637) 830580
- E paulsmuggler@aol.com
- W www.thesmugglersden.co.uk
- St Austell, Sharp's and Skinner's ales; guests
- ☺ Traditional English with global influences
- 400-year-old thatched inn down narrow lane with Elizabethan courtyard

Local ingredients are used as far as possible including all meat and sausages from the butcher in Perranporth. Much of the meat is raised locally, and most of the fresh fish comes from fishing boats operating out of St Ives; herbs are grown in the pub garden. Steak, ale and wild mushroom pie or Newlyn cod in beer batter using Smuggler's Ale brewed by Sharp's are two of the most popular dishes.

Starters always include home-made soup and oven-baked bruschetta with field mushrooms in mustard sauce. Main meals include Smuggler's fish pie of fresh and smoked fish, moules marinière, sausages with horseradish mash, ham, egg and chips, bean and vegetable cassoulet or duck confit with parsnip mash as well as locally-smoked chicken or goats' cheese tart salads, priced from £6.95-£10.75. Char-grilled fillet, sirloin, leg of lamb or pork loin steaks cost from £10.94-£13.95. Sandwiches include Cornish crab, Cheddar and chutney, ham with mustard mayonnaise, smoked salmon, or the club sandwich of chicken, bacon, cheese, salad and mayo plus chips, prices £3.95-£6.50. Desserts include waffle baskets with Cornish ice cream. An annual ale and pie festival is held.

★ Q S V P C

BOOT
Boot Inn
CA19 1TG

- Between A595 and A593
- Daily 11am-11pm
- Bar daily 11am-5pm, 6-9pm; restaurant open Thu-Sat

T (019467) 23224
F (019467) 23337
E enquiries@bootinn.co.uk
W www.bootinn.co.uk

- Black Sheep Best Bitter; Jennings Cumberland Ale; guest beers
- Wholesome, home-cooked meals
- Award-winning, cosy, peaceful pub in a superb location

Formerly the Burnmoor Inn, the Boot is a well-known walkers' pub in the Eskdale Valley, surrounded by Scafell Pike, Harter Fell and Great Gable, and offers comfortable overnight accommodation. The daytime menu is supplemented by a good choice of sandwiches and baguettes. On the evening menu starters include creamy garlic mushrooms topped with grilled Stilton and served with tomato bruschetta, mixed Mediterranean salad, Morecambe Bay shrimps tossed in butter with ginger and celery served with home-made tomato chutney, or hot smoked mackerel on horseradish potato cake. To follow there are local lamb chops, Austrian wienerschnitzel, Boot pie of steak and stout in shortcust pastry, vegetable moussaka or daily specials.

When the restaurant is open you can have the good value set menu: £13.50 for two courses, £18.50 for three. The dishes are slightly more adventurous – maybe smoked venison with rowan jelly or baked apple stuffed with walnuts and Cheddar, followed by baked whole sea bass with fennel and green peppercorn butter or button mushroom and smoked Brie stroganoff on a bed of rice, with home-made chocolate and chilli ice cream for afters.

★ Q S V (Dalegarth) P C

BUTTERMERE
Bridge Hotel
CA13 9UY

- Turn off A66 at Braithwaite, take either Whinlatter or Newland Pass
- Daily 9.30am-11.30pm
- Daily 9.30am-9.30pm

T (017687) 70252
F (017687) 70215
E enquiries@bridge-hotel.com
W www.bridge-hotel.com

- Black Sheep Best Bitter; Theakston Old Peculier
- Cumbrian, British and international cuisine
- Low beamed, traditional bars and dining room in hotel set in the Buttermere Fells, an area of outstanding natural beauty

This hotel offers various dining options to suit all tastes and budgets. In the bar the menu focuses on English and local dishes such as Cumberland sausages, hotpot, Borrowdale trout, salmon from local waters and several vegetarian options. In the dining room a five-course table d'hôte menu is served, enough to satisfy anyone who has built up a hearty appetite on the fells.

A sample menu offers soup to start, perhaps roast tomato, garlic and tarragon, followed by seafood Provençal or sorbet made from local wild strawberries. A choice of four main courses is offered – sliced duck breast plus a confit of leg with honey and lemon glaze, a spicy lamb curry in a filo pastry basket with mint, cucumber and yogurt, medallions of fillet steak on buttered crushed potatoes with mushroom and red wine jus, or poached plaice roulade and lemon peppered julienne vegetables with a tomato dill concasse. All main courses are served with potatoes and fresh vegetables or seasonal salad. To finish there is a selection of desserts or cheeses. The 21-room hotel is ideal for a quiet break with easy walks around Buttermere or Crummock Water or challenging hikes and climbs for the more experienced.

Q S V P C

CROSTHWAITE

☆ Punch Bowl

Lyth Valley, LA8 8HR

- ▶ In southern Lakeland, off A5074
- Daily 12-11pm (10.30pm Sun)
- Daily 12-3pm, 6-9pm
- T (015395) 68237
- F (015395) 68875
- E info@the-punchbowl.co.uk
- W www.the-punchbowl.co.uk
- Barngates Cat Nap, Tag Lag
- ☺ Home-cooked, innovative British cuisine
- After seven months' work this upmarket venue, with stylish accommodation and elegant dining room, reopened in 2005

Acquired from the owners of the Drunken Duck (home of Barngates Brewery), the Punch Bowl was completely refurbished during 2005 to provide nine beautiful, individually designed guest rooms and a formal restaurant for a well-heeled clientele. All food is freshly prepared from local suppliers recognised for good farming practice. In the restaurant starters include ravioli of crab and spring onions with a light shellfish foam, foie gras parfait with bitter chocolate bread, ginger beer jelly and maple syrup, tart tatin of goats' cheese and caramelised onions or halibut poached in olive oil with Dublin Bay prawns, new potatoes, soused cucumbers and vanilla and tarragon vinaigrette. Prices range from £7 to £13 for seared queen scallops.

Main courses all have very imaginative accompaniments – you could try twice cooked rabbit with a honey glaze, rosemary mousse and potato pancake with root vegetables, fillet of Galloway beef with mushroom and tarragon paste, steamed cabbage and pickled walnut jus or seabass fillet with vanilla potato purée, spinach and a crisp shrimp beignet, prices from £14.25 to £25 for lobster. Desserts include a fig tart with walnut flapjack and coffee sorbet or damson gin and vanilla pannacotta with poached plums. Meals are also available in the comfortable bar, starters £5-£7.50, mains £10-£13. S V P C

INGS

☆ Watermill Inn

LA8 9PY

- ▶ Off A591 near Staveley, 2 miles E of Windermere
- Daily 12-11pm (10.30pm Sun)
- Daily 12-4.30pm, 5-9pm
- T (01539) 821309
- F (01539) 822309
- E all@watermillinn.co.uk
- W www.watermillinn.co.uk
- Beer range varies
- ☺ Excellent food produced from locally sourced ingredients
- Attractive, award-winning stone built inn in operation since 1990; a new extension will house its own brewery

In a peaceful setting surrounded by beautiful countryside, the Watermill is an ideal base for touring the Lakes. A former wood mill, it has built up an excellent reputation for real ale and fine food. Locally reared meat includes lamb from Kentmere Valley, Hawkshead pork produced the other side of Lake Windermere, mature Galloway beef and full flavoured Cartmel venison, while fruit and vegetables are supplied by Ribble Farm Fare. The pub's policy is to support local business as much as possible so it buys from Kendal Fisheries, free-range eggs come from Bannerigg Farm and the ice cream is produced by English Lakes.

This all adds up to a varied menu at reasonable prices: expect to pay between £16 and £22 for a full three-course meal. Enticing specials chalked up on the board might be king scallops and gravadlax salmon with chilli and lemon dressing, monkfish and smoked bacon kebabs or goats' cheese and red onion tart for starters followed by venison casserole, wild mushroom stroganoff, South African bobotie (a Moroccan lamb and chilli bean casserole) or local roast lamb chops with honey and mustard glaze. Snacks are available during the afternoon. Q S V P C

LOWESWATER
Kirkstile Inn
CA13 ORV

▶ S of Cockermouth off B5289
☼ Mon-Sat 11am-11pm; Sun 12-10.30pm
🍴 Daily 12-2pm, 6-9pm
T (01900) 85219
F (01900) 85239
E info@kirkstile.com
W www.kirkstile.com
Coniston Bluebird; Loweswater Melbreak Bitter; Grasmoor Dark; Yates Bitter; guests
☺ Rustic dishes with a Lakeland slant
Classic, historic Lakeland inn, local CAMRA Pub of the Year 2003 and 2004

They've been feeding hungry diners for 400 years at the Kirkstile and, since 2003, brewing as well at Loweswater Brewery in an outhouse. Daily home-made soup is always served with a home-made loaf at £3, while other starters might include Mediterranean brochette of hake with peppers and mushrooms on scented rice with a chilli tomato sauce. Main meals on the specials board could be creamy vegetable stroganoff, chicken supreme stuffed with Cumberland cheese wrapped in bacon or local Lakeland rump steak served with Drambuie sauce, prices £6.95-£10.50, and desserts could include a trio of home-made ice creams – fudge, marmalade, rum and raisin – apple and peach crumble or plum meringue pie, all £3.75.

The set menu offers black pudding in beer batter made with their own Kirkstile ale and Crofton Farm goats' cheese baked in filo among the starters. Lakeland steak and mushroom pie has their Melbreak Bitter in the stock, while other dishes are grilled monkfish with trio of capsicum sauces, baked shoulder of lamb with honey and mint or roast Lakeland duck with figs and calvados. Veggie meals include wild mushroom and feta lasagne. Cumberland Rum Nicky made to a 17th-century recipe from dates, orange, ginger and rum with lattice topping is among home-made desserts, all £3.85.

★ S V P C

PARSONBY
Horse & Jockey
CA5 2DD

▶ On B5301, S of Aspatria
☼ Daily 11am-11pm
🍴 Daily 12-9pm
T (016973) 20482
E judeanian@aol.com
W www.horseandjockeypub.co.uk
Jennings Mild, Bitter
☺ Good value, mostly home-made pub food
Friendly roadside pub with flagged floors and exposed beams; look out for the pig collection and the drawings of customers executed by children

You will find nothing flashy or ostentatious on the menu here; the food is plain and homely as befits this friendly, cosy inn. What's more it is extremely good value – the Sunday roast costs just £2.95! In summer many visitors stumble upon the inn when they have lost their way, but are invariably pleased to have found it, especially if they are hungry! Simple starters are soup, prawn cocktail or egg mayonnaise, none of them over £2. Main courses are mostly around £3.75 but go up to £9 for a mixed grill. You may find home-made steak pie, Cumberland sausages, Whitby seafood platter, roast chicken, chilli con carne, gammon steak with pineapple, sirloin steak, deep-fried haddock or poached salmon – and the price includes chips or jacket potato and veg. There is a choice of three curries – chicken masala, beef vindaloo or vegetable – and vegetarians can also choose from cheese and broccoli bake, veggie lasagne or spinach and ricotta cannelloni, all £3.75. On the snack menu there are freshly-cut sandwiches for just £1.50, filled jacket potatoes or various salads, and you can fill up your kids for a couple of quid, providing they are not too busy drawing pictures to add to the portrait gallery. Desserts are available at £1.50.

★ Q S V ♣ P

SANTON BRIDGE
Bridge Inn
CA19 1UX

- ▶ From A595 turn E at Holmrook
- ☼ Daily 7am-11pm
- Ⓨ Daily 12-2.30pm, 6-9.30pm
- T (019467) 26221
- F (019467) 26026
- E info@santonbridgeinn.com
- W www.santonbridgeinn.com
- Jennings Bitter, Cumberland Ale, Cocker Hoop, Sneck Lifter, seasonal
- ☺ Real food from fresh produce; popular Sunday lunch carvery
- Once a mail coach halt, now a comfortable country inn with low beams

With an emphasis on 'proper' food from fresh ingredients, the menu carries a warning about long delays at busy times, but who would want to rush in such a pleasant spot? The menu is served in the bar, Eskdale Room and bistro. Starters, mostly around £4.50, include Greek salad, crab and prawn medley, New Zealand green lip mussels and a classic Caesar salad, while the specials board might offer smoked trout and mackerel with horseradish cream or a trio of smoked chicken, duck and Cumberland sausage with apple and plum chutney.

Main course specials might feature pasta Eliche with crab, prawn, Pernod and cream, Cajun spiced tuna, or organic meats supplied by the farm next door such as lamb's liver and onion on celeriac mash or rib eye steak served with pepper sauce topped with goats' cheese on a bed of roasted vegetables. There is a good choice for vegetarians: maybe grilled Mediterranean vegetable salad with tomato bread or winter vegetable pie topped with celeriac and mashed potato. Main courses are £8 for steak and kidney pie to £15 for a rump steak; on Sunday the excellent carvery with a choice of two roasts is just £6.20. Home-made desserts and local Hartley's ice creams are listed on a blackboard.

S V C

SHAP
Greyhound Hotel
Main Street, CA10 3PW

- ▶ On A6, 1 mile off M6 jct 39
- ☼ Mon-Sat 11am-11pm; Sun 12-10.30pm
- Ⓨ Daily 12-2pm, 6-9pm
- T (01931) 716474
- F (01931) 716305
- E postmaster@greyhoundshap.demon.co.uk
- W www.greyhoundshap.co.uk
- Jennings Bitter, Cumberland Ale; Young's Special; guests
- ☺ Award-winning menu with plenty of Westmorland fare
- 17th-century former coaching inn; popular stopping place for walkers on Wainwright's Coast to Coast

Owners and joint chefs Derrick Newsome and Keith Taylor go to Penrith auction most weeks to source meat on the hoof from neighbouring farms, which is then slaughtered and matured at the nearby abattoir before they prepare it themselves at the pub. A hugely tempting menu has daily changing specials such as black pudding in onion cream sauce, £4, followed by saddle of Shap Abbey Farm lamb with citrus stuffing and Cumberland sausage, red snapper en papilotte with Thai spices, roast loin of Cumbrian pork with apples and apricots, steak and kidney pudding or leek, asparagus and four cheese crumble, priced £8-£12.

The main menu is just as tempting, featuring Fell bred lamb in wine and redcurrant gravy, Shap's championship Cumberland sausage with egg (from Vera's hens next door), pot roast brisket of Fell bred beef cooked with button mushrooms, onions and smoked bacon, steak and ale pie, a 12oz grilled Westmorland sirloin steak and fresh cod in beer batter, priced £7-£13 – half portions are available for children. Home-made desserts are special, too – warm date and walnut tart, sticky toffee pudding, apple crumble and bread and butter pud with apricots and nutmeg, all £4.

S V C

STAVELEY

Eagle & Child

Kendal Road, LA8 9LP

- Off A591 near Windermere
- Daily 11am-11pm; Sun 12-10.30pm
- Daily 12-3pm, 6-9pm
- T (01539) 821320
- F rich@eaglechildinn.co.uk
- E www.eaglechildinn.co.uk
- Beer range varies
- Locally sourced fresh produce creating honest, wholesome fare
- Attractive bar area, lots of memorabilia, garden with river frontage, close to Kentmere Valley

All ingredients are sourced locally, be it from the village butcher and baker, fresh fruit and vegetables from Ambleside or fish from Fleetwood – and constantly changing beers are from local micros. A day's specials could include fresh chicken breast stuffed with Cumberland sausage, wrapped in smoked bacon and served with Cumberland sauce, fresh grilled tuna on roast Mediterranean vegetables, roast beef or lamb dinner with all the trimmings and vegetarian choices such as home-made spinach and wild mushroom lasagne, or cheese, leek and potato bake, prices from £7.95-£10.94 for Barbary duck breast on spring onion potato cake with black cherry and cognac sauce.

The set menu starts with warm salad of local black pudding on mixed leaves with mustard and brandy dressing, or home-breaded Brie wedges on roast vegetable and pesto salad, priced £3.95-£4.95. Main dishes range from Kentmere lamb shank slow braised on mustard mash, Hayton's Cumberland sausage or beef slow cooked in Black Sheep gravy with Yorkshire pudding, to fresh local trout grilled with lemon and prawn butter, home-made fresh spinach and ricotta puff pastry lattice and a half pound rump or sirloin steak char-grilled with wild mushroom and cognac sauce, prices from £7.95-£11.50.

Q S V (Staveley) P C

TROUTBECK

☆ Queen's Head

Townhead, LA23 1PW

- Off A592, less than four miles from Windermere
- Mon-Sat 11am-11pm; Sun 12-10.30pm
- Daily 12-2.30pm, 6.30-9pm
- T (015394) 32174
- F (015394) 31938
- E enquiries@queensheadhotel.com
- W www.queensheadhotel.com
- Beer range varies, mostly local
- Exciting, eclectic menu of modern and traditional with plenty of local flavours
- Historic 17th-century coaching inn with beams and huge open fire

Gorgeous country cooking with everything home made on the premises – black pudding, bread and biscuits for cheese. Head chef Ben Ashworth is creating superb traditional dishes, some with a modern twist, such as braised oxtail and real ale risotto with crispy shallots. At lunchtime try the superb baguettes with fillings including hot smoked salmon at only £4.75, and main dishes such as lamb's liver and pancetta on champ, £6.25-£7.95.

In the evening starters might include home-made black pud topped with foie gras, crab risotto or just a platter of home-made breads, £2.95-£6.95. Steak, ale and mushroom cobbler is among the main courses, as well as crisp pork belly with caramelised Granny Smiths, local venison with roast parsnips and garlic confit, whole shank of Lakeland lamb braised in red wine, pheasant with herbed risotto in cider liquor, salmon supreme with rosti potato and confit tomatoes, priced £7.95-£15.95. Vegetarian dishes could be asparagus and wild mushroom risotto or shallot tart tatin with Thornby Moor goats' cheese and roast beetroot. Home-made children's meals from £3 will gladden Jamie Oliver's heart, and caramelised rice pudding with boozy prunes is just one of the irresistible desserts.

★ V P C

ULVERSTON
Bay Horse
Canal Foot, LA12 9EL

▶ Follow signs for Canal Foot from A590
☼ Daily 9am-11pm
🍴 Tue-Sun 12-2pm; evening restaurant only 7.30 for 8pm
T (01229) 583972
F (01229) 580502
E reservations@bayhorsehotel.co.uk
W www.thebayhorsehotel.co.uk
Greene King Old Speckled Hen; Jennings Cumberland Ale; guest
☺ Sassy bar menu
In a glorious setting on the shore of Morecambe Bay, hard to find but worth wending your way through the industrial estate to get to

Landlord Bob Lyons, former head chef of the Miller Howe, is still here after many years in this Guide, still cooking up magic. Everything is home made from date chutney to soda bread and chunky chips, using plenty of local produce. A bar menu at lunchtime offers rich chicken liver pâté with cranberry and ginger purée, toasted cheese and herb pâté on ciabatta, cherry tomato, black olives and feta cheese on curly endive or deep-fried chilli prawns with sweet 'n' sour sauce, priced £6.25-£7.95.

Main dishes are medallions of pork, leek and Lancashire cheese on Madeira sauce, fresh crab and salmon fishcakes with white wine and herb sauce, grilled Waberthwaite Cumberland sausage with cranberry and apple sauce, Aberdeen Angus steak and kidney pie with home-made puff pastry topping, lamb shank braised in red burgundy, all served with stir-fried vegetables, seasonal salad, new potatoes or home made chips, from £10.50-£12.50. Home-made soup is £3.50 and sandwiches £3.70-£4.45 with fillings such as sugar baked ham or poached salmon with spiced cucumber. A gourmet restaurant menu at night is priced at around £20 for a main dish.

★ Q ❀ S V ♿ C

WESTNEWTON
Swan Inn
CA7 3PQ

▶ On B5301, 2 miles N of Aspatria
☼ Mon & Tue 6-11pm; Wed closed; Thu-Sun 12-2pm, 6-11pm (10.30pm Sun)
🍴 Thu-Mon 12-2pm, 6-8.45pm
T (016973) 20627
E info@theswaninnwestnewton.co.uk
W www.theswaninnwestnewton.co.uk
Yates Fever Pitch
☺ Changing menu based on local produce
Traditional pub at the heart of the community with comfortable 24 seater restaurant, situated in a lovely village that is also home to Yates Brewery

You will not get steak and chips here! In fact they don't cook chips here at all – a bonus for customers who are sensitive to the odour of deep fat fryers spoiling their beer. The no-smoking restaurant serves a limited menu, but it changes every week and innovative dishes are carefully prepared from local ingredients. Everything is produced in house, including the bread and desserts. So for starters, around £4-£7, you may be offered a terrine of smoked and fresh salmon with asparagus and an orange and saffron dressing, mushroom salad with guinea fowl terrine and pickled wild mushrooms, roast Mediterranean vegetables with melted Crofton Hall cheese and balsamic vinegar and tarragon dressing, or an unusual soup such as parsnip and Bramley apple with a hint of ginger.

Mains could include roast haunch of venison on root vegetables with polenta, wild mushrooms and an elderberry game jus, pan-fried Lakeland beef fillet medallions on fondue potatoes with grilled Mediterranean vegetables, or roast rack of lamb on sweet potatoes with ginger stewed plums. A wild mushroom risotto accompanied by roasted root veg or grilled local brill fillets on a tomato and basil fondue with fresh tagliatelle and wilted spinach are the alternatives. Most dishes are priced around £14-15.

★ Q ❀ S V ♿ ♣ P C

ASHOVER

☆ Old Poet's Corner

Butts Road, S45 0EW

- ▶ Off main Chesterfield-Matlock road between Kelstedge and Woolley Moor
- ☼ Mon-Fri 12-2.30pm, 5-11pm; Fri & Sat 12-11pm; Sun 12-10.30pm
- 🍴 Mon-Sat 12-2pm; Sun 12-3.30pm
- T (01246) 590888
- E enquiries@oldpoets.co.uk
- W www.oldpoets.co.uk
- 🍺 Greene King Abbot; guests
- ☺ Home-cooked traditional country fare but also famed for authentic curries
- ◙ Welcoming country pub with oak beams, dried hops and log fires

'All game dishes are prepared using meats provided by the local falconry club – no lead shot in our rabbit pie,' says owner Kim Beresford – and apparently club members drink at the pub too, bringing their hawks with them. Typical specials include game pie with mushy peas, haggis, neeps and tatties, Irish stew with mash, pork hock in honey and mustard, spicy sausage casserole or beef in stout. One of the cooks specialises in Indian food, blending spices and marinades in house for dishes such as chicken balti jalfrezi at £6.95, and adding home grown searingly hot Scotch Bonnet chillis to the chilli con carne.

On the regular menu look for meat and potato pie, beef casserole with suet dumplings, haddock in real ale batter with chips and mushy peas, an 8oz rib eye steak from a local butcher supplying Derbyshire beef, dishes priced £5.25-£9.95 for the big grill of sirloin steak, gammon, pork and lamb chops, pork sausage, liver, kidney, black pudding, fried egg, chips and peas at £12.95. Four veggie choices include home-made cauliflower cheese, cannelloni stuffed with goats' cheese and five-bean chill with basmati rice. Traditional desserts are also home made. House ales Old Poet's and Ashover Gold are brewed by Tower and Leatherbritches breweries.

★ 🏰 Q ❀ S V 🍺 ♿ ⛺ ♣ 🍎 🅿 ⚡ 👪 C

BRASSINGTON

Olde Gate Inne

Well Street, DE4 4HJ

- ▶ Off A5023
- ☼ Tue-Thu 12-2.30pm, 6-11pm; Fri & Sat 12-3pm, 6-11pm; Sun 12-3pm, 7-10.30pm
- 🍴 Tue-Thu 12-1.45pm, 7-8.45pm; Fri & Sat 12-2pm, 7-9pm; Sun 12-2pm
- T (01629) 540448
- E theoldgateinn@supanet.com
- 🍺 Marston's Pedigree; guests
- ☺ Eclectic menu of traditional English meals and dishes and from across the world
- ◙ Grade II listed, ivy clad, unspoilt village inn with three open fires

This 17th-century pub features a black leaded range in the public bar, though it is no longer used for cooking. However, traditional dishes do come from the kitchen including hot lunchtime favourites such as home-made soups, hot pot, cottage and shepherd's pies. There is also a range of imaginatively named baguettes – the Italian Job filled with Black Forest ham, artichokes, sweet peppers, basil and parmesan; Sloppy Joe containing hot chilli and melted cheese; Innkeeper with rare roast beef and melted local Stilton; Submarine of smoked salmon and prawns; the Rustler with a jumbo hot dog, melted cheese and barbecue sauce. Poached salmon salad, Thai fishcakes and dressed crab salad are also on the menu.

In the evening, specials might range from traditional dishes such as beef in porter with horseradish dumplings and fillet steak with pâté in Madeira sauce to Moroccan lamb tagine, navarin of lamb, home made curries, lemon sole rolled round crabmeat and scallops, seafood risotto, home-made vegetarian chilli and lasagne, and the Gate special paella containing king prawns, scallops, clams and mussels. In summer they barbecue well hung steaks, lamb kebabs, Cajun and chicken piri piri, spare ribs and lamb steaks with honey and thyme.

★ 🏰 Q ❀ S V 🍺 ♿ ♣ 🍎 🅿 ⚡ 🥛 C

CROMFORD
Boat Inn
Scarthin, DE4 3QF

▶ Off A6, near Market Place
☼ Mon-Fri 12-3pm, 6-11pm; Sat 12-11pm; Sun 12-10.30pm
(🍴) Mon-Sat 12-2pm (not Tue), 6-9pm; Sun 12-3pm
T (01629) 823282
E debbiewhite77@hotmail.com
W www.theboatatcromford.co.uk
Beer range varies
☺ Traditional pub staples and a curry night, all home cooked
Cosy 18th-century free house with oak beams, open fires and barrel tables

In the bar you will find old favourites such as steak and ale pie, gammon steaks, home-made lasagne and a selection of freshly filled baguettes and jacket potatoes, as well as a constantly changing specials board and curry night every Wednesday. The à la carte menu starts with treats such as grilled black pudding in Cumberland sauce, moules marinière with shallots, white wine and cream, smoked mackerel in a creamy mustard sauce or home-made soup such as leek and potato with a warm roll, prices from £3.50-£4.50.

Main courses could be pork Mombassa (pork fillet and scampi cooked with shallots in creamy Pernod sauce), grilled red snapper on Mediterranean vegetables, grilled haddock on cheesy mashed potato with lemon butter sauce, chicken breast wrapped in bacon with Stilton sauce, grilled sirloin steak with black pepper sauce or pan-fried duck breast in orange and Cointreau sauce, all accompanied with fresh vegetables or salad, prices £8.45-£11.95. Vegetarian dishes at £8.45 include baked red pepper stuffed with vegetable risotto or seasonal vegetables in tempura batter with sweet chilli dip.

Three guest ales often come from local brewers such as Whim or Leatherbritches.

★ S V ♿ (Cromford) ♣ C

DERBY
Olde Dolphin Inn
6-7 Queen Street, DE1 3DL

▶ In city centre, next to the cathedral
☼ Mon-Sat 10.30am-11pm; Sun 12-10.30pm
(🍴) Mon-Sat 11.30am-10pm; Sun 12-6pm
T (01332) 267711
F (01332) 295828
E yeoldedolphin@yahoo.com
Adnams Bitter; Draught Bass; Black Sheep Best Bitter; Caledonian Deuchars IPA; Greene King Abbot, guests
☺ Excellent steak menu plus specials and light meals
Historic, timber-framed pub circa 1530 with beamed interior divided into different areas

Derby's oldest surviving pub is listed in CAMRA's National Inventory of pub interiors of outstanding historic interest. The upstairs steak bar serves a wide selection of cuts of meat, cooked to the customer's liking and served on sizzling skillets; the biggest sellers are the 16oz T-bone and 8oz fillet. Four or five daily specials, priced between £9 and £12, add variety, such as Derbyshire oatcakes filled with goujons of fillet steak in a creamy Stilton sauce served on a medley of pan-fried black pudding, smoked bacon and sliced potatoes, chicken supreme stuffed with minced venison and wrapped in pancetta, served in a creamy leek sauce, and pan-fried wild boar under a fresh rosemary crust, topped with honeyed slices of apple and pear on lyonnaise potatoes with cider gravy.

You can also eat (more cheaply) in the bar where daily specials such as seared tuna steak with roast asparagus and tomato salad or pork steak in black pepper and mushroom sauce cost under £5. Mainstays of the bar menu are special sausages, such as wild boar and orange, or garlic, pork and sage, home-made pies and faggots. This is not the best venue for vegetarians, but they do offer a mushroom pepperpot, served with garlic bread, and hearty snacks.

★ Q S V ♿ ♣ P C

FENNY BENTLEY
☆ Bentley Brook Inn
DE6 1LF

- ▶ On A515 N of Ashbourne
- ☼ Daily 11am-11pm; Sun 12-10.30pm
- Ⓨ Daily 12-9pm
- T (01335) 350278
- F (01335) 350422
- E all@bentleybrookinn.co.uk
- W www.bentleybrookinn.co.uk
- Leatherbritches Goldings, Ashbourne Ale, Hairy Helmet; Marston's Pedigree; guests
- ☺ Good Derbyshire cooking plus sausage, pickles and preserves shop
- Award-winning brew pub with B&B

The inn, long owned by the Allingham family, is a quite remarkable hive of industry, with an old wash house and cold store converted into the Leatherbritches craft brewery in 1993. An in-house butcher's produces sausages, black pudding, salami and home-cured bacon sold in their shop along with biscuits, jam, marmalade and preserves home made to Derbyshire recipes, and a kitchen garden provides fresh herbs, fruit and salad.

Typical dishes include starters such as seafood chowder with a home-made roll, brandied mushrooms in garlic and parsley butter or melon with exotic fruits, all £3.75. Main courses might be roast pheasant with game chips and bread sauce, Linda's home-made Derbyshire oat cakes filled with basmati rice and vegetables (the same oat cakes form part of a brilliant breakfast with their own bacon and sausages), beef fillet in a sauce of home-made wholegrain mustard with cream, pork medallions in cider, apple and double cream sauce, chicken breast stuffed with their own black pudding on a white wine sauce, or lamb's liver in a rich black pepper sauce. Prices from £10.50-£14.50 for the fillet steak. Bar dishes include farmhouse breakfast bake, steak and ale pie, Derbyshire hot pot and vegan stir fry; there's a Sunday lunch carvery.

S V C

HOPE
Cheshire Cheese Inn
Edale Road, S33 6ZF

- ▶ Off A6187
- ☼ Mon-Fri 12-3pm, 6-11pm; Sat 12-11pm; Sun 12-10.30pm
- Ⓨ 12-2pm, 6.30-9pm; Sat 12-2.30pm, 6.30-9pm; Sun 12-8.30pm
- T (01433) 620381
- F (01433) 620411
- E cheshire.cheese@barbox.net
- W www.cheshire-cheese.net
- Black Sheep Best Bitter; Blackpool Barnsley Bitter; Whim Hartington Bitter; guests
- ☺ Traditional pub cooking at reasonable prices
- A free house in the heart of the Peak District with a liquor licence since 1578

Walkers plan their routes around the Hope, where they know they will find plenty of good, wholesome, home-cooked fare. Typical dishes on the specials board might be a giant Yorkshire pudding filled with lamb's liver or sausages in onion gravy at £6.95, chicken and mushroom or steak pies at £7.95, medley of local butcher's sausages or a peppered pork steak with vegetables. Starters include garlic mushrooms, baked potato skins with dips or moules marinière, from £3.95-£6.95.

The set menu offers home-made soup of the day, steak and kidney pudding with new potatoes and vegetables, grilled cod with lemon and cracked black pepper or grilled chicken breast in a leek and Stilton sauce, priced £7.95-£8.95. The Cheshire Cheese mixed grill of rump steak, gammon, lamb chop, pork chop, sausage, black pudding, onion rings, mushrooms, chips and peas is a modest £9.25, while veggie dishes include cream cheese and broccoli bake or mushroom and nut fettuccini. On Sunday there is a traditional home-cooked roast lunch with a choice of pork or beef. Lunchtime snacks include bacon and egg or roast beef sandwiches, ploughman's and omelettes.

★ Q S V C

HULLAND WARD
☆ Black Horse Inn
DE6 3EE

- On A517, midway between Ashbourne and Belper
- Daily 12-3pm, 6-11pm (7-10.30pm Sun)
- Daily 12-2pm, 6-9.45pm (7-9.30pm Sun)
- T (01335) 370206
- Beer range varies
- Extensive menu with particularly good vegetarian selection
- Split-level, multi-roomed drinking area with a central bar and restaurant; low beamed ceilings and quarry tiled floors

This 300-year-old inn is in an elevated village surrounded by picturesque Dales countryside on the edge of the Peak District near Carsington Water. Landlady Muriel Edwin does all the cooking herself – even baking her own cakes and shortbread. Meat comes from a local butcher and Muriel puts all kinds of game on the menu as available. The prices here are extremely reasonable – at lunchtime she always offers one special dish (bangers and mash, prawn curry, battered haddock and chips, for example) for £4.

There is an extensive list of specials that changes frequently, but could include tagliatelle with smoked salmon and lemon sauce, lamb in cashew nut and mint sauce with rice and peas, pork steaks with bacon and sage sauce, pigeon and tomato sauce with farfalle, chicken in white wine and asparagus sauce or sausage and bean chilli hotpot, £5-£8.50. Vegetarians are well catered for here, with at least a dozen choices including the veggie crumbles: Brie, courgette and almond, leek and mushroom or Stilton and vegetable. There are also pasta bakes, Mediterranean vegetable hotpot or feta cheese soufflé pancakes, £7 or less. Lovely puds include seasonal rhubarb or damson crumble, mixed berry sponge pudding and custard and Irish cream chocolate truffle torte, all served with cream or ice cream for £3.

★ Q S V ♣ P C

NEW WHITTINGTON
Wellington
162 High Street, S43 2AN

- Near Chesterfield
- Mon-Sat 11am-11pm; Sun 12-4pm, 7-10.30pm
- Daily 12-2.30pm, 5-7.30pm (not Sun)
- T (01246) 450879
- Camerons Strongarm; Marston's Pedigree; guests
- Traditional pub food
- Friendly village local with tap room, lounge and quizzes

A local pub in all senses, buying meat and vegetables in the village and cooking traditional, value for money pub meals popular with regular visitors. The Wellington is known throughout the area for home-made steak pies, traditional Sunday roasts and beef in real ale stew using Hobgoblin or some other dark brew. Daily changing specials could include liver and onions, cheese and onion pie or chilli with rice, all home made and served with freshly cooked vegetables – all dishes on the specials board are priced £3.50 or two for £6.50. Full marks for their special board for pensioners which always includes a roast dinner and sponge pudding, two courses for £2.70.

Yet another menu offers 'value meals' at £2.25 including toad-in-the-hole or fish 'n' chips with mushy peas, the mushy peas home made every day. A curry night or steak night is held once a month, and there is a wide choice of vegetarian meals with vegetable lasagne the most popular, plus snacks and sandwiches. A Sunday roast dinner is a bargain £3.70, two courses £4.60 and three courses £5.75. Puddings, at just £1.50, include delicious home-made treacle, jam, sultana, lemon and almond sponges. Children get a free ice cream after their meal.

S V ♣ P

OCKBROOK

Royal Oak

55 Green Lane, DE72 3SE

- ▶ Off A52, follow signs to village
- ☼ 11.30am-2.30pm (Sat 3pm), 6-11pm; Sun 11.30am-3pm, 7-10.30pm
- Ⓨ Mon-Fri 12-2pm, 6-8pm (not Tue); Sat & Sun 12-2pm
- T (01332) 662378
- E royaloak_ockbrook@hotmail.com
- Draught Bass; guests
- ☺ Traditional, home-cooked pub meals
- Country pub with five rooms and two beer gardens

A recent CAMRA Country Pub of the Year, the Royal Oak has been in the Hornbuckle family since coronation year and is virtually unchanged since then. Fresh local fruit and vegetables and herbs from the pub's own garden are used in cooking, meat arrives most days from the local butcher and fresh fish direct from Grimsby is delivered on Wednesdays and Thursdays.

As well as the regular menu, specials could include pork chops with apples and cider cream sauce, salmon with whisky cream and roast cod with cherry tomatoes and mozzarella, while 'grandma's steak pie' is a particular favourite. On the fresh fish days cod or haddock are very popular in the pub's home-made beer batter. Steaks, chicken and lamb are often accompanied by sauces, savoury butters or compotes; roast meals are served on Sunday lunchtimes, and the home-made Stilton soup is a favourite during winter. Meal prices range from £4.95-£7.95, with filled rolls as a lunchtime snack from £1.20. There are themed evenings on Valentine's Day and St George's Day, and Christmas dinner is available in December. As well as three constantly changing guest beers from micros, there is an annual beer festival in October.

★ Q ❀ S V ♿ ♣ P C

SUTTON-CUM-DUCKMANTON

Arkwright Arms

Chesterfield Road, S44 5JG

- ▶ On A619 between Chesterfield and Bolsover
- ☼ Mon-Sat 11am-11pm; Sun 12-2.30pm
- Ⓨ Mon-Fri 12-2.30pm, 5-7.30pm (Fri 5.30-8pm); Sat & Sun 12-2.30pm
- T (01246) 232053
- E chadjpr@msn.com
- W http://thearkers.mysite.wanadoo-members.co.uk
- Marston's Pedigree; guests
- ☺ Wholesome pub fare with a good range of snacks
- Mock Tudor fronted free house with a central bar and dining room at the rear; local CAMRA Pub of the Year 2004

A haven for real ale lovers, this pub showcases the products of local micro-breweries such as Kelham Island, Abbeydale and Whim. It hosts two major annual beer festivals and regular mini fests, dedicated to a single brewery. A good selection of home-cooked fare at very reasonable prices is available to accompany your pint. The landlady and her son do the cooking and source their produce locally.

There is a wide choice of bar snacks including filled rolls with salad, under £2, jacket spuds, toasties, burgers and salads. For a more substantial meal you could start with whitebait, garlic mushrooms or soup of the day, then follow with pub favourites such as home-made steak pie served with three veg and chips or potatoes, roast of the day with all the trimmings, giant battered haddock with salad or chips and peas, all under £6. Lamb shank is often on the menu served in a rosemary and red wine sauce and there is always a good selection of grills – steaks from rump to T-bone, gammon and Cajun chicken. For the best choice of home-made dishes you need to go on Friday, although there will always be at least one available. There are some good home-made desserts, too.

★ ❀ S V ♣ P C

SOUTH WINGFIELD
Old Yew Tree
51 Manor Road, DE55 7NH

- ▶ On B5035
- Daily 12-3pm, 5-11pm
- Daily 12-2pm, 5-9.30pm (not Sun eve)
- T (01773) 833763
- Marston's Pedigree; guests
- Extensive range including a speciality Thai and oriental menu
- Friendly country free house, near the magnificent ruins of the 15th-century Wingfield Manor, destroyed during the Civil War

Featuring regularly in CAMRA's Good Beer Guide for its strong support of micro-breweries, the pub also enjoys a good food trade, particularly for the traditional Sunday lunches. It offers several menus, including one just for grills and the popular Thai and oriental selection. With those and the extensive menu of the day, which includes a good vegetarian choice, you would be hard pressed not to find something to your liking here.

Starters, priced £4-£5, include a couple of salads – egg mayonnaise and salmon, and Cajun chicken Caesar – that are also offered in main course portions. Other choices include hot garlic prawns and sliced chorizo with garlic bread, feta cheese filo pastry parcel with sweet chillip dip, marinated king prawn kebabs with garlic mayo and a vegetarian antipasti whose ingredients vary according to availability. Some of the main course dishes, £9-£15, are flagged up as 'fresh from France', such as quail braised in bacon, red wine and cranberry sauce, woodpigeon on black pudding with bacon, apricot and onion stuffing and roast guinea fowl. There's also Moroccan lamb and beef tagine and English favourites such as steak and kidney pud and pan-fried lamb's liver. There are a few fish dishes too, while veggie options include spicy Mexican enchiladas and Tuscan crunchy bean casserole served with salad.

★ Q V P C

YOULGREAVE
George Hotel
Church Street, DE45 1VW

- ▶ Off A6 between Matlock and Bakewell
- Mon-Sat 11am-11pm; Sun 12-10.30pm
- Mon-Sat 11.30am-9pm (8.45pm Sat); Sun 12-7.45pm
- T (01629) 636292
- Bateman XXX; Courage Directors or Greene King Old Speckled Hen; guest
- Hearty, home-made food with game a speciality; fish 'n' chips take away
- Unspoiled, award-winning, three room B&B opposite a 12th century church

The George specialises in game dishes such as roast pheasant and partridge with bacon and cream sauce, rabbit or wood pigeon casserole, jugged hare and, occasionally, venison, priced around £9 including fresh vegetables and potatoes. They try to buy as much meat as possible locally, naming the supplier on the specials board. Duck served either with an orange and Cointreau sauce or on a beetroot confit is popular, as are the beef burgers and pork or lamb with rosemary sausages made by the landlord's son who is a butcher. Both the beef and steak and Old Peculier pies have won awards for being the best in the Midlands, and are available to take away, as is fresh cod in batter with chips at £3.50.

Typical specials could be gammon, braised steak or liver with onions, also available at weekday lunchtimes as smaller portions in a two-course mix 'n' match menu at £6, especially popular with pensioners. Vegetarian meals were bought in until recently but are now home made and include cheesy leeks, vegetable pasta bake, macaroni cheese, mushroom stroganoff and, most popular, a giant Yorkshire pudding filled with a fresh vegetable stew; all soups are veggie from curried parsnip to minestrone. The Sunday roast of beef, lamb or turkey with all the trimmings is £6.50.

★ Q S V ♣ P

BRANSCOMBE
Masons Arms
EX12 3DJ

▶ Signed off A3052, in village centre
☼ 11am-3pm, 6-11pm; weekends and summer 11am-11pm
🍴 Daily 12-2pm, 7-9pm
T (01297) 680300
F (01297) 680500
E reception@masonsarms.co.uk
W www.masonsarms.co.uk
Branscombe Vale Branoc; Otter Bitter, Mason's Ale; Draught Bass; guests
☺ Traditional English with imaginative tweaks using fresh fish and local produce
17th-century coaching inn in National Trust valley a few minutes from sea

A cornucopia of different dishes is produced using local fresh produce by a cooking team that even makes bread, jams and chutneys in this former Devon Dining Pub of the Year. In the bar you will find ploughman's such as Stilton with spicy pickle or honey roast ham with pineapple and chilli ham, and starters from home-cured salmon gravadlax to duck confit pancakes and Branscombe crab bisque at a bargain £4.50. Fish dishes include cod in beer batter, seafood mixed grill, Branscombe crab cakes, salmon, mussel, cod and leek stew or roast seabass. Other dishes might be pork and west country cider (Addlestones) cobbler, seared venison steak with root vegetables and red wine, the popular steak and kidney pudding, chicken and mushroom pie flavoured with tarragon or Devon sausages with red onion gravy and Savoy cabbage, prices from around £9-£12.95. A superb vegetarian choice includes Thai vegetable sour orange curry, spinach and ricotta ravioli, gorgonzola fiochetti, or banana and sultana Indienne with coconut milk. Spiffing desserts range from chilled berry soup with clotted cream to iced nougatine parfait. The children's menu is better than many. House beer Mason's Ale is brewed by Otter.

★ S V P C

BROADHEMBURY
Drewe Arms
EX14 3NF

▶ South of A373 Cullompton-Honition, near M5 jct 28
☼ Daily 11am-3pm, 6-11pm; Sun 12-3pm
🍴 12-2pm, 7-9.15pm
T (01404) 841267
Otter Bitter, Bright (summer), Ale, Head, seasonal
☺ Award-winning restaurant, fish a speciality
Grade II listed pub among whitewashed cottages owned by the Drewe family of Castle Drogo

No frozen food at all is the promise at this foodies' pub, and no exotic fish, either, but the 'largest possible portion' of fresh fish and seafood, all sourced in the west country, served as simply as possible. That could include spicy crab soup or smoked haddock and Stilton rarebit for starters, whole lemon sole with herb butter, half a Cornish lobster with salad and new potatoes, £18, whole Lyme Bay crab, wing of skate with black butter, griddled Cornish sardines, seared tuna salad, whole langoustines with aioli, cod baked with Cheddar and cream or seabream with orange and chilli, all with vegetables or salad, from £13.50 to £15.50.

Fish on the three course dining menu includes fillet of turbot hollandaise, wild sea bass with pesto, John Dory with anchovies and capers, halibut with grated horseradish, sea trout with asparagus and herb butter or red mullet with red pepper chutney, all £17.50. Other main dishes include beef fillet with mushroom sauce or rack of lamb with onion marmalade. Snacks are open sandwiches topped with gravadlax, Brie and bacon, crabmeat mayonnaise, rare beef or sausage of the day, from £5 to £7.25 for a combination. For afters choose between puds such as Mrs Gill's almond cake with rhubarb compote or a selection of west country cheeses.

★ Q V P C

BUTTERLEIGH
Butterleigh Inn
EX15 1PN

▶ West of Cullompton, between the M5 and the A3072
☼ Mon-Sat 12-2.30pm, 6-11pm; Sun 12-3pm, 7-10.30pm
🍴 Daily 12-2pm, 7-9pm (not Sun eve)
T (01884) 855407
F (01884) 855600
E info@dunx.net
🍺 Butcombe Bitter; Cotleigh Tawny; Theakston Best Bitter
☺ Home-cooked menus based on local produce at reasonable prices
◙ 400-year-old Devon cob building in a picturesque village in a lovely rural setting; the dining room is modern

The owners of this charming inn say the only items on the menu that are bought in are the breaded garlic mushrooms and the chips. Quite a claim, but they are in a favoured part of the country – all their meat and vegetables come from local suppliers who sell Devon farm produce. An already varied menu is supplemented by a daily specials list that you are urged to consult before deciding. This may include pan-fried pork chops served on apple purée and topped with mustard sauce, oven-baked barbary duck breast served on poached peaches and glazed with honey, salmon and prawn fishcakes drizzled with a sweet chilli sauce or sun-dried tomato and black olive loaf topped with tomato and basil sauce and Cheddar cheese. There is a good range of steaks and grills, all around £15, or you could try the home-made burgers. If you just want a snack there is a good choice of ploughman's, crusty baguettes and sandwiches, from £4 to £7 for the rump steak baguette. Don't miss the ice cream from Langage Farm, £2.95, or one of the delicious home-made desserts, all under £4: seasonal fruit cheesecake, chocolate bread and butter pudding or lemon surprise.

★ 🏰 Q ❀ 🛏 S V 🍺 ♿ ♣ P ⚡ 👪 C

CHARDSTOCK
George Inn
Chard Street, EX13 7BX

▶ 1 mile NW of A358, between Axminster and Chard, near Tytherleigh
☼ Mon-Sat 12-2.30pm (3pm Sat), 6-11pm; Sun 12-3pm, 7-10.30pm
🍴 Daily 12-2pm, 7-9pm
T (01460) 220241
E info@george-inn.co.uk
W www.george-inn.co.uk
🍺 Branscombe Vale Branoc; Otter Bitter; guests from local micro-breweries
☺ British, both traditional and modern
◙ Grade II listed 15th-century thatched church house in village centre

Using mainly local produce including meat, game in season, fish from Bridport and autumn fruits from rosehips to damsons, home-grown walnuts and crab apples, the George produces the most irresistible fare. Favourites include half a guinea fowl roasted with fennel or basil, mustard rabbit with bacon and thyme, cold game pie or half a shoulder of lamb slow roasted with honey and rosemary. A typical specials board might include starters of calamari with garlic mayonnaise or char-grilled vegetables with balsamic dressing, whole rainbow trout with smoked salmon and whisky, Devon pork and apple hot pot or whole grilled Devon sole, prices £6.95-£13.50.

The set menu includes home-made soup and smoked fish with horseradish cream followed by pork medallions with port and pear sauce at £8.95 or the George fillet tower of fillet steak wrapped in bacon topped with Stilton on beef tomato and field mushroom at £14.95. In the bar you can choose home-made burger, cod in beer batter, bacon and avocado salad with honey dressing, prices £5.25-£6.95. Excellent veggie choices and even vegan dishes are always on the menu, such as pepper stuffed with Moroccan spiced couscous, and home-made puds include baked chocolate tart or treacle pudding.

★ Q ❀ 🛏 S V 🍺 ♣ P ⚡ 👪 C

CULMSTOCK

☆ Culm Valley Inn

EX15 3JJ

- ▶ Off A38 four miles SW of Wellington
- ☀ Mon-Fri 11am-3pm, 6-11pm; Sat 11am-11pm; Sun 12-10.30pm
- Daily 12-2pm, 7-9pm
- T (01884) 840354
- Beer range varies
- ☺ Emphasis on local, organic and free range produce
- Former railway hotel, now a village inn set by the River Culm where it emerges from the Blackdown Hills

Landlord and cook Richard Hartley is dedicated to sourcing not only the best local produce but as far as possible he makes sure it comes from farms and producers that use organic and free range rearing methods – including the ducks, chickens, eggs and cream. Fish and seafood do not travel far either, with mussels from the Exe, live crab and lobster landed locally and fresh fish from Looe in Cornwall. Vegetables and salads are grown locally and the pub has its own herb garden. Just about everything is home made, including the sausages – pork and sage, served with mash for £7.

Many of his imaginative dishes are served in small and large portions: brill served with hand dived scallops and spiced mango dressing, onion risotto with beaten butter and sage, trio of smoked salmon, Lebanese flatbread parcels with roasted squash, feta and pistachios, grilled lobster or chicken liver and brandy parfait. Prices start at £7 for small portions, £9 for large. You can start with a selection of home-made tapas and finish with one of the scrummy home made desserts, all £4, such as pecan and treacle tart, lemon tart, sticky toffee pud, or in summer maybe pavlova with summer fruits or Pimms and strawberry jelly.

Q S V P

DARTMOUTH

Cherub

13 Higher Street, TQ6 9RB

- ▶ Near inner harbour
- ☀ Mon-Sat 11am-11pm; Sun 12-10.30pm
- Mon-Sat 12-2.30pm, 6.30-9.30pm; Sun 12.30-3pm, 6.30-9.30pm
- T (01803) 832571
- W www.the-cherub.co.uk
- Sharp's Doom Bar, Own; Summerskills Cherub; guests
- ☺ Reborn trad British with lots of fresh and smoked fish from the local smokery
- The oldest house in Dartmouth with a small, cosy, oak-beamed bar; a spiral staircase leads to two no smoking restaurants

Last time I was in Dartmouth we failed to get in to the much vaunted New Angel of celebrity chef John Burton-Race. Taking refuge in the Cherub, we were greeted by the welcome sight of a long line of handpumps, and in the cosy upstairs restaurant savoured superb English cooking. My friends enjoyed a huge pork hock casseroled in cider and a spinach, mozzarella and cherry tomato pudding. Fresh fish include lemon sole, John Dory, salmon, seabass, Dover sole, monkfish, cod, trout, crab and mussels, as well as smoked fish from Dartmouth Smokehouse. I chose smoked haddock – used in the well known Cherub smokie with saffron and cream sauce.

The menu changes quarterly but typical starters are duck confit with Victoria plum sauce, Dartmouth smoked salmon with rhubarb and gooseberry chutney or scallops with a black pud and west country ham fritter. Mains include Poole Farm sausages with bubble and squeak, Devon lamb shank braised with orange, redcurrants and honey roast garlic, £7.95-£13.45. At night extra main courses include steak and kidney pudding with Guinness gravy and, in season, Exmoor venison with macerated cherries, parsnip purée and thick game chips.

★ S V C

DODDISCOMBSLEIGH

Nobody Inn

EX6 7PS

- ▶ 3 miles W of A38 at Exeter racecourse
- ☼ Daily 12-2.30pm, 6 (7pm Sun)-11pm
- Ⓨ Daily 12-2pm, 7-10pm
- T (01647) 252394
- F (01647) 252978
- E info@nobodyinn.co.uk
- W www.nobodyinn.co.uk
- Branscombe Vale Nobody's; Otter Ale; guest
- ☺ Amazing cheese list and a wide menu
- ◉ Isolated 16th-century pub with beams and an inglenook fire

An extraordinary range of freshly-cooked dishes created from local produce is served throughout the year – not all at once, but a daily selection from the inn's long list of original recipes. The bar menu includes Nobody soup of chicken stock, vegetables and fruit, crab crumble or roast fennel and Pommery mustard risotto, mainly £4-£5, followed by venison with spiced red cabbage, steak and kidney pudding, Provençal fish stew or wild boar and apple sausages on beetroot mashed potato with onion and cider gravy, priced £6.90-£10.50.

Restaurant dishes might include fresh Brixham crab cakes or smoked eel on potato pancake as starters, fish such as lemon crumbed halibut on sweet potato mash, monkfish in smoky bacon with spicy tomato sauce, or oyster, prawn, squid and cockle pie. Meat dishes, depending on season, might be stuffed brace of quail with fig and apricot sauce, chicken with venison on ratatouille, faggots and mash, or wild boar and wild mushroom pie with tomato and ginger chutney. Vegetarians are spoiled for choice – maybe Beenleigh Blue cheese, leek, chestnut and Roman nut mustard pie or spicy lentil cakes with red onion salsa. But the real glory is the cheeseboard, chosen from over 60 fascinating cheeses, mainly from Devon – a plateful of six in the bar is £6.20.

★ Q ❀ S V P C

EXETER

Well House Tavern

Cathedral Yard, EX1 1HD

- ▶ Opposite Exeter Cathedral
- ☼ Mon-Sat 11am-11pm; Sun 12-10.30pm
- Ⓨ Mon-Sat 12-5.30pm; Sun 12-2.30pm
- T (01392) 223611
- Otter Ale; guests
- ☺ Contemporary pub meals and snacks
- ◉ Well-preserved pub adjoining the Royal Clarence Hotel in a stunning location overlooking the cathedral green at the historic heart of the city

Served throughout the afternoon, the meals here are based on local produce and freshly prepared. Bread is baked in house each morning, while fish comes from Brixham market and cheese is supplied by Paxton and Whitfield. A fairly limited menu is boosted each day by specials and desserts that are chalked on the blackboards. Starters are mostly salads – Greek, chicken Caesar or smoked duck – or there is home-made soup of the day served with a canon loaf. Main course dishes include steaks and grills, bangers and mash, chicken chasseur or pie of the day – for which there is a waiting time of 25 minutes. Prices for mains are from £8.50-£13. Alternatively you could have a pint of prawns for £7.50 or the 'not so traditional' fish in ale batter and chunky Devon chips, £9, or mussels in garlic, thyme and white wine sauce. A trio of pasta dishes is also offered. If you do not want a full meal there is a fair selection of sandwiches and wraps – the grilled Provençal vegetables and goats' cheese is a good veggie choice – and various hot snacks, such as filled jacket spuds for around a fiver or steak baguette with onions, French fries and salad for £8. On Sunday a traditional roast dinner replaces the daily menu.

S V (Exeter Central) **C**

KILMINGTON

☆ Old Inn

EX13 7RB

▶ A35 at Kilmington Cross, 1 mile W of Axminster

Mon-Sat 12-2.30pm (3pm Sat), 6-11pm; Sun 12-3pm, 7-10.30pm

Daily 12-2pm, 6.30-9pm (not Sun eve)

T (01297) 32096

E oldinnkilmington@aol.com

Branscombe Branoc, O'Hanlon's Port Stout; Otter Bitter; St Austell Tinners, Tribute

Traditional English with a soupçon of French; local fresh fish and shellfish

Detached 15th-century Grade II cob and thatched pub steeped in character

The Kilmington uses locally-sourced ingredients. Award-winning Colyton Butchers provides the meat and fresh and smoked trout and salmon come from a nearby trout farm. On the fish menu you will find a pint of smoked prawns, Lyme Bay crab gratin, grilled brill with lemon and dill, red mullet on stir-fried vegetables, monkfish on spicy tomato coulis, Membury trout, wild seabass or hake in lemon butter sauce, prices around £8.95-£11.25.

Starters include French fish soup and black pudding with bacon in cream sauce, main dishes are Colyton sausages with horseradish mash, pan-fried lamb's liver and bacon, rack of lamb marinated in honey and mint, Colyton Butchers' faggots with rich onion gravy or Old Inn port stout stew with dumplings, mainly £8.95-£9.95. Veggie choices include home-made roast vegetable pie. Pasta dishes are smoked fish in a cream and horseradish sauce, chorizo and wild mushroom in cream Dijon sauce or home-cured ham and mushroom carbonara. Home-made desserts could be Eton Mess of raspberries, meringue and chantilly or apple and cinnamon crumble with clotted cream or custard, and there is a platter of west country cheeses. Bar lunches include lovely omelettes and six different ploughman's.

★ Q S V ♿ ♣ P C

LOWER ASHTON

Manor Inn

EX6 7QL

▶ Village is off B3193

Tue-Sat 12-2pm (2.30pm Sat), 6.30-11pm; Sun 12-2.30, 7-10.30pm

Tue-Sun 12-1.30pm, 7-9pm

T (01647) 252304

E mark@themanorinn.co.uk

W www.themanorinn.co.uk

Princetown Jail Ale; RCH Pitchfork; Teignworthy Reel Ale; guest

Home-cooked menu that changes regularly, based on local produce

Small but full of character, this two bar country pub has a delightful little garden affording stunning views of the Teign Valley

Chalked up on boards, this little pub manages quite a large menu, including at least eight different home-made desserts. In fact all the food here is cooked on the premises and varies according to what produce is available locally. This is, of course, particularly true of fish, but you will usually find a fish pie with salad or a trio of fresh fish with new potatoes and usually a beer battered fish with new potatoes and peas (note – no chips served here!). Other tempting main courses include beef casserole made with beer or red wine served with garlic bread, home-cooked ham with egg and jacket potato, chilli tortilla wrap on a bed of lettuce with sour cream, lamb shank and cheese and bacon pasta. Usually a couple of curries will be listed, too. Main courses are all under £9 apart from steaks, £10-£13. Vegetarians are also offered a choice, maybe mushroom curry with rice, £5.95, or tomato, basil and garlic sausages with sautéed mushrooms and mash, £7.95 or ratatouille with garlic bread to wipe around the dish, £6.25. Desserts are all £3.50. For a light meal there is a selection of sandwiches, filled baguettes and jacket spuds or home-made soup.

★ Q V P C

NEWTON ST CYRES
Beer Engine
EX5 5AX

- ▶ Off A377 between Crediton and Exeter, near station
- Mon-Sat 11am-11pm; Sun 12-10.30pm
- Daily 12-2pm, 6.30-9.30pm
- T (01392) 851282
- F (01392) 851876
- E enquiries@thebeerengine.co.uk
- W www.thebeerengine.co.uk
- Beer Engine Rail Ale, Piston Bitter, Sleeper Heavy
- Daily chalked menus based on fresh local produce
- Former railway hotel, now the home of Devon's oldest brewery (established 1983), the single room houses a bar and dining area

The pub is famous for its on-site brewery, one of the reasons it was voted local CAMRA Pub of the Year in 2003. The landlord is equally proud of the food served here. Landlady Jill Hawksley is in charge of the kitchen and buys all her produce locally. The butcher provides information on the farms he uses, greengrocery and fish come from local markets or suppliers and poultry from a nearby farm that uses no hormone or growth stimulants. The cheese is bought from an award-winning producer 200 yards from the pub. Naturally enough the ale is incorporated into several dishes, such as steak in Sleeper pie and wort from the brewery is added to the batter for deep-fried cod and haddock.

The pub usually offers a good range of fresh fish, such as organic salmon, wild seabass, lemon sole and plaice. There is always a choice for vegetarians, too: aubergine bake, spinach lasagne, cheese and pasta bakes. On Sunday lunchtime a traditional roast is served 'family style' with dishes of vegetables, potatoes and gravy put on the table. Most of the desserts are home made or you could try the delicious ice cream supplied by Langage Farm in Plympton.

Q V (Newton St Cyres) P C

PRINCETOWN
Plume of Feathers
Plymouth Hill, PL20 6QQ

- Mon-Sat 10.30am-11pm; Sun 12-10.30pm
- Daily 10.30am (12 Sun)-9.30pm
- T (01822) 890240
- F (01822) 890780
- E pataweir@aol.com
- W www.plumeoffeathers-dartmoor.co.uk
- Princetown Dartmoor IPA, Jail Ale; St Austell Tinners
- Best of British featuring local produce
- Princetown's oldest building with a copper topped bar and slate walls

Using local produce down to the village brewery's ale, the Plume offers both bar snacks and hearty meals, much of it traditional English. The specials board changes more or less on a daily basis with starters such as spiced onion and parsnip terrine, Ardennes pâté, salmon and broccoli fishcakes, Stilton and bacon salad or fresh grilled mackerel, prices around £4-£5. Main meals could be grilled pork loin topped with spicy chorizo, local Dartmoor smoked trout with salad and new potatoes, braised lamb shank in red wine with mashed potato, whole baked mackerel with herbed butter or home-made chicken curry, prices £7-£9.

The set menu provides toasted wholemeal paninis with fillings such as bacon, tomato and mushrooms, sandwiches, jacket potatoes and local hand-made pasties, both chuck steak and vegetable, snacks £3.75-£4.50. Main courses are the Plume ploughman's of home-cooked ham, beef, Stilton and Cheddar, steak and Jail Ale pie with fresh vegetables, chicken and leek steamed pudding, Devon lamb rump with wild rocket and mint sauce, a whole braised lamb knuckle served on mash with wholegrain mustard sauce, local pork and leek sausages or Devon rump steak, £6.50-£9.95. Roast Mediterranean vegetables with herb couscous is popular with vegetarians, treacle pudding with clotted cream is loved by all.

★ S V P C

ROCKBEARE
Jack in the Green
EX5 2EE

- ▶ Close to Exeter airport on old A30
- ☼ Mon-Sat 11am-3pm, 5.30 (6pm Sat)-11pm; Sun 12-10.30pm
- Ⓨ Mon-Sat 11am-2pm, 6-9.30pm (10pm Sat); Sun 12-9.30pm
- T (01404) 822240
- F (01404) 823445
- E info@jackinthegreen.uk.com
- W www.jackinthegreen.uk.com
- Branscombe Vale Branoc; Cotleigh Tawny Bitter; Otter Ale; Greene King Ruddles BB; guests
- ☺ Imaginative mix of trad and modern, 99 per cent organic fruit and veg
- 200-year-old award-winning food-based pub; recently refurbished restaurant

Nine chefs make sure the food is all home cooked and tempting at this former winner of Devon Pub of the Year. Menus change every two months to coincide with seasonal produce, all bought locally, including excellent veggie choices. In the bar main courses could be calf's liver and bacon with onions, braised beef in stout with champ, smoked chicken carbonara with garlic bread, or bangers and mash with onion gravy. Prices from £7.50-£9.50 including vegetables, with rib eye steak £16.50.

In the restaurant starters range from red mullet saltimbocca to caramelised scallops with leeks and star anise orange sauce, prices from £6.50-£8.50. Main dishes could be lamb chump with pine kernels, walnuts and black olives, seared organic salmon with saffron new potatoes or duck breast with honey, cloves and spices, prices £14.50-£15.95. Veggie meals might be tomato, black olive and feta tart tatin or Stilton and baby leek Eccles cake, all £11.50. Sunday lunch with choices such as roast rib eye beef or braised belly pork with aubergine caviar is £17.95 for two courses. Home-made desserts include coconut and ginger rice pud.

S V P **C**

TALATON
Talaton Inn
EX5 2RQ

- ▶ On B3176 off A30 between Honiton and M5
- ☼ Daily 12-3pm, 7-11pm
- Ⓨ Daily 12-3pm, 7-9.30pm
- T (01404) 822214
- Badger Tanglefoot; Fuller's London Pride; O'Hanlon's Yellowhammer; guest
- ☺ Plenty of variety at modest prices
- Traditional pub with real fire, one room for bar and dining

The landlord is also the cook at the Talaton Inn, producing a modestly priced menu with something for everyone on a specials board and set menu that begins with home-made soup, kiln-smoked salmon and trout fillets, smoked chicken, Brie and bacon Caesar salad, soused Orkney herrings with cockles and prawns, priced £3.25-£4.95. Main courses feature prime Devon steaks from £8.25 for rump to £12.95 for fillet, pork and leek sausages with onion gravy in a Yorkshire pudding, home-baked ham, egg and chips, roast of the day with all the trimmings, crispy beef in chilli with sweet and sour sauce, lamb cutlets roasted with rosemary and Madeira, half a roast duck with orange and cointreau or black bean and spring onion, lightly battered calamari with sweet 'n' sour sauce or locally smoked haddock with lemon parsley butter, prices £6.25-£11.95. Vegetarians can choose Quorn sausages in a Yorkie, nut and vegetable roast again with Yorkshire pudding and seasonal vegetables or a three-egg Spanish omelette. Sunday lunch is £6.75 for the main course, £8.75 for two courses. On Monday the over 50s can choose a main course and pud for £3.75, while the mid-week special lunch of two courses at £4.95 is available to all Mon-Fri.

Q S V P **C**

TUCKENHAY

☆ Maltsters Arms

Bow Creek, TQ9 7EQ

- ▶ Signed from A381, Totnes-Kingsbridge road
- Mon-Sat 11am-11pm; Sunday 12-10.30pm
- Daily 12-3pm, 7-9.30pm; all day Sat and in summer
- T (01803) 732350
- F (01803) 732823
- E pub@tuckenhay.demon.co.uk
- W www.tuckenhay.com
- Princetown Dartmoor IPA; guests
- ☺ Inspiring and eclectic daily changing menu with lots of local produce and cheese
- Lively riverside pub on Bow Creek attracting locals, tourists and yachties

You will find great ingenuity and temptation on a different menu every day, featuring local produce from Dartmouth Smokehouse, fresh fish from Brixham, Dartmouth and Plymouth, west country cheeses, free range eggs, meat from the butcher in Totnes and local game in winter – though you could equally find West Indian style goat curry. While the Maltsters has a chef of seven years' standing, landlady Denise Thwaites plans the menus and often makes magic soups and veggie dishes. Just a small sample of the choice of starters might be air-dried ham, smoked duck and chicken with kirsch cherries, seafood soup with plaice, cod, gurnard, clams and oysters, River Fowey mussel chowder, or quails' eggs with guacamole and hummus, priced £3.95-£6.

Main dishes could be whole Dorade bream with lime and sambucca glaze, local sole with lemon and herb butter, fisherman's pie with marlin among fish in the net, wild boar chops pot roasted with cider and calvados, grilled lamb with sloe berry jelly, five spice duckling with honey, or pheasant, venison and rabbit casserole, prices £8-£16 including lovely vegetables. Vegetarian dishes might be potato gnocchi with rocket pesto or butternut squash, aubergine and banana curry. Desserts range from kiwi and tequila fool to ginger sponge pudding. Kids have a real food menu – grilled plaice or salmon fillet, pan-fried chicken breast, pasta in cheese sauce and small portions from the main menu. Former owner Keith Floyd was responsible for the flamboyant B&B accommodation (10 per cent discount for CAMRA members).

Q S V P C

TURNCHAPEL
Boringdon Arms
Boringdon Terrace, PL9 9TQ

- ▶ Turnchapel is signed from A379 on the edge of Plymouth
- ☼ Mon-Sat 11am-11pm; Sun 12-10.30pm
- 🍴 Mon-Sat 12-2pm, 6-9pm; Sun 12-2pm, 6-8pm
- T (01752) 402053
- F (01752) 481313
- W www.bori.co.uk
- 🍺 Butcombe Bitter; RCH Pitchfork; Summerskills BB; Sutton Plymouth Pride; guests
- ☺ Freshly made, hearty food including legendary pies
- ◉ Waterside, character pub attracting locals and sailors; beer festivals are held regularly

The Boringdon is renowned for its giant cod fillets in beer batter made with Pitchfork, and home-made 'legendary' pies with shortcrust topping such as minty lamb, beef and ale, steak and Stilton, turkey and stuffing, pork with apple and cider, cheese and onion, priced £5.25 with chips and mushy peas. However its biggest seller is fish pie of cod and smoked haddock topped with mash, breadcrumbs and cheese at £6.95. Soup such as parsnip and Stilton or leek and potato, served with garlic slices at £3.25, is almost a meal in itself.

A typical choice on the daily changing specials board could be could be Thai chicken flavoured with lemongrass, coriander and coconut milk, home-cooked ham with two eggs and chips, lamb goulash with tomatoes, paprika and garlic bread, Thai salmon steak with sweet chilli sauce, lamb shank with mint gravy, new potatoes and vegetables, beef madras curry or vegetarian caramelised onion and goat's cheese filo tart, prices £5.25-£8.25. Desserts, all £2.95, include treacle sponge, jaffa orange pudding, chocolate fudge cake and chocolate brûlée with custard, ice cream or clotted cream.

★ 🏰 ❀ 🛏 S V 🍺 ♣ 👪 C

UGBOROUGH
Anchor Inn
1 Lutterworth Street, PL21 07G

- ▶ Off B3210 close to A38 10 miles E of Plymouth
- ☼ Daily 11.30am-3pm, 5-11pm
- 🍴 Daily 12-2pm, 7-9pm
- T (01752) 892283
- E enquiries@anchorugborough.co.uk
- W www.anchorugborough.co.uk
- 🍺 Adnams Broadside; Courage BB; Draught Bass; Wadworth 6X; guests
- ☺ Bar meals and an à la carte restaurant with some rather exotic meats on the menu
- ◉ Traditional country village inn with plenty of atmosphere

If you have never tried kangaroo, wild boar, ostrich or bison, now's your chance. At the Anchor kangaroo comes with orange and mint sauce, wild boar is roasted with cider and apple sauce, ostrich barbecued and finished in bourbon while bison is enhanced by a wild berry sauce. Less exotic 'game' includes a brace of quail stuffed with apricot and bacon in a light apricot sauce or venison in sweet mustard sauce, prices all approaching £15. Fish includes sole Veronique, whole lemon sole, trout with almonds, swordfish with rosemary and garlic, monkfish sautéed in garlic butter, salmon and asparagus in creamy lemon sauce, prices £10.50-£16.55. You might start with bacon and banana in mild curry sauce or the happy snapper, that's crocodile kebab with mushrooms, peppers and bacon in barbecue sauce.

Bar food is simpler and cheaper, including Cheddar or Stilton ploughman's around £4.50, toasted ciabatta with fillings from sausage and onion to ham and cheese, or sandwiches from ham and tomato to fresh crab, a bargain at £3.75. There are various filled jacket potatoes starting at £2, steak and kidney pie, chilli with wild rice and the all day breakfast. Rotating guest beers are from Devon micros.

★ 🏰 ❀ 🛏 S V 🍺 ♣ P ⚡ 👪 C

WOODLAND
Rising Sun
TQ13 7JT

▶ Signed Woodland/Denbury off A38
☼ Tue-Sat 11.45am-3pm, 6-11pm;
Sun 12-3pm, 7-10.30pm
🍴 Tue-Sat 12-2.15pm, 6-9.15pm;
Sun 12-3pm, 7-9.15pm
T (01364) 652544
F (01364) 653628
E mail@risingsunwoodland.co.uk
W www.risingsunwoodland.co.uk
🍺 Princetown Jail Ale; guest
☺ Award-winning, mainly English country cooking featuring lovely fish
◉ Delightful, welcoming rural free house with lovely grounds and open fire

The list of local suppliers is as long as your arm, from Dartmouth Smokehouse to Langage Farm cream, fresh fish from Newton Abbot to Luscombe Cider. Superb ingredients are put to good use on an innovative English menu; their pies are nationally renowned and include Devon lamb with lemon and honey, steak and Jail Ale, beef and Devon blue cheese or game with redcurrant jelly, all £7.95. Otherwise the blackboard menu could boast succulent roast belly pork with roast onion mashed potato, locally caught Pollock in batter with home-made chips, a trio of Brixham fish – brill, gurnard and monkfish – with red pepper sauce, honey roast pork sausages from the butcher Chris McCabe with roast onion mash and gravy, superb Devon steaks or simple home-cooked ham with local free-range eggs and hand-cut chips, prices £6.95-£13.50. Veggie dishes are always good and could be Greek-style salad with olives and Vulscombe goats' cheese or vegetable tempura with noodles and sweet 'n' sour dip. Starters might be leek, walnut and Devon blue cheese tart or ham and pork terrine with apple jelly. Do leave room for local cheeses or an excellent dessert.

Q S V P C

Julia Kingsford, who describes herself as chief cook and bottle washer at the Stag's Head in Swalecliffe in Kent, sends this spicy recipe:

SMOKED CATALAN BEEF WITH TOMATO AND BELL PEPPER RICE
Serves 6

For Catalan beef
1 kg (2lb) chuck steak, cut into large chunks
Seasoned flour
Olive oil
1 clove garlic, chopped
150ml (¼ pint) white wine
1½ heaped tsps smoked paprika
250g (9oz) Chorizo sausage, sliced
600ml (1 pint) passata
150ml (¼ pint) chuck stock

For tomato rice
1 large onion, chopped
2 cloves garlic, crushed
2 bell peppers, sliced
Olive oil
125g (5oz) Basmati rice
250g (9oz) chopped tinned tomatoes
Vegetable stock
Salt and pepper

Coat steak in seasoned flour and brown in a deep pan with a little olive oil and the garlic, set aside. Deglaze pan with the white wine, adding the smoked paprika, chorizo, passata and beef stock. Return beef to the pan, bring to simmering point, cover and cook for around 90 minutes; season to taste. When the beef is nearly cooked, prepare the rice by softening the onion with the garlic and sliced peppers in olive oil in a large skillet. Add the washed rice and fry gently, turning, until the rice is opaque. Add the chopped tomatoes with a little vegetable stock and season. Slowly add more stock and let the rice absorb it until the rice is al dente then press into ramekins, turn out and serve alongside the Catalan beef and a mixed salad.

BRANSGORE
Three Tuns
Ringwood Road, BH23 8JH

- Four miles from Christchurch
- Mon-Sat 11.30am-3pm, 6-11pm; Sun 12-10.30pm
- Mon-Sat 12-2.15pm, 6.30-9.30pm; Sun 12-9.30pm
- T (01425) 672232
- E info@3tuns.com
- W www.3tuns.com
- Caledonian Deuchars IPA; Ringwood Best, Fortyniner; Taylor Landlord; guest
- Freshly made bar and à la carte food
- 17th-century thatched pub with exposed beams

All food is freshly made to order from ingredients delivered daily by local suppliers, with bread, pasta and puddings made on the premises. Lunchtime snacks include Welsh rarebit brioche made with cheese and ale, or a Scottish version with smoked salmon and the Three Tuns ploughman's of home-baked ham or mature Cheddar. Pasta freshly made to a traditional Italian recipe includes spinach and ricotta cannelloni, penne with chorizo and chilli, or tagliatelle with chicken or smoked salmon; moules marinière is prepared from rope grown mussels. Main meals include locally-made pork and leek sausages with mash and red wine gravy, fish pie, pan-fried lamb's liver with bacon in sherry cream sauce, tempura battered cod, steak and ale pie or slow roasted lamb shank, priced £7.75-£13.

'Posh nosh' includes starters such as grilled aubergines with mozzarella and tomato, or warm lorraine tart followed by grilled sea bass, roast chump of lamb served pink, grilled Aberdeen Angus fillet, pork loin with roast pear and parsnips with boulangère potatoes or medallions of Balmoral venison with red cabbage parcel, Madeira and blackcurrant sauce. Sunday roast is well regarded, home-made desserts include hot pineapple sponge and brioche bread and butter pud. Q S V P C

BUCKHORN WESTON
Stapleton Arms
Church Hill, SP8 5HS

- Wincanton exit off A303 or A30
- Mon-Sat 11am-3pm, 6-11pm; Sun 12-3pm, 6-10pm
- Mon-Sat 11am-3pm, 6-9.30pm; Sun 12-3pm, 6-9pm
- T (01963) 370396
- F (01963) 371524
- E mail@thestapletonarms.co.uk
- W www.thestapletonarms.co.uk
- Butcombe Bitter; Hop Back Crop Circle; Ringwood Best Bitter, Fortyniner; guests
- Gastropub serving eclectic and traditional fare
- Outstanding village pub, there for the community, with lovely garden

You don't often find organic, home-made beef burgers on a bar menu, but you do at the Stapleton – plain, cheese plus bacon or mushrooms, £4.75-£5.50 in a bun with salad and French fries. Daily changing specials could include starters of chickpea and tahini hummus, chicken liver and green peppercorn pâté or salmon fish cakes, all home made, priced around £4.75. Main courses might be boned saddle of rabbit wrapped in bacon with mustard sauce, peppered venison steak with Guinness sauce, fresh crabmeat and leek risotto, char-grilled swordfish with capers, mint and lemon, or lamb shank in Moroccan spices, priced £8.75-£11.95.

The regular menu offers home-made soup and veggie spring rolls with sweet chilli sauce among the starters, followed by home-made steak and kidney or chicken pie, wild boar sausages with mash, sweet and sour chicken, Somerset ham with double egg and chips, and cod or haddock in home-made batter. A full selection of grills is topped by the full monty at £10.95, and children get real food including home-made chicken nuggets. Desserts from old English sherry trifle to spotted dick cost around £3.50. S V P C

FARNHAM

☆ Museum Inn

DT11 8DE

- Between A354 and B3081
- Daily 12-3pm, 6-11pm (7-10.30pm Sun)
- Daily 12-2pm, 7-9.30pm
- T (01725) 516261
- F (01725) 516988
- E enquiries@museuminn.co.uk
- W www.museuminn.co.uk
- Hop Back Summer Lightning; Ringwood BB; Taylor Landlord
- Multi award winning food pub using fresh local and organic produce
- Part thatched 17th-century inn with flagstone floors and large inglenook

English Inn of the Year 2005 is just one of the awards won by the Museum Inn, whose head chef Mark Treasure gained Michelin stars at his previous two establishments and is winning accolades here. He has sourced local suppliers for fresh ingredients including traditionally raised meat, free range poultry and eggs, game from nearby estates and fish from the south coast, using organic produce where possible.

The menu, printed on brown wrapping paper, changes daily but a sample choice starts with yellow split pea and honey glazed streaky bacon soup, bruschetta of marinated sardines, fishcakes with tartare sauce, wood pigeon, duck and wild mushroom terrine, caramelised onion tart with hot goats' cheese and truffle oil, mozzarella risotto with pine kernels or smoked chicken and pancetta salad, prices from £5-£7.50. The same day's main choices are roast brill with prawns, lemon and basil and potato purée, haunch of venison in red wine with bubble and squeak, 10oz rib eye steak with horseradish butter and hand-cut chips, slow roast belly pork with creamed savoy cabbage or baked tomatoes with zucchini, olives and aubergine, prices £13.50-£16.50. A plate of five cheeses with chutney is £6.50, desserts include tiramisu and iced coffee parfait.

★ Q S V C

SHAFTESBURY

☆ Mitre

23 High Street, SP7 8JE

- In town centre
- Daily 10.30am-11pm
- Mon-Fri 12-3pm, 6-9pm; Sat & Sun 12-9pm
- T (01747) 853002
- E mitre@youngs.co.uk
- Young's Bitter, Special, Winter Warmer, seasonal
- Good selection of meals and snacks
- Smart town pub where you can dine on the three-tiered decking

One of the London brewer's more southerly outposts, Young's acquired the Mitre in 2003 and reopened it after extensive renovations including the decking area. The Mitre offers a good snack menu: alongside chunky sandwiches with plenty of filling options, £4.50, there is a ploughman's board with cheese, ham or sausage, £6.50 and hot open sandwiches served with salad and chips for £5.95, including minted lamb with tzatziki yogurt, Greek feta cheese and salad, a minute steak or sausage.

The main menu starts with 'small plates' priced from £4-£8: smoked chicken and mango salad, Somerset Brie and cherry tomato salad with raspberry vinaigrette, local Dorset dressed crab with citrus mayo and salad, smoked salmon with beetroot chutney and a seasonal soup. 'Main plates' include pub standards such as steaks, burgers, bangers and mash and (local) ham with free-range eggs and chips. You could also try Young's award-winning steak and mushroom pie or the more exotic roasted butternut squash and asparagus risotto with shaved parmesan. Prices range from £7-£10 but many items are available as children's portions – which makes a nice change from the usual breadcrumbed dinosaurs of indeterminable content. For dessert there are Beechdean ice creams, various chocolate confections or summer pudding with clotted cream.

★ S V C

STUDLAND
Bankes Arms Country Inn
Manor Road, BH19 3AU

- Signed from village
- Daily 11am-11pm
- Daily summer 12-9.30pm; winter 12-3pm, 6-9pm
- T (01929) 450225
- F (01929) 450307
- Isle of Purbeck Fossil Fuel, Solar Power, Studland Bay Wrecked; guests
- Fresh, home-made food with notable vegetarian and fish dishes
- Brew pub made of Purbeck stone with own mooring close to Poole harbour; home to Isle of Purbeck brewery

A pub with plenty going for it including its own brewery, August beer festival with over 50 ales and a massive garden overlooking the sea. Renowned for its good food, dishes are freshly made on a changing menu. A sample menu offers vegetarian specials leek and mushroom stroganoff with brandy and cream sauce, Spanish quiche, oven-roasted goats' cheese with salad and chilli sauce, wild mushrooms on fettuccine and vegetable curry of sweet potatoes, butternut squash, courgettes, capsicums and mangetout.

Main courses include chicken supreme in Blue Vinney cheese sauce, lamb, capsicum and coconut curry, game casserole of pheasant, wild boar and wild duck braised in a house ale served with Yorkshire pudding, a genuine spag bol, shank of lamb slow cooked in red wine, lamb and mint sausage with wine and balsamic vinegar sauce flavoured with thyme, moules marinière, as well as fillet and sirloin steak. In addition there is plenty of fresh fish such as pan-fried plaice, swordfish, salmon, halibut, tuna steaks, fresh crab and lobster in season and home-battered tempura prawns. Tempting snacks include hot filled baguettes, ploughman's and large salads. Desserts include fresh fruit and locally made ice cream.

S V C

TARRANT MONKTON
Langton Arms
DT11 8RX

- Off B3082 from Wimbourne or A354 from Blandford
- Mon-Sat 11.30am-11pm; Sun 12-10.30pm
- Mon-Fri 11.30am-2.30pm, 6-9.30pm; Sat & Sun all day
- T (01258) 830225
- F (01258) 830053
- E info@thelangtonarms.co.uk
- W www.thelangtonarms.co.uk
- Ringwood Fortyniner; Langton Bitter; guest
- Large menu of home-made pub favourites, specials and vegetarian dishes
- 17th-century thatched gem in unspoilt Tarrant Valley with rustic public bar

In the bar you can enjoy home-made 'pub favourites' such as steak and ale pie, local Kingston Lacy Red Devon beef roast with home-made Yorkshire pudding and vegetables, Dorset lamb's liver fried with local pork and leek sausages in red wine gravy with mash and vegetables, Dorset chicken breast with peanut and chilli cream sauce and home-cooked honey roast ham, egg and chips, prices £7.20-£8.25. Five home-made veggie dishes include broccoli, Brie and mushroom lasagne, baked aubergine filled with vegetables topped with mozzarella, mixed bean stew or deep fried Brie with home-made mixed fruit sauce.

Light bites include filled baguettes, jackets and ploughman's with three local cheeses. All beef from mince to fillet steak comes from a herd of grass fed Red Devon cattle from the local National Trust Kingston Lacy estate. The restaurant menu changes weekly, sample dishes include ham and butterbean soup or beetroot, ricotta and prawn tartlet followed by roast duck breast with home-made chutney, local loin of venison, steak, oyster and red wine pie, or wild seabass or butternut squash with pine nuts, hummus, sultanas and ginger in filo pastry. Langton Bitter is brewed by Hop Back.

S V P C

WAREHAM
Duke of Wellington

7 East Street, BH20 4NN

▶ In town centre close to town hall
☼ Mon-Sat 11am-11pm; Sun 12-11pm
Ⓨ Daily 12-2.30pm, 6-9.30pm; all day in summer hols
T (01929) 553015
E janetmasson@aol.com
Ringwood seasonal beers; guests
☺ Tempting home-cooked menu and imaginative weekly specials
◙ Popular town centre pub with cosy bar, separate restaurant area and courtyard

Sterling home cooking features on both the weekly-changing specials board and on the set menu, with prices surprisingly low for the sort of dishes presented. A typical specials selection includes minced beef pie in red wine with Dijon mustard under home-made short crust pastry with mash, peas and parsley sauce for £6.95. An oven-roasted Dorset partridge with cherry, onion and brandy sauce is an alternative, as well as Singapore-style chicken noodles with cashews, coconut sauce and salad, spinach and mushroom crêpes flavoured with nutmeg, or monkfish, paprika and cream sauce with wild rice, prices £6.95-£12.95 – dessert of the day might be whisky marmalade bread and butter pudding with cream at £2.95. Fish specials might be whole grilled plaice, lemon and pepper haddock or skate wing with garlic and herb crust.

Main meals on the regular menu are around £5.45-£7.95, including freshly-made omelettes, home-cooked gammon, egg and chips, freshly battered cod, home-made lasagne verde and roast vegetable lasagne, or traditional steak and ale pie. For those with hearty appetites there is the Duke of Wellington special pork shank marinated in honey and mustard at £11.45. There is a good choice of snacks; house beer Duke's Bitter is Isle of Purbeck Fossil Fuel rebadged.

★ Q ❀ S V ♿ ≉ (Wareham) ♣ Ⓟ ⚡ C

Shepherd's pie is a simple dish, but here is the real McCoy made not with minced meat but with lamb shanks. It comes from the Sun Inn at Hook Norton in Oxfordshire.

SHEPHERD'S PIE USING SAUTED LAMB SHANKS

Serves 4

4 lamb shanks
1 onion
1 large carrot
3 sticks celery
3 cloves garlic
2 bay leaves
600ml (1 pint) good meat stock
2 dashes Worcestershire sauce
750g (1½ lb) Desiree potatoes, cooked
Knob butter
Dash of milk
Salt and pepper

Sauté lamb shanks to seal and place in a large pan with the chopped vegetables, crushed garlic and bay leaves, pour over the stock and simmer, covered, until the lamb shanks are tender – around 90 minutes. Remove shanks and simmer stock briskly to reduce by two thirds, add Worcestershire sauce. Remove meat from the shanks, break up, and divide between four small pie dishes. Add a ladleful of stock to each. Mash the hot, cooked potatoes with butter and milk, season with salt and pepper. Pipe the mash on top of each dish and bake in a hot oven (200C/400F/gas mark 6) for around 10 minutes, until the mash is browned.

CARLTON VILLAGE

☆ Smith's Arms

TS21 1EA

▶ Off A177, near Stockton on Tees
Mon 4-11pm; Tue-Sat 12-11pm; Sun 12-10.30pm
Tue-Sat 12-2pm, 6-9pm; Sun 12-3pm
T 01740 630471
E danny_keen@hotmail.com
W www.thesmithscarlton.co.uk
Caledonian Deuchars IPA; guest
High-quality dishes based on locally-sourced ingredients
The bustling bar is a focus for village life at this Victorian pub; the upmarket restaurant is in converted stables

This village pub is a place of contrasts: from the plain public bar where the locals congregate, which can be packed on big match days, to the much cosier lounge bar and upmarket restaurant where award-winning food is served. Most of the ingredients have travelled not much more than three miles, including fruit and veg from a local farm, while fish is provided from a fishmonger who lands his own boats at Hartlepool. Expect to pay around £18 or so for two courses in the restaurant; desserts are all £4.95.

For starters there may be pressed terrine of ham hock with Puy lentils and foie gras wrapped in Parma ham on brioche toast, roast goats' cheese and red onion confit tartlet with toasted almond salad and walnut oil dressing, or smoked haddock and tarragon fishcakes with herb salad and horseradish cream. Mains include confit duck leg with dauphinoise potato, rich French black pudding and red wine sauce, slow cooked beef with celeriac purée, wilted spinach and a wild mushroom and redcurrant sauce, pan-roasted cod fillet with champ mash or locally reared rib eye steak with hand-cut chips and a green Madagascan peppercorn sauce. Vegetarians can ask about the day's dishes. Lovely puds include warm chocolate mousse with pistachio ice cream.

S V P C

CROXDALE

Daleside Arms

Front Street, DH6 5HY

▶ On B6288, 3 miles S of Durham, off A167
Mon-Fri 4-11pm; Sat 11-11pm; Sun 12-10.30pm
Wed-Fri 4-9pm; Sun 11.30am-3pm
T (01388) 814165
E daleside.croxdale1@barbox.net
Beer range varies
Specialises in Euro-Asian cuisine
Sporting ephemera decorate the bar of this comfortable roadside local that was until fairly recently a guest house; it stages frequent beer festivals

Although the Daleside does not serve food at all sessions, it has a strong following from customers who regularly reserve tables. This is no doubt due to the pub's policy of offering special deals for early diners who book. There is a discount when you choose two dishes from one section of the menu (full prices are charged for non-bookers and diners after 8pm). The first part, with a two for £10 deal, lists mostly straightforward pub favourites such as minced beef and dumpling, braised lamb's liver and onions, roast beef and Yorkies or chilli con carne (this carries a heat warning!). The second section, two meals for £12, offers the house special of minted lamb and leek dumpling, braised beef with Yorkshire pud or dumpling, beef in cream pepper sauce and sweet and sour chicken. The third offer, two meals for £14, is great value with choices including a 12oz rump steak, chicken Vesuvius (again, very hot in a rich chilli, tomato and garlic sauce), Thai Massaman beef, chicken Mysore, Mexicana pepper rump steak or beef stroganoff. If you feel really brave you might want to try the jalapeno rump slices – although you are warned that this is possibly the hottest dish in the locality. Whatever you order arrives in generous portions, which is probably why the popular Sunday lunch also comes in a small size, £3, for older people and children.

Q S V P

DARLINGTON
Number Twenty-2
22 Coniscliffe Road, DL3 7RG

- Near the town centre, 100 yards from Binns Department Store
- Mon-Sat 12-11pm (closed Sun)
- Mon-Sat 12-2pm
- T (01325) 354590
- F (01325) 402502
- Village Brewer White Boar; guests
- Contemporary cuisine and great sandwiches
- Spacious, town-centre ale house that specialises in beers from small independent breweries

The home of Village Brewer beers, this ale house is a favourite with CAMRA members for obvious reasons – ten beers on tap at any one time. The award-winning bar with high ceilings and huge windows always feels light and airy, even when crowded. It is an ideal choice for shoppers or town centre workers for a quick bite at lunchtime as it offers a great range of sandwiches made with thick wholemeal bread and served with dressed salad leaves, coleslaw and fries for around a fiver, they are a meal in themselves. Fillings include tandoori chicken, tuna paprika, Brie and cranberry, smoked salmon with cream cheese and chives, grilled sirloin with a mushroom, bacon and tarragon sauce, prawns with Marie Rose sauce or BLT.

Alternatively there are hot toasted muffins with grilled bacon (with or without cheese) or tuna melt, home-made soup or pâté served with chunks of bread. The blackboard also offers daily specials such as chicken breast wrapped in bacon with dolcelatte and brandy cream sauce on butter broccoli tagliatelle, beer-battered cod fillet fish fingers with fresh tartare sauce and proper chips, sirloin steak with dressed salad leaves and chips or pork sausages with tomato and basil sauce and cheese topped mash, £7.50-£9.75.

★ **Q V** ≉ (Darlington) **C**

HEIGHINGTON
Bay Horse
28 West Green, DL5 6PE

- Six miles N of Darlington
- Daily 10am-midnight
- Daily 12-2pm, 5-9.30pm
- T (01325) 312312
- F (01325) 304068
- E info@bayhorseheighington.co.uk
- W www.bayhorseheighington.co.uk
- John Smith's Magnet; Theakston Cool Cask; guests
- Home-cooked menu with good vegetarian and fish choices
- Picturesque, 300-year-old, busy pub with exposed beams and stone walls

Food plays a major role at the Bay Horse although, with up to five real ales to choose from, drinkers are not entirely neglected. The varied menu is supplemented by a daily changing specials board. You know you are in the north-east of England when you encounter a starter of three home-made Yorkshire puddings served simply with home-made gravy (or garlic mushrooms as a vegetarian option), but there is also oriental tiger prawn parcels served with sweet and sour dip, or tomato salad with fresh basil and feta cheese, or you can have a simple bowl of mussels in garlic sauce or prawns in Marie Rose sauce with brown bread and butter.

Fillet steak is a speciality – try it stuffed with Stilton, wrapped in bacon and topped with Stilton sauce, marinated in Cajun spices and pan fried with spring onions or plain grilled with king prawns in garlic butter, £14.75-£17. Fish dishes, £7.75-£11.75, include salmon steak in creamy prawn and mustard sauce, grilled halibut steak, green lipped mussels Italian style in a tomato, oregano, mushroom and white wine sauce or fillet of lemon sole with pan-fried prawns and bacon, while vegetarians are offered mushroom and cashew stroganoff, stir-fried vegetables in a spicy black bean sauce or Parma style courgettes.

★ **S V** P **C**

HIGH HESLEDEN
Ship Inn
TS27 4QD

- ▶ A mile inland from Blackhall via B1281, off A19 at Castle Eden
- ☼ Tue-Thu 6-11.30pm; Fri & Sat 12-2pm, 6-11.30pm; Sun 12-7pm
- 🍴 Tue-Thu 6-9pm; Fri & Sat 12-2pm, 6-9pm; Sun 12-4pm
- T (01429) 836453
- Beer range varies
- ☺ Bar meals and a more adventurous restaurant menu
- Cosy inn featuring an open fire and nautical memorabilia, with an extensive garden

The Crosbys should get an award for sheer hard graft and enthusiasm. When they took on the pub in 2001 it had been shut for over two years and suffered years of neglect before that. In just 12 days they got the place ship-shape and reopened. Since then it has undergone a thorough refurbishment and established a reputation for fine food. Freshly produced meals rely on superb ingredients such as live rope-caught mussels and hand-dived king scallops from the west coast of Scotland.

Mouth-watering special dishes change daily; you may find pan-seared line-caught seabass with toasted king scallops, buttered asparagus and white wine for a reasonable £14, or char-grilled Angus fillet steak on rosti potato topped with game parfait, wild wood pigeon breast and Drambuie jus, £20, or their signature dish of fresh seafood platter: silver gilt bream, salmon, swordfish, lobster tail, king scallops and prawns infused with roast garlic, lemon and saffron butter and a friture of garden herbs, £20. Many main course dishes are under £12, including char-grilled swordfish loin with coriander and wild lime crust, roast coriander lamb chump on Lyonnaise potatoes with tomato, garlic and ginger masala sauce or sautéed duck breast on water chestnut noodles and oriental sauce. Most of the equally inspiring starters cost less than a fiver.

S V P C

OVINGTON
Four Alls
The Green, DL11 7BP

- ▶ Between the A66 and A67, two miles S of Winston
- ☼ Mon-Thu 7-11pm; Fri & Sat 3-11pm; Sun 12-10.30pm
- 🍴 Mon-Thu 7-9pm; Fri & Sat 6-9.30pm; Sun 12-2pm, 7-9pm
- T (01833) 627302
- Tetley Bitter; guest
- ☺ Excellent home-made fare at sensible prices
- Friendly, 18th-century pub with a bar, games room and restaurant, in what is known as the 'Maypole village'

John Stroud, landlord of the Four Alls, says, 'we don't have a chef – just Mum and me' – and good, homely cooking is what he and his Mum produce, based on the best locally-sourced ingredients and freshest vegetables. The menu is kept informal so they can adapt to customers' wishes, so for vegetarians it simply states 'vegetarian dishes and salads available on request - £7.30'. Buying the best quality beef means that the char-grilled steaks are a popular choice here, served with all the trimmings. A 10oz sirloin is £10.50 or a 16oz T-bone £13.25; pepper sauce is an optional extra.

Home-made dishes on the menu include braised beef (slices of prime beef in rich onion gravy), chicken and mozzarella melt, chicken and ham pie, the medium hot house curry and good old steak, kidney and ale pie. Main courses are usually accompanied by market fresh veg, new potatoes and home-made chips for around £7. On Sunday lunchtime food is served for just two hours so the traditional roast is always cooked to perfection and much appreciated by regulars, who reckon it to be 'just like Granny used to make' (not Mum?). The Four Alls has its own micro-brewery but local CAMRA members recommend that if you want to try the beer, phone first as it tends not to last.

Q S V P C

WOLVISTON

Ship

50 High Street, TS22 5JX

- Off A19 at Hartlepool turn
- Daily 12-3pm, 5-11.30pm
- Mon-Sat 12-1.45pm, 5-8.45pm (8.30pm Fri); Sun 12-1.45pm
- T (01740) 644420
- F (01740) 644651
- Caledonian Deuchars IPA, guests
- Good value, varied menu of home-cooked fare
- Once a coaching stop on the main Stockton-Sunderland road, this village pub now serves a more local clientele; it benefits from a secluded garden

The licensee at the Ship is a keen supporter of real ale and changes the guest beer every couple of days. The same dedication is apparent in the kitchen, with meals of generous portions freshly prepared to order attracting diners from a wide area. Prices start as low as £2.75 for a filled jacket potato, while for another pound there are baguettes with hot fillings such as bacon and Brie, beef and gravy or Cajun chicken, with chips and salad. Grills are a popular choice – from £9.50 for a 10oz sirloin up to £14 for a 16oz T-bone with all the trimmings.

Wholesome home-made dishes also feature, such as steak and ale or corned beef pie, mince and dumpling, liver and onions or a giant Yorkie filled with sausage and onion, mince or roast of the day, all priced at around a fiver. There are several fish choices including fresh seabass, Cajun spiced salmon or 'whopper' cod, all around £8, as well as international influences such as beef in black bean sauce, king prawn or chicken Thai green curry, beef stroganoff and chicken tikka, plus a vegetarian dish. At lunchtime children can eat for £3.25 and they are not confined to chicken nuggets – they can choose liver and onion, roast of the day or mince and dumpling, all with fresh veg.

S V P C

The Sun Inn at Feering in Essex is known for its unusual and inspiring Maltese dishes devised by landlady Kim Scicluna. They get lots of rabbits around harvest time, and here is Kim's recipe for a popular Maltese dish. Kim says that in Malta this would be Sunday dinner, or they would cook it the night before and take it to the beach to eat cold with rustic bread.

RABBIT IN RED WINE AND CAPER SAUCE

Serves 4

1 rabbit, jointed
Oil for frying
2 large onions, chopped
4 cloves of garlic, crushed
2 sticks of celery, chopped
2 medium carrots, sliced
5 medium mushrooms, sliced
1 300g tin processed peas, drained
1 400g tin chopped tomatoes
50g (2oz) sugar
1tbsp tomato purée
4 bay leaves
½ tsp dried oregano
2 tbsps capers
300ml (½ pint) red wine

Heat oil in a large pan, add the rabbit pieces and fry until golden on all sides; remove and put to one side. Add to the pan the onions, garlic, celery, carrots and mushrooms and cook until softened. Add all the other ingredients, stirring, finally returning the rabbit to the pan. Bring to the boil, reduce to a simmer, cover and cook for around an hour until the rabbit is cooked through and tender. Serve with hot crusty bread.

ARKESDEN
Axe & Compasses
CB11 4EX

- ▶ Village is between jct 8 and 9 of M11
- Mon-Fri 11.30-2.30pm, 6-11pm; Sat 12-3pm, 6-11pm; Sun 12-3pm, 7-10.30pm
- Daily 12-2pm (2.15pm Sun), 6.45-9.15pm (no Sun eve meals in winter)
- T (01799) 550272
- F (01799) 550906
- W www.axeandcompasses.co.uk
- Greene King IPA, Abbot, Old Speckled Hen
- Award-winning food served in the bar and restaurant
- Partly thatched traditional English inn, situated in tiny village of pretty cottages; a comfortable bar and lounge plus restaurant in converted stables

When the Christous arrived in the UK from Cyprus in the 1960s, they fell in love with Arkesden's beautiful village setting and bought the pub. Little has changed, and you can dine extremely well here, choosing your meal from blackboards in the lounge or from the à la carte menu in the dining room. Expect to pay around £18-23 for two courses in the evening (desserts are all £4), less for bar meals, or £16 for a three-course Sunday lunch. Tempting starters include pan-fried strips of duck breast with scallions and cucumber in a pancake with plum sauce, feta cheese parcels in filo pastry with a sweet cherry tomato and anchovy dressing, avocado pear baked with parma ham and stilton, laced with port or king scallops with mushrooms, white wine and cream, glazed with fresh Parmesan.

Plenty of fish choices grace the main course lists: medallions of monkfish with prawn and lemon parsley butter sauce, whole grilled lemon sole, lightly-grilled sea bass fillets with leek and potato cake or halibut steak stacked with spinach, tomato and cheddar. Meat comes from Burtons in Saffron Walden to make delicious medallions of beef fillet with Drambuie, mushroom and cream, noisettes of grilled lamb with mint and red wine gravy or pork tenderloin topped with ham and cheddar on a creamy mustard sauce.

★ Q S V ♣ P C

FEERING

☆ Sun Inn

3 Feering Hill, CO5 9NH

- ▶ On B1024
- ☼ Daily 12-3pm, 6-11pm (10.30pm Sun)
- 🍴 Daily 12-2pm (Sun 3pm), 6-9.30pm
- T (01376) 570442
- W www.suninnfeering.com
- Beer range varies
- ☺ Exciting bistro-style cooking
- ◙ Fascinating grade II listed building circa 1525 with carved black and white beams

A free house where the food style is as wide ranging as the choice of up to 25 different real ales a week on six handpumps. Possibly the only pub in the land serving Maltese cuisine – landlord Charlie Scicluna is from Malta and his English wife, Kim, is the chef who has produced a fabulous array of food for at least a decade. Extensive bar and blackboard menus are prepared from fresh ingredients, mainly local, apart from the occasional appearance of kangaroo, ostrich, bison and crocodile. Kim's sparkling repertoire includes Maltese dishes such as bragioli (Maltese beef olives), Maltese rabbit with red wine and capers, timpana (Maltese pasta bake) or vegetarian kapunata. Tempting game could be Romany pheasant or stuffed pigeon with apricot sauce.

Traditional choices range from steak and kidney pudding with oyster stout to liver and bacon in Adnams bitter, crofter's lamb casserole, pork chops with apples and walnuts in Crouch Vale bitter, Kentish casserole and haggis with black pudding on whisky sauce. Dishes with an international flavour are Creole beef, Hong Kong lamb and pork in lime and coconut. Eats to gladden a vegetarian might be tomato and walnut casserole, savoury peanut pie, Maltese ricotta and pea pie or cauliflower and leek terrine with orange sauce. Soups and starters are equally tempting, as are desserts such as plum and port crumble, beer tart or Maltese apple charlotte.

★ Q ❀ S V ♿ ♣ ● P C

GOSFIELD

☆ King's Head

The Street, CO9 1TP

- ▶ Centre of village on main road A1017
- ☼ Mon-Sat 12-3pm, 6-11pm; Sun 12-10.30pm
- 🍴 Mon-Sat 12-2.30pm, 6.30-9.30pm; Sun 12.30-7.30pm
- T (01787) 474016
- E enquiries@thekingsheadgosfield.co.uk
- W www.thekingsheadgosfield.co.uk
- Greene King IPA; guest
- ☺ The menu combines the best of traditional and modern dishes
- ◙ Charming, 16th-century pub sympathetically restored retaining period features such as the huge fireplaces

A lot of love and care has gone into the recent renovation of this Tudor pub that has been an integral part of Gosfield village since the reign of Henry VIII. The newly-furnished conservatory dining area is light, airy and comfortable, but you may also eat informally in the bar. The menu offers two or three starters, home-made pies, burgers, bangers and mash or baguettes, toasted panninis and filled jacket potatoes.

The restaurant offers far more variety and some inspired dishes. For starters there could be seared marlin niçoise salad, smoked duck breast salad with raspberry and balsamic dressing or crayfish and celeriac remoulade with tomato and herb salsa, £3.50-£6. Main course choices include duck breast with almond butter sauce, rack of lamb on thick cut potatoes with rosemary cream sauce and sweet potato and pepper timbale, grilled halibut steak with caper and chilli butter, spinach and dauphinoise potatoes, and spicy vegetable enchilada in a tortilla with tomato salsa gratin, £9.50-£14.50. The irresistible dessert menu might offer blueberry crème brûlée, pear, cinnamon and nutmeg crumble, pecan and treacle tart, mango and white chocolate pavlova or rhubarb fool, all £4.50, or there is a cheeseboard for an extra £1.

★ Q ❀ S V ♿ ♣ P C

GREAT EASTON
Swan
The Endway, CM6 2HG

▶ Off B184 Between Dunmow and Thaxted
☼ Mon-Sat 12-3pm, 6-11pm; Sun 12-3pm, 7-10.30pm
🍴 Mon-Sat 12-2pm, 7-9pm; Sun 12-2pm
T (01371) 870359
E theswangreateaston@talk21.com
W www.swangreateaston.co.uk
🍺 Adnams Bitter; guests
☺ Traditional British home cooking with unusual touches
◉ 15th-century free house and restaurant with log burning stove and beams

The Swan prides itself on home-made food down to the chips, ice cream and the chocolate truffles served with coffee. Much of the produce is locally sourced – meat comes from Sweetlands butchers in Great Dunmow, sausages and pork from Priors Hall while fresh fish from Grimsby is delivered daily. As well as bar and restaurant menus there are daily specials such as slow cooked lamb shank with port, redcurrant and rosemary sauce, bacon wrapped chicken breast filled with Stilton, shepherd's pie with thick gravy or steak and ale pie with real chips, priced £8.50 to £12.95.

The bar menu has a good range of sandwiches and filled baguettes, salads, home-made soup, ploughman's or just a bowl of real chips. The main menu offers favourites such as sausages and mustard mash, freshly breaded plaice, honey glazed ham, egg and chips, boeuf bourguignonne, butterflied chicken breast marinated in tequila, lime and Cajun spices, priced £7-£9.95, while a fine fillet steak is £13.75. Sunday offers a choice of four roasts. The favourite veggie dish is mushroom and cashew stroganoff containing oyster, cep, shiitake and button mushrooms. Home-made desserts include mixed berry Passion Pudding. Local guest ales are sourced direct from brewers such as Woodford and Nethergate.

★ ❀ S V ♣ P C

GREAT YELDHAM
White Hart
Poole Street, CO9 4HJ

▶ On A1017
☼ Mon-Sat 11am-3pm, 6-11pm; Sun 12-3pm, 7-10.30pm
🍴 Daily 12-2pm, 6.30-9.30pm
T (01787) 237250
F (01787) 238044
E reservations@whitehartyeldham.co.uk
W www.whitehartyeldham.com
🍺 Adnams Bitter; guests
☺ Modern British food served informally in the brasserie or restaurant
◉ Timber-framed inn built in 1505 with historic interior and big riverside gardens

Head chef John Dicken grew up in a Norfolk pub but trained at the Connaught Hotel, and now cooks up fine cuisine with British and international flavours, buying fresh fish and local produce daily, with asparagus and strawberries from a nearby farm in season. He also puts on beer cuisine evenings for local CAMRA branches, creating dishes such as Puy lentil, bacon and Adnams soup, shank of lamb braised in honey stout, and poached pear with Young's double chocolate stout sauce.

A lunch menu with two courses for £10.50 could start with roast pigeon and wild mushroom salad followed by beef cobbler with horseradish mash. Brasserie starters include halibut gravadlax, open goats' cheese ravioli and roast pumpkin risotto. Main courses might be classic fish pie, grilled Lincolnshire sausages and mash, slow braised lamb shank with swede mash, fish in beer batter or roast rosemary and lemon chicken, priced £9.95-£13.50. In the restaurant starters include seared scallops on black pudding with celeriac purée or red mullet with new potato and smoked bacon salad, going on to seared monkfish on pappardelle pasta, grilled turbot, rump of lamb with sweet potato mash and beetroot tatin, or spinach, plum tomato and caramelised red onion tart, priced £11.95-£16.50.

★ Q ❀ V P C

HEMPSTEAD
Bluebell Inn

High Street, CB10 2PD

- ▶ B1054 between Saffron Walden and Steeple Bumpstead
- ☼ Mon-Fri 12-3pm, 6-11pm; Sat & Sun 12-11pm (10.30pm Sun)
- 🍴 Mon-Fri 12-3pm, 6-9.30pm; Sat & Sun 12-9.30pm
- T (01799) 599199
- E enquiries@thebluebellinn.co.uk
- W www.thebluebellinn.co.uk
- 🍺 Adnams Bitter, Broadside; Woodforde's Wherry; guests
- ☺ Home-cooked food, mainly traditional but with a foreign influence
- ◙ Country inn, birthplace of Dick Turpin

English meat and prize-winning sausages from local butchers, fresh fish from Lowestoft, poultry and game from nearby farms, wild venison from the woods and fruit and vegetables chosen in the market are used to prepare a wide choice on the menu and specials board. Bar snacks include roast pepper stuffed with minted couscous and mango, home-made soup, and baguettes with fillings from home-cooked Suffolk ham to goats' cheese with red onion and olives, £3-£4.50. Bar meals include Suffolk ham with two free-range eggs and chips, three butcher's sausages with onion gravy or beef and ale pie.

The main meals menu offers Moroccan leg of lamb steak with mint yoghurt, chicken breast wrapped in bacon, Portuguese chicken piri piri, Italian chicken with oregano and basil, grilled seabass, large fried seafood platter, baked cod and deep fried haddock in batter, all priced £6.95-£8.95, plus char-grilled steaks. Excellent veggie choices include Mediterranean vegetable pie, mushroom and tomato pasta, veggie sausages with mash or home-made lasagne with spinach, courgettes and sun dried tomatoes. The rare real food menu for children would please Jamie Oliver.

★ 🏰 Q ❀ S V 🍺 🍎 P ⚡ 👪 C

LITTLEBURY
Queen's Head

High Street, CB11 4TD

- ▶ On main road B1383 running through village
- ☼ Daily 12-3pm, 5-11pm
- 🍴 Daily 12-2pm, 6-9pm
- T (01799) 522251
- E info@queensheadinnlittlebury.co.uk
- W www.queensheadinnlittlebury.co.uk
- 🍺 Greene King IPA; guests
- ☺ Quality traditional British home-cooked fare with plenty of specials
- ◙ 14th-century coaching inn with open fire in a picturesque village

They've given up on a printed menu at the Queen's Head where the head cook and landlady change the selection virtually daily to reflect the fresh fish available, cuts of meat recommended by their local butcher, 'or any recipe that inspires us'. Choices include such pub classics as sausage and mash (using the famous local Braughing banger) with roast onion gravy made from the juices of the roast beef, home-cooked ham with local free-range eggs and chips, steak and Greene King IPA pie, home-made soup and chicken liver with cognac pâté, both making a substantial lunchtime snack as well as a starter.

Other dishes could include pan-fried Gressingham or Barbary duck breast with sauces like spicy plum or morello cherry and red wine sauce, or bitter orange and Grand Marnier. There are at least three fish dishes daily, maybe fresh Norfolk mussels with white wine and cream in season, mixed seafood – red mullet, smoked haddock, tuna, salmon and king prawns – on stir fried vegetables and noodles, three grills including home-made Aberdeen Angus burgers and fillet steaks, and a vegetarian dish (tell them if you have a special dietary requirement). Portions are generous and prices reasonable. As well as the IPA there are three guest beers served on the four handpumps.

★ 🏰 Q ❀ 🛏 S V 🍺 ♣ P ⚡ 👪 C

LITTLE CANFIELD
Lion & Lamb
Stortford Road, CM6 1SR

▶ On B1256 Takeley-Little Canfield road, accessible from M11 jct 8
☼ Daily 11am-11pm
Ⓨ Daily 12-10pm
T (01279) 870257
F (01279) 870423
E info@lionandlamb.co.uk
W www.lionandlamb.co.uk
Greene King IPA, Old Speckled Hen; Ridley's Old Bob
☺ Varied menu with good fish choices
◙ Traditional country pub with an extensive garden; the charming beamed bar features a huge fireplace

Kangaroo fillet features on the menu here, and because most of the staff hail from Australia it has become something of a trademark dish. It is one of the few ingredients that incurs air miles – the sausages are from Dunmow and meat from a local butcher who supplies excellent Scotch beef. Fresh fish comes up regularly from Billingsgate market. Diners have a choice here: the bar offers an extensive menu of snacks and traditional pub food such as steak and Ridley's ale pie, beer-battered cod and chips, lasagne, burgers, salads and even roast rib of beef, £9.25. If you wish you can choose from the bar menu but dine in the restaurant, for a cover charge of £2.50.

In the restaurant the two-course fixed price menu is £18.50, three courses £21.50. Starters include Thai crab cakes, saffron risotto, warm leek and Gruyere tart and Cajun chicken Caesar salad. To follow there is supreme of chicken filled with Camembert then wrapped in Parma ham with pesto dressing, magret of duck - breast with red wine and black cherry jus on Parisienne potoatoes, slow braised lamb shank served on creamed potatoes and beef stroganoff. There is a separate listing for the char-grilled steaks (and kangaroo fillet!) and a fresh fish board. ★ Q S V

RICKLING GREEN
Cricketers' Arms
CB11 3YG

▶ Off B1383 near Quendon
☼ Daily 12-11pm
Ⓨ Daily 12-3pm, 6.30-10.30pm
T (01799) 543210
F (01799) 543512
E reservations@cricketers.demon.co.uk
W www.thecricketersarms.com
Burton Ale; Greene King IPA; Jennings Cumberland; guest
☺ Modern British cuisine served in the bar and two restaurants
◙ 18th-century country inn with Japanese style garden overlooking the village cricket pitch

A smart pub with a modern restaurant but a traditional beamed bar where ales, including a weekly guest, are served straight from the barrel. Freshly-prepared food includes, on the lunch menu, home-made soup of the day and baguettes with fillings such as chicken supreme with guacamole accompanied by real chips, priced £5.95-£6.95. Main courses include sausage trio – Boerewors, Toulouse and wild boar – with apple and cider on Dijon mustard mash, crayfish risotto, smoked salmon with truffle champ potatoes, 8oz sirloin steak with Portobello mushroom, tuna loin served rare on chilli and ginger stir fried vegetables, or tamarind glazed duck breast with bok choi potato gratin, prices from £7.95-£14.95.

The à la carte menu might start with pan-fried foie gras on rhubarb and fresh fig compote, warm duck salad or cherry tomato and buffalo mozzarella puff pastry tart, going on to Denham estate fallow venison, pork tenderloin in apple and sage risotto with Armagnac, rack of lamb with polenta and garlic spinach on red lentil purée, pan-fried calf's liver with back bacon and horseradish mash, or steamed wild sea bass, priced £12.50-£15.95; the vegetarian dish could be grilled polenta with ratatouille and spinach served with braised fennel.
Q S V C

ALDERTON
Gardener's Arms
Beckford Road, GL20 8NL

- Near M5 jct 9, off B4077 near Tewkesbury
- Mon-Sat 12-2.30pm, 6.30-11pm; Sun 12-3pm, 6.30-10.30pm Sun
- Daily 12-2.15pm, 6.30-9.30pm (10pm Fri & Sat)
- T (01242) 620257
- Beer range varies
- Home-cooked food, fresh fish and special menu theme nights
- Community pub with something for everyone; beer festivals in May and Dec

All food is home cooked at a free house with weekly changing ales and beer festivals held on the second May Bank Holiday and between Christmas and New Year. All produce is bought locally, with a fresh fish and pie of the week featuring along with daily specials. Dishes could include kangaroo kebab with king prawns on green peppercorn sauce, cod in beer batter with chips and mushy peas, whole baby seabass with roasted red pepper sauce, home-made cod and pancetta fishcakes or lemon sole with lime and parsley butter, prices from £7.95-£11.95.

On the main menu starters include soup with home-made bread at £3.95, home-made chicken liver and game pâté or deep fried goats' cheese parcels with black pudding and mint crème fraîche, £3.95-£4.50. Cotswold lamb steak, chicken breast filled with Roquefort on rosti potato, fillet steak topped with wild mushrooms and Gruyere, calf's liver pan fried with crispy bacon and mini faggots, pork tenderloin with grain mustard sauce and parsnip crisps or simple home-cooked ham, egg and chips with home made piccalilli are among main courses priced £7.50-£11.95. Desserts, £4.95, range from Amaretto crème brûlée with home-made shortbread to sticky toffee pud. Sunday lunch includes a choice of three roasts at £7.95. The pub is happy to cater for any event, offering the same high quality home-cooked food.
S V P C

BLEDINGTON
☆ King's Head
The Green, OX7 6XQ

- Between Burford and Stow-on-the-Wold
- Daily 11-3pm, 6-11pm (10.30pm Sun)
- Daily 12-2pm, 7-9.30pm
- T (01608) 658365
- F (01608) 658902
- E kingshead@orr-ewing.com
- W www.kingsheadinn.net
- Hook Norton Best Bitter, guests
- High quality English cuisine with the accent on locally-sourced produce
- Archetypal English country inn dating back to the 16th century, replete with exposed beams, inglenook and flagstone floors

The King's Head is practically a permanent fixture in CAMRA's Good Beer Guide and has appeared in previous editions of this guide. In an idyllic setting on the village green with a brook, it is the quintessential English country pub. With local real ales, top quality food created by a chef renowned for his flair and inventiveness, and guest accommodation, what more could one ask for? The menus here change regularly as dishes are based on seasonal, mostly local produce. Starters might be scallop and Parma ham brochette with chilli onion marmalade, seared fresh tuna fillet with crispy leeks and ginger and soy sauce, thinly-sliced smoked venison bruschetta with plum chutney, and blue cheese and port pâté with toasted walnuts and crusty bread.

Main courses include a good selection of meat, fish and vegetarian options: shrimp and samphire risotto, roast rack of lamb with carrot and parsnip cake, mustard mash and apricot and thyme jus, char-grilled venison steak with savoy cabbage, sautéed rosemary potatoes and redcurrant and port jus, spicy chickpea cakes with char-grilled red onion and coriander salad and lime and chilli yoghurt, or Brie stuffed chicken breast served with bacon, sugar snap peas and garlic fried potatoes on a skewer. Expect to pay around £4-£7.25 for a starter, £9-£15.25 for mains. ★ Q S V (Kingham) P C

BROAD CAMPDEN
Baker's Arms
GL55 6UR

- Signed from B4081
- Mon-Fri 11.30am-2.30pm, 4.45-11pm; Sat & summer 11.30am-11pm; Sun 12-10.30pm
- Winter 12-2pm, 6 (7 Sun)-9pm; summer 12-9pm
- T (01386) 840515
- Stanway Stanney Bitter; Taylor Landlord; Wells Bombardier; guest
- Traditional, home-cooked food with good pub dishes
- Atmospheric Cotswold stone pub with beams, inglenook and dining room

Expect to find fresh meat and vegetables from local suppliers, salad or veg rather than chips, and heart-warming pub specials here – faggots in gravy, bangers 'n' mash, pork chops in cider, venison in red wine, casseroled beef, salmon fishcakes, lamb shank or duck breast, prices from £6.95-£8.95. At lunchtime there are sandwiches, Cheddar, Stilton or ham ploughman's with warm baguettes, pickles and salad at a bargain £4.75, warm baguettes with fillings such as BLT or sausage and onion, and giant Yorkies with fillings from cottage pie mince to roast beef and gravy or cheese, leek and potato, all £4.95.

Lunchtime and evening starters include home-made soup with warm baguette, goats' cheese with redcurrant jelly, potato skins with cheese and ham sauce, £2.95-£3.95. Main dishes on the set menu are authentic moussaka, chilli con carne and lasagne verdi, steak and kidney pudding, cottage pie with cheese topped mash, smoked haddock with diced hard-boiled eggs in a creamy sauce topped with bubbling cheese, mariner's pie of salmon, cod, smoked haddock and prawns and veggie dishes such as cheese, leek and potato bake or Thai red vegetable curry. Sweets include toffee and banana sponge, fruit crumble and treacle tart, all £3.25.

★ Q S V P

FORD
Plough Inn
GL54 5RU

- On B4077 between Tewkesbury and Stow on the Wold
- Mon-Sat 10am-11pm; Sun 12-10.30pm
- Mon-Fri 12-2pm, 6-9pm; Sat & Sun 12-9pm
- T (01386) 584215
- Donnington BB, SBA
- Excellent for steaks, plus daily specials and fresh fish
- This 16th-century courthouse once had cellar dungeons for prisoners, now it offers three bars with low, beamed ceilings, inglenooks and flagged floors

This charming olde-worlde inn overlooks the racing gallops of trainer Jonjo O'Neill. An enticing menu offers starters including pan-fried button mushrooms and smoky bacon in a fresh herb sauce with crusty bread, spicy crab cakes with a hot and sweet chilli jam, walnut crusted Brie deep fried and served with cranberry sauce or crispy coated whitebait with home-made tartare sauce and salad garnish, up to £5.50. The Plough is popular for its prime Aberdeen Angus sirloin steak – char grilled to the customer's taste and served with all the trimmings, or you could have a char-grilled fillet, glazed with Roquefort butter and a rich red wine and mushroom sauce. Alternatively there might be braised pork shank on a bed of sage mash with cider and apple sauce, half a roast Norfolk duck with caramelised orange and Cointreau sauce, green Thai chicken curry with fresh coriander and basmati rice or a half shoulder of lamb slow cooked in a garlic and rosemary sauce. Main courses range from the home-made steak, ale and mushroom pie, £10, to fillet steak, £15. Consult the blackboard for daily specials, vegetarian options and fresh fish of the day. Home made desserts, £4.50, also change daily.

★ S V C

GLOUCESTER
Café René
31 Southgate Street, GL1 1TP

- Through archway opposite New County Hotel
- Summer 11am-11pm; winter 12-11pm
- Mon-Sat 12-9.30pm; Sun 12-10.30pm
- T (01452) 309340
- W www.caferene.co.uk
- Beer range varies
- Traditional and international with an eclectic choice in the evening
- Real ale pub/café with a relaxed, friendly atmosphere

Freshly prepared, quality food from home-made burgers to real Caribbean lamb curry is on the menu at this pub/eaterie hidden up an alleyway with tables outside and a no-smoking, candlelit dining room. At lunchtime there is an extraordinary array of sandwiches from hot roast pork with crackling and stuffing to mixed Italian meats with Brie, prices £3.50 to £4.95 accompanied by salad. A wide choice of ploughman's includes Cooper's Hill Double Gloucester and smoked mackerel. Home-made Desperate Dan burgers start with the quarter pounder at £4.25 progressing to the Very Desperate (pounder) at £7.25, served with potatoes of the day plus salad.

In the evening expect starters such as home-made soup and home-made chicken liver pâté, veggie Caesar salad, three-cheese salad with anchovies and olives or duck spring rolls, priced £3.25-£4.25. For main courses, the home-made burgers are augmented by grilled rump, sirloin and fillet steaks, £8.75-£13.75. Sample dishes might be Caribbean lamb curry with gungo pea rice, jerk chicken with rice, duck breast with spiced forest fruits, steamed whole bream with ginger and spring onions, pasta such as spaghetti with chicken, bacon and pine nuts or three roast peppers stuffed with savoury rice and mushrooms, prices £5.75-£14.95.

★ S V (Gloucester) C

GLOUCESTER

Fountain Inn

53 Westgate Street, GL1 2NW

- Mon-Sat 10.30am-11pm, Sun 12-10.30pm
- Mon-Wed 10.30am-9pm; Thu-Sat 10.30am-9.30pm; Sun 12-6pm
- T (01452) 522562
- F (01452) 311414
- E peter@fountainglos.co.uk
- W www.fountainglos.co.uk
- Caledonian Deuchars IPA; Fuller's London Pride; Greene King Abbot; Wickwar BOB; guest
- Dishes from around the world
- Busy city centre pub dating from 17th century, flower bedecked courtyard

A surprising home-cooked global repertoire of dishes you don't often see all on one menu. Starting at home, though, traditional starters include home-made soup, ham and cauliflower bake topped with smoked applewood cheese, Stilton fingers in smoked bacon or sautéed chicken livers in choux pastry basket with Cognac, cream and wild mushroom sauce, prices £3.45-£6. British style main dishes include home-made steak and kidney pie with red wine gravy or chicken, leek and bacon pie, pot casseroled lamb with fresh vegetables and minted dumplings, chicken cobbler topped with sage and onion scones, double Gloucester, red onion and chive quiche, freshly battered cod or haddock and chips or home-cooked ham with two eggs and home-made chips, modestly priced at £5.50-£6.25.

From overseas come paella Andalucia, lamb kofta kebabs with couscous and sweet chilli sauce, Tuscan pork casserole with wild mushroom risotto, moussaka, squid ink pasta with smoked salmon and clams, spinach, mushroom and parmesan risotto, and plenty of Mexican sizzling fajitas, all around £5-£6. The children's menu is good – roast dinner at £3.50, home-made chicken nuggets, cheese and tomato pizza with salad or pasta napoli.

★ Q S V (Gloucester) C

HAWKESBURY UPTON

Beaufort Arms

High Street, GL9 1AU

- 1 mile W of Dunkirk jct A46
- Daily 12-11pm (10.30pm Sun)
- Daily 12-2.30pm, 7-9.30pm
- T (01454) 238217
- E mark@beaufortarms.com
- W www.beaufortarms.com
- Beer range varies
- Honest, home-cooked, classic pub food
- Grade II listed Cotswold stone pub, CAMRA Gloucs Pub of the Year 2004

It's a treat to find a pub serving the sort of simple dishes with low prices you hope to enjoy alongside a pint of beer. At the Beaufort Arms they use as much local and seasonal produce as possible including bread from a nearby bakery, Gloucester Old Spot sausages from a Bristol butcher, home-made faggots from the local butcher, game from a local estate, fresh fish from Bristol fish market, salad and herbs grown by one of their cooks whose garden wins awards. As with the beers, 75 per cent from the west country, the aim with the food is to sell out, but they try to keep a core menu of 12 items.

Sample dishes include cheese and onion potato cakes, faggots, peas and chips, ham cooked in the cider ullage, home-made fish cakes, venison casserole, cod in fresh batter or haddock in fresh crumbs, steak and Guinness pie (sometimes Mr Perretts Stout from Wickwar), lamb shank with mint gravy, liver and bacon casserole, or corned beef hash cakes, prices mainly £5.50 or £6.25. Large rib eye or rump steaks are £9.50 and £8.95. On Sunday lunchtimes three roast meats are accompanied by five vegetables including cauliflower cheese at £5.50. Desserts such as crème brûlée with toffeed apples and banoffee cheesecake are locally made.

Q S V P C

LONGFORD
Queen's Head
84 Tewkesbury Road, GL2 9EJ

- ▶ On A38, between Tewkesbury and Gloucester
- ☼ Daily 11am-3pm, 5.30-11pm
- Ⓨ Daily 12-2pm, 6.30-9.30pm
- T (01452) 301882
- F (01452) 524368
- E queenshead@aol.com
- Ringwood Best Bitter; guests
- ☺ Upmarket pub serving award-winning food in its smart restaurant
- Partly timber framed, former blacksmith's forge dating from the 1730s, popular with local drinkers and diners

A good choice for a proper adult night out, smart, casual dress is preferred in the restaurant and children are not admitted. The meals are all freshly prepared to order. Starters are priced around £5: choose from fresh scallops wrapped in lean smoked bacon grilled and served with a drizzle of honey, Irish mussels in creamy white wine sauce, local black pudding steeped in Cognac, topped with Stilton and grilled, home-made herb pancake filled with melted Brie and Bramley apples, or maybe something from the specials list such as smoked salmon and fresh asparagus with mascarpone cheese in a filo pastry parcel.

To follow you could have steak with or without a home-made sauce, beef dishes such as stroganoff served with rice, medallions of beef fillet with Cajun spices and salsa, or pan-fried fillet with fresh tagliatelle in hoisin sauce. However, many customers opt for the pub's famous Longford lamb that simply falls off the bone, or maybe roasted lamb cutlets on a herb potato rosti with redcurrant and rosemary jus. The specials list might offer fresh local venison on a bed of summer fruits or chicken breast stuffed with ripe banana served on a bed of mild curry sauce. Main courses are priced £10-£14 and include a good choice of fish and vegetarian dishes. **V** P **C**

LOWER ODDINGTON
☆ Fox
GL56 0UR

- ▶ Off A430 between Stow on the Wold and Chipping Norton
- ☼ Mon-Sat 11am-11pm; Sun 12-10.30pm
- Ⓨ Mon-Sat 12-2pm, 6.30-10pm; Sun 12-2pm, 7-9pm
- T (01451) 870555
- F (01451) 870666
- E info@foxinn.net
- W www.foxinn.net
- Greene King Abbot; Hook Norton Best Bitter; Wadworth 6X; guest
- ☺ Good food featuring fresh, local ingredients
- Charming, creeper-clad, 16th-century inn with a lovely dining room plus a terrace for outdoor eating and a pretty cottage garden

Flagstone floors, hop-strewn beams and plenty of fresh flowers are characteristic of this lovely old pub, creating an ambience appreciated by visitors. The menu here changes often, according to the availability of fresh, seasonal ingredients, and which fish have been delivered from Cornwall. Starters might include carrot, coriander and ginger soup, gravadlax and dill mustard dressing, charcuterie with cornichon and olives, or wilted rocket, olive and parmesan tart, £4-£5.75.

To follow there could be baked sea trout with creamed leeks and saffron, rib eye steak (plain or with mustard butter), smoked haddock fishcake with chive cream sauce, lamb tagine and couscous or tagliatelle with olive and tomato concasse, £8-£11. In summer there might be chicken, bacon and avocado salad or cold poached salmon with pesto dressing and new potato and spring onion salad, both £8.75. There is a terrific choice of puddings, mostly just over £4: apricot and almond tart, bitter chocolate mousse cake and clotted cream, crème brûlée, mango and passion fruit parfait with kiwi coulis or summer pudding. Local Bennetts ice cream is served in various flavours for £2 per pot. **S V** P **C**

NAILSWORTH
George Inn
Newmarket, GL6 0RF

- Mon-Sat 11am-3pm, 6-11pm; Sun 12-3pm, 7-10.30pm
- Daily 12-2pm, 6.30 (7 Sun)-9pm
- T (01453) 833228
- Moles Tap Bitter; Taylor Landlord; Uley Bitter, Old Spot
- A blend of British and continental with Portuguese influences
- Cotswold local, originally three cottages, facing south over the valley above Nailsworth

Co-landlord David de Sousa brings a touch of Portugal and Madeira to a renowned menu served in both the bar and small restaurant. The house speciality is chicken piri piri, half a boned chicken flavoured in a chilli and garlic marinade then char-grilled, £10.25 with salad or vegetables. Among the starters is the daily home-made soup plus home-made chicken liver pâté, Parma ham with melon, chicken and leek pancake, fresh melon with port or frogs' legs in batter with garlic butter, priced £3.95-£5.95.

Meat dishes include calf's liver with sage butter, lamb's liver with bacon and onion gravy, lamb's kidneys with Dijon mustard and sherry sauce, chicken breast stuffed with wild mushrooms on watercress sauce, home-made cottage pie, duck leg confit on braised red cabbage and rump of English lamb with mustard mash, priced £9.25-£12.75. Rib eye steak in red wine and mushroom sauce is £13.75, char-grilled beef fillet with green peppercorn sauce £16.95. Seabass fillets with sun-dried tomato sauce is on the fish selection, along with tuna steak, rainbow trout pan fried with almonds, and scampi Florentine, priced £11.50-£12.50. Veggie options are penne with mushroom pesto and vegetable pancake. Ten home-made desserts, all £4.50, include caramelised rice pudding with fresh strawberries.

★ Q ❀ S V ♿ P ⚡ C

POULTON
☆ Falcon
London Road, GL7 5HN

- On A417 midway between Cirencester and Fairford
- Mon-Sat 11-3pm, 6-11pm; Sun 12-3pm, 7-10.30pm
- Mon-Sat 12-2.30pm, 7-9.30pm; Sun 12-2pm, 7-9pm
- T (01285) 850844
- E mail@thefalconpoulton.co.uk
- W www.thefalconpoulton.co.uk
- Hook Norton Best Bitter; guest
- Award-winning modern European style
- Traditional Cotswold pub with a stylish and contemporary interior; the skittle alley has been converted to a dining area

Just as I have been bemoaning the lack of decent 'prix fixe' meals in this country that in France allow you to dine well for a reasonable price, up pops the Falcon with its daily-changing £10 two-course lunch menu. A typical day's offerings include roast tomato soup with basil oil, country terrine with home-made onion marmalade and a blue cheese, pear and walnut salad. The main course also has three choices: grilled gammon steak with egg and home-made chips, fillet of Bibury trout, crushed peas and new potatoes and North Cerney goats' cheese in puff pastry with home-made apple and sultana chutney.

The evening menu changes monthly, with daily specials incorporating the best seasonal produce. You might start with crab risotto with crayfish, pan-fried saffron red mullet with ratatouille or duck leg confit with orange and watercress salad, £7-£8.50. To follow is rare breed rib eye steak with chive and black peppercorn butter, herb-crusted roast Cotswold lamb, or maybe monkfish wrapped in Parma ham with sweet potato fondant and curried leeks, £10-£17. Unusual desserts, £5.95, include chilled damson soup with home made ice cream and blackberries.

V ♿ P ⚡ C

PRESTBURY
Royal Oak
43 The Burbage, GL52 3DL

- Near racecourse
- Mon-Sat 11.30am-2.30pm, 5.30 (6 Sat)-11pm; Sun 12-10.30pm
- Daily 12-2pm, 6.30-9pm
- T (01242) 522344
- F (01242) 577344
- E eat@royal-oak-prestbury.co.uk
- W www.royal-oak-prestbury.co.uk
- Archers Best Bitter; Oakham JHB; Taylor Landlord; guest
- Honest, traditional English fare
- A small Cotswold inn in Britain's most haunted village (allegedly)

Real ale and real food are the benchmark at the Royal Oak, where traditional English dishes range from sautéed pigeon breast with ginger and honey to steak and kidney pie with a herb crust or, on the specials board, treats such as fresh scallops and seabass. Favourites include home-cooked, freshly-carved ham with egg and chips, hake and tarragon fishcakes with 'poor man's' caviar, and rump and fillet steaks with brandy and peppercorn sauce. Using local produce including Cotswold game, the set menu offers 'real good soup' with warm bread, baked mushroom filled with Gruyere and Stilton or tomato and olive tapenade crostini among starters priced £3.95-£5.25.

Main dishes are fish pie with caper and nutmeg mash and Vermouth sauce, chicken breast stuffed with Emmental, pork tenderloin with green pepper and satay sauce, priced from £8.95-£10.95. A good selection of home-made veggie choices includes spinach and ricotta parcel with tahini dressing, or goats' cheese, tomato and potato galette. Lunch snacks might be warm ciabatta with Brie and bacon, sausage or Stilton. Sunday roast – leg of lamb or pork and roast sirloin with freshly-grated horseradish sauce – is hugely popular and booking is essential. Desserts range from tiramisu torte to treacle tart. ★ Q S V P C

ROWBERROW
Swan Inn
BS25 1QL

- Signed off A38 1 mile S Churchill crossroads
- Mon-Sat 12-3pm, 6-11pm; Sun 12-3pm, 7-10.30pm
- Mon-Sat 12-2pm, 6.30-9pm (9.30pm Fri and Sat); Sun 12-2pm, 7-9pm
- T (01934) 852371
- E swan_bob@tiscali.co.uk
- Butcombe Bitter, Blonde, Gold; Draught Bass
- Varied, home-cooked menu
- Traditional, convivial country pub created from three knocked-through miners' cottages during the late 1700s

A menu full of choice, mainly home cooked from fresh ingredients. A typical selection from the specials board might be starters of freshly-made smoked haddock mousse, scallops in herb and garlic butter, roast pepper stuffed with rice mushrooms and spring onions, followed by lamb shank braised in stock flavoured with port, redcurrant and root vegetables, pork tenderloin with Stilton, horseradish and cream sauce or whole seabass. The set menu has starters of home-made soup, deep-fried potato shells stuffed with Stilton and walnut, goats' cheese tartlet on Caesar salad or moules marinière, prices from £3.40-£5.25.

Main dishes include the chef's curry of the day, home-made steak and kidney pudding with fresh vegetables and home-made chips, jacket or new potatoes, the Swan home-made pies topped with proper shortcrust pastry – either Scottish beef braised with Butcombe Ale or chicken and mushroom in white wine and cream – baked salmon or simple ham, egg and chips, prices £6.50-£9.25. There is a full range of char-grilled steaks, and a vegetarian choice including ratatouille flan or leek and mushroom potato crumble. You will also find a big selection of ploughman's, jacket potatoes and sarnies. Q S V P C

SLIMBRIDGE
Tudor Arms
Shepherds Patch, GL2 7BP

- ▶ From A38 1 mile beyond Slimbridge village
- ☼ Mon-Sat 11am-11pm; Sun 12-10.30pm
- Sat & Sun and summer throughout opening hours; winter Mon-Fri 12-2pm, 6-9pm
- T (01453) 890306
- F (01453) 890103
- Uley Pig's Ear; Wadworth 6X; Wickwar BOB; guests
- ☺ Home-cooked and varied set menu plus specials board
- Canalside free house down winding road to Wildfowl and Wetlands Trust

They serve a mean soup at the Tudor Arms, using fresh vegetables with lentils or cheese and described by the landlady as 'fantastic'. A local supplier brings fresh vegetables and the butcher provides game as well as meat. Examples from the specials board include beef or pork stroganoff, stuffed peppers or mushrooms, calf's liver with bacon and shallots, chicken or lamb curry, sausages with mash and onion gravy, various game dishes or the popular pies which might be game, steak and mushroom, gammon, leek and chicken or turkey and ham.

On the regular menu starters range from home-made soup with a baguette at £3.25 to three-cheese combo of Camembert, smoked Cheddar and blue, all deep fried. Main meals might be lamb shank with rosemary and onion sauce, fish pie, pork fillet in Stilton and grain mustard sauce or an 8oz sirloin steak with all the trimmings at £9.50. The snack menu offers stuffed paninis, ploughman's of Cheddar, Stilton and ham, and jacket potatoes with choice of fillings. Dishes are home made except the burgers and children's menu. Delicious home-made desserts include the 'to die for' chocolate truffle.

★ S V P C

Kim Scicluna, landlady of the Sun Inn at Feering in Essex, is known for the dishes her husband, Charlie, used to enjoy in his native Malta. But her range is international – here is a beef dish she enjoyed so much on holiday in Slovakia that she now uses the recipe in the pub.

SVICKOVA
Serves 6

1kg (2lb) slices of casserole beef
2 tbsps oil
2 tbsps French mustard
1 tbsp paprika
3 carrots, 1 parsnip, 1 small swede and 1 onion, all finely grated
2 tbsps flour
1 litre (2 pints) beef stock
4 bay leaves
5 whole peppercorns
300ml (½ pint) double cream
2 tbsps white wine vinegar
2 tbsps sugar
175g (6oz) cranberries
Salt and pepper

Pre-heat oven to 180C/350F/gas mark 4. Wash meat and lay flat on clean board. Smear French mustard over one side of the meat, then sprinkle with paprika and repeat with salt and pepper; turn over and repeat. Heat oil in pan, brown meat on both sides, and lay in ovenproof dish. Place grated carrot, parsnip, swede and onion in pan and soften for 5 minutes, add flour and stir well, then slowly add stock stirring all the time until the liquid reaches a brisk simmer and thickens. Add bay leaves, peppercorns, cream, vinegar, sugar, salt and pepper and 75g (3oz) of the cranberries, then pour over the meat. Cover and cook in the oven for 1½-2 hours until the meat is tender, adding remaining cranberries approx 30 minutes before the end of cooking time. Serve with creamed potatoes and green vegetables.

ALTON
Market Hotel
3 Market Square, GU34 1HD

- In market square off Market Street
- Mon-Sat 11am-11pm; Sun 12-10.30pm
- Daily 12-2.30pm, 7-9pm
- T (01420) 549730
- e elainemarketsquare@fsmail.net
- Courage Best Bitter; guests
- Traditional value for money pub grub
- Striking mural in the public bar commemorates Alton's former livestock market; comfortable lounge bar with family area

Landlady Elaine and her helper Donna (whose Yorkshire puddings are said to be the best anywhere) make all the soups, chillis and lasagnes themselves here. Meat comes from the local butcher including his range of interesting, spicy sausages; three types are served with real mash and onion gravy. Also on the specials board you will find dishes of the day, home-made vegetarian eats and desserts.

The basic menu includes home-cooked ham, egg and chips, lasagne with chips, salad or jacket potato, jumbo sausages, cheese, chilli and plain burgers, and cheddar or ham ploughman's with freshly baked roll, salad and pickles. Prices range from £3.10 to £6.35 for chicken balti with naan bread. There are freshly prepared half baguettes with fillings such as tuna, cheese, ham, egg mayonnaise, bacon, egg and mushrooms, sausage and onion or sausage, egg and bacon, priced £2.95-£3.95, or you can just have a chip butty. On Sunday a two-course roast Sunday lunch is only £5.95 (booking advisable), complete with the renowned Yorkshire puddings. Two handpumps serve guest ales.

S V (Alton) C

ANDOVER
Wyke Down Country Pub and Restaurant
Picket Piece, SP11 6LX

- Follow signs to Wyke Down from A303
- Mon-Sat 12-2.30pm, 6-11pm; Sun12-3pm, 6-10.30pm
- Mon-Sat 12-2.30pm, 6-9pm; Sun 12-2pm, 6.30-8.30pm
- T (01264) 352048
- F (01264) 324661
- E p.read@wykedown.co.uk
- W www.wykedown.co.uk
- Exmoor Ale; guests
- Food ranges from simple, fresh bar room dishes to imaginative à la carte
- Converted barn behind old farmhouse in open countryside with extensive facilities including a camping/caravan park

Two chefs, both with more than five years at the Wyke Down, create a wide choice of tempting meals using meat and vegetables from their regular local butcher and greengrocer. Bar food offers a wide choice from fish and chips or Dorset ham with two eggs and chips to smoked chicken with mozzarella and sun dried tomato salad, salmon and broccoli fishcakes with sweet chilli sauce, steak and mushroom pudding with vegetables and potatoes, or half a pound of Scotch sirloin steak, all under £8 apart from the steak. Veggie options could be Bresse Bleu, grape and walnut salad or potato skins topped with peppers, onions and cheese.

In the smart restaurant starters might be home-made chicken liver and green peppercorn pâté, smoked haddock and spring onion fishcake or wild mushrooms with port and tarragon sauce in puff pastry. Pork tenderloin with apricot and sage stuffing, chicken supreme filled with Brie and Camembert, barbary duck breast on rhubarb and plum sauce or grilled tuna with spicy tomato dressing are the main courses, prices from £11.95-£13.95. Veggie choices include their own recipe roast sultana and nut loaf.

★ Q S V P C

BANK
Oak Inn

Pinkney Lane, SO43 7FE

- ▶ Just over a mile W of Lyndhurst
- ☼ Mon-Fri 11am-2.30pm, 6-11pm; Sat & Sun 11am-11pm
- Daily 12-2pm, 6-9.30pm
- T (02380) 282350
- Hop Back Summer Lightning; Ringwood BB; Young's Special; guests
- ☺ Fresh fish, well hung meat, specials and doorstep sarnies
- Welcoming New Forest pub with beer festivals in July and December

Doorstep sandwiches are an ideal accompaniment to a pint at lunchtime, and tasty fillings served in either white or granary bread include tuna and mayonnaise, home-cooked ham and tomato, mature Cheddar and onion, coronation chicken and prawn cocktail, all with a salad garnish at £4.25-£5.75; a ploughman's of award-winning Ashmore farmhouse Cheddar is £6.25. Starters, also sold as light snacks, include a bowl of garlic mushrooms topped with melted cheese, baked Brie with almonds and honey, half a dozen king prawns with garlic butter, or cured meats antipasto with pickles and crusty bread, £4.75-£6.25.

Main meals include Thai spiced salmon fish cakes with sweet chilli sauce, home-cooked ham with two eggs served with salad and fries, local sausages of the week with champ topped with onion gravy, roast lamb shank with champ, a char-grilled rib eye steak cooked in garlic butter, or the Oak's pie of the day, listed with other specials on the blackboard, prices from £6.95-£11.95. Desserts are also listed on the blackboard.

★ S P C

BEAUWORTH
Milburys
SO24 0PB

- ▶ S of A272, 1 mile beyond Beauworth
- ☼ Mon-Fri 11am-3pm, 5.30-11pm; Sat & Sun 11am-11pm
- Mon-Thur 12-2pm, 6.30-9pm; Fri-Sun 12-3pm, 6.30-9.30pm (9pm Sun)
- T (01962) 771248
- F (01962) 771910
- E info@themilburys.co.uk
- W www.themilburys.co.uk
- Caledonian Deuchars IPA; Theakston Old Peculier; Milburys Best; guests
- ☺ Freshly prepared pub food plus à la carte
- 18th-century hilltop inn with a 300-foot well and wealth of beams

This lovely pub is old and traditional but the restaurant was built within the last few years. Milburys offers a tempting mix of traditional pub fare in the bar and South African inspirations in the restaurant. In the bar expect home-made soup, salmon and strawberry salad or moules marinière as starters, priced £3.95-£4.95, followed by main dishes such as hake in beer batter, Durban lamb curry, Nick Harriot's award-winning sausages with mash and onion gravy, or sirloin steak with chips and vine tomatoes, priced £7.95-£11.95. Snacks include a range of filled baps at £3.95 and a £6.95 ploughman's platter of Cheddar, Brie, Stilton, ham, pickles, fruit and salad, at lunchtime only.

The African Oasis restaurant starts with baby Cape calamari, Laangebann chicken livers in peri peri sauce, or Portuguese steamed mussels, £4.25-£5.75. Main dishes include Tannie's Baboti, a traditional South African meal of curried mince meat and raisins, Cape Malay prawn and chicken curry, or rump sosati of rump steak in garlic butter on couscous. More traditional choices might be 'the ever changing game dish', line-caught fish of the day, fillet steak, rack of ribs and home-made spinach pancakes filled with cream cheese, from £9.50-£15.95.

★ Q S V P C

BRAISHFIELD
☆ Wheatsheaf
SO51 0QE

- ▶ Off Romsey-Winchester road
- ☼ Mon-Sat 11am-11pm; Sun 12-10.30pm
- Daily 12-9.30pm (9pm Sun)
- T (01794) 368372
- F (01794) 367113
- E jonesthebeer@btinternet.com
- W www.wheatsheafbraishfield.co.uk
- Beer range varies
- ☺ Eclectic mix of traditional and modern
- Village pub benefiting from wonderful views from its pretty garden, which has a petanque pitch

Landlady Jenny Jones won a Morning Advertiser Pub Chef of the Year award for her seafood gumbo. This dish, something in between a soup and a stew, also comes in chicken and vegetarian versions and is a highlight of a very varied menu. Starters, £4-£8, include oven-baked mussels in tomato, garlic and chilli sauce, hot potted brown shrimps, a salad of chorizo, feta, balsamic strawberries, rocket and grapes (also available in a vegetarian version) and Chinese crispy shredded duck. To follow there is a choice of chicken ragout with tarragon pastry lattice, ham hock with parsley sauce and sticky pineapple or smoked lamb with spiced ratatouille, mostly around £11.

There is always a good range of specials, particularly fish and seafood – baby octopus, calamari or scallops with sweet chilli sauce, rack of lamb and home-made ravioli with light curry sauce are all popular. Jenny buys locally and takes advantage of game in season and brown trout from the River Test, not to mention the eggs from her own chickens and vegetables from the pub garden. Tempting desserts include lemon mousse with caramelised bananas, Armagnac parfait with Earl Grey syrup, chocolate and hazelnut tart with mascarpone and orange marmalade cream, all £4.50. Set menus, available at most sessions, represent excellent value.

★ S V P C

CHAWTON
Greyfriar
Winchester Road, GU34 1SB

- ▶ A32/A31 jct take exit into Chawton village
- ☼ Mon-Sat 12-11pm; Sun 12-10.30pm
- 🍴 Mon-Sat 12-3pm, 7-9.30pm; Sun 12-3pm
- T (01420) 83841
- E bookings@thegreyfriar.co.uk
- W www.thegreyfriar.co.uk
- Fuller's Chiswick, London Pride, ESB, seasonal; guest
- ☺ Fresh home-made food on a daily changing blackboard menu
- 16th-century village pub with low ceilings and exposed beams

Head chef and landlady Frances Whitehead designs her menu around seasonal fresh produce, with fish bought directly from Brixham and an award-winning butcher supplying meat from Scottish and Welsh farms. Preserves are made in the pub's kitchen, as well as interesting vegetable dishes to accompany meals such as spiced red cabbage broccoli with hazelnut and orange butter, carrot and celeriac purée, or roast parsnips with honey and grain mustard. Bar snacks are tapas style including deep fried Brie wedges, sweetcorn fire sticks, lemon peppered scallops, Cajun onion rings, mozzarella melters, spinach and feta goujons, £2 per portion or a sharing platter.

Lunchtime meals include chicken breast with bacon Caesar salad, Cheddar or Stilton ploughman's, home-made beef burger with various toppings, rib eye steak and fresh-baked filled baguettes, £4.95 up to £10.95 for steak. The blackboard specials change every day but a sample evening selection might be gurnard fillet with tomato and olive sauce, gammon steak with bubble and squeak, milk-fed lamb, pork and leek sausages with mash and onion gravy, or filo pastry filled with roast vegetables in butternut sauce. Desserts include crumbles made with fruit from the family garden and home-made meringue nests.

★ Q ❀ S V ♿ P ⚡ 👪 C

EAST STRATTON
Northbrook Arms
SO21 3DU

- ▶ Off A33 between Basingstoke and Winchester
- ☼ Mon-Sat 11am-11pm; Sun 12-10.30pm
- 🍴 Mon-Fri 12-3pm, 6-8.30pm; Sat & Sun 12-10.30pm
- T (01962) 774150
- E info@northbrook-arms.co.uk
- W www.northbrookarms.co.uk
- Gale's HSB; Otter Bitter; guests
- ☺ Good, wholesome pub grub with specials
- Opposite the green in an attractive village of thatched cottages, in good walking country. The skittle alley also has bar billiards

Many of this guide's entries have won food awards, but the Northbrook was nominated for something rather different – the 2005 Winalot Dog Friendly Pub award! It is surrounded by countryside, so many customers drive the few miles out from Basingstoke or Winchester to get some fresh air and then stop off at the pub. There are several eating areas: lounge, Plough bar and dining room (children welcome) or outdoors – ideal for the dog walkers.

You can choose from a 'light bites' menu, which includes basket meals of burgers, sausages or chicken breast served with chips, jacket spuds, ploughman's, sandwiches and toasties. The main menu is also standard pub fare, but nearly all of it is home made, such as the steak and Guinness pie, beer-battered cod and chips and a roasted vegetable lasagne. There is a choice of curries, too. Most dishes are around £7-£9 and on Sunday for £8.95 you can have a roast with all the trimmings (children's portions are also available); if you go on a Wednesday evening you can treat yourself to a half price steak. The menu is always supplemented by home-cooked specials such as sausage and bean cassoulet or teriyaki stir fry. Afterwards you may be tempted by hot chocolate fudge cake or local Judes ice cream.

Q ❀ S V ♿ ♣ P ⚡ 👪 C

HINTON AMPNER
Hinton Arms
Petersfield Road, SO24 0NH

- On A272 between Winchester and Petersfield
- Mon-Fri 11am-3pm, 5pm-midnight; Sat & Sun 11am-midnight
- Daily 12-3pm, 6-10pm
- T (01962) 771252
- Beer range varies
- Home-cooked English food ranging from sandwiches to an à la carte menu
- Welcoming, 17th-century former coaching inn with pleasing decor

The Hinton Arms is more a restaurant than a pub, but you can still get a sandwich or more substantial snack here if you don't want a full meal, and the welcome is extremely warm whether or not you are dining. The beer range may not be quite as extensive as it once was, but it still features local breweries. The food is excellent and the portions are generous – dishes are all freshly cooked on the premises from local produce as far as possible. Game features strongly here with tasty, fruity sauces, such as young roe deer fillets with a damson and cranberry sauce, served with fresh local vegetables and new potatoes. Other popular choices are a half shoulder of lamb with rosemary gravy and redcurrant sauce or fillets of pork with wholegrain mustard sauce. Traditional pub favourites such as the home-made steak and kidney pudding and Thai prawn curry always go down well with the locals. Desserts are all home made but you will need a very sweet tooth to tackle the Toblerone torte or the Mars bar cheesecake! Tasty bread and butter pudding would be somewhat less demanding on the palate.

★ S V P C

MICHELDEVER STATION
Dove
Andover Road, SO21 3AU

- Off A303 near Winchester, alongside Winchester-Waterloo rail line
- Mon-Sat 11.30am-midnight; Sun 12-11pm
- Daily 12-2.30pm, 6-8.30pm
- T (01962) 774288
- F (01962) 774952
- E carl.carley@dsl.pipex.com
- W www.thedoveinn.com
- Fuller's London Pride plus two guests that change frequently
- Good bar snacks, steaks and curries
- The spacious, bare boarded bar and adjacent games room cater for locals, while the hotel and restaurant attract visitors

Local CAMRA members describe the Dove as a 'multi-purpose' pub. It caters well for local drinkers and bikers, as well as visitors to the historic city of Winchester (nine minutes away by train). It also enjoys a good reputation locally as a music venue, with impromptu jazz/blues nights in the main bar. On the food front it is popular for the Sunday carvery, when the gravy is laced with London Pride. This meal is self-service so you can refill as many times as you like, and booking is advised. The monthly home-made curry nights also draw a good crowd.

Straightforward, wholesome food is the order of the day here and half the menu is given over to substantial snacks such as home-made soup with freshly baked bread, £3.75, assorted sandwiches served with chips and salad, filled baguettes, jacket spuds, omelettes and salads. Burgers are home-made, topped with cheese and bacon and served with a special chilli sauce. Main dishes include Glastonbury lamb in mushroom, leek and red wine sauce, £6.75, lamb on the bone with mint gravy, £7.95, liver and bacon casserole and hot chilli con carne, both under £6.

S V (Micheldever Station) P C

SELBORNE
Selborne Arms
High Street, GH34 3JR

- On B3006 in village
- Mon-Sat 11am-3pm, 6-11pm; Sun 12-10.30pm
- Daily 12-2pm, 7-9pm
- T (01420) 511247
- Cheriton Pots Ale; Courage Best Bitter; Ringwood Fortyniner; guests
- Wide choice of traditional dishes using local ingredients including smoked meats
- Ancient building dating back to 1600 with original features near Wakes Museum; extensive outdoor area popular in summer

Interesting dishes with many local touches start with a lightly poached free-range egg on bubble and squeak with chive butter sauce, or cassoulet of portobello mushrooms, both £4.95. Salads, as starters or main courses, include Dorset smoked duck breast with pecorino and pine nuts, while other main dishes might be home-made steak and kidney pie with vegetables, local Toulouse style sausages with mash and onion gravy, home-made curry of the day with rice, half a roast duck with orange and elderflower sauce or penne pasta with tomato fondant sauce, prices £6.50-£9.95, including vegetables.

At lunchtime you can also get light snacks such as ploughman's with English cheese including Ashmore Cheddar, Cornish organic Brie and Yarg, Walda sheep's and Winchester as well as home-cooked Hampshire ham; two cheeses plus crusty bread, celery, salad leaves, pickle, tomato, apple and pear is £5.95, children's portions £4.25. Jacket potato fillings include smoked chicken with avocado in mayonnaise. On Sunday, roast sirloin with Yorkshire pudding and vegetables plus dessert is £7.65, £4.50 for children. There is a daily changing specials board too and, to accompany your food, guest ales from local micros.

★ S V P C

SHALDEN
Golden Pot
Odiham Road, GU34 4DJ

- On B3349, 1 mile N of village
- Daily 12-11pm (10.30pm Sun)
- Daily 12-3pm, 7-10pm
- T (01420) 80655
- E goldenpot80655@aol.com
- Greene King IPA, Ruddles County, Abbot, Old Speckled Hen; guest
- All home-made dishes including fresh seafood, local game and vegetables – lots of vegetarian choices
- Rural pub with ghosts among the regulars

Food that tastes 'as food should taste' is created by landlady and chef Melanie Jane Hatch using fresh herbs and vegetables grown in her own garden as available, meat and well matured steaks delivered daily by the local butcher, and fresh fish and seafood from Newlyn on Fridays and Saturdays. Local game is either garnered by the landlord or three gamekeepers who drink there, including venison, pheasant, partridge, woodcock, rabbit, hare and pigeon for terrines and pies. Other pies might be lamb and cider, steak and mild, pork, cider and pineapple or seafood. Home-made soup such as vegetable broth or ham and lentil might be followed by lamb casserole with mint dumplings or duck simmered with pineapple and honey, prices from £8-£9.50.

The set menu has a really smooth chicken liver pâté with brandy, cream and herbs, smoked haddock, salmon and mackerel pots, half a pint of prawns or feta and courgette parcels, priced £4-£5. Char-grilled fillet, sirloin, rum and T-bone steaks are either plain or served with home-made sauces. There is a choice of home-made pies, all £9, cider-cooked ham glazed with honey and cloves, and vegetarian dishes dreamed up by Melanie such as aubergine and Brie pot with chestnut mushrooms. She also makes desserts from very sherry trifle to bread and brandy butter pudding.

Q S V P C

SHERFIELD ON LODDON
White Hart
Reading Road, RG27 0BT

- ▶ Just off A33
- ☼ Mon-Sat 11am-11pm; Sun 12-10.30pm
- Ⓨ Mon-Sat 12-3pm, 6-9.30pm; Sun 12-9.30pm
- T (01256) 882280
- E whitehartsherfield@youngs.co.uk
- W www.youngs.co.uk
- Young's beer range
- ☺ Freshly cooked, traditional pub food – with a twist
- Friendly, welcoming, 17th-century pub recently acquired and sympathetically refurbished by Young's, with a large garden

The White Hart stands opposite the village green and with the benefit of a large garden it makes an ideal destination for a summer lunch. The meals are all freshly produced in the pub kitchen, concentrating mostly on traditional dishes such as pies (often made incorporating Young's beer), steaks, sausages and mash. Daily specials are often more adventurous; octopus and ostrich have featured in the past, alongside game and vegetarian dishes. At lunchtime a good selection of sandwiches (hot and cold) and ploughman's platters is supplemented by free-range omelettes served with chips and salad, £5/£7.50.

Starters on the main menu include pan-fried mushrooms topped with Stilton sauce, crispy breaded Brie served with Young's chutney, lemon and coriander hummus with toast and crudités and a Greek salad that is also available as a main course, £4/£7. To follow you could have char-grilled duck breast served on bubble and squeak with vegetables and port and honey sauce, £10, pork loin with mustard mash and caramelised apples and leeks, or the chef's own fish pie, both £9. Roasted vegetable crêpes with rich tomato sauce is the vegetarian option. For afters why not try the luxury Jersey ice cream made at a farm in the village.

S V (Bramley) P C

TADLEY
Bishopswood Golf Course
Bishopswood Lane, RG26 4AT

- ▶ 6 miles N of Basingstoke off A340
- ☼ 11am-11pm (9.30pm Mon, winter hours vary); Sun 12-7pm
- Ⓨ Tues 12-2.30pm; Wed-Sat 12-2.30pm, 6-9pm; Sun 12-2.30pm
- T (0118) 981 2200
- F (0118) 940 8606
- E info@bishopswoodgolfcourse.co.uk
- W www.bishopswoodgolfcourse.co.uk
- Beer range varies
- ☺ Traditional bar snacks and à la carte with home-made specials
- Golf clubhouse with lounge and public bars open to all

A (watering) hole in one for real ale and good food at a golf club offering both, and chosen as local CAMRA Club of the Year in 2004. The club's Conifers restaurant specialises in traditional meals with home-made soups, curries, pies and lasagnes, as well as vegetarian dishes. The bar menu offers snacks such as home-made tomato and sweet chilli soup with freshly baked roll, jacket potatoes with fillings from bacon, cheese and mushroom to home-made chilli, burgers and triple decker sarnies. Main courses in the bar include Bishopswood brunch of sausage, bacon, tomato, mushrooms, beans, egg, fried bread and chips for £5.50, home-made chicken curry with rice and naan, freshly made salads and rump steak grill, prices £4.50-£9.50.

In the restaurant main courses include baked salmon fillet with lemon butter, breaded scampi with tartare sauce, a selection of grills culminating in 10oz rib eye steak topped with pâté on Madeira sauce, home-made pork jambalaya (spicy pork with peppers, rice and prawns), home-made steak and ale pie and braised lamb shank, prices £7-£12. On Sundays (booking essential) there is a choice of roast meats, £8.50 for two courses.

S V P C

WHITCHURCH

Red House

21 London Street, RG28 7LH

- Off A34 on B3400
- Mon-Sat 11.30am-3pm, 6-11.30pm; Sun 12-3pm, 7-10.30pm
- Daily 12-2pm, 6.30 (7 Sun)-9.30pm
- T (01256) 895558
- F (01256) 895966
- Cheriton Pots Ale; guests
- Gastropub with award-winning restaurant
- 16th century coaching inn, stone-flagged public bar; large garden popular with families

Described by local CAMRA as a real gem, the Red House stands out from the other seven real ale pubs in Whitchurch for its quality food at reasonable prices, served in the bar, large garden and restaurant. The menu changes often, but a typical selection includes a range of starters such as soup of the day with home-made bread flavoured with garlic and basil butter, sesame-seared tuna carpaccio with honey and mustard vinaigrette and char-grilled pear salad, hand-made tortellini filled with crab, spinach and mascarpone flavoured with roast tomato jus, confit chicken and watermelon with feta and watercress salad, or marinated halloumi with roast peppers, pesto and yoghurt dressing, prices from £4.10-£6.75.

Main courses might be thinly-sliced pork tenderloin with creamed leeks, chorizo and dried Granny Smith apples, ostrich fillet medallions with polenta and Emmenthal fondue and blueberry jus, while steaks include a 16oz rump steak with bacon and mushroom sauce or fillet steak with bacon and Stilton sauce, priced £11.95-£17.25. Fish dishes included roast seabream fillets with prawn panacotta and Puy lentil salsa and seared skate wing with warm gazpacho sauce and confit of Parisienne potato, priced £12.50-£14; a vegetarian dish might be aubergine parmesan with Dutch mozzarella and grilled portobello mushroom.

V (Whitchurch) P C

WINCHESTER

☆ Wykeham Arms

75 Kingsgate Street, SO23 9SG

- Close to Winchester Cathedral and College
- Mon-Sat 11am-11pm; Sun 12-10.30pm
- Daily 12-9pm
- T (01962) 853834
- F (01962) 854411
- Beer range varies
- Contemporary British cuisine with overseas touches
- Traditional, friendly, Georgian inn with three log fires, deluged in memorabilia; food served throughout

The menu here offers offbeat, creative cooking with a changing repertoire of seasonal dishes. At lunchtime that could mean chicken, spinach and apricot roulade with pear and walnut chutney, confit of buffalo mozzarella and plum tomatoes, home-cooked gammon with English mustard and Demerara glaze, char-grilled aubergine and mixed pepper gateau topped with Dijon rarebit, wild mushroom and Stilton risotto, oven baked seabass with Thai vegetable noodles, or a locally-reared Dexter beef open sandwich, prices from £5.75-£7.50.

An evening menu includes home-made soup and starters such as wok-fried honey and harissa beef warm noodle salad, home-cured salmon gravadlax and prosciutto platter or Thai crab mousse, prices £3.75-£6.25. Main dishes might be roast rack of Hampshire Downs lamb, Gressingham duck breast with sweet potato purée and aromatic red cabbage, free-range chicken with chorizo risotto, char-grilled yellow fin tuna with spiced Mediterranean couscous, paupiettes of seabass, king scallops with poached asparagus and saffron cream or a veggie dish such as fresh egg linguine with wild mushroom cream and pine nut salad, prices £10.95-£14.95. The cheese board includes Cornish Yarg, Somerset blue and Long Clawson Stilton with home-made apple and grape chutney.

★ Q V (Winchester) P C

AYMESTREY
☆ Riverside Inn
HR6 9ST

- ▶ On A4110, 18 miles north of Hereford
- ☼ Daily 11am-3pm, 6-11pm
- 🍴 Daily 12-2.15pm, 7-8.45pm
- T (01568) 708440
- F (01568) 709058
- E theriverside@btconnect.com
- W www.theriversideinn.org
- 🍺 Beer range varies
- ☺ Imaginative menus based on English cuisine with an interesting twist
- ◙ Delightfully situated 16th-century inn on the River Lugg; stylish bar areas and good accommodation

The Riverside stands midway along the Mortimer Trail, a 30-mile marked walk through some outstanding countryside. The inn offers a two or three day package with transport, packed lunches, breakfast and dinner. Sounds very tempting, especially when the food here is so good. Meat and cheese are sourced locally, while much of the fruit, vegetables and herbs are produced in the pub's own extensive gardens; it also makes its own preserves.

Sample starters include warm salad of Lugg trout on samphire and new potatoes with summer herb vinaigrette, gâteau of Cornish crab with chive and lime and a tomato dressing, fillet of Herefordshire beef marinated in thyme with balsamic mushrooms, priced from £3.75-£5.25. To follow there might be roasted haunch of local venison with beetroot rösti and blackcurrant jus, herb-crusted local pork tenderloin on caramelised apple and raisin mustard mash with sage jus, or seared fillet of brill on a bed of summer vegetables with a saffron and mussel sauce, priced £9-£15. Vegetarians always have a choice of imaginative dishes, such as spinach, soft cheese and pine nut filo strudel and beetroot and orange risotto with parmesan. Good bar lunches, £4.25-£10, are also available.

★ 🏰 Q ❀ 🛏 S V 🍺 🍎 Ⓟ ⚟ 👪 C

CRASWALL
Bull's Head
HR2 0PN

- ▶ Six miles from Hay on Wye via Forester Road
- ☼ Mon-Sat 11am-11pm; Sun 12-10.30pm
- 🍴 Daily from 12 noon
- T (01981) 510616
- E info@thebullsheadpub.com
- W www.thebullsheadpub.com
- 🍺 Wye Valley Butty Bach; guests
- ☺ English cooking with a modern twist
- ◙ Ancient cider house with wood burning fires and flagstone floors; two elegant dining areas

This beautiful old drovers' inn lies at the foot of the Black Hill, immortalised by Bruce Chatwin's book, in an area that is great for all outdoor pursuits. For the more cerebrally minded the 'Town of Books' Hay on Wye is nearby. The inn may have changed little over the centuries, but its menu has kept pace with modern tastes and new dishes appear regularly on its blackboard. If you only have time for a snack its famous 'huffers' will fit the bill: thick wedges of home-baked seasoned bread, with a choice of fillings too numerous to list, priced from £5.75.

For a more leisurely meal you could try the longstanding favourite, Craswall pie, made with gammon and beef in Butty Bach gravy under a shortcrust pastry lid, or the cider and apple sausages made by the local butcher served on a bed of crushed new potatoes with scrumpy cider gravy. Other enticing dishes are country game casserole with rosemary and paprika dumplings and vegetables, warm black pudding and bacon salad, char-grilled chicken breast with Stilton sauce and local Herefordshire steaks (rump or sirloin). Vegetarians might be offered stuffed sweet peppers glazed with Cheddar cheese and Provençal sauce or wild mushroom tagliatelle. Main courses are priced from around £9 to £14.85 for the best-selling 'mega' mixed grill.

★ 🏰 Q ❀ 🛏 S V 🍺 ⛺ 🍎 ⚟ 👪 C

KENTCHURCH
☆ Bridge Inn
HR2 0BY

- ▶ Off A465 at Pontrilas, follow B4347 to Kentchurch
- Mon & Tue 5-12pm; Wed-Sat 12-2.30pm, 5pm-midnight; Sun 12-3pm, 7-11pm
- Wed-Sat 12-2pm, 7-9pm; Sun 12-2pm
- T (01981) 240408
- F (01981) 240213
- Beer range varies
- ☺ Home-cooked English cuisine with continental influences
- In a beautiful setting overlooking the River Monnow, this olde-worlde pub probably dates back to the 14th century

You can't miss this pub – painted red with bright blue doors and windows – but why would you want to? Recently refurbished, its single bar offers local ales (particularly Wye Valley brews), while the restaurant affords lovely views of the riverside garden where petanque can be played in summer. Landlords David Young and Kevin Shaw share the cooking. They don't bother printing a menu as meals are designed around the produce they buy at the local markets and trusted suppliers. They believe in providing fresh food, not overdressed or overpriced.

Chalked up on the board you might find for starters a warm Brie salad with dill vinaigrette, bacon, black pudding and vine tomato bake, a salad of buffalo mozzarella, parma ham and roasted peaches, or home-made tuna fishcake with asparagus and wine sauce, all under £6. You are unlikely to find a main course costing more than a tenner; a sample selection might include Gloucester Old Spot gammon with local free range eggs, pork fillet in sage and cider sauce, luxury fish pie incorporating salmon, haddock, prawns and mussels, Welsh Black rump steak, a duo of pheasant breasts with honey and mustard sauce and a vegetarian option such as Stilton, leek and walnut pie. A three-course Sunday lunch with plenty of choices is £9.95 (£6 for children).

★ S V P C

LEDBURY
Talbot Hotel
14 New Street, HR8 2DX

- ▶ Off High St crossroads
- Mon-Fri 11am-3pm, 5-11pm; Sat 11am-11pm; Sun 12-10.30pm
- Mon-Sat 11.45am-2.15pm, 6-9pm (9.30pm Sat); Sun 12-2.30pm, 6-8.30pm
- T (01531) 632963
- F (01531) 633796
- E talbot.ledbury@wadworth.co.uk
- W www.visitledbury.co.uk/talbot
- Wadworth 6X, IPA; Wye Valley Butty Bach; guest
- ☺ Specialising in excellent local meat on a traditional British/continental menu
- Historic, half-timbered coaching house that dates back to the 16th century, with a fine oak-panelled dining room

The Talbot hosts the annual Ledbury English Festival, held around St George's Day (23rd April), which promotes the best in local food, beers and wine. A highlight of the event is the competition to promote Ledbury's High Street butchers featuring the Black Pudding Push and String of Sausage Relay! The Talbot itself buys its meat from award-winning Dave Waller, whose sausages appear regularly on the specials board. He also provides the best rib of beef and most succulent loin of pork for Sunday lunch.

The main menu here combines traditional English dishes with some from France and, unusually, Romania, all home cooked. Chef's favourites include supreme of chicken filled with sugar-glazed ham in white wine and Brie sauce, £9.25, savoury pancakes filled with sautéed leeks, mushrooms and sweetcorn in a rich parsley sauce, £7.95, home-made lamb and mint pie with red wine under puff pastry lid, £8.95 and salmon supreme, grilled and served with herbs and sesame oil on a bed of spinach with tomato and basil sauce, £9.75. Excellent steaks can be ordered plain or with sauce, such as Stilton and whisky or brandy and peppercorn.

★ Q S V (Ledbury) C

TARRINGTON
Tarrington Arms
Ledbury Road, HR1 4HX

- ▶ A438 Ledbury-Hereford road, in village
- ☼ Mon-Sat 12-3pm, 6.30-11pm; Sun 12-3pm, 7-10.30pm
- Ⓨ Daily 12-2.30pm, 7-9.30pm (not Sun)
- T (01432) 890796
- F (01432) 890678
- Wood Shropshire Lad; guests
- ☺ Eclectic menu making good use of local produce, exceptional vegetarian choice
- ◙ Fine late-Georgian red brick hotel with two bars, refectory-style restaurant

The home-made vegetarian menu is so splendid at the Tarrington, we'll start there. A choice of eight dishes includes Brie and redberry tart, roast nut cakes with creamy mash on tomato and onion sauce, wild mushroom and pepper risotto and red pepper, spinach and sweetcorn crown, prices from £6.45-£7.95. Bar meals, all home made, include steak pie with potatoes and vegetables, Indian-style chicken curry, pork and cider sausages on mash with onion gravy, freshly beer-battered haddock fillet and grilled D-cut gammon with egg or pineapple, prices around £6.95.

In the restaurant, chef's specials may be muntjak with juniper and port, monkfish tail with shellfish, spinach and tarragon sauce or Hereford sirloin steak at only £9.25. Starters range from trio of home-made crab cakes to steamed mussels in curried cream, followed by home-made fish croquettes on minted mushy peas, oven-baked chicken supreme with wild mushroom and tarragon risotto, trio of fish with chilli and pesto tagliatelle, pork tenderloin on purple sage mash with devilled kidney sauce, again well priced below £9, with rack of lamb on colcannon, £14.25. A lighter selection offers interesting noodle bowls for a fiver, and full marks for the children's menu including prawn and pineapple salad with garlic bread.

★ S V ♣ P C

TITLEY
Stagg Inn
Titley, HR5 3RL

- ▶ On B4355 between Kington and Presteigne
- ☼ Tue-Sat 12-3pm, 6.30-11pm; Sun 12-3pm
- Ⓨ Tue-Sat 12-2pm, 6.30-9.30pm; Sun 12-2pm
- T (01544) 230221
- E reservations@thestagg.co.uk
- W www.thestagg.co.uk
- Beer range varies
- ☺ Modern British cuisine prepared by an award-winning chef
- ◙ Charming, family-run pub, with a small but friendly bar and a pleasant garden

In 2001, landlord Steve Reynolds was the first pub chef to be awarded a Michelin star and he has maintained an excellent reputation by consistently offering innovative dishes prepared from the finest local produce. The blackboard menu in the bar gives an indication of the quality, listing dishes such as crispy duck leg with cider sauce, scallops on parsnip purée, smoked haddock risotto, locally smoked salmon salad with citrus dressing or gammon with apricot sauce for around £8. For a full meal expect to pay around £26 or £15 for a three-course Sunday lunch.

Exciting appetisers include pan-fried foie gras with apple jelly, gingered mushroom and turnip bake, pigeon breast with Puy lentils and bacon, or venison carpaccio. To follow there might be local game such as mallard duck breast with figs and port sauce or partridge with poached pear and potato fondant. Or perhaps a fillet of Herefordshire beef, braised lamb shank with saffron risotto or wild seabass fillet. There is always a vegetarian option. You can finish with a choice from the prize-winning selection of regional, mostly unpasteurised cheeses or imaginative puddings such as chocolate meringue with satsuma cream, caramelised lemon tart with cassis sorbet, passion fruit jelly with Cointreau sauce or cinnamon pannacotta with caramelised apples.

S V P C

WELLINGTON
Wellington
HR4 8AT

- ▶ Turn off A49 at Wellington, quarter mile on left
- ☼ Mon 6-11pm; Tue-Sat 12-3pm, 6-11pm; Sun 12-4pm, 7-10.30pm
- Daily 12-2pm, 7-9pm
- T (01432) 830367
- E thewellington@hotmail.com
- Hobsons Best Bitter; Wye Valley Butty Bach; guests
- ☺ Contemporary British cuisine in the restaurant; low-priced, tasty bar menu
- Victorian village pub with welcoming bar and barn style restaurant

Highly commended in the 2004 Flavours of Herefordshire pub awards, the Wellington majors in local produce including sausages made to its own recipe and a Herefordshire cheeseboard. A short but well thought out bar menu offers home-made soup at £3.75, steak and Guinness pie, cheese and tomato omelette, fish 'n' chips, scrambled eggs with oak-smoked salmon, prawn, avocado and mango salad, pork sausages with mash and onion gravy or sirloin steak sandwich, all with accompaniments modestly priced at £4.95-£6.95.

A sample menu in the no-smoking restaurant starts with warm salad of smoked pheasant breast with raspberry vinegar or crayfish tails with feta, wild rocket and honey mustard dressing, priced from £3.75-£5.75. Main courses might be Herefordshire rib eye steak with red onion marmalade and real chips, crisp belly pork with red onion and mustard mash, Guinness braised lamb shank with champ mash, baked smoked haddock with leek mash and watercress sauce or red onion and balsamic tart, prices £8.75 to £12.95. A Sunday carvery at £11.50 for two courses offers roast local Hereford cross beef or roast leg of free range pork, possibly followed by apple and walnut crumble – or Mars Bar mousse!

S V P C

WOOLHOPE
Crown Inn
HR1 4QP

- ▶ Centre of village, next to church
- ☼ Daily 12-2.30pm, 6.30-11pm (10.30pm Sun)
- Daily 12-2pm, 6.30-9.30pm
- T (01432) 860468
- F (01432) 860770
- Fuller's London Pride; Whittington's Cats Whiskers; Wye Valley Bitter; guest
- ☺ Extensive home-cooked menu catering well for all, especially vegetarians
- Parts of the inn are almost 500 years old; outside is a stone mounting block dated 1520

The menus offered at the Crown are so extensive that it has adopted the practice of numbering the dishes for ease of ordering. However, that is where the similarity to a fast food joint definitely ends. All the food here is freshly cooked to order and the variety of dishes is just an indication of the inn's efforts to please all its customers. So one page of the menu is devoted to smaller appetites, one for vegetarians, with innovative dishes such as nut moussaka with feta cheese topping, and another for children where it is pleasing to see small rump and gammon steaks as an alternative to fish fingers and nuggets.

Starters, £4-£6, include home-made dishes such as potted Stilton with mushrooms, smokies served with granary bread, chicken liver pâté, crab cakes and, of course, soup. There is a good choice of grills and fish to follow, supplemented by a list of home-made main courses including lamb and cranberry casserole, beef bourguignon served in a Yorkshire pud, pork, ginger and apricot casserole, good, old-fashioned rabbit pie or faggots in onion gravy and favourites such as steak, stout and mushroom pie or beef lasagne, all priced around £9. Desserts, £3.95, are also home made: peach and raspberry bakewell tart, forest fruit meringue, chocolate profiteroles with hot chocolate sauce, to name a few.

★ S V P C

The Crown Inn, Woolhope (see page 125)

Rack of lamb gets a Mediterranean touch in this recipe from Henry Taylor of the Tarrington Arms in Herefordshire.

ROAST RACK OF LAMB WITH ROASTED GARLIC, TOMATO SAUCE AND PESTO DRESSING

Serves 4

Roast lamb

4 x 4-bone racks of lamb, trimmed French style
75g (3oz) French mustard
50g (2oz) fresh breadcrumbs
50g (2oz) mixed, chopped herbs (rosemary, thyme and parsley)
Salt and pepper

Sauce

1 head of garlic
Olive oil
Herb trimmings
1 shallot, finely chopped
100ml (3fl oz) white wine
½ litre (1 pint) lamb stock
25g (1oz) mirepoix (onion, carrot, celery, leek)
3 cherry tomatoes
Salt and pepper

Pesto

75g (3oz) Parmesan
50g (2oz) pine nuts
1 large clove garlic
1 bunch basil
150ml (¼ pint) olive oil

Pre-heat oven to 220C/425F/gas mark 7. Season the lamb racks well, then seal in a hot pan with a touch of oil; reserve pan for sauce. Spread each rack with mustard, dip into the mixed herbs and breadcrumbs, then oven roast until pink (rare to medium rare).

To make the sauce, rub the whole head of garlic in olive oil and wrap in tin foil, roast in a hot oven for 15-20 minutes. Sweat herbs with shallot until just coloured in the pan used for sealing lamb, gently add white wine and reduce. Add stock and mirepoix and allow to reduce by one third. Peel warm, roast garlic and crush into a paste with a strong knife, sauté briefly in a hot pan, then add sauce through a fine chinois. Season to taste and add any meat juices from cooked racks, along with the cherry tomatoes.

To prepare pesto, process Parmesan in a blender, add pine nuts and garlic clove, then the basil. While machine is running, slowly pour in the olive oil to give quite a runny texture.

ALDBURY
Greyhound Inn
19 Stocks Road, HP23 5RT

- Village centre, near Tring
- Daily 11am-11pm
- Daily 12-2.30pm, 6.30-9.30pm
- T (01442) 851228
- F (01442) 851495
- W www.greyhoundaldbury.co.uk
- Badger Best, First Gold, Tanglefoot
- Upmarket menu of good quality food
- Small, family-run country hotel, a former coaching inn overlooking the ancient stocks and duck pond in a picturesque little village

Aldbury is a pretty little village not far from the market towns of Tring and Berkhamsted and on the edge of the National Trust's Ashridge Park, which is popular with walkers. The Greyhound is a charming hotel with just eight guest rooms, serving good quality meals from fresh ingredients. At lunchtime filled baguettes, ciabattas and jacket potatoes are supplemented by a selection of dishes such as pasta, mussels, sausages and mash and steak and ale pie, main courses £6-£12, snacks around £6.

The evening menu is more extensive, with starters, £4-£7, such as baby mozzarella with roasted peppers and pesto dressing, king prawns with a tequila and lime dip, smoked duck breast with piccalilli or an oriental platter of prawn toast, chicken, spicy beef and deep-fried won ton to share at £10.50. To follow you could choose from honey and soya glazed duck with vanilla rice, fillet of beef Rossini with château potatoes, roast cod on cheesy mash with mushy peas and tartare sauce, roast rump of lamb with redcurrant jus on minted rosti or wild mushroom risotto with shaved parmesan (also available as a starter). Main courses are £10-£16. The Sunday lunch menu here offers much more than just the traditional roast, with a good choice of starters and main courses as well as snacks.

★ Q S V P C

BUSHEY HEATH
Black Boy
19 Windmill Street, WD23 1NB

- Off Elstree Road near A41 and A4140 via Windmill Lane
- Mon-Sat 12-11pm; Sun 12-10.30pm
- Mon-Fri 12-2.30pm, Tue & Wed 6.30-8.30pm
- T (0208) 950 2230
- E elainemylius@aol.com
- Adnams Bitter; Draught Bass; Fuller's London Pride; Greene King Abbot; guest
- Rustic pub grub plus vegetarian and healthy meals
- Single room back street pub; three times winner of local CAMRA Pub of the Year

There is a set menu here but most diners go for the hearty, delicious specials – at bargain prices – chalked up on the board, all cooked by landlady and landlord Philip and Elaine Mylius. These could include lamb shank with rosemary gravy, creamed potatoes and vegetables, Lincolnshire or Cumberland sausages with sliced, fried apples and onions, mash and gravy, gammon steak with fried egg, sauté potatoes or chips and peas or salad, beef ribs in barbecue sauce with horseradish mash, fried liver with bacon, mash, peas and onion gravy, a giant Yorkie filled with sausages in onion gravy plus mash or chips, or home-made beef madras, chicken korma or lamb pasanda with rice, priced £6.50-£8.95. Extra mature sirloin steak with mushrooms, fried onions, tomato, jacket potato and salad is a snip at £9.50.

Snacks appearing on the specials board are home-made pork and apple or chilli burgers, tomato boats filled with mushrooms, bacon and grated Cheddar plus side salad, a steak sandwich or baguette with mushrooms and melted Stilton, priced £3.95-£5.50.The set menu offers jacket potatoes and sandwiches or baguettes, five other burgers, ham or sausages (including vegetarian), egg and chips, as well as a ploughman's platter of pork pie, Cheddar, bread, pickles and salad.

Q S V ♣ P C

FLAUNDEN
Bricklayers Arms
Hog Pits Bottom, HP3 0PH

▶ Take A404 from jct 18 M25, signed for Flaunden
☼ Daily 12-11.30pm
Mon-Sat 12-3pm, 6.30-9.30pm; Sun 12-4pm
T (01442) 833322
F (01442) 834841
E goodfood@bricklayersarms.com
W www.bricklayersarms.com
Fuller's London Pride; Greene King IPA, Old Speckled Hen; guest
☺ English traditional with French fusion
18th-century flint pub with vine creepers and real log fire

Winner of the 2004/5 Greene King Best Pub Food in South England award, the Bricklayers prepares meals to order from fresh ingredients from local suppliers. The menu changes regularly but typical starters include smoked duck breast with grilled almonds and honey vinegar, a selection of smoked fish with coriander butter – all home-smoked at the pub – foie gras mi-cuit with onion jam, cream of spinach soup and fresh asparagus with hollandaise, around £5-£6. Main courses could be lamb shank with red wine and shallot sauce, breast of chicken stuffed with mozzarella in mushroom and smoked bacon sauce, confit duck leg with honey and sesame jus, quail stuffed with mushrooms on balsamic sauce or fillet of roast seabass in olive oil with sweet red pepper cream sauce – prices from £13 to £15.45 for mature Scotch beef with peppercorn sauce, all accompanied by potatoes but vegetables are extra. Roast lamb, beef or chicken are around £10, and veggie choices include crêpe of Mediterranean vegetables or wild mushroom and vegetable risotto. Tempting puds range from pear in spicy red wine to gingerbread crème brûlée.

★ Q ❀ V P C

MARSWORTH
Anglers Retreat
Startops End, HP23 4LJ

▶ On B489 between Aston Clinton and Ivinghoe
☼ Daily 11am-11pm
Mon-Sat 12-9.30pm; Sun and bank hols 12-7.30pm
T (01442) 822250
E anglersretreat23@aol.com
Fuller's London Pride; Tring's Sidepocket For A Toad; guests
☺ Traditional English with a hint of the unusual
Traditional village pub opposite Startops Reservoir in an area of outstanding natural beauty; garden has an aviary and pets' corner

Here is a pub dedicated to fresh local produce and good beer, including locally-brewed ales promoted at spring and autumn beer festivals. Seasonal ingredients include fresh fruit and vegetables, fish and game such as trout, duck, rabbit, pheasant and partridge – the wild goose casserole is a local delicacy – as well as fresh crayfish served in garlic butter, home-made fruit pies and asparagus grown in Ivinghoe. The menu changes daily, but typical dishes include the local asparagus in garlic butter with Parmesan, and avocado and prawn cocktail among the starters.

Main dishes might be roast belly pork with apple and walnut stuffing, chicken and leek pie, pork fillet in creamy beer mustard and cider sauce, lamb chops with fresh vegetables, sausages with mash and onion gravy, a hunter's platter of ham, cheese, pickle and apple and, for vegetarians, Brie and broccoli or wild mushroom lasagne. Main courses are priced from £5-£6.50 apart from sirloin steak with all the trimmings at £9.50. Typical pub grub, all home made, includes cottage pie, pasty and chips, lasagne, chilli with rice, spag bol or beef stroganoff. Desserts range from brandy snaps filled with fresh strawberries and cream to home-made rhubarb crumble or treacle tart.

★ Q ❀ S V ♣ P C

PRESTON
Red Lion
The Green, SG4 7UD

- ▶ Near Hitchin, village is signed from B651
- Daily 12-2pm, 5.30-11pm (not Tue or Sun)
- Daily 12-2pm, 7-9pm (not Tue or Sun)
- T (01462) 459585
- Young's Bitter; guests
- Varied menu of home-cooked food at reasonable prices, game is a speciality
- A community pub owned by the villagers themselves, this attractive free house stands on the village green

Back in 1984 the Red Lion made the pages of the national press when the villagers raised enough money to buy the pub from Whitbread who planned to turn it into a steak house. The first community-owned pub in the country, it has gone from strength to strength, winning the local CAMRA Pub of the Year award in 2005. With frequently changing real ales and food that is a lot more tasty and varied than any pub chain can manage, it is always popular with locals and visitors too.

Start your meal with one of the hearty home-made soups, £3 – curried parsnip, tomato and fresh chilli, leek and potato or game. Main courses, £5-£8, depend on availability and game features highly in season; there could be half a boned pheasant in red wine, roast partridge, venison casseroled in red wine or rabbit or game pie. Other choices include creamy haddock tart, fresh rod-caught wild trout, fish pie, black pudding and fresh apple stack, pork medallions, lamb's liver and bacon or vegetarian options such as spinach and asparagus quiche or cauliflower and broccoli cheese bake. Home-made puddings are all £3: blackberry and apple crumble, lemon meringue pie and sticky toffee to name a few. Well-filled sandwiches and ploughman's are also available.

S V P

RICKMANSWORTH
Rose & Crown
Woodcock Hill, Harefield Road, WD3 1PP

- ▶ 1½ miles up Harefield Road at top of hill
- Summer 11am-11pm; winter 12-11pm
- Summer 12-11pm; winter 12-3pm, 7-10pm
- T (01923) 897680
- W www.morethanjustapub.com
- Fuller's London Pride; Caledonian Deuchars IPA; guests
- Traditional English cooking with contemporary twists
- Old farmhouse pub with gorgeous garden offering fine views over the Herts countryside

Sister pub to the Village Hall in Chalfont St Peter, also in this guide, the Rose and Crown regularly hosts beer suppers showcasing the ales of a different brewery (see website for events). On a day to day basis, the seasonal lunchtime menu offers starters such as Thai style crab cakes with avocado salsa, grilled goats' cheese slice with caramelised pear and walnut salad or potted chicken liver and foie gras pâté with onion marmalade, £5.50-£6.20. Main courses always include a half pound fresh cod or haddock fillet in home-made beer batter with hand cut chips, £7.90, as well as choices such as char-grilled bangers of the day (turkey sausages at Christmas) and mash with onion gravy, roast cornfed chicken breast with spring onion mash or char-grilled large rib eye steak with Stilton and pepper sauce at £13.90. For vegetarians there is wild mushroom and toasted pine nut risotto at £7.90.

The evening menu changes weekly – a typical selection includes starters such as scallops with ginger butter or potted smoked mackerel pâté with home-made horseradish sauce, £5-£6, followed by garlic and rosemary rack of lamb with rosti potato and redcurrant, char-grilled pork chop with minted peas, apple sauce and thyme gravy or pan roast duck breast with bubble and squeak and raspberry sauce, £10.90-£13.50.

S V P C

ST ALBANS

☆ Portland Arms

63 Portland Street, AL3 4RA

- ▶ Turning off Verulam Road
- Mon 6-11pm; Tue-Thu 12-2.30pm, 5-11pm; Fri-Sun 12-11pm (10.30pm Sun)
- Tue-Sat 12-2pm (3pm Sat), 6.30-9.30pm; Sun 12-4pm
- T (01727) 844574
- E championk2@btinternet.com
- W www.portlandarmspub.co.uk
- Fuller's Chiswick, London Pride, ESB, seasonal
- ☺ Imaginative, award-winning meals created with quality local produce
- Attractive back-street community pub, tastefully refurbished with comfy seating, floral displays outside

This Fuller's house has been transformed since landlady Kim Champion, a chef from New Zealand, took over a few years ago. The pub has won several awards including Fuller's Newcomer of the Year in 2004, and Kim reached the national finals of Pub Chef food awards. She sources fine local ingredients from Childwickbury goats' cheese, produced less than a mile away, to fine home-raised lamb, beef and pork from Hedges Farm in St Albans. A fairly simple lunchtime selection includes excellent open sandwiches and salads such as goats' cheese with olives and char-grilled peppers.

A wide choice in the evening includes a sharing platter of whatever Kim has found in St Albans market such as olives, antipasto, sun-blush tomatoes with ciabatta at £6.25, large cod in home-made beer batter with chips and home-cooked ham with either her exciting salad or eggs and chips – both dishes a snip at £5.25. The monster beef burger is home made to her own recipe, or choose Hedges Farm sausages in a giant Yorkie with wholegrain mustard mash and onion gravy. Pies such as steak and London Pride are unusually topped with filo, or there is kiln roasted salmon from Scotland with crayfish tails, smoked haddock and chive fishcakes, noisettes of Hedges' lovely lamb or superb beef fillet steak, prices £7.25 to £12.95 for generous platefuls. Sunday roasts of Hedges' meat are truly wonderful.

Q ❀ S V ♣ P C

ST ALBANS
White Lion
91 Sopwell Lane, AL1 1RN

- In a side road off Holywell Hill
- Mon-Fri 12-2.30pm, 5.30-11pm; Sat 12-11pm; Sun 12-10.30pm
- Tues-Sat 12-2.30pm, 6.30-9pm; Sun 10am-1pm breakfast/brunch
- T (01727) 850540
- E david@TheWhiteLionPH.co.uk
- Black Sheep Best Bitter; Fuller's London Pride; guests
- Contemporary European menu including fresh fish and seafood
- Beautifully kept listed building with two bar areas and garden close to St Albans Abbey

Landlord David Worcester was previously at St Albans' famous Lower Red Lion before taking over the White Lion in late 2004, persuading a talented local chef to join him. They have put together an upbeat menu of interesting dishes, using excellent fresh fish, meat and vegetables. The menu changes often but a typical selection might be skate wing with wine and caper sauce, tiger prawn and pea risotto, lamb cutlets on pea and mint purée, Aberdeen Angus fillet of beef au poivre, beef fillet stroganoff made properly with gherkins, mushrooms and paprika in a creamy sauce, pasta dishes such as penne arrabiata (tomato, garlic, basil and chilli sauce), and tagliatelli al fredo (creamy mushroom and white wine sauce). Main dishes served with vegetables are priced £6.50-£14.95.

The nachos with home-made chilli con carne, freshly made guacamole, sour cream and melted cheese are seriously good, either as a snack or main course, or there is a mean chicken Caesar salad, and sarnies with fillings from Brie, bacon and black olives to rib eye steak with caramelised onions. From 10am on Sundays, David cooks up a full English breakfast including black pudding and fried bread, Devon smoked kippers, or smoked salmon and scrambled egg on toast.

S V (St Albans Main Line/Abbey) C

TEWIN
☆ Plume of Feathers
57 Upper Green Road, AL6 0LX

- Off B1000 between Welwyn and Hertford
- Mon-Sat 11am-11pm; Sun 12-10.30pm
- Mon-Sat 12-2.30pm, 6-9.30pm; Sun 12-4pm
- T (01438) 717265
- E 8646@greeneking.co.uk
- Greene King IPA, Abbot Ale
- Lively menu using fresh and organic local produce
- 400-year-old coaching inn tastefully renovated in 1997

Food Pub of the Year for Greene King in 2003 and 2004, the Plume of Feathers is food focused throughout its spacious, airy interior. All food, down to chips, is freshly prepared using local and organic produce. It features Tamworth pork, famous Braughing bangers and organic flour from Redbournbury Mill to make the bread; the pub has apple trees and grows its own herbs. Sample starters from an evolving menu could be a selection of home-made organic breads with olive oil at £2.50, cheese and vegetable soup, smoked salmon with Loch Fyne smoked mussels, grilled herring on leaves with citrus dressing, or mussels with red cabbage and white wine sauce.

Main meals include char-grilled Scotch rump steak with hand-cut chips, burger made from properly hung steak with cheese and bacon in organic bread, pan-fried duck breast with peppercorn sauce, and trio of Braughing, wild boar with apple and pork and mustard sausages with mash, prices £8.95-£14.95. Fish lovers might find tempura battered cod, sea-salted whole seabass and salmon supreme with sun-blushed tomato dressing. For vegetarians there are free-range garden herb omelettes or grilled goats' cheese with couscous. To finish, home-made desserts or intriguing cheese – Stinking Bishop, Grandma Singleton, Wigmore, Casel Blue…

Q S V C

TRING
King's Arms
King Street, HP23 6BE

- ▶ Back street pub at the top of Queen Street
- ☼ Mon-Thu 12-2.30pm, 7-11pm; Fri & Sat 12-3pm, 7-11pm; Sun 12-4pm, 7-10.30 pm
- 🍴 Mon-Thu 12-2.15pm, 7-9.30pm; Fri & Sat 12-2.30pm, 7-9pm (9.30pm Sat); Sun 12-3pm, 7-9.30pm
- T (01442) 823318
- F (01442) 890038
- 🍺 Wadworth 6X; guests
- ☺ Original food made to original recipes – no chips
- ◙ Listed Regency pub with largely original interior; frequent local CAMRA Pub of the Year

A pub that successfully tries to avoid conventional pub grub (though bangers 'n' mash, liver and bacon and cottage pie might slip on to the specials board) boasts a menu as good to read as it is to eat. House specials include Mediterranean roast cod, Iranian lamb and orange khoresh, Thai green chicken curry, Turkish adana kebab, Mexican cheese quesadillas, Indian sweet potato cakes and traditional home-made English steak and kidney pudding, prices around £6-£7.

Starters include home-made soup such as carrot with coconut and sweet potato, Greek salad and mushrooms with bacon and Brie; on the snack list are bacon bap, egg and bacon on thick buttered toast, Welsh rarebit, various burgers, salad bowl, sausage and fried onion baguette, a good range of filled baked potatoes including rich Italian tomato sauce with melted cheese and olives, and double decker sarnies. Typical specials could be chicken, bacon and leeks in mustard sauce with new potatoes and vegetables or tagliatelle with mushrooms, Stilton and cream. Desserts range from bread pudding with ice cream to date, almond and honey cake. No smoking at lunchtimes, children are welcome lunchtimes only.

★ 🏰 Q S V ♣ ⚡ 👥 C

TYTTENHANGER GREEN
Plough
AL4 0RW

- ▶ Off A414 between St Albans and Hatfield
- ☼ Mon-Sat 11.30-2.30pm (3pm Sat), 6-11pm; Sun 12-3pm, 7-10.30pm
- 🍴 Daily 12-2pm
- T (01727) 857777
- E theplough@hotmail.com
- 🍺 Fuller's London Pride, ESB; guests
- ☺ Informal pub lunches with a good snack menu
- ◙ Busy rural free house with a notable bottled beer collection; children are welcome in the conservatory and the garden has play equipment

The antithesis of a gastropub, in fact the owners of the Plough do not consider it to be a serious food pub at all, but nonetheless it gets very busy at lunchtime with customers enjoying the good value, wholesome grub. The menu has grown over 21 years to 83 regular dishes (including 12 different omelettes): 'we have an idea, try it ourselves, add it to the menu then find we are unable to delete it due to its popularity'. The self-deprecating Barrowmans say they sell more kebabs than the local kebab shop – an ideal lunchtime snack for around £4. Fry ups are also perennially popular (more mauvaise than haute cuisine they say!).

Their eight daily changing items on the board in the bar are described as 'today's not very specials', however, they might include braised lamb's liver with bacon (served with proper 'lumpy' mash), egg pasta parcels stuffed with mozzarella, tomato and basil, pan-fried Cajun chicken breast with sauté potatoes or various salads such as feta cheese, sweet red onion and black olive, avocado, mozzarella and Parma ham, chicken and spinach or chicken Caesar salad. Specials are usually £7.50-£9.50. You will also find various croques monsieurs, burgers, ploughman's and sandwiches.

🏰 ❀ S V Ⓟ ⚡ 👥 C

HULVERSTONE
Sun Inn
Main Road, PO30 4EH

- Between Brook and Brighstone, half a mile from the coast
- Mon-Sat 11am-11pm; Sun 12-10.30pm
- Daily 12-9pm
- T (01983) 741124
- Beer range varies
- Traditional home-cooked meals with a good range of daily specials
- Traditional thatched 600-year old building at the heart of rural west Wight with a lovely garden

According to local CAMRA members this ancient inn has been restored to its former glory following a few years of uncertainty. As well as being noted for its variety of ales (almost 300 different beers per year), it has also built up a strong following for home-cooked food based on local produce served all day. It boasts one of the most expensive dishes in this guide (although it is doubtful one person would be expected to get through it all) – billed as 'Shell shocked', for just under £40 you will be served a whole lobster on a bed of mussels with calamari rings, scampi, fish goujons and tiger prawns, plus a selection of dips, crusty bread and butter and seasonal salad. Not tempted? There's plenty more to choose from, including specials such as fresh swordfish steak with lemon butter, home-made game and ale pie, giant vol-au-vents filled with creamy chicken, mushroom and tarragon sauce, home-made moussaka or steak, ale and mushroom suet pudding. Other main meals include roast ham, egg and chips, local home-made faggots or bangers and mash, for around £7. There's also a good choice of grills and salads, plus chunky sandwiches or filled jacket potatoes, around £5 for a light meal.

★ Q ❀ S V ♿ ♣ P C

NORTHWOOD
Travellers Joy
Pallance Road, PO31 8LS

- On main Yarmouth-Cowes road (A3020), via Thorness
- Mon-Thu 11-2.30pm, 5-11pm; Fri & Sat 11am-11pm; Sun 12-3pm, 7-10.30pm
- Daily 12-2pm, 6.30-9pm
- T (01983) 298024
- E tjoy@globalnet.co.uk
- Beer range varies
- Good value, straightforward pub food
- Renovated and extended traditional rural pub

A favourite with the island's CAMRA members who have voted it local Pub of the Year five times, it always offers a good variety of eight beers and showcases micro-breweries. On the food front, it serves wholesome, straightforward, home-cooked fare – nothing fancy but all good value. Starters are limited to home-made soup with crusty bread or garlic mushrooms, £2.40 and £3.85. Many of the main courses are just £5.75, such as battered cod and chips, honey roast ham, egg and chips, or home-made steak and kidney pie with veg. Burgers are a bargain £2.60 for a plain beef burger or veggie burger, up to £3.95 for a 'Cyrilburger' with onions, cheese, bacon, mushrooms and egg. From the grill you can have an 8oz rump steak, mixed grill, gammon steak, loin of lamb or garlic chicken for £9 or less. Some interesting seasonal home-made specials are available daily, such as salmon fishcake with herby mashed potatoes, pheasant, bacon and wild mushroom pie, lamb rogan josh with pilau rice, or chicken supreme with rice. Where possible children can have smaller portions of main dishes, or they can pick from the standard fare of chicken nuggets or fish fingers. Varied snacks include a big range of sandwiches plus filled jacket spuds and ploughman's.

❀ S V ♿ ♣ P C

BOUGHTON MONCHELSEA
Cock Inn
Heath Road, ME17 4JD

- ▶ Off B229, S of Maidstone on B2163
- ☼ Mon-Sat 11am-11pm; Sun 12-10.30pm
- 🍴 Mon-Sat 12-2.30pm, 6-9pm; Sun 12-4pm
- T (01622) 734166
- E cockinn@youngs.co.uk
- Young's Bitter, Special, seasonal
- ☺ Interesting, freshly-cooked menu with tempting fish dishes
- Former coaching inn built in 1568 to provide lodgings for Canterbury pilgrims; taken over by Young's in 1999

Some lovely touches feature on the Cock menu, starting with garlic mushrooms en chemise (in a pancake), alongside Irish rope mussels in garlic, white wine and cream, Irish fishcakes of fish, shellfish and potato deep fried and served with garlic butter, dressed crab baked with garlic butter and coarse liver pâté with Cumberland sauce among starters priced £5.95-£7.95. If you are really pushing the boat out, pre-order its famous seafood platter of smoked salmon, oysters, langoustines, king prawns, whelks, clams, cockles, smoked mackerel and mussels – with crab £49.95 for two, with lobster £64.95 for two, or £79.95 for four sharing the combo platter.

Other fish dishes on the main menu include a whole fresh crab mayonnaise as available, seafood paella, oven-roast whole seabass with lemon grass and ginger, salmon in cream and tarragon, rope-grown moules marinière or jumbo cod in Young's beer batter, £11.95-£15.95. Meat dishes include shoulder of lamb pot roasted in red wine and redcurrant, three spicy sausages with mash, char-grilled chicken breast with creamed leeks, spinach and rice, steak, ale and mushroom pie, home-roast ham with egg and chips, £9.95-£14.95. There is a choice of steaks and salads, while vegetarian dishes are on the specials board.

Q ❀ S V ♣ P C

DOVER
Blake's
52 Castle Street, CT16 1PJ

- ▶ Off Marine Parade (A20)
- ☼ Mon-Sat 11.30am-11pm; Sun 12-10.30pm
- 🍴 Mon-Fri 11.30am-2.30pm, 5.30-9.30pm; Sat 6-9.30pm
- T (01304) 209194
- F (01304) 211263
- E book@blakesofdover.com
- W www.blakesofdover.com
- Beer range varies
- ☺ Home-cooked traditional meals with plenty of fresh fish and good vegetarian choice
- Cellar wine bar also sourcing ales from micros nationwide

A cellar wine bar serving at least four cask ales at a time, with a no-smoking restaurant, it offers fresh fish delivered daily from Jackson's of Deal, and special sausages made locally at Tappington Hall. The superb fish menu includes whole Dover sole, lemon sole, plaice and sea bream, fillet of seabass, cod baked in lemon and garlic butter, Scottish salmon poached in white wine with prawns, rainbow trout with stuffing of the day and traditional fish 'n' chips. Prices range from £8.95 to £15.50, with some fish dishes market price of the day. Vegetarian specials might include aubergine, Stilton and pesto stack, veggie Wellington with parsnip chips, or roast Mediterranean vegetables. Meat dishes range from beef in ale pie, Moroccan lamb, chicken breast in Stilton and sherry sauce or with a sage and onion stuffing wrapped in bacon, to home-cooked ham with free range eggs and chips or those special sausages with mash and onion gravy, priced £8.50-£10.95. Rump, sirloin and fillet steaks with home-made sauces are priced £10.05-£15.95. Home-made puds include bread and butter with brandy and apricots, apple and raspberry crumble, and pineapple upside down cake with double cream. The real food children's menu includes small portions of main courses.

Q ❀ S V (Dover Priory) C

EAST MALLING

King & Queen

1 New Road, ME19 6DD

- ▶ Close to M20 jct 4, in village centre
- ☼ Mon-Thu 10.30am-3pm, 6-11pm; Fri & Sat 10.30am-11pm; Sun 12-4pm
- Mon-Sat 11.30am-2pm, 6-9.15pm; Sun 12-3pm
- T (01732) 842752
- F (01732) 529627
- Hook Norton Old Hooky; Marston's Pedigree; guests
- ☺ From baguettes to bar meals and full à la carte including fresh fish and game
- Busy 16th-century whitewashed pub with spacious saloon bar

A Clean Food award-winning pub that often showcases beers from Kent micros, the King and Queen provides a right royal menu. Bar meals include home-made soup of the day, steak and kidney pudding with vegetables, large cod with chips or new potatoes, ham, Cheddar or Stilton ploughman's, freshly carved ham with egg, salad and chips or the pasta dish of the day, prices £3.95-£8.75. Tempting fillings for baguettes and tortilla wraps at £4.25 include smoked back bacon with roast mushrooms, honey-glazed chicken and roast vegetables with cream cheese. Steak grill nights are Monday and Tuesday, and traditional Sunday lunch offers a choice of roasts or fresh fish at £9.95 for two courses.

In the restaurant you could start with baked herrings coated in pesto and oatmeal, warm pasta salad or asparagus roasted with bacon at £4.25-£5. Main courses include roast cod with tomato, basil and garlic sauce, pork medallions with honey, cinnamon, apple and cider sauce, duck and bacon mixed salad with plum dressing, swordfish with smoked cheese and chickpea salad, fillet of beef with black pudding and potato rosti, braised guinea fowl with chorizo or spinach and ricotta mille feuille, mainly £11-£12 with vegetables, rising to £14.95 for the beef.

★ Q S V ♿ ⇌ (East Malling) P C

HALSTEAD

Rose & Crown

Otford Lane, TN14 7EA

- ▶ Near jct 4 M25
- ☼ Mon-Sat 12-11pm; Sun 12-10.30pm
- Daily 12-7pm
- T (01959) 533120
- F (01959) 534120
- E joybrushneed@yahoo.co.uk
- Courage Best Bitter; Larkins Traditional; Whitstable IPA; guests
- ☺ Wide range of home-made meals and snacks plus Sunday roasts
- Two-bar, flint-faced, 1850 grade II listed free house with refurbished bars; bat and trap played in enclosed rear garden

What a good idea – not two sizes of Sunday lunch but three. There is mini for children at £3.50, midi for normal appetites at £5.75 and maxi – or, as landlady Joy Brushneen puts it, 'the Full Monty' – at £8.45, a serious platter including roast beef or pork, roast parsnips and potatoes, new potatoes, Yorkshire pudding, cauliflower, cabbage, carrots, roast onion, swede and carrot mash and gravy. On weekdays expect traditional home-made pub dishes such as steak and kidney or chicken casserole, Cumberland sausage with onion gravy, bacon and cheese omelettes made with free-range eggs, home-made beef burgers, moussaka, beef chilli and chicken tikka masala. Wednesday is fresh fish day when a 'man in a van' from Grimsby brings fresh haddock which is then cooked in real ale batter. Main meals are priced around £5-£7.

Joy is a vegetarian and careful to use only veggie ingredients in veggie dishes which include pasta with various sauces, vegetable tikka, mushroom omelette and an outstanding ploughman's of Cheddar, Stilton and Camembert with crusty bread, celery, salad and pickled onions. A wide range of sandwiches includes ham, salad, BLT or egg, bacon and mushroom. The three frequently changing guest ales are often from micros and cover different ABVs.

S V ♿ P

LADDINGFORD
Chequers Inn

Lees Road, ME18 6BP

- Mon-Fri 12-3pm; Sat 12-11pm; Sun 12-10.30pm
- Daily 12-2.30pm, 7-9.30pm (9pm Sun)
- T (01622) 871266
- Adnams Bitter; Fuller's London Pride; guests
- Good quality, home-cooked food with a varied menu and theme nights
- 15th-century, white weather-boarded, former farmhouse close to Hop Farm

Self-taught chef and landlord Charles Leaver cooks dishes he knows regulars and visitors will enjoy, from classic poached cod with parsley sauce and mash to daily specials which might include king prawns with spicy noodles, duck breast with mango salsa or his original Mediterranean lamb shank. The main menu offers ham off the bone with fried eggs and chips (people travel miles for his hand-cut chips), Cumberland sausage in a large Yorkie with mash, the all day breakfast, spicy pancakes filled with home-made chilli, cod or plaice in light batter, all between £6-£7 with accompaniments. Steaks include rump and fillet, there is a choice of sizzling fajitas, and a good range of vegetarian meals such as mixed vegetable stir fry on noodles. Groups of four plus can order a special paella to their original recipe. Thursday is sausage day with six different types such as pork and hop, and pie days on the first Tuesday and Wednesday of the month range from pork and calvados to steak and stout. There are freshly cut sandwiches (Monday lunchtimes sandwich menu only), and desserts include Chequers chocolate cake of crushed biscuit soaked in brandy and rum, covered with chocolate sauce and topped with desiccated coconut.

S V P C

LENHAM
Dog & Bear

The Square, ME17 2PG

- Signposted off A20, short drive from M20 jct 8
- Mon-Sat 11am-11pm; Sun 12-10.30pm
- Mon-Sat 12-2.30pm, 6.30-9.30pm; Sun 12-7.30pm
- T (01622) 858219
- F (01622) 859415
- E dogbear@shepherdneame.co.uk
- W www.dogandbearlenham.co.uk
- Shepherd Neame Master Brew Bitter, Spitfire, seasonal
- Interesting dishes made with fresh produce
- Village pub built in 1602 with bar areas, restaurant and B&B

Landlord Brian Hogg is a trained chef with 20 years' experience. He ensures everything is made from fresh local produce – all meat can be traced back to the animal itself, and all from Kent. Light bites and starters include coarse pork and liver pâté, warm goats' cheese salad, oriental pancake wrap with crispy duck or home-cured gravadlax. Main dishes could be peppered salmon fillet with tomato salsa, lamb chilli with shallots and mixed peppers, fresh cod in beer batter, pan-fried lamb's liver and bacon, home-made steak and Spitfire or chicken, bacon and leek pie made with shortcrust pastry. Further choices include honey-glazed duck with damson sauce, rump of lamb on rosti potatoes, cold home-baked ham with chips and fried egg, roast topside of beef or leg of lamb, prices from £6.95-£12.95. Kentish rib eye, rump and fillet steak range in price from £11.95-£14.95. A choice of veggie dishes includes field mushrooms stuffed with ratatouille and mozzarella, oriental vegetable stir fry with pak choi, cauliflower and Stilton bake or parsnip, sweet potato and chestnut bake. The highlight of January is the Rabbie Burns tribute with a celebration of Scottish food.

★ S V (Lenham) P C

NORTHBOURNE
Hare & Hounds
The Street, CT14 0LG

- Signed from A256 and A258
- Mon-Sat 11.30am-3.30pm, 6-11pm; Sun 12-3pm, 7-10.30pm
- Daily 12-2pm, 7-10pm
- T (01304) 365429
- F (01304) 369188
- Fuller's ESB; Harveys BB; Shepherd Neame Master Brew, Spitfire; guest
- Home-cooked traditional English food on a weekly changing menu
- Village centre 18th-century pub close to church and cricket ground with open layout, hops around the bar, real fires, large garden

The Hare & Hounds prides itself on good, wholesome food made from local produce including meat sourced from nearby farms by its butcher, fish from Deal fishermen, bread from the baker using organic flour, and all fruit and vegetables grown locally. Ninety per cent of the food is produced on the premises by a team led by Judy Butcher, head chef for 20 years, and includes steak and kidney pie, beef in Guinness, steak simmered in ale with mushrooms, pork in cider, beef chasseur or lamb in port flavoured with rosemary. Main meals cost around £6.95.

Fresh fish might be cod and haddock in batter or plaice in crumbs, while hot snacks at around £4 include tuna melts, spaghetti Bolognese or Irish pork sausages with bubble and squeak. Home-made vegetarian dishes include spinach and onion crêpes in creamy sauce flavoured with nutmeg, marinated lentil and artichoke salad or cashew nut and sesame stir fry. Sunday roasts of beef, lamb or pork with Yorkshire puddings, fresh vegetables and all the trimmings cost around £6.50. On the more sophisticated à la carte evening menu you can choose from lamb shank with butterbean ragout, pork fillet stuffed with prunes in bacon and mushroom sauce, duck confit with plum and ginger sauce, mixed grill or fillet steak Rossini, prices from £10-£14.95.

Q S V P C

PENSHURST
Spotted Dog
Smarts Hill, TN11 8EE

- Off B2176 near Tunbridge Wells
- Mon-Fri 11am-3pm, 6-11pm; Sat 11am-11pm; Sun 12-10.30pm
- Daily 12-2.30pm, 7-930pm; Sun 12-6pm
- T (01892) 870253
- F (01892) 870107
- E thespotteddog@btopenworld.com
- Harveys Sussex Best; Larkins Traditional; guests
- Modern and traditional British with local produce, beer and cider used in cooking
- Grade II listed pub with low beams and three fires, one an inglenook

A pub with a menu that shouts 'eat me', from local free-range eggs on bubble and squeak to mussels with leeks and Chiddingstone cider sauce. Traditional Sunday roasts feature locally-raised Hildenborough pork and lamb from Elliots farm in Penshurst, with other local ingredients including Chiddingstone smoked salmon and gravadlax, East Sussex cheeses and local asparagus. Specials could include whole Dover sole with dressed leaves, baked hake with garlic mayo and duck breast with puréed swede and caramelised shallots.

The menu changes regularly but includes starters such as bread and olives to nibble at 75p, scrambled eggs with fresh crabmeat on brioche, duck liver and orange pâté with home-made grape chutney, or diver-caught Scottish scallops with crispy Parma ham, £4.25-£8.25. Among the regular main courses are Larkin's beer-battered cod and chips with home-made tartare sauce, home-baked ham with free-range egg, chips and home-made piccalilli, venison sausages with mash, honey carrots and red wine gravy, or lamb, rosemary and apricot burger with tzatziki, prices £7.25 to £13.95 for Scotch rib eye steak. Veggie meals might be spinach and ricotta tortellini; there is an interesting choice of sandwiches and real food for children.

★ S V P C

RUSTHALL
Beacon

Tea Garden Lane, TN3 9JH

- ▶ 400 yards off A264, opposite cricket club, just outside Tunbridge Wells
- Mon-Sat 11am-11pm; Sun 12-10.30pm
- Throughout opening hours
- T (01892) 524252
- F (01892) 534288
- E beaconhotel@btopenworld.com
- W www.the-beacon.co.uk
- Harveys BB; Larkins Traditional; Taylor Landlord
- ☺ Freshly-cooked English and continental meals
- Building dating from 1895 set in 17 acres of grounds on an outcrop of sandstone with outstanding views, wealth of architectural features including stained glass windows, oak-panelled bar, ornate plaster ceiling; four room restaurant

Romantic real ale drinkers could actually tie the knot in this pub, and enjoy a splendid wedding breakfast afterwards. A member of Kentish Fare, it uses as much fresh local produce as possible: fish, its speciality, is bought daily. Specials might include Nile perch on prawn ratatouille, pan-seared scallops and tiger prawns with chilli noodles, grilled seabass with herb crust on fish casserole, smoked haddock with Stilton cream and mustard mash, roast pheasant with chestnut and cranberry jus, or pan-fried calf's liver with chive and horseradish new potatoes, prices £13-£15.95.

The bar menu includes mussels mouclade, rosemary and redcurrant lamb fillet, fresh haddock in Guinness and chive batter, pastrami, gherkin and goats' cheese in thick rye bread, seafood kebabs on prawn and pea couscous, as well as pappardelle pasta with wild mushrooms and cream, prices £7.50-£10.25. Jacket potatoes have lovely fillings from roast beef with Stilton to honey-glazed gammon with sweetcorn and celery salsa. The à la carte offers stuffed fresh figs and smoked duck breast with black bean and lime dressing among the starters, then mains from venison fillet with thyme and bitter chocolate sauce to leek, potato and apricot galette with Brie and tarragon sauce.

★ Q S V P C

SEAL
Padwell Arms
Stone Street, TN15 0LQ

▶ From Seal town centre take Park Lane, fork left into Grove Road, follow to Stone Street
☼ Mon-Sat 12-3pm, 6-11pm; Sun 12-3pm, 7-10.30pm
🍴 Mon-Sat 12-2.30pm, 6-9pm; Sun 12-2.30pm, Sun 7-9pm
T (01732) 761532
F (01732) 760008
Beer range varies
☺ High quality, home-cooked British cuisine
Traditional pub in a rural setting amidst orchards, with a conservatory restaurant

The landlord of the Padwell Arms reckons his chef is one of the best in Kent, so why not give his pub a try and see if you agree? Certainly, all the elements of good pub food are here: local ingredients, freshly cooked, with good daily specials and home-made sauces. The chef doesn't produce his own desserts but they are made for the pub by a first class local supplier. Interesting starters include terrine of wild boar and truffles served with fruit chutney, halloumi cheese, tomato and roasted peppers on toasted brioche, oak smoked salmon with bloody Mary dressing, Camembert and Brie medley with Cumberland sauce and a salad of mozzarella, avocado and tomato with basil and balsamic dressing, mostly priced around £6-£7. To follow there is always a daily roast, a choice of steaks, poached salmon, battered cod or fisherman's platter and a choice of veggie options such as ricotta and spinach tortellini, Thai red vegetable curry or salad niçoise. Then there are the pub standbys such as ham or sausage, egg and chips, chicken stir fry and good salads. Main courses are £6.50 to £14 for a steak. On the daily specials list you might find game in season, red wine steak pie, grilled mackerel with rosemary and butter sauce or pan-fried Cajun tuna. There is a sandwich bar with a children's menu.

S V P C

STAPLEHURST
Lord Raglan
Chart Hill Road, TN12 0DE

▶ 1 mile N of A229 at Cross at Hand garage
☼ Mon-Sat 12-3pm, 6-11pm; closed Sun
🍴 Mon-Sat 12-2.30pm, 7-10pm
T (01622) 843747
Goacher's Light; Harveys BB; guest
☺ Traditional bar dishes plus imaginative choices on an elegant menu
Gem of an unspoilt olde worlde rural pub with a hop-strewn bar and two log fires; garden set in orchards

You can start in the bar with plain snacks at plain prices – chilli with rice, macaroni cheese, ham, egg and chips or sausage egg and chips, mostly £5.95, plus sandwiches and baguettes, £2.95-£6.50, or ploughman's at £5.95. There are also seasonal dishes such as home-made asparagus soup, beef and red wine casserole, shepherd's pie or fish pie. But the main menu offers serious temptation – starters including marinated anchovies with apple and potato salad, smoked duck and orange salad, smoked venison with pickled walnut, Mediterranean salad, smoked salmon, and garlic mushrooms, priced £3.95-£5.75. Main courses are priced from £7.50 for vegetarian penne pasta with tomatoes, peppers, olives and cheese, or fish dishes such as poached salmon with lemon and herb sauce, grilled seabass or Dover sole, £9.95-£15.50. Meat dishes are very reasonably priced, mainly under £10, with pork loin on Puy lentils and apple at £8.95, grilled lamb chops, duck breast with port and orange sauce, and even breast of guinea fowl with red wine sauce all costing £9.95; stir-fried beef with peppers and rice is £10.95. A selection of home-made puddings and ice creams all cost £3.95, as do children's meals.

Q V P C

ST MARGARET'S BAY

☆ Coastguard

The Bay, CT15 6DY

- On the beach below White Cliffs
- Mon-Sat 11am-11pm; Sun 12-10.30pm
- Daily 12-30-2.45pm, 6.30-8.45pm
- T (01304) 853176
- E thecoastguard@talk21.com
- W www.thecoastguard.co.uk
- Beer range varies
- Innovative menu of dishes cooked to order from fresh local produce: bread, pâtés, cakes and pickles all made in house
- Closest pub to France in mainland Britain

An active member of Kentish Fare, local produce matters at the Coastguard where all food is freshly cooked to order and no frozen or microwave dishes are served. Local fish and beef, poultry and game are used to create exciting dishes, bread and cakes hand made to traditional recipes. Examples from the daily changing menu might be house pâté flavoured with orange, tarragon and brandy, Kentish pork and game terrine, or samphire with wild garlic and Wensleydale tart, priced £4-£5 as starters.

Main dishes include local fillet steak topped with whisky fried haggis, fresh cod or haddock in Hoegaarden batter, hot devilled crab topped with mature cheddar, local lamb and local ale (Gadd's or Hopdaemon) steamed pudding, roast skate with caramelised onions and capers, fresh Sussex chicken breast with cinnamon, quince and rosewater glaze or poppy seed tarts with smoked haddock and real ale, mainly £7.50-£9. Fresh salsify, porcini and 'tame' mushroom stew with truffle oil with sea salt fried winter greens is one vegetarian choice. The cheeseboard is special, too – unpasteurised artisan cheeses from across the UK, a French cheeseboard based on the north coast, or carefully matched mixture of both at £6.50. Desserts range from dark chocolate stout cake to sticky poached mandarins. Children are allowed in the restaurant only.

Q ❀ S V (Martin Mill) P C

TUNBRIDGE WELLS

☆ Sankey's

39 Mount Ephraim, TN4 8AA

- On A26 opposite Kent and Sussex Hospital
- Daily 11am-11pm (10.30pm Sun)
- Mon-Fri 12-3pm, 6-10pm; Sat 12-10pm; Sun 1-8pm
- T (01892) 511422
- F (01892) 511450
- E crabs@sankeys.co.uk
- W www.sankeys.co.uk
- Harveys BB; Larkins Traditional
- Specialities are shellfish and seafood
- Quirky pub with many classic, continental beers; food served in ground floor bar and cellar brasserie

A pub that modestly claims, 'Our house specialities are without a doubt the finest examples of fresh seafood anywhere in the country'. Judge for yourself with the hand-dressed Cadgwith cock crabs they have been buying for 40 years, £17.50 with salad, fresh Scottish mussels in a choice of Thai with lemongrass and coconut, Indian masala or French white wine marinière style sauces, £6 starter, £8 main, or 'monster' spider crabs served hot in chilli sauce or cold with salad at £16.50. Or there are fresh Newfoundland lobsters, £15 per half or £27 whole served cold, grilled with garlic or thermidor, plus new potatoes and salad, fresh Shetland cod with chips, home-made fishcakes of smoked haddock and salmon in garlic spinach sauce, or whole grilled lemon sole or steamed seabass with soy, ginger and spring onions on noodles. Prices range from £8.50-£11.50. Other mains include braised pheasant with pesto mash, char-grilled rib eye steak or mushroom and goats' cheese lasagne, £9.50-£10.50. For starters the choice is Morecambe Bay potted shrimps, queenie scallops, chilli tiger prawns, fish soup and Cork harbour rock oysters, £7 for half a dozen. On a Sunday, do try the roast rib of beef. This is one of the few UK outlets serving Belgian Trappist Chimay on draught.

★ ❀ S V (Tunbridge Wells) C

AUGHTON
Derby Arms
Prescot Road, L39 6TA

- ▶ Off B5197 between Ormskirk and Kirby
- ☼ Mon-Sat 11.30am-11pm; Sun 12-10.30pm
- Ⓨ Mon-Sat 11.30am-2pm, 5.30-8pm (not Sat eve); Sun 12-3pm
- T (01695) 422237
- E janthelandlady@aol.com
- Beer range varies
- ☺ Good value traditional pub menu plus evening specials
- A perfect country pub that has resisted modernisation and juke boxes, serving a marvellous beer range from micro to larger brewers

You will find plain fare at bargain basement prices on the lunchtime menu where main dishes, including a choice of potatoes and fresh vegetables, cost £2.25-£2.95. Take your pick from lamb or pork chops, steak braised in ale, sausage casserole, liver and bacon, meat balls, steak pie or shepherd's pie, roast chicken breast, gammon and pineapple or chicken curry. Some of these dishes are also on the set evening menu, alongside Westmorland pie and plate steak pie at £3-£3.95, and a 12-oz T-bone steak at an amazing £6.45, but there is also a selection of evening specials. These include chicken Maryland with a pineapple fritter, cod or chicken fillet with wine and mushroom sauce, seafood pie of cod, prawns, smoked haddock and mussels in wine and dill sauce, pork steak with black pudding and cheese sauce, chicken with ginger and honey or braised lamb shank in red wine sauce, prices again very modest at £3.95-£4.95 with salad or vegetables. In addition there are spicy dishes – lamb rogan josh, vegetable korma, lamb bacharica and beef teriyaki – with a choice of rice or potatoes. Sunday lunch provides an all-day breakfast at £3.45, choice of roast lamb, beef, turkey or pork also £3.45 – or those with hearty appetites can have a double roast including apple pie or trifle at £6.95.

★ Q S V P

BISPHAM GREEN
☆ Eagle & Child
Malt Kiln Lane, L40 3SG

- ▶ Off B5246 between Parbold and Mawdesley
- ☼ Daily 12-3pm, 5.30-11pm (10.30pm Sun)
- Ⓨ Daily 12-2pm, 5.30-8.30pm (9pm Fri & Sat); Sun 12-8.30pm
- T (01257) 462297
- F (01257) 464781
- Moorhouses Black Cat; Taylor Landlord; guests
- ☺ Freshly cooked food featuring local ingredients from bar to à la carte menus
- Fine 16th-century local with a stone-flagged floor and wonderful views; annual beer festival in May

Under the same ownership for a decade, this former farm is renowned for its food from curry club and theme nights to inventive à la carte, freshly cooked by two chefs. The bar menu begins with goujons of fresh cod, home-made soup and onion and goats' cheese tart, £3-£5, followed by chicken with chorizo and sun-dried tomatoes on linguini, steak and real ale pie, Cumberland sausage with mash and onion gravy, penne with asparagus and sun dried tomatoes, all £7.50 or £8. On the à la carte you can start with roast Bury black pudding, crispy duck and chorizo salad, queen scallops with garlic and lemon butter, home-made soup or grilled seabass on potato salad, £3.50-£7. The menu is divided into fish and different types of meat – what a sensible idea – and includes grilled seabass with mint couscous, sautéed king prawns and crayfish with Gruyere, char-grilled lamb cutlets with honey and mint glaze, braised lamb shank with mint mash, sirloin steak with roasted vine tomatoes and black olive sauce, Thai beef stir fry, Mr Kelly's pork, garlic and ginger sausages, pan-fried pork with smoked paprika sauce, and breast of Goosnargh chicken with chorizo cream, prices £9-£14. Vegetarian choices, at £8.50, are vegetable korma or mushroom stroganoff.

★ S V P C

BLACKPOOL
Pump & Truncheon
13 Bonny Street, FY1 5AR

- Opposite the police station
- Daily 10.30am-11pm (10.30pm Sun)
- Daily 12-7pm
- T (01253) 751176
- E pumpandtruncheon@aol.com
- Beer range varies
- Home-cooked traditional pub dishes and grills at low prices
- Busy, town centre local, furnished in typical Hogshead style with bare floorboards; note the photos of old Blackpool and the police force

Such is the popularity of the food served at the Pump and Truncheon that in the summer season there is a queue of people waiting for Sunday lunch. They reckon if they had another 20 tables they could fill them all, but that's hardly surprising when a proper roast with three veg and Yorkshire puds costs less than a fiver. All the meat served here is purchased daily from the local butcher and is of the highest quality: steaks, gammon, Cajun chicken and the mixed grill are all highly-rated dishes, prices between £3.95 and £5.25. The meat is also used to make lasagnes, cottage pie, steak pie and curries, prepared on the premises and served three or four times a week. The pub is a magnet for discerning tourists and gets very busy at both lunch and tea time in the summer when customers may have to be patient when waiting for their meals. The food is not the only draw at this local CAMRA award winner; it offers beer discounts to CAMRA members and stages live entertainment during the season as well as horse racing on a Sunday evening.

★ **S V** **C**

CROSTON
Crown Inn
Station Road, PR26 9RN

- Mon-Sat 11.30am-11pm; Sun 12-10.30pm
- Daily 12-9pm
- T (01772) 600380
- Thwaites Mild, Bitter, Thoroughbred, Lancaster Bomber, seasonal
- Casque Mark pub serving traditional home cooking at bargain prices
- Ivy-clad pub offering a warm welcome; comfy lounge and tap room, garden with boules pitch

The Crown not only serves good pubby meals but deserves full marks for a separate pensioners' menu, served Mon-Fri 12-5pm, that offers a smaller portion of dishes on the main menu, £3.50 for one course, £4.50 for two courses or £5.50 for three, including a 4oz rump steak with chips and salad or cod in Thwaites' beer batter with mushy peas and chips. But food is still excellent value on the main menu: Cumberland sausage, mash and red onion gravy, giant cod in Thwaites batter, hand-carved ham with two fried eggs and chips, or chicken and bacon cheesy melt with jacket potato are all around £5-£5.50, while a huge mixed grill is £9.45. On Monday nights you can order two steak dinners for £9.95, on Wednesday night two curries for £8.95, on Friday night two beer-batter cod 'n' chips for £8.95. Sunday roast with all the trimmings is just £4.95. Vegetarian dishes include three-cheese broccoli bake, or a three-cheese ploughman's with Branston and salad at £4.95. Tenants Tony and Rachel Carr took over last year after earning CAMRA awards at their previous pub in Greasby; they gained Cask Marque accreditation within three weeks of arriving at the Crown.

S V (Croston) P **C**

GREAT ECCLESTON
White Bull
The Square, PR3 0ZB

- ▶ In village centre, accessible from M55 jct 3
- Mon-Sat 11am (4.30pm Tue)-11pm; Sun 12-10.30pm
- Wed-Sun 12-8pm
- T (01995) 670203
- Black Sheep Best Bitter; Tetley Bitter; guests
- ☺ Good value, traditional pub fare with interesting daily specials
- Comfortable, village-centre former coaching inn

The landlord of this local CAMRA award winner takes care to offer his customers a range of beer styles. Diners will not be disappointed either, with a varied menu that features good value regular dishes as well as more unusual specials. There is always a home-made soup of the day – could be cream of leek and Stilton, carrot and ginger, celery and nutmeg or cauliflower and bacon – for a mere £1.95. Specials include beef and bean casserole, pork, black pudding and mustard sausages with creamy mash and onion gravy, liver 'n' onions, a fish pie of smoked haddock, whiting and prawns topped with mashed potato, pan-fried fresh salmon with minted hollandaise, or Spanish rice (peppers, onions and rice cooked in a rich tomato sauce topped with cheese and crispy bacon). Vegetarians may find spinach and Brie quiche or vegetable cannelloni on offer. There's always a selection of pasta dishes such as salmon and king prawns in white wine sauce and pan fried chicken tagliatelle, and various salads for around £5-£6. Other choices include sirloin steak, home roast ham with egg and hand-cut chips, and roast beef with gravy in a giant Yorkie with mash and vegetables, £5-£10. Sandwiches, toasties and filled jacket spuds are available for a quick bite for under £4.

S V C

GRIMSARGH
Plough

187 Preston Road, PR2 5JR

- ▶ On main Preston-Longridge road
- ☼ Mon-Sat 11am-11pm; Sun 12-10.30pm
- Ⓨ Mon-Sat 12-2.30pm, 6-9pm; Sun 12-8pm
- T (01772) 652235
- E theploughgrimsargh@hotmail.com
- W www.theplough-grimsargh.co.uk
- Taylor Landlord; guests
- ☺ Award-winning food using local produce from Fleetwood fish to game
- Refurbished pub with original oak beams, open fires, antique furniture, a large public bar and no-smoking area

The Plough covers all angles from village hostelry to destination dining pub in great style, including bowling parties on its own green. Using excellent local produce including fresh fish from Fleetwood six days a week, locally-reared meat, cheese and bread from down the road, landlord and chef Francis McGrath and his co-chef achieve delicious dishes. A typical specials selection might feature venison, rabbit and pheasant pie, roast pork fillet on mustard mash with cider and sage sauce, half a roast Goosnargh duck with rhubarb and ginger compote, rump of Bowland lamb with red wine and mint gravy, the Plough's special fish pie topped with cheesy leek mash or a whole seabass roasted with garlic and parsley butter, mostly £8.95-£10.25. A veggie special might be roast red pepper filled with ratatouille and goat's cheese.

The set menu offers fresh, tasty pub dishes at low prices – lamb's liver and smoked bacon with onion gravy, cheese-topped cottage pie, fresh haddock or jumbo scampi both in beer batter with real chips, slow roast shoulder of lamb with the day's potato dish, or local bangers and mash, £5.45-£9.95. Snacks include Lancashire cheese and home-made chutney. Kids have a good real food menu at £3-£4, and home-made desserts include white and dark chocolate profiteroles and cranberry crème brûlée.

★ ❀ S V ♣ Ⓟ C

HOGHTON
Royal Oak

Blackburn Old Road, Riley Green, PR5 0SL

- ▶ From M65 jct 3 follow signs for Hoghton Tower
- ☼ Mon-Fri 11.30am-3pm, 5.30-11pm; Sat & Sun 11.30am-11pm
- Ⓨ Mon-Sat 12-2pm, 6-9pm; Sun 12-9pm
- T (01254) 201445
- E heric740@aol.com
- Thwaites Mild, Original, Lancaster Bomber, seasonal
- ☺ Good pub food supplemented by interesting specials
- Rural stone pub dating from 1620 on the old Blackburn-Preston road, near the Riley Green basin on the Leeds-Liverpool Canal

This Thwaites tied house regularly stocks the brewery's seasonal beers and is also popular with diners. The pub is free from the intrusions of background music, gaming machines or televisions. In the separate restaurant you will find starters, priced £4-£5.25, including home-made soup, black pudding slices with wholegrain mustard dip and smoked salmon with brown bread and butter. Main courses are mostly pub favourites such as a giant Yorkshire pudding filled with roast beef, roast potatoes and veg, home-baked pies such as cheese and onion or minced beef and onion, steaks, lasagne, home-made chilli and fresh haddock in beer batter with mushy peas; prices range from £7.95 to £13 for an 8oz fillet steak. However, the main attraction here is the specials board, which lists around a dozen daily dishes including three vegetarian options. You might find whole baby leg of lamb, a game pie, mignons of lamb, a curry such as lamb and spinach or home-made steak and stout pie. There is a selection of puddings including ice cream, £2.25, or cheese for £3.75. Lunchtime snacks are also available, including sandwiches (the hot roast beef served on a barm cake with fried onions at £4.95 is a real winner) and filled jacked spuds for around a fiver.

★ Q ❀ S V Ⓟ C

HOGHTON
Sirloin
Station Road, PR5 0DD

- Off A675, near the level crossing
- Daily 12-11pm (10.30pm Sun)
- Daily 12-6pm
- T (01254) 852293
- F (01254) 852389
- E thyme.restaurant@dsl.pipex.com
- W www.thyme-restaurant.co.uk
- Beer range varies
- Excellent menu of award-winning food that changes frequently
- Former coaching inn of rustic charm, replete with oak beams and wood panelling, catering well for the local community as well as passing trade

The pub's name derives from the fact that King James I famously knighted a loin of beef at nearby Hoghton Tower – a plaque above one of the pub's three fireplaces recording the event is frequently snapped by tourists. Sirloin, naturally, features on the menu here: roast sirloin of beef with Yorkshire pudding and all the trimmings is dubbed 'A rise Sirloin'. Other popular choices are char-grilled steak served with thick chips and pepper sauce, or hot hand-carved sirloin of beef served on fresh ciabatta with chips and salad, £5.95-£8.95. Starters could include an imaginative soup such as field mushroom and vine tomato infused with basil and finished with thyme roasted red onions, a slate of tuscan olives served with dipping oils, hummus and crusty bread, seafood salad with home-made ocean sauce or a tartlet of black pudding, leeks and grain mustard topped with herb crumb, £3-£4.50. If you don't fancy the beef to follow you could try salmon, either marinated in lemon grass, honey and soy sauce or poached and served on crushed parsley potatoes with tomato and tarragon dressing, pan-fried chicken breast with red wine sauce or prime cod fillet in real ale batter, all around £7. Puds include sticky toffee, home-made bread and butter or rum and coconut brûlée.

★ Q S V P C

MAWDESLEY
Robin Hood
Bluestone Lane, L40 2RG

- Off B5250 at crossroads between Mawdesley, Croston and Eccleston
- Mon-Sat 11.30-11pm; Sun 12-10.30pm
- Pub: Mon-Fri 12-2pm, 5.30-9.30pm; Sat & Sun 12-10pm (9.30pm Sun)
- T (01704) 822275
- F (01704) 823327
- E info@robinhoodinn.co.uk
- W www.robinhoodinn.co.uk
- Flowers Original, John Smith's Bitter; Taylor Landlord; guests
- Home-cooked English dishes in the bar; more elaborate restaurant fare
- Charming, white painted inn that dates back to the 15th century. Upstairs is Wilsons Restaurant

Good, traditional pub meals are served at the Robin Hood, while upstairs Wilsons Restaurant offers a more inventive, and accordingly slightly more expensive menu. Wilsons is only open in the evenings (not Monday). Both the pub and restaurant have been run by the same family for over 30 years. Starters in the restaurant include tiger prawns in lime, chilli and coconut cream, mussels steamed in a garlic and citrus cream and oven-baked mushrooms stuffed with Brie and pine nuts, £5.50-£7.20. Or you can have tapas dishes, two for £10, three for £12, such as chorizo sausage with mixed peppers, chicken strips tossed in pesto and pine nuts or prosciutto ham with Parmesan.

To follow there is a choice of noisette of suckling pig with black pudding and apple tart on thyme and brandy jus, venison and wild boar sausage with spring onion mash and redcurrant and whisky sauce, slow braised lamb shank in vintage ruby port, oven baked whole loin of cod with buttered spinach and cherry tomato coulis, or green leaf salad with scallops and crayfish drizzled with walnut and tarragon dressing. On weekdays most dishes are offered as two courses for £15.

Q S V P C

AB KETTLEBY
Sugar Loaf
2 Nottingham Road, LE14 3JB

- ▶ On A607, 1 mile N of Melton Mowbray
- Mon-Sat 11am-11pm, Sun 12-10.30pm
- Daily 12-9.30pm
- T (01664) 822473
- Draught Bass; Caledonian Deuchars IPA; Fuller's London Pride; Tetley Burton Ale; guests
- ☺ Home-cooked food from substantial snacks to full meals, served all day
- A Georgian façade fronts this 17th-century former coaching inn; recently refurbished but retaining its character and atmosphere

The landlord (who is also the cook) of this fine old inn gives equal consideration to drinkers and diners, with half of the premises – bar, lounge/dining area and conservatory – devoted to each type of customer. Real ale fans will often get the opportunity to sample local Belvoir Brewery beers, while diners will appreciate the meals, which are all home cooked, of excellent quality and good value. You can opt for a substantial snack of steak and kidney pie, served with chips and fresh veg, fish and chips, sausages and mash or other pub favourites.

In the evening a more extensive menu is offered than at lunchtime, although food is available all day here. Starters that might appear on the specials list are black pudding bake or prawns and smoked salmon with the chef's special sauce. Popular main course choices are honey-roasted duck fillet with plum sauce and pork loin steaks on chive mash with Stilton sauce. Most of the food is prepared on the premises but the desserts are all made especially for the pub by a Café Royal-trained pastry chef. The Sugar Loaf is accessible by public transport, with regular daytime bus connections to Melton Mowbray and Nottingham.

S V ♣ P **C**

BARKBY
Malt Shovel
27 Main Street, LE7 3QG

- ▶ Two miles N of Leicester city, a mile from Syston
- Mon-Sat 11.30am-3pm, 5.30-11pm; Sun 12-11pm
- Mon-Sat 12-2pm, 6-9.30pm; Sun 12-3pm, 5.30-9pm
- T (0116) 269 2558
- E richardcross@btconnect.com
- Beer range varies
- ☺ Food ranges from sandwiches to full meals, with plenty of home-cooked dishes
- Old-fashioned village inn where display shelves are lined with bottled beers; pretty little courtyard for summer drinking

The landlord is one of the shootin' 'n' fishing fraternity, so provides a lot of seasonal ingredients for the pub's special dishes, including local game, trout from Rutland water and even sea fish caught during the pub's sea fishing club expeditions. So if he's been a busy lad you may be able to try pheasant roulade (pheasant breast filled with pâté, wrapped in bacon and roasted with red wine), roast partridge topped with orange and Grand Marnier sauce, trout fillet stuffed with king prawns and baked, or whole baked trout served with lemon and herb butter. The chef also produces his own speciality sausages with venison and red wine.

Other favourite home-produced dishes include boozy beef and Stilton pie in shortcrust pastry, lamb balti, chicken fillet Melton Mowbray (filled with Stilton and wrapped in bacon) and baked marrow filled with summer veg and topped with Applewood smoked cheese. You may find locally made faggots with mushy peas and mash or more exotic kangaroo rump steak topped with a sweet chilli relish. All these are chalked up on a blackboard to supplement the main menu which is much more straightforward: steaks, £8-£12, plus cod, scampi and other pub standards such as home-made lasagne and curry of the day.

★ **Q** **S V** (Syston) ♣ P **C**

MELTON MOWBRAY
Anne of Cleves
12 Burton Street, LE13 1AE

- ▶ Town centre
- ☼ Mon-Sat 11am-11pm; Sun 12-4pm, 7-10.30pm
- 🍴 Daily 12 (12.15 Sun)-2pm, Tue-Sat 7-9pm
- T (01164) 481336
- E theanneofcleves@btconnect.com
- W www.anneofcleves.com
- Beer range varies
- ☺ Freshly cooked meals, different menus lunchtime and evening
- Historic, unspoilt inn, reputed to have once been the residence of Henry VIII's fourth wife

In the home of pork pies it is a shame not to find one among the snacks, but they do offer ploughman's of three local cheeses, ham and haslet (local pork charcuterie) or ham and Stilton, around £5.50, plus hot filled baguettes of lamb, beef and turkey with or without gravy – not forgetting black pudding, sliced and fried with a tangy tomato sauce. The lunchtime menu also offers home-made soup, 'sausage of the moment' with mashed potato and onion gravy, their own recipe lasagne, home-cooked ham, egg and chips, horseshoe gammon grilled with honey, cheese and paprika or plain with two eggs for the less adventurous, tuna and fresh orange salad or pan-fried chicken breast with lettuce, blue cheese, croutons and Caesar dressing, prices £5.50-£7.65. Grilled ribeye and sirloin steaks with all the trimmings are £10-£11.

In the evening there is a wider choice, with duck liver pâté and onion relish, melon with parma ham and spiced ginger among the starters. Main courses include the Cleves sausage made exclusively for the pub by Thompsons of Melton with red wine and onion gravy, Cajun salmon steak, honey and mustard pork with peach compote, and veggie goats' cheese tartlets with stir fry black bean vegetables, priced £6.75-£7.95.

★ Q S V (Melton Mowbray) P C

OADBY
☆ Cow & Plough
Stoughton Farm, Gartree Road, LE2 2FB

- ▶ Off A6 near BUPA Hospital
- ☼ Mon-Fri 12-3pm, 5-11pm; Sat & Sun 12-11pm
- 🍴 Mon-Sat 12-3pm, 6-9pm; Sun 12-5pm
- T (0116) 272 0582
- E enquiries@steaming-billy.co.uk
- W www.steamin-billy.co.uk
- Steamin' Billy Bitter, guests
- ☺ Emphasis on local and organic produce on a modern English menu
- Converted Victorian farm building, decked out in breweriana from old pubs

This is the home of Steamin' Billy beers and licensee Barry Lount is as passionate about the food he serves as he is about the ales: 'We are what we eat – no chicken nuggets or fishy whales here'. Indeed the menu often indicates exactly where ingredients have come from, such as vegetables from an organic producer, award-winning lamb from Thorpe Langton or bison from a herd at nearby Nether Broughton.

The kitchen team produces some innovative dishes; summer starters might include roasted duck pizza with pea shoots and a hint of Chinese five spice, beetroot cured swordfish on cucumber noodles with a blob of wasabi or crayfish and prawn ravioli with fresh dill and a Pernod seafood sauce – or you could simply opt for seasonal soup of the day, prices are all around £5. Sample mains, £12-£15, are rack of lamb rolled with parma ham and baby spinach with a mild roast garlic jus, Wyndham farm chicken and cauliflower bake with a Cheddar and saffron sauce, and loin of organic Gloucester Old Spot with sage and apple port sauce. For fish fans there is pan-fried mackerel with sautéed spring onions or seabass fillet with a salt crust, tomato and fresh thyme sauce; there is always a good veggie option. Yummy home-made puds include vanilla bean and two-berry brûlée and apple, hazelnut and organic maple syrup crumble.

Q S V P C

SILEBY
White Swan
Swan Street, LE12 7NW

- ▶ Off A6 between Leicester and Loughborough
- ☼ Tues-Sun 12-2pm, 7-11pm (not Sun)
- 🍴 Tues-Sun 12-1.30pm; 7-11pm (not Sun)
- T (01509) 814832
- F (01509) 815995
- 🍺 Banks's Mansfield Bitter; Fuller's London Pride
- ☺ Huge range of exciting, freshly-cooked dishes on constantly changing menu
- ◙ Back-street 30s village local with bar and pretty dining room

Award-winning chef Theresa Miller cooks with the passion that has put the White Swan in five editions of this guide, creating an ever-changing menu. Among the starters you could find Parma ham with goats' cheese and walnut salsa, a delicious vegetarian soup, hot garlic and herb bread topped with red onion chutney, black olives and melted Brie or field mushrooms baked with black pudding and Stilton, prices from £3.25-£4.95.

Comfort food might be roast beef and Yorkshire pudding or roast lamb with apricot and nut stuffing, chicken casseroled with bacon, onions, mushrooms and wine, gammon with black pudding, mushroom and fried eggs, beef cobbler cooked in Guinness with Stilton scone topping or roast pheasant breast with lemon and herb stuffing wrapped in bacon, from £6.95-£10.25. Alternatively, there is a scallop, monkfish and prawn cheese soufflé, salmon and prawn pancake, warm salad of smoked chicken with sun blush tomatoes and pine nuts, cod baked in garlic butter with prawns and mussels, and plenty for vegetarians such as mixed vegetable crumble with creamy tomato sauce. A 'skittle alley' menu provides a main course such as faggots and mushy peas or beef and beer casserole with potatoes and vegetables for £5.75 per person including room hire.

Q ❀ S V 🍺 ♿ ⇌ (Sileby) ♣ P ⚟ 👪 C

SOMERBY
Stilton Cheese Inn
High Street, LE14 2QB

- ▶ Off A606 between Melton Mowbray and Oakham
- ☼ Mon-Sat 12-3pm, 6-11pm; Sun 12-3pm, 7-10.30pm
- 🍴 Daily 12-2pm, 6 (7 Sun)-9pm
- T (01664) 454394
- 🍺 Grainstore Ten Fifty; Marston's Pedigree; Tetley Bitter; guests
- ☺ Set menu and specials blackboard all freshly cooked
- ◙ Late 16th-century pub built from the local ironstone with low beams and low doorways, two rooms, one no smoking

It is no surprise that Stilton cheese features frequently on the menu here, including the ploughman's and a sandwich selection. It is also often on the specials blackboard, making an appearance in starters such as baked avocado or field mushrooms stuffed with Stilton, home-made Stilton and cranberry parcels, main courses including chicken and bacon burgers topped with Stilton, chicken and Stilton sausages with mustard mash or Stilton and wild mushroom lasagne.

There are spiffing soups from bacon and broccoli to mulligatawny, and at least two fresh fish from a list including Rutland Water trout with prawn and tarragon butter, haddock in beer batter, monkfish Provençale, lemon sole, scallops, sardines, mussels and seabass. At least five meat specials could include duck breast with orange and ginger, liver, bacon and onions with bubble and squeak, game pie, pork in sage and cider sauce (real draught cider is served here), rack of lamb, suet puddings and hotpots. The veggie choice might be wild mushroom risotto, home-made butternut squash ravioli, pasta and egg Florentine, and several more; main dishes are priced from £6.25-£11.95. Irresistible desserts range from ginger and walnut treacle tart to Bramley apple pie, all £3.25.

★ 🏠 Q ❀ 🛏 S V ♿ ♣ 🍎 P ⚟ 👪 C

SWITHLAND
Griffin Inn
174 Main Street, LE12 8TJ

▶ Off A6 S of Loughborough
Daily 11am-11pm
Daily 12-2pm, 6-9.30pm; Sat & Sun 12-9.30pm
T (01509) 890535
E griffininn@fsmail.net
W www.griffininnswithland.com
Everards Beacon, Tiger, Original; guests
Good, varied menu with seasonal specials
Country pub at the heart of the Charnwood Forest, popular with walkers and cyclists; try your hand at long alley skittles her

This pub is welcoming at any time of year: in winter log fires blaze, in summer there is a delightful patio and gardens, and all year round there is good food to enjoy. The same menu is served in the comfortable bar and the restaurant. As a snack or starter you will find toasted goats' cheese with walnuts, smoked salmon roulade, basil baked tomato with mozzarella, lobster bisque, Stilton cheese and button mushrooms in a puff pastry case, game soup with sherry or soup of the day.

Main dishes, £8-£16, include grilled gammon with black pudding and plum relish, beef stroganoff with rice, rump steak and mussel pie, lamb's liver and bacon with redcurrant and onion sauce, mash and vegetables, Glastonbury lamb hotpot or fillet steak au poivre. Fish dishes include seabass fillet, medallions of monkfish and crayfish sautéed with onions with white wine, cream and mushroom sauce, baked cushion of salmon Cajun style and fried wholetail scampi, while vegetarian options include roasted Mediterranean vegetables and goats' cheese with salad, or linguini with tomato, mushroom and basil. There is always a list of daily specials, more fish dishes and desserts on chalkboards. Snacks such as filled hot baguettes with chips are served and in the afternoon cream teas are available.

★ Q S V P C

WALCOTE
Black Horse
25 Lutterworth Road, LE17 4JU

▶ A mile from M1 jct 20, on A4304
Mon-Thu 12-2.30pm, 5.15-11pm; Fri & Sat 12-11pm; Sun 12-10.30pm
Mon-Thu 12-2.30pm, 6-9.30pm; Fri-Sun 12-9.30pm
T (01455) 552684
W www.theblackhorseinn.co.uk
Greene King Abbot; Oakham JHB; Taylor Landlord; guests
Authentic Thai cuisine at pub prices
Single-bar country free house; small beer garden

In every edition of this guide, the Black Horse has been serving up Thai street food cooked to order for 25 years, long before pubs got into ethnic cuisine. The dishes are all carefully described so you know which are hot or even very hot, starting with the hot Thai curry, chicken, fish or prawn, cooked with spices and herbs in coconut cream, then the very hot prik khing, stir fry of your choice with chilli and special hot basil, while kao phat prik, chicken with fried rice, fresh chillies and garlic, is topped with a fried egg. Khao mu deang is marinated pork leg served in its own juices with boiled rice and a chilli/ginger side sauce; there is a selection of chicken, beef, pork and prawn dishes flavoured with oyster sauce on boiled rice, and the same choice but with noodles and fresh vegetables. Thai fried rice is blended with meat and beaten egg, flavoured with nam pla sauce and topped with a fried egg, and there is the chef's special Thai mixed grill of various meats and livers with salad and Thai sweet 'n' sour sauce, accompanied by boiled rice, meals from £7.25-£8.50. In addition there is a constantly changing specials board, and Thai banquets are available to order for 10 or more.

Q S V P C

WESTON BY WELLAND
Wheel & Compass
Valley Road, LE16 8HZ

- Centre of village
- Mon-Sat 12-3pm, 6-11pm; Sun 12-11pm
- Mon-Sat 12-2pm, Sun 12-9pm
- T (01858) 565864
- Beer range varies
- Old fashioned country cooking offering superb value for money
- 16th-century pub with low, beamed ceilings and real fire in bar

Just the sort of dishes you want to find alongside a range of five constantly changing real ales, and most costing a bargain £4.50. Choose from a long list of good traditional dishes including steak and kidney or roast chicken with stuffing pudding, beef, Stilton and red wine pie, braised beef and dumplings, Cotswold chicken and bacon, Lancashire hotpot, English sausage in onion gravy and – even cheaper at £3.50 – liver and bacon casserole, sausage, egg and chips or pie of the week. There are grills, too, also moderately priced, such as the 16oz mixed grill at £5.50 and, would you believe, for an extra thirty bob you get a 24oz platter. An 8oz pork T-bone in honey and ginger is £4.50, while a 24oz rump steak is a mere £9.50. The meat, all from cattle raised on farms in the Welland Valley, comes from the local butcher Joseph Morris who has an on-site slaughterhouse, while game in season includes rabbit, pheasant, venison and partridge, in what is described as a hunting, shooting and fishing area. Fresh fish could include Rutland Water trout, red snapper, lemon sole, mackerel and mussels. Most desserts are home made, and all bread and baguettes are from a nearby baker.

★ S V

At the olde-worlde White Lion near St Albans Abbey in Hertfordshire chef Margaret Howard dishes up good modern cooking such as this seafood risotto.

TIGER PRAWN & ENGLISH PEA RISOTTO
Serves 4

Knob of butter
4 large raw king prawns
¼ cup brandy
4 tbsps olive oil
2 cups Arborio rice
1 medium onion, finely chopped
1 shallot, finely chopped
½ cup white wine
4 cups chicken stock
75g (3oz) peeled prawns
½ cup blanched English fresh peas
(if frozen do not blanch)
¼ cup flat leaf parsley, chopped
¼ cup Parmesan
Salt and pepper

Melt the butter and sauté the king prawns for three minutes, then flambé with the brandy and set aside. Add the rice, onion and shallot, sauté for 4 minutes, then add wine and stir constantly until absorbed. Add chicken stock half a ladle at a time, stirring until absorbed before you add the next, carry on until all the stock is absorbed and the rice creamy but with a bite in the middle. When all the stock has been added, stir in the peeled prawns and peas and stir while heating through. Remove from the heat, stir in the chopped parsley and Parmesan and season to taste. Top with the king prawns and serve.

COLEBY
Bell Inn
Far Lane, LN5 0AH

- Seven miles S of Lincoln, A607
- Mon-Sat 11.30am-3pm, 5.30-11pm; Sun 12-10.30pm
- Mon-Sat 12-2.30pm, 5.30-9pm (9.30pm Sat); Sun 12-8pm
- T (01522) 810240
- F (01522) 811800
- W www.thebellinncoleby.co.uk
- Beer range varies
- Modern English and French with a separate seafood menu
- Rural stone-built village pub with real fire, bed and breakfast

The Bell always has three real ales on tap and is building up its list of different beers available to accompany fine food, which even includes suckling pig. But to start with the fish and seafood menu: you might begin with moules marinière, a plate of smoked salmon, fishcake with mushy peas and parsley sauce or tempura king prawns, £4.94-£6.50. Main courses include grilled seabass on mushroom, leek and smoked Cheddar risotto, potage of king scallops, langoustines, seabass, salmon and monkfish or grilled haddock on wok-fried cabbage.

The main menu opens with a real Lincolnshire treat, slow cooked pig's cheek with creamed cassoulet sauce, as well as home-made soup and deep fried Brie, £3.50-£4.75. Staying with pork, you could then try the suckling pig with gateau of braised belly pork and black pudding, or Lancashire hot pot, calf's liver on corned beef hash, roast rack of lamb, char-grilled duck breast on sweet potato with bitter chocolate jus, hand-made tagliatelle freshly prepared in the kitchen perhaps with chorizo, peas and pancetta, priced £5.25-£12.50. Rib eye, sirloin and fillet steaks are Aberdeen Angus and are served with home-made chips. Desserts, all home made, range from spiced apple crumble to baked Alaska and the interesting British cheeses arrive with home-made bread.

S V P C

EASTOFT
River Don Tavern
Sampson Street, DN17 4PQ

- In village centre on A161 Goole-Gainsborough road
- Mon & Tue 7.30-11pm; Wed-Fri 5-11pm; Sat 12-11pm; Sun 12-10.30pm
- Wed-Fri 5-9pm; Sat & Sun 12-9pm
- T (01724) 798040
- F (01724) 798974
- John Smith's Bitter; guests
- Majoring on grills with some daily specials and a weekend carvery
- Rural pub with a country inn ambience; the orchard serves as a garden

Situated in the area of north Lincolnshire known as the Isle of Axholme, this country inn displays old agricultural implements and boasts an orchard for an outside drinking area. It hosts a beer festival in the summer. Only open in the evenings except at the weekends, the menu is limited but enticing. It specialises in hot skillet meals and grills, all at very reasonable prices, from simple sausage (Lincolnshire of course), egg and chips for £3 to the Monster 45oz grill for £11.50. If you can't face the full gammon, steak, lamb and pork chop, sausage, chicken, black pudding and egg that this entails, you can pay half the price for a mere 20oz version, without the chicken and black pudding.

Those with more modest appetites can order a plain grilled steak or a sirloin Marlborough with pâté and red wine sauce or Stilton sirloin that comes with a slab of cheese and smothered with a mushroom or white wine sauce. The popular carvery (a choice of three meats for £5.45) is available on Saturday evening and Sunday, until 8pm (or sold out). Vegetarians will be pleased to know that the daily specials board shows a selection of suitable dishes or they can opt for a cheese salad or sandwich.

S V P C

GRIMSBY
Hope & Anchor
148 Victoria Street, DN31 1NX

- ▶ Close to town centre
- ☼ Daily 12-11pm (Sun 10.30pm)
- Ⓨ Daily 12-3pm
- T (01472) 500706
- F (01472) 500708
- Everards Tiger; Fuller's London Pride; Tetley Bitter; guest
- ☺ Eclectic menu from traditional to ethnic
- Modern one-room pub; live entertainment at weekends

The landlord and landlady share the cooking, producing a menu offering plenty of choice using fresh meat, fish and vegetables bought from local suppliers. Starters begin with assorted breads served with olive oil, balsamic vinegar and olives, home-made 'soup of the moment', prawn bayou, Wexford mushrooms in a creamy pepper sauce topped with blue cheese, nachos nibbles and loaded potato skins with bacon, melted cheese and sour cream, prices from £3-£4.35.

Main meals on the set menu are chicken mushroom sizzlers with stir-fried vegetables, chicken New Yorker of char-grilled chicken topped with bacon and melted cheese, wholetail scampi in breadcrumbs with coleslaw and tartare sauce, Lincolnshire sausages with bubble and squeak, steak and Guinness pie served with mash and vegetables, or the Hope & Anchor burger, a half pounder topped with bacon and melted cheese, prices from £7-£8.25. A separate grill menu offers rump steak, pork chop, gammon, lamb cutlets, chicken breast, salmon or king prawns, all at £6.99, with all the trimmings. In addition there are salad bowls, jacket potatoes or big bloomers with plenty of fillings. A chalkboard lists Mexican dishes and specials, while Sunday roast is £7.95 for one course, £8.95 for two and £9.95 for three.

Q ❀ **S V** ♿ ⇌ (Grimsby) **C**

HARMSTON
Thorold Arms
High Street, LN5 9SN

- ▶ Off A607 Grantham-Lincoln
- ☼ Daily 12-3pm (not Mon), 6-11pm
- Ⓨ Tue-Sat 12-2.45pm, 6-8.45pm; Sun 12-2.45pm
- T (01522) 720358
- E enquiries@thoroldarms.co.uk
- W www.thoroldarms.co.uk
- Beer range varies
- ☺ Traditional home-made dishes with local touches and plenty of choice
- Friendly local renowned for its offbeat theme events from swinging safari week to Diwali with Bollywood menu

A Lincolnshire platter of two Lincolnshire sausages, black pudding, potato wedges, grated cheese and apple sauce at £7 features on the lunch menu along with a fish platter plus the fresh fish of the day, butterfly chicken in home-made barbecue sauce, fillet steak at £11.50, or gammon at £7.50 with pineapple and ginger relish, all served with salad, seasonal vegetables and home-made chips or new potatoes. In addition there is a good choice of filled baguettes and sarnies from the Club triple decker to bacon and Brie, and salads including chicken with bacon in a warm dressing, hot or cold prawns with home-made Marie Rose sauce.

In the evening you might start with home-made soup, feta salad, whitebait, smoked salmon with balsamic dressing or goats' cheese with sweet chutney, priced £3-£4.50, followed by a huge mixed grill of fillet steak, pork and lamb chops, liver, kidney, home-made Thorold sausage, tomato and mushrooms at £11.50, lamb shank with mint gravy, beef or mushroom stroganoff, baked mackerel with horseradish cream, pork fillet with fruit and port sauce, duck breast or Barnsley lamb chop with red wine sauce, or liver and onions. On Sundays there is a traditional roast lunch with free cheeseboard in the evening, and Wednesday is fish 'n' chip night.

S V ♿ P **C**

KEADBY
Auld South Yorkshire
Trentside, DN17 3EF

- ▶ Near Keadby Canal, 4 miles from Scunthorpe
- ☼ Mon-Fri 12-11pm; Sat 4-11pm; Sun 12-10.30pm
- 🍴 Mon-Fri 12-2pm, 6-9pm; Sat 5-9pm; Sun 12-5pm
- T (01724) 783518
- Daleside Bitter; guests
- ☺ Traditional home-cooked food; Sunday lunches are popular
- Comfortable pub at the junction of the South Yorkshire Canal and River Trent

This traditional village pub is popular with locals but also attracts plenty of visitors, particularly at the weekend for its live music and Sunday lunch. All the food here is freshly cooked to order, so you may have to be patient at busy times. The good value menu offers mostly traditional pub fare. Starters, £3.50 or less, include prawn and egg mayonnaise, peppered mackerel, Irish mushrooms (served in a brandy and cream sauce), chilli prawns served in hot chilli sauce or deep fried pâté with cranberry sauce – mostly accompanied by brown bread or garlic bread.

To follow there is a good choice of steaks including gammon, sirloin – plain or peppered – and a 16oz T-bone, a bargain £10.95. There are various chicken dishes such as breast stuffed with leeks and Stilton, £8.95, or fillet served in lemon, parsley and butter sauce, £7.95, along with deep-fried fish and chips or poached cod served in a prawn, onion and white wine sauce, £7.95. For a lighter meal there is a choice of omelettes, £4.50 plain, £5 flavoured, meat or cheese salads or filled baguettes served with coleslaw and chips. Desserts from the cabinet are all £2.95.

★ Q S V P C

LINCOLN
Pyewipe Inn
Fossebank, Saxilby Road, LN1 2BG

- ▶ 2 miles W of cathedral, just off A57/A46 junction, on river
- ☼ Mon-Sat 11am-11pm; Sun 12-10.30pm
- 🍴 Mon-Sat 12-9.30pm; Sun 12-9pm
- T (01522) 528708
- F (01522) 525009
- E enquiries@pyewipeinn.co.uk
- W www.pyewipeinn.co.uk
- Charles Wells Bombardier; Greene King Abbot; Taylor Landlord; guest
- ☺ Traditional to exotic menu, changing daily
- 18th-century riverside inn overlooking countryside on edge of Lincoln

Head chef Peter Dodd and his team of five create a wide ranging menu daily from fresh local produce, written up on eight food boards. Starters may include tossed blue cheese salad with grapes and walnuts and deep-fried Brie with fruit chutney, followed by main dishes such as chicken breast stuffed with Stilton wrapped in Parma ham, salmon fillet on mash with lemon butter sauce, red Thai beef curry with rice and salad, fillet steak with Lyonnaise potatoes and Stilton sauce and duck breast on roast vegetables with hoi sin sauce, prices £7.95-£14.95.

On the fish specials board you might find salmon fillet with orange and mustard seed crust, tiger prawns with lime and coriander butter or crayfish tails with tagliatelle. Veggie specials could be mushroom and asparagus risotto topped with parmesan, grilled goats' cheese on salad with deep-fried rocket and balsamic dressing or tagliatelle with sun dried tomatoes and basil pesto. Snacks include dressed crab or rare roasted beef, crayfish tails and marinated artichoke salad, while home-made desserts might be raspberry and mascarpone crème brûlée, banoffee pie, chocolate marquise with amoretti biscuits, fresh fruit pavlova or lemon mousse with fruit coulis, all £3.75.

★ Q S V P C

LOUTH
☆ Masons Arms Hotel

Cornmarket, LN11 9PY

- ▶ Centre of town, off Mercer Row
- Mon-Sat 10am-11pm; Sun 12-10.30pm
- Daily 12-2pm, 6-8.30pm (not Sun-Tue)
- T (01507) 609525
- F (08707) 066450
- E info@themasons.co.uk
- W www.themasons.co.uk
- Bateman XB, XXXB; Marston's Pedigree; Taylor Landlord; guests
- ☺ English cooking supplemented by specials with an international flavour
- A former posting inn dating back to 1725; dine in the bar downstairs or the Art Deco style restaurant upstairs

Sourcing produce locally from excellent suppliers ensures high quality ingredients; here the sausages are provided by National Sausage Champions Fenwicks, who have earned a place in the Guinness Book of Records. Apart from the bangers, the most popular dish here is haddock, fresh from nearby Grimsby, cooked in beer batter and served with home-made chunky chips and salad with the pub's own recipe dressing, £6.95. All the main courses are reasonably priced, nothing over £7 except for the steaks.

Starters are always chalked up daily on a board which also lists some tasty main course options: sample specials include spinach and parmesan mini muffins with tomato chutney, prawn, cod and sweet chilli fishcakes with coriander and spring onion, pan-fried duck breast on butternut squash with red wine sauce, avocado, cherry tomato and basil tartlets with a tomato salsa, pesto crusted salmon fillet on a bed of peppered leeks, and medallions of char-grilled lamb with wine and rosemary jus and parmesan mash. Unlike many pubs, snacks can also be ordered in the evening: sandwiches, baguettes, wraps and jacket potatoes. A hot baguette or wrap with side order of home-made chips will set you back less than £6.

★ S V C

MESSINGHAM
Bird in the Barley

Northfield Road, DN17 3SQ

- ▶ On A159, midway between Bottesford and Messingham
- Daily 11am-3pm, 5.30-11pm
- Tue-Sat 12-2pm, 6-9pm; Sun 12-2.30pm
- T (01724) 764744
- E birdinthebarley.messingham@virgin.net
- Marston's Pedigree, Old Empire; guests
- ☺ Traditional home-cooked pub food
- Spacious, open plan, roadside inn where rural artefacts add to the decor and the atmosphere is relaxed and friendly

Food is given prominence here, but ale lovers will be pleased to know that beer is also accorded due consideration, with tasting notes and a sampling policy. The menu is not at all fancy, just good honest pub dishes or snacks carefully produced using local produce at reasonable prices. To start with you could have melon with seasonal berries, deep fried Camembert with plum and apple chutney, oriental king prawns wrapped in filo pastry with garlic mayo or crispy fried whitebait, prices £1.95-£3.25.

For the main course traditional favourites are again the mainstay, such as cod, chips and peas, braised liver and onions, chicken curry or bangers and mash from award-winning butcher Spelmans. Home-made pies under a shortcrust lid are a speciality here, the fillings vary – consult the specials board for the pie of the day. Most main courses are under £7, but you can have a sirloin steak for £9.95, a fillet for £12.95 or braised minted lamb shank for £8.95. For vegetarians there are mixed vegetable pasta or baked vegetable tartlets, both £5.95. Puddings, all under £3, are home made: sticky toffee, cheesecake, crème brûlée or chocolate pot with cherry ice cream (a rich velvety pure chocolate fondant with a hint of brandy). The ice cream served as an accompaniment or as a selection on its own is from Blyton.

★ Q S V P C

NETTLETON
Salutation Inn
Church Street, LN7 6NP

- ▶ On A46, near Market Rasen
- Daily 11am-3pm, 6pm-1am
- Daily 12-2pm, 6-9.15pm
- T (01472) 851228
- Flowers IPA; Greene King Old Speckled Hen; Taylor Landlord; Wadworth 6X, guest
- ☺ Varied menu of home-cooked food
- Friendly pub, popular with walkers for its proximity to the Viking Way; the large garden is home to various domestic and farm animals

The pub's motto is, 'we do not serve fast food, we serve good food as fast as we can' –an already extensive main menu is supplemented by additional dishes chalked up on a daily basis, as well as a traditional roast on Sunday and monthly themed food nights. Starters range from pâté, prawn cocktail and hot peppered mackerel to home-made soup, £2.30-£3.85. Salads, priced £5-£6, have titles here: Frenchman's (pâté), Countryman's (home-cooked ham with pineapple), Sea Farer's (prawns with Marie Rose sauce) and Gentleman's Special (Stilton with pickles). Sandwiches get the same treatment: the Squire's Choice has roast beef and horseradish, the Cheshire Cat is filled with cheese and pineapple, while the Salutation Special combines bacon, chips and cheese.

Main courses offer a good choice of meat and fish dishes, prices from £7-£12.25, plus some veggie options such as Gypsy Stew (mixed veg in a rich tomato-based sauce), and Old Fashioned Omelette made with English cheese and beer. Steaks include Blue Mountain Fillet topped with Stilton and Fillet au poivre. On the fish front there is pan-fried salmon poached in butter and brandy, fresh Grimsby haddock and wholetail Whitby scampi. For pudding, choose from a variety of bought-in and home-made dishes.

★ S V P

SKEGNESS
Vine Hotel
Vine Road, PE25 3DB

- ▶ Follow Drummond Road from town centre
- Daily 11am-11pm
- Mon-Fri 12-2.15pm, 6-9.15pm; Sat & Sun 12-9.15pm
- T (01754) 610611
- F (01754) 769845
- E info@thevinehotel.com
- W www.thevinehotel.com
- Bateman XB, XXXB; guest
- ☺ Wide choice of home-made traditional dishes
- Newly refurbished 18th-century country inn, beautifully tranquil in lovely gardens, but less than a mile from the town centre

The Vine was once the haunt of Alfred, Lord Tennyson, and considering that the oak panelled bar has changed little since the beginning of the 19th century, he would probably still feel quite at home today. He would certainly recognise some of the traditional dishes served here and would undoubtedly appreciate the local cheeses such as Lincoln Blue and Lincolnshire Poacher washed down with Bateman's ales. Home-cooked meals are served in both the bars, while the restaurant offers an à la carte menu. Bateman's is often used in the popular pies and in the beer batter. Local suppliers provide a high proportion of the vegetables, meat and herbs, although the hotel has its own herb garden for everyday use.

The bar menu offers light dishes such as cold or hot sandwiches, half a dozen salads, various omelettes with chips and salad, filled baked potatoes and pasta dishes such as spaghetti and basil carbonara and spinach and mushroom tortellini for around a fiver. Reasonably priced main courses include the famous pies – steak and ale or Norfolk chicken and mushroom – Lincolnshire bangers and mash, a curry of the day and steaks. There are also popular fish dishes: char-grilled supreme of Scottish salmon with parsley sauce, deep fried scampi or fillet of Grimsby cod in beer batter.

★ Q S V P C

STALLINGBOROUGH
Thatchers Inn
Riby Road, DN41 8BU

- ▶ On A1173, edge of village
- ☼ Daily 11am-11pm
- 🍴 Daily 12-2pm, 6-9.30pm
- T (01469) 561302
- F (01469) 561338
- E grange.hot@virgin.net
- W www.stallingborough-grange.com
- 🍺 Greene King Abbot; Tetley Bitter; guests
- ☺ From traditional to the more exotic with plenty of fresh fish
- ◙ Picturesque thatched country inn steeped in local history

The Thatchers at Stallingborough Grange Hotel serves a wide range of home-cooked food from traditional beef, mushroom and red wine pie to more exotic eats like Thai sizzling king prawns. A top choice, and probably the biggest seller, is fresh haddock deep fried in home-made batter – being near the port of Grimsby there is always fish on the menu and on the specials board, which also offers game in season and more offbeat dishes.

The set menu includes home-made soup of the day, roast Mediterranean and buffalo mozzarella timbale, smoked haddock and pancetta fishcakes, char-grilled chicken Caesar salad, duck, orange and fig pâté or prawns layered in filo pastry with lobster mayonnaise, prices £3.25-£4.50. Main dishes open with fashionable lamb shank served with rosemary and garlic potatoes in roast shallot sauce, feta cheese and oregano stuffed chicken, char-grilled loin of pork with mustard sauce, honey-glazed barbecued chicken, salmon niçoise salad properly made with boiled egg, anchovies and black olives, roast loin of cod with lobster and prawn sauce, rib eye steak and chicken korma with rice and naan bread – all dishes, served with chips or vegetables, priced £7.50-£10. Vegetarian choices include asparagus and pecorino ravioli in cream and white wine sauce with parmesan shavings or vegetable and egg noodles stir fry in creamy coconut sauce.

★ Q ❀ 🛏 S V 🍺 ♿ ♣ P ⚡ 👪 C

THORNTON CURTIS
Thornton Hunt Inn
Main Street, DN39 6XW

- ▶ On A1077, between Wooton and Barton
- ☼ Mon-Sat 12-3pm, 6.30-11pm; Sun 12-3pm, 7-10.30pm
- 🍴 Mon-Sat 12-2pm, 7-9.30pm; Sun 12-2.15pm, 7-9.15pm
- T (01469) 531252
- E peter@thornton-inn.co.uk
- W www.thornton-inn.co.uk
- 🍺 Highwood Tom Wood Bomber County; Taylor Landlord; Tetley Bitter
- ☺ Traditional home-cooked bar menu
- ◙ Award-winning village local with rustic charm close to the ruins of Thornton Abbey

The Thornton Hunt participates in Tastes of Lincolnshire, serving food prepared with as much Lincolnshire produce as possible. The menu features traditional, home-made country dishes such as cottage pie of minced beef and onions with leek, creamed potato and Cheddar topping, steak and ale pie with a Highwood beer (as well as Bomber County the brewery's seasonal ales are served), fisherman's pie of cod, smoked haddock and prawns, lamb hotpot topped with sauté potatoes, fresh haddock in their special beer batter, chicken, ham and leek pie, Lincolnshire sausages with mash and onion gravy, all priced around £7.

Other choices include a mixed grill with sirloin, gammon and pork steaks plus Lincolnshire bangers, home-made chicken madras with coconut and tomato chutney, freshly made three egg omelettes, a ploughman's platter of mature Stilton, Cheddar or Lincolnshire Poacher cheese, or home cured ham, with celery, salad, apple, pickle and a bread roll. Vegetarian choices might be home-made vegetable Cumberland pie, tomato and cheese pasta bake or vegetable madras. Six lovely home-made puds include jam roly poly, sticky toffee and lemon ricotta cheesecake. The children's menu is better than average, and traditional Sunday lunch is popular at £6.95.

Q ❀ 🛏 S V ♿ P 👪 C

EC1: CLERKENWELL
Eagle
159 Farringdon Road, EC1R 3AL

- ▶ Close to Farringdon station
- ☼ Mon-Sat 12-11pm; Sun 12-5pm
- 🍴 Mon-Sat 12.30-3pm (3.30pm Sat), 6.30-10.30pm; Sun 12.30-3.30pm
- T (020) 7837 1353
- Wells Eagle IPA, Bombardier
- ☺ Modern, rustic Mediterranean cooking at London's original gastropub
- One-bar street corner hostelry with stripped wooden floors and tables; cooking visible and entertaining behind the bar; four outside tables

Appetites are still healthy for both eating and cooking real food at London's first gastropub, opened in 1991 and buzzing ever since. Despite its location in central London, the owners have worked at sourcing fresh produce, with deliveries from the brilliant Borough market and direct from Billingsgate fish market. In addition, the pub now buys all its pork and lamb (Gloucester Old Spot and Romney Marsh lamb) from a farm in Essex. But just about the favourite dish is still the Beef Anna steak sandwich – steak marinated Portuguese style in oil, herbs and garlic then cooked in red wine and served in a ciabatta type bread.

With lots of Spanish, Portuguese and Italian influences in food packed with herbs, spices and flavour, there is no set menu – dishes can change even during a sitting. Choices include Portuguese fish or pork stew 'using just about every part of the pig', mixed grilled Mediterranean vegetables such as aubergines, peppers and vine tomatoes served bruschetta style, salt cod, gilt-headed bream, seabass char-grilled with herbs, lamb steaks grilled with oregano and rosemary, and peppery, garlic Napoli sausages. The average spend is around £10 for a main meal. The Eagle continues to show the vitality that has sparked so many imitators since it opened 15 years ago.

❀ **S V** ♿ ⇌ (Farringdon) ⊖ (Farringdon) 👪 **C**

EC1: CLERKENWELL
Jerusalem Tavern
55 Britton Street, EC1M 5UQ

- ▶ Near Farringdon tube station
- ☼ Mon-Fri 11am-11pm
- 🍴 Mon-Fri 12-3pm
- T (020) 7490 4281
- W www.stpetersbrewery.co.uk
- Beer range varies
- ☺ Mostly traditional British food but with some foreign influences
- Tiny pub where self-contained seating areas offer some privacy; bare wood and candlelight lend a medieval feel fitting for such an old house

Even if you are not hungry, if you happen to be in Clerkenwell the Jerusalem Tavern is well worth a visit. It is owned by the idiosyncratic St Peter's Brewery in Suffolk, so you get a chance to try the brewery's unusual beers such as Lemon and Ginger Spiced Ale, Grapefruit beer or its organic bitters, which are served in rotation. The pub is named after the Priory of St John of Jerusalem, founded in 1140, and has occupied various sites in the area – the present building dates from 1720. Its proximity to Smithfield Market is a boon as it allows them to buy meat fresh every day and to select the best organic, locally-produced cuts. They buy British cheeses from Neal's Yard and organic sourdough (the only bread they serve) is purchased daily from St John's Bakery nearby.

The food is mostly traditional pub fare: heart-warming roasts, bangers and mash, and so forth, but some dishes have a distinctly Provençal flavour. All meals are freshly prepared to order. Prices are typically £4.50 for a starter and around £7.50 for a main course. The tavern only serves food at lunchtime and, like many a city pub, is closed at the weekends.

★ 🏰 **Q S V** ⇌ (Farringdon) ⊖ (Farringdon) 👪 **C**

EC1: SMITHFIELD
Bishops Finger
9-10 West Smithfield, EC1A 9JR

- ▶ Near St Paul's and Farringdon tube stations
- ☼ Mon-Fri 11am-11pm
- (Ψ) Mon-Fri 12-3pm, 6-9pm
- T (020) 7248 2341
- E bishopsfinger@shepherd-neame.co.uk
- W www.shepherd-neame.co.uk
- Shepherd Neame Master Brew Bitter, Spitfire, Bishops Finger, seasonal
- ☺ Traditional, home-cooked English fare, sausages are a speciality
- Refurbished in 2005 in Victorian style, with much brass and dark wood furniture; attractive ground-floor bar and upstairs bar/restaurant

Re-opened in November 2005 following a complete refit by Kent Brewer Shepherd Neame, the Bishops Finger is now attracting custom from a growing band of office workers in the area. Indeed, for those who can't bear to be out of touch even during their lunch break, the pub has a new 'laptop' area with wireless broadband internet access. This former Shep's Pub of the Year stands next to Smithfield Market and most of the ingredients for the menu are purchased there, including the 15 different varieties of sausage for which the pub is famous.

The bangers are all served with mash, onion gravy and a choice of mustards, £7.75; unusual flavour combinations include pheasant and tarragon, chicken and asparagus, and pork and spinach. There is also a Thai sausage of pork, lemon grass chilli and Thai rice, the Tunisian with leek, peas, tomato, chillies and paprika and a veggie version with Cheddar and spinach. During refurbishment the kitchen was also updated, allowing them to produce a more varied menu and add daily specials such as pan-fried Dover sole and home-made burgers, plus a steak of the day, £9.95, cooked over hot coals. A good range of sandwiches (including sausage) is available for less than a fiver.

Q ❀ **S V** ♿ ⇌ (City Thameslink)
⊖ (Farringdon/St Paul's) 👪 **C**

EC2: SHOREDITCH
Princess
76 Paul Street, EC2

- ▶ Second right along Old Street from Old Street tube station
- ☼ Mon-Fri 12-11pm; Sat 5.30-11pm; Sun 12.30-5.30pm
- (Ψ) Mon-Fri 12.30-3pm, 6.30-10.30pm; Sat 6.30-10.30pm; Sun 1-3pm
- T (020) 7729 9270
- Fuller's London Pride; Taylor Landlord
- ☺ Mix of Antipodean, modern British and Mediterranean
- Gastropub with food served in pubby downstairs bar and dining room reached by original spiral staircase

A proper pub downstairs buzzing with conversation, and fine dining room up a wrought iron spiral staircase. Chef and joint owner Zim Sutton from Australia provides exciting fare be it the more modestly priced bar menu 'down under' or the original and ever-changing choices upstairs. In the bar – where you can accompany your meal with a cask ale – expect to pay £6-£12 for a main course such as slow roast belly pork with crackling, cod in beer batter with chips, sausage (could be ostrich or pork and ale) with mash, a vegetarian dish such as linguine with tomatoes, olives and basil, baby artichoke risotto or roast walnuts with tomato and marjoram on a pea and pumpkin pilaf. And then there is the favourite sandwich – bacon and rocket. Dishes tend to change weekly in the downstairs bar where on Sunday, when the dining room is closed, a splendid roast served from 1pm includes beef, lamb, cornfed chicken, or roast pork, plus a vegetarian pie, £9.95-£12.95. Upstairs main courses, £10-£15, could include barbecued organic salt marsh lamb rump with chickpeas, coriander and yoghurt, baked monkfish loin with olives and pine nut couscous or pork cheeks braised in milk flavoured with fennel.

★ **S V** ♿ ⇌ (Liverpool Street)
⊖ (Old Street) 👪 **C**

EC4: FLEET STREET
Old Bank of England
194 Fleet Street, EC4A 2LT

- ▶ Near Strand
- ☼ Mon-Fri 11am-11pm
- 🍴 Mon-Fri 12-9pm (8pm Fri)
- T (020) 7430 2255
- E oldbankofengland@fullers.co.uk
- Fuller's Chiswick, Discovery, London Pride, ESB
- ☺ Traditional British pub food
- Originally the Law Courts' branch of the Bank of England trading until 1975, it was acquired and refurbished by Fuller's in 1994

This pub boasts a wonderfully restored interior with beautifully decorated ceilings, a fantastically ornate bar and a fine gallery that can be hired for private functions. The basement contains the original vaults used to store bullion; two safes have been converted as the pub cellars and kitchens but the main vault is still intact and can be visited by prior arrangement, along with the alleged site of the infamous pie shop owned by Sweeney Todd's mistress. Believing that the barber butchered his customers in the tunnels and vaults below the pub before they were cooked and sold in the pies adds a certain frisson to this Fuller's Ale and Pie House, but all the wares sold today contain far more wholesome ingredients!

The home-made pies are the mainstay of the menu: steak with Fuller's ale, chicken, bacon and leek or vegetarian sweet potato and goat's cheese, as well as potato-topped shepherd's and fisherman's pies. Alternatively, there is a variety of traditional pub dishes such as bangers and mash, liver and bacon, and beer-battered cod, chips and peas. Most main courses are around £7-£8; lamb shank served in red wine jus with mashed potato and braised root veg is the most expensive dish at £9.95. There is also a good range of hot and cold sandwiches.

★ **V** ⊖ (Temple) **C**

W1: MAYFAIR
Guinea
30 Bruton Place, W1J 6NL

- ▶ Just off Berkeley Square
- ☼ Mon-Fri 11am-11pm; Sat 6.30-11pm; closed Sun
- 🍴 Mon-Fri 12.30-2.30pm; Sat 6.30-11pm
- T (020) 7409 1728
- W www.theguinea.co.uk
- Young's Bitter, Special, seasonal
- ☺ High quality grills and seafood, three-times UK steak and kidney pie champions
- Young's house famed worldwide with a front bar dwarfed by the fine dining restaurant at the rear; clientele includes celebrities and politicians

There is no arguing with the quality of the suet crust pastry topped steak and kidney pie at the Guinea, originally created by licensee Carl Smith. In 1991 it won the UK S&K pie competition the first of three times, culminating in the title Steak Pie of the Century in 2000, and best pie in the Restaurant magazine awards in 2005. Enjoy it for £8.50 in the bar where it runs out rather quickly. Sandwiches such as the triple decker Mirabeau with main ingredient Aberdeen Angus sirloin steak, once voted best sandwich in Britain, are also available.

Or push the boat out in the famous Guinea Grill, renowned for beef sourced exclusively from Aberdeenshire and the Orkney Islands, hung for 28 days, prices starting at £17.50 for the Guinea mixed grill, or a 16oz rib eye steak on the bone, rising to £27 for a 12oz fillet steak. Other Scottish delicacies include Loch Fyne salmon with a crab galette, £10.50 as a starter, and Scottish smoked salmon. In the grill that famous steak pie, either kidney or mushrooms, costs £11.50 but is twice the size of most pies. Other main courses include hot smoked chicken Caesar salad, braised lamb shank with clapshot and bubble and squeak, pan-fried Shetland sea trout with crayfish sauce, and whole seabass, £12.50-£18.50. Snacks are served at lunchtime only.

❀ **S V** ⊖ (Green Park/Oxford Circus/ Bond Street) **C**

W1: MAYFAIR
☆ Windmill
6-8 Mill Street, W1S 2AZ

- ▶ Close to Oxford Circus, off Conduit St between Regent St and Bond St
- ☼ Mon-Fri 11am-midnight; Sat 11am-4pm; closed Sunday
- 🍴 Mon-Fri 12-9.30pm (2.30pm restaurant); Sat 12-3.30pm
- T (020) 7491 8050
- W www.windmillmayfair.co.uk
- 🍺 Young's Bitter, Special, seasonal
- ☺ Outstanding traditional pub food in the bar, they ring the changes in the restaurant
- ◙ Large downstairs bar with sunken dining room and upstairs restaurant

Sister pub to Young's house the Guinea close by, the Windmill has a wider and more 'pubby' selection of bar food, including that same prize-winning steak and kidney pie served here at £6.95, with other pie choices such as cheese, potato and spring onion with apple chutney, or smoked salmon, potato and egg pie. Main dishes, all home made, include roast free-range loin of pork with crackling and apple sauce, calf's liver and bacon with onion gravy, freshly baked ham with two free-range eggs and home-made chips, lamb and herb burger with cucumber, mint and yoghurt dip, freshly battered fish and roast cod with herb crust, prices £6.95-£9.50.

There is a different special every week day, so on Monday it is beef and mushroom pie with horseradish mash, Tuesday roast free-range chicken with chorizo and new potato stew, Wednesday lamb and apricot casserole with garlic dumplings, Thursday roast rib of beef with thyme roast spuds and Yorkshire pudding then, on Friday luxury fish pie of salmon, cod, prawns and oysters. There is a lovely selection of veg to accompany though they do charge extra – savoy cabbage, glazed carrots, broccoli, broad beans with sage and lovage, £2.95 for a dish of four. You can end with a pudding or fine English cheese board including Colston Bassett Stilton.

S V 🍺 ⊖ (Oxford Circus/Bond Street) ⚡ **C**

WC2: COVENT GARDEN
Lamb & Flag
33 Rose Street, WC2E 9EB

- ▶ Between Leicester Square and Covent Garden tube stations
- ☼ Mon-Sat 10am-11pm; Sun 12-10.30pm
- 🍴 Daily 12-3pm
- T (020) 7497 9504
- 🍺 Beer range varies
- ☺ Simple pub food on a limited menu
- ◙ Historic, atmospheric pub in Covent Garden; meals are served in the upstairs bar of this tall, narrow building

Licensed during the reign of Elizabeth I (although probably not on its present site), the Lamb and Flag claims to be the oldest tavern in Covent Garden. It certainly carries some history, with one famous incident being the vicious attack in Rose Alley on poet John Dryden in 1679, apparently instigated by the mistress of Charles II for scurrilous verses he wrote about her behaviour. In terms of food, the pub still serves probably pretty similar fare to what was available in Dryden's day.

The menu changes slightly every day but is mostly centred around a daily roast, probably beef or lamb, plus a few other straightforward dishes, such as chicken and mushroom or steak and ale pie and something with sausages – either a casserole with mashed potato or spicy Cumberland bangers with chips and beans. There's always a dish for vegetarians, maybe a quiche with salad and French bread or cauliflower cheese, and there might be a fish pie with prawns. Nothing is likely to cost more than around £6.50, and if you just want a snack there are filled jacket potatoes for £4.50. You have to ask at the bar for the day's desserts, a mere £2.50 – all in all very good value for central London.

★ 🏛 **S V** ⊖ (Covent Garden/Leicester Square) 👪 **C**

WC2:HOLBORN
Seven Stars
53 Carey Street, Holborn, WC2A 2JB

- ▶ Behind Royal Courts of Justice
- ☼ Daily 11.30am-11.30pm
- 🍴 Daily noon-9.30pm
- T (020) 7242 8521
- Adnams Bitter, Broadside; guests often include Harveys
- ☺ Eclectic selection satisfying customers' demands and whims of TV chef and cookbook writer Roxy Beaujolais, the proprietor
- Grade II listed, built 1602; one of London's oldest pubs

Happily for drinkers and trenchermen, this small freehouse with two narrow rooms built during the last year of Elizabeth I's reign survived the Great Fire which destroyed much of the locality a decade later. Chef/proprietor Roxy Beaujolais arrived from Oz in '73 and has since been chef for the Royal Shakespeare Co as well as a former presenter on BBC TV's 'Full On Food'. The blackboard menu changes daily, frequent choices including charcuterie with sourdough mustard, char-grilled sirloin, dill cured herring and potato salad, or Napoli sausages with sliced pork belly and cauliflower puree. Two or three specials include dishes such as lamb steak with barley, roast chicken with a warm bread salad of ciabatta, rocket, chives, redcurrants and pine nuts in a vinaigrette including chicken stock, char-grilled, boned quail with polenta, Portuguese pork with clams, home-made sausages and ground steak chilli mole with a touch of chocolate. Fish might include baked sea bream or shrimp tea – potted shrimps with a wedge of lemon and sprinkling of cayenne; vegetarian choices tagliatelle with gorgonzola. Or you might find country scramble - scrambled eggs with smoked ham, chives, potato, parsley and thyme served with sourdough. In 2005 the pub expanded into a tiny wig shop and still displays legal wigs in its window.

★ Q S V ⊖ (Holburn/Temple) C

An irresistible version of bangers 'n' mash using local wild boar sausages comes from Dougie Muir, chef at Greyfriars bar, Perth, in Tayside.

ROMANY STYLE WILD BOAR SAUSAGES
Serves 4

12 wild boar sausages
Oil or butter for frying
1 large onion, diced
4oz (100g) button mushrooms, quartered
25ml (1 fl oz) dry white wine
150ml (¼ pint) gravy
20 fronds fresh rosemary
1 tsp chopped chives
Salt and pepper

Pre-heat oven to 220C/425F/gas mark 7. Seal and brown sausages in a little oil or butter in a frying pan, transfer to a casserole. Add onions and mushrooms to pan and fry quickly for 1 minute, douse with white wine, add the gravy and bring to the boil. Add rosemary and pour sauce over the sausages. Place the uncovered dish in a hot oven and cook for 20-25 minutes, turning the sausages once or twice. When cooked, taste the sauce and adjust seasoning. Just before serving add the chives. At Greyfriars, the sausages are accompanied by grain mustard mash and a side dish of pickled red cabbage.

E3: BOW

☆ Morgan Arms

43 Morgan Street, E3 5AA

- ▶ Two minutes' walk from Mile End underground station
- ☼ Daily 12-11pm (10.30pm Sun)
- 🍴 Mon-Sat 12-3pm, 7-10pm; Sun 12-4pm
- T (0208) 980 6389
- E morgan@arms.fsworld.co.uk
- 🍺 Adnams Bitter; Taylor Landlord
- ☺ Modern European and British cuisine on a regularly changing menu
- ◙ Stylish gastropub with old fashioned features

Winner of the Evening Standard Pub of the Year award in 2005, this popular venue offers an eclectic choice of freshly-prepared food. The lunch menu changes every six weeks, while the evening menu can vary from day to day as only a limited number of each dish is prepared daily in the pub kitchen. The lunchtime snacks are an ideal match for real ale, for instance crispy roast pork open sandwich with apple sauce, treacle-glazed baked ham with home-made piccalilli, chunky chips and free-range eggs, beer-battered fish and chips or crumbled goats' cheese, garlic crouton and French bean salad, £5.50-£8.

In the evening you could start with chicken and pistachio terrine, onion marmalade and brioche toasts, ravioli of wood pigeon, game broth and herb salad, baked Brie in brioche with cep stuffing and roast tomatoes or devilled whitebait with tartare sauce. To follow, perhaps an unusual fish stew, grilled grey mullet fillet or sea bream (served with steamed choy, Asian salad and sticky rice), or roast lamb chump with stuffed aubergine, white polenta, spinach and tomato-olive jus, crisp belly pork with pea risotto, pea shoots and mangetout or a brioche calzone with mozzarella, ceps, leeks and courgettes as a vegetarian choice. Two courses will set you back around £21.

❀ **S** 🍺 ♿ ⊖ (Mile End) ⚡ **C**

E8: HACKNEY

☆ Dove

24-28 Broadway Market, E8 4QJ

- ▶ Near London Fields
- ☼ Mon-Sat 12-11pm, Sun 12-10.30pm
- 🍴 Mon-Fri 12-3pm, 6-10pm; Sat 12-10.30pm; Sun 12-10pm
- T (0207) 275 7617
- F (0207) 254 2770
- E info@dovefreehouse.demon.co.uk
- W www.belgianbars.com
- 🍺 Beer range varies
- ☺ Eclectic selection of dishes, many including Belgian beer
- ◙ Free house with bohemian, candlelit atmosphere; separate dining area

This free house serves four different real ales monthly and a far wider selection of Belgian bottled beers including Trappist, Abbey, Gueuze, witbiers, 'golden' beers, fruit beers, seasonal, regional and special beers. Even better, the beers are used in cooking innovative dishes that feature on both the set menu and specials board.

Its famous sausages are made exclusively for the Dove by Mrs O'Keefe's to the pub's own recipe, including mixed game with dried apricots, thyme and Frambozen (raspberry beer), pork with fennel seeds, sweet basil and Leffe Blonde, Thai chicken with ginger, coriander, chilli and Hoegaarden, all £8.95 served with onion gravy and a choice of plain, cheddar, spring onion or bacon mash. Burgers also include beer, such as ostrich with roast oranges and Delerium Tremens, wild boar with spiced apple and cherry beer, beef with pearl barley, horseradish and Leffe Brun or a veggie burger of field mushrooms, oats and chickpeas with De Koninck, all £5.95 served in focaccia with salad, gherkins and mustard onions. Dove pies are a steak and button mushroom plate pie cooked with Leffe Brun topped with sweet potato and parsnip crisps, or spinach with caramelised, red onions; Belgian dishes include mussels with Hoegaarden and Flemish fish stew.

♨ **Q** ❀ **V** 🍺 ⊖ (Bethnal Green) ⚡ 👪 **C**

E11: WANSTEAD
Nightingale
51 Nightingale Lane, E11 2EY

- Central line to Wanstead or Snaresbrook
- Daily 10am-midnight (11.30pm Sun)
- Daily 10am-4pm
- T (0208) 530 4540
- F (0208) 530 4683
- E rontale@hotmail.com
- Beer range varies
- Varied menu of home-cooked meals and snacks
- Lively, old-fashioned community pub popular with locals; prides itself on good service, good beer, good food

The landlord at the Nightingale describes his pub as a 'traditional back-street boozer' – but this description is a little disingenuous as it boasts a palatial sitting room with plush curtains and upholstered seats, and an excellent menu. What's more there can't be many back-street boozers that offer a choice of 10 different champagnes, ranging from a £20 Louis Dornier to 35 quid for a bottle of Bolly. The food is based on locally-sourced produce; the pub is fortunate enough to be the meeting place for a local allotment society so it benefits from a constant supply of good, organic veg.

The 'big breakfast' starts at 10am, moving on to lunchtime menus that offer a mix of traditional pub food and international dishes. The 'sizzlers' are renowned in the area – served with rice, chips or garlic bread and salad, they come in several varieties: Cajun chicken, beef or mussels with oyster and black bean sauce, king prawn and garlic, or a mixed sizzler, £7-£!2. There is a good choice of deep-fried fish – cod, plaice, lemon sole or haddock or a seafood platter with chips or potatoes and veg. Other pub favourites include curries, chilli con carne, lamb shank and liver and bacon, £5.75-£9. Vegetarian dishes are available as well as salads, filled jacket potatoes, sandwiches, rolls and baguettes.

★ ❀ **S V** ⊖ (Snaresbrook/Wanstead) ♣ **C**

E14: LIMEHOUSE
Grapes
76 Narrow Street, E14 8BP

- Accessible via DLR to West Ferry
- Mon-Fri 12-3pm, 5.30-11pm; Sat 12-11pm; Sun 12-10.30pm
- Bar: Mon-Sat 12-2pm (2.30pm Sat), 7-9pm; Sun 12-3.30pm Restaurant: Mon-Fri 12-2.15pm; Mon-Sat 7.30-9.15pm
- T (0207) 987 4396
- F (0207) 987 3137
- Adnams Bitter; Marston's Pedigreee; Taylor Landlord; guest
- Bar meals plus seafood restaurant upstairs
- Warm, cosy, riverside inn with a small deck offering good Thames views; described by the landlady as a 'real old East End boozer'

Steeped in history, The Grapes is the inn loosely disguised as the Six Jolly Fellowship Porters in Dickens' Our Mutual Friend. Local supplier Tradewinds, based on the Isle of Dogs, provides the fresh fish and seafood as well as the delicious Hoad's Korkers sausages and Maris Piper potatoes used to make possibly the best chips in town. In the bar you can have home-made lobster bisque, a pint tankard of shell on prawns with brown bread and butter, home-made fish cakes with caper sauce, fresh fish and chips, poached salmon or dressed crab, £4.25-£7.75. Alternatively there are pub favourites bangers and mash, salads, ploughman's and sandwiches, and a traditional roast lunch is served Sunday.

Upstairs, the menu is almost exclusively fish and seafood (vegetarians, vegans and meat eaters can be accommodated with 24 hours' notice). Starters include smoked fish platter, seafood salad, whitebait, pickled herrings, potted shrimps prepared to the pub's own recipe or whole dressed crab, £4.25-£8. Most of the main course fish is offered at market prices – seabass, supreme of halibut or monkfish. There is a choice of sauces to accompany the fish. Good home-made puds might be apple crumble or bread and butter pudding, £3.25.

★ ❀ **S V** (West Ferry DLR) ♣ **C**

N1: ISLINGTON
Barnsbury
209-211 Liverpool Road, N1 1LX

▶ A few minutes' walk from Upper Street
☼ Mon-Sat 12-11pm; Sun 12-10.30pm
Ⓨ Daily 12-3pm, 6.30-10pm
T (020) 7607 5519
F (020) 7607 3256
E info@barnsbury.co.uk
W www.thebarnsbury.co.uk
⊟ Fuller's London Pride; Taylor Landlord; guest
☺ Modern European
◙ Gastropub renovated in 2004 when the name changed to Barnsbury; horseshoe bar with bare floorboards; tables outside on decking for al fresco dining

Seasonal menus offer plenty of temptation starting at lunchtime with starters or snacks such as chorizo 'al infierno', eggs Benedict with English bacon, three-cheese soufflé or Italian charcuterie, prices £3.50-£5.50. Main courses might be steak sandwich with Caesar salad and chips, salmon and tarragon fishcakes, a selection of house antipasti, porcini and ricotta ravioli with artichokes and pine nuts or grilled swordfish steak with pesto and caperberries, prices £8.50-£10 with chips, new potatoes, sugar snap peas or salad.

In the evening you might start with seabass ceviche, Bayonne ham with celeriac remoulade, chicken liver and foie gras parfait or grilled asparagus with Parmesan, £4.50-£6. Main courses include some lunchtime choices plus honey-glazed duck confit with mustard mash and Portobello mushrooms, roast chump of lamb with flageolet beans and herb yoghurt dressing, veal chop with provolone and tomato crust, prices £9.50-£14.50 with accompaniments. Sunday lunch includes roast rib of Herefordshire beef with Yorkshire pud and horseradish, roast free-range chicken with sage and onion stuffing, or roast English lamb with rosemary crust. Desserts might be chocolate pot with warm cherry compote, French apple tart with butterscotch sauce, or lemon mousse brûlée.

⛬ ❀ S V ♿ ⊖ (Angel) ⚟ ⚣ C

N1: ISLINGTON
☆ Crown
116 Cloudesley Road, N1 0EB

▶ North of Angel tube station
☼ Daily 12-11pm (10.30pm Sun)
Ⓨ Mon-Fri 12-3pm, 6-10pm (10.30pm Fri); Sat 12-10.30pm; Sun 12-9pm
T (020) 7837 7107
E crown.islington@fullers.co.uk
⊟ Fuller's Discovery, London Pride, guest
☺ Home-made, good quality, gastropub food
◙ The Crown is in a listed Georgian building in a quiet, residential street

The Crown's menu focuses on mainly British dishes prepared in the kitchen from fresh ingredients, featuring mostly British produce, especially meat and cheeses. The result is simple, effective cooking that allows the quality of the ingredients to shine. The menu changes daily, but here is an autumnal sample. For starters there might be buffalo mozzarella with peaches, hazelnuts and basil oil, mackerel and orange salad, tuna fishcakes with watercress sauce, or smoked duck breast and figs on rocket with soy ginger dressing, prices around £5-£6 except the soup, £3.95.

Main courses include leg of lamb steak with minted pears, dauphinoise potatoes and red wine jus, red snapper on risotto with chilli sauce, char grilled 12oz T-bone steak with chips and shallot cream sauce, crab linguine with basil and red chilli or Brie and asparagus quiche with green bean and beetroot salad. Mains are £8-£14, vegetables extra. Afterwards you could have white chocolate and raspberry cheesecake, strawberry flan with chantilly cream or chocolate pancake with vanilla ice and Baileys, £4-£5.50, or share a plate of cheese, chutney and crackers for £8. On Sunday there is a traditional roast with all the trimmings for £10.50. A short list of snacks includes beef and Guinness pasty, eggs and bacon on toast, or sweet roasted vegetables with focaccia and black bean hummus.

★ ⛬ Q ❀ S V ♿ ⇌ (Highbury & Islington) ⊖ (Angel) ⚟ ⚣ C

N1: ISLINGTON
Duke of Cambridge
30 St Peter's Street, N1 8JT

- Daily 12-11pm
- Daily 12.30-3pm (3.30pm Sat & Sun); 6.30-10pm (10.30pm Sat)
- T (020) 7359 3066
- E duke@dukeorganic.co.uk
- W www.dukeorganic.co.uk
- Organic beer range varies
- Traditional British with Mediterranean influences; all organic produce on a menu that changes twice daily
- The UK's first organic pub; spartan wood and whitewashed decor in its bar and restaurant; no music or games machines

This most unusual pub uses only organic produce, and this environmentally-friendly philosophy is carried through in everything they do, so recycling and green energy sources are important to the business. The first pub in the UK to achieve Soil Association certification, it also operates a fish purchasing policy that is approved by the Marine Conservation Society. All bread, pickles and ice cream are home-made.

The blackboard menu, chalked up twice daily, offers uncomplicated, seasonal dishes. On the winter menu you might find a salad of bitter greens, capers and lemon, celeriac, chickpea and cabbage soup, or tagliatelle with lemon cream, parsley and Parmesan, £3-£6.50, or if you are feeling extravagant, half a dozen oysters with shallot vinegar for £9. To follow there could be a vegetarian stew, boiled ham hock with mash and savoy cabbage, grilled herring fillets with Puy lentils and mustard sauce, venison steak with spinach, chips and redcurrant jus or herb-crusted salmon fillet on butter bean and chorizo stew, £6.50-£14.50. Puddings, £5, include apple pie with cinnamon custard, treacle tart with cream or chocolate tart and ice cream. Alternatively a plate of three cheeses is £7.50. Children are positively encouraged here and offered small portions from the menu.

Q ❀ **S V** ⊖ (Angel) **C**

N1: ISLINGTON
Island Queen
87 Noel Road, N1 8HD

- Few minutes walk from Angel tube station
- Mon-Sat 12-11.30pm; Sun 12-11pm
- Daily 12-10.30pm
- T (020) 7704 7631
- Fuller's London Pride; guests
- Imaginative menu both traditional and contemporary with plenty of snacks and dishes to share
- Listed building with original features and real fire

At this popular food pub the aim is to serve freshly made meals within 20 minutes, though they warn it could take a little longer at busy times. A carefully designed brasserie-style menu starts with home-made soup of the day at £3.80, followed by 'lights and sharing' dishes such as potato wedges with sautéed mushrooms and Stilton or cheese and chorizo, quesadilla with spinach, tomato and huntsman's cheese, fresh calamari with salad and lime, skewered chicken in yakatori sauce, £3.50-£5.50, or a sharing butcher's meat platter at £8.90. Lively sandwiches include Moroccan chicken with minted crème fraîche, pork and leek sausage with roast red onion in ciabatta bap, cod fish fingers with lime mayo on ciabatta or Welsh rarebit, £4-£5.

Mains might be warm spinach, mushroom and feta salad, ham hock in BBQ sauce on mash, chicken and stuffing pie with sautéed potatoes and mangetout, spicy sausage casserole, coq au vin with new potatoes and fresh vegetables, roast vegetable and pine nut rigatoni, or gnocchi with ham, tomato and oregano sauce, £6.50-£9.50. Extras include home-made potato wedges with chilli mayo, mash of the day or a mixed salad, while calorific desserts are bread and butter pudding with cream, chocolate puddle pudding with vanilla ice cream, apple and blackberry crumble, or tarte tatin with vanilla pod ice cream.

★ ❀ **S V** ♿ ⊖ (Angel) P **C**

N1: ISLINGTON
Mucky Pup
39 Queen's Head Street, N1 8NQ

- ▶ Off Essex Road
- ☼ Mon-Sat 12pm-1am; Sun 12-10.30pm
- Ⓨ Daily 12-10pm (9pm Sun)
- T (020) 7226 2572
- E themuckypup@woof.co.uk
- W www.muckypup-london.com
- Greene King IPA; Sharp's Eden Ale
- ☺ Speciality 'hot rocks' dishes plus comfort snacks and Sunday roasts
- Friendly, back street local; the elusive (especially in London) front room with a bar

Just a stone's throw from Camden Passage in trendy Islington, the Mucky Pup comes as something of a surprise. Not only is it rare in London to find a pub that welcomes dogs (winner of the Dog's Trust Most Dog-Friendly Pub in the UK award), but it also offers something out of the ordinary in the food stakes, too: 'hot rocks' cooking. Diners are presented with a volcanic stone that has been heated in the oven for 6-8 hours (don't touch!), along with their choice of fish, poultry, meat or vegetables to cook at the table. Steaks, chicken, barramundi fillet or aubergine and portobello mushrooms can be cooked plain or with a 'rub' such as garlic and rosemary, Thai, Mediterranean herbs or piri piri.
Accompaniments are included in the price: a sauce for the meat plus potato wedges, jacket spud, mash or rice, £7.50-£13.50. There are also 'special rocks': halloumi and Mediterranean veg, lamb leg steak, swordfish steak and scallops, £8.95-£12.95, and sizzling sarnies: paninis with potato wedges and salad garnish, £5.50-£7.50. Another innovation here is the 'start and share' dishes – you choose two for £3.75 then pay £1.25 for any extras, tapas style: choices include cream cheese filled jalapenos, mini veg samosas and spring rolls, rosti feta parcels and calamari.

❀ **S V** ♿ ⇌ (Essex Road) ⊖ (Angel) ♣ **C**

NW1: CHALK FARM
Queens
49 Regents Park Road, NW1 8XD

- ▶ Over bridge from Chalk Farm tube
- ☼ Daily 11am-11pm
- Ⓨ Daily 12-3pm, 7-10pm
- T (020) 7586 0408
- F (020) 7586 5677
- E mail@thequeens49.fsnet.co.uk
- W www.geronimo-inns.co.uk
- Young's Bitter, Special
- ☺ Modern European with contemporary twists
- Gastropub with dining room, outside drinking space

A tempting menu of bright ideas features a lunch deal of £5 or £10 for a meal and a drink. A typical lunchtime menu includes rock oysters with spicy dressing, prosciutto and green olives, salt and pepper squid with chilli jam, bubble and squeak with avocado and poached egg, prices £5.95 to £6.95. Mains could be open steak sandwich with roast tomatoes, bacon, chilli jam and chips, battered whiting with fat chips, confit duck leg with honey and celeriac, or crisp fried potato cake with curried lentils, cucumber and coriander salad and minted yoghurt, or cod in beer batter with fat chips, £7.25-£10.95.

Some dishes cross over to evening when you might also find starters of home-made chicken sausage with balsamic vinegar and pecorino or carpaccio of yellow fin tuna and crumbed prawns. Main dishes at night include roast acorn-fed black pork cutlet from Pays Basque with artichokes, red plums and smoked garlic sauce, cassoulet of scallops and salt cod with chorizo, char-grilled sirloin steak with hand-cut chips and roast courgettes, or braised lamb shank with warm potato and chorizo salad on caramelised onion pizza, prices £12.95-£14.50. Monthly four-course crab dinners are £26.50, and they do a great Sunday roast.

❀ **S V** ♿ ⊖ (Chalk Farm) 👪 **C**

NW1: PRIMROSE HILL

Lansdowne

90 Gloucester Avenue, NW1 8HX

▶ South of Chalk Farm tube
☼ Mon 5-11pm; Tue-Sat 12-11pm; Sun 12-10.30pm
🍴 Mon 7-10pm; Tue-Sat 12.30-3pm, 7-10pm; Sun 12.30-3pm, 7-9.30pm
T (020) 7483 0409
F (020) 7586 1723
E thelansdowne@hotmail.co.uk
🍺 Caledonian Deuchars IPA; Everards Tiger
☺ Modern British and Mediterranean
◉ End of terrace Victorian pub close to Primrose Hill; laid back, cosy boozer with dining room upstairs

A daily changing menu in the smart upstairs dining room features imaginative modern bistro-style home prepared dishes. A typical day's selection might include spiced red lentil soup with Greek yoghurt, home-cured bresaola with rocket, capers and Parmesan, pigeon and port terrine with red onion chutney, a salad of feta, radish, pousse and pomegranate with sweet lemon dressing or pan-fried sardines on toast with watercress, priced £5-£7.

Main courses include trendy pork belly, here as a confit with prunes, potatoes and bacon lardons, a Welsh cawl-style lamb neck hotpot with carrots and potatoes, poached sea trout with crushed herb potatoes, spinach and sorrel hollandaise, whole roast mackerel with rosemary new potatoes and tapenade or polenta with roast pumpkin, buffalo mozzarella, and a dressing of walnut and mustard fruit, prices £10-£14. Desserts could be treacle tart with crème fraîche, hot chocolate fondant with double cream, cinnamon brûlée, pear poached in saffron with Greek yoghurt and nuts or a clementine sorbet, all £4.50-£5. The ice cream choice includes vanilla, pistachio, stracciatelli or cardamom, all £4.50, and in addition there is a plate of cheese selected from the Aladdin's cave that is Neal's Yard, served with oatcakes at £6.

🏰 ❀ **S V** ♿ ⇌ (Euston) ⊖ (Chalk Farm) 👪 **C**

NW3: HAMPSTEAD

☆ Holly Bush

22 Holly Mount, NW3 6SG

▶ Off Heath Street, up Holly Steps
☼ Mon-Sat 12-11pm; Sun 12-10.30pm
🍴 Mon-Fri 12-4pm, 6-10pm; Sat & Sun 12-10pm (9pm Sun)
T (020) 7435 2892
F (020) 7431 2292
🍺 Adnams Bitter, Broadside; Fuller's London Pride; Harveys BB; guest
☺ Atlantic inspired, beer-based funky food
◉ Grade II listed multi-roomed pub built from stables in early 19th century, attracting a wide spectrum of locals and visitors

'We use beer as others use wine,' is the heartening promise from the Holly Bush, a pub full of character in a colourful area. Rabbit in pilsner, roast chicken in paprika and ale sauce, beef and Harveys BB pie are just some of the treats available. Cheese comes mainly from Dorset, butter straight from a farm, and the cooks bake sourdough bread most mornings. The menu changes seasonally but typical dishes might be chicken, Fuller's London Pride and mushroom pie with cheddar mash, duck and cherry beer sausages with red onion and Scotch marmalade, rabbit in pilsner with mustard, salt marsh lamb cutlets with hazelnut and rosemary stuffing (organic lamb is from farms in Wales and Hertfordshire), and organic salmon with creamed spinach pie. Wild mushroom and smoked tofu pie flavoured with dill and sour cream or vegetarian sausages with mash and non-meat red onion gravy are just two veggie choices, prices from £8.50-£14. Smaller plates include rarebit made with Adnams Broadside, lamb rillettes with red onion marmalade and toast, oak smoked mackerel with celeriac and apple salad, or a pint of prawns. Home-made desserts, all £5, are sticky toffee pudding, hot chocolate with quince and single malt whisky fondant, or bread and butter pudding.

★ 🏰 ❀ **S V** ⊖ (Hampstead)

SE1:SOUTHWARK

Anchor & Hope

36 The Cut, Southwark,SE1

- Mon 5-12pm; Tues-Sat 11am-midnight; closed Sun
- Mon 6-10.30pm; Tues-Sat 12-2.30pm, 6-10.30pm
- T (020) 7928 9898
- Charles Wells Eagle IPA, Bombardier; guest
- Gastropub serving fresh, seasonal European food; no bookings
- Street corner pub with large downstairs room decorated in 'roast beef red', dining and drinking areas divided by curtain

A newish gastropub attracting rave reviews with no set menu but dishes constantly changing, even between lunchtime and evening. Cooking is both innovative and traditional with shared dishes a popular feature. The sort of starters you might find include duck hearts on toast, devilled sprats, pea and ham soup, pigeon terrine with cornichons, or beetroot with horseradish and watercress. Main courses, £8-£15, might include slow cooked lamb shoulder with gratin dauphinoise 'for around five people', rib of beef with chips and béarnaise sauce for two, cassoulet with duck, Toulouse sausage and pork belly in an earthenware dish for two, whole roast seabass with fennel, olives and aioli for two. Single dishes for those of us who want it all to ourselves could be rabbit with mustard, bacon, prunes and swede, skate with lentils and green sauce, grilled soles with anchovy butter, plus vegetarian choices like braised chicory and ceps with wet polenta topped with melted St James cheese or Stinking Bishop cheese and potato pie in puff pastry. There is a cheeseboard of traditional British cheeses, and tempting desserts might be spiced apple, pear and prune cake with custard, quince and apple pie, nectarine and almond tart or chocolate and hazelnut cake with ice cream and chocolate sauce.

S V ♿ (Waterloo) ⊖ (Southwark/Waterloo) **C**

SW3: CHELSEA

Pig's Ear

35 Old Church Street, SW3 5BS

- Off King's Road
- Daily 12-11pm
- Bar daily 12.30-3pm, 7-10pm; dining room Tue-Fri 7-12pm; Sat 7-10.30pm; Sun 12-4pm
- T (020) 7352 2908
- E hello@thepigsear.co.uk
- W www.thepigsear.co.uk
- Uley Pig's Ear; guest
- Porcine pleasures on traditional and modern English menu
- Nicely renovated Victorian corner house

Pig's Ear is cockney rhyming slang for beer, so that's what the owners called this Victorian pub when they acquired it in 2004, and shortly afterwards found themselves in the final of the London Evening Standard Pub of the Year. Then they discovered Uley brew a beer called Pig's Ear, and chef Ashley Hancill (he's worked for Marco Pierre White and Gary Rhodes) suggested they go the whole hog – literally. So there are both pig's ears and pig's trotters on the menu, the ears cured in brine then long simmered in chicken stock, sliced, crumbed and fried, the trotters boned and given a spicy stuffing; also thick slices of Gloucester Old Spot belly pork in broth, and Tamworth pig pork chop. On Sundays pork shoulder is slow roasted overnight with an incredibly crisp crackling – and not forgetting the pork scratchings.

But there's plenty more on daily changing menus such as, in the bar, broad bean and lettuce broth, English asparagus with poached duck egg, Irish rock oysters with shallot relish and stout, and roast monkfish with bitter leaves, main courses £6.50-£7.50. Upstairs, in an immaculate dining room, you might find lamb's tongue with lamb's lettuce and anchovy croutons or squid salad with confit lemon and pine nuts among the starters, roast rump of salt marsh lamb or almond crusted plaice.

Q S V ♿ ⊖ (Sloane Sq, S Kensington) **C**

SW6: FULHAM

☆ White Horse

1 Parsons Green, SW6 4UL

- ▶ Off New King's Road
- ☼ Daily 11am-11pm (10.30pm Sun)
- Ⓨ Throughout opening times
- T (020) 7736 2115
- F (020) 7610 6091
- E whitehorsesw6@btconnect.com
- W www.whitehorsesw6.com
- Adnams Broadside; Brakspear BB; Fuller's ESB; Harveys BB; Oakham JHB; Rooster's Yankee; guests
- ☺ Brilliant, eclectic food from comfort to contemporary
- Mecca for beer enthusiasts, large three-sided bar and separate restaurant

The famous White Horse at Parsons Green, run by the indefatigable beer and food enthusiast Mark Dorber, is the template for all pubs. Not only is the food outstanding, and the kitchen brigade enthusiastic about cooking with beer but, following the Belgian tradition of marrying beer with fine food, different beers are recommended to accompany dishes on the menu.

So a typical food selection, with Mark's recommendations, might be roast plum tomato, pancetta and Wigmore tart with rocket salad (Moinette Blonde), Formans smoked salmon salad (Trappiste Orval), pork belly, apple and thyme terrine (Westmalle Tripel), roast pumpkin salad with pine nuts and goats' cheese (Duvel), cep and green onion risotto (draught De Koninck), salt and lemon pepper squid with Chinese cabbage, bok choi and sweet chilli dressing (draught Hoegaarden), pork sausages and mash with cabbage and beer onion gravy (draught Adnams Broadside), Bank Farm venison and wild mushroom casserole (Schlenkerla smoked beer), salmon fishcake with creamed leeks and rocket (Schneider Weisse wheat beer), or pheasant roast supreme and confit leg with savoy cabbage and bread sauce (Rochefort 10), prices £6.75-£11.25.

S V ≠ (Putney) ⊖ (Parsons Green) C

SW10: WEST BROMPTON

☆ Chelsea Ram

32 Burnaby Street, SW10 OPL

- ▶ Close to Chelsea Harbour
- ☼ Mon-Sat 11am-11pm; Sun 12-10.30pm
- Ⓨ Mon-Sat 12-3pm, 6.30-10pm; Sun 12-3.30pm, 7-9.30pm
- T (020) 7351 4008
- Young's Bitter, Special, seasonal
- ☺ Gastropub much praised by foodies
- Back street pub with a friendly atmosphere, mainly open plan; opens 10am for early afternoon Chelsea FC home ties

A Young's house and stylish gastropub offering an inventive monthly menu plus daily changing specials, well executed by a talented kitchen brigade. A typical selection includes starters such as roast Portobello mushrooms with sage and scrambled eggs on toasted focaccia, wood pigeon, quail's egg and Puy lentil salad, smoked haddock and potato tart with creamed leeks, smoked salmon wrapped prawns with dill sour cream, chicken Caesar salad and fresh daily soup, £4-£6.90. Mains could be pork and leek sausages with spinach, mash and onion gravy, the Chelsea Ram salad of chicken, bacon, feta and cherry tomatoes, salmon fishcake with chunky tartare sauce and green beans, five spiced duck breast with red cabbage, leek and chorizo pie, grilled lamb cutlets with spicy ratatouille and mint salsa verde, sea bass with piri piri king prawns and Swiss chard, fillet steak with spinach confit tomato and chunky chips.

Prices range from £8.50 for a veggie dish such as peppers stuffed with wild rice, peas and mozzarella to £14.90 for the fillet steak or £26.90 for two people sharing rib of beef with dauphinoise potatoes, french beans and béarnaise sauce. Desserts include Bramley apple galette with toffee apple ice cream, sticky toffee pudding with butterscotch sauce and crème fraîche, or a big cheeseboard for two.

S V ⊖ (Earls Court) C

SW13: BARNES
Red Lion
2 Castelnau, SW13 9RU

- Mon-Sat 11am-11pm; Sun 12-10.30pm
- Mon-Fri 11am-3pm, 6-10pm; Sat 11am-10pm; Sun 12-10pm
- T (020) 8748 2984
- Fuller's London Pride, ESB, seasonal
- Modern British and continental with a bit of a twist and nice beery touches, plus great Sunday roasts
- Attractive Fuller's house with a lovely garden

A pub that boasts no frozen food, chips hand cut in the kitchen, and excellent produce from fresh vegetables to beef for the burgers sourced from a farm in Oxfordshire. Sunday lunch is especially popular when roast rib of beef is served medium rare, carved to order, with fluffy home-made Yorkshire puds and a rich gravy that takes a week to prepare. Or there is shoulder of lamb braised for hours in red wine with redcurrants and fresh mint, as well as a whole chicken stuffed with sage and onion for diners to carve at the table, all with four fresh vegetables and roast potatoes, followed by a trolley of home-made desserts. Specials change daily, but could include trout with lime and parsley butter or speciality sausages with savoy cabbage, mash and London Pride gravy, not forgetting old-fashioned classics such as omelette Arnold Bennett.

The set menu includes full English breakfast, served until 1pm, at £6, as well as starters/snacks such as home-made pâté with Honey Dew ale chutney, coarse coriander and lime hummus or ploughman's with Double Gloucester and Somerset Brie, £4.75-£6.50. Main courses range from chicken and leek pie on mash to Mediterranean vegetable tart, plaice goujons with mushy pea purée, char-grilled gammon with Caerphilly cauliflower cheese or rib eye steak, £7.95-£11.95. Children are allowed during the day only.

V (Barnes) C

SW18: WANDSWORTH
The Freemasons
2 Wandsworth Common Northside, SW18 2SS

- Daily 12-11pm (10.30pm Sun)
- Mon-Sat 12-3pm, 6.30-10pm; Sun 12.30-4pm, 6.30-9.30pm
- T (020) 7326 8580
- F (020) 7223 6186
- E thepublandlordltd@btinternet.com
- W www.freemasonspub.com
- Everards Tiger; Taylor Landlord
- Modern British and European cooking
- Upmarket, stylish gastropub

The menu perhaps shouts gastropub but the dishes are alluring and well executed, and well priced for food of this quality. The menu changes, but a typical selection always includes soup of the day with home-made bread as well as starters such as Caesar salad with anchovies, parmesan and croutons, smoked chicken with bacon and avocado, cured salmon fillet with palm heart and piquillo pepper frittata, focaccia bruschetta with grilled aubergine, baked sweet potato, roast peppers and melted goats' cheese, Parma ham and rocket salad, wok-fried Spanish chorizo with soft poached egg and salad, or grilled tiger prawns with truffle potato, crème fraîche salad and sweet chilli sauce, prices £3.75-£6.75.

Mains may include Cumberland sausages with spring onion mash, green beans and onion gravy, roast butternut squash risotto with filled mushrooms, spinach and mascarpone, pan-fried seabass with garlic and saffron broth, grilled hoi sin pork chop with Stilton new potatoes, sautéed cavolo nero and apple sauce, char-grilled lamb, mint and olive burger with salad and French fries, pan-baked chicken breast with roast spring onion and sweet potato mash, finishing with char-grilled rib eye steak with potato and onion rosti and red wine jus, ranging in price from £9.25-£11.50. There are side orders of chunky chips, olives with home made bread, nachos with tomato sauce and melted cheese, hummus with Turkish bread or chicken liver pancetta and shallot pate.

V (Clapham Junction) C

SW18: WANDSWORTH
Le Gothique

Royal Victoria Patriotic Building, Fitzhugh Grove, SW18 3SX

▶ Off Trinity Road
☼ Mon-Sat 11am-midnight
🍴 Mon-Sat 12-3pm, 6-10.30pm
T (020) 8870 6567
E marklegothique@aol.com
W www.legothique.co.uk
Shepherd Neame Spitfire, Bishops Finger; Ballard's Best, Nyewood Gold
☺ French country cooking full of flavour prepared by a French chef
Housed in a grade I listed Victorian Gothic masterpiece surrounded by lawns

Le Gothique prefers to be called a 'posh pub' rather than a 'gastropub', and the team that started the enterprise in 1985 – Mark Justin and Joanne Thorp with Jean-Marie Martin in the kitchen – celebrated 20 years in 2005. The rustic French cuisine has gone from strength to strength, supplemented by duck and lamb from their small holding in Hampshire, and with three real ales served as well as 12 vintage Armagnacs. They make all their own pâtés and terrines such as rabbit at £5.75, and soups such as the Mediterranean fish or Jean-Marie's real French onion inside a crusty cottage loaf at £5.25, not forgetting home-made apple and raisin chutney.

At lunchtime the menu is simpler, offering croque monsieur or madame, wild boar sausages with mash, creamy mushroom risotto with Parmesan, Arbroath smoked haddock with white wine, cream and prawns, moules marinière, and the plat du jour, prices £4.50-£7.95. The à la carte is more extensive including starters such as snails and mushrooms with garlic, cream and Pernod and Loch Fyne Scotch whisky smoked salmon, main courses include pan-fried seabass with prawns on spinach, duck breast with potato dauphinoise, skewered red snapper and tiger prawns or pasta with sun dried tomato, artichoke hearts, black olives and parmesan, £8.95-£14.95.

★ ❀ **S V** ♿ ⇌ (Clapham Junction) P 👪 **C**

SW18: WANDSWORTH
King's Arms
96 Wandsworth High Street, SW18 4LB

- Mon-Sat 11am-11pm; Sun 12-10.30pm
- Mon-Sat 12-3pm, 6.30-9.30pm; Sun 12-4pm
- T (020) 8874 1428
- Young's Bitter, Special, Waggle Dance or Winter Warmer
- Modern gastro with imaginative menu plus daily specials
- Spacious pub with a garden and private function room

All food is freshly prepared on the premises daily including two flavoured breads and fresh pasta. Even bangers and burgers are home made and the chefs cater for special diets. Typical daily specials include tempura cod with pea purée and chips, roast red pork with a noodle and vegetable broth, roast lamb with galette potato and swede purée, or bruschetta of artichoke, sun dried tomato and pesto, all £6.95 apart from the lamb at £10.95.

The main menu changes every six weeks, typical starters being confit lamb with haricot bean and thyme purée, home-made taglierini, crab and chive broth with seared scallops, Caesar salad with soft boiled egg and anchovies, or home-made soup of the day, £3.95-£6.95. A selection of main courses might be braised oxtail wrapped in pastry with garlic mash and fried foie gras, calf's liver with sweet potato purée and crisp pancetta, roast hake wrapped in prosciutto with minted broad bean and tomato vierge, Cumberland sausage with caramelised onions and grain mustard mash, rib eye steak with real chips or vegetarian pea and okra pilaf with home-made onion and coriander bhaji, prices £7.95-£10.95. Side dishes include home-made falafel and hash browns; desserts range from treacle tart with clotted cream to meringue and berry compote with pineapple crisp.

S V (Wandsworth Town) (East Putney) C

SW19: WIMBLEDON
Crooked Billet
15 Crooked Billet, SW19 4RQ

- Near Wimbledon Common
- Mon-Sat 11am-11pm; Sun 12-10.30pm
- Mon-Fri 12-3pm, 6-10pm; all day Sat & Sun
- T (020) 8946 4942
- Young's Bitter, Special, seasonal
- Good combination of traditional and eclectic
- Traditional pub on the edge of Wimbledon Common dating back to 1509 as a brewery and inn though rebuilt in 1776; open fires in bar and restaurant

The landlady and her chef dish up freshly-cooked pub food with some thoughtful touches at budget prices for the area. Starters and salads include home-made soup, tiger prawns in lemon, garlic and tarragon butter, warm chicken, bacon and mango salad, baked goats' cheese and avocado gratin, nachos with chilli salsa with dips and jalapenos, buffalo mozzarella, tomato and red onion salad or a rich duck pâté with orange, chutney and oatmeal biscuits, £3.95-£6.25. In addition two people can choose three items to share on a 'Billet Board' for £8.95 from a list including Blue Stilton, mature Cheddar, Somerset Brie, duck and orange pâté, poached salmon, roast beef, honey roast ham and chicken breast, accompanied by Young's real ale chutney, salad, apple, grapes, celery and crusty bread.

Hot meals include pork and leek sausages on mustard mash, haddock in Young's beer batter with chips, chicken, Brie and bacon stack on colcannon potatoes, grilled salmon with tarragon sauce, vegetables and new potatoes, tagliatelle with spinach and blue cheese sauce and toasted pine nuts, sirloin steak with horseradish butter, chips, grilled tomato and fried onion, prices from £7.25. Desserts range from chocolate fudge brownie to the daily hot fruit crumble, and sarnies both hot and cold are served with salad.

★ S V (Wimbledon) (Wimbledon) C

SW19: WIMBLEDON

Rose & Crown

55 High Street, SW19 5BA

- Mon-Sat 11am-11pm; Sun 12-10.30pm
- Mon-Fri 12-3pm, 6-10pm; Sat & Sun 12-10 (9pm Sun)
- T (020) 8947 4713
- E roseandcrown@youngs.co.uk
- Young's Bitter, Special, Waggle Dance or Winter Warmer
- Stimulating mix of traditional and eclectic
- Traditional Young's house in Wimbledon High Street with real fire, garden and B&B accommodation

Landlady Nichola Green is also the chef, creating a menu that offers an especially tempting choice of salads and lighter meals. Favourites include home-made soup such as broccoli or leek and potato, flat mushrooms with Swiss cheese and roast cherry tomatoes on toasted ciabatta, salads in both small and main meal portions – Caesar, tomato of plum, cherry and sunblush with red onion and basil oil, or wild rocket and Parmesan – plus smoked haddock and salmon kedgeree, poached salmon with new potatoes and asparagus salad or hummus, tzatziki and taramasalata with hot pitta, prices £3.95-£8.95.

Main meals include the ever popular deep-fried fresh fish of the day in Young's beer batter with chips and minted pea purée, chicken, leek and mushroom pie, Cumberland sausage with caramelised onion, mash and thyme gravy, the Rose and Crown home-made burger (plain or cheese), smoked haddock with chives, mash, poached egg and grain mustard sauce, or wild mushroom risotto, prices £6.95-£9.95. Typical specials might be a smoked salmon platter or eggs Benedict, and main courses include Young's champion steak and kidney pie, South African baboti, or Swiss open sandwich of steak and mushrooms on roast red onion ciabatta. A generous Sunday roast of beef or chicken with all the trimmings is £10.

S V (Wimbledon)
(Wimbledon) C

KEW

Coach & Horses

8 Kew Green, TW9 3BH

- Accessible from M4 via Chiswick roundabout
- Daily 11am-11pm
- Mon-Sat 7-9.30am (breakfast), 12-2.30pm, 7-9.30pm; Sun all day
- T (020) 8940 1208
- F (020) 8978 8787
- E coachandhorse@youngs.co.uk
- W www.coachhotelkew.co.uk
- Young's Bitter, Special, seasonal
- Traditional menu with good fish specials and Sunday roasts
- This former coaching inn has a lovely oak panelled restaurant

Kew Gardens offers a wonderful day out, but all that walking and fresh air certainly builds up an appetite, so what better way to end a visit than with a meal at the Coach and Horses, just five minutes' stroll away? The home-cooked menu kicks off with mackerel on an onion bread crouton with horseradish potato salad, home-made fish cakes, duck liver pâté with foie gras or crostini saladette – bruschetta and tapenade toasts on salad leaves with pesto dressing. Steamed mussels in shallot and cream sauce and English nachos (real chips topped with chilli beef, guacamole and soured cream – also available as a veggie option) come in small portions, £5.25, or large, £9.50. To follow there is prime Scottish beef from the Buccleuch estates, duckling breast with a confit leg accompanied by pear poached in red wine, vegetable timbale and redcurrant and horseradish glaze, or simple burgers, liver and bacon and Cumberland sausage, around £8.75-£13 up to £22.50 for a fillet steak. Fish is a speciality – featuring whatever the chef chooses from the fishmonger that day – simply grilled or steamed on a bed of fresh veg, with a choice of three sauces, served separately. The pub offers a good all day bar menu.

★ S V (Kew Bridge)
(Kew Gardens) P C

RICHMOND
Marlborough

46 Friars Stile Road, TW10 6NQ

- Off Richmond Hill
- Daily 12-11pm (10.30pm Sun)
- Mon-Thu 12-3pm, 5.30-9.45pm; Fri & Sat 12-9.45pm; Sun 12-9pm
- T (020) 8940 0572
- Fuller's London Pride; guests
- Limited but nonetheless interesting menu with good vegetarian options
- Former hotel with a relaxed atmosphere; modern furnishings including comfy sofas blend with stained glass panels and open fires

The Marlborough boasts the largest pub garden in Richmond, complete with its own bandstand, so it is a good choice for a sunny day. The pub itself is very comfortable too, and is no-smoking throughout. The menu is fairly limited but the dishes on offer are not run of the mill pub grub. Snacks include skewered chicken in yakatori sauce, tomato, basil and Cheddar soup served with toasted ciabatta, home-made potato wedges topped with Cheddar and chorizo or a dish of olives and feta cheese served with ciabatta, £3.50-£5.50. The sandwiches for under a fiver are out of the ordinary, too, served on fresh Italian breads, with fillings such as roast pepper and cheese melt, chicken with tarragon mayo, Suffolk sausage with red onions or fish fingers with lime mayonnaise.

Main courses include spinach and mushroom gnocchi in tomato and herb sauce, warm Portobello mushroom and feta salad, mixed bean cassoulet with couscous, and smoked haddock fishcakes served with home-made wedges and baby spinach. More down to earth are the 8oz Angus burger and rib eye steaks. Prices are £6.50-£10.50. Just three desserts are on offer, but all delicious: bread and butter pudding with cream, chocolate puddle pudding or apple tarte tatin served with vanilla pod ice cream.

Q S V C

RICHMOND
White Swan

26 Old Palace Lane, TW9 1PG

- Near Richmond Green
- Mon-Sat 11am-midnight; Sun 12-11pm
- Mon-Sat 12-3pm, 6-10pm; Sun 6-9pm
- T (020) 8940 0959
- F (020) 8332 2423
- E r.grant@fluidpubs.com
- W www.fluidpubs.com
- Fuller's London Pride; Greene King Old Speckled Hen; Wells Bombardier
- Upmarket, modern European style cuisine
- Lovely riverside inn dating back to the early 19th century when it was built to serve local artisans

The pub may have been built to cater for local tradespeople and craftsmen but it now serves a more affluent community and its menus reflect modern tastes. It is the boast of the chef that he only regularly buys in two items for the pub's kitchen – filo wrapped tiger prawns and ice cream. Fruit and vegetables are sourced locally, and some of the herbs and spices now come from the pub's own nearby allotment. The menu changes daily, but typical starters might be a vegetable soup such as cream of fennel and tarragon, grilled, herb-filled Portobello mushrooms, char-grilled lamb kofte served with sour cream, deep-fried whitebait with lime mayo and warm salad of smoked duck with Parma ham, £4-£6.

A choice of eight or nine main courses is supplemented by slightly more expensive special dishes, such as seared venison steak on sticky red cabbage, £13, or whole grilled seabass on wilted pak choi, £14. Other main courses, £8-£13, include char-grilled chicken breast with grilled goats' cheese, Scottish beef braised in Guinness with dauphinoise potatoes, rack of Welsh lamb on butter bean purée with caramelised shallots and pan-fried Cornish mackerel fillets with salsa verde and anchovy. Vegetarians may find roasted butternut squash risotto or stuffed Spanish tomatoes.

Q V (Richmond) (Richmond) C

W4: CHISWICK

George & Devonshire

8 Burlington Lane, W4 2QE

- South side Hogarth roundabout, A4/A316
- Mon-Sat 11.30am (12 Sat)-11pm; Sun 12-10.30pm
- Daily 12-3pm
- T (020) 8994 1859
- E georgeanddevonshire@fullers.co.uk
- Fuller's Chiswick, London Pride, ESB, seasonal
- Mainly English with international touches
- One of two pubs next to Fuller's Griffin brewery, with a separate public bar and saloon

Good, wholesome food at surprisingly low prices for the area – most main dishes are around £5-£7. But you can eat even more cheaply from the lighter section, with sandwiches ranging from mature Cheddar with plum and apple chutney to grilled chicken with avocado and crisp bacon, £3.25-£4.95, filled jacket potatoes, proper nachos of spicy salsa, jalapenos, Cheddar and guacamole, £4.95 to share, and traditional ploughman's of Cheddar and goats' cheese, home-cooked smoked ham or smoked salmon and prawns, or a bowl of chunky chips with cheese and bacon for £2.15.

Main meals include that delicious ham with two fried eggs and chips, fish in ESB beer batter, Lincolnshire sausages with chive mash and onion gravy, chicken Caesar salad, home-made chicken and mushroom pie with seasonal veg and mash, or grilled chicken with sautéed mushrooms and asparagus, mash and onion gravy, £4.95-£6.95. Vegetarian choices include warm goats' cheese, roast pepper and pine nut salad with basil oil or tagliatelle with grilled asparagus and roast peppers in pesto with toasted pine nuts. A good burger selection offers beef with cheese and crispy bacon, grilled chicken with avocado and tomato, beef with goats' cheese and roast peppers or a giant mushroom with asparagus and goats' cheese.

★ Q ❀ S V ⊖ (Turnham Green) P ⚮ C

W6: HAMMERSMITH

Brook Green Hotel

170 Shepherd's Bush Road, W6 7PB

- 5 minutes' walk from Hammersmith tube
- Mon-Thu 7am-11pm; Fri-Sun 8am-midnight
- Mon-Sat 12-3pm, 6-10pm; Sun 12-4pm, 6-9pm
- T (020) 7603 2516
- F (020) 7603 6827
- E brookgreen@youngs.co-uk
- W www.brookgreenhotel.co.uk
- Young's bitter, Special, seasonal
- Tasty, traditional home-made pub grub at reasonable prices
- A modernised 'gin palace' retaining many original features

A pub serving delicious food – for several years Young's has generously hosted the AGM of the British Guild of Beer Writers at the Brook Green – last year's buffet was ab fab. For plainer occasions, you can snack on home-made soup, fishcakes with parsley sauce, steamed mussels with garlic, shallots and cream, or nachos with chilli beef, guacamole and salsa, £3.50-£6.75. Main dishes include fresh fish in Young's beer batter with hand-cut chips, Cumberland sausages or grilled liver and bacon with mash and onion gravy, home-made chicken kiev pan-fried with bacon in garlic butter, a half pound rump steak with hand-cut chips and onion rings, cheese glazed penne and roast vegetable bake or ploughman's with Cheddar and Stilton, £5.50-£8, or £9.50 for steak. Veggie or meat platters are a popular idea – the vegetarian has mini vegetable kievs, hot mozza melts, spinach and feta goujons, Camembert samosa, onion rings, breaded mushrooms and dips; the meat includes bacon and cheese straws, chicken spring rolls, BBQ wings, mini kievs, BBQ ribs, mushrooms, onion rings and dips – both priced £9.50 for two sharing or £15 for four. There are salads and paninis, and breakfast too, as this is a hotel with 14 en-suite rooms at reasonable rates.

Q ❀ S V ♿ ⊖ (Hammersmith) ♣ C

W8: KENSINGTON
Windsor Castle
114 Campden Hill Road, W8 7AR

▶ Nearest tube is Notting Hill Gate
☼ Daily 12-11pm (Sun 10.30pm)
🍴 Mon-Sat 12-4pm, 5-10pm; Sun 12-9pm
T (020) 7243 9551
Beer range varies
☺ Extensive, mainly British menu
◙ Unusually for London this Dickensian pub boasts a beautiful garden where barbecues take place most summer days

The beers change frequently here, so does the menu (generally once a month). If you want a light meal you are always likely to find ciabatta with enticing fillings such as smoked English ham with Brie, salmon with cream cheese and dill or hummus and roasted peppers, £5-£6, or other snacks such as goats' cheese crostini and even half a dozen oysters, as available.

The pub buys all its lamb from a family-run farm in Snowdonia and serves it as lamb chops with mash, roast veg and redcurrant sauce, £10.50, lamb and mint burger, £7.50, or lamb and mint sausages. The bangers are just one of a wide range, including wild boar and apple and beef and tomato, served with mash and onion gravy for £9. There's always a fish of the day, plus fish and chips, £9.50 and mussels steamed in cream and white wine for £7.95. Enticing salads include crayfish or chicken Caesar and a Greek salad. Chicken dishes might include breast wrapped in bacon, stuffed with mozzarella and basil with spicy couscous or creamy chicken and leek penne pasta. A traditional roast lunch is served on Sunday and barbecues take place throughout the summer. Puddings (some home made) are £4.50, including sticky toffee squares, fruit crumble, squidgy chocolate pud and cheesecake.

★ ❀ **S V** ♿ ⇌ (Notting Hill Gate) ⊖ (Notting Hill Gate) ♣ **C**

BRENTFORD
Weir Bar & Dining Room
22-24 Market Place, TW8 8EQ

▶ Just of the High Street
☼ Daily 12-11pm (Sun 10.30pm)
🍴 Mon-Fri 12-3pm, 7-10pm; Sat & Sun 12-10pm
T (020) 8568 3600
F (020) 8758 0892
E info@theweirbar.co.uk
W www.theweirbar.co.uk
Adnams Broadside; Fuller's London Pride; Greene King Old Speckled Hen
☺ Modern European menu that changes frequently
◙ Contemporary style with a relaxed atmosphere, but smart dress required

The Weir, so named because its garden overlooks the Grand Union Canal, places great emphasis on high quality food and drinks – its wine list is extensive. Food is delivered freshly on a daily basis, sourced from local suppliers as far as possible. It offers a different menu for lunch and dinner, the lunch menu listing lighter dishes. For starters there is salt and pepper squid served with roasted chilli sauce or moules marinière with home-made bread or maybe soup, followed at lunch by grilled goats' cheese salad with walnut vinaigrette, free range stir-fried chicken with chilli and basil rice or spaghetti and clams with chilli and rocket, all £7-£8.

In the evening some of the same starters appear alongside perhaps warm chorizo, potato and bean salad with poached egg, £7.50, or smoked salmon with orange dressing and avocado pâté. To follow there may be organic cod and champ with crisp pancetta and red wine sauce, five spice corn fed chicken and Asian salad, wild mushroom spaghetti with spinach and truffle oil or roasted pork belly and crackling with spring onion mash, all £11-£12. Make sure you leave room for one of the spiffing puds, £5-£6 – chilled lemon soufflé or cardamom panna cotta with stewed rhubarb.

Q ❀ **S V** ♿ ⇌ (Brentford) ⊖ (South Ealing) **C**

TEDDINGTON

☆ Teddington Arms

38-40 High Street, TW11 8EW

- Five minutes from A316
- Daily 12-11pm (Sun 10.30pm)
- Mon-Fri 12-3pm, 6-10pm; Sat & Sun 12-9pm
- T (020) 8973 1510
- F (020) 8973 1511
- E enquiries@teddingtonarms.com
- Adnams Bitter; Brakspear Bitter; Fuller's London Pride; Young's Bitter plus two guest beers
- Modern English, all freshly prepared
- Once a tyre depot, now a cool, modern pub; the bar tends to be noisy, but the restaurant is quieter

The pub opened in 2003 and has been well received locally, quickly earning a listing in CAMRA's Good Beer Guide. The bar leads through to the lounge area furnished with sofas and rugs and the no-smoking restaurant where an exciting menu is served at reasonable prices. Starters range from £4 to £7, including pan-fried king scallops with hazelnut and coriander butter, char-grilled asparagus with Parmesan and sea salt, chicken liver parfait with red onion marmalade and warm toasts, or charcuterie – a selection of cured meats and garnishes. Or two can share a whole baked Camembert, served with dipping croutons, for £8.50.

There is a good choice of risottos and pastas served as a starter or main course, £5/£9, such as artichoke and swimmer crab risotto with shaved Parmesan or fettucini with Gorgonzola and spinach. There is always a pasta of the day and a fish of the day, while other mains are rib eye steak with mustard mayo, oven-roasted duck breast with sweet potato purée, pan-fried halibut fillet with baby leeks and salsa verde or moules marinière with hand-cut chips. Again, a twosome can share a 22oz rib of beef on the bone for £23.

S V ♿ ⇌ (Teddington) **C**

At the romantic Grade I listed turreted 'posh pub' Le Gothique on Wandsworth Common in London, French country cooking is at the heart of the menu. This soup in a loaf is the signature dish of one of the team, Jean-Marie Martin.

SOUPE A L'OIGNON AU POT ANCIENNE

Serves 6-8

50g (2oz) butter
2 tbsps vegetable oil
1kg (2lb) large onions, thinly sliced
1 tsp salt
Bottle basic red wine
1 litre (1 pint) beef and chicken stock, mixed
75g (3oz) flour
6-8 small crusty cottage loaves
Grated Gruyere

Melt butter and oil in a frying pan, stir in the onions with salt and continue stirring occasionally for 20-30 minutes or until golden brown and caramelised. In a deep saucepan, heat the red wine with the mixed stock, then stir in the cooked onions. Simmer for a further 30-40 minutes before mixing the flour with a little cold water until smooth, then adding slowly to the pot, stirring all the time. Slice the tops off 6-8 cottage loaves and scoop out the bread, leaving at least 1 cm (half inch) as lining. Pour in the soup, top with grated Gruyere, replace the top and serve piping hot.

BIRTLE
Pack Horse Inn
Elbut Lane, BL9 7TH

- ▶ On the old Bury-Rochdale road, opposite Fairfield Hospital
- Daily 12-11pm
- Daily 12-9.30pm (9pm Sun)
- T (0161) 764 3620
- F (0161) 762 4796
- E briandferris@aol.com
- Lees Bitter, seasonal beers
- ☺ Varied menu that changes seasonally, plus freshly-prepared daily specials
- Traditional country inn with a small bar with open fire, restaurant and conservatory; the south-facing patio and garden are popular in summer

Owned by Manchester brewery JW Lees, this rural pub is close to a network of footpaths and bridleways so is frequented by walkers and riders as well as locals. The standard menu, which changes with the seasons, features pub favourites such as chilli, home-made lasagne and a curry of the day, all around £7, plus a good choice of steaks and snacks. This is supplemented by a more adventurous specials menu where you might find starters for around £5 of smoked mackerel with horseradish, mushroom and Stilton 'knots' with a garlic mayo dip or a vegetarian platter of Indian savouries with mint yogurt dip. To follow there could be fish such as grilled tuna steak with stem ginger sauce, noodles and salad or a medley of monkfish, salmon and cod with a creamy prawn and dill sauce. Meat dishes might be pork steak with walnut stuffing and wholegrain mustard sauce, lamb 'Henry' with pepper sauce or pan-fried duck breast with orange sauce. There is usually a good choice of desserts for around £3.50, including pear and almond tart, banoffee pie, a hot pudding of the day or a pavlova with strawberries and raspberry coulis for two to share. A two-course roast on Sunday costs £9.95.

Q S V P C

CHEADLE HULME
Church Inn
90 Ravenoak Road, SK8 7EG

- ▶ On A5149
- Mon-Sat 11am-11pm; Sun 12-10.30pm
- Mon-Sat 11.30am-2.30pm, 5.30-8.30pm; Sun 12-7.30pm
- T (0161) 485 1897
- F (0161) 485 1698
- Robinson's Hatters, Old Stockport, Best Bitter, seasonal
- ☺ Cosmopolitan selection with plenty of choice
- Cheadle Hulme's oldest pub has been a Robinson's house since 1830. Cottage style exterior with two comfy lounges and small vault

With food served both in the bar and Edwardo's restaurant, the Church Inn provides a full menu plus daily blackboard specials. Snacks include sandwiches on white or brown, toasted, or the club triple deckers, priced from £3.75-£5.75. You can start with the day's home-made soup, Ed's home-made smooth chicken liver pâté laced with brandy and port, squid rings in crisp batter with garlic mayo dip, button mushrooms in garlic butter topped with Brie then grilled, or chicken satay Malaysian with rice and salad, £3.25-£5.50.

On the set menu, main courses are fresh salmon supreme with Bearnaise sauce, home-made pie of the day, lightly-fried breaded plaice, cod in batter with home made tartare sauce, chips and mushy peas, Ed's special Tex Mex recipe chilli with rice, Thai green chicken curry with oriental spices, lemongrass, fresh coriander and cream, chicken supreme in cracked black peppercorns finished with cream and brandy, grilled 10oz sirloin steak or gammon. All main courses include fresh vegetables and potatoes, and are priced mainly from £7.50-£9, or £12.50 for the sirloin steak. Veggie dishes are home made, such as fresh mushrooms cooked with mixed peppers in wine, cream and brandy served on rice or Thai vegetable curry.

★ Q S V (Cheadle Hulme) P C

HEATON CHAPEL
Hinds Head
Manchester Road, SK4 2RB

▶ From A6 follow Denby Lane, then 300 yards to Manchester Road junction
☼ Mon-Sat 11.30am-11pm; Sun 12-10.30pm
🍴 Mon-Fri 12-3pm, 6-9pm; Sat 12-9pm; Sun 12-5pm
T (0161) 431 9301
F jay@hindshead.co.uk
🍺 Boddingtons Bitter; John Smith's Bitter; Taylor Landlord
☺ Traditional English with a touch of the more exotic
◙ Quiet local with garden on the edge of Stockport

A varied selection starts with an interesting range of bar snacks, including toasted ciabatta sandwiches with fillings such as roast vegetables topped with melted goats' cheese and balsamic dressing or tuna with shallots, cherry tomatoes and melted cheddar, around £4. Then there are 'light bites' – home made 6oz beef burgers with cheese, bacon or chilli in toasted sesame buns, traditional steak pie with chips and mushy peas, haddock, curry or bangers and mash with sautéed leeks and gravy, £5-£6.

On the main menu, you can start with home-made soup of the day, Cajun potato wedges with dipping sauce, home-made pâté, tiger prawns in white wine, lime and sweet chilli sauce or moules marinière, £2.95-£5.95. Grilled seabass with wok-fried vegetables drizzled with lemon and basil oil is on the main menu, along with three char-grilled lamb cutlets on mint mash, chicken stroganoff in a mushroom, wine, mustard and cream sauce on basmati rice, pork chop in Calvados sauce, and pan-fried duck breast with hoi sin sauce on spring onion mash, prices from £7-£10. There is a choice of steaks – gammon, rump and sirloin – while vegetarians might choose penne in tomato, Parmesan and mozzarella sauce or mixed vegetable fajitas. Traditional Sunday roast lunch is £5.95-£9.95 for one to three courses.

Q ❀ S V 🍺 ♿ P ⚡ 👪 C

HEATON NORRIS
Nursery
Green Lane, SK4 2NA

▶ Off A6
☼ 11.30am-3.30pm, 5.30-11pm; Fri & Sat 11.30am-11pm; Sun 12-10.30pm
🍴 Daily 12-2.30pm; Fri & Sat eve until 8pm
T (0161) 432 2044
E nurseryinn@hydes37.fsnet.co.uk
🍺 Hydes Mild, Bitter, Jekyll's Gold, seasonal
☺ Home cooking on a traditional theme at reasonable prices
◙ Classic, unspoilt 1930s gem; traditional vault with its own entrance, wood-panelled lounge for diners

This former national CAMRA Pub of the Year is enhanced by its quality home cooking in the caring hands of chef Dave Langfield and landlady Susan Lindsay. Specials could include steak and kidney and other home-made pies and fresh fish. The set menu offers roast beef and Yorkshire pud, roast chicken with stuffing, gammon, egg and chips, or freshly made omelettes, all with potatoes and fresh vegetables, from £4 up to £6.50 for a half pound sirloin steak. There are plenty of snacks such as home-made soup, open sandwiches including home-roasted ham, hot baguettes such as cheese and tuna melt, and jacket potatoes with eight different fillings. Delicious puddings follow – hot chocolate fudge cake, sherry trifle, ginger sponge and ice cream sundae (and milk shakes).

The evening menu is only served on Fridays and Saturdays until 8pm, with daily changing dishes possibly including fillet steak with Dave's home-made sauces, lamb shank in red wine with rosemary, char-grilled chicken filled with parma ham and Gruyere, wild mushroom pancake in vermouth sauce, or naturally smoked haddock on spinach topped mash with a poached egg, prices £6.95-£10.95. Evening desserts may be raspberry and Drambuie cranachan or cassis royale. The pub holds Stockport Council's food safety award.

★ Q ❀ S V 🍺 ♿ ♣ P ⚡

LYDGATE

☆ White Hart Inn

51 Stockport Road, OL4 4JJ

- At the A669/A6050 jct
- Daily 12-11pm (10.30pm Sun)
- Mon-Sat 12-3pm, 6-9.30pm; Sun 1-9.30pm
- T (01457) 872566
- F (01457) 875190
- E booking@thewhitehart.co.uk
- W www.thewhitehart.co.uk
- Lees Bitter; Taylor Landlord; Tetley Bitter; guests
- Award-winning modern British and European cuisine
- Spacious, stone-built free house dating from 1788 boasting impressive views; contemporary restaurant, rustic brasserie, newly-built Oak Room for private events

This lovely inn offers a variety of possibilities for diners – bangers and mash washed down with a pint of JW Lees' finest in the Barn Room, à la carte meals in the traditionally designed, homely brasserie or the smart, contemporary restaurant, or a dinner dance in the beautiful Oak Room. Chef John Rudden just keeps on winning awards. His inspired menus change frequently, but you could start with fresh Carlingford Loch oysters with red wine shallot vinegar, Demlane mussels with Asian spices, beef fillet carpaccio with smoked pepper piperade or baked crottin of goats' cheese and red pepper with a pear and balsamic salad. Expect to pay around £6-£7, then £13.50-£17 for the main course which might be braised lamb shank with chorizo couscous, confit duck leg with choucroute, cassoulet beans and cured duck, grilled fillet of plaice with a mussel and sun blushed tomato broth and straw potatoes or braised beef skirt with roasted vegetables and horseradish dumplings. Vegetarians could try roast butternut squash and cumin tagliatelle or herb risotto with griddled aubergine and halloumi. Wonderful desserts include steamed chocolate pud with strawberry yogurt ice cream, banana and saffron parfait or damson and sweet ginger pie.

S V P C

MARPLE BRIDGE

Lane End Inn

2 Ley Lane, SK6 5DD

- From Marple Station take Lowerfold, turn right on Glossop Rd, top of the hill
- Tue-Thu 12-2.30pm, 4.30pm-midnight; Fri-Sun 12pm-midnight
- Tue-Thu 12-2.30pm, 5-8pm; Fri-Sun 12-7pm
- T (0161) 427 5226
- Caledonian Deuchars IPA; guests
- Wholesome, home-made food served with masses of steamed vegetables
- Spacious, stone pub benefiting from lovely country views; children are welcome with play areas for them; the old local photos are worth a look

It is a long uphill climb here from Marple Station a mile away, but fortunately when you get to the pub you will be rewarded with enormous portions of food. Happily for the fainthearted or not so nimble visitor the Glossop-Hazel Grove bus passes the door. All the main course meals come with great platefuls of healthy steamed vegetables – they usually cook seven or eight at each session – or if you prefer you can have salad, plus chips or potatoes.

The regular menu normally includes roast beef and Yorkshire pud, home-made lasagne and pies of various fillings, liver and onions, braised steak, half a roast chicken, lemon and garlic chicken fillet, or chicken stuffed with Brie and asparagus served with white wine sauce, lamb cutlets, griddled pork steaks and chilli con carne. All are priced at around £6.75. Steaks are good value too: prime fillet or a 16oz rump or T-bone for £9.50; an 8oz sirloin or rib eye for £8.50. There are always some special dishes on, such as horseshoe gammon, egg and pineapple, home battered cod, chips and mushy peas or roast lamb. Children can choose from their own menu, and snacks such as burgers and sandwiches are also served.

★ Q S V (Marple) P C

STOCKPORT
Arden Arms
23 Millgate, SK1 2LX

▶ Behind Asda in town centre
☼ Mon-Sat 12-11pm; Sun 12-10.30pm
Mon-Fri 12-2.30pm; Sat & Sun 12-4pm
T (0161) 480 2185
E steve@ardensarms.com
Robinson's Hatters, Best Bitter, Old Tom (winter), seasonal beers
☺ High quality, simple pub lunches with a cosmopolitan flavour
Grade II listed pub with handsome bar, tiled lobby, grandfather clocks, two fires and superb snug; local CAMRA Pub of the Year 2004

Landlord and chef Joe Quinn has been at the Arden for five years; previously he ran successful Manchester restaurant The Café. Here he provides food at lunchtimes only, dishing up an interesting range of budget snacks and specials. There is always home-made soup of the day at £2.50 (or just a cup for 75p), freshly-made sandwiches including smoked salmon for £3.25, special hot sandwiches on ciabatta from roast peppers and mozzarella to sirloin steak with caramelised red onions, and the all day breakfast of three scrambled eggs and smoked salmon on toast at £5.25.

The home-made specials board changes daily, a sample selection includes goats' cheese and red pepper crêpe with salad and pan fried potatoes, steak and ale pie with onion gravy, mash and roasted vegetables, Thai red chicken curry with basmati rice and prawn crackers or Cajun style cod with spinach and mango salsa served with roast vine tomatoes, prices from £6.25-£7.95. Joe serves a roast on Sundays. Desserts change daily, all £3.25, maybe sticky toffee pudding, Dutch apple crumble or banana and toffee sponge. Produce, meat and fish are sourced from local suppliers with cheese from local farms via Stockport market.

★ Q S V ♿ ⇌ (Stockport)

STOCKPORT
Tiviot
8 Tiviot Dale, SK1 1TA

▶ In town centre
☼ Mon-Sat 11am-11pm; Sun 12-4pm
Tues-Sat 11.30am-2.30pm
T (0161) 480 4109
Robinson's Unicorn, Hatters, Old Tom
☺ Traditional pub fare, all home made
Old-fashioned pub run by friendly, long serving licensees; central bar serves four rooms – a lively vault, long room with table football, lounge and dining room

Though the pub has been run by the same family for more than 40 years, landlady Jill Woolley only started the catering side fairly recently and already the Tiviot is gaining a reputation for good, wholesome, home-made food. Jill describes the menu as very traditional, with a choice of three roast lunches (beef with Yorkshire pudding, lamb and mint sauce, turkey and stuffing), braised steak, home-made steak, chicken, ham and leek or cheese and onion pies, all with real short crust pastry toppings, and liver and onions. All main courses are a bargain £4 complete with fresh vegetables such as mashed carrots with swede, green beans, cauliflower cheese, roast potatoes, crisp chips or mash.

Also very popular are the roast meat muffins – giant teacakes with hot roast beef and onions, pork and stuffing or turkey and cranberry sauce, accompanied by chips and salad at only £2.50. Snacks also include toasties, jacket spuds, baguettes and burgers, around £2-£3. Despite the low prices portions are generous, but do try and leave room for one of the tempting desserts, all priced £2.75. Food is served Tuesday to Saturday lunchtime only.

★ S V ♿ P C

WEST DIDSBURY
Metropolitan
2 Lapwing Lane, M20 2WS

- Corner of Burton Road and Lapwing Lane near Withington Hospital
- Mon-Sat 11.30am-11pm; Sun 12-10.30pm
- Mon-Thu 12-9.30pm; Fri & Sat 12-10pm; Sun 12-9pm

T (0161) 374 9559
F (0161) 282 6544
E barry_lavin@the-metropolitan.co.uk
W www.the-metropolitan.co.uk

- Caledonian Deuchars IPA; Marston's Pedigree; Taylor Landlord
- Modern British cooking with traditional Sunday lunches and evening à la carte
- Former Victorian railway hotel with a traditional interior and wood fires, outside bar in summer

Plenty of choice is offered by the kitchen team, providing quality bar and à la carte restaurant food. The daytime menu from 12-6pm starts with home-made soup, goats' cheese and cheddar pâté or warm chorizo and potato salad with orange and mint dressing, £3.50-£5.25. A salad, pasta and risotto section includes Caesar salad with fresh anchovies, goats' cheese and pancetta or gnocchi and mozzarella gratin, while mains range from the traditional (Cumberland sausages with mustard mash) to the modern (chicken, halloumi and red pepper stack), prices from £8.50 to £12.95 for sole with prawns.

Some dishes reappear on the evening menu, where you will also find starters such as sautéed chicken livers with bacon, hand-dived scallops with pancetta and dandelion salad or fennel carpaccio with Parma ham and truffle oil. Main courses at night include lamb rump in yoghurt and saffron marinade with pilau rice, roast loin of venison with roast artichokes, chorizo and tiger prawn risotto with red beans, tagine of monkfish and duck leg confit – and, for vegetarians, skewers of char-grilled halloumi and Mediterranean vegetables with rice and hot red pepper chutney, £8.95-£12.95. From 5-7pm, two courses are £6.95.

★ S V C

WORTHINGTON
Crown Hotel
19-21 Platt Lane, WN1 2XF

- Off A5106 between Wigan and Chorley
- Daily 12-11pm (10.30pm Sun)
- Mon-Fri 12-2.30pm, 5.30-9.30pm; Sat 12-9.30pm; Sun 12-8.30pm

T (01257) 421354
F (01257) 428981
E dan@thecrownatworthington.co.uk
W www.thecrownatworthington.co.uk

- Beer range varies
- Good variety of home-cooked dishes, excellent value fixed-price menu
- Country inn in rural Lancashire that has been given a new lease of life; meals are served in the bar and no-smoking conservatory/restaurant

A rare outlet for the local Mayflower Brewery, the Crown offers beers from micro-breweries all around the country. It is also well worth a visit for the food, based on locally-sourced produce, including fish from Fleetwood and properly hung beef from nearby farms. In fact steaks are one of the specialities here; on its 'butcher's block' menu you can build your own steak meal, choosing your own cut (priced per 100 grams), length of cooking, sauces and extras.

The fixed price menu offers excellent value for money at a mere £5.95 for a main course plus £2.50 each for starters and desserts. You could begin with smoked mackerel mousse, deep-fried Welsh goats' cheese, a trio of shellfish (cockles, mussels and prawns) or pan-fried black pudding on crushed potato with tomato and horseradish sauce. To follow there is a choice of gammon steak, a trio of home-made bangers and mash, pan-fried lamb's liver, poached fresh haddock fillet, a daily roast or butternut squash and spinach risotto as a veggie option. Home-made puddings include a daily fruit pie, chef's choice of hot pudding and – something rarely encountered on a menu these days – real home-made creamed rice pudding, served with cream, jam or syrup.

Q S V C

LIVERPOOL
Everyman Bistro & Bars
5-9 Hope Street, L1 9BH

- Hope Street links the two cathedrals
- Mon-Sat 12-midnight (2am Fri & Sat); closed Sun
- Mon-Sat 12pm until shortly before last drinks orders
- T (0151) 708 9545
- F (0151) 709 3515
- E bistro@everyman.co.uk
- W www.everyman.co.uk
- Cains Bitter; guests
- A mix of British and international dishes
- Busy cellar bar and restaurant beneath the theatre where drinkers and diners mingle

Head chef Tom Gill leads a team of six creating a great variety of good value, award-winning dishes. All the meals are produced from scratch from the very best ingredients sourced daily from local markets, farmers and specialist suppliers, many of whom number among Rick Stein's 'Food Heroes'. Dishes are cooked in small batches and displayed buffet style, so your selection is reheated by microwave. The menu changes twice a day, combining traditional dishes such as shepherds pie, home-cooked outdoor reared ham with new potatoes and Aberdeen Angus beef braised in beer, with more adventurous offerings - maybe Moroccan lamb couscous or roast paprika chicken with chorizo mash. The bistro is popular with vegetarians – Tom maintains that the secret of good vegetarian food is to allow natural flavours to stand up for themselves, not to try and disguise the fact that no meat is in the dish –with the result that many meat eaters also choose his veggie dishes, particularly the sweet potato and spinach curry and the Lancashire cheese, leek and potato bake, perfect with a glass of real ale. Two pastry chefs provide a dazzling array of traditional puds and modern classics making good use of seasonal fruit. Excellent snacks, pizzas, fresh salads and soups (try the Indonesian chicken) are also served.

S V (Lime Street) (Central)

LIVERPOOL
Fly in the Loaf
13 Hardman Street, L1 9AS

- Mon-Thu 12-11pm; Fri & Sat 12pm-midnight; Sun 12-10.30pm
- Daily 12-7pm
- T (0151) 708 0817
- F (0151) 706 0895
- E thefly@manx.net
- Okells Bitter, seasonal; guests
- Straightforward pub food plus varied snacks and salads
- Bakery refurbished with ecclesiastical fittings; attracts a good cross section of customers from students to theatregoers

'No flies in the loaf' was the slogan of the bakery that became the Fly, hence the name. Opened by Okells Brewery in 2004, it is the second Manx Cat inn on the mainland. Meals are served throughout the day until early evening; the Sunday roasts are highly recommended. For a reasonable price of £7.50 for two courses or three for £8.25 there's a choice of three starters, roast meat, chicken or a vegetarian choice and indulgent desserts such as Irish cream liqueur cheesecake with ice cream or chocolate fudge cake with cream.

Main meals the rest of the week major on good, home-made traditional pub grub such as a curry of the day, home-made burger topped with bacon, pineapple and cheese, steak and Okells pie with proper chips and seasonal veg or fresh cod fillet in beer batter with mushy peas, all £6.50 or less. A good range of salads is also on offer, such as tuna and mixed olives, coronation chicken, salmon fillet and prawns or peppered sirloin strips with melted Stilton. The range of sandwiches is also varied – fillings include roasted herby vegetables, chipolata sausages in honey and herbs, prawns in Creole mayo, tuna and cheese melt or the classic BLT, all priced £2.75-£3.95 in brown or white bread or an extra £1.10 for a baguette.

S V (Liverpool Lime Street) (Central) **C**

RABY
Wheatsheaf Inn
Raby Mere Road, CH63 4JH

▶ Off B5151 (accessible from M53 jct 4)
☼ Daily 11.30am-11pm
Ⓕ Daily 12-2pm, 6-9pm (not Sun & Mon eve)
T (0151) 336 3416
F (0151) 353 1976
Caledonian Deuchars IPA; Greene King Old Speckled Hen; Tetley Bitter; Theakston Best Bitter, Old Peculier; Wells Bombardier; guests
☺ Extensive bar menu plus excellent restaurant, the Cowshed
Historic, thatched pub with an inglenook and suntrap garden; meals can be enjoyed in the bar or the award-winning restaurant

Possibly the oldest pub on the Wirral, the 'Thatch', as it is known locally, is very popular with CAMRA members for its choice of no fewer than nine cask ales. The bar menu is extensive too –toasties come in almost 50 varieties based around fillings of cheese, bacon, black pudding, ham and tuna, for around £3-£4.50. Other 'light bites' also double as starters, such as duck parfait (terrine with Cumberland sauce and warm toast), soup of the day and salads. Main courses include pub favourites such as cod or plaice and chips, steak and ale pie, a mixed grill, gammon steak, or various omelettes. The specials board lists a fish, pasta and roast of the day. Meat is all sourced locally and the Sunday lunch special, £12.95 for three courses, offers a choice of four roasts as well as grilled sirloin steak or fish of the day.

The Cowshed restaurant is pricier but offers fine dining: starters of fresh figs and peach salad, Loch Fyne gravadlax or smoked black pudding with oyster mushrooms can be followed by fillet steak royale, pan-fried barbary duck breast with honey and ginger or plum sauce, wok-fried Caribbean chicken or lamb Henry (braised shoulder with redcurrant and apricot sauce), plus good fish and grills, £13-£17. Children are allowed at lunchtimes only.

★ Q S V C

Fish is a speciality at the Lighthouse Inn, Walcott in Norfolk where they serve locally landed fish in home-made batter. Here is their recipe for fresh salmon.

SALMON FILLET WITH WHITE WINE AND PARSLEY SAUCE
Serves 4

4 portions salmon fillet
2 whole fresh lemons
1 tbsp black peppercorns
1 bunch fresh parsley
50g (2oz) firm margarine
50g (2oz) plain flour
½ tsp dry mustard powder
600ml (1 pint) milk
300ml (½ pint) medium dry white wine
Salt and pepper

Place salmon fillets, one lemon cut into wedges, black peppercorns and a third of the parsley into a deep frying pan with enough water to barely cover. Bring to simmering point and cook gently for around 5 minutes until just cooked. Meanwhile, melt the margarine in a saucepan, add the flour and mix in, cooking gently until all the margarine has been absorbed. Add the dry mustard powder and gradually pour on the milk, stirring continuously to prevent lumps. Still stirring, slowly squeeze in the juice of the second lemon, add the wine and as much finely-chopped parsley as you like, season and remove from the heat. Place salmon fillets on four warm plates, lightly coat with the sauce and serve the remainder in a sauceboat. Garnish with lemon twists and sprigs of parsley, and serve with new potatoes and fine green beans.

BARFORD
Cock Inn
Watton Road, NR9 4AS

- 7 miles W of Norwich on B1108
- Mon-Sat 12-3pm, 6-11pm; Sun 12-3pm, 7-10.30pm
- Mon-Sat 12-2pm, 6-9pm; Sun 12-2.30pm, 7-9pm
- T (01603) 757646
- Blue Moon Easy Life, Sea of Tranquillity, Hingham High, seasonal
- Freshly-made bar snacks and full à la carte with fish a speciality
- Home to Blue Moon Brewery; wood burner in public bar; bowls green and croquet lawn

As well as brewing real ales, the Cock serves up some fine food to go with them. The daily changing fish selection is especially tempting with choices such as fish pie of salmon, prawn and cod, Indonesian style red snapper, baked trout fillets cooked with cherry tomatoes, prawns, mushrooms and herbs, tuna with black olive mash, skate wing with caper cutter, or Barford cod in Blue Moon beer batter, prices from £8.95 up to £14.95 for a whole Dover sole. Meat dishes might be Downham duck with rich plum sauce, grilled pork chop with mushroom, bacon and Stilton sauce, venison steak with cassis or chump of lamb with port and redcurrant gravy, £11.95-£13.95, and £8.95 for a vegetarian choice such as Thai green curry or gnocchi.

The bar menu features gammon with local eggs and chips, £4.95, pie of the day such as steak and kidney or game in winter, cottage pie with fresh vegetables, haddock and spring onion fishcakes with white wine sauce or tagliatelle with smoked salmon and crayfish in cream sauce, prices £5.75-£6.95. Snacks include a full choice of baguettes and sandwiches from £3.95 up to £5.95 for rump steak with onion, and hot pitta filled with Greek salad and beef marinated in soya and ginger or roast Mediterranean vegetables. The traditional Sunday roast is £6.95.

S V P C

BRANCASTER STAITHE
Jolly Sailors
Main road, PE31 8BJ

- A149 between Hunstanton and Wells-Next-the-Sea
- Mon-Sat 11am-11pm; Sun 12-10.30pm
- Daily 12-9pm
- T (01485) 210314
- E jayatjolly@aol.com
- W www.jollysailors.co.uk
- Brancaster IPA, Old Les; Woodforde's Wherry; guest
- Home-made, fresh pub food with plenty of local and seasonal produce
- 18th-century pub with two restaurants and large beer garden; home to Brancaster Brewery

With its own micro-brewery and a growing reputation for both good food and decent ale, the Jolly Sailors, dating back to 1789, has gone from strength to strength over recent years, and now claims the largest food output on the Norfolk coast. It has a public bar, two restaurants and beer garden with children's play area. Menus are written up on chalk boards, changing according to the season, but with an emphasis on fresh local fish. A typical selection includes Brancaster Brewery beer-battered haddock, Norton Creek oysters baked in chilli sauce topped with Stilton, locally smoked cod, whole grilled Brancaster seabass, Norfolk wild mushrooms and red pepper pasta, feta cheese with black olive and sun dried tomato salad, slow braised lamb shank with mash, and Wells sausage served with mash and onion gravy. Meat, including fine rump steaks, comes from local butcher and grazier Arthur Howells. One of the most popular dishes at the pub is its version of moules marinière cooked with local mussels, white wine and double cream. Booking is advisable on summer evenings when the pub gets extremely busy. Cider is available in summer only.

★ Q S V P C

BRANCASTER STAITHE
☆ White Horse
PE31 8BY

- On A149 coast road between Hunstanton and Wells-Next-the-Sea
- Mon-Sat 11am-11pm; Sun 12-10.30pm
- Daily 12-2pm, 7-9pm
- T (01485) 210262
- F (01485) 210930
- E reception@whitehorsebrancaster.co.uk
- W www.whitehorsebrancaster.co.uk
- Adnams Bitter; Fuller's London Pride; Woodforde's Wherry; guests
- Modern British cuisine with flair
- Excellent seaside pub and award-winning hotel on the beautiful Norfolk coast; cosy front bar with log fire; superb sea views

Chips are hand cut, all bread, pasta, ice creams and sorbets home made, everything is freshly prepared on the premises using local Norfolk ingredients, including meat reared and slaughtered locally, at this renowned inn. Menus change monthly but with daily extras – typical starters might be haddock chowder with poached egg, half a dozen local oysters, Cyril's Brancaster Staithe mussels in cream and wine sauce, Letzer's local smoked salmon, or sweet potato and cumin soup, £3.95-£7.95.

Main courses might feature roast cod with wild mushrooms, poached halibut with hand-dived scallops, black bream with fresh herb linguine, best end of English lamb with colcannon potatoes, steamed steak and onion pudding or corned beef hash on toasted muffin with fried egg and capers, mostly £9.25-£12.95. The roast fillet of beef with rosti potato, spinach purée and roast salsify is £17. Vegetarian starters include plum tomatoes with Norfolk goats' cheese and lemon oil, or pepper tempura with chilli dipping sauce, main dishes, parsley tagliatelle with slow baked tomatoes, asparagus and wild mushrooms. Home-made puds, all £4.50, include steamed rum and raisin sponge with apple ice cream or lemon tart with sweet pickled raspberries.

S V

ELSING
Mermaid
Church Street, NR20 3EA

- Take North Tuddenham turn from A47, follow signs to Elsing
- Mon-Fri 12-3.30pm, 7-11pm; Sat 12-3.30pm, 6-11pm; Sun 6.30-10.30pm
- Mon-Fri 12-2pm, 7-9pm; Sat & Sun 12-2.30pm, 7-9pm
- T (01362) 637640
- Adnams Broadside; Wolf Golden Jackal; Woodforde's Wherry; guests
- Traditional English home-prepared meals, ingredients sourced locally
- 17th-century free house in the upper Wensum Valley, modernised interior has main bar with games area, pool table and brick fireplace

Farmers' markets and local suppliers provide the vegetables for the Mermaid, while locally-raised meat including fine steaks comes from a butcher two miles away. Good old-fashioned dishes usually on the menu include gammon joints cooked on the premises, steamed steak and kidney roly poly, cottage pie, liver braised with onions and Stilton and walnut tarts for vegetarians – the walnuts from the tree in the car park. The cooks are the landlord and landlady Helen Higgins and Kevin Wills – Kevin says the traditional dishes are inspired by what they ate as children and favourite recipes from his mum.

A 'tropical' garden behind the pub, with all sorts of exotic plants, is a popular place to eat in summer. Snacks are served in the bar, and there is a no smoking restaurant where children are welcome. All cask ales come from East Anglian breweries, with the house beer brewed by Wolf in Attleborough. To walk off your meal, visit the 14th-century church opposite, which boasts the widest unsupported nave of any parish church in England, as well as interesting brasses and an octagonal font with an ornate canopy.

S V C

FOULDEN
White Hart Inn
White Hart Street, IP26 5AW

- 2 miles off A134 Thetford to King's Lynn
- Mon-Thu 11am-3pm, 5-11pm; Fri & Sat 11am-11pm; Sun 12-10.30pm
- Daily 12-2.30pm, 7-9pm
- T (01366) 328638
- Greene King IPA, Abbot; guests
- Traditional British cooking with international influences; plenty of fresh fish and local produce
- Family-run, flint-built, village free house surrounded by woodland; real fire and wooden beams

Using barley-fed beef from the local butcher, fresh fish from the Norfolk coast every Wednesday, and local fruit, vegetables and free range eggs, landlady Ann Moss dishes up a sterling menu. Daily changing specials could be black pudding with fried apples in cider, beef and dumplings in real ale, pork sausages with Cumberland sauce, goats' cheese and spinach omelette, Greek lamb stew with feta, teriyaki beef or roasted vegetables on couscous.

Set menu starters include avocado with prawns, four wedges of deep fried Brie with redcurrant jelly, deep-fried king prawns with chilli dip or fresh melon served with port or prawns, priced £3.75-£4.75. Main meals include steak and kidney pudding with potatoes and vegetables, home-baked ham with free-range egg, chips and peas, deep-filled steak and ale pie topped with short crust pastry, £6.50 with potatoes and vegetables, cod or haddock in batter and pan-fried salmon with honey and ginger sauce, prices from £5-£8.50. A wide range of grills includes rib eye, fillet, sirloin, T-bone and gammon steaks, £9.95-£13.95. Omelettes made from three free-range eggs are especially good value – cheese, ham, mushroom and Stilton or prawn, with chips and peas, around £5. Sunday lunch is popular and the over-60s lunch club is held on the first Wednesday of every month.

S V

GAYTON
Crown
Lynn Road, PE32 1PA

- B1145, 5 miles from King's Lynn
- Mon-Thu 12-2.30pm, 6-11pm; Fri & Sat 11-11pm; Sun 12-10.30pm
- Mon-Thu 12-2pm, 7-9pm; Fri-Sun 12-9pm
- T (01553) 636252
- E crownath2wf@supanet.com
- Greene King XX Mild, IPA, Abbot, Old Speckled Hen; guest
- Lunchtime buffet and bar snacks, evening à la carte
- Thriving, friendly village pub with a variety of small drinking areas, log fire in winter; West Norfolk CAMRA pub of the Year 2004

The best of both worlds – an inexpensive, hot buffet and no-frills snacks at lunchtime, good daily specials, and an imaginative à la carte with better than average vegetarian dishes at night. Starting with bar meals, there is home-made soup daily at £3.25, a selection of sandwiches in freshly baked bloomers at £2.75 served with crisps and salad, ploughman's of mixed cheese, fresh haddock in batter, home-baked ham, free range eggs and chips, or home-made steak and kidney pie, prices £4.95-£6.95. Daily specials include old-fashioned favourites such as liver and bacon in red wine, steak and kidney pudding, honey glazed rack of lamb, Lancashire hot pot and a seasonal game dish – generally partridge, pheasant, teal or pigeon, prices £8.30-£8.95.

On the à la carte, you could start with grilled halloumi and crispy bacon, savoury crêpe of the day, duck liver pâté or local mushrooms in Stilton, prices around £4. Those veggie dishes include aubergines stuffed with vegetables topped with cheese. Fish dishes range from fresh plaice in crispy batter to black bream or Dover sole, £9.85-£12.95, and meat includes grills, Stilton-stuffed chicken, duck breast with raspberry sauce and quarter leg of lamb slow roasted with onions and garlic, from £9.65 to £12.95 for fillet steak.

★ Q S V C

HARPLEY

Rose & Crown

Nethergate Street, PE31 6TW

- Harpley is signed off A148 between King's Lynn and Fakenham
- Daily 12-3pm, 6.30-11.30pm
- Daily 12-2pm, 6.30-9.30pm
- T (01458) 520577
- E john.carol@mail.com
- Courage Directors; Greene King IPA, Abbot; guest
- Inventive, high quality, varied menu at reasonable prices
- Classic country pub, warmed by real fires

The Rose and Crown is close to Houghton Hall, renowned for its herd of white deer and peacocks, and well worth a visit before lunch at the pub. Interesting sandwiches include grilled halloumi and mint mayo, grilled aubergine and feta, or Peking duck, hoisin sauce and spring onion salad, all priced at £4.50. More substantial dishes range from home-cooked ham or free range egg and hand-cut chips to chicken Caesar salad with fresh anchovies or mushroom stroganoff with wild rice, £6.25-£8.25. All the food here is home cooked from locally-sourced produce.

The main menu offers some truly inventive dishes: whitebait with orange and home-made tartare sauce, grilled goats' cheese crumpet with onion marmalade, sweet cured herring with apple and caper salad or moules marinière, £5.25 or under for starters. To follow, vegetarian options include triple stack quesadilla with beans, jalapenos, salsa, cheese and guacamole, grilled halloumi with spaghetti Vicenza and mushroom chow mein. For fish and meat eaters there is a choice of Goan monkfish curry with spicy brinjalli rice, pan-fried red mullet fillets with three bean colcannon and salsa rosso, veal chop with gnocchi Romanov, roast belly pork with pink peppered mash and sweet and sour apple or lamb kofta meatballs with apricot and almond couscous, £6.25 to £15 for fillet steak.

Q S V P C

ITTERINGHAM

☆ Walpole Arms

The Common, NR11 7AR

- B1354 from Aylsham, first right after Blickling Hall
- Mon-Sat 12-3pm, 6-11pm; Sun 12-3pm, 7-10.30pm
- Mon-Sat 12-2pm, 7-9.30pm; Sun 12.30-2.30pm
- T (01263) 587258
- F (01263) 587074
- E goodfood@thewalpolearms.co.uk
- W www.thewalpolearms.co.uk
- Adnams Bitter, Broadside; Woodforde's Wherry; guest
- Multi award-winning gastropub with Michelin recognition and renowned chef creating exciting dishes from local produce
- 18th-century oak-beamed country pub with a romantic restaurant

Andrew Parle (ex Terence Conran and Alastair Little restaurants) is head chef, most recently winner of the Morning Advertiser regional Gastropub of the Year 2005. Changing the menu on a daily basis, in winter Andrew generally opts for stews and game, in summer looks to the Med for inspiration, regularly featuring local produce such as Morston mussels and venison from Gunton Hall.

Starters such as sweet potato and fennel soup with Israeli couscous, pigeon, pheasant and hare terrine with home-made chutney, home-cured gravadlax or breadcrumbed parsnip chips with mustard and honey mayonnaise are £5-£6. Main courses might include bolito misto of pork belly, chicken, ham and smoked sausage with salsa verde, haddock in beer batter with hand-cut chips, tripe braised with chorizo and chickpeas, or Morston mussels in cider, onions and thyme, prices from £10.50-£12.50. Vegetarian dishes could be feuillette of Swiss chard, mushrooms and gruyere or bulgar wheat and halloumi kibbi. On the snack menu you might find smoked sprats with granary bread and ham, eggs and real chips.

★ Q S V P C

KENNINGHALL
Red Lion
East Church Street, NR16 2EP

▶ Just off village centre
☼ Mon-Thu 12-3pm, 6.30-11pm; Fri-Sun 12-11pm
🍴 Daily 12-2pm, 7-9pm
T (01953) 887849
Greene King IPA, Abbot Ale; Woodforde's Wherry; guests
☺ Home-cooked traditional and oriental dishes featuring local meat and produce
Grade II listed, pink painted 18th-century inn with many original features; main bar with wood floors and old photos, garden with bowling green

With many awards for its real ale (Norfolk and Norwich CAMRA Pub of the Year, Country Mild Pub of the Year), the Red Lion is further enhanced by landlady Mary Berry's cooking. On her snack menu she provides a cheese ploughman's, or farmer's with the addition of ham, steak sandwich and chips, home-cooked ham, egg and chips, filled jacket potatoes and baguettes.

As well as a constantly changing specials board there is a full set menu with everything cooked to order. It offers starters such as the unusual rabbit satay with peanut sauce, smoked duck salad and home-made soup, £3.95-£4.95, followed by main courses including seafood pancakes, char-grilled tiger prawns in ginger, garlic and chilli, Pacific game fish escolar or salmon and roast pepper fishcakes, £8.95-£11.95. Meat dishes include beef and mushroom pie with a Guinness stock, char-grilled local sausages with mustard mash and onion gravy, chicken breast marinated in lime and chilli then char grilled, rack of pork ribs with barbecue sauce, £7.95 to £9.95, grilled steaks and mixed grill of sirloin steak, local sausages, bacon, and lamb cutlet, £8.95-£11.95. If you are really hungry go for the 32oz rump steak at £19.95!

★ Q ❀ S V P C

LARLING
Angel Inn
NR16 2QU

▶ Just off A11, 1 mile S of Snetterton
☼ Mon-Sat 10am-11pm; Sun 12-10.30pm
🍴 Mon-Thu 12-2pm, 6.30-9.30pm; Fri 12-2.30pm, 6.30-10pm; Sat 12-10pm; Sun 12-9.30pm
T (01953) 717963
F (01953) 718561
Adnams Bitter; guests
☺ Wide choice of excellent home-cooked fare from traditional to Indian to snacks
Excellent pub popular with local farming committee and Norwich City FC supporters; beer festival every August

Using local produce, the Angel achieves a huge range of dishes all prepared on the premises, from hearty snacks such as home-made beef burgers, ploughman's toasties, Welsh rarebit or home-cooked ham with egg and chips to soups such as broccoli with cheese or tomato and orange. Main dishes might be a trio of pork loin steaks served 'farmer style' with mushrooms, onions and potatoes in herb butter, or tournedos Dubois – prime fillet steak in Stilton, cream, Madeira and green peppercorn sauce. Popular fish dishes include the Angel's special fisherman's crumble combining fresh cod, haddock, salmon, prawns and pasta in cheese sauce under paprika flavoured crumble, or fresh salmon and asparagus in home made crêpes with tarragon sauce, main meals around £7.50-£10. A good selection of home-made veggie choices includes cannelloni filled with fresh spinach and ricotta. Indian dishes are lamb balti and chicken korma. There are also daily specials such as deep-fried cod or haddock in crisp Adnams Bitter batter, or steak and pig's kidney pie containing real ale, topped with home-made shortcrust pastry. Four ever changing guest ales include beers from micro-breweries such as Orkney, Wolf and Iceni.

★ Q ❀ S V ♣ P C

NORWICH
Coach & Horses
82 Thorpe Road, NR1 1BA

- ▶ 400 yards from station
- Mon-Sat 11am-11pm; Sun 11-10.30pm
- Mon-Sat 12-9pm; Sun 11am-8pm
- T (01603) 477077
- E info@thecoachthorperoad.co.uk
- W www.thecoachthorperoad.co.uk
- Chalk Hill Tap, CHB, Dreadnought, Flintknapper's Mild, Old Tackle; guests
- ☺ Fine fare from snacks to main meals and Sunday roasts with plenty of fish
- Coaching inn dating from 1811, the large bar has several drinking areas; home to Chalk Hill Brewery

The home of Chalk Hill Brewery often uses its own wide range of ales in pies and casseroles, as well as produce from local suppliers, with all meat of British origin. The interesting pub grub menu is brilliant value, including large, warm pittas with fillings from smoked salmon and scrambled egg to pesto, mushrooms and mozzarella, under £5, juicy 6oz steak sandwich with salad at £5.25, giant jacket spuds with all sorts of fillings from £3-£4, 100 per cent beef burgers with chips 'chipped on the premises' with toppings from £5-£6, home-made vegetarian 'beastless burgers', home-made fish cakes with sauté potatoes at £5.70, and those hand-cut chips served in large portions plain or with toppings from Old Tackle beer gravy to sweet chilli, £2-£2.50.

There are also plenty of specials: home-made soup such as mushroom and tarragon or tomato and basil, home-made pies or casseroles, and always home-made veggie specials such as flat mushrooms filled with sun blush tomatoes, and mozzarella with crisp crumb and Parmesan topping. Fish specials are especially popular from the traditional, such as cod, tuna and haddock, to the exotic, maybe Nile perch or escolar. Sunday sees the traditional roast – beef or pork with all the trimmings and beer gravy.

S V (Norwich) P C

STOW BARDOLPH
☆ Hare Arms
PE34 3HT

- ▶ Off A10, two miles from Downham Market
- Mon-Sat 10.30am-2.30pm, 6-11pm; Sun 12-2.30pm, 7-10.30pm
- Daily 12-2pm, 7-10pm
- T (01366) 382229
- F (01366) 385522
- W www.theharearms.co.uk
- Greene King IPA, Abbot, Old Speckled Hen; guest beer
- ☺ Wholesome bar meals and more adventurous specials and restaurant meals
- Beautiful, ivy clad pub in an idyllic setting in a quiet Norfolk village; elegant restaurant; children welcome in conservatory

Visitors to this lovely, archetypal village pub will find excellent ales and wonderful food as well as a warm welcome in the atmospheric bar, especially in winter when a bright fire blazes in the hearth. A choice of award-winning bar meals, daily specials, the restaurant's three-course set menu at £22.50 (served Mon-Fri) or à la carte caters for all appetites and tastes. On the table d'hote menu you will find smoked sprats with horseradish dip, Cajun chicken and avocado, risotto cakes or melon with yogurt to start, followed by chicken breast topped with peppers, spring onions and mascarpone and oven-baked pork fillet with pear and thyme stuffing, slow-cooked lamb shank, turkey breast marinated in coriander, chilli and lime, vegetarian puff pastry parcel, or fish of the day. Vegetarians are well catered for, with a choice of six starters and seven main courses, including jalapeno poppers filled with cream cheese and deep fried, sweet pepper and chilli tart tatin, nut cutlets with a spicy chilli dip, and ravioli filled with mozzarella, goats' cheese, black olives and tomatoes. If you go à la carte expect to pay £5-£7.50 for a starter and a minimum of £14.50 for the main course. All the food is freshly cooked using locally sourced ingredients. Some children's portions are available, including the Sunday roast.

★ S V P C

TERRINGTON ST JOHN
Woolpack
Main Road, PE14 7RR

- ▶ On A47 between King's Lynn and Wisbech
- Mon-Sat 11.30am-2.30pm, 6.30-11pm; Sun 11.30am-2.30pm, 7-10.30pm
- Mon-Thu 12-2pm; 6.30-9pm; Fri & Sat 12-2pm, 6.30-9.30pm; Sun 12-2pm, 7-9pm
- T (01945) 881097
- F (01945) 881242
- W www.wool-pack-inn.co.uk
- Wells Eagle; guests
- ☺ Good home-cooked pub favourites plus innovative specials
- Historic three-storey pub dating back to the late 19th century; a traditional village inn featuring modern geometric prints and specially commissioned glass panels

Australian landlady Lucille Carter ensures that any event is celebrated in style, and there is nearly always a good excuse for a party here, so it may not be the best place for a quiet, intimate meal, however the home-cooked food is excellent. As well as the head chef whose specialities are Thai, Indian and Chinese food there is a full-time vegan cook who produces top notch vegetarian dishes, including an alternative to the traditional Sunday roasts. Two specials boards, chalked up daily, always offer a fresh fish dish.

The regular menu lists house favourites such as chicken and bacon tower in a creamy peppercorn sauce, grilled lamb cutlets with rosemary, garlic and redcurrant glaze in minted jus, honey and mustard roast gammon and steak and kidney suet pudding; while fish lovers can choose from pan-fried red snapper or fresh tuna, Whitby scampi and chips, or a Thai fish curry. Main courses are mostly £7-£10; children are offered half portions of some dishes. Hot and cold desserts are freshly prepared every day (not all in the pub's kitchen); sugar-free and diabetic options are also available. Indeed, with notice the chef can rise to any culinary challenge whether for dietary reasons or because a customer would like something different.

S V P C

THORNHAM
Lifeboat Inn
Ship Lane, PE36 6LT

- ▶ A149 from Hunstanton, left into Church Street in Thornham village
- Daily 11am-11pm
- Daily 12-2.30pm, 6.30-9.30pm
- T (01485) 512236
- F (01485) 512323
- E reception@lifeboatinn.co.uk
- W www.lifeboatinn.co.uk
- Adnams Bitter; Greene King IPA; Woodforde's Wherry; guests
- ☺ Tempting, imaginative food featuring local produce, especially fish
- 16th-century smugglers' alehouse on the North Norfolk coast retaining original features including oil-burning lamps: 'children, dogs and muddy boots welcome'

I have eaten memorably in the Lifeboat but not on my most recent visit when, after painstakingly moving enough chairs to an abandoned little table, we realised there were many, many to feed before us... well, it was New Year's Day. But I'll be back for mussels, crabs, oysters and lobsters from the local fishermen, and fresh fish in beer batter. With menus changing daily, you might start with soup such as butternut squash, sweet potato and leek, Cromer crab with salad in seafood dressing, or fried mullet with sweet chilli sauce, £3.95 to £5.25. Main courses in the bar could be home-made chicken and mushroom fricassée topped with short crust pastry and mash, roast crispy duck with pecan and cranberry stuffing, shepherd's pie with cheesy mash, local venison sausages with olive mash and red onion gravy, seared marlin loin with noodles, fillet of bigeye Trevally with shellfish risotto or game casserole in cider with apricots, all accompanied by vegetables at £8-12.95. Desserts change daily, too – how about winterberry meringue, lavender pannacotta, chocolate and Guinness sponge, hazelnut torte, or banana fritters with butterscotch sauce, all £3.90 with cream, custard or ice cream?

★ S V P C

WALCOTT

Lighthouse Inn

Coast Road, NR12 OPE

- ▶ On B1159
- Mon-Sat 11am-11pm; Sun 12-10.30pm
- Daily 11am (12 Sun)-10.30pm
- T (01692) 650371
- E thelighthouseinn@amserve.net
- W www.lighthouseinn.co.uk
- Adnams Bitter; guests
- Wide ranging menu of interesting, home-made food including locally-landed fish
- Large pub on Yarmouth-Cromer coast road; free house since 1989 with bar, dining room and covered terrace

Steak and kidney pies made to the Lighthouse's special recipe are famed at the inn, the pastry made on the premises, served with fresh vegetables, potatoes or home-made chips (over a ton a week), and delicious gravy of meat juices and red wine, £7.25 or £8.95. Fresh locally-caught fish delivered daily includes cod in two sizes, plaice and haddock, cooked as you like it and served with those hand-cut chips or jacket potato. Home-made lasagne is also special here, with even the béchamel sauce freshly made.

On the specials board you might find mussels in white wine, cream and garlic sauce, fresh salmon with white wine and parsley sauce, Cromer crab, fresh lobster, seabass and more, depending on the catch and season. The set menu also offers a wide choice of steaks – rump, sirloin, fillet and T-bone in various sizes – ploughman's of ham, Stilton, Cheddar or smoked mackerel, and a wide choice of sandwiches and baguettes. Bar snacks include various burgers, around £3-£4, and bowls of chips or potato wedges. An ethnic selection includes Malaysian beef rendang, prawns in sweet chilli sauce, chicken balti, korma and tikka masala. A huge fireworks display with hog roast is held on the first Friday in November.

S V P C

WARHAM ALL SAINTS

☆ Three Horseshoes

Bridge Street, NR23 1NL

- ▶ Centre of village
- Daily 11.30am-2.30pm, 6-11pm (10.30pm Sun)
- Daily 12-1.45pm, 6-8.30pm
- T (01328) 710547
- Greene King IPA; Woodforde's Wherry; guests
- Local produce cooked Mrs Beeton style – a chip free zone
- Norfolk flint pub dating from 1725 with 1920s gas lights and CAMRA National Inventory interior

Inspired by Mrs Beeton and without a deep fat fryer in the place, landlord and chef Iain Salmon dishes up fine, traditional meals in generous portions using local produce. 'All our food tends to be as our mothers or grandmothers cooked – plain and straightforward,' says Iain. Meals are seasonal, with a typical blackboard selection including soups such as 'car park nettle', local mussel, curried parsnip, Warham crab and samphire or cream of vegetable, all £3.25. Other starters could be home made Stilton or chicken liver pâté, or cheese-stuffed mushrooms.

Main dishes are pub food at its best – country lamb and vegetable stew with dumplings, toad-in-the-hole, fried liver and onions, mussels in cider, grilled Narborough trout with almonds, skate wing, and cod in parsley and wine sauce. Pies include savoury mince, Norfolk turkey, lamb and cranberry, and pork with apricots or sage and onions, prices are £7-£7.50 including potato dish of the day, a root vegetable and a green vegetable. Dearer pies at £8.20 include veg and steak and kidney, beef and horseradish or beef with venison and wine. A sample veggie dish is parsnip, butter bean and cheese bake. Desserts, all £3.25, might be golden syrup sponge, bakewell tart or chocolate syrup sponge. On the set menu, starters include Mrs Beeton's potted cheese and home-soused herrings.

★ Q S V P

WINTERTON-ON-SEA
Fisherman's Return
The Lane, NR29 4BN

- ▶ On B1129 8 miles N of Great Yarmouth
- Mon-Fri 11am-2.30pm, 6-11pm; Sat 11am-11pm; Sun 12-10.30pm
- Daily 12-2pm, 6.30-9pm
- T (01493) 393305
- E fishermans-return@btopenworld.com
- W www.fishermans-return.com
- Adnams Bitter, Broadside; Greene King IPA; Woodforde's Wherry, Norfolk Nog; guests
- Mainly traditional English with some continental additions
- 300-year-old brick and flint village inn

The Fisherman's offers a set menu of snacks and just a few main meals, but the main action here is on the specials board. A typical day's choices include starters such as spicy aubergine soup with coriander chutney, game and pork terrine with port jelly, moules marinière and local Winterton smoked salmon, £3.50-£6.25. Main dishes are local cod with caper and mushroom sauce with new potatoes, smoked haddock mornay and salad, boozy beef pie with Norfolk Nog, chicken cooked with lime and coriander on wild and basmati rice with salad, or venison sausages with mash and onion gravy; the veggie choice is stuffed peppers on Italian tomato base, sauté potatoes and salad, main meals £7.75-£10.25. Dessert choices are sticky toffee pudding, chocolate layer cake, pecan pie and local ice creams.

Available every day on the set menu are savouries from button mushrooms with oregano and garlic to individual cottage or fish pie, £3.75-£5.75, filled jacket potatoes, toasted sandwiches and Stilton or Cheddar ploughman's for £5.50. Main dishes include a seafood platter of shellfish and white fish, seafood omelette with prawns and smoked salmon or, fisherman's omelette which contains not fish but bacon, onion and mushrooms topped with cheese.

★ Q S V P C

WOODBASTWICK
Fur & Feather
Slad Lane, NR13 6HQ

- ▶ Off B1140 near Norwich, follow tourist signs to Woodforde's Brewery
- Summer Mon-Sat 11.30am-11pm; Sun 12-10.30pm; winter Mon-Sat 11.30am-3pm, 6-11pm; Sun 12-10.30pm
- Daily 12-2pm (3pm Sun), 6-9pm
- T (01603) 720003
- F (01603) 722266
- W www.thefurandfeatherinn.co.uk
- Woodforde's range
- Traditional, hearty home-made pub grub
- Thatched pub in row of converted farm cottages; Woodforde's brewery tap

Woodforde's award-winning ales (served on gravity from casks set into the wall, no handpumps on the bar) are used to great effect in rib-sticking rural dishes that come in generous portions. You can start with home-made soup, smoked salmon and scrambled eggs, rich game pâté with port and redcurrant sauce or smoked chicken breast with crispy bacon, Stilton and walnuts on rocket and cherry tomatoes, £3.75-£5. Main dishes include Nog Cobbler of beef in Woodforde's Norfolk Nog with traditional Norfolk savoury scone topping, chicken, leek and Eastern Ale pie and home-made steak and kidney pudding, each over a pound in weight or, for vegetarians, field mushroom and caramelised onion suet pudding. Locally-made bangers come with mash, bacon snaps and Woodforde's Wherry gravy, there is venison pot roasted in red wine served in a giant Yorkshire pudding, crispy pork belly with braised red cabbage, and the Bastwick half-pound burgers, specially made for the pub, topped with prawns or melted Applewood Cheddar and crispy bacon, prices including fresh vegetables £8-10. Also for vegetarians there is gnocchi in rich goats' cheese and red pepper sauce, char-grilled Med veg and herb couscous. Baguettes and sandwiches are available, and a choice of delicious puds.

S V P C

ARTHINGWORTH
Bull's Head
Kelmarsh Road, LE16 8JZ

- ▶ Off A508
- Mon-Sat 12-3pm, 6-11pm; Sun 12-10.30pm
- Mon-Sat 12-2.30pm, 6-9pm; Sun 12-8.30pm
- T (01858) 525637
- F (01858) 525640
- E thebullshead@btconnect.com
- W www.thebullsheadonline.co.uk
- Everards Tiger; Wells Eagle; guests
- ☺ Traditional home-cooked food plus an à la carte menu at weekends
- Large 1850s brick village pub with log fires and pub games, L-shaped bar with beamed ceiling, B&B rooms, separate restaurant

Here's a first for me, goose Wellington – goose breast wrapped in pastry served with red wine gravy – at a more than reasonable £9.95. In fact, all the à la carte menu is good value, with starters such as honey-baked goats' cheese, game terrine, crab salad and bacon-wrapped black pudding around £4-£5, main dishes including Mediterranean seafood and rice parcel, home-made steak and ale pie, roast Gressingham duck breast, stuffed tandoori chicken or home-cooked ham, egg and chips from £6.95-£8.95.

Daily deliveries of fresh produce include meat from a local butcher with his own abattoir and eggs from a local farm. Sunday sees a three-course roast meal for £10.95, and the pub hosts speciality evenings which have included Thai, Italian and Australian, when crocodile was on the menu. Senior citizens' lunches are served on Tuesday lunchtimes at £4.95 for a starter and main course (bookings only). All desserts are home made, apart from ice cream, and cost £3.95 for chocolate croissant bread and butter pudding, iced fruits of the forest brûlée, mixed berry crumble and profiteroles. Children can have small portions of main meals and special diets can be catered for.

★ Q S V P C

ASHTON
Chequered Skipper
The Green, PE8 5LD

- ▶ From Peterborough take left turn off A605 roundabout at Oundle
- Mon-Fri 11.30am-3pm, 6-11pm; Sat 11.30am-11pm; Sun 12-10.30pm
- Mon-Sat 12-2pm (2.30pm Sat), 6.30-9.30pm; Sun 12-3pm, 7-9pm
- T (01832) 273494
- Beer range varies
- ☺ Menus change frequently depending on whatever takes the chefs' fancy from fresh ingredients
- Idyllic thatched pub with a modern oak interior

The menus here are based on fresh, local and seasonal produce so they vary accordingly and reflect whether the chefs feel like creating something with a British, Italian, French or Spanish influence. Favourite starters include Scotch smoked salmon served with prawns and dill flavoured mayo, baked Brie wrapped in parma ham with salad, or a warm salad of black pudding, chorizo and potato, all £4.95. Typical main courses are roast rack of lamb with red wine and rosemary jus and dauphinoise potatoes, breast of chicken with bacon and onion rösti with Stilton and mushroom sauce, pan-fried lemon sole with crushed new potatoes and garlic shallot sauce, and wild mushroom risotto. Prices range from £9.25 for the vegetarian dish to £14.95. Desserts, all £4.25, offer the traditional – apple and pear crumble with custard or poached pear with raspberry sorbet – and the more exotic such as pineapple and coconut mousse cake, or you can finish with cheese and biscuits for £5.50. For Sunday lunch there is a choice of roasts – beef, pork or leg of lamb with all the trimmings – or alternatively a kebab of marinated tuna or Thai style vegetable curry, all £9.25. Tasty hot bar meals, jacket spuds and filled ciabattas are also served.

Q S V P C

DENFORD

Cock

High Street, NN14 4EQ

- Off A508, near M1 jct 15
- Mon-Fri 12-3pm (not Mon), 5.30-11pm; Sat 12-4pm, 6.30-11pm; Sun 12-4pm, 7-10.30pm
- Mon-Sat 12-2pm (not Mon), 7-9pm; Sun 12.30-2.30pm
- T (01832) 732565
- W www.cock-inn.co.uk
- Draught Bass; Flowers Original; Potbelly Aisling; guests
- Bar meals lunchtime, à la carte evenings, includes authentic Indian cooking
- Pretty Nene Valley pub with beams and roaring fire close to river

A destination dining pub, the Cock works hard to maintain its reputation with everything from bar snacks to à la carte at night cooked to order from fresh ingredients. At lunchtime the bar menu features home-made soup such as wild mushroom, tomato and basil or cauliflower and Stilton, steak and potato Irish pie (made with stout), filled baguettes, jacket potatoes, cheese or ham ploughman's or ham, egg and chips, hot meals around £4-£6.50.

Evening meals are usually eaten in the restaurant, where garlic prawns make a popular starter, as do mussels in season and home-made salmon fishcakes, £3.75-£5.95. Main courses include the sensational châteaubriand with fried onions, mushrooms, chips and peppercorn/Stilton sauce, £25.95 for two sharing, roast rack of English lamb with redcurrant sauce and stir-fried vegetables at £11.95, pork tenderloin with Old Rosie cider, and vegetarian choices such as Mediterranean omelette or cheese and vegetable crumble. Then there is the genuine Indian menu served Wednesday-Friday nights, with prawn purris and samosas, followed by chicken, lamb or prawn korma, rogan, madras, jalfrezi and bangalore plus pilau using best Derdahni basmati rice, and choice of naan breads. But Sunday is traditional – roast beef, loin or pork and chicken (child-sized portions available).

Q S V C

MIDDLETON CHENEY
New Inn
45 Main Road, OX17 2 ND

▶ On A422, 1 mile E of M40 jct 11
☼ Mon-Thu 12-3pm, 5-11pm;
Fri & Sat 12-11pm; Sun 12-10.30pm
🍴 Daily 12-2.30pm; 7-9.30pm (not Sun)
T (01295) 710399
E newinn@pipemedia.co.uk
W www.newinn.tablesir.com
🍺 Adnams Broadside; Fuller's London Pride; Hook Norton Best Bitter; Wadworth 6X; guests
☺ Home-made pub food with good grills
◉ Traditional stone-built village pub, dating from the 17th century, where you can play Aunt Sally in the extensive garden

The New Inn has a small kitchen, but from it two cooks produce a good range of home-made fare, aided in the evenings by students from the local catering college who bring ideas for new dishes. Customers are also invited to contribute – one of the regular's recipes for scrumpy chicken proved so popular it now often appears on the menu. Most ingredients come from local suppliers and farmers' markets, including free range meat and poultry, although the beef is Orkney Gold from the Scottish islands, delivered by the local butcher who prepares all the steaks and roasts for the pub. Sausages come from the landlord's sister's farm a few miles away.

Home-made starters include mushrooms in cream and garlic, soup or chicken liver pâté, all under £4. An 8oz rump or sirloin is £10.50/ £11.75 while the mixed grill is also under £12. Other main courses are good value – only the fish dishes, grilled trout with lemon butter or poached salmon with hollandaise, cost more than £7. A choice of veggie options is offered alongside the traditional liver and bacon, bangers and mash and Guinness stew with dumplings. Good home-made puds – cherry pie, apple crumble and bread and butter pudding – are supplemented by bought-in favourites such as death by chocolate, all £3.25.
★ ▲ Q ❀ V ♿ ♣ P ⚡ 👪 C

PYTCHLEY
Overstone Arms
Stringer Hill, NN14 1EU

▶ Off A43/A14
☼ Daily 12-2.30pm, 7-11pm
🍴 Daily 12-2pm, 7-9.30pm
T (01536) 790215
F (01536) 791098
🍺 Beer range varies
☺ Good choice of home-cooked dishes
◉ Large, stone village pub with a small bar and no smoking restaurant, benefiting from extensive gardens

The 2005 edition of the Good Beer Guide noted that the Overstone Arms was a 'much improved pub'. That is certainly true of the restaurant where booking is now advisable. The menu is extensive enough to appeal to all tastes and certainly won't break the bank. Starters cost around £3.50-£4.50 and include some tasty combinations such as honeydew melon with fresh fruit and a sharp lemon sorbet, fillet of smoked mackerel with horseradish sauce, crispy cauliflower florets with a tomato and garlic dip or deep fried Camembert with cranberry and redcurrant coulis. Steaks, served plain or with a sauce, are only served in the evening, but there is a still a good choice of dishes at lunchtime with most main courses around £7 or £8 (fillet steak is £14.25). Vegetarians are well catered for with Thai vegetable schnitzel, tortellini formaggio filled with five cheeses, garlic mushrooms sautéed with onions and served in white wine and cream sauce on rice, or Stilton and chestnut pâté served with salad and a jacket spud. There's plenty of fish, too: haddock royale (deep fried with cheese, prawns and mushrooms) or smoked fish mornay, while grilled rainbow trout is served with almonds or a prawn and watercress sauce. Other home-made favourites include steak and Guinness pie, chilli con carne, chicken curry and beef and Stilton pie topped with puff pastry. Desserts, £3.50 change daily.
★ ▲ Q ❀ S V 🍺 ♿ P ⚡ 👪 C

RAVENSTHORPE
Chequers
Chequers Lane, NN6 8ER

- Off A428
- Daily 12-3pm, 6-11pm
- Daily 12-2pm, 7-10pm
- T (01604) 770379
- F (01604) 771152
- E chequers@ravensthorpe.net
- Fuller's London Pride; Greene King IPA; Jennings Bitter; guests
- Extensive menu of meals and snacks, plus daily specials
- Grade II listed building, with bar, dining room and a games room where you can play Northants skittles

Set in a pretty village, the Chequers is ideally situated for visitors to local attractions – Coton Manor, Holdenby House Gardens and Althorp Park, the Spencer family home, are all within three miles. The full menu is served on Tuesday to Saturday evenings, but the extensive lunch and bar menu, plus daily specials served at other times are more than adequate to cater for most appetites. Steaks are a popular choice here, available in three sizes from 8oz to 16oz, plain or with sauces, priced from £9.50-£15.45, and fresh fish features on midweek evenings.

Starters, all under £4, include several mushroom dishes: with creamy garlic sauce, topped with Stilton cheese or with Cheddar cheese, prawns and herbs, then grilled. Or you could opt for jalapeno peppers filled with cream cheese or seafood such as whitebait, scampi or butterfly king prawns. On the main course specials board you might find roast pheasant, chicken curry or salmon supreme hollandaise, while the regular menu offers roast lamb shank and mint sauce, roast duck or mixed fish platter for two to share, plus five or six veggie options, mostly around £8.50. Leave room for pudding – home-made specials and cheese selections are displayed on the board, or there are various ice cream confections.

★ S V P C

WOODNEWTON
White Swan
22 Main Street, PE8 5EB

- In the village centre, 15 minutes' drive S from A47
- Tue-Fri 12-2.30pm, 6-11pm; Sat 12-11pm; Sun 12-10.30pm
- Tue-Sun 12-2pm, 6.30-8.30pm
- T (01780) 470381
- Adnams Bitter; Draught Bass; Fuller's London Pride; guest
- Extensive menu supplemented by daily specials, all home made
- Village pub with one long room divided into drinking and dining areas by a wooden partition

Coco the Clown used to drink at the White Swan and in his memory Bateman's brews a special house beer for the pub, Coco's Wisdom. The real ale here is complemented by real food; the regular menu of home-cooked dishes changes monthly and lists some 20 main courses and six starters, but that's not all. A daily 'limited editions' blackboard gives another eight choices, varying from the traditional – short crust pie of the day, beer battered fish of the day with chips – to the exotic, and always including a veggie option.

Sample dishes from a summer menu are, for starters, smoked salmon terrine with citrus mayonnaise, trio of cold meats (salami, chorizo and parma ham) with tomato and onion chutney and oriental king prawns topped with plum sauce, priced £3.50-£4.75. Mains, costing £6-£9.50, included oven-roasted duck breast with lemon and coriander pickle and buttered leeks, hot chicken salad (chicken tossed in honey and cashew nuts), pork tenderloin strips topped with hoi sin and spring onion sauce on a bed of stir fried veg and rice, and goats' cheese, mozzarella and tomato ravioli. There is usually a choice of five home-made desserts to finish including an interesting cheesecake. The pub hosts monthly gastronomic themed evenings, with decorations to reflect the cuisine – be it Mexican, French or Thai.

★ Q S V P C

DIPTON MILL

☆ Dipton Mill Inn

Dipton Mill Road, NE46 1YA

- 2 miles S of Hexham on B6306 towards Whitley Chapel
- Mon-Sat 12-2.30pm, 6-11pm; Sun 12-3pm, 7-10.30pm (summer only)
- Daily 12-2.30pm, 6.30-8.30pm
- T (01434) 606577
- Hexhamshire Devil's Elbow, Shire Bitter, Devil's Water, Whapweasel, Old Humbug; guest
- Good variety of home-made food and an excellent cheese board
- This small, welcoming pub is the tap for Hexhamshire Brewery; the large garden has a stream running through it

Cotherstone, Coquetdale, Chevington, Kielder, Cuddy's Cave – these are just a few of the 14 cheeses, mostly from local dairies, that feature on the special cheese menu here. Reason enough to visit this charming little pub whose home brewed beers, which delight in equally evocative names, are also a must to sample, and terrific when paired up. However, you should come with an appetite for more than just cheese and ale, as the food here is all home cooked from local ingredients and served with fresh veg at very reasonable prices – few places these days can provide a bowl of home-made soup, a dessert or freshly-made sandwich for under two quid. Soup, perhaps carrot and celery or spiced parsnip, is the only starter offered here. Haddock baked with tomato and basil, lamb leg steak in wine and mustard sauce, pork fillet with apple, orange and ginger or steak and kidney pie are just some of the hearty main courses you may see listed, all around £5 or £6. Vegetarians also have a good choice – tagliatelle with a creamy basil sauce and fresh Parmesan, ratatouille and couscous. Delicious desserts could include plum crumble, chocolate rum truffle torte or raspberry roulade.

Q S V

GREAT WHITTINGTON

Queen's Head Inn

NE19 2HP

- Tue-Sat 12-2.30pm, 6-11pm; Sun 12-3pm
- Tue-Sat 12-2pm, 6.30-9pm; Sun 12-2pm
- T (01434) 672267
- Black Sheep Bitter; Hambleton Bitter
- Fresh local produce on a European style menu – no frozen ingredients
- Reputedly the oldest inn in the county, this charming pub and restaurant at the heart of Hadrian's Wall country is popular with tourists

This 15th-century pub is the only regular outlet in Northumberland for Hambleton Brewery – sample the ale brewed specially for the pub in front of a roaring fire in the friendly bar before your meal. All the meat, game and fish served here is sourced locally and delivered daily for the head chef to prepare himself, while scallops and salmon are from the Shetland Isles. A set lunch menu, £11.50 for two courses, starts with deep-fried black pudding with beetroot relish, warm ciabatta bread with smoked mackerel and mustard dressing, melon, pâté or home-made soup. To follow there are steak and game casserole, roast pork loin with apple tartlet, salmon and herb fishcakes with mustard sauce, Cumberland sausage and mash or roast vegetable and sweet pepper pasta.

The more extensive à la carte menu offers additional starters such as smoked chicken on orange and hazelnut salad, pan-fried king scallops with bacon and green bean salad or cornets of smoked salmon filled with prawns in a lemon and chive dressing, £7-£8. Mains include fresh halibut fillet with tomato and fennel scented fume; pork tenderloin on orange and onion marmalade with black pudding fritters, and sirloin steak with a king prawn and mushroom kebab, £10-£19. Home-made desserts include the chef's signature dish of iced nougatine.

★ V P C

HALTWHISTLE
Black Bull
Market Square, NE49 0BL

- In town centre, off A69 between Carlisle and Hexham
- Daily 12-11pm (closed Monday in winter)
- Daily 12-2pm, 6-9pm (not Sun eve)
- T (01434) 320463
- E haltwhistlebull@aol.com
- Beer range varies
- Varied menu based on seasonal local produce with good fish selection
- Compact, olde-worlde pub, free from background music

Somewhat surprisingly for a rather northerly town, Haltwhistle claims to be at the geographic centre of Britain. Something else one wouldn't automatically associate with Northumberland is champagne, but at the Black Bull they have had the inspired idea of offering a bucks fizz brunch on Sunday – a generous meal of gammon, Cumberland sausage, mushrooms, black pudding, egg and sautéed potatoes washed down with a glass of orange juice and champagne, for just £5.95. Wednesday evening is another good time to visit as it is steak night, with prices from £5.25 to £8.95 for an 8oz steak with all the trimmings.

At other times the pub serves an imaginative menu that changes often as it is based on locally sourced produce. All meals are cooked to order so individual diets can easily be catered for. Starters, £4-£6.25, might include black pudding and apple tower topped with Stilton and Cumberland sauce, goats' cheese on a balsamic crouton with red onion marmalade or king prawns marinated in fresh ginger and lime butter. To follow there may be haddock fillet with prawns and mozzarella, local trout fillets with fennel and horseradish sauce, roast partridge stuffed with pear, wrapped in parma ham, lamb shank with redcurrant and port sauce or Mexican stuffed peppers as a veggie choice, £8.25-£15.

Q S V (Haltwhistle) C

HAYDON BRIDGE
General Havelock Inn
9 Ratcliffe Road, NE47 6ER

- On A69, 7 miles W of Hexham
- Tue-Sun 12-2.30pm, 7-11pm (10.30pm Sun)
- Tue-Sun 12-2pm, 7-9pm
- T (01434) 684376
- F (01434) 684283
- E generalhavelock@aol.com
- Beer range varies
- A mix of modern European and local dishes from locally sourced ingredients
- Overlooking the River Tyne, this 18th-century inn has a fresh, modern feel

If you simply cannot decide what to choose on the pub's extensive menu you could do worse than follow the locals. Chef and proprietor Gary Thompson lists the following dishes as his top sellers: moules marinière, cullen skink (natural smoked haddock in a leek, potato and milk broth), beef, Guinness and wild mushroom stew served with creamed potato, and seabass on ratatouille with fresh pesto. For dessert, favourites are bread and butter pudding with apricot compote, or a trio of home-made ice creams (delicious flavours to tempt you include burnt almond and honey, crème de menthe, dark Belgian chocolate, hazelnut or marmalade).

The pub offers different bar menus in summer and winter, so lighter dishes such as cheese croquets with dressed salad or salmon and asparagus quiche are replaced with local game pie or Cumberland sausage with onion gravy and mash. Bar meals are priced between £6 and £7, filled baguettes and sandwiches are always available. In the evening the dinner menu is offered at £20.25 for two courses, £22.75 for three or even £25 for four; you could start with tuna and aubergine cannelloni or baked field mushrooms filled with bacon, shallots and smoked cheese. Mains include pan-fried port tenderloin with brandied prunes, roast marinated duck leg, steak or fish of the day.

★ Q S V (Haydon Bridge) C

HEDLEY ON THE HILL
Feathers
NE43 7SW

- S of A695
- Mon-Fri 6-11pm; Sat 12-3pm, 6-11pm; Sun 12-3pm, 7-10.30pm
- Tue-Fri 7-9pm; Sat & Sun 12-2.30pm, 7-9pm
- T (01661) 843607
- E mo.thefeathersinn@virgin.net
- Mordue Workie Ticket; guests
- Home-cooked food on a blackboard menu that changes weekly
- Unspoilt, cosy pub with stone walls, exposed beams and fires in both bars, set in a hamlet high above Tyne Valley

Described in CAMRA's Good Beer Guide as an outstanding pub, possibly because the annual mini beer festival at Easter culminates with an uphill barrel race where the winner is rewarded with real ale! Or maybe it is for the views over three counties. In our book it is definitely for the food: though limited to a few choices for each course, quality and freshness are guaranteed and all produce comes from local suppliers. Everything is home made – even the ice cream – and the weekly changing menu always offers three imaginative vegetarian dishes (one suitable for vegans). Favourites include cannelloni bean cakes with chilli and tomato salsa, roasted red pepper and Gruyère tart, and spinach, tomato, garlic and cheese lasagne, all around £8. There are veggie options to start with, too – perhaps soup or mozzarella, plum tomato, olive and pesto salad, while meat eaters could pick country pâté or smoked chicken Caesar salad, all under £5. Main course choices for meat eaters might be moussaka, honey roast ham with mango chutney, pork casserole with orange, celery and leeks, fish pancake, beef braised in wine and brandy or Cumberland sausage and mash, prices £8-£10.50. Good puds are all £4.50 including the aforementioned delicious ice cream, ginger pudding and lemon brulée tart.

★ Q S V

LOW NEWTON BY THE SEA
Ship Inn
Newton Square, NE66 3EL

- Off B1340, park in village car and walk down hill into hamlet
- Mon-Fri 11am-3pm, 8 (6 Fri)-11pm; Sat 11am-11pm; Sun 12-10.30pm
- Daily 12-2.30pm, 7-8pm (opening and meal times may vary seasonally)
- T (01665) 576262
- Beer range varies
- Good, plain, local ingredients, always home cooked
- Lovely old pub, set within a row of whitewashed fishermen's cottages by the village green, almost on the beach

The Ship is easier to access by foot along the Northumberland coastline than by road (drivers must park in the village car park). If the sea air has given you an appetite, this is the place to be, although the Ship can be busy, even in winter, so you may have to wait for your food to be cooked. At lunchtime there are soups, salads, toasted sandwiches and snacks such as fishcakes and Craster kippers, followed by home-made apple crumble for afters.

The evening menu is fairly limited, too, but high quality and changing daily according to what is available. Most of the meat comes from free range stocks at New Barns Farm in Warkworth, the fish is brought in by the day boats at Amble and Boulmer and the lobster is landed just yards from the pub. Typical starters are kipper pâté with oatcakes, potted crab with chilli and garlic butter, grilled goats' cheese with tomato and basil, and grilled peppers on pine nut and rocket salad with parmesan, prices from £3 to £7.25 for king scallops. There are usually two fish, meat and vegetarian main courses to choose from, such as grilled lobster, wild sea trout cutlets, fresh local crab, free-range duck breast with wild rice and plum sauce, Mexican hot beans with wild rice and salad, and venison steaks in red wine sauce. Most main courses are £7-£11.50 (lobster £22.50).

★ Q V

OLD HARTLEY
Delaval Arms
Beresford Road, NE26 4RL

▶ On A193 between Whitley Bay and Blyth
☼ Daily 12-11pm
🍴 Daily 12-3pm, 6-8pm (not Sun)
T (0191) 237 0489
Wylam Gold Tankard; guests
☺ Good selection of snacks, traditional pub fare and daily specials
Village pub that serves its local community well

Sunday lunches are a speciality here – there is always a choice of beef, lamb, pork or turkey breast, all served with home-made Yorkies and available in three sizes (X Large £5.25, adults £4.50 and children £3.25). The food here is cooked to order, mostly sourced from local suppliers, and offered at very reasonable prices as befits a village community pub. Dishes on the daily specials board, served with roast potatoes and three veg, are only £3.25, while various salads are available from £3.50. Unusually, any of the main meals can be ordered as a salad, such as the seafood medley, £4.75, or char-grilled salmon, £4.75. Other main course favourites are chicken tikka masala, chicken kiev or battercrisp cod. A plain sirloin steak will only set you back £5.25. If you don't want a full meal, there is a good range of hot sandwiches (stotties) such as beef, lamb and mint, hot pork with apple or stuffing or sausage, £2.25. For the same price you can have a quarter pounder beef burger and all are served with chips or salad. Desserts, all £2.25, come with custard, ice cream or cream.

★ P

SLALEY
Travellers' Rest
NE46 1TT

▶ On B6306, a mile N of the village
☼ Daily 12-11pm (10.30pm Sun)
🍴 Daily 12-3pm, 5-9pm
T (01434) 673231
E info@1travellersrest.com
W www.1travellersrest.com
Black Sheep Best Bitter; guest
☺ French bistro-style cooking executed with loving care
Licensed a century ago, this 300-year-old stone inn started out as a farmhouse; now refurbished but retaining its large open hearth and flag floors

Children are welcome at the Travellers' Rest – the garden boasts a rustic adventure playground that will keep them amused for ages. Most ingredients are sourced locally – some of the beef comes from a herd in a field near the pub and herbs are freshly picked from the landlady's herb garden. The lunch menu includes a good choice of sandwiches, warm filled baguettes and omelettes as well as steak and mushroom pie, grilled salmon with hollandaise sauce or oven-baked breast of duck, £5.75-£10.25. A traditional roast is prepared daily, price £6.50 or £3.50 for a half portion.

In the evening, starters range from home-made soup, £3.75, to king prawns sautéed in butter, garlic and herbs, £5.50. Other choices might be duck and leek Chinese pancakes with plum sauce, smoked haddock in cream sauce on tomatoes or egg Florentine (poached egg and spinach covered in hollandaise sauce served on a toasted muffin). Main courses include lamb fillet on sautéed potatoes with a mint jus, char-grilled slices of venison on potato rosti, oven-baked cod fillet topped with scallops and scampi in a fish cream sauce, a choice of pasta dishes and a veggie option, plus steaks or mixed grill, £8-£13.50. Desserts at £3.95 feature chocolate bread and butter pudding and lemon tart.

★ Q S V P C

STANNINGTON
Ridley Arms
NE61 6EL

- ▶ Off A1, 5 miles S of Morpeth, 8 miles from the airport
- Mon-Sat 11.30am-11pm; Sun 12-10.30pm
- Daily 12-9.30pm (9pm Sun)
- T (01670) 789216
- F (01670) 789315
- E g.reilly@fsmail.net
- Black Sheep Best Bitter; Jennings Cumberland Ale; Taylor Landlord; guests
- ☺ Excellent choice of well-cooked British classics
- Large, traditional, stone and slate multi-roomed pub

Ramps and wide doors in this Fitzgerald-managed house make it easily accessible for all visitors, and the well thought out menu ensures that it enjoys a good food trade. Several of the starters and light bites are offered in two portion sizes, either £4 or £8, such as steamed mussels in white wine, parsley and garlic cream, lamb koftas with cucumber and red onion raita, halloumi wrapped in red pepper with lemon and chilli and crab linguini with chilli, lemon, garlic and parsley. Other interesting appetisers include ginger prawns with asparagus and honey mayo dressing or fennel, feta and sun-blushed tomato salad with softly boiled egg.

Main courses are mostly pub favourites such as bangers and mash, steak, red wine and mushroom pie or curry of the day, all around £8, and steaks, £11.50-£15, plus £2 for a sauce. To add variety there is a list of house specialities, £8-£9, perhaps duck breast skewer with lemon pepper marinade and watercress salad, sticky honey mustard chicken skewer with Greek salad, rump steak burger with chimi churri pepper chutney, and grilled tandoori chicken or garlic king prawns both served with a salad of mango, radish, cucumber and rocket. A daily specials board offers additional choices.

Q S V P C

Here's a short, sweet dessert recipe from the Admiral Rodney Inn at Berrow Green near Martley in Worcestershire.

WHITE CHOCOLATE & LAVENDER TART
Serves 4

350g (12oz) shortcrust pastry
320g (10oz) white chocolate
200ml (7 fl oz) double cream
100ml (3.5 fl oz) milk
A few sprigs of fresh lavender
2 eggs and 2 egg yolks

Preheat oven to 140C/275F/gas mark 1. Roll out the pastry and cut to fit 4 tart cases; bake blind. Melt the white chocolate slowly in a glass bowl over a saucepan of simmering water. Heat double cream, milk and lavender together and leave to infuse for 30 minutes. Reheat milk and cream and mix with chocolate using a spoon, not a whisk, so as not to get bubbles. Mix together the eggs and egg yolks, add to the chocolate mix and strain. Use to fill tart cases and bake above the centre of the oven for approx 10 minutes until barely set and shiny.

KIMBERLEY
Nelson & Railway
12 Station Road, NG16 2NR

- ▶ Next to Hardys & Hansons Brewery
- ☼ Mon-Sat 11am-11pm; Sun 12-10.30pm
- Mon-Fri 12-2.30pm, 5.30-9pm; Sat 12-9pm; Sun 12-6pm
- T (0115) 938 2177
- Hardys & Hansons Bitter, Olde Trip, seasonal
- ☺ Traditional pub food, mainly home made, perfect with H&H Nottinghamshire beers
- Immaculate, traditional local run by the same family for more than 30 years

The Nelson is renowned for the sort of simple, no frills pub grub at bargain prices that is the antidote to gastropubs. The menu is basically unchanged since the last edition of this guide six years ago, and so are the prices. On the set menu home-made soup of the day with a roll and butter is only £1.60, while main dishes include home-made steak and kidney pie with seasonal vegetables, a 'sausage feast' of beef and tomato bangers, minted lamb and pork with garlic served with Yorkshire pudding, onion gravy, peas and mash, an extra large cod fillet in home-made batter, a three-egg omelette (ham, cheese, mushroom or Spanish) with chips or jacket potato – all around £5. An 8oz sirloin steak with mushrooms, tomatoes, peas and sauté potatoes is only £6.90, and so is the monster mixed grill of lamb chop, gammon, sausage, lamb's liver and black pudding, also served with mushrooms, tomatoes and chips. There is a home-made vegetarian special of the day and substantial Cheddar ploughman's. Bar snacks include cottage pie of minced beef topped with mash and melted cheese, and hot roast beef or pork in a Notts cob at £1.90. You can get a chip butty for £1.30 and puds such as fruit crumble or treacle sponge. A daily specials board is slightly more adventurous, but still in keeping.

S V P C

LOWDHAM
World's End
Plough Lane, NG14 7AT

- ▶ Just off A6097
- ☼ Mon-Thu 12-3pm, 5.30-11pm; Fri-Sun 12-11pm
- Daily 12-2.30pm, 6.30-8.30pm (not Sun eve)
- T (0115) 966 3857
- Mansfield Cask; Marston's Burton Bitter, Pedigree
- ☺ High quality, home-cooked British dishes
- White-painted village inn dating from the mid-18th century; cosy interior, large garden with a fine floral display in summer

The fish night held on the last Thursday of the month is so popular that it is often booked up two months in advance by customers who enjoy something more than just cod 'n' chips (although that is available) – dishes might include trout fillet with spinach and prawns, salmon with fennel and orange or tuna supreme with mango and chilli salsa, all at around £8 or £9. The pub also hosts special themed evenings such as a Trafalgar weekend in 2005, while Burns' Night, St George's and St Patrick's Day are celebrated annually.

Most of the food here is cooked to order from locally sourced produce – indeed they grow their own herbs and some fruit, while customers provide other home-grown fruit and vegetables. The à la carte menu of steaks, grills and fish is supplemented by an extensive list of specials, including pan-fried duck breast with blackberries in port, £11.95, lamb's liver with bacon and onions, £7.50, and beef and Guinness casserole, £8.95. Vegetarians are offered a pie of Brie and broccoli in garlic sauce or vegetable moussaka. Desserts are all £3.45, some home made. There is a good value menu for senior citizens on weekday lunchtimes, £3.85 or £5.10 for two courses, as well as an extensive snack menu.

★ Q S V (Lowdham) P C

LOWER BAGTHORPE
Shepherds Rest
Wansley Lane, NG16 5HF

- ▶ Two miles from jct 27 of the M1 towards Heanor
- Daily 12-11pm (10.30pm Sun)
- Mon-Sat 12-2pm, 6-9pm (not Mon); Sun 12-3pm
- T (01773) 811337
- E ed1clarke@yahoo.co.uk
- Caledonian Deuchars IPA; Greene King Abbot; Wells Bombardier; guest
- ☺ Home-made food, good steaks, fish and daily specials
- Traditional 17th-century pub, reputedly haunted, with exposed beams and open fires, extensive gardens and rural views

The laudable aim of the owners of this family-run pub is to exceed customers' expectations and provide items not on the menu if at all possible. As the menu is fairly extensive, this is probably a rare request. All the usual pub snacks are supplemented by home-made daily specials and a full à la carte menu. All the fish is delivered fresh from Grimsby, sausages are prepared for the pub by a local butcher and the honey roast ham is cooked in house. The Sunday carvery is so popular they regularly have to turn customers away, so booking is recommended.

To begin you could have black pudding stack (layered with bacon, mushrooms and tomatoes), home-made soup or pâté, deep fried Brie with cranberry dip or maybe the chef's scallops and tiger prawns pan fried in garlic butter from the specials board. There is a good choice of steaks from 8oz sirloin to 24oz rump, plus gammon, mixed grills and 'surf and turf' (rump with scampi). On the specials list you might find game birds, home-made pies or piggyback chicken (breast stuffed with cheese and wrapped in bacon). Vegetarians have three choices plus omelettes and children can have small portions of many of the dishes. Expect to pay £12-50-£20 for two courses; desserts are £3.95.

★ Q S V C

NOTTINGHAM
Fellows, Morton & Clayton
54 Canal Street, NG1 7EH

- ▶ Just S of Broadmarsh shopping centre
- Mon-Thu 11am-11pm; Fri & Sat 11am-midnight; Sun 12-10.30pm
- Mon-Sat 11.30am-9pm; Sun 12-6pm
- T (0115) 950 6795
- F (0115) 9539 838
- E sales@fellowsmortonandclayton.co.uk
- W www.fellowsmortonandclayton.co.uk
- Caledonian Deuchars IPA; Camerons Castle Eden Ale; Fuller's London Pride; Taylor Landlord; guests
- ☺ Pub favourites at reasonable prices in the bar or gallery restaurant
- Large, converted warehouse on split levels with beer garden overlooking the canal

This attractive canalside warehouse conversion, ten minutes from the town centre, houses the first pub brewery in Nottingham. Snacks and light meals are available until 5pm (except Sunday), with a good range of sandwiches, burgers, jacket spuds and wraps with enticing fillings such as roasted tomato, feta and olives, Brie and onion marmalade for around £5.

The main menu kicks off with eggs Benedict, home-made salmon fish cakes, creamy garlic mushrooms, Brie parcels with sweet chilli and onion marmalade or a seasonal pâté. There is always a good choice of main course salads such as char-grilled chicken and bacon, niçoise, Greek or Caesar salad and steaks. Alternatively there are traditional dishes such as steak and kidney pie, while more innovative combinations include grilled butterfly chicken breast with Spanish chorizo and melted mozzarella in roasted pepper, tomato and basil sauce, haddock fillet grilled with smoked salmon and served with scallops, mussels and prawns in a fresh dill and tomato sauce, marinated pan-fried pork fillet with sage and leek mash or spinach and green pesto macaroni with Parmesan and garlic bread. Starters are mostly around £3, mains £7.

V (Nottingham Midland)
(Canal St Tram) C

NOTTINGHAM
Falcon Inn
Canning Circus, NG7 3NE

▶ At junction of A52 Derby Road and A610 Alfreton Road
☼ Daily 12-midnight (11pm Sun)
Ⓨ Mon-Sat 12-2pm, 5-11pm; Sun 12-11pm
T (0115) 978 2770 (pub),
T (0115) 978 4422 (restaurant)
F (0115) 973 8090
E falconinn@tennantsuk.com
W www.thefalconinn.co.uk
Adnams Bitter, Broadside; Wells Bombardier; guests
☺ Contemporary Indian cuisine and snacks
Small, traditional, friendly pub popular with locals; the 30-seater Turmeric Indian restaurant upstairs offers home delivery

Claiming to be Nottingham's first curry pub, Indian cuisine is the main focus here, although freshly-baked baguettes and toasties are available at lunchtime except on Sunday when a proper roast lunch is served. A range of appetisers is offered to start with, from £1.95-£3.75, served with fresh salad. Along with the popular bhajis and samosas you could have bengan paneer (aubergine in a mild sauce, topped with melted cheese), tandoori king prawns or chicken, kebabs or tikka dishes.

Main meals are all served with popadam, chutney and pilau rice. Meat or fish is cooked in the full range of Indian methods: vindaloo, madras, korma, dupiaza, jalfrezi, rogan josh, balti. There is also a list of 'tandoori sizzlers' – chicken tikka, lamb tikka, fish or prawns – cooked in a traditional clay tandoor oven. You could opt for one of the chef's specials, which include vegetarian dishes such as sabzi special and palak paneer (spinach and cheese cooked in a medium sauce), chicken tikka nantara (cooked in karahi with prawns, garlic, ginger, green chillies, herbs and spices) or their popular tandoori lamb masala. Main courses are £5.25-£8.95.

★ Q ❀ S V C

NOTTINGHAM
☆ Kean's Head
46 St Mary's Gate, The Lace Market, NG1 1QA

▶ Directly opposite St Mary's Church in the Lace Market
☼ Mon-Sat 10am-11pm; Sun 12-10.30pm
Ⓨ Daily 10am (12pm Sun)-10pm
T (0115) 947 4052
E keans.head@btinternet.com
Bateman XB; Castle Rock Harvest Pale, Elsie Mo; guests
☺ English and authentic Italian recipes, everything home made
Smart but cosy pub in the heart of the Lace Market; soft background jazz music

Landlady Charlotte Blomeley was taught to cook by an Italian and her mother, now living in Italy, sends recipes. All her Italian ingredients come from a local supplier who imports directly from Italy (except for the pizza dough that is made at the pub – along with the focaccia and all the cakes and pies served here). Meat and sausages are from a butcher in Beeston, Stilton is from Colston Basset and pork pies from Mrs King's in Melton Mowbray; fish and vegetables (often organic) are delivered daily.

Small dishes, such as antipasto, suppli (fried risotto balls with mozzarella and basil) and caponata melanzane (slow-cooked aubergines with olives, pine nuts and tomatoes served with focaccia) are mostly around £3-£4. Imaginative sandwich fillings such as salami, artichoke and roasted peppers, grilled courgette and sun dried tomato, smoked baked ham with green salad or Stilton with home-made plum chutney are all £3.95. A pizza is £4.75 with extra toppings for 50 pence each. The vegetarian goats' cheese, roasted vegetable and polenta pie is popular. A good selection of specials may include penne with fresh figs and parma ham in cream and parmesan sauce, £6.95 or fresh lightly poached turbot with a piquant sauce, £11.25. Home-made desserts include baked peaches stuffed with chocolate, £3.95.

S V ♿ ⇌ (Nottingham) ⊖ (Lace Market Tram) C

CAULCOTT
Horse & Groom
Lower Heyford Road, OX25 4ND

- ▶ On B4030 between Middleton Stoney and Lower Heyford
- ☼ Mon-Sat 11am-3pm, 6-11pm; Sun 12-3pm, 7-10.30pm
- Daily 12-2.30pm, 7-9.30pm
- T (01869) 343257
- Hook Norton Best Bitter; guests
- ☺ The speciality sausage menu offers 12 varieties of O'Hagans sausages
- Cosy little country-cottage style pub that always has three guest beers on tap

O'Hagans speciality sausages are one of the main attractions at the Horse and Groom. For £7.50 you get a plateful served with a choice of mash or chips, peas or baked beans. Made with real skins and proper cuts of meat with no added preservatives or monosodium glutamate, these could be the best bangers you will ever taste. You can opt for a traditional style such as the herby Oxford or the Spanish chorizo from a 600-year-old Catalan recipe, or the more recent invention: chicken flavoured with orange and walnut.

If you are not a sausage fan then consult the specials board for a good range of alternatives. Starters include home-made soup, grilled sardines or perhaps mussels in white wine, garlic and cream. Main courses such as Cajun spiced chicken or pork tenderloin wrapped in Parma ham are joined by seasonal specials – look out for roast wild duck or partridge – and a vegetarian choice, maybe home made ratatouille. The pub also offers a good bar menu with a big selection of toasted sandwiches (the 8oz steak at £6.30 is the most expensive, others are generally under £4), jacket spuds or ploughman's. Home-made desserts include sticky banana toffee pudding, apple pie or very sherry trifle.

★ Q ❀ S V ♿ ⇌ (Lower Heyford) ♣ C

CHADLINGTON
Tite Inn
Mill End, OX7 3NY

- ▶ Off A361, approximately 2 miles S of Chipping Norton
- ☼ Tue-Sun 12-2.30pm, 6.30-11pm
- Tue-Sun 12-2pm, 7-9pm
- T (01608) 676475
- F (0870) 7051251
- E willis@titeinn.com
- W www.titeinn.com
- Doombar; Ramsbury Bitter; guests
- ☺ A mix of traditional and more imaginative dishes
- Local CAMRA Pub of the Year 2005, with superb views in an area of outstanding natural beauty

Susan and Michael Willis have owned and run the Tite Inn as a free house since 1986. Susan, in charge of the kitchen, ensures that all food is freshly prepared and sourced locally wherever possible – she buys her unusual duck sausages from a local butcher. The lunch menu is more limited than the evening version, but includes a good choice of sandwiches in French or granary bread. Main courses on the lunch menu are all priced around £8-£9 and could include babotie (a sweet and spicy meat loaf) with mixed salad, warm, chicken bacon and avocado salad or the veggie option – brazil nut loaf with a fresh tomato sauce.

The Sunday lunch menu is more varied as is the daily evening menu with a wider choice of starters such as spinach and feta samosas with cranberry sauce or king prawns in filo pastry with a sweet chilli sauce, both under £5.50. Main courses include boeuf bourguignon and mash, £9.95, slow braised lamb shank in a wine and rosemary sauce, £12.95, or a couple of fishy choices for under £9. Desserts such as meringue glacée with toffee sauce or 'posh' bread and butter pudding are all home made or you can opt for a selection of local and country cheeses.

Q ❀ S V ♿ ⇌ (Charlbury) ♣ P C

CHIPPING NORTON

☆ Chequers Inn

Goddards Lane, OX7 5NP

- ▶ Next to the theatre in the town centre
- Mon-Sat 11am-11pm; Sun 12-10.30pm
- Mon-Sat 12-2.30pm, 6-9.30pm; Sun 12-5pm
- T (01608) 644717
- F (01608) 646237
- E joshreid@supanet.com
- W www.chequers-pub.co.uk
- Fuller's Chiswick, London Pride, ESB, seasonal
- ☺ Varied menu includes some Thai dishes and a good vegetarian and vegan selection
- Award-winning town-centre pub dating from the 16th century; its beamed interior is divided into four seating areas and a no-smoking restaurant

The pub's restaurant was formed by covering an open courtyard and provides a light, airy contrast to the traditionally-styled bar areas. All the food is carefully prepared in the pub kitchen, even the beef and ham for the sandwiches is home cooked. Ingredients are sourced locally and incorporate organic and seasonal produce wherever possible. The pub is renowned for its vegetarian and vegan dishes which include wild mushroom risotto or mixed bean mussamen – a medium spiced Thai curry.

The lunch and evening menus vary with the seasons, supplemented by a daily specials board. Starters, priced at £5.50 or under, include roast vegetable terrine with Parmesan crisp and herb oil, rocket, orange and pine nut salad with Parma ham, and chorizo frittata accompanied by garlic open cup mushrooms and spinach pesto. Main courses range from a simple home-made beef burger with chips and salad for £5.95 to steamed seabass fillet, with an intriguing accompaniment of asparagus with ginger, plus a hot, sour sauce and jasmine rice, £11.95. Other imaginative combinations are roast lamb shank with dauphinoise potatoes, sweet roasted bell peppers and braised celery, and Gloucester Old Spot pork fillet, served with red onion potato cake with a fig and balsamic reduction.

★ Q S V ≠ (Kingham) C

CHURCH ENSTONE

Crown Inn

Mill Lane, OX7 4NN

- Take B4030 turn off A44 at Enstone
- Mon 6-11pm; Tue-Sat 12-3pm, 6-11pm; Sun 12-3pm
- Tue-Sat 12-2pm, 7-9pm; Sun 12-2pm
- T (01608) 677262
- W www.crowninnenstone.co.uk
- Hook Norton Best Bitter; Shepherd Neame Spitfire; guest
- Simple food on a daily changing menu, specialising in fresh fish and seafood
- 17th-century free house on the edge of the Cotswolds surrounded by walking country

Award-winning chef Tony Warburton hates clichés – especially on his menu which is chalked up twice daily. He likes his customers to know exactly what to expect when they order. And without doubt those expectations will be amply satisfied, whether you choose to dine in the slate-floored conservatory, the beamed dining room or traditional bar. Using game from nearby estates and other local seasonal produce, Tony serves up simple but mouth-watering dishes.

His chalkboard lists starters such as fishcakes with chilli and coriander mayo, grilled courgettes and chorizo salad with Parmesan, both under £6, or the more extravagant king scallops and bacon salad at £7.85. For the main course you can be assured of a straightforward dish such as lamb's liver with bacon, mash and onions or the more unusual goats' cheese omelette which comes with chips and salad, both priced at £7.95. Other choices might be fillet of haddock under a sun-dried tomato and cheddar crust, £10.50, or grilled gammon served with bubble and squeak and free-range poached eggs for £8.50. Be sure to leave room for pudding – all home made at a single price of £4.50 – you could be tempted by the caramelised pear tart with pear purée and vanilla ice cream, raspberry and mascarpone cheesecake or an old favourite, crème brûlée.

★ S V C

DEDDINGTON

Deddington Arms

Horsefair, OX15 0SH

- On Banbury-Oxford road
- Daily 11am-11pm; Fri-Sat 11am-1am
- Daily 12-2, 6-9.30pm (9pm Sun)
- T (01869) 338364
- F (01869) 337010
- E deddarms@oxfordshire-hotels.co.uk
- W www.oxfordshire-hotels.co.uk
- Caledonian Deuchars IPA; Greene King IPA; Tetley Bitter; guests
- Traditional English food served in the bar or candle-lit restaurant
- 16th-century coaching inn overlooking the market square of a medieval village, now offering accommodation in stylish rooms

Air conditioning makes the hotel's no-smoking restaurant a very comfortable place to dine in all seasons, although traditionalists may prefer the flagstone-floored bar warmed in winter by an open fire. Both offer varied, home-cooked dishes and hotel guests can also order room service from the bar menu. Several starters on this menu are offered in larger portions as main courses, for example the Thai barbecue duck salad, London Pride and grain mustard rarebait or the Bantry Bay mussels steamed in white wine and garlic. Main courses range from beer-battered haddock at £7.50 to rib-eye steak at £13.25. Various sandwiches with French fries are offered for a quick bite to eat.

The more upmarket restaurant has a menu to match: starters include sea of scallops with carrot butter sauce and plumped sultanas, £7.25, or croutton due chevre lentil salad with hazelnut viniagrette, £6.25. For the main course loin of venison with celeriac colcannon and Irish stout reduction, or monkfish bourguignon with bacon, baby onions and red wine sauce; prices range from £13.75 to £17.75. Look out for special music evenings when you can dine along to jazz or traditional Irish music.

★ S V P C

GREAT TEW
Falkland Arms
OX7 4DB

- Off A361 on the B4022 between Chipping Norton and Banbury
- Mon-Sat 11.30-2.30pm (3pm Sat), 6-11pm; Sun 12-3pm, 7-10.30pm (all day Sat and Sun in summer)
- Mon-Sat 12-2pm, 7-8pm; Sun 12-2pm
- T (01608) 683653
- F (01608) 683656
- E sjcourage@btconnect.com
- W www.falklandarms.org.uk
- Beer range varies
- Simple, traditional fare
- The jewel in a perfectly preserved Cotswold village, this pub boasts an inglenook and stone-flagged floors worn smooth through centuries of use

This historic building dates back 500 years and is picture-postcard perfect. If you want to eat here your best bet is to go at lunchtime. In the evenings they only serve food in the charming but tiny dining room, which seats 12 people, and booking is essential. At lunchtime meals are also available in the bar or the delightful garden, where children are welcome. Ploughman's come with cheese, gammon or pâté, baguettes are filled with sausage and onion, Brie and apple, chicken mayo or other combinations, while jacket spuds are offered with a choice of four fillings: prices start at around £4. More substantial dishes are listed on the specials board such as spicy vegetable jambalaya or smoked haddock and herb chowder.

A sample evening menu offers a delicious starter of avocado and crayfish salad with lime and coriander, or grilled goats' cheese salad, followed by spinach and mushroom risotto or salmon fillet with honey-roasted parsnips. Desserts are home made – the Falkland version of crème brûlée is flavoured with lemon and thyme – or you can opt for a plate of English cheeses.

★ Q V (Banbury) C

HOOK NORTON
Gate Hangs High
OX15 5DF

- Due N of Hook Norton village towards Sibford Ferris
- Mon-Fri 11.30am-3pm, 6 (5 Fri)-11pm; Sat 11.30am-11pm; Sun 12-10.30pm
- Mon-Fri 12-3pm, 6-10pm; Sat & Sun 12-10pm
- T (01608) 737387
- E gatehangshigh@aol.com
- W www.gatehangshigh.com
- Hook Norton Best Bitter, Old Hooky; guest
- Varied menu of home-cooked dishes plus specials and a daily fish menu
- Attractive beamed bar where a fire burns in the inglenook; pleasant restaurant and garden; refurbished, en-suite guest rooms

With a menu that covers traditional and international cuisine, and an emphasis on local produce, the Gate aims to please all-comers. Children are well catered for and if nothing appeals on the main menu you can consult the specials board and the fish menu that are chalked up daily. Starters, £3-£7, include home-made soup, mushrooms stuffed with spinach and topped with goats' cheese, a fruit salad of hot bacon, banana and pineapple, bruschetta with hot chorizo, pesto and Parmesan, black pudding with bacon and potato rosti and a poached egg or king prawns in garlic butter.

Main courses are mostly £9-£13.50, a little more for fillet steak. A sample menu might read: rack of lamb in garlic butter, half a roast duck with leeks and marmalade, pork fillet with mushrooms, cream and sherry sauce, lamb's kidneys with bacon and onion, steak and wine pie or fillet of beef wrapped in pastry with mushroom and wine sauce. All the desserts are home made. Barbecues are held in summer and the pub is open for lunch on Christmas day (book early). The pub is set in lovely countryside and makes a good base for visiting Oxford, Stratford-on-Avon and Blenheim Palace.

★ Q S V C

HOOK NORTON
Sun Inn
High Street, OX15 5NH

- ▶ Turn off A361 at Milcombe, follow signs to Hook Norton
- Daily 11am-3pm, 6-11pm
- Daily 12-2pm, 6.30-9.15pm
- T (01608) 737570
- F (01608) 737535
- E joyce@thesuninn.fsnet.co.uk
- W www.the-sun-inn.com
- Hook Norton Best Bitter, Old Hooky plus rotating Hook Norton Beers
- ☺ Based on locally-sourced, fresh ingredients
- Unashamedly old-fashioned country inn; bar has its own dining area, no-smoking candlelit restaurant

Situated in the same village as the brewery, the Sun serves Hook Norton's fine ales to accompany its home-cooked fare and even includes the beer in some of the dishes – its fresh haddock in Hook Norton batter is a long-standing favourite. Although both the chefs trained in Michelin kitchens, their preference is for a simpler style of cooking, as befits a traditional rural pub. There is no compromise on standards and the use of fresh local ingredients means that the specials board changes twice weekly and the main menu is regularly revised.

Starters range from £3.50 for home-made soup of the day to £6.50 for oriental crispy duck salad served with hoisin dressing and pancakes, with home-cured salmon (gravadlax) or home-made pâté with toasted onion bread in the mid price bracket. Main courses have some unusual accompaniments – sweet and spicy cherry pepper, potato cake infused with basil and pesto cream sauce, £10.95, makes a pleasant change from the ubiquitous veggie lasagne. The introduction of fusion-style dishes to the menu has proved popular – Thai mussels, and King Scallops Hoisin now feature regularly on the specials board. In summer you can dine out in the pretty patio garden.

S V C

RAMSDEN
Royal Oak
High Street, OX7 3AU

- ▶ Centre of village
- Mon-Sat 11.30am-3pm, 6.30-11pm; Sun 12-3pm, 7-10.30pm
- Throughout opening times
- T (01993) 868213
- F (01993) 868864
- Butts Barbus Barbus; Hook Norton Best Bitter, Old Hooky plus rotating guests
- ☺ Modern English and French cuisine
- Comfortably furnished, traditional pub dating back to the 17th century, in the same hands for the last 18 years

The proprietors of the Royal Oak have a policy of sourcing all ingredients used in their kitchen from a maximum radius of 25 miles, using small specialist suppliers and organic produce as much as possible. Their menus are therefore seasonal and based on availability of supplies. The bar menu offers steaks and home-made burgers from the char grill, alongside old favourites such as steak and mushroom pudding, £11.95, or pie of the week, £7.95. In the spacious restaurant, which opens onto a courtyard, you could start with oven-baked baby Brie with a tomato and herb crust, served with crudités or maybe brochette of monkfish with a lemon butter sauce. Starters are all priced under £6.

For the main course, the loin of organic local pork might be accompanied by a casserole of mixed beans, Tuscan style, or you could opt for confit of duck served with green Puy lentils and honey, Cognac and redcurrant sauce, both priced at £12.95. Desserts at £4.25 are chalked up on the blackboard. The Royal Oak is very much a pub serving food rather than a restaurant with beer – at lunchtime a good snack menu offering ploughman's or hearty sandwiches is available in the main bar, which boasts an inglenook fireplace and is free from intrusive games machines or background music.

★ Q S V C

SWALCLIFFE
Stag's Head
The Green, OX15 5EJ

- On B4035, 6 miles W of Banbury
- Tue-Sat 12-2.30pm, Mon-Sat 6-11pm; Sun 12-4pm
- Tue-Sat 12-2.15pm, 7-9.30pm; Sun 12-3pm
- T (01295) 780232
- F (01295) 788977
- Hook Norton plus two guests
- Quality home cooked food using local produce
- At the centre of a historic and picturesque village, this 15th-century, thatched pub features an inglenook and a delightful garden

Taking over from previous owner and chef, Julia Kingsford, Tracey Kingsford's emphasis is on high quality home cooked food (no relation, just coincidence). All produce usedin the dishes is sourced locally from around Oxfordshire including meat and eggs from the farm next door. Herbs are freshly picked from the pub's own garden.

The menu kicks off with starters including warming soups, pates and whitebait which are priced from £3.95 to £5.00. For your main course choose from cottage pies, lasagne, steaks with or without sauces, mixed grills, fish in Hook Norton beer batter and the current favourite, the 'Stag's Head Burger' which includes parma ham and stilton served in Foccaccia. Prices range from £6.95 to £13.00. A weekly specials board offers further choice as well as themed food nights. Snacks are also available.

Save room for the mouth watering desserts which include crumbles with cream, custard or both, tarts, lemon meringue pies and pavlovas, priced from £4.25.

S V C

Described by the Sunday Sun as 'to die for', this is a recipe for sticky toffee pudding interestingly incorporating Camp coffee, sent by Lucy Irving, landlady of the Travellers Rest in Slaley, Northumberland.

STICKY TOFFEE PUDDING WITH BUTTERSCOTCH SAUCE
Serves 6-8

225g (8oz) butter
225g (8oz) brown sugar
8 eggs, beaten
450g (1lb) self-raising flour
2 tsps bicarbonate of soda
4 tbsps Camp coffee
600ml (1 pint) boiling water
500g (1lb) chopped dates

Butterscotch sauce
75g (3oz) unsalted butter
100g (4oz) soft brown sugar
75g (3oz) granulated sugar
450g (1lb) golden syrup
300ml (½ pint) double cream
Few drops vanilla essence

Pre-heat oven to 150C/300F/gas mark 2. Cream butter and sugar together in a bowl, stir in the beaten eggs then the flour. In a separate bowl, mix together the bicarbonate of soda and Camp coffee, add the boiling water, then stir in the dates. Combine contents of both bowls. Line a deep tray with greaseproof paper, pour in the mixture, and bake for 90 minutes.

To make the sauce, heat butter, all the sugar and golden syrup in a pan for 10 minutes, stirring. Continue to heat while pouring in the cream, then add a few drops of vanilla essence, and continue stirring until the sugar has fully dissolved.

BILLINGSLEY
Cape of Good Hope
WV16 6PG

- ▶ On Cleobury Mortimer road, 7 miles from Bridgnorth
- ☼ Mon-Fri 12-3pm, 6-11pm; Sat & Sun 12-11pm
- (¶) Mon-Fri 12-3pm, 6-9pm; Sat & Sun 12-9pm
- T (01746) 861565
- E jwaddison1@aol.com
- Banks's Bitter; Enville Ale; Hobson's Best Bitter; guests
- ☺ Good quality English at reasonable prices; steaks are a speciality
- Set deep in the countryside, this friendly pub's reputation for good food makes it worth the effort to seek out

The Addisons took over the pub in 2002, refurbished the restaurant and kitchen, and quickly achieved a good following for its food. A visit is an absolute must for dedicated carnivores – a whopping 32oz rump steak will set you back £14.95 – the same price that you would pay in many a restaurant for something a quarter the size. All is not lost if you are vegetarian however, as home-made vegetarian curry and lasagne are always on the menu, as well as something seasonal on the specials board such as chestnut, parsnip and sweet potato bake. Other dishes on the board might include poached haddock on spring onion mash with wine and mushroom sauce, oven-roasted cod or rolled rack of lamb with chestnut and shallot stuffing.

Starters are mostly pub favourites such as garlic mushrooms, hot garlic prawns or filled potato skins, all under £4. The list of steaks is most impressive, with a range of rumps from 7oz up to 32oz, including Rossini rump served with pâté and red wine sauce and an 8oz sirloin with Stilton sauce. Alternatives include a massive 'he man' grill, lamb chops, home-made pies, cod in batter and salads. If you can manage a dessert, consult the blackboard.

★ Q S V P C

BRIDGNORTH
Fox Inn
46 Hospital Street, WV15 5AR

- ▶ On main A442, directly opposite turn to Bridgnorth Low Town
- ☼ Mon-Wed 5-11pm; Thu & Fri 12-3pm, 5-11pm; Sat & Sun 12-11pm
- (¶) Mon-Wed 5-9.30pm; Thur & Fri 12-3pm, 5-9.30pm; Sat & Sun 12-9.30pm
- T (01746) 769611
- F (01746) 761736
- E lewiscresswell@virgin.net
- W www.foxinnbridgnorth.co.uk
- Enville Ale; Fuller's London Pride; Holden's Bitter
- ☺ Contemporary English food
- Coaching inn that has undergone a stylish refurbishment but remains friendly

Food at the Fox is contemporary in style, but balanced with classical elements. The menus change regularly; the specials boards reflect the availability of seasonal produce. For a light meal, choose from fresh ciabattas with fillings such as steak with Shropshire blue or Camembert, red onion and spinach; if you prefer you can opt for an open toasty with chorizo, cheese and basil or rarebit of Shropshire blue.

The starters list offers inventive combinations, such as slices of lobster tail with strawberry velouté dressing and red chard salad, marinated salmon with nutmeg, white balsamic and fennel slaw or terrine of smoked bacon, chorizo and pimento with watercress and basil salad, £4-£7. Equally interesting are the main courses: double-baked wild mushroom and tarragon soufflé with avocado and ginger salad and toasted brioche soldiers, seared monkfish and scallops with mango and pineapple salsa and toasted cashew and artichoke salad, gâteau of pork tenderloin, sun dried tomato and oyster mushroom stuffing, with apple and calvados cream, £11-£15. Stylish desserts include iced bitter chocolate parfait with lavender and chilli syrup.

★ S V (Bridgnorth) P C

COALBROOKDALE
Coalbrookdale Inn
12 Wellington Road, TF8 7DX

- Opposite the Enginuity Museum
- Daily 12pm-midnight (10.30pm Sun)
- Daily 12-2.30pm, 6-9pm
- T (01952) 433953
- E tudorhotels@aol.com
- W www.coalbrookdaleinn.co.uk
- Beer range varies
- Home-cooked food with a Gold Healthy Eating award
- Unspoilt by progress, this Grade II listed inn retains its early Victorian character, without intrusive juke box or games machines

Coalbrookdale was at the cradle of the developing Industrial Age and the pub was built to serve iron workers in the 1830s. Now a pleasant suburb of Telford, the village is worth a visit for its heritage museums (the Enginuity Museum is a hands-on experience for children). Nearby, the striking Open Air Museum of Steel Sculptures is also fascinating. You can dine in the bar or restaurant, and all the meals are home cooked from local produce, with an emphasis on healthy dishes, including vegetarian choices.

Starters include salsa mussels with warm, crusty bread, Thai fish cakes with a sweet chilli dip and warm smoked duck and bacon salad with hoi sin sauce, mostly around £5. To follow, pub favourites such as steak and ale pie and succulent steaks vie for your attention with pork tenderloin in a caramelised shallot white wine sauce, chicken enchiladas with side salad or home-made chips, sautéed duck breast with a choice of sauces, filo pastry parcels filled with tomato and goats' cheese, served with red pesto or oven-baked sea bass with langoustines, olive oil and citrus juices, prices from £7-£13. Home-made desserts, £4, include the chef's signature dish of Baileys Irish cream cheesecake, as well as apple and rhubarb crumple and hot chocolate fudge cake.

★ S V P C

HEATHTON
Old Gate Inn
WV5 7EB

Off B4176 between Wolverhampton and Bridgnorth
Daily 12-2.30pm, 6.30-11pm (10.30pm Sun)
Daily 12-2pm, 6.30-9pm
T (01746) 710431
F (01746) 710131
E oldgateinn@aol.com
W www.oldgateinn.co.uk
Enville Ale; Greene King Abbot; Taylor Landlord; guests
Good quality home-cooked food with daily specials
Busy rural inn dating back to the 16th century; garden with children's play area

A good daily specials list supplements an enticing, home-cooked menu that is a mix of pub favourites and more up to date recipes. Starters, £4-£5, include home-made soup, king prawns in garlic butter, smoked salmon and cream cheese roulade and perhaps specials of warm goats' cheese salad and spicy chicken wings with a blue cheese dip. A good selection of fish normally appears on the specials board, such as baked salmon fillet with honey and Jack Daniels glaze, grilled seabass fillets, whole grilled Brixham plaice or lemon sole or fresh haddock in beer batter with French fries.

Other specials, £9-£14, may include braised lamb shank in a rich minted gravy, fillet steak strips in a cream and paprika sauce with rice timbale or the popular chicken breast wrapped in bacon topped with cheese and served on a bed of coleslaw. Fillet and sirloin steaks, plain or with sauces, are always available. Yummy puds are all £4.50: sticky toffee pudding, warm ginger sponge with stem ginger sauce, mandarin and Cointreau trifle, banana and butterscotch crumble, to name a few. For a light meal there are wraps at £5.95, such as marinated duck, spicy chicken or roasted vegetable.

★ S V C

IRONBRIDGE
Golden Ball
1 Newbridge Road, TF8 7BA

Just off Madeley Bank
Daily 12-11pm (10.30pm Sun)
Mon-Thu 12-2.30pm, 6-9pm; Fri & Sat 12-9pm; Sun 12-8.30pm
T (01952) 432179
F (01952) 433123
E matrowland@hotmail.com
W www.goldenballinn.com
Everards Tiger; Hook Norton Old Hooky; guests
Home-made dishes chalked up daily on a blackboard
Multi-roomed pub set in spectacular countryside, stocking Shropshire ales alongside Belgian bottled beers

Although Ironbridge was the birthplace of heavy industry in the UK, it is now a tranquil spot with no less than 10 fascinating museums. At the heart of this World Heritage Site sits the Golden Ball, the oldest pub in the area. It was built as a brewhouse in 1728 and this original part of the building, still housing the pump that provided water for the beer, is now the restaurant.

All the dishes are home made based on fresh produce from local suppliers. The menu, which is chalked up daily, always includes a fish dish and a vegetarian option. Starters on a sample menu include grilled goats' cheese on mixed leaves with sweet pimento coulis for £5 or crayfish tails on fennel salad marinated with lemon and olive oil for £5.50. Main courses might be kangaroo rump served with forest mushrooms and garlic cream, £14, while vegetarians are offered a fricassée of wild mushrooms with spinach, garlic and sage for £9.50. The most expensive main dish, at £16, is fillet steak on a sweet onion marmalade topped with Brie. Home-made desserts are all £4.50. Booking is recommended for the restaurant.

★ S V C

MUCH WENLOCK
George & Dragon
2 High Street, TF13 6AA

- In the town centre
- Daily 12-11pm (10.30pm Sun)
- Mon-Sun 12-2pm, 6-9pm (not Wed or Sun)
- T (01952) 727312
- Hobsons Town Crier; Greene King IPA, Abbot; Taylor Landlord; guests
- Good quality, traditional British cuisine with daily specials
- Grade II listed 18th-century building at the centre of a small market town, with intimate bar and cosy restaurant

Very much a focal point for the people of Much Wenlock, this historic inn offers a warm welcome to all visitors. Sandwiches and light meals are served at lunchtime, including ham and Shropshire blue cheese rarebit with diced celery, apples and walnuts, filled jacket potatoes and ploughman's with various cheeses or home-baked ham, all for around a fiver. A full menu of freshly-cooked dishes is served five evenings a week, supplemented by daily specials. Starters include home-made soup, Stilton and walnut pâté and garlic mushrooms with crusty bread, or on the specials list there may be crispy coated Camembert, grilled goats' cheese or fried black pudding on caramelised red cabbage, £4.25-£5.25.

Main courses, £9-£16, include home-baked ham with parsley sauce, breast of chicken in apricot, mead and cream sauce, fillet of poached salmon in dill and white wine or home-made Thai chicken curry with all the trimmings, while the specials board might offer a pie of venison marinated in red wine, roast duck breast in plum sauce, roasted Barnsley chop or grilled trout with ginger and prawns. Heart-warming home-made puds are all £4.25: sticky toffee, bread and butter or fruit crumble. Take time to admire the landlord's collection of some 350-plus water jugs.

★ V C

SHIFNAL
☆ Odfellows
Market Place, TF11 9AU

- In centre of town, signed off M54 jct 3 and 4
- Mon-Thu & Sat 12-3pm, 5.30-11pm; Fri & Sun 12-11pm
- Mon-Sat 12-2.30pm, 7-10pm; Sun 12-6pm
- T (01952) 461517
- F (01952) 463855
- W www.odleyinns.co.uk
- Beer range varies
- Modern British with emphasis on locally produced meat
- A wine bar rather than a pub; airy, open plan former coaching house

The odd spelling of Odfellows is because it is one of three houses owned by Odley Inns. Although it calls itself a wine bar, it does offer a good choice of real ales on handpump from local breweries such as Salopian, Wood and Batham. It also stocks some Belgian beers and draught cider. On the food front, great care is taken to source free-range meat and eggs of the highest quality and the same attention is paid to vegetarian dishes – meat substitutes will not do here, recipes are based on fresh vegetables.

The menu changes with the seasons – a typical spring selection offers starters such as devilled lambs' kidneys on toast, Moroccan prawn briouat or spinach and ricotta gnocchi with tomato and garlic sauce, all for around £5. Main courses range in price from just under £10 to £14, with tasty choices such as Gressingham duck breast with pomegranate molasses and walnuts, marinated lamb steak with chickpea and cumin mash, sweet potato crisps and salsa verde, or haricot vert and walnut rissoles with Puy lentils and feta as a veggie option. Home-made sweets are all priced at £3.75 and fair trade coffee is served. A simple lunch menu has good sandwiches, burgers and omelettes made with free range eggs.

V (Shifnal) P C

STOTTESDEN
☆ Fighting Cocks
1 High Street, DY14 8TZ

- Between Cleobury Mortimer and Bridgnorth
- Mon-Fri 6-11pm; Sat & Sun 12-11pm
- Tue-Sat 7-9pm; Sat and Sun 12-2pm
- T (01746) 718270
- Hobsons Best Bitter, Town Crier; guests
- Wholesome, home-made dishes with no fixed menu
- Fine community pub, deep in the Shropshire countryside, that attracts visitors from far and wide for its atmosphere, ales and food

This gem of a village pub enjoys a good reputation for its food, but visitors should note that it is closed weekday lunchtimes. It doesn't bother with a printed menu – dishes depend on fresh local ingredients and vary depending on what is available – and are chalked up daily. Typical starters are smoked duck breast with peach chutney, feta cheese and olive platter, organic smoked salmon mousse and home-made soup or pâté, all under £5. To follow there might be lovely old-fashioned favourites such as braised oxtail with cinnamon and red wine or beef in ale with horseradish dumplings. Other choices are pork T-bone with wholegrain mustard mash and black pudding, sausage cassoulet with red wine, local mutton curry with rice or red Thai pork. There is always a fresh fish dish, maybe organic salmon with pesto sauce. Main courses are mostly £8.95 apart from locally produced lamb or beef steaks which go up to £12. The pub is well known for its home-made pies: steak and kidney or Guinness, chicken and leek or lamb, mint and red wine, all £7.95, and there is a good choice for vegetarians such as red pepper and bean tagine, homity pie, smoked ricotta, or leek and potato pie. Super home-made puds, £3.95, include raspberry charlotte, chocolate torte and eve's pudding.

V C

WORFIELD
Dog Inn
Main Street, WV15 5LF

- 5 miles from Bridgnorth, turn off A454 opposite Vauxhall garage
- Mon-Sat 12-2.30pm, 7-11pm; Sun 12-3pm, 7-10.30pm
- Daily 12-2pm, 7-9.30pm
- T (01746) 716020
- Courage Best Bitter; Theakston Mild; Wells Bombardier
- Upmarket restaurant food or simple lunchtime snacks
- Quaint English two bar village pub in a secluded spot off the main road

The Dog is a typical English village pub, but the lounge has been extended to provide an attractive dining area where daily specials are chalked up on a blackboard to complement the main menu. The popular tapas platter of various cold meats, fish, olives and bread can be served as a starter or snack for two people, £9. The specials board always shows a good variety of fishy starters such as white anchovies with sliced garlic and olive oil, smoked salmon soup or spicy sardines with salad, all under £5.

For main courses, with prices ranging from £8.50 to £18.50 for fillet steak, the two cooks conjure up a mix of local recipes and more exotic fare, all freshly prepared. Traditionalists might go for the rabbit casserole, faggots in gravy or 'blanks and fries', an old Shropshire dish of sautéed pieces of gammon served with broad beans, new potatoes and parsley sauce, while vegetable tortilla or tuna steak with sesame oil and soy sauce might appeal to those with more Mediterranean tastes. A proper roast lunch is served on Sunday. Families are welcome and a basic children's menu is provided.

Q S V C

ASHCOTT

☆ Ring O' Bells

High Street, TA7 9PZ

- Turn N off A39 for village, pub is by the church
- Daily 12-3pm, 7-11pm (10.30pm Sun)
- Daily 12-2pm, 7-10pm
- T (01458) 210232
- E info@ringobells.com
- W www.ringobells.com
- Beer range varies
- All dishes made from scratch in the pub using local ingredients
- Run by the same family for 17 years, this village pub hosts regular quizzes and skittles competitions

The Ring O' Bells makes good use of local specialities on its menu and this policy is carried through into the bar, which always has Somerset draught cider from Wilkins and usually a beer from Ashcott's Moor Beer Co. Cider and ale often make an appearance in the home-cooked dishes: scrumpy chicken is served in a creamy cider sauce with apples or as a pie, while ale is incorporated with cheese and onion to make a delicious soup. Honey and cider syllabub is a lovely light dessert, and Somerset Brie is used to make fritters served with cranberry sauce as a starter.

The regular menu is supplemented by daily specials. Starters include seafood ramekin with salad garnish or cheese-topped ratatouille with granary bread (also available as a main course). Another vegetarian choice is the gypsy vegetable casserole with apricots, chickpeas and mildly spiced tomato sauce. A daily curry is joined by a fresh fish dish of the day, while on Sunday there is always a choice of beef and another roast meat. Main course prices are £6.50-£12.50 but smaller portions are available for less. Ice cream sundaes at £4.25 include the unusual 'tropical maelstrom' of ginger ice cream, ginger, pineapple and cream; other desserts are listed on the blackboard.

★ Q S V C

ASHILL

Square & Compass

Windmill Hill, TA19 9NX

- Off A358 between Taunton and Ilminster
- Mon-Sat 12-2.30pm, 6.30-11pm (closed Tue-Thu lunchtime); Sun 12-3pm, 7-10.30pm
- Daily 12-2pm (not Tue-Thu), 7-9.30pm
- T (01823) 480467
- E square&compass@tiscali.co.uk
- W www.squareandcompasspub.com
- Draught Bass; Exmoor Ale; St Austell HSD
- Wide range of home-cooked meals plus sandwiches
- Inviting pub overlooking the Blackdown Hills in a designated area of Outstanding Natural Beauty

Chris and Janet Slow have owned the pub for seven years and in that time have built up a reputation not only for good food, but also as a popular music venue; acts booked for 2005 included Dr Feelgood, the Animals and Hazel O'Connor, as well as a clutch of well-established tribute bands (check with the website for upcoming dates). The kitchen staff prepare all the meals and try to avoid buying anything in. The home-made steak and ale pie is renowned, but equally tasty are the steaks, served plain or with cream-based sauces and the traditional Sunday roasts, £6.95. A specials board lists seasonal dishes such as game pie, fresh fish and usually a chicken dish, perhaps with a creamy Stilton and bacon sauce, or you could try a trio of local sausages served with red wine and onion gravy. Main courses range in price from just £5.95 to £14, while home-made puds are all a very reasonable £3: banoffee pie, fresh fruit pavlova, apple pie and treacle tart are usually available. You may dine in the pub itself or in the extensive garden. Apart from the real ales listed above, the pub also serve a house beer, Windmill Hill Bitter, from Interbrew and the occasional guest beer.

★ Q S V C

BAYFORD
Unicorn Inn
BA9 9NL

- One mile E of Wincanton on old A303
- Mon-Sat 12-3pm (not Mon), 7-11pm; Sun 12-3pm, 7-10.30pm
- Daily 12-2pm (not Mon), 7-9pm (not Sun)
- T (01963) 32324
- W www.theunicorninnbayford.com
- Draught Bass; Butcombe Bitter; guests
- Generous portions of home-cooked food; fish is a speciality
- Sympathetically modernised former coaching inn retaining many original features including flagstone floors, beams, open fireplace and a hidden well

Landlord Jon Waite and his wife Jo, who is also in charge of the kitchen, have built up a fine reputation for the Unicorn by providing good value home-cooked food in generous portions – 'no-one ever leaves this pub hungry,' they say. They specialise in fresh fish, with dishes that reflect what is available at the time: skate, ling, plaice, Torbay sole or monkfish. One of their home-made dishes is an unusual fish cassoulet, making a tasty change from the spicy sausage version that is often available. Another special recipe is the Unicorn sizzler that can be based on beef, king prawn or served as a vegetarian option. Meat from a local butcher is used in lasagne, curries and casseroles or simply grilled. Soups served here are always home made, vegetarian and gluten free – indeed, Jo will always do her best to fulfil customers' dietary requirements.

All the starters come in large portions: the prawn cocktail is highly praised and another favourite is whole prawns in garlic and chilli. An extensive choice covers pâté, garlic mushrooms, halloumi, and seafood such as mussels or sardines. For customers who have left room for dessert there are old favourites such as fruit crumble, lemon sponge or ice creams. The Unicorn gets busy on Wincanton race days.

S V P C

BRADFORD ON TONE
White Horse
Regent Street, TA4 1HF

- Off A38, between Taunton and Wellington
- Mon-Sat 11.30am-3pm, 5.30-11pm; Sun 12-3pm, 7-10.30pm
- Daily 12-2pm, 6.30-9pm
- T (01823) 461239
- E donna@pmccann1.wanadoo.co.uk
- Cotleigh Tawny; guests
- Traditional home-cooked dishes, supplemented by theme nights showcasing Thai, Mexican, French or Italian cuisine
- Situated opposite the church in a beautiful village of thatched houses

The White Horse is a true community local with the added bonus of serving excellent food. Villagers come here not only to drink in the friendly bar, but also to use the shop and post office in the outbuildings. The pub also offers traditional entertainment, with its bar billiards table and skittle alley. The 65-seater restaurant serves a simple menu at lunchtime and à la carte in the evenings when specials might include venison with a wild mushroom and brandy sauce, oven-baked duck breast with a plum and balsamic compote or maybe Mexican chicken – pan-fried breast topped with a chunky tomato and chilli sauce finished with 'afterburn' cheese. A popular dish is the 'famous half shoulder of lamb' served with redcurrant and rosemary jus – a single portion that might grace a family table on a Sunday lunchtime for £13.95. The pub offers a good choice of fish, especially on Friday lunchtime, which can be served fairly plain or dressed up: plaice fillets come with a ginger butter sauce and rainbow trout with lemon crumble and coriander and lime dressing. A proper Sunday lunch is served with a choice of three roast meats. And if you are a fan of exotic food, look out for the special themed evenings when the menu concentrates on dishes from any corner of the globe.

Q S V P C

BURNHAM ON SEA
Dunstan House Inn
8-10 Love Lane, TA8 1EU

- Take jct 22 off M5 and follow signs for town centre
- Mon-Sat 11am-11pm; Sun 12-10.30pm
- Mon-Thu 12-2.30pm, 6-9.30pm; Fri & Sat 12-9.30pm; Sun 12-9pm
- T (01278) 784343
- E dunstanhouseinn@youngs.co.uk
- Young's Bitter, Special, Waggledance
- Home-cooked pub food
- Spacious roadside pub recently refurbished to provide a new garden room. There is seating and a children's play area outside

It is not everyone who can cope with the sometimes gargantuan portions that are served up in some pubs. Many older people in particular do not have the same appetites they had in their youth, but at the same time hate to waste food. So it is pleasing to see on the Dunstan House menu that its traditional roast dinners of beef, lamb or chicken come in a choice of sizes: giant, £7.50, regular, £6.25 and small £4.75. There is a good choice of lighter dishes too: filled ciabatta rolls served with salad garnish and chips, ploughman's, filled jacket spuds (the roasted vegetable and mozzarella sounds particularly tempting) and a couple of salads – prawn or Caesar with chicken and smoked bacon.

The main menu is typical pub fare, but all good quality and prepared on the premises at reasonable prices. For example oven-baked mushrooms, home-made pâté and moules marinière are all priced at £3.75 for starters (although again a choice is given of a whole pint of mussels for £6.25). Most main courses are priced under £8 except for the steaks that are listed on a blackboard. A couple of dishes are suitable for vegetarians, such as the oven-roasted beef tomatoes packed with an asparagus and lemon risotto. This Young's tied house, far from its London base, caters well for families.

S V C

CHEWTON MENDIP
Waldegrave Arms
High Street, BA3 4LL

- At village centre on A39 between Bath and Wells
- Mon-Sat 11.30am-2.30pm, 6-11pm; Sun 12-10.30pm
- Mon-Sat 12-2pm, 6-10pm; Sun 12-9pm
- T (01761) 241384
- E waldegravearms@aol.com
- W www.waldegravearms.co.uk
- Butcombe Bitter; guests
- Extensive menu ranging from sandwiches to monster steaks
- Attractive main road pub benefiting from an award-winning garden and good value accommodation on the edge of the Mendips

Landlady Sue Clarke leads a team of four in the kitchen to produce an extensive menu from fresh produce. Friday is fish day when there is an amazing choice of up to 10 different types of fish, cooked to customers' requirements – battered, breaded or what you will. Fish also features on the regular menu, and a separate list is devoted to grills and steaks that range in size from the 10oz rump, £9.95 to a 24oz T-bone at £14.95 or the monster mixed grill for the same price. Sauces are an extra £1.50.

There is a good choice of starters; it is a long time since I have seen egg mayonnaise on any menu in the UK, it is about due for a revival. This contrasts with more modern additions, such as the tempura sweet and sour vegetables, £3.95. Main courses offer similar variety, again with old favourites such as liver, bacon and onion, £6.45, offered alongside lighter choices such as three-egg omelettes with a variety of fillings for £5.95, plus a daily specials board. The popular 'real chips' go down well with all the dishes. Sandwiches, snacks and ploughman's start at £2.95 and there is also a children's menu. Bookings are taken for the popular Sunday lunch which is served all day.

★ S V C

COMPTON MARTIN
Ring O' Bells
Main Street, BS40 6JE

▶ On A368 between Blagdon and West Harptree
☼ Mon-Sat 11.30am-3pm, 6.30-11pm; Sun 12-3pm, 6.30-10.30pm
🍴 Mon-Thu 11.30am-2pm, 6.30-9pm; Fri & Sat 11.30-3pm, 6.30-9.30pm; Sun 12-2pm, 6.30-9.30pm
T (01761) 221284
E roger@ring47.freeserve.co.uk
Butcombe Bitter, Blonde, Gold; guests
☺ Local fish and meat plus good salads and snacks at reasonable prices
Atmospheric country inn with good family facilities

The Ring O' Bells has something for everyone: real ales from owners of the pub - Butcombe Brewery, a pretty garden, an attractive family room with toys provided to keep children amused and, above all, a menu to suit all tastes at reasonable prices. Fish features prominently here: trout from a nearby lake is delivered most evenings by one of the regulars, while another local takes a monthly trip to Weymouth and brings back his catch – it could be pollock, bass, ling, cod or one of the many flat fish from that part of the coast. Meat comes from a nearby abattoir, delivered by a local butcher. A favourite dish was created for the pub by landlady Jackie Owen - her Butcombe beef is a simple but tasty affair of diced beef, onion, carrots and herbs stewed for three hours in Butcombe Bitter, priced at £6.50. The pub offers a particularly good choice of salads, £5.50-6.95, with Wiltshire ham, coronation chicken, topside of beef or a mixed platter of all three meats. Ploughman's come with cheese or meat while snacks such as omelettes or filled jacket spuds are always popular. Children have a choice of the usual sausages or burger and chips or they can have a reduced portion of most of the main dishes.

★ Q S V ♣ P C

CROWCOMBE
Carew Arms
TA4 4AD

▶ Off A358, approx 10 miles from Taunton and Minehead
☼ Daily 11am-3.30pm, 6-11pm
🍴 Daily 12-2pm, 7-10pm
T (01984) 618631
F (01984) 618428
E info@thecarewarms.co.uk
W www.thecarewarms.co.uk
Exmoor Ale; guest
☺ Modern English cuisine featuring fresh fish and game
Quiet village inn with a 60-seat restaurant and six en-suite guest rooms; a good base for walking the Quantocks

Even if you are not planning to dine, the Carew Arms is definitely worth a visit. Why? Because it is listed on CAMRA's National Inventory of Pub Interiors of Outstanding Historic Interest. Some sympathetic renovations have been undertaken and work is ongoing as parts of the building date back 500 years, however its flagstone floored public bar remains untouched. Great emphasis is placed on freshness with fish delivered up to three times a week.

Seasonal game, such as rabbit, pheasant and venison comes from local shoots and delicious smoked products (including duck) are supplied by Dartmouth Smokehouse.

All dishes are cooked to order. You can enjoy a 'grazing bowl' while you wait – a dish of olives and a couple of snack items for £1 per head. Starters tend to be 'fishy'; the king scallops in hot garlic butter and the mussels are both also served as a main course. Meats are generally grilled or pan fried (the chicken breast comes with bubble and squeak), although some more unusual variations are offered such as 'rack and black' – Exmoor lamb with black pudding or pork chops served with soy sauce and pak choi. Main courses are priced from £8.75.

★ Q S V ≋ (Crowcombe Heathfield) P C

CULMHEAD
Holman Clavel Inn
TA3 7EA

- Quarter of a mile off B3170, about 5 miles S of Taunton
- Mon-Sat 12-11pm; Sun 12-3pm, 7-10.30pm
- Daily 12-2pm, 7-9pm
- T (01823) 421432
- E richard_cara@hotmail.com
- Butcombe Bitter, Gold; guests
- Main menu specialises in fish and seafood; good range of snacks
- Unspoilt country inn, undisturbed by TV or piped music, but allegedly haunted by the ghost of a defrocked monk

Collectors of trivia will be interested to know that the inn's unique name is due to the lintel or clavel that rests above the fireplace, made of holm oak. Despite rumours of a ghost, visitors are assured of a warm welcome from Richard Lawrence and his wife Cara (in charge of the kitchen). Cara sources all her meat and vegetables locally – the fish is delivered several times a week from Brixham, while the shellfish comes from aptly named Beer. An extensive 'lighter bites' menu offers everything from home-cooked ham with free-range eggs and chips to chicken balti, cod and chips and beef burgers, plus a good range of baguettes and salads. With starters priced at £3.50-£5.50 (for half a pint of shell-on prawns) and mains all under £6.50, they are great value for money. Steak and mushroom pie is a firm favourite and it is not only vegetarians who enjoy the popular home-cooked veggie pastas. The main menu is more inventive with starters such as sweet potato, leek, chickpea and Parmesan soup or grilled sardines with oregano, olive oil, lemon and garlic. Main dishes include a mixed fish platter with an olive oil sauce, Malaysian chicken or Thai spiced lamb. Desserts are displayed on a blackboard. Most dishes are home made, including the soups and the bread.

★ Q S V C

HALSE
New Inn
TA4 3AF

- Signposted off the A358 between Taunton and Minehead
- Daily 12-2.30pm, 6.30pm-Close
- Daily 12-2pm, 7-9.30pm
- T (01823) 432352
- E amanda@newinnhalse.co.uk
- W www.newinnhalse.co.uk
- Halse Hop; guests
- A mix of traditional British dishes and fresh fish
- Free house dating back to the 17th century with oak-beamed bar, candlelit dining room and skittles alley

The award-winning New Inn is more than just another country pub with good food – this one also has its own brewery, set up in 2003. Their beers are currently being brewed by an expert from the nearby Exmoor Brewery.

All produce is sourced locally and their chef, Sara Duddridge, who, being vegetarian herself, always makes sure that a wide range of meat-free dishes are available on the menu.

The lunchtime and evening menus differ with the former including the local's favourite, steak and guinness pie for £8.50 as well as beer battered cod (made using their own beer) at £7.95. Lunchtime prices range from £5.50-£8.95. The evening menu is priced from £8.50-£15.95 and includes Somerset-reared fillet steak (£13.95), fresh fish and local game. The daily-changing specials board increases the choices available. A two-course Sunday roast is excellent value at £9.95.

All desserts are home-made and priced at £4.50. These include a selection of cheeses with the pub's own chutney, marmalade bread and butter pudding and local ice creams.

Q S V C

HINTON BLEWITT
Ring O' Bells
Upper Road, BS39 5AN

- ▶ Turn off A37 at Temple Cloud, follow lane for approx two miles, turn left at T-junction
- Mon-Fri 11am-3pm, 5-11pm; Sat 11am-3pm, 6-11pm; Sun 12-4pm, 7-10.30pm
- Mon-Fri 12-2pm, 7-10pm; Sat & Sun 12-2.30pm, 7-10pm
- T (01761) 452239
- F (01761) 451245
- E jonboy2ringer@aol.com
- W www.ringobells.net
- Butcombe Bitter; guests
- Honest pub fare served in generous portions at reasonable prices
- Free house in a picturesque village, set on the green with stunning views

Cook Gill Grivas' husband is Greek, so it is hardly surprising that the specials board at the pub often displays dishes from his homeland – a summer favourite is moussaka with Greek salad. Gill says that all but one (which one, we wonder?) of the main meals served here are freshly prepared on the premises. The meat all comes from the Whistley herd nearby and other ingredients are sourced locally as much as possible. Two of the most popular choices on the menu are beef marinated in Guinness, served in a giant Yorkshire pudding and served with chips and vegetables, £8.95, and chicken breast stuffed with Stilton with a white wine sauce, £8.25. Vegetarian options include mushroom stroganoff with rice, or vegetable and cheese bakes, both around £7. All the main courses come in hearty portions, so you may not need a starter, but you could be tempted by the filo-wrapped king prawns or the garlic mushrooms on toast. Traditional puds, priced at £3.50, are supplemented by specials chalked up on the blackboard. Hinton Blewitt lies between the Mendip Hills and the Chew Valley and the pub is a popular stopping place for walkers and cyclists.

S V P C

KINGSBURY EPISCOPI
Wyndham Arms
Folly Road, TA12 6AT

- ▶ 3 miles N of A303 between Yeovil and Taunton
- Mon-Sat 12-3pm, 6.30-11pm; Sun 12-3pm, 7-10.30pm
- Daily 12-2pm, 7-9.15pm
- T (01935) 823239
- E mail@wyndhamarms.com
- W www.wyndhamarms.com
- Fuller's London Pride, Worthington's Bitter; guests
- Good, honest pub food supplemented by plenty of daily specials
- Centuries old hamstone inn with open fires, flagstone floors, an extensive garden and courtyard seating

There are several reasons to visit the Wyndham Arms, apart from its delicious food. This thriving village pub, frequented by cyclists and walkers on the Somerset Levels, is home to the Wyndham Blues and Roots Club and regularly features international artists. The pub also has a skittles alley and an increasingly rare bar skittles table. As for the food, an ample menu covers all tastes and appetites. Starters such as whitebait, crispy mushrooms and prawn cocktail come in small and large sizes. Home-made standards such as cottage pie, chilli con carne, steak and kidney pie and curries (daily varieties are chalked on the blackboard) are priced at around £7. All the meat comes from Somerset raised animals; the pork and eggs are free range and the ham is cooked on the premises. Every day up to 10 specials are also prepared in the pub kitchen, such as local faggots or chops, pasta bakes or stuffed chicken breast. The desserts, for around £3-£4, are mostly based on ice cream – such as banana split or fruit sorbets – although an exception is the chocolate fudge cake which is made from a west country recipe. Sandwiches, ploughman's, salads and snacks are always available and a children's menu is provided.

★ S V P C

LONG SUTTON

☆ Devonshire Arms

TA10 9LP

- ▶ Leave A303 at Podimore roundabout, follow A372 to Langport, turn left after 4 miles to Long Sutton
- Daily 12-3pm, 6-11pm
- Daily 12-2.30pm, 6-9.30pm
- T (01458) 241271
- F (01458) 241037
- E mail@thedevonshirearms.com
- W www.thedevonshirearms.com
- Hop Back Crop Circle; Teignworthy Reel Ale; guests
- Modern British cuisine; home-made pies
- Grade II listed former hunting lodge at the heart of the Somerset Levels, on an idyllic village green

With nine well-appointed, en-suite bedrooms this makes an ideal base for exploring the countryside. Visitors who enter expecting a traditional country hotel are however in for a surprise as the interior and the menu are both surprisingly modern. On the starters menu you may find home-cured salmon with wonton wafers, pickled cucumber and lime crème fraîche, £5.35, or Thai tiger prawn fish cakes served with beetroot, ginger and sesame dressing, £4.95. Even the soup is out of the ordinary: sweet potato with rosemary is a typical combination.

The main courses offer readily recognisable dishes but with interesting variations, such as rump of lamb, marinated before roasting and served with ginger and vanilla chutney sauce, £15.25, or the fillet of salmon that comes with a lobster, sweet pepper and sesame dressing, £13.95. A favourite with customers is the slow roasted shoulder of Somerset beef served with caramelised root veg and red wine cooking liquor. A lighter menu is available at lunchtime, sandwiches come in any combination of three fillings from a long list that includes black pudding, char-grilled chorizo and marinated anchovies.

S V P C

MIDDLEZOY

George Inn

42 Main Road, TA7 0NN

- ▶ One mile from A372/A361 jct
- Mon-Fri 12-2.30pm (not Mon), 7-11pm; Sat 12-3pm, 7-11pm; Sun 12-3pm, 7-10.30pm
- Tue-Sat 12-2pm, 7-9pm; Sun 12-2pm
- T (01823) 698215
- E wilzoy@btopenworld.com
- Butcombe Bitter; guests
- Good quality pub food, monthly curry night
- Village pub, dating from the 17th century, with original stone-flagged floor, exposed beams and open fireplaces

Beer festivals are a regular feature at this pub that fully deserves its frequent entry in CAMRA's Good Beer Guide. Independent breweries are showcased here and the pub prides itself on aiming to stock two beers a week that customers have not tried before. Landlady Sonya Enright takes the same care in the kitchen and always has a good selection of dishes to supplement the standard menu. Sausages from a local butcher are often featured, venison being a particular favourite, while the steaks come from herds raised nearby.

Starters will usually include a home-made soup of the day, alongside more unusual offerings such as crispy jalapeno peppers stuffed with cream cheese or battered calamari rings, all under £4. The main courses are equally good value; one day's specials included lamb shank with new potatoes and vegetables for £6.95, broccoli and stilton pie with salad, or cod and chips with mushy peas, both £4.95, and chicken madras for £5.50. Home made chillis and curries (including a vegetarian version) are always on the menu, and a special curry evening is held on the first Saturday of the month. Sonya always offers a couple of vegetarian choices, such as broccoli and cream cheese bake served with salad. All the desserts are priced at a very reasonable £2.75.

★ Q S V P C

MOORLINCH
Ring O' Bells
Pit Hill Lane, TA7 9BT

- Off A39 between Bridgwater and Glastonbury
- Mon 5-11pm; Tue-Sat 12-11pm (may close afternoons if quiet); Sun 12-10.30pm
- Mon-Fri 12-2pm (not Mon), 6-9pm; Sat 12-3pm, 6-9.30pm; Sun 12-3pm, 6-8.30pm
- T (01458) 210358
- E cliveringers@btinternet.com
- Beer range varies
- Mix of traditional pub fare and home-made dishes
- Large public bar and lower lounge that serves as a restaurant

Landlady Trish Gill openly admits that much of the extensive menu is based on frozen or ready prepared dishes. However, since taking over the pub in 2002 (when all the meals were bought in), she has increased food sales dramatically by combining good value pub grub with several of her own home-made dishes. She takes care to source fresh meat from local suppliers, her Sunday roasts are cooked on the day and all the soups are home made.

Each week Trish plans the menu based on what is in season, customers' favourites and any special offers. Beef stew and dumplings, liver and bacon casserole and valentine of pork served with cider and apple sauce are just some of the home-made dishes appreciated by regulars, alongside veggie options such as vegetable Stilton bake. 'Surf & turf' is another popular choice – an 8oz rump steak served with scampi and all the trimmings. There is a choice of salad, peas or fresh vegetables to accompany main meals, none of which costs more than £10.95. On the dessert front, banoffee pie and treacle tart are perennial favourites as well as the banana Tia Maria (made to the pub's own recipe). Puddings are all a bargain £2.50, served with a choice of cream, custard or ice cream.

Q S V P C

MUDFORD
Half Moon Inn
High Street, BA21 5TF

- On A359
- Daily 12-11pm
- Daily 12-10pm (9.30pm Sun)
- T (01935) 850289
- F (01935) 850842
- E enquiries@thehalfmoon.co.uk
- W www.visitwestcountry.com/thehalfmoon
- RCH Hewish IPA, Pitchfork, East Street Cream
- Varied menu of freshly cooked food served all day
- A five-year restoration programme has retained and enhanced the character of this 17th-century inn; large courtyard

Renovation work here has significantly upgraded the facilities. The old skittle alley and log store have been sympathetically converted to provide en-suite bedrooms and the spacious cobbled courtyard is a lovely spot in summer. A high quality menu is the icing on the cake. Tasty appetizers, all under £6, include prime smoked salmon with king prawns served with lime and dill mayonnaise, warm savoury tartlet filled with spinach salsa, pine nuts and goats' cheese or king prawns with lemon grass and noodles wrapped in filo pastry and served with a sweet chilli dip. To follow, pub favourites such as steak and kidney pie or home-made curry or chilli can be had for around £9, while more inventive choices cost a little more: barbary duck, for example, served with black cherry and cointreau sauce, or braised lamb shank with redcurrant and rosemary jus. For fish lovers there may be smoked haddock with cheese and chive mash, mornay sauce and a poached egg, fresh salmon with saffron and crayfish tail cream sauce or seafood thermidor. The pub also offers a good range of steaks, £10-£16. Puddings are all £3.95: ginger and lemon cheesecake, fresh fruit pavlova, apple and sultana crumble to name a few.

★ Q S V P C

PORTISHEAD
Windmill Inn
58 Nore Road, BS20 6JZ

- ▶ Portishead is off M5, jct 19. Take the coast road out of town
- ☼ Mon-Sat 11am-11pm; Sun 12-10.30pm
- Daily 12-9.30pm (10pm Fri & Sat)
- T (01275) 843677
- E jeff@thewindmill.wanadoo.co.uk
- W www.thewindmillinn.org
- Butcombe Gold; Draught Bass; Courage Best Bitter; RCH Pitchfork; guests
- ☺ Wide ranging menu from snacks to steaks and home-made specials
- Spacious free house on three levels; the pretty terrace overlooks the Severn estuary

Handy for the golf course and coastal footpath, the Windmill is an ideal choice for golfers and walkers who have built up an appetite. If hunger strikes during the afternoon you can take advantage of the pub's 'early bird' offer – order a main course between 3pm and 7pm (6pm Sat, not Sun) and you can choose a free dessert from an extensive list that includes ice cream sundaes, fruit crumble of the day or Belgian chocolate torte. Or you may just want to enjoy a sandwich or snack such as a filled jacket potato with your pint.

The main menu concentrates mostly on pub standards such as home-made steak, mushroom and ale pie, while a char grill offers steaks, mixed grills or gammon. There are a few more exotic items: the lamb shanks are prepared Moroccan style with olives, chickpeas and couscous, and four or five vegetarian choices are generally listed on the menu including goats' cheese and sun dried tomato ravioli or mild curried sweet potato and spinach bake. You can start with something fishy – maybe the prawn and smoked mackerel salad or cod and pancetta fishcake, or play safe with the home-made soup. The blackboard listing a good range of daily specials is always worth consulting.

❀ S V ♿ P ⚐ C

SALTFORD
Bird in Hand
High Street, BS31 3EJ

- ▶ Bottom of the High Street
- ☼ Daily 11am-3pm, 6-11pm
- Daily 12-2.15pm (2.30pm Sun); 6.30-9.30pm
- T (01225) 873335
- F (01225) 874774
- E mbaker000@btclick.com
- Beer range varies
- ☺ Home-cooked pub food supplemented by more adventurous daily specials
- Converted in 1869 from two cottages, the pub is in the original part of Saltford village that was mentioned in the Domesday Book

A committed team of cooks at the Bird in Hand caters for three different menus entitled 'Our Lunchtime Spread', 'Our Evening Spread' and a third 'Sunday Spread'. Most of the dishes, including quiches, curries and steak and ale pies, are made in house and the bread is freshly baked every day. The hams are cooked locally and served off the bone, while other meat, fish and vegetables all come from local suppliers.

The Bird in Hand concentrates mainly on pub favourites such as ham, egg and chips for £5.50, chicken kiev or fish and chips for under £7. A traditional roast is served every day, with a selection of meats on Sunday. They feel no meal is complete without one of their 'delicious desserts' that are listed on a board – strawberry pavlova might be a summer choice or bread and butter pudding for a winter warmer. Children are well catered for – apart from the usual bangers and beans, they are also offered a pasta dish of the day or curry and rice, both £3.50. Saltford is an interesting village; after your meal you could amble down to the River Avon or visit the site of one of the oldest brass mills in the country a little further on.

★ Q ❀ S V ♿ ♣ P ⚐ C

WELLS
Crown at Wells
Market Place, BA5 2RP

- ▶ Follow signs for Wells Market Place
- ☼ Mon-Sat 10am-11pm; Sun 10.30am-10.30pm
- Daily 12-8pm
- T (01749) 673457
- F (01749) 679792
- E eat@crownatwells.co.uk
- W www.crownatwells.co.uk
- Butcombe Bitter, Blonde; guests
- ☺ Varied menu to suit all tastes and pockets
- 15th-century inn at the heart of England's smallest city

The Crown is ideally situated right in the centre of the city. It serves three slightly varying menus depending on the time you visit. Hungry guests in the afternoon can pick from the 'afternoon delights' menu that is served in the Penn Bar between 2pm and 6pm, when you can order anything from a simple sandwich or a more exotic toasted Italian panini – all around £3.95 - to a main dish such as lasagne, cod and chips or even a beef casserole. A similar but more extensive version of this menu is served at lunchtime, with main courses priced between £5.50 and £7.50, while on Sundays roast beef is available, too. The same dessert menu is served throughout the day and evening, all priced at £4.25, and offering such delights as warm almond tart with praline ice cream and frangellico sauce, or rum pannacotta with fresh vanilla pod and rhubarb coulis.

Starters on the evening menu can also be served as a light meal: smoked haddock and salmon fishcake with a horseradish and lemon mayonnaise or baked asparagus with marinated artichoke hearts and melted pecorino cheese. Main course specials, priced between £9.95 and £14.95, include steamed pavé of salmon with pak choi, rice and creamy Boston chowder or, for vegetarians, wok-fried chunky vegetables with a teriyaki sauce on steamed rice.

S V (Castle Cary) **C**

WELLS
☆ Fountain Inn & Boxer's Restaurant
1 St Thomas Street, BA5 2UU

- ▶ 50 yards from the cathedral at Tor Street jct
- ☼ Mon-Sat 12-2.30pm, 6-11pm; Sun 11am-3pm, 7-10.30pm
- Daily 12-2.30pm, 7-10pm
- T (01749) 672317
- F (01749) 670825
- E eat@fountaininn.co.uk
- W www.fountaininn.co.uk
- Butcombe Bitter; Courage Best Bitter
- ☺ Award-winning home-cooked dishes
- Built during the 16th century to house workers constructing the cathedral

The Fountain's excellent reputation has been built up over the years by Sarah and Adrian Lawrence who arrived in Wells in 1981 and fell in love with the city. Their secret is finding the right staff, and in the kitchen talented chef and manager Julie Pearce comes up trumps by sourcing the finest local produce. The set lunch menu, £7.50 for two courses or £9.75 for three, is particularly good value: one day's dishes include deep-fried mushrooms stuffed with blue cheese and served with a garlic dip, or a warm salad of chicken, smoky bacon and pine nuts on mixed leaves, followed by four main course choices including a vegetarian option.

The evening menu is somewhat more adventurous; tempting starters include smoked salmon timbale filled with cream cheese, tuna and lime and drizzled with a citrus vinaigrette or a duck and cranberry terrine accompanied by a red onion, orange and juniper relish. For the main course you might consider pork tenderloin stuffed with dates and bacon, or the goats' cheese and roasted red pepper cannelloni under a pesto crust – vegan dishes can also be prepared on request. Desserts include chestnut and orange roulade, and chocolate and cinnamon bread and butter pudding. You can dine in the bar or restaurant.

S V (Castle Cary) P **C**

BROCTON
Chetwynd Arms
Cannock Road, ST17 0ST

- ▶ On A34, between Stafford and Cannock
- ☼ Mon-Sat 11.30am-11pm, Sun 12-10.30pm
- Daily 12-9.30pm (8pm Sun)
- T (01785) 661089
- Banks's Original, Bitter; Marston's Pedigree; guest
- ☺ Good quality pub food with an emphasis on home-made specials
- Two-roomed pub where the busy public bar caters for drinkers and games players while the comfortable lounge accommodates diners and drinkers

The Chetwynd Arms is part of the national Woverhampton and Dudley brewing conglomerate and as such offers the extensive company menu common to many of its pubs, with a lot of ready prepared dishes. However, tenants Keith and Karen Horton go to great lengths to offer tasty, home cooked alternatives, which account for a quarter of their main course sales. So we shall ignore the standard breaded scampi and ubiquitous lasagne and tell you instead about the proper food to be found here. Ranging in price from £6.50 to £13.50 for a main course, you may find any of the following: slow roasted Barnsley lamb chop in mint and cranberry gravy, sizzling chicken with stir-fried vegetables in black bean sauce, beef stroganoff, pan-fried fillet steak finished with a leek, Stilton and red wine jus or chicken breast stuffed with Brie, wrapped in bacon and served with white wine and mushroom sauce. In season the specials board will also list pheasant, partridge, duck or goose from local shoots, and pan-fried venison steak with a port, red wine and wild mushroom sauce often features. The Hortons are adventurous with their spuds too, offering a range of accompaniments such as bubble and squeak, dauphinoise, garlic roasted potatoes or mash with various flavourings.

❀ S V ♣ P C

BURTON ON TRENT
Devonshire Arms
86 Station Street, DF14 1BT

- ▶ Near station, half a mile from town centre
- ☼ Mon-Thu 11.30am-2.30pm, 5.30-11pm; Fri & Sat 11.30am-11pm; Sun 12-3pm, 7-11pm
- Mon-Sat 12-2.15pm, 5.30-8pm
- T (01283) 562392
- Beer range varies
- ☺ Good value pub fare
- Friendly, Grade II listed, 19th-century pub with a small public bar, larger lounge and patio featuring a fountain

This popular, welcoming pub offers traditional, good value pub grub. If you just want a snack you could choose a jacket spud with a variety of fillings or hot or cold sandwiches. Or perhaps a wrap, £3.95-£4.25, served with seasoned potato wedges – either chicken, steak or veggie plus salad and dressing. Main meals are pretty much standard pub fare, but are all freshly prepared and cooked on the premises. You could go the whole hog and choose the all day breakfast – a real plateful for £4.65, or try the faggots, £4.95, or succulent lamb shank in a red wine and rosemary sauce, £5.99. They don't go in much for fresh veg here – most dishes are simply accompanied by chips, mash or peas – although there are four vegetarian choices including a lasagne, a curry and a selection of salads. The grills have the additional trimmings of onion rings, tomato and mushrooms, too; mixed grill (rump steak, gammon, lamb cutlet, bacon and pork sausages) is a mere £5.95, while surf 'n' turf – an 8oz rump and 12 pieces of wholetail scampi – is £7.49.

★ ❀ S V (Burton on Trent)
♣ P C

COLTON
Olde Dun Cow Inn
High Street, WS15 3LG

- ▶ The village is near Rugeley, midway between Stafford and Lichfield
- ☼ Mon-Fri 12-3pm, 5-11pm; Sat & Sun 12-11pm
- (food) Throughout opening hours
- T (01889) 584026
- E brian@dun-cow.com
- W www.dun-cow.com
- (beer) Draught Bass; Wadsworth 6X; guests
- ☺ Straightforward pub food, freshly prepared
- ◉ Former coaching inn with original beams and inglenook

Landlady Victoria Winter has been in charge of the kitchen for 15 years, from where she cooks up all the traditional pub favourites, based on fresh local produce. Starters, from around £2, include home-made soup, king prawns or crudités. Main courses start at £5.95 for home-made steak and kidney pie, lasagne or half a spit-roasted chicken, and go up to around a tenner for steaks – rump fillet, sirloin or T bone – served with the usual trimmings of mushrooms and onion rings. If you'd like a sauce to go with it – mushroom and brandy, black peppercorn or the more unusual Stilton and walnut – it is £2 more. There is a good selection of fish dishes such as plaice stuffed with prawns and mushrooms and coated with breadcrumbs, crispy cod bake or simply jumbo cod cooked in batter. These are all priced between £5.95 and £6.95 and supplemented by other fish choices on the specials board. Fruit crumble occasionally appears as a home-made option on the dessert menu, otherwise there are ice creams and other ready-prepared sweets. The pub is handy for the Staffordshire Way, so if walking has given you an appetite why not pop in, or enjoy the delightful beer garden.

★ Q ❀ S V ♿ ⇌ (Rugeley) ♣ P C

ENVILLE
Cat Inn
Bridgnorth Road, DY7 5HA

- ▶ On A458 near Stourbridge
- ☼ Mon & Tue 12-3pm, 7-11pm; Wed-Sat 12-3pm, 6.30-11pm; Sun 12-6pm
- (food) Mon-Sat 12-2.30pm, 7-9.30pm (not Mon); 12-3pm Sun
- T (01384) 872209
- E guy@theenvillecat.co.uk
- W www.theenvillecat.co.uk
- (beer) Beer range varies
- ☺ Hearty, traditional fare, all prepared on the premises
- ◉ Cosy, four-roomed 16th-century pub full of olde-worlde charm, with open fireplaces and many original features

Recognised as the unofficial tap for the Enville Brewery, the Cat still gives prominence to its beers but new owners Guy and Michelle Ayres also seek out guests from local breweries further afield. They have given the restaurant a boost, too. Chief cook Michelle aims to provide good value, old-fashioned meals just like Mum used to make, served in hearty portions. One of her best sellers is ham with two free-range eggs: the ham, honey roasted on the premises, is an ideal accompaniment to Enville Ale brewed with honey. Another favourite is Michelle's home-made steak pie – the meat is cooked slowly in the ale with herbs and a hint of onion then topped with shortcrust pastry and served with mash and fresh veg. Both dishes cost around £6.50. Specials cost a little more, but are a little more adventurous, such as pork fillet medallions with cider and thyme sauce, salmon fillet with lemon and dill sauce or chicken supreme with bacon and Brie sauce, all priced at £7.95. The most expensive dish is lamb shank with caramelised onions for £9.25. Fresh soup is made daily and a clutch of home-made desserts for around £3-£3.50 round off the meal nicely. Excellent sandwiches and snacks are also available.

★ Q ❀ S V ♣ P C

GREAT HAYWOOD
Clifford Arms
Main Road, ST18 0SR

- ▶ Centre of village, 200 yards from Bridge 27 of Trent & Mersey Canal
- ☼ Mon-Fri 12-3pm, 5-11pm; Sat 12-11pm; Sun 12-10.30pm
- Ⓨ Daily 12-2pm, 6-9pm
- T (01889) 881321
- E cliffordarms@tiscali.co.uk
- Draught Bass; Greene King Old Speckled Hen; Worthington's Bitter; guests
- ☺ Wide variety of meals and snacks, some home made
- Village pub with large bar, no-smoking restaurant and garden

The menu here has been designed to provide customers with a wide choice of good quality, unpretentious meals at reasonable prices. The robust portions suit the many walkers and cyclists from the Trent & Mersey Canal towpath or visitors to the National Trust's Shugborough Estate nearby. Children are welcome if dining and a menu is provided for them. Many of the dishes are bought in, but from good quality suppliers, and supplemented by regular specials such as lamb casserole with Stilton dumplings, beef in brown ale with root vegetables, smoked haddock and spinach bake or pork hock with apple and sage.

The main menu is divided into various headings: there is a limited selection of starters, mostly priced at £3.75, offering garlic mushrooms or red chilli and ginger chicken goujons and mayo. Snacks include pub favourites filled jacket spuds, egg and chips or ploughman's. A good selection of steaks follows, priced between £9 and £12, then a section called 'Home and Abroad' which contrasts good old British liver and onions with beef stroganoff or beef in black bean sauce; prices from £6 to £9. 'Spicier meals' covers curries, baltis and Thai dishes, while the vegetarian section is self explanatory. Puds are all around £3.

❀ S V ♿ ♣ P C

HOAR CROSS
Meynell Ingram Arms
Abbots Bromley Road, DE13 8RB

- ▶ One mile E of the A515 at Newchurch
- ☼ Daily 12-11pm
- Ⓨ Daily 12-2pm, 7-9pm
- T (01283) 575202
- F (01283) 575788
- E themeynell@btinternet.com
- Marston's Pedigree; Taylor Landlord; guests
- ☺ An extensive menu with an international flavour caters for all tastes
- Built as a farmhouse on the Earl of Shrewsbury's estate, this unspoilt village pub has an intimate restaurant

The enterprising staff at this pub keep a database of 450 regular diners to send them details of their special theme nights, which are normally booked up within days of being announced. This alone shows how popular the pub's award-winning Deerpark Restaurant is. Customers come back again and again to sample the imaginative menus that change with the seasons. All the dishes including soups and desserts are prepared in house; game comes from nearby estates and Needwood Farm Ice Creams provides sorbets and ices.

Starters, which range in price from £3.50-£7, include inspired dishes such as pear and Stilton filo parcel with home-made Cumberland sauce and confit duck leg pancakes with spring onion, cucumber and plum compote. All main courses come with fresh seasonal vegetables, starting at a very reasonable £7.45 for an unusual vegetarian choice such as caramelised banana shallot and thyme tarte tatin with ratatouille and red onion marmalade. You could try the pan-roasted duck breast, £11.95, or roasted haddock under a hazelnut crust for £8.95. From the grill a fillet steak is £16.95 or braised lamb shoulder on a casserole of puy lentils £14.50. Sweets include rich chocolate truffle torte and home-made fruit cheesecake.

★ ❀ S V ♿ P C

HYDE LEA
Crown Inn
ST18 9BG

▶ Off M6 at jct 13 (A449), two and a half miles from Stafford
☼ Daily 12-11pm (10.30pm Sun)
🍴 Mon-Sat 12-2pm (not Tue), 6-8pm; Sun 12-3pm
T (01785) 253332
E info@thecrownhydelea.co.uk
W www.thecrownhydelea.co.uk
Banks's Original, Bitter; guests
☺ Country style pub food at very reasonable prices
Welcoming family-run village pub with a no-smoking lounge for diners that opens onto the garden

This homely, comfortable pub serves its community well: as there is no village shop it also sells convenience items. Owners the Masseys like to support local businesses, so fruit and veg come from the markets and meat is supplied by Phil Eldershaw, a butcher in nearby Penkridge. Jenny Massey makes most of the dishes herself but buys pies from another Penkridge butcher, Russells. You can have a light snack here for as little as £1.75, or a three-course meal for under a tenner. The regular menus are updated regularly and specials added on a daily basis. One blackboard is dedicated to vegetarian choices such as roasted vegetable lasagne or creamy vegetable kiev.

There is nothing fancy here, just good honest steak and kidney pies, faggots, liver and onions, cottage pie and so forth. Specials might include a curry or ham, egg and chips, even venison on occasion. Puddings again are old favourites such as treacle sponge or apple pie, all served with custard or ice cream. If you go for Sunday lunch you are in for an inexpensive treat with a choice of three roast meats and all the trimmings for a fiver. A bargain £2.95 lunch for the over 50s is available every Monday and Thursday.

★ Q ❀ S V ♣ P

KINGS BROMLEY
☆ Royal Oak
Manor Road, DE13 7HZ

▶ On the crossroads at the village centre
☼ Daily 11.45am-3pm, 6-11pm
🍴 Daily 12-3pm, 6-9.30pm
T (01543) 472289
E shropshall@btinternet.com
Marston's Pedigree; guest
☺ Varied menus produced by an award-winning chef
Quiet country village pub and restaurant warmed by open fires

In 2002 chef Matthew Shropshall was a finalist in the Publican's Pub Food Awards in the Pub Chef of the Year category. His signature dishes are now a feature of the menu at the Royal Oak. You could start with crab cakes with a sweet chilli dip or Thailand dim sum mini food parcels with dipping sauce, smoked salmon and scrambled egg on warm toast with lemon and tomato sauce or crab, prawn, avocado and mango stack with a lime and coriander dressing, all under £5. To follow there are 'quick dishes', £6.50-£9, such as sirloin steak, lamb madras curry, cod fillet or classic steak and ale pie. Presumably the 'signature dishes', £7-£17, take a little longer but are worth the wait: marinated duck breast with apricot and lime jus, pot roasted fillet steak with smoky bacon, garlic and morel sauce, poached black halibut in lemon grass, pan-fried scallops in light saffron and thyme sauce, lamb with mustard crust and seared plum tomato and mint pesto or the interesting sounding combination of sirloin steak with banana and peppercorn sauce. There are also vegetarian options such as roasted vegetable lasagne or wild mushrooms and brandy with a creamy sauce in filo pastry, surrounded by a rich tomato sauce.

★ Q ❀ S V ♣ P C

KINVER
Vine Inn
1 Dunsley Road, DY7 6LJ

- Off A449 between Wolverhampton and Kidderminster
- Mon-Sat 11.30am-11pm; Sun 12-10.30pm
- Mon-Fri 12-2.30pm, 6.30-10pm; Sat 12-10pm; Sun 12-9pm
- T (01384) 877291
- Beer range varies
- The Waterfront Restaurant offers a varied freshly-cooked menu
- Updated Victorian canalside pub with a terrace to watch the boats go by

In July 2004 a long development and refurbishment programme was finally finished at the Vine, which saw the opening of the new Waterfront Restaurant. It has proved very popular, particularly for its set menu of main course, dessert (a choice of three dishes for each course) and coffee or tea at £10.95, while the Over 60s club offers a 20 per cent discount on weekday meals lunchtime and evening. On the main menu starters range from home-made soup of the day for £3.25 to warm smoked duck, orange and watercress salad or smoked salmon timbale for £4.75. Flavoured Italian flatbreads are £3.25, enough for two to share.

Main courses are very varied, from humble steak, mushroom and Enville Ale pie, £7.95, to the more exotic Caribbean chicken (breast stuffed with banana, wrapped in bacon and served on a mild korma sauce). Other home-cooked choices are the chef's famous pot-roasted Shrewsbury lamb cooked with root veg and served on a bed of mash, £10.45, and confit of duck – two crispy legs also with rice timbale and an orange and brandy sauce. Several fish dishes, a good choice of steaks and a couple of veggie options complete the picture. Desserts feature staples such as apple pie and bread 'n' butter pud, but you could be tempted by Baileys cheesecake.

S V P C

MEAFORD
George & Dragon
ST15 0PX

- On the A34 in the village, near Stone
- Daily 11am-11pm
- Daily 12-2pm, 6.30-9.30pm
- T (01785) 818497
- F (01785) 812134
- E robert.quinn2@btopenworld.com
- Burtonwood Bitter, Top Hat; guests
- Good home cooking: Sunday lunch offers five meat options plus a vegetarian alternative
- Characterful inn in a beautiful village, handy for the Wedgwood visitor centre and other pottery factory shops

Conveniently situated for the M6 motorway (between junctions 14 and 15), the Domesday listed Meaford lies at the heart of the pottery industry and is near to many tourist attractions such as Shugborough Hall, Trentham Gardens and Alton Towers. The award-winning George and Dragon attracts visitors from far and wide and the Quinn family's reputation for good home-cooked food has spread rapidly in the eight years they have been in charge here.

The menu divides into starters, fish main courses, vegetarian, grills and pan-fried dishes, with a good selection under each heading. Choose from red snapper baked in salt crust or seafood tagliatelle, roast medallions of pork, noisettes of lamb or large mixed grill, all served with interesting garnishes. Main course prices range from £9.45 to £14.25, although you will pay less for a vegetarian dish such as cherry tomato and onion tartlet or tagliatelle of mushrooms and fine herbs, both under £9. In the evening a list of specials appears usually featuring a fish and a chicken dish, as well as their own 'fillet steak stacker', the steak cooked to order and filled with Orkney black pudding and coated in an Islay malt whisky sauce for £11.75. The traditional Sunday lunch provides good choice and value – three courses for £8.25.

V P C

NEWTON REGIS
Queen's Head
Main Road, B79 0NF

- ▶ Two and a half miles from M42 jct 11
- ☼ Mon-Sat 11am-2.30pm, 6-11pm; Sun 12-2.30pm, 6.30-10.30pm
- 🍴 Daily 12-2pm, 6-9.30pm
- T (01827) 830271
- E rhodesqueens@aol.com
- Draught Bass; guests
- ☺ Traditional home-cooked British food
- Popular 400-year-old village pub situated by the duck pond; a proper community local where pool, darts and dominoes are played

The price you pay for a traditional Sunday roast lunch at a pub is always a good indication of the sort of value for money you can expect. At the Queen's Head the roast of the day with all the trimmings will set you back just £5.50 (or £3.95 for a child's portion), and most of the main dishes on the menu are similarly priced. The food here is very straightforward, probably the most exotic dish on offer is the Japanese-style breaded king prawns with a hot chilli dip. Apart from that there is just good home cooking, such as grilled Barnsley chops, gammon steaks with pineapple, roast breast of duck, or steaks provided by a butcher in Sutton Coldfield – a mere £4.95 for an 8oz rump, rising to £8.50 for an 8oz fillet, although you might find a 24oz T-bone on the specials board for £12.50. The blackboards are definitely worth a look as you will find whole fish at market prices or maybe dressed crab, poached salmon fillet, smoked haddock or smoked salmon, all priced between £5.50 and £7, or perhaps a seafood platter or 'surf 'n' turf'. Roast minted shoulder of lamb, whole gammon hock with parsley sauce, curry, home-made pies and vegetarian choices are also chalked up, along with home-made desserts of the day.

★ Q ❀ S V ♣ P C

SALT
☆ Holly Bush Inn
ST18 0BX

- ▶ In the village, 4 miles from Stafford
- ☼ Daily 12-11pm
- 🍴 Daily 12-9.30pm
- T (01889) 508234
- F (01889) 508058
- E geoff@hollybushinn.co.uk
- W www.hollybushinn.co.uk
- Adnams Bitter; Marston's Pedigree; guest
- ☺ Traditional British cooking at its best
- Licensed since 1610, the building dates back to 1190; the oldest part is still thatched but much altered internally

The Holly Bush must have won just about every pub food award going – even its website has won a prize. This is no surprise when you see the care and dedication that goes into sourcing ingredients for a menu that boasts 80 per cent of its dishes are based on British recipes and produce. The main exception to this is the seafood which changes with the seasons and may include exotic fish as available. The owners care about 'food miles', too - they can name many of the individual farms and producers, such as ice cream from a Jersey herd two miles away, free-range eggs from Rodbaston College and cheese from Fowlers of Earlswood – the oldest cheese making family in England.

All this results in a menu of surprisingly affordable dishes, with starters priced at £3.50 or less and no main course (apart from steaks) over £8.50. To begin you could try innovative dishes such as warm watercress, potato and bacon salad or Earlswood cheese in forest blue stuffed pears or pan-fried cheese with redcurrant sauce. Mains are thoroughly traditional: slow cooked lamb and barley stew or braised venison with chestnuts and celery; a daily vegetarian dish is also provided. Home-made sweets vie for your attention with Earlswood cheese to finish the meal; desserts start at £3.25, an individual cheeseboard is £4.25.

★ Q ❀ S V ♿ P C

SHENSTONE
Fox & Hounds
44 Main Street, WS14 0NB

- ▶ Village is midway between Lichfield and Sutton Coldfield
- ☼ Mon-Fri 12-3pm, 5-11pm; Sat 12-11pm; Sun 12-10.30pm
- 🍴 Mon 6-9pm; Tue-Sat 12-2pm (3pm Sat), 6-9.30pm; Sun 12-4.30pm
- T (01543) 480257
- E kendorgardner@aol.com
- Adnams Bitter; Highgate Dark; Marston's Pedigree; Taylor Landlord
- ☺ Varied menu with Monday steak night
- Recently refurbished Grade II listed pub with a 16th-century traditional snug

Not only has the pub itself been recently redecorated throughout but the restaurant has been transformed by a new chef from London's National Theatre. On Monday evening the pub offers steaks and nothing else, from £6.95 for a 6oz rump to £12.99 for a whacking 32oz hip bone (rump), with a free glass of wine or beer. During the rest of the week the full menu is available. Appetisers include plenty of seafood dishes, such as hot fillet of mackerel with a fennel and tarragon sauce, breaded lobster tails with lemon oil and pepper dressing, or two people can share the 'Combo' – a big platter of crispy mushrooms, potato wedges, onion rings and chicken goujons. The Combo is £6.95, other starters are under £4.

The main menu is very varied, ranging from steaks to poultry, fish and vegetarian options – mushroom stroganoff or broccoli and tomato pasta bake, both £7.95. The chef's house specials, cooked to order, include wild boar steak with a rich braised Chinese cabbage, grilled fillet of red snapper coated with lemon, parsley and butter served with ratatouille, or locally shot pheasant in season accompanied by a rich game and red wine sauce and button mushrooms. Main courses range from £7.95 for lasagne to £14.95 for tournedos Rossini.

★ Q ❀ S V ♿ ⇌ (Shenstone) P C

STOKE ON TRENT
Plough
147 Etruria Road, Etruria, ST1 5NS

- ▶ From A500 (Queensway) take A53 to Leek and follow signs for city centre, pub is opposite Grosvenor Casino
- ☼ Daily 12-2pm (not Sun), 7pm-midnight
- 🍴 Mon-Sat 12-2pm (not Sun), 7-9pm
- T (01782) 269445
- Robinson's Hatters, Unicorn, Double Hop, seasonal beers
- ☺ Specialises in steaks as well as hot sandwiches at lunchtime
- Country-style eating house in the city centre, adorned with old pictures and bric a brac

The ambition of proprietors Rob and Jane Ward is to establish the Plough as a modern classic – a high quality, independent steak house. In 12 years they have certainly cemented their reputation, catering at lunchtime mostly for local business customers and in the evening to guests from much further afield. At lunchtime their 'famous' hot sandwiches are more than adequate to set you up for the afternoon. Served on granary bread with salad and hand-cut chips, most are based on steak or bacon but you could have garlic chicken or a vegetarian version. If you want a proper meal you could have old favourites steak, egg and chips, £6.50, fish and chips or steak and ale pie, both £5.60.

For a full three-course blow out go in the evening when you could kick off with smoked bacon and garlic mushrooms, Brie wedges or soup of the day. The difficulty comes with deciding which of the 10 steak dishes to choose from, not to mention the lamb, pork or chicken alternatives. The menu tends not to change much apart from the occasional special dish, which will be listed on the blackboard alongside current prices. For dessert there are traditional puds, speciality ice creams, or cheesecakes.

S V ♿ ⇌ (Etruria) P C

TUTBURY
Olde Dog & Partridge
High Street, DE13 9LS

- Off A511, centre of village
- Mon-Sat 11am-11pm; Sun 12-10.30pm
- Daily 12-10pm (9pm Sun)
- T (01283) 813030
- F (01283) 813178
- E dogandpartridge@thespiritgroup.com
- Courage Directors; Marston's Pedigree; guests
- Freshly-cooked English dishes and frequently changing specials
- Charming olde worlde pub, dating back to the 14th century, offering good hospitality

This lovely, half-timbered pub served as a coaching inn during the 18th century on the Liverpool to London road, and it continues to satisfy travellers' needs today. Those who only have time to stop for a snack will find a good choice of sandwiches or focaccia, hot filled baguettes, jacket potatoes or light meals such as moules frites (Bantry Bay mussels in cream and white wine sauce with chips and mayo) or Aberdeen Angus burger, £3.75-£7.65.

Those with time to enjoy the full menu could start with lamb kofta with tzatziki, smoky chicken, pear and walnut salad, Somerset Brie crostini served with roasted plum tomatoes and apple and onion chutney, or mushroom rarebit with Stilton. Starters are all under £5.50. Next you could have seafood pie under a puff pastry lid, chicken Camembert served with Dijonnaise sauce, duck with braised red cabbage and bacon and onion sautéed potatoes, blackened Cajun salmon fillet, served on a bed of couscous with a tzatziki dressing or roasted pepper timbales (filled with mushrooms, tomatoes and sweet potato then topped with Stilton and served with a plum tomato sauce). Traditionalists could opt for bangers and mash, fish and chips or beef and ale pie. Main courses are from £6.25-£14 for a fillet steak. Desserts are chalked up on a board.

S V (Burton & Hatton) P C

WATERHOUSES
George Inn
Leek Road, ST10 3HW

- On A523 between Leek and Ashbourne
- Mon-Thu 11am-2.30pm, 5.30-11pm; Fri-Sun 11am-11pm (10.30pm Sun)
- Mon-Thu 12-2.30pm, 6.30-9.30pm; Fri-Sun 12-9.30pm
- T (01538) 308804
- E andy@george-waterhouses.com
- W www.george-waterhouses.com
- Fuller's London Pride; Wadworth 6X; guest
- Home-cooked bar and restaurant food with an Italian influence
- Village pub on the edge of the Peak District National Park, 10 mins from Alton Towers

If Alton Towers does not appeal, how about this for a day out? Leave your car at the George and cycle up the designated track into the beautiful Manifold Valley then return to the pub for dinner. You will not be disappointed in either the scenery or the food. English and Italian influences combine to offer a varied, home-cooked menu. There is a good choice of pastas – the pescatori is based on green lipped mussels, while the vegetarian penne is sautéed with courgettes, broccoli and sun dried tomatoes and finished with flaked parmesan. As a main course pasta is £7.95 or £4.50 as a starter. Other appetisers include honeydew melon with seasonal fruits, home made chicken liver pâté with orange dressing, or fishy dishes such as whitebait, king prawns or pan-fried Dover sole, £5.95. Fish appears as a main course, too, with whole seabass or bass fillets, plus 'catch of the day' mostly priced around £14.95. Otherwise there are six meat dishes, with Italian flavours cropping up in chicken pancetta – breast wrapped in bacon, pan fried and served with lime coriander sauce, £10.95. Or how about pork escalopes Calvados - escalopes with black pudding and melted Brie accompanied by an apple Calvados sauce. The George also serves sandwiches and cream teas.

S V P C

WRINEHILL

☆ Crown Inn

Den Lane, CW3 9BT

▶ Just off A531, midway between Crewe and Newcastle under Lyme

☼ Mon-Sat 12-3pm (not Mon), 6-11pm; Sun 12-4pm, 6-10.30pm

Ⓨ Mon-Fri 12-2pm (not Mon), 6.30-9.30pm; Sat 12-2pm, 6-10pm; Sun 12-3.30pm, 6-9pm

T (01270) 820472

E mark_condliffe@hotmail.com

Adnams Bitter; Marston's Burton Bitter, Pedigree; Taylor Landlord; guest

☺ Generous portions on a monthly-changing menu with good veggie options

Family-owned village free house warmed by an inglenook fire

Owned by the Davenhill family for nearly 30 years, home-cooked food plays a big role in the pub's continuing popularity. Mother and daughter co-owners, Sue and Anna, are both vegetarians, which ensures there is always a good choice of non-meat choices such as red pepper Moroccan style – filled with savoury couscous, mixed Mediterranean veg and pine kernels with a piquant tomato sauce, or Caribbean bean casserole – beans simmered with vegetables in a rich garlic, thyme and tomato sauce.

The chef meanwhile has his own favourites, such as slow-roasted lamb shank with fresh rosemary and garlic gravy, and salmon and monkfish kebabs, chunks of fish skewered with tomatoes, mushrooms, lemon and lime and baked with a sharp citrus and coriander glaze. Local ingredients are used as much as possible, including the sausages; cheese comes from the Staffordshire Cheese Company in Leek and delicious ice cream from a Jersey herd in Stafford. The main menu concentrates on steaks and meat dishes, priced from £6.95 for plaice and chips to £14.50 for a fillet steak. For a light meal there are open baps with a variety of tasty toppings such as a 4oz fillet steak, prawns or tuna with lemon mayo, served with salad or home-made coleslaw for around a fiver.

★ Q ❀ S V ♿ P C

ALDEBURGH
Mill Inn
Market Cross Place, IP15 5BJ

- Mon-Sat 11am-11pm; Sun 12-10.30pm
- Daily 12-2.30pm, 7-9pm
- T (01728) 452563
- E drink@themillinn.com
- W www.themillinn.com
- Adnams Bitter, Broadside, seasonal
- Home-cooked meals based on local produce especially fish
- Lovely two-bar pub with a small restaurant, opposite the 17th-century Moot Hall and just yards from the sea

For a genuine seafaring pub you should come to the Mill Inn. Frequented by local fishermen and the lifeboat crew (the landlord is a member) you will hear plenty of tales here and even the odd sea shanty. You won't get fresher fish than that supplied from the fishermen's huts on the beach opposite where the fishing boats are pulled up to await the tide. Cod, skate, Dover sole, monkfish, local crab and lobster regularly feature on the menu. If you don't have time for anything else you should at least try a crab sandwich washed down with a pint of Adnams from the brewery a few miles up the coast.

Prices are very reasonable here, with most dishes between £4.25 and £7.25. The fish comes in various guises: fish bake, seafood lasagne and, of course, traditional fish and chips. Otherwise there is usually a good range of pub favourites: steak and ale pie, gammon steak, home-made curry, cottage pie, large filled Yorkies, ham or sausages with egg and chips, meat lasagne and a home-made vegetarian dish of the day. The mouth-watering steaks are provided by local butchers and farms. All the meals are home cooked using local produce as far as possible. The guest accommodation, with sea views, is popular here.

★ ❀ 🛏 **S V** ⊞ ♿ ⚟ **C**

BECCLES
Bear & Bells
11 Old Market, NG34 9AP

- ▶ In the town centre, near the bus station
- Mon-Sat 11.30am-3pm, 5.30-11pm; Sun 12-3pm, 7-10.30pm
- Mon-Sat 11.30am-2pm, 5.30-9pm; Sun 12-2pm, 7-9pm
- T (01502) 712291
- E bearandbells@aol.com
- W www.bearandbells.co.uk
- Adnams Bitter; Greene King IPA; guests
- Varied menu featuring locally sourced ingredients
- Friendly Victorian pub not far from the river. Beamed ceilings in the charming bar and restaurant are hung with tankards

A regular entry in CAMRA's Good Beer Guide, this pub is an adult haven as no children are admitted and there are no intrusive games machines. Renowned for fine ales and wholesome food based on locally sourced ingredients, it serves an abundance of game. The specials menu changes weekly and offers a choice of at least six dishes for each course, all home made.

Starters at £4.95 include roasted onion soup, mackerel fishcake with horseradish crème fraîche, home made pheasant pâté with onion marmalade, goats' cheese and chard tartlet and dressed Cromer crab. Suffolk is famed for its pork and the favourite main dish here is pork loin on red cabbage with cider gravy. Alternatively, choose from roast duck leg on bubble and squeak, steak and kidney pud, roasted seabass with mushrooms, oven baked filo parcel with goats' cheese and red pepper or T-bone steak, all £9.95, veg extra. If you have room you could sample local cheeses with home made chutney, hot chocolate soufflés or maybe vanilla cheesecake, all £3.95. If you do not want a full meal there is a good choice of special sandwiches, such as steak or tuna melt, £6-£8.

★ 🏛 **Q** ❀ **S V** ⊞ ♿ ⇌ (Beccles) ♣ 🍎 Ⓟ ⚟ **C**

DUNWICH
Ship Inn
St James Street, IP17 3DT

- Mon-Sat 11am-11pm; Sun 12-10.30pm
- Daily 12-3pm (6pm Sat & Sun), 6-9.30pm
- T (01728) 648219
- Adnams Bitter, Broadside; Mauldons seasonal
- Varied menu that also caters for children
- Dating in part to Tudor times, it has a spacious bar, dining room and conservatory; the garden boasts an ancient fig

After a bracing walk along the beach a visit to the Ship is very welcome, with its cosy wood-burning stove in winter. A different menu is available at lunchtime and in the evening. During the day it offers soup, snacks or basic hot dishes such as fish and chips, a vegetarian dish, sausages or a meat dish of the day. There is a choice of plougman's or salad, both served with ham, cheese, quiche, mackerel or pâté. All main dishes are under £7 apart from prawn or crab salad which is £8. Puddings are £3.45, ice cream £2.65.

The evening menu is a little more varied: you could start with bacon and walnut salad or black pudding with apple cider and wholegrain mustard sauce, or something fishy such as whitebait or smoked trout with horseradish cream, £6.25. Main courses are all accompanied by stir-fried vegetables and chips or new spuds. Fish is given prominence with plaice, cod and scampi all served deep fried, and a special fish dish is chalked on the blackboard, from £9.25. Meat choices are gammon or steak, chicken in lemon and pepper sauce or pork in peach and Madeira sauce, while vegetarians can opt for pasta, chalked daily on the board, spinach flan or butter beans in barbecue sauce, all served with a mixed salad. Home-made puds are £4.25.

★ S V P C

ERWARTON
Queen's Head
The Street, IP9 1LN

- Follow signs for village from B1456
- Mon-Sat 11.30am-3pm, 6.30-11pm; Sun 12-3pm, 7-10.30pm
- Daily 12-2pm, 7-9.30pm
- T (01473) 787550
- Adnams Bitter; Greene King IPA; guests
- Extensive menu with lots of home-cooked specials
- Overlooking the river, this heavily beamed pub has a spacious bar displaying seafaring pictures and maps; bar billiards can be played

Handy for walkers on the Shotley Peninsula, the food at the Queen's Head will satisfy most appetites. Starters are mostly standard pub fare: home-made soup of the day, prawn cocktail, whitebait or home made pâté, all priced at £4.50 or less. Thereafter the menu covers all tastes: from steaks, local ham or sausages to curry, moussaka and Japanese-style prawns adding an international flavour. There is a good choice of fish including a seafood platter that combines hake, plaice, scampi, scallops and cod. Main course prices range from just over £7 to around £11 for steaks.

The best bet, though, is to consult the specials board for home-made dishes. There may be a shortcrust pie such as sausage and walnut, turkey and apricot or, of course, steak and kidney. Or try one of the casseroles – beef and ale or Somerset pork, both served with herb dumplings. Local seasonal game is used to good effect: there might be pheasant or rabbit casserole, or roast partridge with redcurrant, port and rosemary sauce. Fish dishes are added as available, perhaps smoked haddock Florentine or a fish casserole, and there is a separate board for vegetarian options. Sweets, such as pecan pie and sticky toffee pavlova, and cheese and biscuits are all under £4.

★ Q S V P C

FRAMLINGHAM

☆ Station

Station Road, IP13 9EE

- ▶ On B1116 towards Woodbridge, accessible from A12
- Daily 12-2.30pm, 6-11pm (7-10.30pm Sun)
- Daily 12-2pm, 6-9pm
- T (01728) 723455
  framstation@btinternet.com
- Earl Soham Gannet Mild, Victoria Bitter, Albert Ale, seasonal beers
- ☺ Imaginative, modern British food
- Simply furnished, railway themed pub, gets its name from the station that used to stand next door but closed in the 1950s

Snacks and a limited menu can be enjoyed at lunchtime, but the main event here is the evening meal. Landlord and chef Mike Jones has quickly established a reputation for great cooking based on fresh, local ingredients. His menu varies with the seasons and features around half a dozen starters and no more than 10 main courses. A summer menu might include starters such as an unusual roast plum and cardamom soup, fishcakes made with salmon and cod, flavoured with dill and served with a sweet mustard dressing, thinly-sliced marinated kipper with cucumber relish, and grilled aubergine, rocket and parmesan salad, around £4.95. The list of main courses, £9-£10.50, includes three fish dishes – sea bream, skate wing and salmon – as well as roast pigeon breasts served on celeriac purée with spiced cherries, pan-fried lamb's kidney with bacon and sage and Dijon mustard, slow roasted belly of pork with braised Puy lentil ragoût and, as a vegetarian choice, wild mushroom and tarragon risotto with goats' cheese and young spinach. All the food is freshly cooked to order. You will need to leave room for dessert as it might be a delicious pear and almond tart with pistachio ice cream or dark chocolate star anise mousse cake.

★ Q ❀ S V P C

HOLTON

Lord Nelson

Mill Road, IP19 8PP

- ▶ Village centre, opposite the green
- Mon-Sat 11.30-3pm, 6.30-11pm; Sun 12-3, 7-10.30pm
- Daily 11.30am-2pm, 6.30-9pm
- T (01986) 873275
- Adnams Bitter; Shepherd Neame Spitfire; guests
- ☺ Simple, straightforward home cooking
- Traditional village local decorated with Nelson memorabilia and seafaring artefacts; large garden

This is a homely, family-run village inn with food to match – nothing too fancy here, just good honest grills and pub staples, plus a few daily specials. If you just want a snack to go with your pint, there are good value hot sandwiches, £2.25-£4.50, such as bacon and egg, BLT or rump steak (with mushrooms, tomatoes and fried onions), and you can have a basket of chips for £1. Meat and vegetables all come from local suppliers and the grills are particularly good value: a 12oz rump with all the trimmings or five lamb cutlets with kidney are both £7.75; for dedicated carnivores the enormous mixed grill is just £8.25. Other main courses include Cumberland sausage and mash, chilli beef (the landlord's special recipe), steak, kidney and mushroom pie cooked in ale, Suffolk ham, egg and chips or local smoked haddock with lemon and parsley butter, fresh veg and potatoes – you'll get change from £7 for any of these dishes. Puddings, again, are pub favourites such as spotted dick or syrup sponge with custard or chocolate fudge cake with cream. The pub is particularly popular for Sunday lunch when booking is recommended.

Q ❀ S V P

HORRINGER
Six Bells
The Street, IP29 5SJ

- ▶ On A143 between Haverhill and Bury St Edmunds
- ☼ Daily 11.30am-11pm
- 🍴 Daily 12-2pm, 6.30-9pm
- T (01284) 735551
- 🍺 Greene King IPA, Abbot; guests
- ☺ No fixed menu but a changing mix of traditional and modern dishes
- ◉ Attractive 18th-century pub with a relaxed atmosphere in a beautiful village setting with its own garden

The Six Bells stands right next to the National Trust property of Ickworth House and Gardens, well worth a visit before dropping in to the pub for a bite to eat. There is no printed menu here; fresh dishes are chalked up on the blackboard and changed on a daily basis according to what seasonal ingredients are available. Starters often include old favourites such as prawn cocktail, garlic bread with cheese or chicken goujons, priced between £3-£5. To follow there is usually freshly battered cod, very sensibly served in three portion sizes between £5 and £11, or you could have a steak – rump, sirloin or gammon – or maybe a pork tenderloin dish for around £9. Perhaps surprisingly in these days of gastropub dining, lasagne, served with chips and salad, remains one of the most popular choices – possibly because it is home-made and tastes so good – and chilli also goes down well. The blackboard will usually show four or five vegetarian options and a variety of home-made puddings such as spotted dick or treacle pudding for £4, or a selection of ice creams for a fiver. The pub stages popular theme nights showcasing international cuisine.

★ ♛ ❀ 🛏 S V ♿ 🍎 P ⚡ 👪 C

KETTLEBURGH
Chequers
The Street, IP13 7JT

- ▶ Off B1116 near Framlingham
- ☼ Daily 12-3pm, 6-11pm
- 🍴 Daily 12-2pm, 7-9.30pm
- T (01728) 723760
- E info@thechequers.net
- 🍺 Greene King IPA, Elgood's Black Dog Mild; Shepherd Neame Spitfire; guests
- ☺ Straightforward, freshly cooked pub food served in the bar or restaurant
- ◉ Village pub in a delightful location with a garden leading down to the River Deben

According to local CAMRA members the Chequers is the third pub to inhabit this favoured site – the previous one burnt down in 1912 – and at one time the Deben Brewery stood next door. Landlady Debbie Germain is in charge of the kitchen here, producing wholesome snacks and meals, including a £5 menu served only in the bar. This offers quite a list of heart-warming fare such as a giant Yorkshire pud filled with local Revett's sausages, mash and onion gravy, battered cod, cauliflower cheese and chips, salmon fishcakes or seafood risotto with salad.

The à la carte menu is available in the bar or restaurant. For starters the choice includes rosemary and garlic crusted Brie with salad and cranberry sauce, crispy bacon and Stilton salad, breaded mini squat lobster tails with tartare sauce or Cajun chicken fillet strips on salad with croutons, all £4.50 or less. To follow you can choose a steak, with or without sauce, a fish dish such as fisherman's pie, breaded plaice fillet or grilled whole rainbow trout, or a vegetarian dish, either Brie, pesto and cherry tomato filo tart or roasted vegetable tourte. Other main courses are braised lamb shank, hunter's chicken, pork loin steak, honey roast duck breast, steak and Guinness pie or chicken tikka masala. Most dishes are around £9, and there is a board for daily specials.

♛ Q ❀ 🛏 S V 🍺 ♿ ⛺ ♣ P ⚡ 🍷 👪 C

LAVENHAM

☆ Angel

Market Place, CO10 9QZ

- ▶ On A1142 between Bury St Edmunds and Sudbury
- ☼ Mon-Sat 11am-11pm; Sun 12-10.30pm
- Daily 12-2.15pm, 6.45-9.15pm
- T 01787 247388
- F 01787 248344
- E angellav@aol.com
- W www.theangelhotel-lavenham.co.uk
- Adnams Bitter, Broadside; Greene King IPA; Nethergate Suffolk County
- ☺ Home-cooked traditional English menu with continental flair
- Atmospheric 15th-century, family run inn overlooking the market cross in possibly the finest medieval village in England

Lavenham is a bit of a tourist honeypot so the Angel enjoys a busy trade in its well preserved bar and restaurant. Meals are also served in the delightful garden at lunchtime. The food is prepared on the premises from fresh ingredients by a team of four chefs; both the lunchtime and dinner menus change daily. Examples of starters are butternut squash and sweet potato soup, game terrine with Cumberland sauce or tomato salad with feta cheese and basil, priced between £4 and £7. At lunchtime a selection of light dishes is offered, such as grilled herring fillets in oatmeal with mustard sauce, cottage pie or tomato, goats' cheese and basil tart, all under £7. Home-cooked gammon salad is also usually available.

Main course choices, depending on the season, could include pheasant breast with roasted vegetables and wild mushroom sauce, £11.95, braised shank of lamb with redcurrants and rosemary, £10.95, a fish dish such as grilled skate wing with herb and lime butter and a veggie number such as baked aubergine with courgette, cauliflower and coconut topping, £8.95. All main courses come with a selection of mixed vegetables or salad. Home-made desserts, all £4.25, include a selection of hot or cold options such as steamed syrup sponge pud, lemon meringue roulade or apricot and passion fruit syllabub. The pub has eight comfortable guest rooms.

★ Q S V P C

LIDGATE
Star Inn
The Street, CB8 9PP

- ▶ On B1063 Clare road, 7 miles from Newmarket
- ☼ Daily 11am-3pm, 6-11pm
- Ⓨ Mon-Sat 12-2pm, 7-10pm; Sun 12-2.30pm
- T (01638) 500275
- E tonyaxon@aol.com
- Greene King Old Speckled Hen
- ☺ Varied menu of Mediterranean dishes
- Beamed 16th-century village inn warmed by open fires

The Star offers an interesting mix: a quintessentially English pub run by a cosmopolitan staff from Poland, Australia and South Africa under the direction of landlady Maria Axon, whose Spanish origins give the menu here a special quality. The majority of dishes are either Spanish or at least Mediterranean in flavour – even the lambs' kidneys are cooked in sherry and, of course, you can enjoy a glass of wine to match, maybe a Rioja or ValdepeÀas, or the lesser known Ribera del Duero or Rueda.

At lunchtime there is a dish of the day or the set menu and Maria provides a good choice for vegetarians. You may consider taking a Spanish-English dictionary with you to translate the menu, as it lists such evocative sounding dishes as fabada asturiana (a kind of bean stew) and boquerones (anchovies). Starters, all under £6, include Catalan salad, Mediterranean fish soup, carpaccio of salmon or venison alongside the more familiar smoked salmon and avocado, or prawns in garlic. There is a good main course choice of fish and seafood such as scallops, salmon and hake, all prepared to Spanish recipes, and of course paella, while meat dishes include venison in port, lamb steaks in blackcurrant or even wild boar in strawberry sauce. Main courses cost £14.50-£16.50, desserts are all £4, and £4.50 for the cheeseboard.

★ V P C

ST PETER SOUTH ELMHAM
St Peter's Hall
NR35 1HQ

- ▶ Off A144 between Bungay and Halesworth
- ☼ Mon-Sat 11am-11pm (closes 3-6pm winter); Sun 12-10.30pm
- Ⓨ Daily 12-2.30pm, 7-9pm
- T (01986) 783115
- F (01986) 782505
- E stuart@stpetersbrewery.co.uk
- W www.stpetersbrewery.co.uk
- St Peter's Organic Best Bitter, Golden Ale
- ☺ Good English cooking from light meals to fine dining
- Medieval hall (circa 1280) with moat and gardens; the interior features antique furnishings and fittings, the restaurant is in the Great Hall

St Peter's Hall is no ordinary pub. It is worth taking some time to admire the carved façade and the gardens or pop into the brewery shop. For all its grandeur (the hall is Grade II listed) you can enjoy an informal bar meal here. Meals are freshly prepared from local ingredients – some from the greenhouse and herb garden.

Starters range from peppered mackerel compote with spring onion, horseradish and potato, or home-made game pâté, to various salads – crisp bacon with egg, croutons and Stilton and red wine dressing, smoked salmon, or Stilton, grapes and spicy olives. To follow the choice includes steak pie made with St Peter's organic ale, bangers and mash, wild mushroom risotto and a couple of fish choices, £9-11. Moreish desserts include blueberry cheesecake with mango coulis, treacle and sultana pud and mulled wine timbale with a fresh fruit compote. Wednesday at the Hall is fish and chip night.

The evening menu in the more formal restaurant offers suitably sophisticated dishes such as smoked and fresh salmon compote or a selection of Italian meats to start. To follow there might be roast pheasant, sirloin steak Rossini or haddock with pesto and Parmesan crust.

★ Q S V P C

WALBERSWICK
Anchor
Main Street, IP18 6UA

- ▶ Village is on B1387
- ☼ Summer daily 11-11pm; winter 11am-4pm, 6-11pm
- 🍴 Mon-Sat 12-3pm, 6-9pm; brunch at weekend
- T (01502) 722112
- W www.walberswick.ws/anchor
- Adnams Bitter, Broadside, seasonal
- ☺ Rustic seasonal dishes with good vegetarian choices
- Three cosy bars plus a 50-seater restaurant and large garden

Mark Dorber, who famously runs the White Horse in Parsons Green, London, and his wife, Sophie, who used to be the innovative chef there, took on the Anchor as a new venture in late 2004, continuing their commitment to linking beer with food. Here they are able to use vegetables and herbs from their allotment, grown in accordance with Soil Association organic guidelines, on an evolving menu that grows more adventurous over time.

Typical dishes include home-made soup at £4.50, pork sausages and mash with cabbage and beer onion gravy, salmon fishcake with green beans and lemon butter (recommended Adnams Bitter), warm stew of chorizo, planchada bean and pork knuckle, or rib-eye steak sandwich with garlic butter, grilled green tomatoes and hand-cut chips. Main courses are all £8.75 apart from the steak at £12.75. Good veggie choices include roast pumpkin and butternut salad with pine nuts, goats' cheese and red onion, Lancashire cheese and caramelised onion tart with mixed leaves (Bitburger Pils recommended), and wild mushroom risotto cake with buttered spinach and red pepper pesto, £6.75-£8.25. Side orders encompass spicy potato wedges with sour cream or bacon and cheese, and rocket salad with parmesan.

Q S V C

A gorgeous, refreshing, and alcoholic dessert for hot weather comes from Andrew Parle, the chef of the Walpole Arms at Itteringham in Norfolk.

MELON GRANITA WITH PINK GRAPEFRUIT
Serves 4

1 good size sweet Ogen, Cantaloupe or Galia melon
300ml (½ pint) sugar syrup made by boiling together 400ml (½ pint) of water and 225g (8oz) sugar
2 shots vodka
1 pink grapefruit
Springs of mint

Remove melon flesh, discarding seeds, and puree in a blender, add cooled sugar syrup and vodka. Pour into a metal or ceramic bowl and freeze. Whisk mixture briefly every 20 minutes as it begins to set, whisking more often as it gets thicker. When it is a thick slush, transfer to a smaller container and freeze. Segment the grapefruit. Finely shred some mint leaves and scatter over. Serve in chilled glasses, layering scoops of the granita with the minted grapefruit segments.

ALBURY HEATH
King William IV
Little London, GU5 9DG

- ▶ Just S of A25, between Shere and Albury
- ☼ Daily 11-3pm, 5.30-11pm
- 🍴 Mon-Sat 12-2pm, 7-9pm
- T (01483) 202685
- Archers Best Bitter; Flowers IPA; Greene King Abbot; Hogs Back TEA; guests
- ☺ Good, honest pub food
- 16th-century pub retaining original features such as flagstone floor, inglenook and exposed beams

The landlord of this two-bar pub insists that they don't make a big deal about food at the William IV; what they offer are straightforward meals that go down nicely with a pint or two of its excellent ales. They don't even bother with a proper menu, just chalking up what is available on a blackboard, which they feel is much more appropriate in a country inn than any pretentious 'gastro nosh'.

There are a few starters but these are more usually bought by customers as snacks, such as filo wrapped king prawns, deep fried whitebait or home made pâté and toast. Main courses, again, are fairly limited, but all home cooked to order, such as ham off the bone served with egg and chips or battered cod and chips, both £7.95, home-made steak and kidney pie for £8.50 or an 8oz steak for £10.50. Puddings are treated, like starters, as a bit of an adjunct, but there may be seasonal dishes, such as an autumnal apple crumble, and old favourites including bread and butter pudding.

Situated in a quiet lane adjoining extensive woodland in a popular walking area, ramblers could do a lot worse than stopping off here for a snack or meal in the dining room.

★ Q ❀ S V ≡ (Gomshall) ♣ C

BOUNDSTONE
Bat & Ball
15 Bat & Ball Lane, GU10 4SA

- ▶ Take Upper Bourne Lane off Sandrock Hill Road, 2 miles from Farnham centre, or footpath signposted via steep steps off Shortheath Road
- ☼ Mon-Thu 11am-3pm, 5.30-11pm; Fri & Sat 11am-11pm; Sun 12-10.30pm
- 🍴 Mon-Sat 12-2.15pm, 7-9.30pm; Sun 12-3, 6-8.30pm
- T (01252) 792108
- F (01252) 794564
- E info@thebatandball.co.uk
- W www.thebatandball.co.uk
- Hogs Back TEA; Young's Bitter; guests
- ☺ A mix of traditional English and dishes from other cultures
- Excellent free house with a large garden

It may take some perseverance to find the pub the first time you visit, however you will be well rewarded by a menu that changes every six to eight weeks and is based on local produce.

All the main courses and desserts are made in the pub kitchen, with just a few of the starters bought in. Starters (also offered as light lunches) could include home-made pâté – either smoked mackerel, lemon and horseradish or chicken liver and brandy – avocado with crab, mango, mild spices and mayo, or mussels in a rich tomato, herb and wine sauce. Recipes for the dips are inspired by landlady Sally's travels: frijolemole (chick pea, chilli, lime and coriander) and baba ghanoush (aubergine, garlic and yogurt) from the Middle East are both served with pitta bread. Starters are mostly around the £5-£6 mark, while mains range from £7.50 for a salad to £13. Main courses include Moroccan lamb shank with apricots, fruits and spices served on couscous, fajita stuffed with spicy stir fried beef with avocado salsa, or charred aubergine and coconut curry. For the British palate there are home-made pies, a rich farmhouse beef stew or pot-roasted partridge in season.

Q ❀ S V ♿ ♣ P C

BOUNDSTONE
Sandrock
Sandrock Hill Road, GU10 4NS

- ▶ From A325, take School Hill and follow straight on to Sandrock Hill Road
- ☼ Daily 12-11pm (10.30pm Sun)
- 🍴 Daily 12-2.30pm, 6.30-9.30pm (not Sun)
- T (01252) 715865
- E info@thesandrock.com
- W www.thesandrock.com
- 🍺 Batham Best Bitter; Cheriton Pots Ale; Hop Back Summer Lightning; guests
- ☺ Varied menu with monthly theme nights
- ◙ Small, friendly semi rural local

Despite being a vegetarian herself, landlady and head chef Carol Haime takes enormous pleasure in experimenting with new recipes and unfamiliar ingredients and caters for any diet – for a dedicated vegan customer she provided a completely raw meal, including avocado, pine nut and herb pâté and papaya with honey and rose petals. At lunchtime choose from a range of chunky sandwiches: everything from roast beef and horseradish to feta cheese and sundried tomatoes, or smoked salmon and salad, priced from £2.75-£5, or you could have warm ciabatta or pitta bread with various fillings. Other staples include ham, egg and chips.

The evening menu changes regularly, with starters from £4.95; favourites include fried haloumi with caper vinaigrette, garlic and herb chicken salad with basil dressing, grilled goats' cheese on garlic panini, Thai broth and dressed Devon crab with citrus mayo and crusty bread. Main courses, £9-£16 may include Scottish fillet steak stuffed with mushrooms and pâté wrapped in parma ham, Conwy salt marsh lamb with pea and mint champ and braised red cabbage, Cornish monkfish Wellington, or seasonal game such as whole roast pheasant with smoked bacon and spring onion stuffing. The puds are good, too, such as carrot cake with clotted cream ice cream or rich chocolate pot with Grand Marnier.

♛ Q ❀ S V ♣ P ⚇ C

DORMANSLAND
Old House at Home
West Street, RH7 6QP

- ▶ Behind village church off the High Street
- ☼ Daily 11.30am-3.30pm, 6-11pm
- 🍴 Daily 12-2pm, 7-9pm (not Sun)
- T (01342) 832117
- F (01342) 837247
- 🍺 Shepherd Neame Master Brew Bitter, Best, Spitfire
- ☺ Home-cooked pub fare with a good choice of specials
- ◙ Friendly, old fashioned, unspoilt village pub with an open fire in the beamed lounge

Handy for Lingfield Park races, the pub attracts many visitors as well as being a focal point for villagers, who gather in the cosy side room to chat and play darts. Children are welcome in the dining room, although the basic kids' meals at £5 are perhaps a bit pricey. A good choice of home-made specials is served at lunchtime and in the evening.

A typical day's specials list kicks off with home-made soup of the day and the pub's 'crunchers' – toasted French bread with a variety of toppings, such as prawns with stilton or a mix of tomato, mushroom, onion, garlic butter and cheese, for around £5 or so. To follow there may be home-made spicy corned beef hash served with a fried egg and sauté potatoes, home-made fisherman's pie (three types of fish under cheese topped mash), tagliatelle served with a Stilton, mushroom and cream sauce or pan-fried lamb's liver, bacon and onions; main courses are mostly under £9.

The snack menu includes home-made burgers, chilli, ploughman's and sandwiches. In the evening an additional menu offers a bigger range of starters such as Thai style prawns or deep-fried Brie, followed by a choice of steaks and grills, prices up to £17.25 for the 16oz T-bone, and a vegetarian dish such as mushroom stroganoff. Home-made desserts are all £3.95.

★ ♛ Q ❀ S V 🍺 ♿ ⇌ (Dormansland) ♣ P ⚟ ⚇ C

FOREST GREEN

☆ Parrot

Horsham Road, RH5 5RZ

- ▶ From A29 in Ockley take B2126
- ☀ Daily 11am-11pm
- Ⓨ Mon-Sat 12-3pm, 6-9.30pm (10pm Sat); Sun 12-4pm
- T (01306) 621339
- Beer range varies
- ☺ Exciting menu featuring modern and traditional dishes using their own farm produce
- Quaint, extended old pub facing village green with friendly village bar, inglenook, modern dining room and extensive gardens

Charles and Linda Gotto have run four excellent Young's pubs in London, supplying them with produce from their Home Farm near Dorking. They now run their own free house where the menus feature their rare breed livestock - Shorthorn beef, lamb from Suffolk sheep and Middle Whites pork. They cure pork for hams and bacon, have a small smoker, and make biltongs and pork scratchings sold in the bar. They are also the sole user of extra virgin olive oil from the Brolio estate in Chianti.

The changing menu reflects local produce – starters such as potted pork with parsley, spiced pigeon breast or wild mushrooms with Madeira, priced £4-£5.50. Main courses could be rump of Home Farm lamb or char-grilled sirloin steak with hand-cut chips, rabbit and shallot stew with pancetta dumplings, steak and oyster pie, herb-baked sea bass in mussel chowder, roast Middle White pork belly, guinea fowl with dauphinoise potatoes or gnocchi with dolce latte, £8.75-£14.50; more dishes using meat from the farm are on a separate board. Puds range from dark chocolate meringue tart to fresh fruit fudge crumble, and the £5.50 cheeseboard boasts Isle of Mull cheddar, local Norbury Blue and Cornish Yarg with biscuits and grapes. If you like the sound of the food you can celebrate your wedding breakfast here.

★ S V P C

HURTMORE

Squirrel Inn

Hurtmore Road, GU7 2RN

- ▶ Just off A3 at the Norney/Shackleford/Hurtmore junction
- ☀ Mon-Sat 11am-11pm; Sun 12-10.30pm
- Ⓨ Mon-Sat 12-2.30pm, 6.30-9.30pm (Fri & Sat 10pm); Sun 12-2.30pm, 7-9pm
- T (01483) 860223
- F (01483) 860592
- E info@thesquirrelinn.co.uk
- W www.thesquirrelinn.co.uk
- Fuller's London Pride; guests
- ☺ From traditional British to modern continental
- Inviting bar plus two lounge areas and a large garden

When Nigel Wilkes acquired the Squirrel in 2000 it was in dire need of some TLC, which he administered so successfully that it instantly became a favourite with locals and visitors alike, the 13 guest rooms are often fully booked. His food, based on local produce, is always popular. Everything (apart from ice cream and scampi on the kids' menu) is either home cooked or made locally for the pub.

The menu is sensibly divided into smaller plates, costing around £4-£6, and larger plates, £9-£14. Under the first heading you will find tasty offerings such as goats' cheese crostini with onion marmalade and Cumberland sauce, char-grilled chicken and pineapple skewers with rocket salad and tomato salsa, mushrooms sautéed in a creamy Cajun sauce or pan-fried duck livers with lardons, black pudding and mixed leaf salad. Larger plates include standards such as steak and mushroom pie and honey roasted ham or egg and chips, but also a Mediterranean vegetable cobbler, char-grilled lamb kebab with onion salad, sweet chilli and mint mayo and chips, and Thai red chicken curry. Daily specials are offered while good puds include caramelised lemon tart with citrus sorbet and chilled chocolate soufflé with orange shortbread.

S V ♣ P C

MICKLEHAM
King William IV
Byttom Hill, RH5 6EL

- ▶ Off A24 southbound, accessible from M25 jct 9
- ☼ Mon-Sat 11am-3pm, 6-11pm; Sun 12-10.30pm
- Mon-Sat 12-2pm, 7-9.30pm; Sun 12-5pm
- T (01372) 372590
- Adnams Bitter; Badger First Gold; Hogs Back TEA; guest
- ☺ Wholesome fresh produce with good vegetarian and fish options
- Originally the ale house for Lord Beaverbrook's staff, this family-run free house has a lovely terraced garden with views over the Mole Valley

The King William makes an ideal watering hole for cyclists and walkers as tracks and footpaths are abundant in this area at the edge of the North Downs (the pub is on the regular 465 bus route). Chris Grist, proprietor and main chef, produces good home-made food from fresh ingredients. He offers a choice of fish and vegetarian dishes and a traditional roast is served throughout Sunday afternoon. Chris insists this is a pub, not a restaurant, so simple fare is always on offer such as jumbo sausages in French bread and salad for £6.95. Starters are only served in the evening.

The blackboard menu changes with the seasons: typical dishes are seafood pie under a mozzarella and mustard crust, fillet steak in a wild mushroom and cream sauce, lamb gigot with savoy cabbage and mash or the perennial favourite, steak and kidney pie. Game features in season. Prices range from £9.95 to £16 for the steak. A couple of specials are added each day, such as Brie, leek and cranberry filo parcel or seafood penne with salad, both £8.75.

Apart from the chocolate fudge cake all the desserts, £4.25, are home made, such as toffee banana bread and butter pudding, treacle and pecan toffee tart or a seasonal fruit crumble.

★ Q ❀ S V C

NEWDIGATE
Surrey Oaks
Parkgate Road, RH5 5DZ

- ▶ Off A24 1 mile from Newdigate village on road to Leigh
- ☼ Mon-Fri 11.30am-2.30pm, 5.30-11pm; Sat 11.30am-3pm, 6-11pm; Sun 12-3pm, 7-10.30pm
- Daily 12-2pm; Tue-Sat 6.30-9.30pm
- T (01306) 631200
- E ken@surreyoaks.co.uk
- W www.surreyoaks.co.uk
- Caledonian Deuchars IPA; Harveys Sussex Best Bitter; Taylor Landlord; guests
- ☺ Meals, all home made, are listed on the specials board
- 16th-century country pub retaining its inglenook and other period features

The 'Soaks', as it is affectionately known, is much appreciated by CAMRA members for its support of micro-breweries, and has been rewarded several times with the local Pub of the Year award. Various drinking areas each attract their own group of regulars, while diners can enjoy snacks in the bar or consult the specials board in the dining room.

A typical day's offerings might start off with Stilton and celery soup, cheese soufflé with cheese dip or smoked salmon mousse with granary toast – all home made; other starters such as Brie wedges, whitebait and smoked salmon are also always available. To follow there is usually a choice of pan-fried dishes such as pork escalope with Dijon mustard sauce, calf's liver and bacon, lamb steak with redcurrant and fresh rosemary jus or swordfish steak with dill sauce. Local sausages, a vegetarian quiche and probably another veggie option are always on the board. Prices are £4-£5 for starters and £7.50-£11 for mains. Desserts, all £3, include apple and blackberry pie, tarte au citron, banoffee pie and chocolate fudge cake. The bar snack menu includes ploughman's and hot dishes such as steak pudding.

★ Q ❀ S V P C

OCKLEY
King's Arms Inn
Stane Street, RH5 5TS

- On A29, 9 miles from M25
- Mon-Sat 11am-2.30pm, 6-11pm; Sun 12-3pm, 7-10.30pm
- Mon-Fri 12-2pm, 7-9pm; Sat & Sun 12-2pm, 7-10pm
- T (01306) 711224
- Draught Bass; Flowers IPA; Greene King Old Speckled Hen; Marston's Pedigree
- Good home cooked food with some Spanish dishes
- Well-preserved 500-year-old free house with beamed bar, attractive restaurant and high quality en-suite guest rooms, close to Gatwick Airport

The King's Arms benefits from a good game supplier and people drive miles for its home-made game soup in season. Pheasant stuffed with Stilton, wrapped in bacon and served with a red wine and mushroom sauce is another favourite and the game pies are particularly popular. Meat is sourced locally: the steaks, including gammon, are served char-grilled. Chicken breast is also cooked this way, then topped with prawns and melted cheese as chicken Atlantis. Curries are all home made and the second chef, who is Spanish, makes a fine authentic dish of meatballs served with garlic mushrooms. Another favourite with customers is the shoulder of lamb slow roasted in honey and mustard but this is not for dainty appetites.

Vegetables are delivered daily from Covent Garden and the pub is unusual as it steams all vegetables freshly to order. Fish comes in daily, too, so the menu will vary according to what is available. It may be fresh whole sea bass roasted with herb butter, mackerel pan-fried with lemon and capers, baked cod with a mushroom and tarragon sauce topped with cheese, or salmon simply steamed with a dill and cucumber sauce. Summer barbecues and spit roasts are served in the garden.

★ Q S V ≠ (Ockley) P C

OCKLEY
Old School House (Bryce's)
Stane Street, RH5 5TH

- On A29, 8 miles S of Dorking
- Daily 12-3pm, 6-11pm
- Daily 12-2.30pm, 6.30-9.30pm
- T (01306) 627430
- F (01306) 628274
- E bryces.fish@virgin.net
- W www.bryces.co.uk
- Fuller's London Pride; Gale's Best; Harveys Sussex Best Bitter
- Specialises in high quality fish and seafood
- Former school house provides spacious but intimate dining

How does hot smoked rainbow trout fillet on a salad of chicory with black treacle and juniper berry dressing, followed by slivers of Shetland salmon and calves' liver on warm black pudding, potato and pear salad with pear cider and mustard cream sound? If this is a little extravagant for your tastes, the chef will happily cook any of the fish on his menu quite simply without added ingredients. Other inspired starters are carpaccio of yellow fin tuna, Loch Fyne queenie scallops on buttered spinach, and white fish and crab soup.

To follow there might be pan-fried fillets of plaice with glazed kumquats and mache salad, hake fillet under a brioche and fennel crust on celeriac purée with orange balsamic syrup, or medallions of monkfish with stuffed squid and a soy, ginger and pineapple dressing, all beautifully presented. And if none of these fish dishes tempt you, there are always some meat dishes on the specials board and a vegetarian menu is available.

Award-winning chef and proprietor Bill Bryce has taken the sensible decision to offer his restaurant menu at a set price of £22 for two courses or £27.50 for three – the desserts are chalked up on a blackboard. Bryce's also offers an excellent bar menu featuring some simpler fish dishes, steaks and open sandwiches.

S V ≠ (Ockley) P C

STAFFHURST WOOD
☆ Royal Oak
Caterfield Lane, RH8 0RR

- Just S of Oxted
- Mon-Sat 11am-11pm; Sun 12-10.30pm
- Daily 12-2.30pm, from 6pm
- T (01883) 722207
- Beer range varies
- Weekly changing menu of traditional dishes
- Excellent rural free house that serves the local community and is popular with ramblers; the large garden benefits from good views

Denise Eckersley, landlady and chief cook at the Royal Oak, draws inspiration for her home-cooked dishes from Mrs Beeton's cookbook, observing that, 'the British Empire was so vast, the world was the Victorian cook's oyster'. That particular seafood does not feature on the pub's sample menu, but it does have fish delivered daily, so you might be offered king scallops St Jacques with sugar snap peas, poached brill fillet with prawn and spinach mousse or lobster and crayfish tart.

There are often fishy starters, too – could be deep fried whitebait, a Nordic platter of smoked salmon, prawns and sweet cured herring, or a spicy fish soup. Other starters include devilled kidneys, baked avocado with garlic mushrooms and brie, and a Roquefort pine nut and spinach tart. There's always a vegetarian option.

All meat comes from farms within a 10 mile radius, and game from local estates, so you may find minted lamb steak with sweet potato Lyonnaise, crisp belly pork stuffed with black pudding and served with bubble and squeak, topped with a fried egg, rabbit and wild mushroom pie with mustard mash, or whole wild duck with strawberry and Cointreau sauce. Apart from steak, main courses are generally under £14, accompanied by fresh veg or salad. The only frozen ingredient purchased is ice cream; desserts are often made with locally grown fruit.

★ S V (Hurst Green) P C

WEYBRIDGE
British Volunteer
Heath Road, KT13 8UT

- Mon-Sat 11am-11pm; Sun 12-10.30pm
- Mon-Sat 12-3pm, 6.30-10pm; Sun 12-4pm
- T (01932) 847733
- F (01932) 858300
- E stevecurry42@hotmail.com
- Black Sheep Best Bitter; Fuller's London Pride; guests
- Standard pub fare, freshly cooked
- Traditional pub with a lively but welcoming atmosphere, frequented by sports fans

Good value, straightforward pub fare is on offer at the British Volunteer, freshly prepared in the kitchen and supplemented by curries, fish and pasta dishes that are chalked up on a daily basis. It offers sandwiches, £2.50, and baguettes, £3.95, with no less than 16 fillings to choose from: Stilton and onion, smoked salmon and cream cheese, Cajun chicken, to name just a few – you can even have a traditional chip butty here. Other snacks, £3-£5.50, include filled jacket spuds, toasted panini, ploughman's, scampi with brown bread and butter or Welsh rarebit, £3.25.

The most expensive main course is the fillet steak, with a choice of pepper, Diane or blue cheese sauce, for £8.95. Other dishes include old favourites such as bangers and mash, shepherd's pie or chilli con carne, all under £6. Omelettes are made with eggs from nearby Gribbles Farm and can be flavoured with cheese, ham, mushrooms or smoked salmon, £5.45, or you could go for the 'blue plate special', a traditional fry up (the HP sauce is provided on the table!). Beefburgers, supplied by the local butcher, come with bacon, cheese and chips for £6.95. For something slightly spicier there is Cajun chicken breast or goulash of beef with paprika and caraway seed, served with rice and sour cream.

S (Weybridge) C

BLACKHAM
Sussex Oak
TN3 9UA

- ▶ On A264, midway between East Grinstead and Tunbridge Wells
- ☼ Sun-Thu 10am-12.30am; Fri & Sat 10am-1.30am
- 🍴 Daily 11am-3pm, 6pm-9.30pm
- T (01892) 740273
- E vijayandmaeve@tiscali.co.uk
- 🍺 Shepherd Neame Master Brew Bitter, Best Bitter, Spitfire
- ☺ Good home-cooked food, often with an Asian or Irish influence
- ◉ Friendly rural community pub

A past local CAMRA Pub of the Year, the pub is well worth a visit at any time for a quiet pint in convivial surroundings. Why not enjoy a freshly-baked baguette to go with it: enticing fillings include chicken tikka with mint yogurt, pork sausages and mustard, egg mayonnaise, home-cooked roast beef or bacon, Brie and cranberry, £4.50-£6.25. But you must also sample the excellent home-cooked menu where for starters you could have asparagus tartlet with feta cheese, sun dried tomatoes and red pepper purée, Brie wedges, breadcrumbed and deep fried, served on raspberry coulis, baked mushroom stuffed with pâté, with bacon and cream or king prawns in tempura batter with sweet chilli dip. To follow you may be tempted by the Indian combo: minced lamb bhoona in a tortilla, a mini chicken breast fillet tikka style, onion bhajiya, poppadom and samosas. Or perhaps a vegetable curry, made to landlord Vijay's mother's own recipe with no less than 10 different vegetables, or 'Sussex Oak Signature' – chicken breast pieces marinated and served in a nutty masala sauce to Vijay's recipe with rice and naan bread. Alternatives include baked rump of lamb with red wine, rosemary and redcurrant jus, pasta penne in a concasse of sweet peppers, onions, tomatoes, brandy and cream or a sirloin steak, £7.50-£12.75.

♔ Q ❀ S V 🍺 ♿ ⇌ (Ashurst) ♣ ● P ✂ ⁂ C

BRIGHTON
Basketmakers Arms
12 Gloucester Road, BN1 4AD

- ▶ Close to Brighton station
- ☼ Mon-Sat 11am-11pm; Sun 12-10.30pm
- 🍴 Mon-Fri 12-3.30pm, 5.30-8.30; Sat 12-3.30pm; Sun 12-4pm
- T (01273) 689006
- F (01273) 682300
- E dowds@hamsey.fsnet.co.uk
- 🍺 Gale's Butser, Best Bitter, HSB, Festival Mild, seasonal; guests
- ☺ Renowned for its massive home-made burgers and good value dishes
- ◉ A rare locals' pub in the North Laines area, describing itself as a traditional pub with modern ideas. Handy for the Theatre Royal

At the Bastketmakers the menu has been developed over the years by successive cooks, maintaining a home-made ethic. It boasts several 'signature dishes' including the massive home-made burgers – with a warning that you have to be very hungry to tackle chips as well! Served with mild chilli relish a burger costs £2.60, plus £1 for chips; a vegetarian version is also available. Friday is fish day and the locally caught cod or haddock in home-made beer batter is hard to beat in terms of value, £4.95, or taste, especially when accompanied by a pint of ale. One dish that it truly claims as its own is the 'basket banger', a large sausage made locally and flavoured with Gale's HSB Bitter, served with rashers of bacon and onions in a locally baked baguette – a meal in a sandwich.

The menu carries a huge range of sandwiches and baguettes, £2.25-£3.50, with everything from salami or tomato and onion to hot salt beef on granary or Brie and gammon, with plenty of fillings for vegetarians. Ploughman's, salads and filled jacket potatoes are also served as a light meal. Other good value specials include spicy beef chilli, £3.60, pan-fried tuna steak with fries and peas, £4.75, a rump steak for under a fiver or 6oz sirloin for £6.

★ ❀ V ⇌ (Brighton) ⁂ C

COLEMANS HATCH

☆ Hatch Inn

TN7 4EJ

- Just off B2110
- Mon-Fri 11am-3pm, 5.30pm-11pm; Sat & Sun 11am-11pm
- Daily 12-2.30pm, 7-9pm
- T (01342) 822363
- E nickad@bigfoot.com
- Harveys BB; Larkins Traditional; guests
- Award winning, freshly prepared food based on locally sourced produce
- Quintessential English country pub at the entrance to Ashdown Forest (Winnie the Pooh country); the cosy, low beamed bar has an open fire

Originally three workers cottages built in the 15th century, the pub is popular with walkers in the Ashdown Forest. Although the interior is traditional in its layout and furnishings a novel feature is an original pair of British Airways Concorde seats. Food here is in demand, and booking for evening meals essential. Expect to pay in the region of £27 for a three-course meal, or around £7 for a superior snack such as a crayfish tail and roquette sandwich, a ploughman's lunch with smoked applewood or Cornish yarg or a jacket potato filled with smoked salmon.

Appetisers might include home-made 'baby' chicken pie with Szechuan pepper sauce, roast Mediterranean vegetables finished with grilled Brie and balsamic syrup, fresh Shetland Isle mussels marinière style or a salad of avocado and crayfish tails. Main course dishes, cooked to order, have interesting accompaniments, so char-grilled barbary duck breast comes with spiced egg noodles, hoi sin and citrus, roast tenderloin of pork is served with crushed celeriac with caramelised apples and cider sauce and char-grilled calves' liver is set on a sweet potato purée with a rich red wine onion sauce. Irresistible desserts include fresh almond and pear pudding with hot chocolate sauce and rhubarb and apple crumble with custard and stem ginger ice cream.

★ V C

DANEHILL

☆ Coach & Horses

School Lane, RH17 7JF

▶ Half a mile off A275, 1 mile E of village
☼ Daily 12-3pm, 6-11.30pm (10.30pm Sun)
🍴 Daily 12-2pm, 7-9pm
T (01825) 740369
Harveys BB; King Horsham Best Bitter; guests
☺ Uncomplicated, modern British cuisine from good ingredients
◉ Rural, two bar free house, popular with diners and drinkers. The garden has a children's play area but the patio is for adults only

The landlord describes the Coach and Horses as a 'proper pub' however, because of its remote location, it has to provide top quality food so that customers feel their journey is worthwhile. In an area that is abundant with good produce, the lamb is particularly good here – you can see the flocks from the front door of the pub. The food is mostly British fare with the odd European classic such as coq au vin or moules frites.

The menu in the spacious restaurant is supplemented by daily specials, usually three each for the first two courses and a couple of desserts. Typically on the menu you might find pancetta risotto, sautéed field mushrooms with home-made tagliatelle, ham hock and puy lentil terrine with ginger brioche, char-grilled local smoked salmon and parmesan salad, roasted red pepper soup, or slow roast tomato and asparagus on toasted brioche, £5-£6.50. To follow there could be rib eye steak with onion confit and home-made chips, spicy crab linguini, pea and broad bean risotto with shaved parmesan, beetroot marinated salmon with lemon basil salad and crème fraîche, fillet of black bream with bacon and sautéed salsify or grilled chicken breast with red pepper and onion confit, £9.25-£14.25. Delicious open sandwiches are offered for smaller appetites.

★ ❀ V ♣ P C

EAST HOATHLY

King's Head

1 High Street, BN8 6DR

▶ Off A22 at the centre of village near Lewes
☼ Mon-Sat 11am-11pm; Sun 12-4pm, 7-11pm
🍴 Mon-Sat 12-2.30pm, 6.30-9pm (9.30 Fri & Sat); Sun 12-2.30pm, 7-9pm
T (01825) 840238
F (01825) 880044
E kingshead1648@hotmail.com
1648 Original, Signature, seasonal; Harveys BB; guest
☺ Good variety of home-cooked English dishes
◉ Former coaching inn dating from 1760; the 1648 Brewery operates from the stables

A brilliant match has taken place at the King's Head – home-brewed beers to accompany the home-cooked meals. The 1648 brewery opened at the pub in 2003 and now produces two regular ales alongside more unusual seasonal brews – depending when you go you may find beers brewed with honey, wheat or smoked barley and ginger. The good food is also dependent on the seasons as the chefs rely on fresh local produce, so for example moules marinière will only appear on the menu when the fishmonger at Newhaven recommends the mussels.

They aim to provide six or eight daily specials here; could be Sussex smoked natural haddock in cheese sauce, venison in red wine pie, fillet of beef stroganoff, fillet of salmon in garden chive cream sauce, half a roast duck in plum sauce, dressed crab or half rack of lamb with mint and redcurrant sauce. There is usually a good choice of salads and various curries, including a vegetarian option, all made with their own curry base incorporating fresh ginger. They use 1648 ale in the fish batter and also make their own chicken kiev. Expect to pay around £7 for a main course, more for a steak. A choice of omelettes made with free-range eggs cost £5-£6.40. The Sunday roast is popular here.

★ Q ❀ S V P C

WHATLINGTON
Royal Oak

Woodmans Green, TN33 0NJ

- On A21 between Robertsbridge and Sedlescombe
- Tue-Sat 11am-11pm; Sun & Mon 12-10.30pm
- Mon-Sat 12-2pm, 6.30-9pm; Sun 12-9pm
- T (01424) 870492
- W www.whatlington.com
- Harveys BB; guest
- Good quality, home-cooked English dishes and various snacks
- Attractive, white weatherboarded inn where the olde-worlde, split level interior retains its exposed beams and a large inglenook

At the Royal Oak they uphold the ancient tradition of wassailing, when the health of the apple tree is toasted with cider. Other traditions are important here, too, such as serving fine ale and food. The varied menu caters for all tastes and it is good to see that children are offered smaller portions of some main courses alongside the usual chicken nuggets and fish fingers. For starters, £3.75-£5.25, you could have Sussex smokie (smoked haddock in cheese sauce), deep fried whitebait with a lemon and tarragon mayo, blackened Cajun chicken kebab, goose liver pâté or garlic bread topped with bacon and Brie.

Main courses, mostly £8-£9, are fairly traditional: home-made steak and kidney pud, half a roast shoulder of lamb, pan-fried fillet of pork with tarragon and mustard sauce, lamb's liver with bacon and onion gravy or home-made chicken curry. Fish lovers can choose fillet of salmon with Noilly Prat and chive cream sauce, fillet of cod with a Welsh rarebit topping or home-made fish pie, while veggie options include mushroom stroganoff, pancakes filled with feta, spinach and mushrooms or puff pastry tart with red onion, Brie and thyme. Leave room for lovely puds, all £3.50, such as summer pudding or dark chocolate and Tia Maria torte.

★ S V P C

WITHYHAM
Dorset Arms

TN7 4BD

- On B2110, between Hartfield and Groombridge
- Daily 11.30am-3pm, 6-11pm
- Daily 12-2, 7.30-9pm
- T (01892) 770278
- E pete@dorset-arms.co.uk
- W www.dorset-arms.co.uk
- Harveys Pale Ale, BB, seasonal beers
- Good, home-cooked food from bar snacks to full restaurant meals
- Dating back to the 15th century, the cosy bar has oak floors and a large fireplace; a no-smoking saloon bar leads through to the restaurant

This attractive village pub lies close to the Ashdown Forest and is popular with walkers, who can stop off for a pint of local Harveys ale and a snack or relax and enjoy a full meal in the restaurant (booking is advised at weekends, especially in summer). Meals, from locally-sourced produce, are all cooked to order. A three-course menu is offered for £18.95, including coffee and mints. A sample menu might include, to start, home-made soup of the day, smoked salmon, melon and fruit cocktail, mushrooms in garlic, white wine and cream or prawn cocktail. Typical main courses are fillet steak strips in peppercorn, cream and brandy sauce, chicken breast with bacon and leeks in a cream and cider sauce, pan-fried pork fillet in caramelised onion sauce, roasted duck breast with stuffing and cherry Amaretto sauce, half shoulder of English lamb with red wine gravy and mint sauce. Fish options include pan-fried seabass fillet with parsley butter, seared scallops with bacon and onions or salmon fillet poached in white wine with julienne vegetables. For vegetarians there is a creamy vegetable risotto topped with parmesan cheese. For a £2 surcharge you can have fillet steak tournados. A mouth-watering selection of desserts changes daily.

★ S V P C

DONNINGTON
Blacksmith's Arms
Selsey Road, PO20 7PR

- ▶ On B2201, 2 miles S of Chichester
- ☼ Daily 11am-3pm, 6-11pm
- Daily 12-2.30pm; 6-9.30pm (not Sun or Mon eves Jan or Feb)
- T (01243) 783999
- Fuller's London Pride; Greene King Abbot; Oakleaf Bitter; Wells Bombardier; guest beer
- Freshly cooked food from fine ingredients, noted for fish
- Cottage-style 17th-century pub that attracts drinkers and diners in equal numbers; large safe garden with children's play equipment

Traditional decor is combined with modern touches to create a cosy, comfortable atmosphere in which to dine; meals can be taken in the bar or adjoining restaurant area. Everything is cooked to order and the fresh fish, delivered daily, is especially recommended – depending on availability you might find wild seabass, bream, skate, John Dory, gurnard, mussels or local crab chalked up on the specials board.

The regular menu carries starters such as duo of smoked fish salad, wild mushroom forestière, warm chicken chorizo and tomato salad, tempura battered pork or home-made soup, £5-£7.50. Non fishy specials include pheasant with braised red cabbage and celeriac mash, duck breast with wild mushroom sauce or rosemary marinated lamb cutlets, plus the vegetarian dish of the day. Other favourites include steak and hand-cut chips, chicken breast wrapped in serrano ham with watercress and white wine sauce, pork loin on celeriac mash, olde English pork sausages on spring onion mash; main course prices are mostly around £10-£14. Light lunches include ham, egg and chips, Thai chicken curry or home-made burgers, while on Sunday, fish pie and a vegetarian alternative supplement the traditional roast, two courses for £12. All puddings are home made, including summer pudding, sherry trifle or rhubarb crumble. ★ 🏠 Q ❀ S V ⛽ ♿ 🍎 🅿 👪 C

EARTHAM
George
Brittens Lane, PO18 0LT

- ▶ Off the A27 or A285, 3 miles E of Chichester
- ☼ Mon-Sat 11am-11pm; Sun 12-10.30pm
- Daily 12-3pm, 6-9.30pm
- T (01243) 814340
- F (01243) 814725
- Arundel Gauntlet; Greene King Ruddles County; King Horsham Best Bitter; guests
- Traditional hearty British fare and good fresh fish
- Attractive old country inn at the village centre with plenty of room for both drinkers and diners; its large garden is an asset

A recently revamped menu offers over 20 main course dishes based largely on local produce. The meat is all free range or organic – the lamb comes from a farm in the village. Vegetarians are well catered for – in winter heart-warming dishes include roasted root vegetable crumble – while fish dishes on the specials board change on a daily basis. Lunchtime snacks include open Danish sandwiches, ploughman's and filled baguettes or, for a more substantial dish, pub favourites such as lasagne, bangers and mustard mash and steak and kidney pie, all £8.25. In winter the home-made crockpots are popular at £5.95 – lamb stew with herb dumplings, coq au vin or chilli con carne, served with crusty bread.

On the main menu you could start with potted Sussex smokies with cheese-flavoured mash, spicy vegetable filo wraps with hoisin sauce, devilled lamb's kidneys on toasted olive bread or chicken liver and cognac pâté with onion marmalade, £4.25-£5.75. To follow there is a choice of rich game casserole in a large Yorkshire pudding, free range pork chops on ratatouille and diced potatoes in tomato sauce, stir-fried calf's liver and bacon in onion gravy with sauté potatoes or slow-braised half shoulder of lamb, prices around £11. Home-made puds including fruit crumbles are all £3.95.
🏠 Q ❀ S V ⛽ ♿ ♣ 🍎 🅿 🚭 👪 C

EAST ASHLING
Horse & Groom
PO18 9AX

- On B2178 between Chichester and Rowlands Castle
- Mon-Sat 12-3pm, 6-11pm; Sun 12-6pm
- Mon-Sat 12-2.15pm, 6.30-9.15pm; Sun 12-2.30pm
- T (01243) 575339
- F (01243) 575560
- E info@thehorseandgroomchichester.co.uk
- W www.thehorseandgroomchichester.com
- Harveys Pale Ale; Hop Back Summer Lightning; Young's Bitter; guest
- High quality, home-cooked British dishes
- Skilfully extended 17th-century inn with flagstone floor, large fireplace with a working range, old settles in the bar and a comfortable restaurant

Voted Pub of the Year in 2005 by local CAMRA members, this lovely old pub offers a varied menu of good food in hearty portions. You could start with home-made soup, deep fried Brie, duck pancake in plum and hoisin sauce or a salad of warm chicken, bacon and avocado. Good fish dishes include whole baked seabass in parsley butter, smoked haddock in creamed spinach, salmon steak in watercress sauce or whole grilled plaice; or there are lamb cutlets, pork fillet in cider marinade, rack of lamb in honey sauce, calves' liver and bacon in red wine sauce or a choice of steaks. Vegetarians are not forgotten – there may be a pasta with sun-dried tomatoes, peppers, mushrooms and mozzarella or baked aubergine with courgette and herb crumb.

Tempting home-made puds could be lemon and ginger crunch, apple and berry crumble, blackberry cobbler, bread and butter pudding or, for chocoholics, death by chocolate. If you are just passing through there is a comprehensive snack menu – baguettes, filled jacket spuds, ham, egg and chips – and there is a children's menu. Overnight en-suite accommodation is available in oak-beamed rooms in a converted flint barn.

★ Q S V P C

FERRING
Henty Arms
2 Ferring Lane, BN12 6QY

- In the village, N of level crossing
- Mon-Wed 11-3pm, 5.30-11pm; Thu-Sat 11am-11pm; Sun 12-4pm, 6.30-10.30pm
- Daily 11.30am-2.15pm, 6.30-9.15pm
- T (01903) 241254
- F (01903) 503796
- E hentyarms@hotmail.com
- Caledonian Deuchars IPA; Fuller's London Pride; Greene King Ruddles County; guests
- Mostly home-cooked pub fare with a good choice of daily specials
- Friendly village pub where the public bar is used for darts, pool and watching TV; the quiet lounge has a no-smoking dining area

The pub benefits from a large garden that is used as the venue for its annual beer festival, timed to coincide with the vintage bus running day from Worthing. A proper village pub that hosts a Sunday quiz, it also offers good food, ranging from sandwiches, ploughman's and snacks to full meals. Owners the Carlyles, who hail from Cornwall, make their own Cornish pasties, and they buy fresh fish from local seafront suppliers.

For starters, £3.25-£4.75, you could have smoked haddock and spring onion fish cake, vegetable pakora with hot chilli sauce and salad, a Thai selection (red curry chicken samosa, green curry chicken parcel, vegetable spring roll and mango chutney), Sawadee tempura king prawns marinaded in ginger and garlic, or salmon shantie (salmon in cream sauce with broccoli and herbs, breadcrumbed and served with salad). The specials board always offers a wide choice of fairly traditional dishes, so you will often find rib eye steak, Stilton and broccoli quiche, fresh grilled plaice or cod, a half shoulder of lamb, steak and kidney or steak and mushroom pie, salmon and dill lasagne, gammon with egg or pineapple, or barbecued chicken breast with bacon and cheese. Main courses are around £7, £10.50 for steaks.

Q S V P C

LAMBS GREEN
Lamb Inn
RH12 4R6

- Near Rusper, 2 miles N of A264
- Mon-Sat 11.30am-3pm, 5.30-11pm; Sun 12-4pm, 7-10.30pm
- Mon-Sat 12-2pm, 7-9.30pm; Sun 12-2.30pm, 7-9pm
- T (01293) 871336
- F (01293) 871933
- E info@thelambinn.info
- W www.thelambinn.info
- King Horsham Best Bitter, Red River
- Freshly-cooked meals based on seasonal, local produce; British with a modern twist
- Brewer WJ King's first tenanted pub was renovated and reopened in 2003, featuring stone flags and exposed beams

At the Lamb they claim to be able to trace every cut of meat back to the original animal: all the meat and game comes from individual farmers. Fish is delivered daily from the south coast. Everything on the menu is home made, even the mayonnaise and tartare sauce, and their own ham is cooked on the premises. The cheese board features only select English cheeses from small producers. With all this attention to detail they still manage to keep prices reasonable: starters under a fiver and many main courses under a tenner.

The bar menu offers a good choice of ploughman's for £5.50, salads and ham, egg and chips. Starters on the main menu include grilled New Zealand green lipped mussels with garlic butter topped with cheese, tiger prawns in filo pastry with a sweet chilli and hot soy dip or guacamole served with toasted pitta bread. Next up, there is tenderloin of pork in honey, cream and cider sauce with apple compote, breast of chicken Neapolitan topped with mozzarella cheese, fresh dressed crab, whole seabass or plaice, or filo pastry basket filled with mushrooms in a creamy wine and thyme sauce. Puddings are all £4.25: apple and raspberry crumble, sticky toffee pud or banoffi pie.

★ Q S V P C

MANNINGS HEATH
Dun Horse Inn
Brighton Road, RH13 6HZ

- On A281 between Horsham and Cowfold
- Daily 11am-11pm
- Mon 12-2.30pm; Tue-Sat 12-2.30pm, 7-9.30pm; Sun 12-3pm
- T (01403) 265783
- W www.dunhorseinn.co.uk
- Fuller's London Pride; Taylor Landlord
- Straightforward, home-cooked pub food
- Recently-refurbished roadside pub with secure garden for children; note the stained glass windows promoting Rock Ales

Children are welcome here, both inside and in the garden, and one of the two guest rooms has family accommodation. The saloon bar has been extended to provide more dining tables as the food here is growing in popularity. The menu concentrates mainly on pub staples, but all the meals are home made and special dishes are added on Friday and Saturday evenings. So, to start with you would find soup, pâté, mozzarella salad, warm goats' cheese, garlic mushrooms and platters of smoked salmon or fresh prawns. To follow, chilli con carne, cod and chips, steak and ale pie, ham, egg and chips, bangers and mash are the mainstays of the menu, with weekend specials of lemon chicken salad, rib eye steak, pork and apple Stilton pie, mushroom stroganoff, calf's or lamb's liver and bacon, mushroom and spinach lasagne, and mushroom and bacon pasta bake. Puds are straightforward too: chocolate slice, apple crumble, fruits of the forest gateau and ice creams. On Sunday lunchtime there is a traditional roast and on summer weekends barbecues are hosted in the garden; special themed evenings are also a regular feature. At lunchtime a selection of sandwiches is also available.

★ Q V P C

NUTHURST
Black Horse Inn
Nuthurst Street, RH13 6RS

▶ Four miles S of Horsham between A281, A24 and A272
☼ Mon-Fri 12-3pm, 6-11pm; Sat 12-11pm; Sun 12-10.30pm
Ⓣ Mon-Fri 12-2.30pm, 6-9.30pm; Sat & Sun 12-9.30pm
T (01403) 891272
E clive.henwood@btinternet.com
Fuller's London Pride; Harveys BB; King Horsham Best Bitter; guests
☺ Traditional pub meals, mostly home made
Split-level, 17th-century village pub retaining many original features including flagstone floors and an inglenook

Guest beers at the Black Horse generally showcase local breweries, such as Welton or Hepworth, and local produce is also featured in home-made dishes prepared to order in the pub's new state of the art kitchen. The menu starts off with home-made soup of the day, pâté, goats' cheese with tomato tatin, moules marinière, and a trio of fish terrine, £3.50-£6.50. Just half a dozen choices are listed on the regular main course menu, but they cover all tastes: chicken breast stuffed with Stilton, wrapped in bacon and poached in red wine, roasted lamb shank, thinly sliced calves' liver with bacon and onion juice and mash, whole sea bass grilled in olive oil with oregano, a 12oz sirloin with all the trimmings and a vegetarian choice of tortilla wrap with roasted Mediterranean vegetables topped with goat's cheese and tomato chutney, prices from £11-£15. There is also a lighter bites menu of home-made pub favourites such as Sussex ham, egg and hand cut chips, chilli con carne, plaice fillet and chips, vegetarian pizza or pie of the day (see specials board) in shortcrust pastry, all priced £8.50 or less. For a quick snack the pub offers freshly baked baguettes or ciabattas with fillings for £5.95.

★ Q ❀ S V P C

WARNHAM
Sussex Oak
2 Church Street, RH12 3QW

▶ Just off A24, opposite parish church
☼ Daily 11am-11pm (10.30pm Sun)
Ⓣ Mon-Sat 12-2.30pm, 6-9.30pm; Sun 12-8pm
T (01403) 265028
F (01403) 265128
E info@thesussexoak.co.uk
W www.thesussexoak.co.uk
Adnams Bitter; Fuller's London Pride; Young's Bitter; Taylor Landlord; guest
☺ Hearty British fare from locally sourced produce, plus a good snack menu
Spacious, 16th-century village pub with beamed interior complete with inglenook; no-smoking restaurant and large garden

To keep up with customer demand the owners of this popular country pub now offer meals seven days a week. In summer they also host barbecues in the garden. They rely on local suppliers for fresh produce for the kitchen and the menus change with seasons. A typical winter meal could start with home-made soup or pâté, warm salad of pan-fried black pudding, bacon and new potatoes in garlic, moules marinière with crusty bread, warm goats' cheese and honey-glazed smoke duck salad or platters to share such as the Mediterranean Meze of taramasalata, houmous, olives, marinated char-grilled vegetables and pitta bread.

The list of mains might include pan-fried venison steak with winter berries and cinnamon, mixed grill or char-grilled steaks, braised lamb shank on root veg with mash and parsnip chips, home-made fish pie or mushroom stroganoff with herb rice. There is always a fish choice or two and a curry. Two courses cost around £12-£17, some dishes are available as smaller portions. Desserts, all £3.95, are chalked up daily, while a selection of local unpasteurised cheeses, fruit and biscuits is £4.95.

★ Q ❀ S V (Warnham) P C

WARNINGLID

☆ Half Moon

The Street, RH17 5TR

- ▶ On B2115, 1 mile from A13 and 6 miles from Haywards Heath
- Mon-Sat 11.30am-2.30pm, 5.30-11pm; Sun 12-10.30pm
- Tue-Sat 12-2pm, 6-9.30pm; Sun & Mon 12-2pm
- T (01444) 461227
- Black Sheep Best Bitter, Harveys BB; Shepherd Neame Spitfire; guests
- ☺ Home-cooked food with a good selection of daily specials
- Attractive Grade II listed brick and stone pub dating back to the 18th century

Landlord and chef Jonny Lea bought the Half Moon in February 2005 and has been slowly building up food trade since then. All meals are prepared here and considerable effort goes into searching out good local produce. In the evening, steaks supplied by the butcher in nearby Partridge Green supplement the menu. There is always a good choice of delicious special dishes, such as braised lamb shank with red cabbage and gratin potatoes, barbary duck breast with plum sauce, pan-fried pork fillet with apple mash and mustard sauce, or tandoori chicken breast with coconut sauce and pilau rice. Fish specials include haddock and prawn fishcakes with lemon crème fraîche, pan-fried halibut steak with red pepper coulis, gilt head bream fillets with fennel and onion dressing or king scallop and chorizo salad. Vegetarians might be tempted by Greek salad with marinated feta and lemon dressing or a tower of aubergine, beef tomato and goats' cheese with fresh tomato sauce. Main course specials are mostly in the £8.50-£14 price range; dishes on the regular menu cost slightly less and include favourites such as battered cod fillet and home-made beef burger spiced with chilli, cumin and coriander. Various ploughman's are £5.95 or there are filled freshly-baked ciabattas for under £5.

★ Q ❀ S V C

WORTHING

Hare & Hounds

79-81 Portland Road, BN11 1QG

- ▶ Town centre, N of Montague Street pedestrian area
- Mon-Sat 10.30am-11pm; Sun 12-10.30pm
- Mon-Thu 12-2.30pm, 6-8.30pm; Fri & Sun 12-2.30pm; Sat 12-5pm
- T (01903) 230948
- Arundel Gold, ASB; Greene King Old Speckled Hen; Fuller's London Pride; Young's Bitter; guest
- ☺ Good value, home-made pub food prepared with artistic flair
- Friendly, cosy pub with plenty of nooks and crannies, surrounded by former fishermen's cottages

The Hare & Hounds provides everything a proper pub should – a good choice of real ales and a varied menu supplemented by daily specials at reasonable prices. The meals are freshly made, with ingredients mostly coming from butchers, greengrocers and fishmongers within walking distance of the pub. Lunchtime customers tend to be local workers or shoppers so they try to offer a fairly speedy service – the chicken club sandwich, home-made soup and 'doorstep' sandwiches always go down well – but in the evenings they aim to be more relaxed. Vegetarians are well catered for with several choices for around £5: wild mushroom risotto, deep-fried carrot and coriander goujons, crispy coated goats' cheese with tomato and onion salad, macaroni cheese or a four-egg omelette. There is home-cooked ham with double egg and chips, and other home-made dishes such as chilli con carne served with rice and nachos, cottage pie (plain or topped with cheese and bacon and served with chips), lasagne served with garlic bread and salad garnish or a pie of the day with seasonal veg. Main courses are mostly around £7. Fish and chips is recommended, as is the good value Sunday roast. Tuesday evening diners can enjoy live jazz.

★ ❀ S V ♿ C

KENTON BANK FOOT
Twin Farms
22 Main Road, NE13 8AB

- Mon-Sat 11am-11pm; Sun 12-10.30pm
- Daily 12-9pm
- T (0191) 286 1263
- Caledonian Deuchars IPA; Taylor Landlord, guests
- Excellent choice of classic British dishes
- New pub, built in traditional style on the site of an old farm; the large open-plan space has alcoves for privacy and is warmed by two open fires

The pub is a new build by Fitzgerald, the same small company that owns the Green at Wardley, also listed in this county. It aims to give its outlets the individuality you might expect at a free house, with plenty of guest beers and good food – not just a standard pub group menu. Starters and light bites on offer include butternut squash macaroni cheese and halloumi wrapped in red peppers with lemon and chilli (both suitable for vegetarians), asparagus, Serrano ham and taleggio tart, steamed mussels with tarragon crème fraîche, devilled crab cakes with garlic mayo and French country salad. All cost less than £5, and some are also available in large portions. To follow there is a choice of Moroccan chicken with saffron couscous, gammon steak with colcannon and redcurrant sauce, tandoori-spiced salmon with cucumber, pear and radish salad or pub favourites with a slight twist: cottage pie with cheddar and parsnip mash or bangers and mash with mustard gravy and apple wedges. House specialities include lentil nut kofta skewer with spiced pepper salsa and coriander raita, sticky honey, tomato and mustard chicken with Greek salad and tandoori steak burger with mint dip and kachumbar piccalilli. Expect to pay £8-£9 for a main course or up to £17 for a 16oz T-bone steak with sauce.

Q S V (Kenton Bank Foot)
P C

NEWBURN
Keelman
Grange Road, NE15 8NL

- Follow signs for the country park
- Mon-Sat 11am-11pm; Sun 12-10.30pm
- Daily 12-9pm
- T (0191) 267 1689
- F (0191) 267 7387
- E admin@biglampbrewers.co.uk
- W www.biglampbrewers.co.uk
- Full Big Lamp range
- Traditional pub meals with good range of sandwiches
- Converted Grade II listed pumping station; a mix of traditional and contemporary styles; adventure playground for children

Situated on the Coast-to-Coast cycleway and the Hadrian's Wall Path, Keelman's is the ideal spot to quench your thirst as it is the tap for Big Lamp Brewery on the same country park site. Food is served all day on a regularly changing menu. For a light bite there is a good choice of hot or cold sandwiches: roast beef and gravy, tuna melt panini, peppered steak, and cheese, mushroom and spring onion baguette number among the hot options, all under £5.

For starters, dipping food features highly – chicken goujons with chilli dip, breadcrumbed king prawns and seafood sauce, and the Keelman combo: a platter of goujons, garlic mushrooms, spicy prawns and potato wedges with various dips for £8.85 for two to share. Main courses are good value, mostly around £5 or £6, with home-made favourites such as beef and ale or chicken and mushroom pie, and mince and dumplings. Vegetarians have an interesting choice of spiced mushroom and aubergine tagine, wild rice, spinach and honey roast, or pear, Gorgonzola and walnut tart, as well as several pasta dishes. From the grill you can order a 10oz rump or sirloin, £8/£10, rainbow trout or the king size grill for £10. For Sunday lunch there is a choice of beef or lamb for £5.95, £3.95 for children.

S V P C

NORTH SHIELDS
☆ Magnesia Bank

1 Camden Street, NE30 1NH

- High on the bank side above fish quay
- Mon-Sat 11am-midnight; Sun 11.45am-11.30pm
- Mon-Sat 12-9.45pm; Sun 12-8.45pm
- T (0191) 257 4831
- F (0191) 258 6847
- E kate@magnesiabank.com
- W www.magnesiabank.com
- Beer range varies from local micros
- Regional food using local produce
- Family-owned community local

Full of enthusiasm and vigour, the Magnesia Bank is an absolute one off. Ingredients for the kitchen comes from interesting local producers. These include Belsay Barns Farm supplying lamb and beef exclusively to the pub. 'Every bit of the animal is used, from pressing the tongue, making rich stock from the bones, suet from round the kidneys, soup from the tails and even our own corned beef,' says landlady Kate Slade. Fruit, vegetables and herbs are delivered daily by a nearby greengrocer; fish and shellfish from the quay five minutes away.

All these fine ingredients are used in a changing menu of dishes such as beef and Black Sheep ale pie, home-made Italian style burgers, pan-fried turbot, Parma monkfish with crispy noodles, peppered venison steak, or a half shoulder of the farm lamb baked with leeks, rosemary and redcurrants. Prices are around £5. A large fillet of locally caught fish in home-made batter served with home-made chips is a favourite here, as is the juicy rib eye local beef steak with tomato and red onion salad and chips for a budget £8.95.

Dee Slade's famous puds have won her a national dessert of the year prize in the Publican awards, with treats such as banana and ginger crumble, chocolate layer meringue, kiwi and strawberry pavlova with ginger syrup or peach and brandy cheesecake.

S V (North Shields Metro) C

NORTH SHIELDS
Shiremoor House Farm

Middle Engine Lane, NE29 8DZ

- N of North Shields and just E of the A19
- Mon-Sat 11am-11pm; Sun 12-10.30pm
- Daily 12-9.30pm
- T (0191) 257 6302
- Mordue Workie Ticket; guests
- Classic British dishes a speciality
- Converted from derelict farm buildings, the pub retains many original features

This Fitzgerald's house is an award-winning conversion of derelict stone farm buildings where many original features have been preserved, including the conical, raftered 'gin gan' that now serves as a restaurant. Meals can also be taken in the bar, terrace and garden. Along with a varied menu, the pub also offers an extensive selection of guest ales. The Shiremoor is popular for its traditional roasts and generous portions of food. The specials list changes daily. For starters, £5-£6, you might find oven-baked field mushrooms with spring onion salad, chef's pâté and Greek style feta salad. Main course dishes major on traditional favourites, but you could find oven-baked fillet of salmon with jacket potato wedges, spicy sausages with fresh vegetables, medallions of beef and rogan josh, served with both rice and fries. Main courses are mostly £6-£10. For dessert, £3-£4, you could be tempted by French apple tart, Belgian chocolate torte or plum frangipane. Children are welcome to eat here; why not combine your meal with a trip to the nearby Stephenson's Railway Museum where you can see 'Billy', a forerunner to the Rocket, and take a ride on a steam train.

★ Q S V P C

WARDLEY
Green
White Mare Pool, NE10 8YB

- ▶ On A184 towards Newcastle at B1288 jct
- ☼ Mon-Sat 11am-11pm; Sun 12-10.30pm
- Daily 12-9pm
- T (0191) 495 0171
- Greene King Ruddles County; Taylor Landlord; guests
- ☺ Varied selection of home-cooked dishes
- The plush, Victorian-style bar only opens in the evenings, but the spacious lounge and highly regarded restaurant are open all day

A pub that from the outside looks like a bungalow and is situated close to a motorway junction might not seem the most likely prospect for good food, however the Green enjoys a respectable following for the meals served in its stylish brasserie. It is also an oasis for real ale fans in an area that is something of a good beer desert.

Many of the starters on the menu can also be ordered as a substantial snack or as a main course portion, such as tempura prawns with mint, chilli and mango salsa, Indian spiced couscous with chickpeas and herb salad, penne pasta with blue cheese, leeks and button mushrooms, chilli mussels, spicy Thai crab cakes with a mango chilli salsa or lemon chicken Caesar salad. Enticing main courses, mostly £8-£9, include slow cooked lamb shank with ratatouille and basil mash, cider apple sausage casserole with buttered veg, grilled aubergine, goats' cheese and tomato burger, hot smoked salmon fishcakes with wilted greens and fish cream or a curry of the day with rice and coriander flatbread. The menu also lists specialities from the grill: skewered tandoori chicken with Caesar salad, duck breast satay, grilled halibut with three bean salad and crispy prosciutto or steaks, served plain or with a sauce, including an unusual sweet and sour onion butter.

Q ❀ S V ♿ ♣ P ⚤ C

Hungry train spotters and commuters can enjoy both fine food and up to eight cask beers on Platform 2 at the West Riding Licensed Refreshment Rooms in Dewsbury, West Yorkshire. The inspired cook is Mary Tidswell who sends this recipe using local black pudding.

SAUSAGES WITH BLACK PUDDING CAKE IN A RICH TOMATO SAUCE
Serves 4

8 of your favourite sausages
1 large onion, chopped
225g (8oz) black pudding, chopped
340g (12oz) puff pastry
1 egg, beaten, for glazing

Tomato sauce

1 medium onion, chopped
450g (1lb) ripe plum tomatoes, skinned and de-seeded
2 tbsps tomato purée
1 dsp brown sugar
Salt and pepper

Pre-heat oven to 220C/425F/gas mark 7. Place sausages in roasting tin and roast for 20-30 minutes. Sauté chopped onion gently until cooked, then mix with the black pudding. Roll out the puff pastry, cut into four rounds, place a quarter of the black pudding mix in the centre of each, seal and glaze with the beaten egg. Place on a greased oven tray in the oven above the sausages, cook for 15-20 minutes until risen and golden brown.

To make the tomato sauce, fry the onion until golden in a little olive oil, add the tomatoes, tomato purée and brown sugar then simmer until thick and pulpy. Season to taste and serve with the sausages and black pudding cakes.

DEPPERS BRIDGE
Great Western
CV47 2ST

- At B4451 and B4452 jct, 10 minutes' drive from M40 jct 12
- Daily 12-11pm
- Daily 12-9pm
- T (01926) 611977
- Adnams Bitter; Black Country Bradley's Finest Golden, Pig on the Wall; guests
- Varied bar menu supplemented by daily specials every evening
- Large rural, roadside pub converted from a former railway station and stationmaster's house

A pub for rail buffs, the Great Western boasts a 20-ton train outside on part of the remaining track, however this is for nostalgic reasons only as it is no longer operational. If you ask nicely, though, the bar staff might compensate by operating the model railway that runs around the pub. Food is served right through until early evening. During the day you can choose from the traditional bar menu that offers a good choice of steaks, fish dishes, lasagne and other favourites, including a bargain three-course meal for £4.95.

In the evening, home-made specials are chalked up to supplement the regular menu, with more adventurous offerings such as duck and bacon casserole, black pudding stack and the chef's own Shackerdale chicken. Main courses are mostly around £7.95. There's a choice of starters including a sharing platter of food to dip, such as fish goujons, chicken pieces, breaded mushrooms. The specials board usually carries some heart-warming home-made desserts, maybe apple pie or crumble or bread and butter pudding, priced around £3.50. On Sundays the traditional roast features a choice of three or four meats, £6.95 for the main course.

S V C

FENNY COMPTON
Wharf
Wharf Road, CV47 2FE

- On A423 between Banbury and Southam
- Daily 10.30am-11.30pm
- Daily 12-3.30pm, 5-9.30pm
- T (01295) 770332
- E thewharfinn@hotmail.co.uk
- Beer range varies
- Varied menu ranging from sandwiches to steaks plus daily specials
- Recently refurbished canalside pub with a modern, stylish interior

A good choice for a summer's day, one wall of the pub is a vast window offering magnificent views over the hills, while the large, west-facing canalside garden has a children's play area and is perfect for watching the sunset. Canal memorabilia feature in the newly refurbished interior that includes a couple of snugs with comfy sofas (and possibly the resident dog) and a no-smoking restaurant with unusual galleried drinking area.

The Wharf's menu changes seasonally every three or four months and the majority of dishes on offer are home made and represent good value. The meat comes from local butchers and the speciality sausages, faggots and steaks are particularly recommended. The meat is put to good use in home-made pies, stews with dumpling, hotpots and soups. There is a good choice for vegetarians as well as fresh fish dishes. A specials board changes daily with the philosophy of 'when it's gone it's gone'. Although some items are bought in, there are always home-made puddings. Apart from the big garden, the pub has a three acre field where they grow all their own herbs and mushrooms.

Q S V C

LONG ITCHINGTON
Harvester
6 Church Road, CV47 9PE

- ▶ Off A423, by the church
- ☼ Mon-Sat 12-3pm, 6-11pm; Sun 12-4pm, 7-10.30pm
- 🍴 Mon-Sat 12-2pm, 6-10pm; Sun 12-2.30pm, 7-10pm
- T 01926 812698
- E harvester@longitchington.org.uk
- W www.theharvesterinn.co.uk
- Hook Norton Best Bitter, Old Hooky; guest
- ☺ Simple, but well cooked fare
- Unspoilt country village pub built as two cottages in the 19th century, with a small games room and restaurant

Not to be confused with the pub chain eatery, this Harvester is a veteran of CAMRA's Good Beer Guide having clocked up 21 consecutive entries. The restaurant is small but seats 28 comfortably and is popular for Sunday lunch, when booking is advised. The food here is fairly simple but always well cooked, based on local produce as much as possible. Steaks come from a butcher in Lutterworth but the fillet is delivered whole so it can be trimmed in the kitchen to ensure quality. Fresh fish such as Dover sole or seabass is offered when it is available at a good price to give customers value for money.

You might start your meal with baby sweetcorns in garlic butter, egg mayonnaise with prawns or chef's pâté with warm toast, all £3.80. To follow the steaks can be served simply grilled or you can opt for one of the pub's specialities: fillet steak Rossini, served on a crouton, topped with pâté and red wine sauce, £13.50, or maybe sirloin chasseur in a white wine sauce with onions, mushrooms, tomato and tarragon. Pork scallopi à la Marsala is tenderloin cooked in butter and rosemary and coated in Marsala sauce for £10.50, or you could try lamb chops Bar-Man grilled and garnished with tomato, bacon and mushrooms. Sweets or cheese to finish cost £2.95.

❀ S ♿ ♣ P C

NAPTON
Bridge at Napton
Southam Road, CV47 8NQ

- ▶ On Oxford Canal, 2 miles from Southam on A425 to Daventry
- ☼ Winter Tue-Sat 7.30am-3pm, 6-10.30pm (11pm Fri & Sat); Sun 12-3pm. Summer daily 12-3pm, 6-10pm (11pm Wed-Sat)
- 🍴 Winter Tue-Sat 7.30-11am, 12-2pm, 6-9pm; Sun 12-2.30pm. Summer Mon-Sat 7.30-11am (not Mon), 12-2pm, 6-9pm; Sun 12-2.30pm, 6-8.30pm
- T 01926 812466
- E tim@schlapfor.fsnet.co.uk
- W www.thebridgeatnapton.co.uk
- Beer range varies
- ☺ Old English traditional with international extras
- Three bars, large garden, play area and magnificent views of Oxford Canal

The Bridge opens at 7.30am most mornings to provide breakfast before going on to the lunch session starting at noon. You'll find starters such as Bantry Bay mussels, Whitby creel prawns, and starter of the day on the specials board. Main meals on the specials board could be traditional favourites such as beef and ale pie containing half a pound of beef, venison casserole with red wine and juniper berries, golden apple duck with honey and spice finished with brandy, liver and bacon casserole, fillet steak and mushroom Wellington, old English fish pie or 'narrowboats in the winding hole' – a big Yorkie filled with Cumberland sausages in beer and thyme gravy. More exotic choices could be Singapore lamb and mango curry, Spanish chicken with red and green peppers and chorizo, chicken and seafood paella, salmon in champagne with pink peppercorn sauce or veggie choices such as Brie, basil and sun-dried tomato cheesecake. On the regular menu look for smoky fisherman's crumble, stuffed roast salmon with balsamic vinegar sauce and butternut squash bake. On weekday lunchtimes only there are baguettes and jacket spuds with a variety of fillings.

Q ❀ S V P C

NORTHEND
Red Lion
Bottom Street, CV47 2TJ

- ▶ Signed off B4100 Bawbury-Leamington, opposite army camp
- ☼ Tues-Fri 11.30am-3pm, 6-11pm; Sat 12-3pm, 6-11pm; Sun 12-3pm, 7-10.30pm
- Tues-Sat 12-2pm, 6-9pm; Sun 12-2pm, 7-10.30pm
- T (01295) 770308
- Taylor Landlord, guest
- ☺ Home-cooked traditional and overseas dishes
- Idyllic rural pub close to Burton Dassett Hills Country Park with a warm welcome for locals and ramblers; wonderful views from the garden

A homely menu of freshly-made meals embraces the traditional and more exotic. Snacks include home-made soup, Warwickshire ham with egg and chips, choice of omelettes and burgers and ploughman's, priced £3.50-£5. Starters including specials might be black pudding and smoked bacon in mustard sauce, Thai prawns in filo, smoked salmon with scrambled eggs, avocado, mozzarella and tomato salad, deep-fried whitebait with garlic mayo or fresh mussels, all £4.50 or £5. Fish dishes are fresh market fish of the day in beer batter, vol au vents filled with monkfish and prawns, grilled swordfish with garlic butter or plaice topped, interestingly, with bananas and mango, prices from £8.25-£12.50. Meat meals could include Indonesian chicken curry, lamb's liver and bacon, chicken filled with cream cheese and spinach wrapped in bacon, rabbit casseroled with cider, steak and ale pie, chicken and asparagus crêpes and grilled gammon or rib eye steaks, prices £8.25-£10.50. Vegetarian choices, all £8.25, might be Thai vegetable curry or mushroom stroganoff with rice and salad. Desserts, all £3.95, include crème brûlée, chocolate rum pots, banoffee pie or home-made meringues with cappuccino ice cream and chocolate sauce.

S V P C

STOCKTON
Crown Inn
8 High Street, CV47 8JZ

- ▶ In village centre
- ☼ Daily 12-11pm
- Daily 12-2.30pm, 6-9pm
- T (01926) 812255
- Adnams Broadside; Ansells Mild, Bitter; Tetley Bitter
- ☺ Good value home cooking with 'early bird' and other special offers
- Village pub at the heart of the community, fielding dominoes, darts and pool teams and home to a pétanque club that plays in Germany and France

This is a proper village pub that offer good food at reasonable prices. Its senior citizens' menu is £4.75 for three courses, while the Sunday lunch is so popular that they have two sittings, £7.50 for one course, rising to £9.75 for three courses. Other offers include an early bird menu (two meals from a choice of five) for £6.25 on Tuesday to Thursday evenings between 6 and 7.30pm, curry and chilli night every Tuesday – a choice of home-made curry or chilli and a pint for just £4.50 – and on Wednesday you can have a choice of three home-made pies (one vegetarian) plus a pint for the same price.

If you want to splash out and choose from the main menu, this won't break the bank either with starters around £3 and steaks starting at £6.75 for an 8oz rump going up to £10.95 for a 12oz sirloin or 16oz T-bone. If you and a guest order two steaks with pepper sauce you get half a carafe of wine thrown in. All the meat comes from Joseph Norris in Leicestershire and fruit and veg from a supplier in the village. There is a daily specials board and home-made puddings, including crumbles and other dishes made from apples and pears from their own trees.

S V P C

WARMINGTON
Plough Inn
Church Hill, OX17 1BX

- ▶ Off B4100 between Gaydon and Banbury
- ☼ Mon-Sat 12-3pm, 6-11pm; Sun 12-10.30pm
- 🍴 Mon; Tue-Sat 12-2.30pm, 6-8.30pm; Sun 12-2.30pm
- T (01295) 690666
- E ploughwarmington@aol.com
- Beer range varies
- ☺ Old-fashioned menu of home-cooked meals
- Genuine single bar free house dating back to the 16th century in a village that boasts a 'sloping' duck pond

CAMRA's 2006 Good Beer Guide describes the Plough as a 'real gem' with a warm, welcoming atmosphere enhanced in winter by an open fire. Popular with locals, especially for the good beer range, ramblers and cyclists, the pub's motto is, 'Goode olde menu, goode olde real ales and goode olde-fashioned pub'. Well maybe the 'olde' doesn't quite ring true as the ales are turned over quickly and the food is certainly fresh – most of the meals are prepared by the owner's octogenarian mum, and only an ungracious son would refer to her as olde!

Mrs Powell concentrates on good value, no-nonsense home cooking, offering all the usual pub favourites such as steak and kidney pies, tasty stews and liver and bacon. You'll need a good appetite to tackle her large mixed grill, and you should not miss the chance to sample her popular pork pie made with belly of pork in proper watercrust pastry. In summer she adapts to the season and offers dishes with a Mediterranean flavour, with recipes from Italy or France. Her puddings are also all home cooked. Visitors with an interest in history should note that the pub dates from the Civil War period and stands on the edge of Edgehill Escarpment.

★ Q S V P

WARWICK
Cape of Good Hope
66 Lower Cape, CV34 5DP

- ▶ Next to Cape Top Lock on Grand Union Canal
- ☼ Mon-Sat 12-11pm; Sun 12-10.30pm
- 🍴 Daily 12-2.30pm, 6.30-9.30pm
- T (01926) 498138
- W www.capeofgoodhope.co.uk
- Fuller's London Pride; Greene King Abbot; Tetley Bitter; guests
- ☺ Home-cooked meals with fresh fish a speciality
- Small, friendly pub dating back to 1800 with a traditional public bar and lounge bar; hosts live music

At the Cape of Good Hope you'll find a warm welcome, good food and real ale, including house beer Lock, Stock and Straight from the Barrel brewed by Weatheroak. Fish is the specialty here, direct from Billingsgate, with fish steaks cooked in garlic butter or lemon juice and served with salad, chips, new potatoes or rice. More fish dishes are fresh cod 'n' chips, salmon, whole trout and halibut as well as New Zealand mussels with whole king prawns cooked in wine and garlic butter, prices £5.25-£8.75.

Traditional pub meals, prepared by the landlady, include fresh baguettes or doorstep sandwiches containing hot steak and mushrooms, beef and onion or bacon and Brie, and large jacket potatoes with various fillings. Main meals are home-made steak and kidney pie packed with meat with one of those huge puff pastry toppings, lamb shank with red wine gravy and colcannon mash, a 14oz rump steak and Cape Fear – a large mixed grill platter of gammon, steak, lamb and pork chops, sausage, liver, kidney, black pudding, mushrooms, onion rings and two eggs, prices from £6.75 up to £13.95 for mixed grill (not available lunchtimes). Sunday roast of beef or pork is £5.95. In winter some meals are two for the price of one from 6.30-7.30pm.

★ ❀ S V ♣ P C

AMBLECOTE
Robin Hood Inn
196 Collis Road, DY8 4EQ

▶ On A4102, off A491 between Stourbridge and Wolverhampton
☼ Mon-Fri 12-3pm, 6pm-midnight; Sat & Sun 12-midnight
🍴 Mon-Sat 12-2pm, 6-9pm; Sun 12-4pm
T (01384) 821120
🍺 Batham Bitter; Enville Ale; Everards Tiger; guests
☺ Varied menu of good quality home-cooked food at reasonable prices
◙ Popular community local with nine comfortable guest rooms; started life in the 1830s as a beer house

The Robin Hood bears the distinction of being the first pub to sell Enville Ale (the brewery owner lived nearby). The story goes that the first barrel was completely emptied before the day was half done. Still an Enville house, its ale remains the biggest seller, but is just one of normally seven beers on tap at this friendly hostelry. These days, however, the pub is also popular for good value, home-cooked meals and snacks, served in the comfortable bar, warmed by an open fire, or the split-level restaurant that can cater both for large groups or candlelit suppers à deux.

The menu offers a wide choice – here are some of the customers' traditional favourites: Robin Hood pie (beef in Guinness gravy), minted lamb casserole served in a giant Yorkie, home-made faggots with mushy peas, rainbow trout in a white wine and mushroom sauce and griddled steaks. You could opt for something spicier, such as Cajun chicken breast in a sweet chilli dressing or Szechuan chicken stir fry with a spicy oriental sauce, or maybe a seafood pasta in a creamy cheese sauce. A proper roast is served in the restaurant on Sundays, while classic puddings and desserts are always available.

★ ♔ Q ❀ 🛏 S V 🍺 ♿ ♣ ● Ⓟ ⚡ 👪 C

BARSTON
Bull's Head
Barston Lane, B92 0JU

▶ Off M42 Solihull exit towards Warwick
☼ Mon-Fri 11am-2.30pm, 5-11pm; Sat 11-11pm; Sun 12-10.30pm
🍴 Mon-Sat 12-2pm, 7-9pm; Sun 12-3pm
T (01675) 442830
🍺 Adnams Bitter; Hook Norton Best Bitter; guests
☺ Good choice of freshly-made daily specials on a traditional menu
◙ Beamed village pub dating back to 1490 with two bars warmed by open fires; the restaurant is in the oldest part of the building

A frequent local CAMRA Pub of the Year winner, the Bull's Head serves good quality food with an emphasis on daily specials. Lunchtime customers are offered a limited but satisfying menu of hot or cold sandwiches including sausage baps, ploughman's, filled jacket potatoes and hot dishes such as bangers, eggs and chips. In the evening the specials board comes out to supplement the usual pub fare of grills – fillet or rump steak, gammon or trout – home-made lasagne and other favourites. On the board you will find starters such as grilled sardines, a smoked fish platter or Caesar salad, £4-£5, or you could choose prawn cocktail, whitebait or home-made soup from the regular menu. Main course specials always include one or two fresh fish dishes and home-made pies, plus other seasonal options such as venison or maybe calves' liver. Main courses, including vegetables, are £8-£9. Two or three home-made desserts vary with the time of year, such as summer fruit pudding, a seasonal crumble, blackberry and apple pie or bread and butter pudding. Desserts are £3.65 or ice cream £3.50. ★ ♔ Q ❀ S V 🍺 Ⓟ ⚡ 👪 C

BARSTON
Malt Shovel
Barston Lane, B92 0JP

▶ Nr jct 5 M42 between Easton and Barston
Mon-Fri 12-3.30pm, 5.30-11pm; Sat 12-11pm; Sun 12-7pm
Mon-Sat 12-2.30pm, 6.30-9.30pm; Sun 12-4.30pm
T (01675) 443223
W www.themaltshovelatbarston.com
Wells Bombardier; Fuller's London Pride; Greene King Old Speckled Hen
Modern British and Mediterranean cuisine using plenty of local produce
Country pub and restaurant with log fires, pretty garden for outside eating

A classy operation with prices to match at a pub and restaurant with an exciting menu, a former AA seafood restaurant of the year, and recommended by both Rick Stein and Antony Worrall Thompson. On the specials board typical starters, priced £5.95-£7.50, could be home-made porcini ravioli with smoked salmon, crispy parsnip pockets with walnut whip or naturally smoked haddock risotto with poached egg, followed by main dishes such as pan-fried seabass with linguine and cherry tomatoes, roast cod fillet on Bombay potato or Cornish crab cakes with tomato and mango salsa, £15.95-£16.95.

The main bar menu offers starters from soup of the day or tomato, red onion and feta salad to pan-fried quail with capers and red wine sauce, £3.95-£6.50. Then comes a range of dishes served as starters at £6.50 or mains at £10.95, such as kidneys, bacon and field mushrooms on toast or blackened chicken and Caesar salad. Main dishes include leek and Dolcelatte tart, fresh cod in batter with fat chips and pea purée, Chardonnay-poached free range chicken with spring vegetables, chilli and salt roasted pork with wok-fried greens, Braised English lamb with Bombay potatoes and ratatouille or Scottish rib eye steak with dauphinoise potato and wild mushrooms, prices from £10.50-£14.95.

V P C

DORRIDGE
Railway
Grange Road, B93 8QA

▶ On B4101 between A41 and A3400
Mon-Fri 11am-3pm, 4.30-11pm; Sat 11am-11pm; Sun 12-10.30pm
Mon-Thu 12-2pm, 5.30-9pm; Fri & Sat 12-2pm, 5.30-9.30pm; Sun 12-9pm
T (01564) 773531
Draught Bass; M&B Brew XI; guests
Home-cooked, good value, traditional pub food, game a speciality
Originally two 19th-century cottages, this popular local pub has been in the same family for four generations

With landlady Janet Watson in charge in the kitchen, plenty of fresh, seasonal produce features in her cooking, especially local game in winter – partridge cooked in cider, pheasant casseroled in red wine with vegetables, roast wild duck with orange sauce or venison steak either braised in red wine sauce or 'in a nest' in a huge Yorkshire pud. Home-made chicken liver pâté is among the starters, and a daily specials board shows the day's game dishes in winter, as well as main meals such as fillet steak, cod in beer batter, seabass with lemon and parsley sauce, smoked haddock with creamed potatoes and mild horseradish sauce, roast loin of pork with crackling, home-made chicken and mushroom pie, locally-made faggots with mash and home made chilli, specials around £4.95-£6.95.

On Sundays Janet always serves lamb shank braised in red wine or roast chump of lamb alongside roast beef and Yorkshire pudding. But there is a set menu, too, always offering fresh soup of the day, home-made steak and kidney pie with chips and peas at £4.95, double lamb chops with potatoes and vegetables, gammon, rump, sirloin or T-bone steaks, medium hot chicken or vegetable madras curry, simple double egg, chips and beans plus hot or cold baguettes and sandwiches.

Q S V (Dorridge) P C

LOWER GORNAL
Fountain
8 Temple Street, DY3 2PE

- Close to Lower Gornal bus station
- Mon-Sat 12-11pm; Sun 12-10.30pm
- Mon-Thu 12-2.30pm, 6-9pm; Fri & Sat 12-9pm; Sun 12-5pm
- T (01384) 242777
- F (01384) 242779
- E fountain@fountain.freeserve.co.uk
- Enville Ale; Everards Tiger; Greene King Abbot; Hook Norton Old Hooky; RCH Pitchfork; guests
- From good pub grub to à la carte
- Superb Black Country free house welcoming visitors and regulars alike

Dudley CAMRA Pub of the Year two years running, the Fountain proudly serves nine real ales, three Belgian beers and 20 of George Gale's fruit wines alongside dishes made with vegetables, meat and other produce all from shops within a mile. Bestsellers include boozy beef pie in Old Hooky stock, £5.95 with accompanying vegetables, home-cooked ham served in generous slices with two eggs, chips and vegetables, £5.25, pork and leek sausages and local faggots with mushy peas, both supplied daily by the butcher.

On the set menu you will find tuna steak in lime and coriander, an authentic home-made curry and light bites from three-egg omelettes to filled jacket spuds. At the other extreme is the Fountain Feast which claims to be the biggest mixed grill ever: steak, lamb and pork chops, gammon, lamb's kidney, pig's liver, sausage, bacon, black pudding, fried egg, mushrooms, onion rings, grilled tomato and chips, all for just £11.95. A specials board, dubbed 'more upmarket', features fresh fish, vegetarian and international dishes, £7.99-£14.99. At lunchtime workers choose from a wide selection of baguettes served with chips and salad. The landlord generously draws attention to four other CAMRA-listed hostelries in Lower Gornal – 'must be the capital of real ale in the Midlands, or England!'

S V P C

NETHERTON
Olde Swan
89 Halesowen Road, DY2 9PY

- On main Dudley-Old Hill Road
- Mon-Sat 11am-11pm; Sun 12-4pm, 7-10.30pm
- Mon-Sat 12-2pm, 6-9pm; Sun 1-2pm
- T (01384) 253075
- Olde Swan Original, Dark Swan, Entire, Bumble Hole, seasonal
- Freshly-cooked meals with some lovely local touches
- Brewery tap for Olde Swan; a gem of a traditional Victorian pub with a front bar, rear snug and separate restaurant

At the home of the Olde Swan micro-brewery they use its beers to create some stalwart dishes such as steak, kidney and ale pudding cooked in Dark Swan, £5.95, and tasty fresh haddock in home-made beer batter with chips and mushy peas at £6.95. Other traditional dishes include lamb shank braised with pearl barley, loin of lamb with black pudding en croute, pork sautéed with wild mushrooms in a creamy mustard sauce, and Olde Swan traditional Black Country faggots with mash, mushy peas and onion gravy, £5.95-£9.75.

If you want something more adventurous, try pan-fried duck supreme rubbed with ginger and cinnamon on stir-fried vegetables, home-made meat balls in spicy tomato sauce or Cajun style butterfly chicken. There is a tempting veggie choice too – caramelised pear, pecan and Stilton filo parcels, roast red peppers stuffed with buffalo mozzarella, sun-dried tomatoes and basil, or goats' cheese and Med vegetables en croute, £6.25-£7. At lunchtime snacks include interesting sarnies such as chicken and lemon mayo in ciabatta from £2.25-£3.95, a hot pork doorstep sandwich with home-made sage and onion stuffing at £1.95, and filled jacket potatoes. Main dishes include the beer battered haddock, steak, kidney and Dark Swan pie, and a substantial ploughman's of pork pie, roast ham and mature cheddar.

★ Q S V P C

WEST BROMWICH
☆ Vine
152 Roebuck Street, B70 6RD

- ▶ Near M5 jct 1
- Mon-Thu 11.30am-2.30pm, 5-11pm; Fri-Sun 11.30am-11pm
- Throughout opening hours
- T (0121) 553 2866
- F (0121) 525 5450
- E post@thevine.co.uk
- W www.thevine.co.uk
- Beer range varies
- Tandoori barbecues, curries and baltis, plus English meals
- A veritable Tardis: a tiny snug, smoke room and back bar open into a spacious glass-roofed extension and a further dining area

The Vine claims to have the only indoor Tandoori barbecue in the West Midlands, and very impressive it is too. The barbecue operates weekdays 5.30-10.30pm and from 1pm on Saturday and Sundays. Individual items are priced between £2.50 to £3.50: chicken or lamb tikka (off the bone), methi chicken tikka, pork steak, spicy spare ribs, piri piri chicken. There are fish options, too – spiced hake or trout. Alternatively, on Thursday there is a spit roast of spicy chicken.

Curries and baltis on the main menu are all home made and very reasonably priced, £3.50-£4.75, including chicken, lamb, prawn, vegetable or mixed curries, plus vegetarian dishes such as aloo gobi (potato and cauliflower) and tarka dhall (mixed lentils). There is a long list of chef's specials: tandoori chicken bhuna, mhakni chicken, goat curry (on the bone), tikka balti, lamb saag or rogan josh and claypot chicken, mostly priced under £5 apart from the king prawn masala, £6.20. All dishes are served with rice, chips, naan, chapatti or porrota. Side dishes such as samosas, popadoms and a selection of chutneys and pickles are extra. They also offer a menu of basic pub favourites (steak and kidney pie, deep fried scampi) for those not tempted by the Indian cuisine.

❀ **S V** ⊖ (Kenrick Park Metro) **C**

WEST BROMWICH
Wheatsheaf
379 High Street, Carters Green, B70 9QW

- ▶ By clock tower
- Daily 11am-11pm
- Daily 12-3pm
- T (0121) 553 4221
- F (0121) 533 7080
- Holden's Mild, Bitter, Golden Glow, Special; guest
- Simple pub food in generous portions at very reasonable prices
- Handsome pub with a long front bar, comfortable lounge and rear patio; the atmosphere is relaxed and friendly

This popular pub gets particularly busy when West Bromwich Albion are playing, when you are likely to find the menu supplemented by Black Country favourites such as 'grey peas 'n' bacon' or faggots and peas. All the food here is straightforward pub grub and none the worse for that. It is all home cooked and the prices are unbeatable: main meals are just £3! The menu includes dishes such as lasagne, chilli con carne and leek and spud pie, alongside other mainstays such as fish and chips, liver and onions, an all day breakfast and bangers and mash (the 'gourmet' bangers are locally produced with a choice of pork, Cumberland or pork and leek).

The specials board might offer a salad such as prawn and salmon or a home-made soup – perhaps carrot and coriander or broccoli and Stilton. The traditional Sunday lunch, served with fresh veg, is the same bargain price of £3. For a quick bite there's a good variety of baguettes with fillings such as chicken and mayo, sausage and Stilton (referred to as a posh hot dog), coronation chicken or ham and mustard for £2, or filled jacket spuds, served with salad garnish and coleslaw for £2.50.

S V ♿ ⊖ (Dartmouth St Metro) ♣

WOLVERHAMPTON
☆ Great Western
Sun Street, WV10 0DJ

▶ Opposite now disused GWR station in city centre
☼ Mon-Sat 11am-11pm; Sun 12-3pm, 7-10.30pm
Ⓨ Mon-Sat 11.45am-2.15pm
T (01902) 351090
Batham Best Bitter; Holden's Mild, Bitter, Golden Glow, Special; guests
☺ Simple but terrific Black Country snacks to go with Black Country ales
Outstanding, listed historic railway pub, a tribute to the days of steam; past national CAMRA Pub of the Year

Last year – shock horror – they raised their prices at the Great Western, but you won't need a credit card (just as well, they don't take them) as the dearest dish on the menu is still only £5.75. This is a railway pub from the great days of rail travel, the only Wolverhampton outlet for both Batham's and Holden's beers, offering typical Black Country snacks. Black Country means meat, and they've been getting superb meat from the same local butcher for 16 years. Served in a twinkling are 'gray payes' (pigeon peas) simmered with bacon at £1.40, double butcher's faggots and chips at £2.95, and traditional Midlands jumbo cobs crammed with home-roasted pork and crackling or roast beef – the whole joints go in the oven first thing in the morning.

If you want something more ambitious try a slice of the superb plate steak pie with chips and peas for £4.25, home-made chilli and chips, prawn and tuna salad, sausage or gammon, egg and chips priced from £3.80 to £5.75 for a huge piece of fresh cod in home-made beer batter with chips and peas. This is not a place where a vegetarians would feel at home, but those wanting to admire the splendid building and quaff fine Midlands ales can tuck into a ploughman's platter, jacket potato filled with cheese or beans, or the excellent chip butty at £1.50.

★ ❀ S ♿ ⇌ (Wolverhampton)
⊖ (Wolverhampton) P

WOLVERHAMPTON
Newhampton
19 Riches Street, WV6 0DW

▶ Twenty minutes' walk from town centre
☼ Daily 11am-11pm
Ⓨ Daily 12-9pm (5pm Sun)
T (01902) 745773
F (01902) 746747
Caledonian Deuchars IPA; Courage Best Bitter, Directors; Fuller's London Pride; Greene King Abbot; Theakston Old Peculier; guest
☺ Home-cooked meals with good specials and always a vegan choice
This newly refurbished local has rooms for all purposes: bar, smoke room, pool room, function room, bowls pavilion; a popular venue for folk and other music

The Newhampton boasts a surprisingly large garden with facilities including a boules piste and bowling green. If you just want a snack while watching a game, there are hot pork or beef rolls, served with hand-cut chips or salad, £2.95, or paninis, £3.50, with various fillings such as chicken curry and mango, all day breakfast, Cajun steak or roasted red peppers and hummus (suitable for vegans). There is always a vegan main dish too, such as red dragon pie, £5.95, a blend of aduki beans, soy sauce, fresh herbs and tomatoes, topped with mash.

All the meals including daily specials are freshly prepared here, prices from £4.95-£7.95. Favourites include scrumpy chicken (fillet stuffed with fresh basil, wrapped in smoked bacon and poached in cider and cream sauce), lamb curry, fresh fillet of organic salmon stuffed with prawn and herb butter, poached with lemon and dill and served in white wine sauce. Other choices include sirloin steak, Cumberland bangers and mash and its own version of Welsh rarebit: a blend of Cheddar, Directors Bitter, caramelised red onions, mustard and Worcester sauce. The pub offers a good, healthy children's menu – how refreshing – and puddings always include a vegan recipe.

Q ❀ S V ♿ C

BRADFORD-ON-AVON
Bunch of Grapes
14 Silver Street, BA15 1JY

- ▶ Off A363
- ☼ Mon-Sat 12-11pm; Sun 12-10.30pm
- Daily 12-2pm, 7-9.30pm (9pm Sun)
- T (01225) 863877
- E (01225) 866776
- E thegrapesboa@aol.com
- Young's Bitter, Special, seasonal
- ☺ Traditional home-cooked meals sourcing local ingredients
- Welcoming, town centre pub with grapevine growing over the front; upstairs restaurant

Let's start back to front with puds, because landlord and chef Mark Williams admits to a sweet tooth and says he particularly enjoys making the desserts. 'I'm a bit old-fashioned and like to use such greats as Mrs Beeton, Delia Smith and Mary Berry for cakes and pastries,' he says. 'Some, like Baileys cheesecake and sticky toffee pudding, have been on the menu for the past seven years as any time I mention replacing them I'm met with threats of bodily violence from the customers!' Others, all £3.95, are pecan pie, spiced apple crumble cake and bread and butter pud, plus gorgeous Marshfield Farm ice creams in eight flavours.

Main courses include traditional favourites such as steak and kidney pie flavoured with ale, bangers from the Sausage Shop in Bath and home-made salmon fishcakes with lemon butter sauce, prices £6.95-£8.95. More exotic choices include grilled tuna niçoise, chicken breast wrapped in bacon covered in mozzarella and spicy Cajun chicken with piri piri potato wedges. Fine steaks – sirloin, rib eye and fillet – come from their long time butcher in Broughton Gifford, while a good veggie selection includes Greek spinach and feta pie and roast Mediterranean vegetable and mozzarella lasagne. Portions are generous at this Young's house, and there is a Sunday carvery.

★ ❀ **S V** ⇌ (Bradford-on-Avon) ✂ **C**

BRINKWORTH
Three Crowns
SN15 5AF

- B4042 between Malmesbury and Wootton Bassett
- Daily 11am-3pm, 6-11pm
- Daily 12-2pm (3pm Sun); 6-9.30pm
- T (01666) 510366
- W www.threecrowns.co.uk
- Archers Village; Camerons Castle Eden; Fuller's London Pride; Greene King IPA; Wadworth 6X; guest
- English and continental mix to chef's own style, rich cream sauces a speciality
- Traditional village local dating to 1801

The Three Crowns has been in every issue of this Guide since chef and proprietor Anthony Windle won the Pure Genius Pub Food national title in 1989, and has gone on to win many more awards. Lunch snacks include unusually good jackets with lavish salad and fillings from smoked chicken to Wiltshire ham or trio of local bangers, £7.95, generous ploughman's platters and double decker rolls. A sample menu offers half a roast duck with cassis, redcurrant jelly and cream sauce, Somerset wild boar, rack of English lamb with pear and rosemary jelly, pork tenderloin with red wine sauce and crispy cheese dumplings, chicken supreme filled with prawns and Stilton wrapped in puff pastry, or roast partridge with a fruit stuffing on pâté topped crouton. Home-made pies include steak and kidney in rich beer gravy, lamb and mint with white wine or chicken, ham and mushroom. For a taste of the wild try slices of kangaroo, venison and ostrich in a secret marinade, griddled then served with a sun dried tomato and wild mushroom sauce, flamed in brandy and finished in cream. Prices range from £14.95-£19.95. There is fresh fish from home-made seafood pie to Thai style halibut supreme and whole Cornish lobster, while delectable puds include home-made strawberry and champagne ice cream.

S V P C

HEYTESBURY
Angel Coaching Inn
High Street, BA12 OED

- Mon-Sat 11am-11pm; Sun 12-10.30pm
- Daily 12-2.30pm, 7-9.30pm
- T (01985) 840330
- F (01985) 840931
- E admin@theangelheytesbury.co.uk
- W www.theangelheytesbury.co.uk
- Greene King IPA, Morland Original, Wadworth 6X; Greene King guest
- Gastropub specialising in fine steaks with imaginative specials and carefully sourced local products and ingredients
- Beautifully restored 16th-century village hostelry with beamed ceilings and open fires

Renovated and reopened in 2004 by celebrity chef Antony Worrall Thompson (who designed the menu but rarely cooks there) and Tim Etchells, creator of the BBC Good Food Show, the Angel concentrates on food but also welcomes drinkers. Worrall Thompson is picky about steaks and these are splendid, sourced from Castle Brae in Scotland and, more locally, Pentsworth Farm, all hung for 35 days and served cooked to your liking with hand-cut chips, salad and Bearnaise sauce, £14.95-£19.95.

A two-course bar lunch/supper Mon-Fri lunchtime at £8 is especially good value, offering home-made soup, black pudding and bacon salad or half a pint of shell-on prawns as starters followed by gnocchi with wild mushroom sauce, herring roes on toast or chicken breast with creamed leeks. The main menu starts with 'nose to tail' terrine with rhubarb chutney, honey-roasted parsnip soup with parsnip crisps and home-cured venison and foie gras cappacio, £4.95-£8.95. Main dishes include shepherd's pie with savoy cabbage, Boyton Farm Tamworth pork sausages with mash and onion gravy, free range pork fillet with sauerkraut and black pudding croquette or roast rump of English lamb with leek and tomato fondue, £7.95-£14.95.

Q S V P C

HOLT

☆ Tollgate Inn

Ham Green, BA14 6PX

- On B3107, between Bradford-on-Avon and Melksham
- Tue-Sat 11.30am-2.30pm, 5.30-11pm; Sun 12-3pm
- Tue-Sat 12-2pm, 7-9.30pm
- T (01225) 782326
- F (01225) 782805
- E Alison@tollgateholt.co.uk
- W www.tollgateholt.co.uk
- Beer range varies
- Menu with the wow factor, modern English with Mediterranean feel, using only local produce
- Gem of an old village inn; now a gastro pub but drinkers welcome

A real food pub, local produce includes fish daily from Brixham, special breeds beef from Church Farm, pork and free range chickens from Newent Farm, game shot nearby including rabbit, pigeon, pheasant, mallard and partridge, and cheese from the famous Cheese Board in Bradford-on-Avon. So what do they do with these fine ingredients? Apart from winning Wiltshire Taste of the West pub 2004, chef Alexander Venables (previously of Lucknam Park where he gained a Michelin star) creates dishes that provoke an 'ooh' just to read the menu.

The menu changes daily but starters may include parsnip, leek and lemon soup with onion bhaji, confit of duck leg with spiced Chinese leaves, twice baked smoked haddock and ham soufflé, roast scallops wrapped in Wiltshire bacon or salt and pepper belly pork deep fried with tartare sauce and lemon, prices £4.50-£6.50. Traditional beef Wellington is among the main courses: fillet of beef topped with mushroom duxelle in rich home-made puff pastry with Madeira sauce, at £16.95. Also there are roast duck breast on butter fondant potato with cherry sauce, sea trout steamed in Earl Grey tea with minted hollandaise, poached brill with lobster and green peppercorn mousse on shellfish sauce, or chestnut mushroom and herb ravioli on endive, blood orange and celery salad, from £12.50-£16.50. Desserts include iced Marsala custard parfait with poached figs preserved in Marsala. The cheese board is inspiring; chutneys, pickles, pasta, bread and ice cream all made by the team.

Q S V P C

KILMINGTON
Red Lion
BA12 6RP

- ▶ On B3092 to Frome, 3 miles N of Mere
- Mon-Sat 11.30am-2.30pm, 6.30-11pm; Sun 12-3pm, 7-10.30pm
- Daily 12-1.50pm
- T (01985) 844263
- Butcombe Bitter; Butts Jester; guests
- Wholesome, home-cooked meals and snacks served lunchtimes only
- Homely, welcoming 15th-century local with warming log fires

'No fancy sauces or decoration, but good, wholesome food, well presented and fresh,' is the promise at the Red Lion. The only bought in item on the menu is the Cornish pasty. Choices include home-made soup of the day at £1.20 (60p extra for a good hunk of white or wholegrain bread), followed by steak and kidney pie, game pie enriched with brandy, fish pie of white fish and prawns, or lamb and apricot pie, all topped with home-made shortcrust pastry, priced £4.45-£4.95 with fresh vegetables and potatoes. They are rather proud of their home-made lasagnes, both beef and vegetarian, served with baked potato and salad at £6.75.

Examples of daily specials include home-cooked ham with fried egg, beans and potatoes, cottage pie with bread from the local baker, or chicken casserole in a rich stock flavoured with peppers and mushrooms served with vegetables, all priced £5.95. The Cornish pasty comes with salad, baked beans and jacket potato, or you can just have jacket potato with fillings from cheese and ham to tuna with salad from £2.40. There are fresh sandwiches, and ploughman's from home-cooked ham to Stilton, at this National Trust owned pub on an isolated stretch of road near Stourhead Gardens.

★ Q S V P

MALET ARMS
Newton Tony
SP4 0HF

- ▶ 1 mile off A338
- Mon-Sat 11am-3pm, 6-11pm; Sun 12-3pm, 7-10.30pm
- Mon-Sat 12-2.30pm, 6.30-10pm; Sun 7-9.30pm
- T (01980) 629279
- F (01980) 629459
- E maletarms@hotmail.com
- Palmer IPA; Stonehenge Heel Stone; Wadworth 6X; guests
- Fresh, home-cooked food chalked on blackboards
- Ancient country pub with low beams and open fire

The menu is chalked up on the blackboard daily, the dishes are described as simple and healthy-ish, using fresh produce in season as far as possible. In winter that means game (occasionally shot by chef Noel Cardew who is also the landlord), especially venison, pheasant and pigeon, and fresh fish throughout the year; also in evidence is plenty of locally smoked produce including fish and meat. Home-made curries are popular, likewise Sunday roasts served from October to April only.

The pub is named after a local family well represented in the nearby churchyard – appropriately as desserts are to die for! They are a big feature of the menu (explaining the 'ish' on the end of healthy), all made by landlady Annie Cardew to both old English recipes and from further afield including Australia and the USA. Among the favourites are stepmother's tart, Canterbury pudding, all kinds of baked cheesecakes, treacle tart and steamed sponge puddings with bitter orange marmalade the most popular. Food is served in two comfortable bars and the restaurant. The Wadworth 6X is always served from the wood, and it's worth noting that Butts Barbus Barbus is often a guest ale.

★ Q V P C

NORTH WROUGHTON
Check Inn
Woodland View, SN4 9AA

- In a cul-de-sac, cut off by the M4 between jct 15 and 16
- Mon-Thu 11.30am-3pm, 6-11pm; Fri & Sat 11.30am-11pm; Sun 12-10.30pm
- Daily 12-2.30pm, 6.30-9pm
- T (01793) 845584
- F (01793) 814640
- E information@checkinn.co.uk
- W www.checkinn.co.uk
- Beer range varies
- Good value, home-cooked food
- Built as farm cottages in 1825, this genuine free house has a recently landscaped garden with a floodlit petanque court

Between 1980 and 1996, the pub suffered badly with 15 different licensees, but since becoming a free house under new ownership in 1996 many improvements have been made, including a modern extension providing a spacious no-smoking area. In 2005 the hard work was rewarded by winning CAMRA South-West regional Pub of the Year. The same care and dedication that has seen the pub's fortunes turn around are also evident in the kitchen where home-cooked, wholesome fare is produced at reasonable prices.

All the soups are made on the premises and some dishes, such as steak and ale pie and beer battered cod, incorporate real ale, while Thatcher's cider is used for a delicious cider and wholegrain mustard sauce to accompany grilled pork tenderloin. Wiltshire hams are cooked on the premises and traditional ham, egg and chips, £5.50, is one of the most popular dishes. Vegetarian meals and special dishes are produced daily. The Sunday carvery, £7.95 for starter and main course, always has home-made puddings to follow, often using apples and blackberries from the pub garden. In the winter hotpot nights are a feature and other special meals are produced to commemorate events.

S V C

ROWDE
☆ George & Dragon
High Street, SN10 2PN

- On A342, 1 mile outside Devizes towards Chippenham
- Mon 7-11pm; Tue-Sat 12-3pm, 7-11pm; Sun 12-4pm
- Tue-Sat 12-2.30pm, 7-9.30pm; Sun 12-4pm
- T (01380) 723053
- E thegandd@tiscali.co.uk
- Beer range varies
- Freshly cooked English dishes, specialising in seafood
- 14th-century country inn dominated by a fine stone fireplace

This delightful old inn in the Vale of Pewsey is worth a visit in summer for its bijou garden or in winter to sit by the open fire in the low beamed bar. The food is unpretentious but well presented. The meat and game are all sourced locally, but one of the main attractions here is the fish and seafood, delivered daily from Cornwall and chalked up on boards in the bar. You might find seabass, lemon sole, John Dory, lobster, scallops or mussels prepared as moules marinière.

The menus are kept deliberately concise, but enticing. Starters, for example, could be home-made soup, £5, or avocado and prawn salad with lemon and dill mayonnaise or double baked cheese soufflé, both £7. These are followed by 'Individuals', either served as a light dish or main course, priced around £7 or £9.50, such as bubble and squeak with black pudding and fried egg, devilled lambs' kidneys with grainy mustard mash or wild mushroom risotto with Parmesan. Main courses include roast chicken breast with dauphinoise potatoes, fillet steak with roasted shallots and brandy cream sauce or pan fried calf's liver with garlic butter, £12.50-£17.50. Save some room for dessert: treacle tart with clotted cream, chocolate bread and butter pud, or iced rum and raisin fudge parfait with hot chocolate sauce, all £5.

★ Q S V C

WANBOROUGH
Harrow
High Street, SN4 0AE

- 5 miles from M4 jct 15
- Mon-Sat 12-3pm, 6-11pm; 12-3pm, 6-11pm
- Daily 12-2pm, 7-9pm (not Sun eve)
- T (01793) 790622
- F (01793) 791942
- E paul@theharrowinnwanborough.com
- W www.theharrowinnwanborough.com
- Adnams Bitter; Wadworth 6X; guests
- Good value meals using local produce, mainly traditional English
- Thatched country pub, the oldest in the village, with two inglenooks with enormous log fires

The Harrow was a brew pub in the 19th century and today the interior is essentially unchanged. Dating from 1637, the pub has a long and fascinating history that includes ghosts and apparitions, and has been used by the BBC as a location for period filming. It has also featured on TV for its food, including Yes Chef in 2003, and the food remains of a very high standard. The emphasis here is on fresh food daily from locally sourced produce, so the menu changes frequently, reflected in daily specials.

A sample menu from head chef Derek Fisher includes boneless rack of lamb stuffed with black pudding served with blackcurrant sauce, home-made steak and kidney pudding, chicken supreme stuffed with smoked cheddar wrapped in bacon with a ham and asparagus sauce and 'catch of the day' fresh fish. Simple fish 'n' chips is the pub's best selling dish. From the char grill comes a range of steaks from rump to fillet cooked to your liking, and in summer there is an outside barbecue. Vegetarian choices, snacks and desserts are also on the menu. A wide choice of guest beers makes a happy accompaniment to the many dishes.

★ Q S V P C

WINTERBOURNE MONKTON
New Inn
SN4 9NW

- Signed from A4361 Devizes-Swindon road, N of Avebury
- Tue-Fri 11.30am-3pm; Sat 11.30am-11pm; Sun 12-3pm, 7-10.30pm
- Tue-Sat 12-2pm, 6.30pm onwards; Sun 12-2pm
- T (01672) 539240
- F (01672) 539150
- E enquiries@thenewinn.net
- W www.thenewinn.net
- Beer range varies
- Real food by a wizard from Oz
- Traditional country inn with swords and weapons decorating the bar

The New Inn proprietors also own a restaurant in Australia. Chef Michael Webb has returned from Down Under after working there last year, bringing some Pacific Rim hints to the menu. At lunchtime the main courses, priced £5.50 to £6.75, include roast pepper, caramelised onion and feta frittata, chicken penne with sun dried tomatoes and spinach, Wiltshire ham with egg and chips, proper Greek moussaka made with lamb, aubergine and hint of mint, or sweet potato, cashew and spinach curry with steamed wild rice and citrus yoghurt.

In the evening starters include Thai fishcakes with coriander and sweet chilli or penne with tomato, fresh mushrooms, herbs and Parmesan. Main courses might be game sausages with home-made tomato chutney and mash, fish in beer batter, braised lamb shanks in red wine with herb mash, coconut and red curry chicken with wild rice, porterhouse steak pan seared on a new potato, courgette and mushroom ragout or pepper crusted pork medallions with pearl barley and sweetcorn risotto and cider apple sauce, prices from £8-£10. Among the puddings is a tantalising take on death by chocolate – wicked chocolate fruit and nut loaf.

S V P C

ABBERLEY
Manor Arms
Netherton Lane, WR6 6BN

- ▶ B4202 off A443 between Tenbury Wells and Worcester
- ☼ Mon-Fri 12-3pm (not Mon), 6-11pm; Sat 12-11pm; Sun 12-10.30pm
- 🍴 Daily 12-2pm (not Mon), 6-9pm
- T (01299) 896507
- E info@themanorarms.co.uk
- W www.themanorarms.co.uk
- 🍺 Flowers IPA; Hook Norton BB; Timothy Taylor Landlord; guest
- ☺ Comprehensive choice from sandwiches to a la carte and fresh fish
- ◉ Traditional village pub with friendly atmosphere and open fire

Bangers are so good at the Manor (supplied by Heart of England of Birmingham) there is a separate sausage board with a choice of half a dozen varieties, different mashes and flavoured gravies – typically venison and red wine sausage with horseradish mash and onion gravy, £7.50. The bar menu offers a traditional selection such as home-made beef or vegetable lasagne, pie of the day, sweet and sour chicken, all £7, or home-made soup of the day with bread for £2.50. The grill menu also uses Heart of England meat, including especially good steaks from £8-£14; the a la carte board features game, some local, chicken, beef and lamb dishes, and fresh fish from Eric the Fish of Kidderminster – typical choices are Scotch venison medallions with wholegrain mustard mash and mushroom, garlic and herb sauce or seared scallops with pink peppercorn, prawn and tarragon sauce, both £14. Main courses come complete with fresh seasonal vegetables and new potatoes, or chips and salad. Vegetarian meals are available, and specific dishes can be pre-ordered. Cask ales served in the pub often feature in the pie of the day and casseroles.

★ Q ❀ S V ♿ ♣ Ⓟ C

BERROW GREEN
☆ Admiral Rodney
WR6 6PL

- ▶ Pub signposted off B4197
- ☼ 11am-3pm (not Mon), 5-11pm; Sat 11am-11pm; Sun 12-10.30pm
- 🍴 12-2pm (Sun 2.30pm), 6.30-9pm
- T (01886) 821375
- F (01886) 822048
- E rodney@admiral.fslife.co.uk
- W www.admiral-rodney.co.uk
- 🍺 Wye Valley Bitter; guests
- ☺ Local ingredients, snacks and a la carte
- ◉ Cosy and immaculate 17th-century inn

At the Admiral Rodney they go the extra mile to get fresh food – though leagues away from the sea they get fish couriered in boxes overnight from Fowey in Cornwall for their well-regarded fish dishes. Vegetables come from Mill Farm and Birmingham market, asparagus in season from the Vale of Evesham, herbs, damsons and other fruit from neighbours' gardens. Ninety five per cent of food is home made starting with soup, always vegetarian, from roast beetroot with a swirl of basil oil to cauliflower and cider.

Sample fish starters are Bantry Bay mussels steamed in beer with leeks and bacon, scallops on minted mash and tiger prawns with home-made citrus dressing, all £5.50; main course fish specials are walnut crusted halibut steak with parsnip cream, whole roast trout with almond and lime mayonnaise, black bream with lime, chillis and potato, pan-fried monkfish with watercress and garlic crushed potato - prices £10-£12.95. Other starters could be pan-fried lamb's liver with smoked bacon, cured beef with sweet and sour chilli shallots, all around £5, while meat main courses could include roast duck breast with spinach mash and orange Grand Marnier sauce, pork tenderloin with caramelised onion and apricot and thyme sauce or steaks with hand-cut chips. Delectable desserts include coconut rice pudding with pineapple sorbet and black molasses, and there are Shropshire cheeses.

★ Q ❀ S V ♿ ♣ Ⓟ C

BIRLINGHAM
Swan Inn
Church Street, WR10 3AQ

- ▶ Near M5, off A4104 near Pershore
- ☼ Daily 12-3pm, 6.30-11pm (Sun 10.30pm)
- 🍴 Mon-Sat 12-2.30pm, 6.30-8.30pm; Sun 12-2.30pm
- T (01386) 750485
- E information@theswaninn.co.uk
- W www.theswaninn.co.uk
- [pump] Banks's Bitter; guests
- ☺ Traditional English cuisine, with plenty of fish, specials and vegetarian dishes
- ◙ 16th-century thatched black and white free house

With around 200 guest beers a year, the Swan is as keen on real ale as home-cooked English food (and plenty of it) using as many locally-sourced products as possible. Popular dishes include game from Bredon Hill during winter such as pheasant or rabbit in cider, lamb and leek casserole or a big beef and guest ale pie. Fish dishes are important – specials include seafood pie, brill with lemon and dill, poached salmon and freshly battered cod. During the May and September beer festivals head chef Marion New puts her huge paella pan into action cooking for 60 at a time.

Sample dishes might be Jerusalem artichoke soup, £3.25, pan-fried shark with Thai pepper sauce, spicy cottage pie with salad and chips, thick cut gammon steak with fried egg and chips, pheasant breasts in cranberry and orange sauce with seasonal vegetables or seafood risotto of shark, salmon, haddock and prawns. Main courses are priced from £6.95-£9.95 for a half pound sirloin steak. Veggie options could be mushroom, red pepper and blue cheese pasta or aubergine stuffed with spicy ratatouille and there are regular theme meals from Burn's Night to Chinese New Year. Desserts include sticky date and banana sponge and pear and almond tart.

★ ♔ Q ✿ S V [pump] ♿ ♣ [apple] Ⓟ ⚟ ✂ 👪 C

BROADWAY
Crown & Trumpet
Church Street, WR12 7AE

- ▶ On the road to Snowshill
- ☼ Mon-Fri 11am-3pm, 5-11pm; Sat 11am-11pm; Sun 12-10.30pm
- 🍴 Mon-Fri 12-2.15pm, 6-9pm; Sat & Sun 12-3pm, 5.30-9pm
- T (01386) 853202
- E info@cotswoldholidays.co.uk
- W www.cotswoldholidays.co.uk
- [pump] Greene King Old Speckled Hen; Hook Norton Old Hooky; Taylor Landlord; Stanway ales
- ☺ Seasonal and local dishes
- ◙ 17th-century Cotswold stone inn with homely atmosphere

Genuine pub food, all prepared on the premises at modest prices, including local recipes – and seasonal beers brewed exclusively for the pub by Stanway Brewery. Ploughmans include Cheddar, Stilton, ham or Cotswold Cheddar with onion and chives, proper pies such as Evesham pie of beef in rich stock topped with local plum sauce, Worcester pie of minced beef flavoured with Worcester sauce, country chicken with apples and cider, beef and Guinness or steak and kidney, all under £7 with fresh vegetables and potatoes. Faggots are made by the local butcher, Evesham bubble and squeak is wrapped in Savoy cabbage served with new potatoes in cream and chive sauce, bangers 'n' mash are with pork or lamb sausages, and four sorts of omelette are all made with three eggs. Other choices include grilled lamb cutlets with rosemary, chicken breast in wild mushroom sauce, or cooked with basil, ginger and orange juice and the sirloin or rump steak specials with all the trimmings. Snacks include tortilla wraps, filled pitta bread or scrambled egg and smoked salmon on toast. Scrummy puds – all home made – include rhubarb crumble, treacle tart and jam roly poly, just over £3.

★ ♔ Q ✿ 🛏 S V [pump] ♿ ♣ Ⓟ 👪 C

HANLEY BROADHEATH

Fox Inn

WR15 8QS

- On B4204
- Mon-Thu 5-11pm; Fri-Sun 12-11pm (Sun 10.30pm)
- Thu-Sat 6.30-10pm
- T (01886) 853189
- Batham Best Bitter; Hobsons Best Bitter; guests
- Authentic Thai food cooked by Thai landlady
- 16th-century grade II listed black and white building

On three evenings a week landlady Phannipha Lawson transports diners to her native Thailand in this very English pub's Phannipha Thai Restaurant. Though most ingredients are sourced locally, she imports some specialist herbs and spices direct from Thailand to create exciting ethnic dishes, both eat in and take away. You could start with chicken tom yam soup, Thai fish cakes, deep fried pork in won-ton pastry, Thai style battered prawns and chicken satay, priced £3-£4. Main dishes all arrive with egg-fried or plain boiled rice and, as everything is cooked to order, you can ask for it to be less spicy or hotter as you prefer. The selection includes chicken, beef, tiger prawns or vegetables either in Thai green curry or stir fried with ginger, red chillies and spring onions, sweet and sour seabass, chicken or beef Panang curry with kaffir lime leaves, put prik pao which is chicken, beef or tiger prawns cooked with onions, chillies, asparagus and medium hot prik pao paste, garlic chillies with bamboo, put ka-nah noodles, special Penang seabass, prawn and broccoli stir fry in oyster sauce, and much more. The Fox is a real community pub where excellent ales and an annual beer festival allow you to judge for yourself just how well beer goes with Thai food.

★ V P C

KNIGHTWICK

☆ Talbot

WR6 5PH

- On B4197, 400 yards from A44 junction
- Daily 11am-11pm
- Daily 12-2pm, 6-9pm
- T (01886) 821235
- F (01886) 821060
- E admin@the-talbot.co.uk
- W www.the-talbot.co.uk
- Hobsons Best Bitter; Teme Vally This, That
- Home grown and even wild food on exciting, daily changed menu by culinary sisters Annie and Wiz Clift
- Part 14th-century family owned hotel on the Teme with own brewery

The emphasis here is on organic and locally produced ingredients. Cards in the bar list all the local suppliers be it cheese, eggs, game, rabbit, meat, organic vegetables and even walnuts. You may have heard Wiz Clift talking about unusual vegetable gardens on Radio Four and her own is growing all sorts of leaves, fruit and vegetables to serve to customers. They make their own bread, preserves, black puddings and raised pies.

Sample dishes are pig's head brawn (head and trotters poached all day in the Aga), venison carpaccio, pan-fried scallops with sweet and sour lime, ham hock terrine and crab bisque with fiery mayo among the starters. Moving on, choose if you can between Jerusalem artichoke, mushroom and red onion risotto, steak and kidney pudding, brill fillet with spinach and red lentil dahl, loin of Herwick lamb stuffed with red onion, herbs and lamb forcemeat or fresh organic salmon in saffron and mussel bouillabaisse with local wild garlic. And how's this for a dish description? Fillet of beef and crepinettes is oxtail long simmered in the pub's own Talbot ale with vegetables, herbs and trotters then stripped from the bones, mixed with julienne of carrots, leek and celeriac wrapped in pig's caul, served alongside seared slices of beef fillet. Main courses from around £7-£14.

S V P C

PENSAX
Bell
WR6 6AE

- ▶ Outside village on B4202, Clows Top-Great Witley road
- Mon-Sat 12-2pm (not Mon), 5-11pm; Sun 12-10.30pm
- Mon-Sat 12-2pm (not Mon), 6-9pm; Sun 12-3pm
- T (01299) 896677
- Hobsons Best Bitter; guests
- Simple, wholesome meals using local produce at reasonable prices
- Popular pub with L-shaped bar, snug and separate no-smoking dining room. Pew-style seating and wood burning stove in bar

This former West Midlands CAMRA Pub of the Year stocks a good range of guest beers from local micros including Teme and Wye Valley, and two real ciders or perries such as Westons Old Rosie and Herefordshire Country perry. These make splendid accompaniments to the meals cooked by landlady Trudy Greaves which feature local produce and suppliers where possible – including organic potatoes and vegetables grown across the road in season. On her specials board you will find meals such as beef in ale or chicken and leek pie, veggie or beef lasagne, sausages with mash and onion gravy, all at a bargain £4.95.

The main menu offers a selection of fresh fish, mainly £8.95, local Herefordshire steaks priced £11.50-£13.50, gammon steaks, and chicken with cream and cranberries or wrapped in bacon and cheese, all £8.95. The local butcher's home-made faggots with chips and mushy peas or lamb's liver with bacon and onions are both £6.95, with sausage, chips, egg and beans at £6.50 and vegetarian choices at £7.50. Meals are served with a choice of rice, jacket potatoes, chips and salad or vegetables, while children can have small portions at £3.95-£4.95. Children are allowed in the snug and no-smoking dining room or the back garden which boasts wonderful views.

★ Q S V P C

UPTON-UPON-SEVERN
White Lion Hotel
21 High Street, WR8 OHJ

- ▶ On A4104, not far from M5J8
- Daily 11am-11pm
- Daily light lunches in bar, 7-9.30pm in restaurant
- T (01684) 592551
- F (01684) 593333
- E jon@whitelionhotel.biz
- W www.whitelionhotel.biz
- Greene King Abbot; guests
- Quality cooking, traditional British with cosmopolitan hints
- Well known 500-year-old hostel featured in the novel Tom Jones

While you can get light bar meals and even afternoon tea, the main thrust of the cuisine is the a la carte restaurant in the evening where the meals are tempting if rather pricey. Starters include toasted Welsh rarebit with pancetta and quail's egg, salmon, scallop, lobster and king prawn roulade, butternut squash risotto with black truffles, monkfish and scallops skewered with rosemary, saffron couscous with smoked trout, Roquefort cheese soufflé, Finnan haddock fish cakes with tomato and garlic sauce or home-made soup of the day, prices £3.75-£6.95. On the meat side, main courses include collops of wild venison with oriental marmalade, duck confit with plum and peppercorn compote, roast rump of lamb with minted peas and faggots, Italian style suckling pig with apple sauce, peppered pheasant supreme with leeks, beans and mushrooms, prices from £13.55 rising to £16.75 for medallions of beef fillet with wild mushrooms and Puy lentils. Fish could be assorted seafood with saffron sauce in crispy pastry, monkfish collops with chilli, ginger, mango and crispy noodles or pan-fried seabass with garlic ratatouille. Home-made desserts ranging from pear tartin to chocolate and cointreau crème brûlée are just under £5. Some 500 different guest beers a year are served.

Q S V P C

DRIFFIELD
Bell Hotel
46 Market Place, YO25 6AN

- ☼ Daily 10am-midnight
- Daily 12-1.30pm, 7-9.30pm; bar meals 7-9.30pm
- T (01377) 256661
- F (01377) 253228
- E bell@bestwestern.co.uk
- W www.bw-bellhotel.co.uk
- Beer range varies
- ☺ Traditional English at lunchtime, English and French fare in the evening
- Historic town-centre coaching inn with long wood-panelled bar, antique furnishings and paintings

A buffet is served at lunchtime – what a good idea – featuring traditional English home cooking at a bargain £5.25, including roast duckling in orange sauce, steak and mushroom pie, pork in creamy spring onion sauce, lamb with rosemary, salad selection or, for an extra 25p, sugar-baked ham with pineapple. The bread is home made and comes with home-made soup of the day, £2, or ploughman's, £3. All food is cooked freshly on the premises, pastries as well as bread at their in-house bakery.

In the dining room, evening meal starters range from tomato and vegetable or pea and mint soup, to buffalo mozzarella with tomato, basil and pesto dressing, or avocado with onions, garlic, tomatoes and Tabasco. Main courses include poached Scottish salmon with citrus sauce, grilled plaice fillet with Parmesan and breadcrumb crust, roast Gressingham duck breast with blackcurrant and cinnamon sauce, grilled lamb cutlets with Cumberland sauce and, the most popular dish, pan-fried pork medallions with sherry, paprika, Worcester sauce and sour cream, created by head chef John Darlington. Those staying overnight are offered local honey and marmalade with their breakfast. Beers often include those of Wold Top, Hambleton or Highwood, but other micros are featured too.

★ Q S V (Driffield) P C

DUNSWELL
Ship Inn
Beverley High Road, HU6 0AJ

- ▶ On old Beverley-Hull main road
- ☼ Mon-Sat 11am-11pm; Sun 12-10.30pm
- Mon-Sat 11am-7pm; Sun 12-3pm
- T (01482) 859160
- John Smith's Bitter; Taylor Landlord; guest
- ☺ Traditional pub food and a good snack menu
- White painted roadside pub on the old main road between Hull and Beverley; originally served river traffic – hence the name

With its log fires and convivial atmosphere, the Ship is described in the 2006 Good Beer Guide as homely, and that description could apply equally well to its menu. Straightforward, home-cooked food is available at a very reasonable price – the Sunday lunch here with a choice of meat and fresh veg is just £4.50. Weekdays you will be able to fill up on home-made curry, steak and ale pie, haddock and chips or an all day breakfast for under £6. The most expensive items on the menu are an 8oz sirloin steak or a mixed grill, both served with onion rings and mushrooms for just £7.25. Vegetarians are offered a choice of omelettes, lasagne or mushroom stroganoff for around £5. Daily specials are chalked up on a board. Hot snacks include filled jacket potatoes, all under £3, and hot baguettes, with steak or chicken (Cajun, garlic or plain) served with chips and other accompaniments for £3.75. Meat or cheese salads, served with chips or a jacket spud, are £4.25. Traditional puds – apple crumble or pie, hot chocolate fudge cake or treacle sponge come with custard, cream or ice cream for £2.20.

★ S V ♣ P C

FLAMBOROUGH

☆ Seabirds

Tower Street, YO15 1PD

- First pub on left on entering Flamborough
- Mon-Fri 12-3pm, 7-11pm; Sat & Sun 12-3pm, 6-11pm
- Mon-Fri 12-2pm, 6.30-9pm; Sat & Sun 12-2pm, 6.30-9.30pm
- T (01262) 850242
- John Smith's Bitter; guest
- Traditional home-cooked food plus full à la carte menu
- Refurbished under new owners in 2003 to give a clean, contemporary look; close to spectacular cliffs and RSPB bird sanctuary

The philosophy at this good old-fashioned seaside pub is good beers – the guest is usually from a local micro – and good food, using the best local produce including fish from Flamborough Fish and English meat from Smiths the Butcher, enhanced by herbs and salad grown in the pub garden. Traditional lunchtime fare includes home-made pies that sell as fast as they can make them, along with liver and onions, local pork and leek sausages with caramelised onions, cottage pie with cheese topping, beef and Guinness casserole with dumplings and home made chilli.

Fresh fish is extremely popular including crab and lobster in season plus dishes ranging from home-made prawn thermador to free-range egg omelettes with prawn and mushroom. Fish choices in the à la carte restaurant include whole Dover sole, fresh haddock in beer batter, lemon sole and Whitby scampi, prices from around £7-£8 to current market price for lobster and Dover sole. Soup is always home made as are desserts such as bread and butter pudding, lemon and coconut sponge, Bakewell tart, fruit crumble and Eve's pudding. Sundays are very busy with up to a dozen specials always including three roasts – booking is advisable for the no-smoking restaurant. Children are allowed in the restaurant only.

Q S V C

KILHAM

☆ Old Star

Church Street, YO25 4RG

- Accessed from A614 and B1249
- Mon-Wed 5.30-11pm; Thu & Fri 12-2pm, 5.30-11pm; Sat & Sun winter 12-2pm, 5.30-11pm; summer 12-11pm (10.30pm Sun)
- Daily 5.30-9pm; Sun lunch 12-2pm
- T (01262) 420619
- John Smith's Bitter; Taylor Landlord; guests
- Tempting home-made menu featuring some gorgeous, old-fashioned dishes
- Village pub in the heart of the Wolds, full of character with open fires and dark panelling

'Some of the fish specials will have been swimming in the sea that morning,' states a pub hot on local produce – Wolds butchers and farms provide the game, poultry, eggs and smoked salmon. In summer, salad, vegetables and herbs are fresh from the pub's garden. The restaurant is no smoking – apart from a magnificent inglenook fireplace! – offering traditional meals including 'signature' dishes honey and mustard glazed roast belly pork with crispy crackling, red sage and apply gravy, Old Star lamb shank marinated in wine then cooked with mint, rosemary and honey on roasted root vegetables, and steak and mushroom pie, the meat slowly braised in a guest ale, with a proper shortcrust pastry topping, all £7-£8.

Other dishes sound just as tempting, such as Scottish cullen skink of smoked haddock in a broth with chunky potato, onions and prawns served with the pub's lemon and parsley loaf, Gibson's award-winning Cumberland sausages and black pudding in mustard sauce on bubble and squeak, steamed steak and kidney pudding with a pot of traditional mushy peas and rich onion gravy, fresh haddock in beer batter with home-made tartare and parsley sauce or slow-roasted joint of brisket on sage mash – prices up to £8.95. Lovely veggie dishes include roast pepper stuffed with bean, leek and sun-dried tomato risotto.

★ Q V C

LUND
Wellington Inn
19 The Green, YO25 9TE

- On B1248 near Driffield, 10 minutes N of Beverley
- Mon 6.30-11pm; Tue-Sun 12-3pm, 6.30-11pm
- Tue-Sat 12-2pm, 6.30-9pm; Sun 12-2pm
- T (01377) 217294
- Black Sheep Best Bitter; John Smith's Bitter; Taylor Landlord, guest
- Good quality, home-cooked modern English cuisine
- Situated by the village green in picturesque Lund, this smart, upmarket inn has stone-flagged floors, beamed ceilings and a candlelit restaurant

The A3-sized sample menu we received from the Wellington Inn is a miniature work of art, with a beautifully illustrated border depicting a wealth of rustic ingredients for the dishes served here. This is altogether a stylish place, serving high-quality home cooked food, with some imaginative dishes to choose from. For starters you could have salad of fresh crab and avocado with bloody Mary dressing, £6.50, Loch Fyne king scallops with garlic and smoked bacon risotto and pesto, £8.95, or glazed sweet potato and goats' cheese terrine with caramelised banana, honey and sesame dressing, £6.95. If you prefer something simpler, there is home-made soup or grilled sardines with garlic butter, £4.95.

Main courses, priced £14-£18, include baked fillet of locally caught seabass on sweetcorn and crab fritter with roast red pepper sauce, fresh monkfish deep fried in chilli and beer batter with chips and sweet and sour sauce, or roast cod on chilli and chorizo risotto. Meat dishes are Gloucester Old Spot belly pork, chicken breast stuffed with Irish blue cheese on char-grilled vegetable ratatouille or sautéed medallions of beef fillet with tomato, rocket and Parmesan salad and home-made chips. No vegetarian main courses feature on the menu.

S P C

SUTTON UPON DERWENT
St Vincent Arms
Main Street, YO41 4BN

- Off B1228 from York
- Mon-Sat 11.30am-3pm; Sun 12-3pm, 7-10.30pm
- Daily 12-2pm, 7-9.30pm
- T (01904) 608349
- Fuller's Chiswick, London Pride, ESB; Taylor Landlord; Wells Bombardier; guest
- Quality pub food with a wide range of dishes to suit all tastes
- Friendly country village inn run by the same family for many years; striking multi-roomed whitewashed building

Daily changing specials offer plenty of excitement, from breast and confit of guinea fowl with Puy lentils and thyme at £11 or belly pork on bubble and squeak mash with onion gravy at £10.50 to fresh lobster either grilled with garlic butter or cold with salad at £18. Starters could be honey-smoked salmon, crevettes in garlic butter or carpaccio of beef with Parmesan and white truffle oil, all around £5. Other main dish specials might be pecan-crusted tuna on noodles, slow braised lamb shank with red wine and rosemary, duck breast with orange and Grand Marnier sauce or monkfish and king prawn curry, £9.50-£12.

The lunchtime bar menu offers splendid sandwiches including home-roasted ham teamed with Cheddar and Victorian chutney in fresh-baked crusty bread with salad, £3.50-£5, plus hot ciabatta filled with chicken, chorizo sausage and home-made chilli jam. Main meals include home-made steak, ale and mushroom pie with real shortcrust topping, haddock and chips with mushy peas and home-made lasagne, all around £8. Set menu starters are home-made soup, seared scallops on celeriac or egg en cocotte with leeks and mushrooms, followed by Thai chicken filled with coconut wild rice, rack of lamb with herb crust, a big mixed grill at £9, salads and fillet steaks, £7-£13.50, plus home-made desserts.

Q V P C

BECK HOLE
Birch Hall Inn
YO22 5LE

- ▶ 1 mile N of Goathland off B169
- ☼ Winter Tue-Sat 11am-3pm, 7.30-11pm (not Mon); Sun 12-3pm, 7.30-10.30pm; summer 11am-11pm; Sun 12-10.30pm
- Ⓨ Throughout opening hours
- T (01947) 896245
- E glenys@birchhallinn.fsnet.co.uk
- W www.beckhole.com
- Black Sheep Best Bitter, guests
- ☺ Short, simple, wholesome menu
- A tiny, unique gem dating back to 1860s, only two licensees in 80 years

What is the Birch Hall doing in a foodies' guide? It only serves pork pies and butties! But how good they are, and how delicious with a pint of Black Sheep in this legendary little pub with a small shop selling things such as boiled sweets dividing the bar from the snug, all doll's house size. I once visited with Derek Cooper to record a radio programme on his 'Necessary Pleasures – the perfect pub' and we agreed the food was perfect to the hostelry.

Let landlady and cook Glenys Crampton describe it: 'Our food is very simple as befits the pub. Butties are one quarter of a large wholemeal stotty baked specially for us by long-established family bakers Bothams of Whitby. We offer Cheddar, corned beef, farmhouse pâté or home-roasted ham as fillings with a dash of pickle or mustard. Radfords supplies the ham which is cooked slowly in our Rayburn. It also provides our pork pies, and special individual turkey and ham pies – the best this side of heaven! Yes, you guessed. Served with pickle. I make the scones, and our famous beer cake using whichever beer is on the pumps, so sometimes light or sometimes rich and dark if it's a porter week...'

★ Q ❀ S V

BILBROUGH
Three Hares
Main Street, YO23 3PH

- ▶ Off A64 between York and Tadcaster
- ☼ Daily 11am-11pm (10.30pm Sun)
- Ⓨ Mon-Sat 12-2.30pm, 6.30-9pm; Sun 11am-4pm
- T (01937) 832128
- Black Sheep Bitter; John Smith's Bitter; Taylor Landlord; guest
- ☺ Local traditional produce and flavours with a bit of pzazz
- Gastropub with meals served in immaculate bars and stylish restaurant

Dishes and produce are rooted in the North of England, provenance on the menu. For instance, you can start with Andrew Race's peat smoked salmon, followed by Bleiker's black pudding with onion relish, or the house speciality, a platter of meats including cured brisket, ox tongue, honey roast ham, potted pork, home-made pickles and piccalilli with crusty bread; also soup of the day such as cauliflower with fresh sorrel and parsley oil.

Starters are priced from £4.25 rising to £8.50 for the meat platter, but some can also be ordered as main courses. To follow, choose from Whitby fish pie with mashed potato and Wensleydale cheese, corn fed breast of chicken with garden pea mash, button onions and carrot juices, an authentic Yorkshire meat and potato pie with mushy peas and Henderson's relish, Masham sausages and mash, priced £8.25-£9.75.

On the evening menu you also find fish soup with 'wicked' mayonnaise, potted shrimps with mace butter and toasted soda bread, or ham hock and foie gras terrine with pease pudding among the starters. Main courses at night also offer Nidderdale lamb hotpot with pickled red cabbage and grills including aged rib eye Yorkshire beef with real chips. Guest ales include brews from local micros such as Hambleton and Daleside.

❀ S V P C

BREARTON
Malt Shovel
Main Street, HG3 3BX

- Off B165 between Knaresborough and Ripley
- Tue-Sun 11.45am-3pm, 6.30-11.30pm (10.30pm Sun)
- Tue-Sun 12-2.30pm; Tues-Sat 6.30-9pm
- T (01423) 862929
- Black Sheep BB; Daleside Night Star; Theakston BB; guests
- Seasonal menu using local ingredients as far as possible
- Unspoilt 16th-century pub with original partitions, oak beams, open fire and oak linen-fold bar

Good, wholesome food is the boast of the Malt Shovel, using the best local ingredients available at the time, flavoured with herbs from the pub garden. Most of the goodies are on an extensive blackboard offering eight meat, eight fish and eight vegetarian dishes; alongside this is another board holding six daily specials, depending on best buys from the fishmonger and butcher. Food is as seasonal as possible including choices such as Cajun chicken or red snapper with mango salsa in summer, while winter sees game pie and the ever popular sausage, mash and onion gravy.

A basic menu of traditional eats at modest prices is also provided, including steak and ale pie, lamb curry, chicken with tarragon sauce, beef lasagne, seafood gratin, poached Scotch salmon, haddock and chips and salads such as smoked salmon or seafood. Main dishes are priced £5.95-£8.20, though char-grilled sirloin and rib eye steaks are dearer. Vegetarian dishes, all around £5.75, include spinach and mushroom lasagne, cheese or tomato omelettes, ploughman's of Cheddar and blue Wensleydale, potato and tomato curry or blue cheese and red onion tart, and there is a good sandwich selection. All desserts are home made including apple crumble, sticky toffee pudding and toffee nut meringue.

★ Q S V P

CARLTON-IN-CLEVELAND
Blackwell Ox
Main Street, TS9 7DJ

- Just off A172, 3 miles S of Stokesley
- Mon-Sat 11.30am-11pm; Sun 12-10.30pm
- Daily 12-2pm (3pm Sun), 5.30-9pm
- T (01642) 712287
- F (01642) 712292
- E blackwellox@netcomuk.co.uk
- W www.theblackwellox.co.uk
- Black Sheep Best Bitter; Tetley's Bitter; guest beers
- Extensive, authentic Thai menu, plus some traditional English dishes
- Cosy village pub with several rooms, warmed by open fires in winter

The Ox is more than just a village pub; its extensive grounds house a camping and caravan park, two beer gardens and a play park for children. The pub employs a team of native Thai chefs who between them produce a long list of authentic dishes for customers to choose from – the starters alone run to some 20 options, including three different soups, and several king prawn dishes, such as breaded pancakes and Thai spice king prawns, or the landlord's recommendation of home-made king prawn spring rolls. There are two or three English alternatives, too, and most are priced at under £4.

To follow, there are dishes based on lamb, pork, beef, chicken and seafood as well as traditional noodle recipes such as Phad Thai (fried noodles with diced chicken and king prawns) and Rad Nha Gai (stir-fried noodles topped with chicken, vegetables and creamy bean sauce). Main courses are mostly around £8, although vegetarian options, of which there are plenty, are a bit cheaper, for example, Massaman vegetable curry or stir-fried vegetables in black bean sauce are both £6.65. Some Thai dishes are also offered as children's portions for under £4. If you really do prefer English food, you can choose from steaks, two or three fish dishes and pub standards such as lasagne.

★ S V P C

CARLTON MINIOTT
Vale of York
YO7 4LX

- 50 yards from Thirsk station
- Daily 12pm-2am
- Mon-Sat 12-2pm, 5.30 (Sat 7)-9pm; Sun 12-2.45pm
- T (01845) 523161
- Black Sheep Bitter; John Smith's Bitter; Taylor Landlord
- Bar snacks, a la carte menu and Sunday lunchtime carvery
- Large family friendly, family owned village local near Thirsk racecourse

Using beef and veal from the local farmers' market, pork, bacon and ham from Wensleydale, fresh haddock and vegetables from local suppliers, the Vale of York cooks up several different menus including the early evening list when everything costs £3.95 – bacon chop with fried egg, deep-fried fish cakes, meatballs, liver in onion gravy, jumbo sausage in batter or the York burger with cheese, all including chips, mash and peas.

The griddle menu offers pork fillet medallions, lamb leg steak, 13-15oz buffalo rump steak, gammon and rib eye, priced £6.95-£12.95, with the giant mixed grill £13.95. On the fish menu is fresh haddock in batter, pan-fried monkfish and king prawns with spring onions and capsicum, seafood platter and tuna pasta bake, all served with side salad, lemon, fresh veg, chips or new potatoes, £6.95-£11.95.

The vegetarian menu provides savoury cheesecake with garlic bread, three cheese pasta bake, wild rice with spinach and honey served with garlic bread and salad or broccoli cream cheese bake with fresh vegetables, all under £7. Lastly, on the bar snack menu, there are filled Yorkshire puds, hot meat stottie with gravy, filled jacket potatoes, assorted sarnies and toasties with a small portion of chips and side salad, cheese and beefburgers.

S V C

CRATHORNE
Crathorne Arms
TS15 0BA

- Half mile from A19, take Yarm turn off
- Mon-Fri 11.30am-2.30pm, 5-11pm; Sat 11am-11pm; Sun 12-3pm, 7-10.30pm
- Mon-Sat 11.45am-1.45pm, 5.30-9.30pm; Sun 12-1.45pm, 7-9pm
- T (01642) 701931
- Black Sheep Best Bitter; Hambleton Bitter
- Good traditional fare using locally sourced produce wherever possible
- A gem of a pub in typical Yorkshire farmhouse, on Lord Crathorne's estate, known to locals as Free House Farm

Two separate menus for lunchtime and evening use local produce as far as possible including fresh fish daily from Hartlepool, beef and lamb mainly from local markets and vegetables brought daily by the local greengrocer. At lunchtime you could start with home-made soup or creamy Stilton mushrooms, £2.95 and £3.95, followed by main courses all at a bargain £5.50 – home-made pie of the day, sausage and mash with onion gravy, home-made fishcake with parsley sauce, roast of the day with Yorkies, potatoes and vegetables, or the Crathorne home-made cheese burger with chips and salad. Lamb's liver and bacon with sage mash, fresh fish of the day, pork fillet stroganoff, a trio of lamb chops with rosemary gravy or king prawn and fresh crab salad are priced £7.50-£8.50.

In the evening starters range from home-made liver and whisky pâté with Oxford jelly to fresh Scottish mussels or a stack of field mushrooms and black pudding, £4.95 - £5.95. Mains include grilled salmon with a sauce of prawns, sweet chilli and mango, fresh local crab, prawn and poached salmon salad, mixed fish kebab with Kenyan hot chilli sauce, drunken chicken with Stilton and port, steak, kidney, oyster and Guinness pie or pan roast duck breast with apple, ginger and honey, around £12-£14, plus a wide selection of charcoal grilled steaks.

★ Q S V C

CRAY
White Lion Inn
BD23 5JB

- On B6160 N of Buckden
- Mon-Sat 11am-11pm; Sun 12-10.30pm
- Daily 12-2pm, 5.45-8.30pm
- T (01756) 760262
- F (01756) 761024
- E admin@whitelioncray.com
- W www.whitelioncray.com
- Moorhouses Premier; Taylor Landlord; guests
- Traditional dishes made to original recipes using local produce, vegetarian dishes are especially innovative
- Rural gem popular with walkers and cyclists; original oak beams, cosy log fire, stone flagged floors

Generous portions of home-prepared food: meat comes from two local butchers, trout and smoked trout from a nearby trout farm, local Wensleydale is in the ploughman's. Six specials daily might be T-bone steak, Normandy pork fillet cooked with cider, apple and cream, chicken in a creamy sauce combining three different mustards, veal Wellington, oven-baked red snapper with sweet chilli dressing or venison steak with marmalade and port, prices from £6.95-£11.95.

At lunchtime a fairly simple menu offers a small selection of evening dishes plus giant home made Yorkies filled with steak and mushrooms, or Cumberland sausages and onion gravy, £4.50-£5. Evening dishes, mainly around £8, include Dales lamb chops or duck breast with raspberry and redcurrant. All soups are home made including broccoli and Stilton or bacon and lentil. Veggie dishes are especially popular, such as cashew and mushroom loaf with sherry sauce or Sicilian lasagne – and vegetables are interesting, too, from oven roasted root vegetables to sweet red cabbage or parsnip dauphinoise. Traditional Sunday lunch is served, and home-made puds could be jam roly poly, lemon syllabub or a proper baked egg custard tart.

★ Q V P C

CROPTON
New Inn
YO18 8HH

- Cropton signed off A170 between Pickering and Kirkbymoorside
- Mon-Sat 11am-11pm; Sun 12-10.30pm
- Daily 12-2pm, 6-9pm
- T (01751) 417330
- F (01751) 417582
- E info@croptonbrewery.co.uk
- W www.croptonbrewery.co.uk
- Cropton Endeavour, Two Pints, Scoresby Stout, Uncle Sam's, Balmy Mild, Monkmans Slaughter; guests
- Traditional British cooking enhanced with beers from the brewery
- Cosy bar welcomes locals and visitors in beautiful area; November beer fest

This family-run inn boasts its own fine micro brewery but offers a huge selection of beers from other micros. The New Inn is equally committed to real food, including fish, vegetarian and regional dishes, using quality ingredients from the area and its own herb garden. The ring of speciality sausage is made with the brewery's own Two Pints Bitter, while the steak and ale pie has award-winning Scoresby Stout in the stock.

In the no-smoking restaurant you might start with home-made soup, garlic bread with chorizo, local black pudding in a skillet with home-made apple sauce and creamy peppercorn coating, oak smoked trout from Pickering, salmon cured at the pub, haddock cakes or Yorkshire feta, priced £3.50-£4.75. Tempting main courses include chicken breast stuffed with Wensleydale cheese on red wine and onion sauce, smoked duck breast glazed with honey on leek and stem ginger, Dales lamb joint in red wine, mint and redcurrant gravy, or pheasant breast with home-made pâté en croute, all served with real, home-made chips, or new potatoes and vegetables, £8.50-£11.95. Fish includes Whitby cod and scampi, veggie dishes lentil patties with curry sauce and broccoli and Stilton quiche – plus real food for kids!

S V P C

EAST WITTON
Cover Bridge Inn
DL8 4SQ

- On A6108, three quarters of a mile N of village
- Mon-Sat 11am-11pm; Sun 12-10.30pm
- Daily 12-2pm, 6.30-9pm
- T (01969) 623250
- E enquiries@thecoverbridgeinn.co.uk
- W www.thecoverbridgeinn.co.uk
- Black Sheep Bitter; Taylor Landlord; Theakston Old Peculier; guests
- Wholesome, traditional home cooking using local meat and vegetables
- Splendid 15th-century inn on the banks of the River Cover, with wealth of original features including an impressive fireplace

On a good, traditional menu, the Cover Bridge's most famous meal is ham, eggs and chips – a juicy gammon steak, two free range eggs, generous portion of home-made, hand-cut chips and peas at £8.75. There are also fine home-made pies – steak or chicken and ham, both £7 – home-made lasagne, pork loin in cream and Stilton sauce, half a roast chicken, trout and cod, or lamb chops, priced £6.75-£8.75 including potatoes or real chips, salad or fresh vegetables. Sirloin and fillet steaks are dearer, but reasonable, at £10 and £11, while the big mixed grill is £12.50.

If you just want a snack you can have a bowl of chips, sausage, egg and chips, ploughman's with four Wensleydale cheeses or cold meat salad, while a choice of sandwiches (lunchtime only) includes home-boiled ham. Soups such as ham and tomato or leek and potato are home made and so are desserts – maybe sticky toffee pudding or apple crumble. A heroic Sunday lunch of roast beef or pork is accompanied by Yorkshire pudding, roast and boiled potatoes and three fresh vegetables. Vegetarians choose from vegetable and cheese crunches, veggie burger, veggie korma with naan bread, or cannelloni in cheese and tomato sauce.

★ Q S V C

EGTON BRIDGE
Horseshoe Hotel
YO21 1XE

- Down hill from station, bear right
- Daily 11.30am-3pm, 6.30-11pm
- Daily 12-2pm, 7-9pm
- T (01947) 895245
- Black Sheep Best Bitter; John Smith's Bitter; guests
- Home-cooked food, traditional and continental
- Country inn on North Yorkshire moors in quiet valley on River Esk

Walking in the National Park up on the moors should whip up an appetite for a hearty pie or casserole at this delightful old inn also offering B&B. Traditional dishes, fresh fish and seafood are all home cooked using local meat, vegetables, game, sausages and cheese – and during summer the hotel's own home-grown salads and herbs.

As well as the set menu there are daily specials; sample starters include warm pigeon breast salad with red wine vinegar, wild mushroom risotto, asparagus and feta tartlets, the day's home-made soup or duck and orange sausages with rhubarb chutney. Main dishes on the specials board always include a pie or casserole of the day, warm tuna salad with chilli dressing, crayfish in cream and garlic sauce or chicken and crab wrapped together in puff pastry.

The regular menu offers warm bacon and blue cheese salad, home-made chicken liver pâté, crab cakes with sweet chilli dip or warm bacon and blue cheese salad, starters priced £3.20-£5.20. Fish pie of white and smoked fish with prawns is among the main dishes as well as home-made lasagne, chicken breast stuffed with cheese and wrapped in smoked bacon, prices from £7.50-£8.50, plus sirloin steak at £13.50. Generous sandwiches include home-baked ham and roast topside.

★ Q S V (Egton Bridge) C

FADMOOR
Plough Inn
Main Street, YO62 7HY

- ▶ 2.5 miles N of Kirbymoorside
- ☼ Mon-Sat 12-2.30pm, 6.30-11pm; Sun 12-2.30pm, 7-10.30pm
- 🍴 Mon-Sat 12-1.45pm, 6.30-8.45pm; Sun 12-1.45pm, 7-8.30pm
- T (01751) 431515
- 🍺 Black Sheep Best Bitter; Tetley Bitter
- ☺ Traditional and modern British cooking with imaginative touches and plenty of fresh fish
- ◙ Olde-worlde village pub with snug, open fires, beams and pretty dining room

There is a daily specials board, but the set menu is quite special enough. You can start with home-made leek, tomato and basil or classic caramelised French onion soup with locally baked flavoured bread, award-winning local black pudding on mushroom and white wine risotto, chicken liver pâté with home made fruit chutney or Loch Fyne salmon gravadlax, priced £5-£6. Main courses start with steak and ale pie with short crust lid at £8.50, continuing through slow roasted lamb shank on leek and potato mash, sliced confit belly pork on shallot and apple risotto with cider and cream sauce, chicken breast stuffed with Irish Cashel blue, to steaks including rib eye topped with home-made chutney and blue Stilton or beef Wellington with rich Madeira sauce at a reasonable £12.95.

The separate seafood menu includes kippers topped with poached egg, pan-seared king scallops with wild mushrooms and sweet chilli, seafood paella, grilled sea bass, cod and pancetta fishcakes with chilli and ginger dip or fresh Whitby haddock in a light, crisp batter, £5.95-£11. A two-course set menu lunchtime and evening (not Sat eve or Sun lunch) is a bargain £12.95 with a choice of six home-made starters and six main courses. Ten tempting desserts include caramelised lemon tart with red orange ice cream or lemon curd Bakewell with vanilla custard.

Q ❀ S V 🍺 P ✗ C

KIRBY HILL
Shoulder of Mutton
DL11 7JH

- ▶ Off A66, 4 miles SW of Richmond
- ☼ Mon-Fri 6-11pm; Sat & Sun 12-3pm, 6-11pm (Sun 10.30pm)
- 🍴 Wed-Fri 7-9pm; Sat & Sun 12-2pm, 7-9pm
- T (01748) 822772
- E info@shoulderofmutton.net
- W www.shoulderofmutton.net
- 🍺 Black Sheep Best Bitter; Daleside Bitter; Jennings Cumberland Ale; guests
- ☺ Home-cooked traditional bar meals and more adventurous restaurant menu
- ◙ Ivy-clad, olde-worlde inn benefiting from a beautiful setting

In the tiny, picturesque village of Kirby Hill, surrounded by moorland and dales, the pub, with five en-suite bedrooms, makes an ideal base for exploring Yorkshire's national parks. The meals here are based on seasonal market produce so the menus vary accordingly, with all meals cooked to order; here are a few samples of the tasty dishes you can expect to find on offer.

To start you might try warm kidney and crispy bacon salad, Parma ham with melon and black peppered strawberries, garlic mushroom and bacon crêpes, oak-smoked salmon with a bouquet of prawns, mussel, bacon and potato chowder or cullen skink. Next up there may be roast duck breast on apple compote with plum and orange sauce, fillet steak with mushrooms and Stilton sauce, chicken breast with aubergine, tomatoes, parma ham and grilled smoked cheese, mint and honey marinated lamb cutlets with a minty mushroom sauce, or seasonal roast venison. There is always a vegetarian option and fish dishes such as grilled halibut with asparagus and bacon. Starters are £5-£7, mains £9.50-£13.50, including fresh vegetables; a selection of home-made desserts is offered to finish your meal. Home-made bar meals are also available from £5.95.

★ Q ❀ V 🍺 ♿ P ✗ C

KNARESBOROUGH
So! Bar & Eats
1 Silver Street, HG5 8AJ

▶ Next to bus station on High Street
☼ Daily 11am-11pm (10.30pm Sun)
🍴 Daily 12-9.30pm
T (01423) 863202
E rob@appetiteforlife.freeserve.co.uk
Black Sheep Best Bitter; guests
☺ Modern British and fusion cooking with a twist
Spacious, open, bistro-style bar with relaxed seating, ranging from giant bean bags to a conventional dining area

The So! Bar serves food all day – you can drop in for a pint of ale and a plate of cheese, or a full meal. Cooking everything to order means the chefs can cater for particular dietary needs and will happily adapt a dish to customers' individual requirements – just ask. Most items can be cooked in children's portions, too.

Three regular menus are offered: at lunchtime there are pub classics such as sausage, egg and chips (with bangers from the local butcher), haddock and chips, ploughman's, plus an impressive list of sarnies and salads. The main menu, available all day, is extensive, as are the descriptions of the dishes, so it could take a while to decide what to order. Starters, £3.25-£7.95, include crab toasties, a tart of roasted shallots and onions, and skewers of chicken marinated in coconut milk, lime, chilli, mint and garlic then char grilled and served with pancakes. The Seconds selection includes main dishes from £7 to £13, such as curry pie, char-grilled lamb on buttered spinach and mash (So!'s signature dish), pastas, warm fish and chip salad and steaks. There is also a selection of plates to share. The Specials menu lists around eight dishes which change daily. Leave room for Afters – or you may regret missing the poached cherries in kirsch, served with mascarpone and brandy snaps, £3.75 or the lemon and raspberry ripple tart, £4.95.

S V ♿ ⇌ (Knaresborough) 🚭 👪 **C**

LASTINGHAM
Blacksmith's Arms
Front Street, YO62 6TL

▶ N of A170, 8 miles from Pickering
☼ Winter Mon-Thu 12-2.30pm, 6-11pm; Fri-Sun and summer 12-11pm
🍴 Daily 12-2pm, 7-9pm
T (01751) 417247
Theakston Best Bitter; guests
☺ Traditional home-cooked food with a Yorkshire dialect, in generous portions
Warm and friendly stone-built wayside inn within National Park area

An extensive menu is freshly prepared on the premises as far as possible, using local produce. Chef Glen Collinson is particularly renowned for her steak and ale pie made with tender, locally reared beef cooked in Theakston's Best Bitter, with a proper short crust pastry topping, and her Yorkshire hot pot served in a giant Yorkshire pudding. Other main courses, from £7.95, include slow roasted lamb shank, home-made lamb and mint pie, jumbo cod in Glen's special beer batter, Whitby scampi with chips and roast of the day with Yorkshire pudding and all the trimmings.

A weekly changing specials board offers local game including venison in season – a pub speciality – along with lamb, beef and fish dishes plus several vegetarian options – adaptable to special dietary needs. The lunchtime snack and sandwich menu from £3.65 includes home-made soup, wholemeal open sandwiches and toasted paninis with various fillings, stuffed jacket potatoes and a cheese ploughman's with crusty bread. Starters include garlic bread, deep fried Brie with cranberry dip and spicy chicken wings. If you can manage a home-made dessert, choose from bilberry pie, old-fashioned treacle tart, Blacksmith's Angel (meringue ice cream) or hot chocolate fudge cake.

★ ❀ 🛏 **S V** ♿ ♣ 🚭 👪 **C**

OLD MALTON
Wentworth Arms
111 Town Street, YO17 7HD

- 200 yards off A64 Malton bypass
- Daily 11am-11pm
- Daily 12-2pm, 6-9pm
- T (01653) 692618
- E pklwray@aol.com
- Beer range varies
- Wholesome food cooked to order with emphasis on English cooking, traditional and modern
- Ivy clad rural coaching inn dating back to early 18th century

'We don't believe in messing with the ingredients, we allow the quality of the meat, fish or vegetables to be recognised,' is the philosophy at the Wentworth Arms where the chefs use local suppliers for fresh produce and seek out what is good and in season. As you have a right to expect in this county, the Yorkshire puddings are home made with fillings from onion gravy to roast beef, priced £3.75-£6.25 with vegetables. Starters could be home-made soup with freshly baked bread, black pudding layered with grape chutney on a crisp crouton, fresh salmon, tuna and spring onion fishcakes or Brie in home-made batter, priced £3.25 to £4.75.

Daily specials include monkfish with vermouth sauce, breast of duck with port and raspberry sauce, seafood risotto, Mediterranean wild rice and honey bake, Stilton and vegetable crumble or game pie with home-made pastry crust. Main courses on the lunch menu include wholetail scampi and fresh haddock from nearby Whitby in a light beer batter, steak and ale pie, three good bangers on mash with red wine and onion gravy, and on the evening menu, chicken supreme, 12oz braised lamb shank with blackcurrant and rosemary sauce, fish of the day and sweet chilli pork loin. Most main courses are under £7 including vegetables; rump and fillet steaks £10.95 and £12.95. Constantly-changing beers include many from local micros.

Q S V P C

OSMOTHERLEY
Golden Lion
6 West End, DL6 3AA

- One mile off A19 at A684 jct
- Mon-Fri 12-3pm, 6-11pm; Sat 12-11pm; Sun 12-10.30pm
- Daily 12-3pm, 6-9.30pm
- T (01609) 883526
- F (01609) 884000
- Hambleton Bitter; John Smith's Bitter; Taylor Landlord; guest
- Varied menu of home-cooked dishes
- Old stone pub overlooking the village cross; the single bar room is used mainly for dining and there is an upstairs restaurant

Osmotherley is a popular spot with tourists, surrounded by walking country. The pub's varied menu is produced by an established team of six in the kitchen. For starters there is a choice of four tasty soups, £3.95, three vegetarian options including goats' cheese and red pepper terrine with onion and apricot relish, ten fishy dishes such as fresh grilled sardines in olive oil, deep-fried soft shell crab with lime mayonnaise, calamari with tartare sauce and lemon, and fillets of mackerel marinated in olive oil, red chilli and onions, prices from £5.25-£7.95. Meat options include spicy pork ribs, bresaola (cured beef) with rocket and fresh Parmesan, or Parma ham with melon or avocado – all under £6. There is also a choice of pastas, risottos and salads.

Main courses, £9-£14, are listed in categories, so under meat there is calf's liver, lamb casserole and beef stroganoff to name just a few; fish dishes include pan-fried cod, salmon fishcake with spinach and cream sorrel sauce, or grilled sea bass; there is a selection of home-made burgers, all £6.50, vegetarian dishes and chicken, such as charcoal-grilled poussin or coq au vin. Desserts, all £3.95, are scrumptious – middle eastern orange cake with marmalade cream, poached pear in wine with hot chocolate sauce and home-made vanilla ice cream, or very sherry trifle.

Q V C

PICKHILL

☆ Nag's Head

YO7 4JG

- ▶ One mile E of A1, 5 miles from Leeming
- Daily 11am-11pm
- Daily 12-2pm, 6-9pm
- T (01845) 567391
- F (01845) 567212
- E reservations@nagsheadpickhill.freeserve.co.uk
- W www.nagsheadpickhill.co.uk
- Black Sheep Best Bitter; Hambleton Bitter, Theakston Black Bull; guests
- ☺ A mix of modern and traditional dishes
- Comfortable country inn, caters well for visitors yet the public bar is still well supported by locals

The CAMRA award-winning Nag's Head is a well established Yorkshire Dales inn that has been run by the Boynton brothers for over 30 years. For a light lunch you can choose from a delicious selection of toasted sandwiches, with salad and optional fries, including smoked salmon and scrambled eggs on focaccia, Brie with grapes on ciabatta or goats' cheese and roasted Mediterranean vegetables on pain rustique.

The main menu is equally varied: starters, £3.50-6.95, often include interesting combinations such as carpaccio of duck with walnut and blue cheese salad and bitter orange compote, warm salmon and prawn mousse with coriander cream sauce or simpler dishes such as devilled whitebait or poached smoked haddock. To follow, vegetarian options such as mixed bean chilli with spicy onion couscous start at £8.95, going up to £15.95 for grilled fillet of wild salmon, with asparagus and hollandaise sauce. In between, there's slow roasted shoulder of lamb, casserole of wild rabbit with herb dumplings, pork fillet wrapped in dry cured bacon with noodles and wild truffle oil, or pan-fried pigeon breast on cauliflower cream mash. Lovely puds include poached figs with peach compote and sweet mascarpone or vanilla and rum panacotta with mango coulis, both £4.50.

Q S V P C

STOKESLEY

☆ Spread Eagle

39 High Street, YS9 5AD

- ▶ Behind town hall
- Daily 11am-11pm
- Daily 11am-9.30pm (8.30pm Sun)
- T (01642) 710278
- E spreadeagle@qnetadsl.com
- W www.thespreadeagle.net
- Banks's Original; Camerons Strongarm; Marston's Pedigree; guest
- ☺ Quality menu with a wide choice of home-cooked farmhouse fare
- Homely 18th-century coaching inn with real coal fire

The pub does not believe in using fancy sauces to mask the taste of its fresh meat; hardly surprising as the family owners also have their own butcher's shop, Adlington's of Stokesley, and their own pedigree Madewell herd of sheep supplying lamb. All fish comes from local supplier Hodgsons of Hartlepool, there is local game in season, and popular organic vegetable soup is made with produce from the farmers' market.

The most popular dish is shoulder, loin or leg of lamb simply braised very gently for several hours. Steaks too, of course, are hugely popular and prices, from just £10.40 for a 12-16oz rump or £10.90 for an 8oz fillet, reflect that they have cut out the middleman. Fish dishes might be plaice or haddock or cod in batter, whole tail Whitby scampi, pan-fried tuna, halibut or swordfish, poached trout, sea bass, monkfish in white wine and mustard sauce or home-made seafood lasagne, again all good value from £6-£8. Other meat choices might be pork or lamb chops, half a chicken, duck breast or Cumberland sausages, while pies include rabbit, steak and ale, game, turkey and ham, mince or corned beef, around £6. There are several vegetarian choices – pasta broccoli bake, vegetarian curry or lasagne, and choice of omelette; a three course Sunday lunch is £9.50.

V C

SUTTON IN CRAVEN
☆ Dog & Gun
Colne Road, Malsis, BD20 8DS

- ▶ From A629 Keighley-Skipton, take A6068 towards Burnley
- ☼ Mon-Fri 12-3pm, 5-11pm; Sat & Sun 12-11pm (10.30pm Sun)
- 🍴 Mon-Fri 12-2pm, 5.30-9pm; Sat & Sun 12-9pm
- T (01535) 633855
- E dogandgun@btinternet.com
- 🍺 Timothy Taylor Golden Best, Dark Mild, Porter, BB, Landlord; guest
- ☺ Extensive range of quality, freshly prepared meals with some tempting ideas, offering good value for money
- ◉ Rural roadside inn with large car park

Chef and landlord Ross Walker and his wife Anita took over the Dog & Gun three years ago with the aim of providing top quality, home cooked food (everything freshly prepared apart from a couple of desserts), and they are succeeding. 'I consider our menu to be simple, unpretentious and largely traditional in style. We do not spend hours garnishing plates as I feel that the food should look as good as it is,' says Ross. Judge for yourself – specials might be sea bass, steak fillet 'old England', moules marinière, beef stifado or chicken with goats' cheese, parma ham and wild mushroom sauce.

On the set menu starters – all under £3.95 – include home-made salmon fish cakes, mushroom and stilton pepperpot or home-made soup at only £1.95. Pub classics include savoury meat pie of the day, trio of different local sausages with mash, onion and mushroom gravy, or home made lasagne, £3.60-£4.25. Pan-fried liver and bacon, chicken caesar salad or lamb shank braised in Taylor's beer with root vegetables are priced £5.90-£9.95. Char-grilled steaks support Yorkshire farming, while fish includes fresh haddock in Taylor beer batter or lemon sole Ricardo. Vegetarians will find plenty to tempt, and there is real food for kids.

⛫ ❀ S V 🍺 ♿ ♣ Ⓟ ⚡ 👪 C

WELL
Milbank Arms
Church Street, DL8 2PX

- ▶ Near Bedale
- ☼ Daily 12-3pm, 6.30-11pm
- 🍴 Tue-Sun 12-2pm, 6.30-9pm
- T (01677) 470411
- 🍺 Black Sheep Bitter; Tetley Bitter; guest
- ☺ Traditional dishes and grills with fresh fish
- ◉ Family-run village inn offering a warm welcome

Local produce is high on the list at the Milbank Arms, with all vegetables from local suppliers, fish fresh daily from Carricks of Snape. The menu begins with a comprehensive range of starters, priced £3.95-£4.95, followed by traditional choices such as steak and ale pie made with Rudgate beer, or liver and bacon with leek mash and gravy. Grills include rump, sirloin, rib eye and fillet steaks, served with home-made onion rings, mushrooms and tomato, priced £10.95-£14.95.

Other main courses always include two pork dishes, two lamb dishes and three chicken choices, as well as vegetarian meals, prices ranging from £7.50 to £15.95. All desserts are made in house, and there is a children's menu – the pub is a 'whole family' destination. 'We aim for middle ground somewhere between standard pub grub and fine dining at reasonable prices,' says the landlord who is also proud of his wine list where there are plenty of options under a tenner and no bottle costs more than £20. With three handpumps on the bar, a guest ale is often available.

★ ⛫ Q ❀ V ♿ Ⓟ ⚡ 👪 C

YORK
Maltings
Tanners Moat, YO1 6HU

- ▶ Turn left out of York station, 5 minute walk, below city wall
- ☼ Mon-Sat 11am-11pm; Sun 12-10.30pm
- Ⓨ Mon-Fri 12-2pm, Sat & Sun 12-4pm
- T (01904) 655387
- E info@maltings.co.uk
- W www.maltings.co.uk
- Black Sheep Best Bitter; guests
- ☺ Simple, value for money fare in huge portions
- Small, idiosyncratic city-centre pub, regularly winning awards, serving York's finest selection of micro-breweries' beer

The Maltings kitchen is famously known as the Dragon's Pantry, 'in honour of the landlady Maxine Collinge whose temper is legendary when under pressure (she has a small kitchen)…' Chips are home made, heroically peeled and cut by Joan who often does 16 stone in a day – all food is freshly prepared on the premises. Maxine's chilli is so hot that the menu carries a health warning! It also carries little snippets such as, 'If you'd like to complain our suppliers are Dick the Veg and M&K the Butcher' (phone numbers supplied), or 'We don't serve kids, so don't ask for one'.

Apart from the chilli, other main meals include boozy beef pie, roast chicken, gammon, haddock, lasagne and ham with egg and chips, sausage with beans and chips, all at around a fiver. Snacks include jacket potatoes with a choice of eight fillings 'or anything else you'd bloody well like', filled toasties, bowls of plain chips or cheesy chips, chilli chips, curry chips and boli chips – 'we call them snacks but we know you won't eat for a week' – and a good range of sandwiches on brown, white or crusty French bread. Chicken, beef, tuna and ham salads are all just under a fiver.

Q S V ⇌ (York) **C**

YORK
Masons Arms
6 Fishergate, YO10 4AB

- ☼ Mon-Sat 11am-11pm; Sun 12-10.30pm
- Ⓨ Daily 12-9.30pm
- T (01904) 646046
- F (01904) 635894
- E masonsarms@tiscali.co.uk
- John Smith's Bitter; guests
- ☺ Home made and wholesome including huge roast dinners
- Traditional, friendly town pub popular with tourists and residents alike

When my son was at York University living on snacks, he tolerated the occasional parental visit if we took him to the Masons for his Sunday lunch, a great roast platter with around six different vegetables. You can eat in all three bars, but it was always tough to snaffle a table – other students (and their professors) all made a beeline for the place, too.

Four female cooks in the family-run pub make traditional dishes from fresh produce, down to the hand-cut chips. Dishes on the regular menu include fresh cod or haddock and chips, pork, leek and sage sausages with mustard gravy, Cumberland sausages with onion gravy and mash, or the famous roasts – turkey with all the trimmings, beef or lamb, all with fresh vegetables and new and roast potatoes and Yorkshire pudding. Other choices are two thick slices of slow roast belly pork topped with two slices of black pudding, chunky apple sauce with orange zest and spices plus veg including red cabbage and mashed swede, chicken breast with prawns, tomato and basil sauce, salmon and potato salad, or warm chicken Caesar salad, all priced around £6-£7.50. Vegetarian dishes range from broccoli and Stilton pie to vegetables of the day in Yorkshire pudding. There is a full range of steaks, and plenty on the specials board with home made rabbit and cider pie a favourite.

★ **S V** P **C**

CUBLEY
Cubley Hall Hotel

Mortimer Road, S36 9DF

- ▶ Off A616, just S of Penistone
- ☼ Daily 11am-11pm
- 🍴 Daily 12-10pm
- T (01226) 766086
- F (01226) 767335
- E cubley.hall@ukonline.co.uk
- Tetley Bitter, Imperial, Burton Ale; guest
- ☺ Extensive menu supplemented by daily specials
- A moorland farm dating from the 17th century, now a flourishing country hotel and restaurant retaining lovely features such as the mosaic tiled hall floor

Set in its own four acre grounds, with gardens and a children's play area, this former Victorian gentleman's residence caters for drinkers, diners and visitors exploring the Peak District. There is a separate restaurant in the converted barn that is often used for functions but is open all day on Sunday for a traditional carvery. The pub itself serves a good bar menu offering everything from club sandwiches and warm filled baguettes for less than £5 to a full three-course meal. There is also a selection of freshly baked pizzas including a calzone, £4.50-£7.75, and seasonal salads.

Main course dishes include home-made Cubley beef and ale pie, chilli chicken with roasted cashews and oriental vegetables in garlic soya sauce served with sweet chilli noodles, a classic risotto with woodland mushrooms, tomatoes, spinach and Parmesan topped with a softly poached egg, grilled salmon fillet and a variety of pasta dishes. Daily main course specials are chalked up on a board followed by home-made desserts; puddings on the main menu are all £3.95, including Bakewell tart, steamed sticky toffee pudding, chilled lemon posset with pistachio ice cream and rich chocolate tart with mango coulis.

S V (Penistone) P C

HATHERSAGE
Plough Inn
Leadmill, S32 1BA

- ▶ On B6001, 1 mile SW of Hathersage
- Mon-Sat 11am-11pm, Sun 12-10.30pm
- Mon-Fri 11.30am-2.30pm, 6.30-9.30pm; Sat 11.30am-9.30pm; Sun 12-9pm
- T (01433) 650319
- F (01433) 651049
- E sales@theploughinn-hathersage.com
- Adnams Bitter; Theakston Best Bitter, guests
- Extensive menus offering a mix of traditional and modern European dishes
- Charming, privately-owned inn dating back to the 16th century, set in nine acres of grounds bordering the River Derwent; the cosy bar has a log fire

Situated near Chatsworth House and Haddon Hall, the Plough is an ideal place to stop for day-trippers or for overnight guests as it offers comfortable accommodation. You can enjoy your meal in the cosy bar with log fires or relax in the intimate restaurant which has its own, slightly more expensive menu. Meals are all freshly cooked to order and there is plenty of choice – home-cured herrings with leek and bacon salad and soft boiled egg, tataki of tuna with bok choi, soy ginger and lemon dressing, seared foie gras with home-made sweet pickle or perhaps asparagus with mushroom vinaigrette are just some of the dozen starters, £3.50-£8. Bar meals include a daily roast for £7.95 and a dish of the day at market price.

In the restaurant expect to pay around £14 for chicken breast with wild mushroom risotto and red wine jus, poached beef fillet with horseradish rosti, spinach and a shallot jus, roast breast of pheasant with root veg mash, served with its braised leg meat, pan-fried seabass with braised red cabbage, morels and port jus and a couple of veggie options such as pithivier of Provençal vegetables and cream cheese with tomato sauce.

★ Q S V (Hathersage) P C

LANGSETT
Waggon & Horses
Manchester Road, S36 4GY

- ▶ Exit 35A from M1 N
- Daily 12-3pm, 6.30-10.30pm
- Tue-Thu 12-2pm, 6.30-8.30pm; Fri & Sat 12-2pm, 6.30-9pm; Sun 12-2pm
- T (01226) 763147
- W www.langsettinn.com
- Acorn Barnsley Bitter; Taylor Landlord; guests
- Good Yorkshire platefuls, excellent value
- Welcoming, Grade I listed pub on the edge of the Peak District with a lovely garden and terrific views; B&B for walkers and holidaymakers

The Waggon and Horses has a reputation for making the best meat and potato, and bilberry pies in Yorkshire, served in hearty portions at value for money prices. These two classic Yorkshire treats have been served at the pub by the Battye family for the past 25 years, along with the renowned Sunday lunch of roast beef and Yorkshire pudding.

All produce is locally sourced, the simple menu offering starters such as freshly-made soup with warm bread, chicken liver pâté flavoured with fresh orange and Grand Marnier served with wholemeal toast, and tuna and grapefruit cocktails. Individual pies include the famous meat and potato served with mushy peas and pickled red cabbage, a steak pot pie with red wine gravy and fresh vegetables, and chicken and asparagus pie with spuds and seasonal vegetables. There is also flan of the day, lasagne with salad or garlic bread, chilli con carne with rice and garlic bread, award-winning sausages from the local butcher or English gammon steak served with egg, tomato, mushrooms and chips. For vegetarians there is mushroom stroganoff with wild rice and fresh leaf salad. Snacks include sandwiches or just a portion of chips. Puds range from that popular bilberry pie with cream or ice cream to a proper sherry trifle or peach melba.

Q S V P C

MARSDEN

Tunnel End Inn

Waters Road, HD7 6NF

- ▶ Off A62, follow road/canal from station towards Standedge Visitor centre
- ☼ Summer Mon-Fri 12-3pm, 5-11pm; Sat & Sun 12-11pm (10.30pm Sun); winter 5pm (8pm Mon)-11pm
- 🍴 Thu-Sun 12-3pm; Fri & Sat eves
- T (01484) 844636
- ⊞ Black Sheep Best Bitter; Taylor Landlord; Tetley Bitter; guests
- ☺ Simple, traditional choices genuinely home made
- ◙ Welcoming country pub near Huddersfield Canal in the heart of the Pennines

Landlady Beverley Earnshaw dishes up real pub food at budget prices, using meat from a local farm shop, fresh fruit, vegetables and fish from local suppliers. The menu changes frequently but starts with home-made soup such as potato and leek with a bread roll at a bargain £2.50, home-made chicken liver pâté with salad and toast, garlic mushrooms or garlic slices. Main meals include three home-made pies – steak and ale, chicken and leek (both with new potatoes or chips, broccoli, carrots and peas), or meat and potato with mushy peas, giant Yorkshire pudding filled with liver, onions and gravy, or tagliatelle with pesto and mushroom sauce, £4.95-£6.95. Slightly dearer is the half faced gammon with egg, pineapple, vegetables and chips or new potatoes, sirloin steak or the mega mixed grill containing just about everything, prices £8.25-£10.95.

Sandwiches, in brown or white with chips and salad, including home-roast beef and chicken, are all £3.50. Home-made desserts are treacle or jam sponge, sticky toffee pudding, apple pie or crumble, all with cream, ice cream or custard at £3.25. The Sunday roast of beef with Yorkshire pudding, roast potatoes, cabbage, carrots and peas and real gravy is £6.25. Food times vary – phone to check.

★ ♛ Q ❀ 🛏 S V ⊞ ♿ ≠ (Marsden)
♣ ● ⚡ ⊓ 👪 C

ROYDHOUSE
Three Acres Inn
HD8 8LR

▶ 5 miles S of Huddersfield between Emley, Shelley and Kirkburton
☼ Daily 12-3pm, 6-11pm
🍴 Daily 12-2pm, 6.30-9.30pm
T (01484) 602606
E 3acres@globalnet.co.uk
W www.3acres.com
🍺 Black Sheep Bitter; Taylor Landlord; Tetley Bitter
☺ Eclectic menu featuring modern British cuisine with offbeat touches
◉ 19th-century drovers' inn with open fire; known as the 'inn, restaurant and grocer' because it also sells speciality foods

Even the sandwich menu is highly tempting at the Three Acres – with a dozen mouth-watering choices including steak cooked to your specification in toasted olive and tomato bread with sweet pepper marmalade topped with mustard and horseradish butter, hot Toulouse sausage with Dijon mustard and caramelised peppers on onion bread, or toasted hot ham and Brie with real ale chutney. On the main menu, starters and light meals include Thai crab and lemongrass broth, French onion soup baked in the oven, home-made black pudding on a stew of chorizo, butter beans, tomato and cumin, mackerel fish cake with horseradish or smoked haddock kedgeree crêpe, prices £5-£6.95.

At the 'oyster bar' go for fresh rock oysters with black bean, ginger and chilli sauce, fresh tuna tataki in Asian herbs with lime and wasabi, home-cured gravadlax, fresh lobster cocktail or Cornish crab on asparagus and samphire. Main dishes include steak, kidney and mushroom pie with grain mustard pastry topping, confit of duck leg on sweet potato and onion tatin with braised peas and bacon, fresh haddock in sun blush tomato and basil batter with real chips, monkfish and king prawn saffron risotto and much more. Prices are around £14-£16.

★ 🏛 ❀ 🛏 S V 🍺 ♿ P 🚭 👪 C

SHEFFIELD
Fat Cat
23 Alma Street, S3 8SA

▶ In city centre next to Kelham Island industrial museum
☼ Mon-Thu 12-3pm, 5.30-11pm; Fri & Sat 12-11pm; Sun 12-3pm, 7-10.30pm Sun
🍴 Daily 12-2.30pm, 6-7.30pm
T (0114) 249 4801
W www.thefatcat.co.uk
🍺 Kelham Island Bitter, Gold, Easy and Pale Rider; Taylor Landlord; guests
☺ Noted for vegetarian and vegan food
◉ Real ale stalwart, home of Pale Rider, CAMRA's Supreme Champion Ale 2004; large beer garden

Well known to local CAMRA members as home to Kelham Island Brewery, the micro that produces fine ales in general and national winner of the Great British Beer Festival in 2004, the Fat Cat is more widely famed among diners for its award-winning vegetarian and vegan food. For 25 years the kitchen has specialised in home-cooked food on a small menu that changes weekly, always offering a meat, fish, vegetarian, vegan and gluten-free dish. Voted Vegetarian Food Pub of the Year by Pub Food magazine in 2001, and local Bargain Food Pub of the Year five times in the past nine years, main meals cost just £3.50, or £4 for Sunday lunch with meat or vegetarian roasts.

A typical menu might include a filling lentil soup followed by steak pie with potatoes, peas and gravy, leek, potato and mustard pie with vegetables, spicy mushroom and red bean casserole with rice and salad, chicken and tomato casserole, quiche or ploughman's; for afters, jam roly poly and rhubarb crumble served with custard. Other popular dishes are vegetable cobbler, pork and pepper casserole, Mexican mince and ham with mustard sauce. Sandwiches are of the doorstep variety and there are barbecues in summer. Morning Advertiser Cask Ale Pub 2004.

★ 🏛 Q ❀ S V 🍺 ♿ 🍎 P 🚭 👪

SHEFFIELD
Plough Inn
288 Sandygate Road, S10 5SE

▶ Take A57 Sheffield-Manchester, turn left at Crosspool, opposite Hallam FC
☼ Mon-Thu 12-3pm, 5-11pm; Fri-Sun 12-11pm (10.30pm Sun)
Mon-Sat 12-2.30pm, 6-9pm; Sun 12-3pm
T (0114) 230 1802
Draught Bass; Caledonian Deuchars IPA; Taylor Landlord; Wadworth 6X; guests
☺ Freshly made from local produce – magnificent six-course banquets
Welcoming pub facing Hallam FC serving seven ales on handpump and gravity

Look out for the Plough's twice-monthly themed six-course 'gourmet' dinners at just £12.95 a head. You're in for a treat – a St Patrick's Day feast, for instance, started with Irish stew with soda bread, followed by Dublin Bay prawns with scallion salad, then pork and Guinness sausages on colcannon, then steak and Guinness pie, a dessert of Irish whiskey and bitter chocolate mousse followed by Irish cheese and biscuits finishing with coffee! All produce comes from local suppliers, all soups and desserts are home made, with meat and fish dishes cooked to order.

On the set lunch menu you could start with roast tomato soup or gazpacho, then enjoy smoked haddock and cod fishcakes, pan-fried gnocchi with sun-dried tomatoes and cheese, chicken pasta with basil sauce, cottage pie with vegetables, all £5.50. Snacks include fresh cut sarnies from chicken tikka to boiled ham, or hot pork with apple sauce and hot roast beef with onion. In the evening, starters also include goats' cheese tart and oak-smoked salmon, with main courses such as braised lamb shank with rosemary gravy on garlic mash, liver, onions and bacon, Plough chicken, bacon and feta salad, balti chicken, moules marinière or rib eye steak with choice of sauces, prices from £5.50-£9.50. Desserts are tangy lemon tart with ice cream, chocolate brownies with cream or apple crumble.

Q ❀ ♿ ♣ P ⚟ 👪 **C**

SHEFFIELD
Riverside Café Bar
1 Mowbray Street, S3 8EN

▶ At junction of Mowbray St and Corporation St (A61)
☼ Mon-Fri 12-11pm; Sat 7-11pm; Sun 12-6pm
Mon-Fri 12-3.30pm; Sun 12-4pm
T (0114) 281 3621
F (01140 281 3622
Beer range varies
☺ Snacks and varied meals including excellent vegetarian options
Modern gastro pub with minimalist interior by the River Don; French windows along one wall open to a sunny terrace

Chef Martin Wood owns and runs this contemporary bar and is in charge of the kitchen. Meals are mostly served at lunchtime although there is a Thai night on Thursday. All produce is purchased on a daily basis from local markets and suppliers, so the meals are as fresh as possible. Martin also employs a specialist vegetarian chef so the daily specials board might feature char-grilled Mediterranean vegetables with salsa verde alongside roast cod with spinach and watercress salad and split pea compote, thick pork and leek sausages in rich onion gravy topped with a mini Yorkie, Riverside hotpot (chicken, leek and ham in a creamy sauce, topped with sautéed potatoes) and steak and ale pie. There is always a good selection of classic salads such as Caesar, Greek, chicken and bacon, and Creole prawn salad, prices from £4.95. A good choice of cold or hot sandwiches includes pan-fried rump steak or BLT served with coleslaw and fresh spinach, rocket and cress salad or chips for around £5. Burgers also feature on the menu – 8oz beef, chicken or vegetarian, £5.25-£3.75. On Sunday the carvery offers a vegetarian option alongside the traditional roast meats.

❀ **S V** ♿ ⊖ (Shalesmoor) ♣ ⚟ 👪 **C**

SHEFFIELD
☆ Wig & Pen
44 Campo Lane, Cathedral Quarter, S1 2EG

- ▶ In the city centre, behind the cathedral
- Daily 11am-11pm
- Daily 12-9.30pm (restaurant); 12-11pm for tapas
- T (0114) 276 3988
- F (0114) 276 3977
- E info@wigandpensheffield.com
- W www.wigandpensheffield.com
- Abbeydale Moonshine; guest
- ☺ Extensive tapas selection in the bar plus à la carte restaurant meals
- After five years as an Irish bar, the Wig and Pen has been reborn as a stylish, award-winning bar and restaurant

The bar at the Wig and Pen follows the Spanish tradition of offering a variety of small tapas dishes such as olives, nuts and fresh bread with oil and balsamic vinegar for dipping, or prepared plates including stuffed vine leaves and mint mayo, red peppers stuffed with tuna, marinated sardines or anchovies, bruschetta with salsa and parmesan or chorizo picante, £1.50-£3.50 per dish.

The European influence continues in the restaurant where starters include ballotine of confit duck and strozzapreti pasta (tossed in ricotta, walnuts and marjoram with a hint of chilli), but you could opt for British classics such as west country faggot, Yorkshire fish cake or cockles and mussels, £4.50-£7. To follow there is rack of Yorkshire lamb, braised pork cheek with flaked ham hock and parsley sauce, or rib eye of beef with potato and swede fondants and wilted spinach. Vegetarians could choose polenta bruschettas topped with aubergine, olive capponatta and buffalo mozzarella, or roasted stuffed courgettes, while fish includes grilled fillets of mackerel with potato rosti, grilled peppers and braised fennel or roast fillet of sea trout. Mains are priced from £9-£14.50. Yummy puds include dark chocolate delice with cassis sorbet and cocoa bean jelly and plum upside down cake.

V C

STANNINGTON
Robin Hood
Greaves Lane, S6 6BG

- ▶ W of Sheffield off A57 and A6101
- Mon & Tue 5-11pm; Wed-Sat 12-11pm; Sun 12-10.30pm
- Mon & Tue 5-8pm; Wed-Sat 12-8pm; Sun 1-4pm
- T (01142) 344565
- E robinhood.loxley@virgin.net
- Beer range varies
- ☺ Quality meals entirely home made using local produce and game in season
- Rural, family run pub close to the Peak District

Tempting dishes are created here by a chef who makes everything from the beef and chicken burgers on the children's menu to fresh pasta and pork and apple sausages, using produce from local suppliers such as butcher Ray Woodhead and Morris Fishmongers. The pub is famed for its meat and potato pies, either £6.95 standard size or £7.95 for one big enough for two. There is no set menu; dishes are chalked on a frequently changing board, including starters such as home-made soup, pickled herring on crème fraîche and rocket or sweet potato cake with spinach and goats' cheese fondue.

When a regular brought in wild mallard it was served as honey-glazed breast with confit leg on a parsnip purée; other dishes could include home-made fishcakes with wilted spinach and white wine sauce, a half pound fresh cod fillet in beer batter, corned beef hash topped with a poached egg at £5.25, the Robin Hood half pound burger, roast cod wrapped in pancetta on potato purée, or vegetarian choices such as vegetable pasty with wild mushroom pickle and curly kale. Mains average £7, up to £11.95 for sirloin steak. The Sunday carvery of roast beef, pork, lamb and turkey including a dozen fresh vegetables is £7.95 for adults, £5.95 children. Beers are often from local micros such as Acorn, Kelham Island and Salamander.

Q S V P C

STRINES
Strines Inn
Bradfield Dale, S6 6JE

▶ Near Sheffield, 2 miles from A57 before Ladybower reservoir
☼ Summer Mon-Sat 10.30am-11pm, Sun 12-10.30pm; winter Mon-Sat 10.30am-3pm, 6-11pm; Sun 12-10.30pm
Ⓨ Summer daily 12-9pm; winter 12-2.30pm, 6-8pm
T (0114) 285 1247
Kelham Island Bitter; Marston's Pedigree; guest
☺ Simple, inexpensive home-made meals
Isolated pub dating from 1275, though most of the building was added later

Unpretentious, all home-cooked food is served here, down to the pâté and soup. Starters include a giant Yorkshire pudding (Strines gives new meaning to the word giant) with onion gravy, smoked mackerel, and garlic mushrooms, £3.95. Among the main dishes the giant Yorkie is back, this time filled with your choice of beef, pork or sausages, accompanied by fresh vegetables, roast potatoes and gravy at £6.95, or the veggie version with cheese or parsley sauce and vegetables, a pound cheaper.

You will also find liver and onions, Mediterranean vegetable hot pot (in another giant Yorkie), the pie of the day with roast potatoes and fresh veg, and Thai mushroom noodles, all £6-£6.95. A giant mixed grill of steak, pork chop, lamb chop, gammon, liver, kidney, sausage and egg with mushroom and chips is £9.75. Fresh fish of the day is on the blackboard, there is a good range of salads and steaks, while snacks include filled jackets, paninis – ham and cheese, bacon and Stilton, roast beef, roast pork – and burgers. It's good to see real food for youngsters at only £3.25, including sausages, home-made pie, spag bol or a small filled Yorkshire pud. Desserts include home-made apple pie and treacle sponge, £3.30, plus luxury ice creams.

★ Q ❀ S V ♿ P C

TICKHILL
Carpenter's Arms
Westgate, DN11 9NE

▶ On regular bus route from Doncaster, Sheffield and Worksop
☼ Tue-Sat 12-11pm; Sun 12-10.30pm
Ⓨ Tue-Sat 12-2pm, 6-8pm; Sun 12-3pm
T (01302) 742839
Black Sheep Best Bitter; Jennings Cumberland Ale; John Smith's Bitter
☺ Good, home-cooked pub favourites in generous portions
Cosy front lounge, adjoining bar and large, no-smoking conservatory where children are welcome

A great pub for a summer evening, the Carpenter's boasts a large, award-winning garden with a crazy golf course – ideal for keeping the children amused while you enjoy a pint in the sunshine. Summer meals are a big hit here too; their salads are splendid – a generous plateful of fresh produce. All the main meals are prepared in the pub kitchen without relying on processed foods, with everything freshly cooked just like mum used to make. The steak and ale pie is a particular favourite, as is the fish that is bought fresh from Edinburgh, in portions so large some call it 'whale and chips'.

The meals are all good value, but on Wednesdays older people get a special deal of a main course followed by ice cream or coffee for £4.95. Home-made desserts such as sherry trifle, fruit crumble or cornflake pie (reminiscent of school dinners) are sometimes available. There is also a hearty snack menu of paninis, nachos and filled jacket potatoes. On Sunday lunchtime booking is essential for the traditional roast that replaces the regular menu, with a choice of lamb or beef for £5.95.

★ ❀ S V ♣ P

BINGLEY
Brown Cow
Ireland Bridge, BD16 2QX

- 100 yards along B6429 from A650 jct
- Mon-Fri 12-3pm, 5-11pm; Sat & Sun 12-11pm
- Daily 12-2.15pm, 6-8.45pm
- T (01274) 564345
- F (01274) 565505
- E prestt@aol.com
- Timothy Taylor Golden Best, Dark Mild, Best Bitter, Landlord, seasonal; guests
- Genuine home-made fare, both traditional and overseas, with especially good vegetarian selection
- Food-based, riverside pub near three and five-rise canal locks

Not only Timothy Taylor's full range, but a wonderful variety of changing guest ales from breweries such as Goose Eye, Kelham Island, Sarah Hughes, Ossett, Daleside and Derwent provide a great opportunity to partner fine beers to all kinds of dishes. The home-cooked food includes starters such as a daily soup, crab cakes or seasonal pâté, followed by main courses including braised liver with sausage and onions, steak and ale pie, chicken and ham pie, chicken and bacon pasta, knuckle of lamb with roast vegetables, Yorkshire pudding with sausages, onion gravy and vegetables, red Thai chicken curry on pilau rice or Mexican chicken pancake, prices from £5.95-£6.95.

Fish includes fish 'n' chips in Taylor's ale batter, salmon in mint marinade, sole stuffed with crabmeat and scallops and king prawn chilli stir fry, while grills start with rump steak and expand to the big Brown Cow mixed grill at £11.95. Six vegetarian dishes include leek and parsnip bake, spinach and ricotta cannelloni, vegetable masala, red pepper and spinach lasagne and veggie quiche of the day. There are salads, too, including bacon with Brie, Thai cod and prawn fishcakes, warm chicken and bacon or Chicken Caesar. Former local CAMRA pub of the season.

★ Q S V (Bingley) P C

BRADFORD
Fighting Cock
21 Preston Street, BD7 1JE

- 1 mile from town centre, off Thornton Road
- Daily 11.30am-11pm
- Daily 12-2.30pm
- T (01274) 726907
- Fuller's London Pride; Old Mill Bitter; Phoenix White Monk; Timothy Taylor Landlord; guests
- Home-made, inexpensive comfort food
- No frills ale house

A combination of cheap 'n' cheerful food and speedy service makes this a popular destination for locals at lunchtime. The food is renowned for its quality – made with fresh ingredients from local markets, and all cooked on the premises. Joints of beef and ham, for instance, are home-cooked, the beef roasted, the ham boiled then oven glazed with honey and Dijon mustard. Home-made soups include leek, broccoli, carrot and coriander and tomato and basil, only £1.10 with bread or £2.60 for soup and a sandwich – the sandwiches are made to order and what you can't eat wrapped up to take away.

Lunchtime dishes include home-made chilli with granary bread, shepherd's pie with cheese topping, chicken tikka masala with pitta, beef stew served with bread, large Yorkshire puddings with various fillings from roast beef or stew to chilli, and vegetarian chilli, prices £2.60 to £3.75. There are plenty of snacks, too: ploughman's lunch of beef, ham, cheese, pork pie and salad at £3.95, regular and special sandwiches starting at £1.95 leading up to the big docker's wedge stuffed with beef, ham, cheese and salad for £3.70, pie and peas at £1.50 or jacket potatoes with all sorts of fillings, £2.20. With 12 real ales including changing guests, real cider and Belgian bottled beers, there is plenty to drink with your food at Bradford CAMRA Pub of the Year 2004.

S V C

BURLEY WOODHEAD
Hermit Inn
LS29 7AS

- ▶ From Ilkley, moor road towards Menson – 3 miles off A65
- Mon-Sat 11.30am-3pm, 5.30-11pm; Sun 12-10.30pm
- Mon-Sat 11.30am-2pm, 5.30-8.30pm; Sun 12-2.30pm
- T (01943) 863204
- John Smith's Bitter; Taylor Landlord; Tetley Bitter; Theakston BB
- ☺ Traditional English with a twist - the chef is known in the area for his fish dishes
- 300-year-old stone built hostelry in hamlet on Ilkley Moor

Named after an 18th-century resident of Burley moor, the pub serves hearty and traditional food using local produce – meat is from the nearby butcher's, the morning's fish from Fleetwood. Fresh haddock in batter and halibut steaks are readily available while other dishes appear as specials, such as Italian fish stew or smoked haddock and prawn crumble. Further specials might be savoury suet puddings, home-made pies such as corned beef and potato or chicken, mushroom and ham or duck breast with honey and spring onions, chicken with leeks and Stilton, smoked salmon and chicken roulade, pork loin with cider and apples.

Two separate dining areas are both no smoking, with food served throughout at lunchtime, in the evening dining room only. The main menu provides chilli-spiced crab cakes and cheese and broccoli melters among the starters, priced £2.25-£2.95. Main meals include home-made steak, Guinness and mushroom pie, authentic chicken tikka masala, Mississippi style chicken breast, double pork chops, American style corned beef hash, roast of the day, salads and vegetarian choices, mainly £6-£7. Steaks are dearer though, with a good value mixed grill at £10.95. A traditional roast Sunday lunch is served.

★ Q ❀ S V ♿ P ⚡ 👫 C

CLECKHEATON
☆ Commercial
33 Bradford Road, BD19 3JN

- ▶ On A638 nearly opposite town hall
- Daily 12-11pm (Sun 10.30pm)
- Daily 12-2pm (Sun 3pm)
- T (01274) 878745
- W www.thecommercialinn.com
- Tetley Bitter; guests
- ☺ Traditional menu with weekly specials
- 1830s stone town pub with cosy snug, retaining some original features

Some regulars eat most days at the Commercial, and who could blame them? Using fresh meat, vegetables, eggs and bread delivered by the same local suppliers over many years, landlady Vivien Laycock dishes up great home cooking at low prices every lunchtime. There are weekly specials such as venison and red wine pie with mashed potato and (joy) buttered cabbage, braised steak and onions in Yorkshire pudding, or something more exotic such as chicken in lime and coriander sauce with rice and stir fry vegetables.

But the set menu is also tempting – roast beef, pork or lamb with all the trimmings, steak and Black Sheep ale pie topped with shortcrust pastry, Cumberland sausages in a big Yorkie with mash and loads of gravy, her own recipe chicken curry and chilli con carne, or three-egg omelettes – prices £4.95-£5.25. A good range of sandwiches includes the famous home roast silverside of beef or leg of pork at £3.15, and there are filled jacket potatoes plus 'loaded' chunky chips with toppings. Sunday lunch with a choice of four roasts plus minced beef and onion suet roly poly is £7.50 for two courses, £8.75 for three. Desserts range from 'very spotty' spotted dick to baked jam roly poly with custard and key lime pie. No smoking at lunchtime only.

★ S V ♿ P ⚡ 👫

DEWSBURY

☆ West Riding Licensed Refreshment Rooms

Railway Station, Wellington Road, WF13 1HF

- ▶ On platform 2, Dewsbury Station
- Mon-Sat 11am-11pm; Sun 12-10.30pm
- Mon-Fri 12-3pm; Tues & Wed 6-9pm
- T (01924) 459193
- F (01924) 450404
- E info@wrlrr.demon.co.uk
- W www.wrlrr.co.uk
- Black Sheep Best Bitter; Taylor Landlord; guests
- ☺ High quality, good value home-cooked meals including vegetarian and vegan
- Reclaimed railway waiting rooms on Trans-Pennine rail ale trail

Food and ale so good you're bound to miss your train – though you can eat and drink at Dewsbury Station even if you're going nowhere. Carefully prepared with fresh ingredients from local producers, lunch menus change daily and always include several vegan and vegetarian options, summed up by the Guardian as 'simple food cooked with a generous heart…at possibly Yorkshire's finest pub'.

Popular dishes include sausage and leek hotch potch, honey mustard pork, shepherd's pie with parsnip mash and cabbage, lamb and mint pie, oriental beef noodles and salad, garlic lemon chicken legs on colcannon, salmon fish cakes with lemon butter sauce and sausage and black pudding cake with rich tomato sauce (recipe in guide). Vegetarian meals included roast sweet potatoes with mushrooms and spinach, mushroom pots with filo topping, spicy bean burgers, mushroom curry in naan bread and spinach pasta with aubergine and tomatoes. Main meals cost just £3.25-£4.50. Tuesday night is pie night, Wednesday night curry night. The 'pub' celebrated its 10th anniversary in 2004, and serves up to eight real ales at a time including Yorkshire micros, a local mild and one from the Anglo Dutch Brewery.

★ S V (Dewsbury) P

HAWORTH

Haworth Old Hall

Sun Street, BD22 8BP

- ▶ Eight miles W of Bradford, 3 miles S of Keighley
- Daily 12-11pm (10.30pm Sun)
- Mon-Sat 12-3pm, 5.30-9pm; Sun 12-4pm, 5-8pm
- T (01535) 642709
- F (01535) 647857
- W www.hawortholdhall.co.uk
- Jennings Bitter, Cocker Hoop, guests
- ☺ Traditional British cooking with an extensive menu
- Tudor manor house with much of its character preserved, including stone floors, mullioned window and a huge fireplace

In stunning countryside, and because of its Brontë connections, Haworth is one of the most visited villages in the Pennines and the pub can get very busy at the weekend. It offers an extensive menu, starting with a good range of hot and cold sandwiches and ciabattas and a basic children's menu. The evening menu carries a few more choices than at lunchtime.

For starters choose from tropical prawn cocktail, Thai fish bites, deep fried Brie, moules marinière (small or large portions) or Old Hall's black pudding (three slices with bacon and tomato in a creamy white wine and mustard sauce), all under a fiver. In the evening there's also duck breast, fig and walnut salad, trio of melon and wild berry coulis or Greek salad. Red wine features in a lot of dishes here – chicken, lamb and beef steak are all braised to produce heart-warming dishes. Other main courses, £7-£11.50, include steaks, roast rack of lamb, medallions of beef fillet and pork fillet Calvados. Roast beef is served every day and there is a daily curry. Fish lovers will find hot salmon, dill and cucumber salad, pan-fried king prawns or a catch of the day; for vegetarians there is a choice of cherry tomato and red onion croute or mushroom stroganoff.

S V (Haworth) P C

JACKSON BRIDGE
Red Lion
Sheffield Road, HD9 7HB

- On A616 above the village
- Daily 12-11pm (10.30pm Sun)
- Mon-Sat 12-2pm, 6-8.30pm (not Mon); Sun 1-4pm
- T (01484) 683499
- E enquiries@the-red-lion-inn.com
- W www.the-red-lion-inn.com
- Adnams Bitter; Caledonian Deuchars IPA; Greene King IPA; Tetley Bitter; guest
- Home-cooked fare; mostly traditional British dishes
- Victorian coaching inn with a central bar, beamed lounge and dining room

The Bells took over the Red Lion in August 2003 and the following summer they were awarded Pub of the Season by local CAMRA. A simple lunchtime specials menu offers a limited choice of traditional pub dishes, two courses for £6.95, or three courses for another £1. Alternatively you can have sandwiches, a ploughman's or hot snacks, all at very reasonable prices.

In the evening there are various starters for around £3-£4, such as breaded mushrooms, black tiger prawns sautéed in olive oil and garlic or a mixed platter of chicken goujons, Thai battered prawns, or potato wedges, all served with dips. To follow there is a good choice of steaks, with or without sauces, supplied by the local farm shop, £8.95 for a plain 8oz rump to £13.25 for a fillet with sauce. House specialities, £7-£9.50, include Spanish chicken, braised lamb shank with redcurrants and rosemary, home-made steak and ale pie or veggie options such as Brie and broccoli pithivier or mushroom tortellini. There is a choice of four fish dishes including salmon fillet with hollandaise sauce, £7.95. Desserts, all £3, are old favourites such as treacle sponge, hot chocolate fudge cake or toffee banoffee. On Tuesday and Friday evenings enjoy live jazz and blues piano.

★ S V C

LEES MOOR
Quarry House Inn
Bingley Road, BD21 5QE

- At mini roundabout A629/A6033 jct take Bingley Road
- Daily 12-3pm, 7-11.30pm (Fri & Sat midnight)
- Daily 12-2pm, 7.30-10.30pm
- T (01525) 642239
- Timothy Taylor Golden Best, Best Bitter, Landlord; Tetley Bitter
- Local traditional dishes and fresh fish using seasonal and market produce
- Converted farmhouse with extensive views run by same family since 1982; three-times local CAMRA Pub of the Season

Celebrating 20 consecutive years in CAMRA's Good Beer Guide, the Quarry House remains a beacon for well-kept real ale – Timothy Taylor's range – and real food. A sample selection from the specials board might be bacon-wrapped grilled black pudding with spiced fruit chutney, hot chorizo sausage with sautéed new potatoes, pork tenderloin in cider cream sauce with bramley apple purée, pan-fried duck breast with cherry brandy sauce, fillet steak on bubble and squeak, chicken supreme filled with cream cheese, chives and mushrooms wrapped in bacon, rib eye steak with teriyaki and ginger sauce or the local butcher's pork and leek sausages on cheese mash with onion gravy.

On the fresh fish board you could find grilled Portuguese sardines, butterfish on a bed of leaf spinach, fresh haddock in crisp beer batter, oven baked grouper with peppers or cod loin marinated in Italian style herbs. Veggie choices might be halloumi cheese with cherry tomato and black olive sauce or field mushrooms topped with spinach and tomato risotto. In addition the set menu offers a full selection of grills and steaks, £6.25-£13.95, and Yorkshire meat and potato pie. A four-course Sunday lunch with roast topside, locally-reared pork leg and lamb is £10.95 for adults, £5.95 children.

★ S V P C

OAKWORTH
Grouse Inn
Harehills Lane, BD22 0RX

▶ Follow B6142 through Oakworth
☼ Daily 12-11 (10.30pm Sun)
🍴 Daily 12-9 (8.30pm Sun)
T (01535) 643073
E greatfood@grouse-inn.co.uk
W www.grouse-inn.co.uk
🍺 Timothy Taylor Golden Best, Best Bitter, Landlord; guest
☺ Comprehensive selection of English, Mediterranean and more
◙ Rural pub with log fires close to Oakworth Valley steam railway

The Grouse Inn does serve grouse, plus plenty more locally shot game – teal, snipe, woodcock, wild duck, pigeon, rabbit, hare, pheasant and partridge. All bread is home made on the premises, along with freshly prepared soups, desserts, pickles, chutneys, pâtés and real Yorkshire puddings. A daily changing specials board featuring fresh produce offers fish four times a week, meat five, and cheese – they're obviously counting – twice a week. Sounds like rationing!

Starters include home-made soup, Cajun chicken with spinach salad and field mushrooms with crisp bacon topped with melting Brie. Regular main dishes are a large slice of the home-made pie of the day, real home-made sausages with cheddar and chive mash, seafood royale, roast of the day with Yorkie, beef stew braised with bacon topped with horseradish dumplings, prices around £8-£9. There are veggie choices, and kids' meals include roast dinner, lasagne, sausage and mash and home-made chips. 'We cook from the land to table and from moor to table in an hour,' is the promise at the Grouse, with meals costing from £5.95-£15. And in good weather you can eat on a large patio with stunning views over the moors.

♛ ❀ **S V** 🍺 ♿ ⇌ (Oakworth Valley Steam Railway) ♣ ● Ⓟ ⚡ 👪 **C**

RIPPONDEN
Old Bridge Inn
Priest Lane, HX6 4DF

▶ M62, J22, on River Ryburn over bridge from parish church
☼ Mon-Fri 12-3pm, 5.30 (5 Fri)-11pm; Sat & Sun 12-11pm (Sun 10.30pm)
🍴 Daily 12-2pm, 6.30-9.30pm (not Sat & Sun)
T (01422) 822595
W www.porkpieclub.com
🍺 Timothy Taylor Golden Best, Best Bitter, Landlord; guests
☺ Modern English with a touch of tradition
◙ Picturesque pub dated 1307 by humpback bridge on Calderdale Way

With true Yorkshire logic, the Old Bridge is the home of the Pork Pie Club but you won't find pork pies on the menu – instead the landlord kindly allows a little group of pork pie fanciers to bring in prime specimens for tastings (read all about it on their fascinating website). What you will find are rather more offbeat eats including starters such as smoke-cured salmon pikelets with dill and lime crème fraîche, devilled Whitby crab with a touch of Thai spice, black pudding and halloumi salad with pineapple and star anis glaze, as well as home-made soup, £3.50-£4.75.

Main meals might be slow roast shoulder of lamb with red wine, honey and rosemary served on champ, smoked haddock and spinach pancakes with cream and Parmesan, salmon steak wrapped in Black Forest ham on dill, lemon and rocket couscous, Greek style shepherd's pie, Gressingham duck breast with apricot, honey and fennel or hot smoked sea bass on mung bean wilted spinach and potato, plus a traditional meat and potato pie, prices £7-£9.95. The dearest dish is prime beef fillet on potato dauphinois with exotic mushrooms, at £11.75, and vegetarians could find Mediterranean vegetable and goats' cheese wraps, £6.75. All home-made puds are £3.50.

★ ♛ **Q** ❀ **S V** ♿ Ⓟ ⚡ 👪 **C**

WALES

CADOXTON
Crown & Sceptre Inn
Main Road, SA10 8AP

- On A4230 near Neath centre
- Monday 5-11pm; Tue-Fri 12-3pm, 5-11pm; Sat 11-11pm; Sun 12-10.30pm
- Tue-Sun 12.30-2.30pm, from 5.30pm
- T (01639) 642145
- E crownandsceptreinn@tiscali.co.uk
- W www.crownandsceptreinn.co.uk
- Draught Bass; Tomos Watkin OSB; guest
- Freshly-cooked, home-made meals including traditional Welsh dishes
- Former coach house near Neath town centre and tourist attractions, popular with local community

The inn's stables have been converted into a restaurant that has earned an excellent reputation for its fine food including Welsh and Italian dishes. Starters range from home-made soup, £3.25, to king prawns in a garlic, herb and white wine liquor, £5.25; or there is oak-smoked Scottish salmon with a wasabí cream, or a warm salad of chorizo sausage with new potatoes and chive mayonnaise. Main courses feature local produce: Welsh lamb noisettes on a bed of lyonnaise potato in a rich minted jus, and Welsh black steaks, either a fillet or a sirloin cooked to your liking, served plain or with a peppercorn cream sauce or port and blue cheese sauce, £14-£17. Roast loin of English pork comes with creamed potato and Marsala sauce, while chicken breasts can be simply sautéed and served in a white wine sauce or stuffed with char-grilled red peppers, Welsh goats' cheese and fresh thyme then pan roasted, both £10.95. Pasta and fish dishes, such as fresh cod fillet wrapped in pancetta and served with Neapolitan sauce, are priced at around £9. The vegetarian tartlet glazed with Welsh goats' cheese is £7.25. Desserts include hand-made chocolate and orange Italian gateau or tipsy red berry trifle, both £3.95. A popular bar menu to suit all tastes as well as daily specials are served in the lounge.

Q V (Neath) C

MACHEN
Nant y Ceisiad (White Hart)
CF83 8QQ

- 100 yards N of A468 at W end of village
- Mon-Fri 11.30am-3pm, 6pm-midnight; Sat 12-midnight; Sun 12-10.30pm
- Daily 11.30am-3pm, 6-10pm
- T (01633) 441005
- Beer range varies
- Traditional pub food
- Independent free house with four guest beers; rambling old building incorporates panels and fittings from the liner Empress of France

A typical pub menu features simple dishes at modest prices, starting with home-made soups that may be oxtail, leek and potato or spring vegetables, priced £2.25 with a roll. Other starters are deep-fried whitebait, pâté such as duck and orange or chicken liver and bacon, deep-fried mushrooms and prawn cocktail. The daily specials board offers pub classics including cottage pie, meat and potato pie or steak and ale pie, liver and bacon or sausages and mash with vegetables at around £5, though small gammon or small fish meals (favoured by pensioners) come in at just £2.99 at lunchtime. There is a good selection of decent steaks, 8oz rump or sirloin, 12oz T-bone, 8oz fillet, priced £8.50-£14.95 will full accompaniments, or the big 16oz mixed grill at £11.50.

The set menu also offers omelettes made freshly to order starting at £4.10, with fillings of your choice from cheese or ham to gammon with pineapple or egg and chips, plus half a roast chicken, home-made lasagne and a selection of bought-in curries including Welsh Dragon and lamb and leek. There are salads, filled jacket potatoes and ploughman's. Sunday lunch offers a choice of roast topside beef and Welsh lamb plus either pork or turkey with all the trimmings at £5.50 a plateful.

★ S V C

PONTYPRIDD

☆ Bunch of Grapes

Ynysangharad Road, CF37 4DA

Mon-Sat 11am-11pm; Sun 12-10.30pm
Mon-Sat 12-2.30pm, 6.30-9.30pm; Sun 12-3.30pm
T (01443) 402934
E info@bunchofgrapes.org.uk
W www.bunchofgrapes.org.uk
Wye Valley HPA; guests
Gastropub offering modern British cuisine featuring locally-sourced ingredients
Friendly pub close to the town centre; now serves its own ales after opening the Otley Brewing Co in July 2005

Everything is freshly made on the premises, from the bread to the speciality desserts by the pub's French chef, with as much produce as possible sourced locally including meat from the butcher with his own abattoir selling only locally farmed livestock. And the pub is now building up a repertoire of dishes using its own beer after opening the Otley Brewing Co last year – though cooks also have a range of 30 bottled beers from round the world to choose from.

The menu changes frequently but sample dishes include starters such as home-made soup or grilled mackerel fillet with cucumber salsa, light meals from laver bread with Talgarth ham to home-made Welsh beef burgers from only £2.80, and excellent sandwiches such as caramelised red onion with melted Celtic blue cheese. Lunchtime main meals might be char-grilled swordfish at £8.50 or a hearty mixed grill with hand-cut chips at £12.95. Veggie dishes are equally impressive – Thai style noodles with pak choi, straw mushrooms and Thai aubergine in sweet chilli sauce, or kebab of summer vegetables on truffle oil mash. In the evening you might also expect steamed seabass with lemongrass, chilli and galangal on lime-scented rice, pan-fried Barbary duck with vanilla and celeriac mash and spiced rhubarb sauce, or char-grilled Welsh sirloin steak.

♨ Q ❀ S V ⊞ ♿ ♣ ● Ⓟ ⚟ ⚇ C

Martin Mitchell has won countless awards at the Johnsburn House pub in Balerno near Edinburgh. Here is his recipe for rather special sausages.

BEEF, WILD MUSHROOM & TARRAGON BANGERS WITH POTATO PURÉE, ONION MARMALADE AND BALSAMIC GRAVY

Serves 8

1kg (2lbs) Maris Piper potatoes
100ml (3½ fl oz) extra virgin olive oil
1kg (2lb) Scottish minced beef (not too lean)
500g (1lb) mixed wild mushrooms
250g (8oz) unsalted butter
1 kg (2lb) onions
2 tbsps fresh, chopped tarragon
150ml (¼ pint) sweet Madeira
500g (1lb) pig's caul
1 tbsp brown sugar
250ml (½ pint) good, aged balsamic vinegar
500 ml (1 pint) excellent reduced stock
1 carrot, 1 courgette, 1 leek, 1 small celeriac, 1 medium parsnip all shredded, deep fried and kept warm on absorbent paper
Salt & pepper

Cook potatoes, season, and make into purée with the olive oil. Process beef in food processor. Slice mushrooms, saute in butter with half a chopped onion, reduce down, add Madeira, reduce down till almost dry, season well with salt and pepper, add tarragon when cooled slightly and mix into the beef. Form into 16 sausages, wrap in pig's caul, cling film and tin foil then steam in a cool bamboo steamer for 30 minutes. Peel and slice the rest of the onions, sweat in a little butter, reduce until light brown, add sugar and half the balsamic vinegar, reduce to marmalade consistency and season. Let sausages cool slightly then fry in oil and butter to caramelise. Place circle of potato in centre of a hot plate, and top with 2 crossed sausages. Add onion marmalade to reduced stock and pour over. Top with fried vegetable garnish.

ABERGAVENNY

Angel Hotel

15 Cross Street, NP7 5EN

- ▶ Town centre, near market
- Daily 11.30am-2.30pm, 6-11pm
- 12-2.30pm, 6.30-10pm
- T (01873) 857121
- E mail@angelhotelabergavenny.com
- W www.angelhotelabergavenny.com
- Draught Bass; Brains Rev James; guests
- Mix of contemporary and traditional British dishes
- Popular town centre coaching inn with real ale in the atmospheric Foxhunter Bar, with interesting local paintings and open fire

Local produce is very important at the Angel and includes home-reared venison, lamb, beef, pork, sausages and free range eggs from the Welsh Venison Centre, Bwlch, stone oven baked breads from Malvern, Black Mountain Smokery salmon and kippers, home-reared Gloucester Old Spot pork plus clotted cream from Bower Farm dairy, farmhouse cheese from Bath, game from Llanarth estate and fresh fish 'from named Cornish boats'. With it they cook up sheer temptation, such as chef/director Mark Turton's signature dish of papardelle with rabbit and Guinness broth. Fish is seasonal but could include crayfish risotto, grilled scallops and squid with chorizo, poached organic salmon or seared red mullet with seabass and saffron poached vegetables, prices from £9.60-£12.

Meat dishes might be lamb navarin with mash and cauliflower, Gressingham duck breast with redcurrant, BBQ pork ribs with cider vinegar slaw or loin of Gloucester Old Spot with cabbage and sage gravy. Egg dishes include a Spanish omelette made with home salted cod, while vegetarians might enjoy wild mushroom risotto or Tuscan vegetable stew with beans, cabbage and pesto. Desserts include Scotch pancakes with whisky ice cream and caraway seed parfait with orange compote.

S V (Abvergavenny)
P C

CLYTHA

☆ Clytha Arms

NP7 9BW

- ▶ On B4598 3 miles from Raglan and 6 miles from Abergavenny
- Tue-Fri 12-3.30pm; Mon-Fri 6-11pm; Sat 12-11pm; Sun 12-10.30pm
- Tue-Sun 12.30-2.30pm; daily 7-9.30pm
- T (01873) 840206
- W www.clytha-arms.com
- Draught Bass; Felinfoel Best Bitter; Hook Norton Best Bitter; guests
- Award-winning food
- Old dower house set in beautiful, extensive grounds near the River Usk, with four en suite guest rooms

A frequent local CAMRA Pub of the Year, the Clytha has won several food awards. Always a part of the annual Welsh Beer and Cheese Festival and the Welsh Cider Festival, ciders and perries are also on tap. The bar snack menu - already comprehensive with everything from smoked salmon and scrambled eggs, wild mushrooms in an omelette or ragoût, to faggots in beer and onion gravy or wild boar sausages, £6-£8.50 - also now offers a selection of tapas chalked on the blackboard at £3.50 a dish. All meals are home cooked, mostly from local ingredients (although the fish is from Cornwall); regular customers often exchange game for beer!

The restaurant offers some inspired combinations; for starters there are leek and laverbread rissoles with beetroot chutney, £6.50, oysters in beer batter with Thai sauce for £7.25, or bacon, cockles and fresh pasta. Mains include pork tenderloin and black pudding kebab with apples and Calvados, £15 and fillet steak with Madeira and cèpes. A trio of fish is served with beurre blanc, while sewin comes with crab, crayfish and laverbread, both £15.50. A set menu is served daily: £16.95 for two courses or £18.95 for three, with several choices. Refreshing desserts include tequila and citrus iced soufflé, or pavlova with tropical fruit.

Q S V P C

PANTYGELLI

☆ Crown

Old Hereford Road, NP7 7HR

- ▶ Off A465, 4 miles north of Abergavenny
- Mon 6-11pm; Tue-Fri 12-2.30pm, 6-11pm; Sat 11-3pm, 6-11pm; Sun 12-3pm, 6-10.30pm
- Daily 12-2pm, 7-9pm
- T (01873) 853314
- E crown@pantygelli.com
- W www.thecrownatpantygelli.com
- Draught Bass; Brains Rev James, Hancock's HB; guests
- ☺ Traditional home-made dishes supplemented by more adventurous specials
- Family owned, welcoming rural pub benefiting from superb views of the Skirrid Mountain from an attractive terrace

Chef Mark previously worked for Marco Pierre White and now, with two assistants, cooks all meals at the Crown to order, from fresh ingredients. Light meals are served at lunchtime: home-cooked ham salad with chips, home-cured salt beef in a mustard sauce with mash, marinated herring niçoise or a platter of meat antipasti served with roasted red peppers and olives. Non-meat starters include leek and potato mornay and penne pasta served with red pepper, olive and tomato sauce.

In the evenings a good selection of starters is usually boosted by several specials such as bresola ham and parmesan served on mixed leaves, a salad of squid and chorizo, or home made terrine with sticky onion jam, mostly around £5. The specials board may list oriental crispy pork served with crunchy spring onion salad in a peanut and soy dressing as a starter for £4.75 or main course, £9.50. Other main course specials are Welsh lamb served on roasted fennel, chilli and garlic accompanied by an exotic fruit sauce, magret of duck with balsamic flavoured Puy lentils, red peppers and pancetta ham, salmon fillet with a red pepper and paprika dressing, or how about chump of free range Welsh pork on a bodega ham wrapped saffron risotto with tomato, olive and red pepper sauce (a mouthful to say let alone digest!). Home made desserts, all £4, include passionfruit and lemon posset and chocolate pots with praline topping.

★ Q S V ● ♿ ♣ P C

SKENFRITH
Bell
NP7 8UH

- B4521, halfway between Abergavenny and Ross-on-Wye
- Mon-Sat 11am-11pm; Sun 12-10.30pm
- Daily 12-2.30pm, 7-9.30pm
- T (01600) 750235
- F (01600) 750525
- E enquiries@skenfrith.co.uk
- W www.skenfrith.co.uk
- Breconshire Golden Valley; Freeminer Bitter; Taylor Landlord
- Modern English and Welsh cuisine
- 17th-century coaching inn with open fire and B&B accommodation in unspoilt village

Head chef Kurt Fleming recently retired from the Welsh Olympic culinary team. The Bell is a pub that 'tries to minimise food miles', from free range eggs ('great double yolkers for breakfast') to venison, pheasant, partridge, pigeon and rabbit shot by the landlord, perry pears, quinces and medlars from the landlord's orchard, fish from Abergavenny fish market – not forgetting Hywel in the village growing organic salad just for the Bell! Dishes with a local flavour include cawl, leek tart, home cured Welsh whisky gravadlax, lavabread, Welsh Black sirloin and Usk sewin.

Starters and light meals include cream of broccoli and blue cheese soup, home-grown basil and goat's cheese pannacotta, or locally smoked duck with hoisin mayo, prices from £4.50-£7. Lunchtime main courses include roast black bream with black olive tapenade, wild mushroom risotto cake or grilled Welsh sirloin with mustard hollandaise, £14.50-£16. Evening starters could be chicken and pepper mousse wrapped in proscuito or ham hock and apricot terrine, around £6.50, maybe followed by roast duck with chorizo and butterbean cassoulet or red onion, tomato and goats' cheese tart, £14-£17. Bread and chips are home made, likewise puds such as pineapple tarte tatin with Madagascan ice cream, all £5.50.

Q S V P C

TINTERN
Cherry Tree Inn
Forge Road, NP16 6TH

- Off A466 at Royal George Hotel
- Daily 12-11pm
- Mon-Sat 12-3pm, 6-9pm; Sun 12-3pm, 6-8pm
- T (01291) 689292
- E Steve@thecherrytree.co.uk
- W www.thecherry.co.uk
- Hancock's HB; guests
- Honest home cooked fare
- Over 30 years in Good Beer Guide; four ensuite B&B rooms, shop and post office

It's so rare to find real food on a children's menu – even in pubs in this Guide – that I'll mention it first. Jamie Oliver would be thrilled to bring his kids to eat at the Cherry Tree where they could choose roast chicken with fresh vegetables, pasta with tomato and basil sauce and grated cheddar, home-made pizza, home-cooked ham or cheese salad with fries, and home-made freshly battered cod bites, prices £2.95-£3.95.

Adults will be tempted, too, by a lunch menu with starters such as wild boar pâté or pea and ham soup, followed by main courses including cod in fresh batter, gammon, egg, pineapple and chips, tandoori chicken, or rib eye steak with salad and home-made fries, priced £5.95-£7.95. There are as many, if not more, veggie choices from Mediterranean olive, feta and couscous salad to sweet pepper and sundried tomato quiche, not forgetting mixed cheese ploughman's, all £5.95. Filled jacket spuds include wild red salmon and mayo.

Sunday lunch offers a splendid choice – Sunday roasts all £5.95 of local Welsh beef and Yorkshire pudding, roast lamb or chicken with all the trimmings, nut cutlets with sherry gravy, butcher's faggots and mustard mash, liver and bacon casserole, tuna and king prawns on fresh tagliatelle or tomato, basil, celery and sweet potato casserole with caraway dumpling. The supper menu changes daily.

Q S V P C

TINTERN
Moon & Sixpence
Monmouth Road, NP16 5SG

- In the village on A466, 7 miles from Chepstow race course
- Summer 11-11pm; winter Mon-Thu 12-3pm, 5.30-11pm; Fri & Sat 12-11pm; Sun 11-10.30pm
- Daily 12-2.30pm, 6-9pm; summer cream teas 12-6pm
- T (01291) 689284
- F (01600) 860322
- E info@themoonandsixpence.co.uk
- W www.themoonandsixpence.co.uk
- Beer range varies
- Good value, traditional pub fare
- Multi-roomed pub featuring an unusual natural spring fed indoor pond

The Moon and Sixpence was recently taken over by the Zsigos who also run the Good Beer Guide listed Lion Inn at nearby Trellech. Their commitment extends to all aspects of their business, including the meals served at the Moon, where the food is proper pub fare rather than anything exotic.

Vegetarians are very well catered for here, with a menu devoted to home-made meat-free dishes, such as leek and mushroom pasta, vegetable kiev, mushroom stroganoff and rice or vegetable curry, all around £6-£7. Three-egg omelettes are also on offer – plain for £6 or with various fillings for £6.40, and fish dishes, such as cod and chips or salmon supreme in a white wine and dill sauce.

The snack menu lists a fair choice of filled baguettes or jacket spuds, plus ploughman's, salads and good old fashioned basket meals such as scampi or home roasted chicken and chips for around a fiver. The main menu offers all the usual pub favourites, again all home made, including steak and kidney pie, liver, bacon and onions, chilli with rice or a curry of the day and a good choice of steaks and grills. Prices range from £7 to £13.95 for a massive mixed grill.

★ ❀ S V Ⓟ ⅍ C

This recipe comes from the Lion Inn at Trellech in Gwent where you're sure of a warm Hungarian welcome. Don't reduce the amounts as it will affect the recipe – however, it does freeze well.

HUNGARIAN PAPRIKA CHICKEN
Serves 10-12

Oil for frying
2 medium onions, finely diced
3 cloves garlic, finely chopped
8 tsps paprika
1 tsp chilli powder
1 tsp ground black pepper
1 tsp medium curry powder
½ tsp ground ginger
1 cup hot water
30 chicken drumsticks
1 large tin chopped tomatoes
100g (4oz) tomato purée
Hot chicken stock
3 green and 2 red peppers, sliced into strips

To serve
Plain boiled rice
Sour cream

Pour a little oil into a large, heavy based saucepan and lightly fry the onions until soft but not coloured, stir in garlic and gently fry. Add paprika and cook for two minutes stirring constantly to prevent burning, add chilli powder, black pepper, curry powder and ginger with hot water, stir and bring to a simmer. Add the chicken drumsticks and stir to coat in the sauce. Add the chopped tomatoes and tomato purée, then enough hot chicken stock to just cover. Finally, add the pepper and bring to the boil. Reduce to a very gentle simmer, cover and cook for around an hour, until the chicken is tender and cooked through, the sauce thick and aromatic (during cooking top up with a little hot water if needed).

To serve, place three drumsticks on cooked rice, top with pepper slices, cover with a generous ladle of sauce and a large dollop of sour cream.

TRELLECH

☆ Lion Inn

NP25 4PA

- ▶ B4293 between Chepstow and Monmouth
- Daily 12-3pm, 6 (7 Mon, 6.30 Sat)-11pm; closed Sun eve
- Daily 12-2pm; eves, until 9.30pm
- T (01600) 860322
- E tom@lioninn.co.uk
- W www.lioninn.co.uk
- Beer range varies
- Award-winning, home-made food with Hungarian dishes a speciality
- Busy pub close to three ancient Trellech standing stones; Grade II listed, exposed beams, large dining area

The cooking landlord and landlady Tom and Debbie Zsigo use local suppliers including a Chepstow butcher sourcing meat from his family farm, not forgetting Orchard cider from Brockweir and regular beers from Bath Ales, Archers or Wye Valley. The pub is well known for Hungarian specials such as peasant dish rakott krumpli of potato and Hungarian sausage baked in sour cream, chicken breast stuffed with apricot, cherries and cheese, sweet peppers filled with minced pork and rice, turkey Budapest and paprika chicken, £9.75-£12.75, plus specially imported hot pickled peppers.

But there is plenty more to please, from home-made bar meals such as lasagne, cottage pie, freshly cooked filled baguettes or ham, egg and chips, to a specialist fish board, Thai curry board, and endlessly changing specials – lamb with port and cranberry, pan fried red snapper, Russian style monkfish, South African game grill, pork in sweet and creamy pickle, kedgeree, kangaroo steak or duck breast in cherry sauce, to name a few. The veggie section includes secret recipe Welsh and Buck rarebits, home-made hot pot, Brittany slice (home made cheese and tomato pasty) or nut Wellington Provençale. Not all credit cards are accepted. Limited wheelchair access.

★ Q S V P C

USK

Nag's Head Inn

Twyn Square, NP15 1BH

- ▶ 1 mile from A449
- Mon-Sat 11am-2.30pm, 5.30-11pm; Sun 12-3pm, 6.30-10.30pm
- Daily 12-2pm, 6-9.30pm
- T (01291) 672820
- F (01291) 673770
- W www.nagshead-usk.co.uk
- Brains Buckley's BB, SA, Rev James
- Traditional British known for game, but good vegetarian choice too
- Delightful, 500-year-old hostelry, family run for past 40 years; main bar with beams and old pictures, snug with etched windows

The Nag's Head is especially known for its game dishes, such as pheasant cooked in port, half a guinea fowl with wine and fig sauce, brace of quail, boned and filled with home-made stuffing, wild boar steak with apricot and brandy sauce, priced from £13-£15. All home-cooked using local ingredients where possible, other special dishes include fresh Scotch salmon, simply poached, Scotch pies, a 10oz veal chop with grilled tomatoes and mushrooms or five fat crevettes cooked in their shells with garlic butter.

The regular menu offers frogs' legs in Provençal sauce or escargots with garlic butter among the starters, plus a pint of prawns, home-made soup with hot buttered toast, fresh grilled sardines, avocado with smoked salmon, from £3.90-£6. Main meals include home-made rabbit pie at £8 with potatoes and fresh vegetables, the renowned steak pie for £7, ham platter of cold, home-cooked ham or cod in batter. The vegetarian selection is better than many – Glamorgan sausage of cheese and leek, with chilli relish, vegetable pancakes, pepper boats filled with rice, pine nuts and mushrooms or the splendid Llandenny bake - layers of carrot and orange, cauliflower cheese with mustard, minty peas, mushrooms with garlic on a spicy apricot sauce, all £7.95.

★ Q S V C

BEGUILDY
Radnorshire Arms
LD7 1YE

- On B4355
- Mon-Sat 9am-12.30am; Fri & Sat 9am-1am
- Daily 7-9pm plus Sunday lunch
- T (01547) 510634
- E peter@angle1.demon.co.uk
- Fuller's London Pride; Tetley Bitter; guest
- Traditional dishes using fresh meat and vegetables
- 15th-century drovers' inn with real fire

All dishes are freshly prepared and cooked to order, salads locally sourced, and local meat bought daily –there is no frozen meat on the menu. Sample main courses could be a lamb hock in mint gravy with vegetables, salmon in lemon butter with salad or vegetables, deep-fried lemon pepper haddock with peas, beef fajitas with cheese topping and salad, 10oz Welsh gammon steak with egg or pineapple, and a choice of beef steaks – 10oz Welsh sirloin or 8oz Welsh fillet – accompanied by chasseur, hollandaise or pepper sauces at £1.50 extra. Main meals, accompanied by new potatoes, fries or jacket potato, are priced at £6.95 up to £12.95 for fillet steak. The vegetarian choice includes potato, cheese and leek bake or Stilton and vegetable crumble, both with salad or vegetables, at £6.95. There are also curries – vegetable dopiaza or chicken madras – both with pilau rice and naan bread at £6.95. A selection of desserts includes Bramley apple pie, summer meringue nest, raspberry and hazelnut roulade, chocolate 'lumpy bumpy', banana split, rum and raisin pudding with rum sauce, or Scotch pancakes with maple syrup, most served with cream or ice cream or both, all £3.25. Roast Sunday lunches also use fresh local chicken or joints of meat, again with fresh vegetables.

★ Q V P

BUILTH WELLS
Greyhound Hotel
3 Garth Road, LD2 3AR

- On A483
- 11am-midnight (winter Mon-Fri 11am-3pm, 6-11pm); Sun 12-11pm
- Daily 12-2.30pm, 6.30-9pm
- T (01982) 553255
- Fuller's London Pride; Greene King Abbot; guest
- Traditional pub food plus a curry board and Sunday carvery
- Early 20th-century hotel with open-plan bars and large function room

Two specials boards display rather different styles of food – curries on one, traditional dishes on the other. Home-made specials change regularly but could include a full rack of barbecued ribs, pork chop and chips, lamb hotpot with potatoes and vegetables, seafood platter, sweet 'n' sour pork or chicken with rice, braised lamb shank or pan-fried seabass, prices £5.75-£10.95. The curries are bought in from a local producer and include chicken vindaloo, balti, and dopiaza as well as vegetable dhansak.

The set bar menu offers home-made soup such as leek and potato, Stilton and broccoli or carrot and coriander, served with a roll at £2.90, followed by main courses starting at £4.25 for a quarter chicken with chips and peas, Cajun or garlic chicken breast, home-made cottage pie or steak and ale pie, haddock in batter with chips and peas, freshly-made ham, cheese or mushroom omelettes, and 10oz rump or gammon steaks. Prices rise to £11 for a 12oz sirloin steak with all the trimmings. Snacks include filled jacket potatoes, baguettes and toasted sandwiches. Desserts change daily, some home made, such as apple pie or crumble and rice pudding. A two-course Sunday carvery at £6.50 always offers beef plus another roast with fresh vegetables and all the trimmings.

Q S V P C

CWMDU
Farmers Arms
NP8 1RU

- ▶ On A479, 3 miles from Crickhowell
- ☼ Daily 12-3pm (4pm Sat & Sun), 6-11pm
- 🍴 Daily 12-2pm, 6-9.30pm
- T (01874) 730464
- E cwmdu@hotmail.co.uk
- W www.thefarmersarms.com
- 🍺 Felinfoel Double Dragon; Shepherd Neame Spitfire, Uley Pig's Ear; guest
- ☺ Modern European plus traditional lunches
- ◉ Farmhouse-style country inn in the Black Mountains with exposed beams

The menu at the Farmer's Arms is based on simple but imaginative cooking using locally sourced ingredients in keeping with a traditional pub. Fresh fish comes from Swansea, fresh vegetables from Swansea market. Starters include home-made soup with fresh-baked bread, field mushrooms baked with bacon lardons and garlic butter, home-smoked salmon wrapped round crabmeat with dill mayonnaise, and tempura king prawns with sweet chilli sauce, prices from £3.95-£6.50. There is a fine selection of prime Welsh steaks – 10oz sirloin, 14oz rib eye or 16oz T-bone – priced £12.50-£15.95, and grilled Swansea Bay seabass with herb and lime butter, £14.50.

The chef's special dishes might be rack of new season Welsh lamb in season served pink on tarragon mash with port and redcurrant jus, baked fillet of Cornish halibut on fresh seafood stew, roast local duck served on noodles with ginger, Cointreau and soy sauce or salmon poached with lemongrass, garnished with mussels, £12.95-£14.50. A three-course Sunday lunch at £12.95 starts with Welsh cawl or sweet pepper and goats' cheese parfait, followed by roast Welsh sirloin, leg of Breconshire lamb, rare breed Shropshire pork with crackling or spinach, tomato and goats' cheese tart, followed by tarte citron or steamed pecan and maple pudding.

★ 🏰 ❀ 🛏 V 🍺 ⛺ ♣ 🅿 ⚡ 👪 C

GARTH
☆ Garth Mill
LD4 4AS

- ▶ Near Builth Wells on A483 to Llandovery
- ☼ Mon-Sat 11am-11pm; Sun 12-10.30pm
- 🍴 Throughout opening hours
- T (01591) 620572
- E dave@pigsfolly.fsnet.co.uk
- W www.pigsfolly.co.uk
- 🍺 Beer range varies
- ☺ True pub food using their own produce
- ◉ The mill, formerly a brickyard, was renovated by the present owners in 2000 and now includes a pub, restaurant, function room, B&B and farm shop

A pub cum small holding owned by Dave and Debbie Lang with farm shop where they make their own sausages in 70 flavours, cure their own ham and bacon, produce their own meat pies and grow their own herbs. They use only locally-sourced meat alongside their own pork in cooking and fresh bread is made by a nearby baker. This outstanding produce features in the all day breakfast of sausage, bacon, egg, mushrooms, beans, fried bread, potato cake, toast and tea or coffee at £4.95 (served until 6pm). Starters or light lunches include fresh mushrooms stuffed with goats' cheese, home-made pâté and soup, or king prawns with Dave's sauce, £2.95-£3.50.

As well as daily specials there are favourite pub meals, all home made, such as steak and ale pie, beef pudding, pork pie, lamb and leek pasty, liver and onions or hand-made faggots at £4.50-£5.95. Other main courses include pork fillet on sweet potato cake with salad, pan-fried chicken topped with cheese and banana, cod in home-made batter with proper chips, or simple ham, egg, salad and chips, £6.50-£8.50. There are Welsh beef steaks – 16oz rump, 10oz sirloin, 8oz fillet or T-bone – all priced £10.50 including real chips, salad and mushrooms. Veggie choices include cauliflower or macaroni cheese, tomato and basil pasta, or mushrooms stuffed with peppers and scrambled eggs with salad.

❀ 🛏 S V 🍺 ♿ ⛺ ⇌ (Garth) ♣ 🍎 🅿 ⚡ 👪 C

HUNDRED HOUSE
Hundred House Inn
LD1 5RY

- On A483 near Llandrindod Wells
- Mon-Sat 10am-midnight; Sun 12-10.30pm
- Daily 12-2pm, 6-9pm
- T (01982) 570231
- Brains SA; Wood Parish; guests
- Good home cooking with plenty of fish to choose from
- Former drovers' inn benefiting from fine views of the surrounding uplands; the cosy bar features an original tiled floor

Licensee and cook Roger Philip has spent a few years in Portugal, and this influence can be tasted in the fish dishes that are a speciality on his otherwise fairly traditionally British menu. He buys the fish every week from a chap in town so it could be any one of a dozen varieties – whatever takes his fancy at the time – then he cooks it with wine, garlic and herbs in authentic Portuguese style.

All the main dishes here are home made: various pies, curries and lasagnes. Roger also offers five different cuts of steak including rib eye and T-bone. Vegetarians are in for a rare treat here with a choice of around six dishes including vegetable curry, sweet parsnip and potato bake, broccoli and cheese bake and mascarpone lasagne. Roger has also created a new starter with vegetarians in mind: sliced mushrooms in a creamy garlic sauce topped with grated cheese and browned under the grill. Main courses range in price from £6.50 to £12.50 for the fillet steak, while desserts, again home made and varying with the seasons, are all priced at £3.50. While you are waiting for your meal to be cooked you can read the detailed explanation in the bar of a 'hundred' – an Anglo Saxon administration division of a shire.

★ S V P C

LLANGATTOCK
Vine Tree Inn
NP8 1HG

- S of Crickhowell
- Daily 12-3pm, 6-11pm
- Daily 12-2.30pm, 6-10pm
- T (01873) 810514
- Fuller's London Pride; guests
- Freshly cooked meals from local ingredients; good for fish and game
- 400-year-old pub with an attractive riverside garden

The pub is geared more towards diners than drinkers and is so popular that it is advisable to make a reservation for dining. The emphasis is on home-cooked dishes made from fresh, mainly local produce including game. Fish, however, is delivered from Cornwall and Portsmouth. Interesting specials change daily and the main menu is pretty impressive, too. Refreshing melon and tangerine cocktail, smoked trout, mushrooms in garlic and chilli, black tiger prawns in tempura batter and tuna and tomato salad are just some of the suggestions for starters, all under £6. To follow there is a good range of steaks including fillet stuffed with pâté in port wine sauce, £13.25 or £16.25 according to weight, a couple of speciality chicken dishes – breast stuffed with prawns on a bed of seafood sauce, or chicken Cymru in white wine, tomato and mushroom sauce – and plenty of game, such as roast pheasant in a royal game sauce or venison in red berry casserole. Monkfish in creamy leek and Pernod sauce, £12.40, or trout in chive sauce, £9.95, number among the many fish options, while vegetarians will always find four or five dishes. A traditional roast lunch is served every Sunday for £6.50.

★ Q S V P C

PENYBONT
Severn Arms
LD1 5UA

▶ On A44, centre of village
Daily 11am-2.30pm, 5.30-11pm
Daily 12-2pm, 6.30-9.30pm
T (01597) 851224
F (01597) 851693
E owen@severnarms.fsnet.co.uk
Brains Rev James; Courage Directors; Theakston Best Bitter
Mostly traditional pub meals with a choice of specials
The spacious bar, with a large open fireplace, opens onto gardens overlooking the River Ithon; quiet, secluded restaurant

This 19th-century former coaching inn used to be a major halt for travellers between Hereford and Aberystwyth and continues to provide excellent hospitality. It has 10 en-suite bedrooms and guests enjoy free fishing rights on six miles of the River Ithon. The restaurant offers a variety of freshly-prepared dishes. To start with you could have home-made soup of the day or pâté, deep fried goats' cheese with cranberry sauce, salad of pear, stilton and walnuts, smoked trout fillet, prawn cocktail or creamy garlic mushrooms, mostly £4-£5. To follow the 'chef's selection' includes pork and apricot or beef with wholegrain mustard and cream sauce with vodka kick, both £13.25, or griddled lamb steak with red wine and mint gravy, £10.95. Or there are steaks, home-made steak and kidney pie or cottage pie, and fish options. Grilled chicken is a popular choice with toppings of bacon, pineapple and melted cheese, Stilton and mushrooms, hot salsa and cheddar or honey and mustard, all £6.95. Vegetarians have a good selection, too: Mediterranean lasagne, bean chilli and rice, chickpea and cauliflower curry, spinach and ricotta cannelloni or ratatouille crumble, all £5.95. Desserts include sherry trifle, hot chocolate fudge cake and fruit pie and custard, all £3.25.

S V P C

RHAYADER
Crown Inn
North Street, LD6 5BT

▶ Town centre
Mon-Sat 11am-11pm; Sun 12-10.30pm
Daily 12-2.15pm, 6-9.30pm
T (01597) 811099
E thecrownrhayader@btinternet.com
W www.thecrownrhayader.co.uk
Brains Dark, Bitter, Rev James, seasonal
Value for money, freshly-cooked traditional pub food
Atmospheric 16th-century hostelry with much of the original timber preserved

The menu of good quality pub fare is augmented by specials of the day which could be pork loin in mustard and cream sauce, salmon fillet cooked with wine and cream, liver and onion casserole, swordfish fried in herb and garlic butter, smoked mackerel with horseradish and lemon or authentic curries including lamb jalfrezi, beef balti or madras, chicken korma or tikka masala. All meat comes from a nearby butcher who sources locally, while fresh fish is from Cardiff's indoor market.

Starters on the set menu include home-made soup and king prawns in peppery garlic sauce, followed by steak, kidney and mushroom pie, haddock in batter, home-cooked ham with egg and chips, lamb shank in minted gravy or chicken cacciatora, that's breast fillet with tomato, wine, mushrooms, bacon and onions, £5.75-£9.50. There are pot meals at £5.95 – savoury mince with potato slices topped with cheese, chilli or lasagne. Grills range from gammon, egg, sausages and all the trimmings at £5.95 to a 12oz sirloin or 8oz fillet of local beef at £12.50. Vegetarians might choose mushrooms cooked with onions, Dijon mustard, brandy, red wine and cream served with rice or chips, £6.50, or the popular ploughman's made up of Welsh cheeses served with French bread, chutney, pickled onions, salad and coleslaw at £4.75.

★ Q S V C

DYSERTH
New Inn
Waterfall Road, LL18 6ET

- On B5119 intersection from A5151
- Daily 12-11pm
- Daily 12-9pm
- T (01745) 570482
- Banks's Original, Bitter; Marston's Burton Bitter, Pedigree
- Wholesome British pub food plus sizzling skillets
- Attractive, popular pub offering great views of the Dyserth waterfall; a single bar serves four cosy areas plus a large secluded garden

Situated by Dyserth's historic church and waterfall, the pub enjoys a good reputation for food; in summer you can eat out in the secluded garden. The varied menu kicks off with warm goats' cheese croquette with cranberry compote, sautéed garlic mushrooms with Stilton, breaded whitebait with granary bread, or steamed mussels in garlic, tomato and white wine sauce (also available as a main course); on the specials board there might be baked Brie, black pudding fritters or Scottish smoked salmon. Starters are all under a fiver.

Then you can opt for one of the 'sizzling skillets': minted lamb strips, chicken Cajun or Chinese style or a prime Welsh steak, all served with salad and home-made coleslaw for £8-£10. Alternatively there is a choice of home-made chicken curry, 'monster' lamb Henry slow roasted on buttered mash, or spinach and ricotta cannelloni in rich tomato sauce as a veggie option. Main course salads include poached salmon and asparagus or home-roasted ham and pineapple with baby beetroot, while specials include fillet steak, peppered rump, a mixed grill, chicken roulade or poached salmon. A good selection of snacks is served until 3pm every day: baguettes, sandwiches and wraps, filled jackets, salads or omelettes, mostly under £5

★ S V C

HAWARDEN
Fox & Grapes
6 The Highway, CH5 3DH

- On B5125, just off A55
- Daily 11am-11pm
- Mon-Sat 12-2.30pm, 5.30-8.30pm; Sun 12-8pm
- T 01244 532565
- E lancescally@hotmail.com
- W www.foxandgrapes.co.uk
- Caledonian Deuchars IPA; Courage Directors; John Smith's Bitter; guest
- Home-made, traditional pub fare and special dishes created with flair
- Friendly, community-minded local near Hawarden Castle

The pub has built up its reputation for good quality meals by ensuring that everything is home made – even the chips. They use the freshest locally-sourced ingredients delivered daily and take great care with the presentation of their dishes. A menu of traditional pub favourites – steaks and grills, fish and chips – is supplemented by more adventurous daily specials. Starters could include home-cooked ham with cream cheese and apricots on a bed of mixed leaves, chicken liver pâté with sun-dried tomato toast and cranberry and onion marmalade or broccoli and Stilton tart.

One of the most popular main course dishes is continental pork – medallions flamed in brandy with Stilton and peppercorn cream sauce – while other specials are smoked haddock fishcakes with parsley sauce, lamb hotpot with mushy peas, red cabbage and crusty bread, highland chicken (char-grilled fillet topped with haggis in a whisky cream sauce), rib eye steak topped with Stilton and herb crust or Mediterranean vegetable lasagne. Expect to pay around £12-14 for two courses, but save room for pudding: lemon meringue pie, knickerbocker glory, rhubarb and apple crumble or sticky toffee pud with butterscotch sauce might be on offer. On Sunday there is a good choice of roasts, £8.95 for two courses.

★ S V (Hawarden) C

HENDRERWYDD
☆ White Horse
LL16 4LL

- 600 yards E of B5429, 1 mile S of Llandymog
- Tue-Sat 12-3pm, 6-11pm; Sun 12-3pm
- Tue-Sat 12-2.30pm, 6-9.15pm; Sun 12-2.30pm
- T (01824) 790218
- F info@white-horse-inn.co.uk
- W www.white-horse-inn.co.uk
- Beer range varies
- Modern European cuisine on a rolling menu, plus good bar snacks
- Charming, rural 17th-century inn in the Vale of Clwyd with public bar and games room; main meals are served in a comfortable dining area

Landlady and head chef Ruth has an unusual take on local produce – she picks much of it herself from hedgerows as she likes to use nature's flavours in her sauces and accompaniments, such as the blackberry sauce she serves with the duck, and elderflower infused gravy to go with pork. Other dishes might be flavoured with crab apple cheese or rowan berry jelly and she plans to experiment with rosehips. Her rolling menu means she can add new dishes according to availability of seasonal produce and she offers some inspired choices.

To start with there might be ruccola salad with Spanish pear and Parmesan, smoked goose breast with fig salad and chutney, fresh black Conwy mussels or crumbled sardines (fresh fillets topped with tarragon and butter crumble). Exciting main dishes include kleftico exohiko (slow cooked, Greek-style lamb stew), venison Wellington (fillet wrapped in filo pastry with sage, thyme, mushroom and bacon stuffing), butternut squash with Moroccan spiced veg and red onion marmalade, wild seabass with smokey cep sauce or medallions of fillet steak with field mushrooms and organic spinach in a garlic cream sauce. To finish there are Welsh or French cheeses, and wonderful desserts such as lemon posset with grilled figs, or home-made pannacotta with fresh raspberries. Expect to pay around £20 for two courses.

Q S V P C

MELIDEN
Miners Arms
23 Ffordd Talargoch, LL19 8LA

- ▶ On A547 Prestatyn to Ghuddlan road
- ☼ Daily 12-11pm (11.30pm Sun)
- Ⓣ Wed-Sat 6.30-9pm; Sun 12.30 on
- T (01745) 852005
- F (01745) 855314
- Marston's Burton Bitter, Pedigree; guests
- ☺ Varied menu of good local produce, mostly home-made dishes
- ◙ Friendly pub dominated by a wood burning stove that warms the stone-floored lounge and snug; the spacious dining area is on a lower level

Once the pay office for the last working lead mines on the North Wales coast, the owner and head chef has worked hard to build up a reputation for home-cooked fare, sourcing all the produce himself to ensure quality. Starters include whitebait with crispy salad and tartare sauce, grilled goats' cheese crouton with roast Mediterranean vegetables, Bury black pudding and Lancashire cheese salad topped with a poached egg or maybe whole dressed Anglesey crab (if available). To follow there is usually a good choice of simply grilled fish such as seabass, red snapper, plaice fillet, or a mixed seafood platter and straightforward cod and chips. Steaks are always available or you might be tempted with pan-fried Cumbrian venison steak with red wine sauce and black cherries, corn fed chicken breast in Parma ham with creamy leek sauce or oven roasted Gressingham duck breast. For vegetarians there's leek and mushroom crumble, mushroom and red pepper stroganoff or roasted Mediterranean veg topped with goat's cheese. Two courses will set you back around £15. Yummy desserts include home-made meringue with marinated forest fruits, bread and butter pudding or a chocolate choice of the day. Puddings are all £3.50, or you could finish your meal with a selection of Welsh cheeses for £5.

V ♿ P **C**

RHEWL
Sun Inn
LL20 7YT

- ▶ From Llangollen take Horseshoe Pass road for 1½ miles then left onto B5103 for 2 miles
- ☼ Tue 12-2.30pm, 6-11pm; Wed 6-11pm; Thu-Sat 12-2.30pm, 6-11pm; Sun 12-10pm
- Ⓣ Throughout opening hours
- T (01978) 861043
- Beer range varies
- ☺ Simple, honest pub food
- ◙ This 14th-century drover's cottage is a gem, comprising three rooms with a wealth of exposed beams warmed by open fires; situated in the Dee Valley, the garden looks on to the Llantysilio Mountain

This delightful little pub, four miles from Llangollen, is frequented by anglers and walkers who stop off here to enjoy beers from regional or small breweries and to fill up on homely fare. This is no gastropub, but all the dishes on the limited menu are prepared to order from mostly local produce. Home-made chicken curry, lasagne or beef and beer pie cost around £7, or for the same price you can have roast pork or beef with Yorkshire pudding, a gammon steak or fish and chips. You'll pay a bit more for steak braised in red wine, an 8oz sirloin or local rainbow trout. There is also a choice of ham or cheese salad, ploughman's, quiche or a vegetable lasagne. The pub serves a traditional roast lunch all day Sunday, £5.50 or £7.25 with a sweet. There is a standard children's menu (fish fingers, sausage, burger, egg or chicken nuggets and chips) for around £3.50, but possibly the filled jacket potatoes would provide a healthier alternative for £4.35. Ice cream sundaes feature on the desserts list, plus fruit pies or chocolate fudge cake with cream. While waiting for your meal you can amuse yourself playing chess on the unusual wall-mounted board.

★ **Q** ❀ **S V** ♿ ♣ P **C**

CONWY

☆ Groes Inn

LL32 8TN

- ▶ Two miles from Conwy Castle via B5106
- Daily 12-3pm, 6-11pm
- Daily 12-2pm, 6.30-9pm
- T (01492) 650545
- F (01492) 650855
- E thegroes@btinternet.com
- W www.groesinn.com
- Tetley's Bitter, Burton Ale
- English and Welsh traditional dishes enhanced by the chef's creative flair
- Dating from 1573, the Groes was the first licensed house in Wales; beautiful location

When a pub takes the trouble to bake its own bread and produce its own ice cream you can be sure that the rest of the food is of the highest quality. And it helps if you don't have to go too far to find superb ingredients. Here, the Welsh lamb is reared on the salt marshes and game comes from nearby estates, while crab, plaice, wild salmon, oysters and mussels all come from the waters around Conwy and Anglesey.

The menu kicks off with 'small meals and starters', ranging from £3.95 for home-made soup of the day to sizzling garlic prawns at £6.95. Or you could choose creamy smoked haddock with a crisp Parmesan topping, asparagus and Parma ham salad with blue cheese dressing or butternut squash and sage ravioli with oil, lemon and black pepper dressing. There is a choice of ploughman's, sandwiches or a Danish open sandwich with smoked fish. Main course 'favourites' include a choice of steaks, Anglesey gammon and eggs, Welsh lamb served in shepherd's pie or braised shoulder, and the chef's own chicken curry. There are plenty of fish dishes: haddock, prawn and mushroom pie, poached fresh salmon and a couple of seafood platters. Daily specials are chalked up in the bar. Desserts include white chocolate and vanilla bean panacotta, bara brith (Welsh fruit bread) and the delicious home-made ices at £4.50.

★ S V P C

GLANWYDDEN

☆ Queen's Head

LL31 9JP

- ▶ Follow Penrhyn Bay sign from A470, 1 mile
- Mon-Sat 11am-3pm, 6-11pm; Sun 11am-10.30pm
- Mon-Sat 12-2pm, 6-9pm; Sun 12-9pm
- T (01492) 546570
- E enquiries@queensheadglanwydden.co.uk
- W www.queensheadglanwydden.co.uk
- Tetley Bitter, Burton Ale; guest
- Award-winning food with hearty dishes and Welsh flavours
- Old village pub lovingly cared for

Proprietor and award-winning chef Bob Cureton says uncompromisingly: 'All our food is home made; our products are sourced locally.' These include Great Orme lobsters, Conwy mussels topped with oak-smoked Llanrwst cheddar or cooked with cider and sage, trio of local sausages, Welsh rack of lamb, dressed Conwy crab, plenty of game from the area, Welsh belly pork and black pudding with cider and mustard on braised cabbage, or oxtail cooked with pickled walnuts in Guinness.

The set menu boasts Provençal fish soup, melon with blackcurrant sorbet, pea and mint risotto or salmon, crab and coriander fishcakes among starters priced £3.95-£5.95. Fish dishes include smoked haddock in cream with tomato and Parmesan, monkfish and king prawn kebabs with coconut sauce, baked cod topped with Welsh rarebit and chunky chips, selection of grilled local fish with dill butter sauce or a whole seafood platter, prices £9.25-£16.50. Hearty meat dishes include roast rib of Welsh beef with Yorkshire pudding, leg of Welsh lamb with mint sauce, loin of pork with crisp crackling and apricot and nut stuffing, lamb's liver sautéed with smoked bacon, and green Thai chicken curry with scented rice, all around £9. Veggie dishes might be mushroom and blue cheese vol-au-vent or stir-fried spaghetti topped with rocket, Parmesan and roasted pine nuts.

V P C

LLANDUDNO
King's Head
Old Road, LL30 2NB

- Behind the tram station at the bottom of Great Orme
- Daily 12-midnight (11.30pm Sun)
- Daily 12-2.30pm, 6-9pm
- T (01492) 877993
- E steve@kingshead99.fsnet.co.uk
- Beer range varies
- Traditional pub fare with char-grilled food a speciality
- The oldest pub in Llandudno, its bar dominated by an open fire. The suntrap patio boasts award-winning floral displays

Situated right by the tram stop, the 300-year-old King's Head is an ideal place to stop for a pint and a bite after riding on Britain's only cable-hauled tramway or walking on the Great Orme. The dining room displays artefacts from the old Great Orme mines, worth a look while waiting for your meal to be freshly cooked. If you are lucky with the weather you can dine alfresco on the delightful patio. Using local produce as far as possible, the pub specialises in char-grilled meats at reasonable prices – the rump will set you back just over £10 for a whopping 16oz steak, or you could choose sirloin, fillet, rib eye or a T-bone. Sauces for the steaks are all home made. The pub is also popular for its Tex-Mex dishes, Thai style curries and seafood; you may find red snapper on the menu for around £10. If your tastes are more traditional you will enjoy the gold award-winning sausages or the steak 'n' ale pie made with Guinness and real ale, both around £8; fresh soup is prepared daily. A proper roast lunch is served every Sunday for £7. If you dine on a Wednesday evening you could join in the regular quiz, which is always well attended.

★ V C

LLANELIAN-YN-RHOS
White Lion Inn
LL29 8YA

- Off B5383, next to church
- Tue-Sat 11.30am-3pm, 6-11pm; Sun 12-10.30pm
- Tue-Sat 12-2pm, 6-9pm (9.30pm Fri & Sat); Sun 12-9pm
- T (01492) 515807
- E info@whitelioninn.co.uk
- W www.whitelioninn.co.uk
- Marston's Bitter, Pedigree; guests
- Traditional home-cooked food with a modern twist
- Family run inn near Colwyn Bay with slate floored bar, tiny snug and lounge

The varied menu features fresh local produce with meat, fish, fruit and vegetables delivered daily, game from local shoots in season, speciality breads from a local bakery and award-winning produce such as sausages from Edwards Butchers of Conwy. The range of home-made specials changes daily, including pear, Stilton and leek tart with red onion chutney, salad and new potatoes, seabass on saffron rice, fresh cod in batter with chips and mushy peas, steak and kidney pie, roast Welsh lamb shank or Mr Edwards' pork and leek sausages on mustard mash with onion gravy, prices from £7.95-£9.50. T-bone steak or fillet with sauce are dearer at around £16-£17.

The main menu offers starters such as deep fried Welsh goats' cheese, fresh mussels in garlic and white wine, home-made soups or warm black pudding and smoked bacon salad at a bargain £2.95-£4.75. Main courses include slow braised best steak in Guinness gravy, fresh grilled plaice with lemon butter or the roast of the day, £5.25-£8.50. Veggie choices might be roast Mediterranean vegetables topped with goats' cheese or roast capsicum filled with marinated vegetables. Sandwiches range from simple cheese and pickle to smoked bacon and cheese melt.

★ Q S V C

ST GEORGE
Kinmel Arms
The Village, LL22 9BP

▶ Travelling W on A55, take exit after Bodelwyddan
Tue-Sat 12-3pm, 7pm (6.30 Sat)-11pm; Sun 12-5.30pm
Tue-Sat 12-2pm, 7pm (6.30 Sat)-9.30pm; Sun 12-4pm
T (01745) 832207
F (01745) 822044
E info@thekinmelarms.co.uk
W www.thekinmelarms.co.uk
Moorhouses Black Cat; Tetley Bitter; guests
Award-winning gourmet food with a continental flavour
17th-century listed inn set in rural tranquillity on a hill overlooking the sea

Artworks by proprietor Tim Watson are displayed at this pub that describes itself as a 'restaurant with rooms' – the rooms in question being four luxurious, individually designed suites. The food is of equally high quality, all freshly prepared from local produce by a team of five. Menus change seasonally, supplemented by blackboard specials. The lunch menu lists a range of salads, including smoked duck and chèvre chaud.

Starters are mostly around £5, and some may be ordered as a main course too, including chicken Caesar salad, porcini raviolini or prawns and salmon bound together with lemon and tarragon mayonnaise and served with salad. Veggie starters include baked aubergine layered with basil, cherry tomatoes and Parmesan, and grilled asparagus on home-made walnut bread. To follow, there is roasted risotto cake flavoured with pea pesto, mushrooms and fresh spinach, osso bucco piedmontaise (slowly braised veal joint), duck leg confit cassoulet with spicy sausages and beans, or marinated rack of lamb, all around £10. Steaks and various fish dishes complete the main menu. Beautifully presented desserts are listed on blackboards.

V P C

TREFRIW
Old Ship/Yr Hen Long
High Street, LL27 0JH

▶ On B5106
Mon-Fri 12-3pm, 6-11pm; Sat & Sun 12-11pm (10.30pm Sun)
Daily 12-2.30pm, 6-9pm
T (01492) 640013
F (01492) 641108
E rhian.barlow@btopenworld.com
W www.the-old-ship.co.uk
Banks's Bitter; Marston's Pedigree; guests
Home-cooked food with some lovely traditional country dishes
Half-timbered former customs house dating from the 16th century

Award-winning chef Rhian Barlow, previously in this Guide as cook at another Welsh pub, took over the Old Ship in 1999 and has worked hard to turn it into a traditional real ale and good food house. Using as much local produce as possible, including fine bangers from the butcher opposite, she prepares all the food herself. She even makes her own pickles and chutneys – a feature of the ploughman's alongside her favourite Welsh cheese, Goran Glas from Anglesey.

Examples from the specials board might be braised rabbit with prunes and Conwy beer – she uses lots of ale in cooking – grey mullet on garlic mash with mussel stew, cheese-topped shepherd's pie with oven roasted veg, or vegetable dauphinoise with salad, £7.50-£9.95. The evening menu offers starters such as home-made soup, smoked haddock with prawns or feta and olive salad, £3.20-£4.50. Main courses include pepperpot beef with ginger, half a shoulder of Welsh lamb baked with redcurrants and rosemary, salmon with Welsh mustard sauce or spinach tortellini in mushroom and red pepper sauce, £7.95 to £12.95 including vegetables. Home-made puds at £3.70 could be bara brith butter pudding, raspberry brûlée, chocolate truffle torte or citrus cheesecake with kumquats.

★ S V P C

CAPEL BANGOR
☆ Tynllidiart Arms
SY23 3LR

▶ On A44, 5 miles E of Aberystwyth
Mon-Wed 11am-3pm, 5-11pm; Thu-Sun 11am-midnight
Daily 12-2.30pm, 6.30-9.30pm
T (01970) 880248
F (01970) 880929
Cwrw Gwynant; guests
Home-cooked, gastropub menu
Open plan bar with a restaurant upstairs; the outside terrace offers fine views

This village pub is home to possibly the smallest commercial brewery in the world. The house beer, Cwrw Gwynant, goes on sale at the weekend and usually sells out quickly. Fortunately supplies from the kitchen are more reliable, but the menu is also based on local products. The chef is happy to cook alternatives to the listed dishes on request, provided he has the necessary ingredients, but most customers will find something to suit their taste as daily specials supplement the already varied menu.

To start there's Brie and mango parcels, pan-fried garlic mushrooms, spicy Thai tiger prawns with caramelised banana in a coconut sauce, and home-made crab cakes or scallops for seafood lovers, all under £5.50, or you could be extravagant and go for the aromatic crispy fried duck breast at £6.85. Welsh meats feature in main courses, often with innovative accompaniments, such as rack of lamb served on a sweet potato mash with parsnip fritters or black beef strips in a creamy mustard sauce with turmeric rice or horseradish mash. Wild Atlantic salmon comes with marinated cherry tomatoes and lemon couscous, while supreme of chicken is filled with leeks, wrapped in Cambrian ham and served with Stilton sauce. Prices range from £8-£13. The cheese board offers four Welsh cheeses and home-made desserts are £3.95.

★ Q S V P C

LLANDEILO
Angel Hotel
62 Rhosmaen Street, SA19 6EN

▶ Centre of town on A483
Mon-Sat 11am-3pm, 6.30-11pm; closed Sun
Mon-Sat 11.30am-2.30pm; 6.30-9.30pm
T (01558) 822765
F (01558) 824346
E capelbach@hotmail.com
W www.angelbistro.co.uk
Evan-Evans BB; guest
Good quality menu with inspired special dishes
Refurbished pub that has retained its olde-worlde charm

This pub has some interesting features: walled gardens, the Capel Bach (Small Chapel) bistro and an unusual, lavishly decorated function room designated Yr Eglwys (the Church). The food is out of the ordinary, too, with tempting specials and a fresh fish board. For starters you might find seared chicken and pepper salad with pineapple salsa, lemon and garlic pan-fried king prawns, a warm savoury cheesecake with apple and balsamic dressing, mussels steamed with coconut milk or cured duck breast on warm orange salad, mostly priced around £5.

To follow there could be char-grilled ham steak with rich cranberry, orange and port gravy, topside of Welsh lamb with forcemeat and apricots in white wine sauce, barbary duck breast on roasted sweet potato and red pepper in gooseberry sauce or pan-fried tuna steak and seafood medley in lime zest butter. Vegetarian options include roasted garlic and mushroom lentil loaf with honey and red wine jus or broccoli and roasted pepper roulade stuffed with cream cheese. Main courses are mostly £11-£15; steaks and fish are priced on the day. The dessert menu deserves some attention: brandy snap baked with lemon mousse and raspberries, French apple tart on sticky toffee sauce or peach melba crème brûlée, all £4.75.

S V (Landeilo) C

PRENGWYN
Gwarcefel Arms
SA44 4LU

- ▶ Between Cardigan and Lampeter on A475, 2 miles E of Horeb crossroads
- ☼ Daily 12-12.30am (1.30am Fri and Sat; 10.30pm Sun)
- 🍴 Daily 12-3pm, 6-9.30pm (bar snacks 12-9.30pm)
- T (01559) 362720
- F (01559) 362339
- E gwarcefelarms@aol.com
- W www.gwarcefelarms.co.uk
- Brains Buckley's Best Bitter, guests
- ☺ Freshly-prepared meals based mostly on locally-sourced produce
- The friendly atmosphere makes this a popular stop for tourists as it lies between the Cambrian Mountains and the coast

Under new management, the Gwarcefel has won the approval of local CAMRA members for its real ales, and now it features in this guide, having gained a good reputation for its food. Meals are freshly prepared and cooked to order on the premises by an experienced chef who is happy to adapt dishes to individual tastes. The restaurant offers à la carte dining including steaks, salads and vegetarian dishes plus around six specials and home-made desserts that are displayed daily.

A typical menu might offer prawn cocktail, home-made pâté and soup – perhaps leek and potato – to start with, then a trio of lamb cutlets with redcurrant and rosemary gravy, pork loin steaks with red wine, bacon and mushroom sauce, baked cod fillet and garlic roasted vegetables with tomato sauce or mushroom, or Brie and spinach parcel with hot cranberry sauce. On Sunday a traditional roast is served all day with a choice of three meats, from £5.50 for one course to £8.50 for three courses. Home-made desserts include rum and raisin cheesecake with cream or ice cream, apple pie and custard or sherry trifle. Welsh ales are sold here but, more unusually, you could select a Welsh wine to accompany your meal.

Q S V P C

TALYBONT
White Lion (Llew Gwyn)
SY24 5ER

- ▶ On village green, 7 miles N of Aberystwyth, 11 miles from Machynlleth
- ☼ Mon-Sat 11am-11pm; Sun 12-10.30pm
- 🍴 Daily 12-3pm, 6-9pm
- T (01970) 832245
- F (01970) 832658
- E Maureen.bumford@btconnect.com
- Banks's Original, Bitter; guest
- ☺ Home-cooked food with good local fish and seafood
- Recently refurbished, the no-smoking extension features a fascinating display of local history, but the public bar is the heart of this friendly pub

Buses from Aberystwyth and Bangor stop right outside this small hotel that has happily been enhanced by refurbishment in 2004; the no-smoking dining area is to the rear. Landlady Maureen runs the kitchen and serves a fairly limited but well thought-out menu. All the trout, crab and lobsters served here are caught by one of her regular customers. Sausages are made locally and come in a variety of flavours – lamb with apricot or mint, venison, pork and leek or pork and garlic – to be served traditionally with mash and onion gravy; the local butcher also provides Welsh sirloin and lamb, the latter cooked with honey and served on minted potato mash with peas and cherry tomatoes.

The trout, which she marinates in lime and coriander and serves with cherry tomatoes and lemon couscous, is one of her most popular dishes. Other favourites are home-made lasagne with smoked haddock and prawn, and red peppers stuffed with salmon and tuna in Stilton sauce, served with couscous. Steaks come with all the usual trimmings or there is strips of Welsh beef in a mustard and cream sauce with mash. For two courses expect to pay around £14. For an extra treat ask about the monthly evenings of Welsh poetry and music, held on a Friday.

S V P C

SCOTLAND

ANCRUM
Cross Keys Inn
The Green, TD8 6X

- On B6400, off A68 3 miles N of Jedburgh
- Mon-Thu 6-11pm; Fri 5pm-1am; Sat 12-midnight; Sun 12-11pm
- Mon-Sat 6-9pm, Sun 12-11pm
- T (01835) 830344
- E ancrumxkeys@ukgateway.net
- W www.ancrumcrosskeys.co.uk
- Broughton ales; guests
- Trad pub and bistro
- Old fashioned, friendly village local almost untouched for a century

Last 'modernised' during a Jedburgh Brewery refit in 1906, this was the first pub in Scotland to receive an internal preservation order from the Borders council. The landlord/chef also preserves traditional cooking, featuring game such as venison, pheasant, salmon and duck in season in dishes like honey and Drambuie marinated pheasant breasts with roast vegetables, or venison steak oven roasted with a wild berry and port sauce.

You might also find chicken stuffed with haggis then wrapped in bacon in a white wine and parsley sauce, smoked haddock with leeks and pasta, pork chops with black pudding in cider sauce, chicken korma in a mild creamy sauce with pilau rice and naan bread or simple braised steak and onions. Prices range from £6-£9, with surf 'n' turf, a locally raised 10oz sirloin steak topped with king prawns, at £14.50.

Among the starters are home-made soup of the day, deep fried Brie with port and orange sauce, creamy garlic mushrooms on toast, potato longboats with prawns Marie-Rose, chicken liver pâté and black pudding with Drambuie sauce. All sausages and burgers are home made, and the specials and desserts are chalked up daily on the blackboard.

★ S V C

AUCHENCROW
Craw Inn
TD14 5LS

- On B6438, follow signs from A1
- Mon-Fri 12-2.30pm, 6-11pm; Sat 12-midnight; Sun 12.30-11pm
- Daily 12-2pm, 6-9pm
- T (01890) 761253
- E info@thecrawinn.co.uk
- W www.thecrawinn.co.uk
- Beer range varies
- Wide ranging menu featuring local produce
- Welcoming, family-owned 17th-century country inn with log-burning stove

An eclectic menu cooked by the chef/owner mixes a generous amount of Scottish flavours with the more far flung, and presents a bar menu worthy of a restaurant. In the bar you might start with home-made soup at £2.75, smoked salmon from the famous Loch Fyne smokery or a traditional Greek salad with feta and olives. To follow, choose from a rich beef cassoulet of Aberdeen Angus and smoked bacon in red wine, game casserole of rabbit, hare, venison, duck and pheasant served with sauté potatoes at a very game £8.75, spicy fish stew of both fish and shellfish in white wine and cream, salmon and dill fishcakes and chips or, for vegetarians, Brie, Cheddar and redcurrant tart. Main courses are around £8.75.

Moving into the restaurant, platters of both whisky-cured Speyside smoked salmon and Italian meats with feta and olives are among the starters. Main courses include Aberdeen Angus steaks, char-grilled pork loin steaks with prune and calvados sauce, pheasant breast stuffed with apricots, apple and raisins or chicken breast stuffed with haggis and wrapped in bacon with Drambuie sauce. Prices range from £14.50 to £17.95 for fillet steak. Specials include teriyaki pork loin with cabbage and chilli salad and poached rib eye steaks with pomme purée.

★ Q S V C

MELROSE
Burts Hotel

Market Square, TD6 9PL

▶ On B6374
☼ Daily 12-2pm, 5-11pm
Ⓨ Daily 12-2pm, 6-9pm
T (01896) 822285
F (01896) 822870
E burtshotel@aol.com
W www.burtshotel.co.uk
Caledonian Deuchars IPA, 80/-; Taylor Landlord; guests
☺ Innovative bar food
Elegantly-decorated bistro, cheerful lounge bar

The bar food at Burts, a family-run hotel close to Melrose Abbey, would grace many restaurants. You might start your supper with freshly-prepared soup and home-made bread, chicken liver parfait with red onion marmalade, sea bass roulade or smoked chicken Caesar salad, priced from £2.95-£5. Then move on to baked sole with mussel and prawn chowder, pork with caramelised onion and parsley sausages on colcannon, maize-fed chicken stuffed with black pudding, rump of lamb with hot pot potatoes and pickled red cabbage, freshly crumbed scampi tails or home-made Aberdeen Angus beef burgers. Vegetarian choices are roast Portobello mushroom with fresh pasta and artichoke sauce or baked bell pepper stuffed with Stichill cheese, pine nuts and couscous. Salads include mustard-baked gammon and Scotch beef served rare. Main dishes range from around £8-£11, £14-£16 for grilled Scottish steak hung for at least 21 days. Snacks include an excellent range of sandwiches and baguettes.

The restaurant is pricey but the food is exceptional, offering a taste of the Borders, such as Teviotdale cheese wrapped in smoked salmon then deep fried with whisky marmalade or loin of Border lamb rolled round wild mushrooms and spinach, with a kidney in the middle.

S V P C

PAXTON

Cross Inn

TD15 1TE

- ▶ Off B6460, Paxton is signed from A1
- Tue-Sun 11am (12.30pm Sun)-2.30pm, 6.30pm-midnight
- Tue-Sun 12 (12.30 Sun)-2.30pm, 7-9.30pm
- T (01289) 386267
- E ivisowd@aol.com
- Beer range varies
- Modern English and European style cuisine, all home cooked
- Renovated village pub, recently reverted to its original name following restoration of the cross outside; comfortable dining room

Sunday lunch at the Cross is a real treat: a choice of five starters, including Berwick crab salad, then either roast lamb or beef, or both together! Or you could opt for local pheasant breast in red wine and mushroom sauce, or baked in a pie with beef steak, Cumberland sausages or baked trout. Main courses are from £7-£9, puddings are £3.50 if you can manage one.

The regular menu is similarly varied, mixing traditional and continental dishes, so you could kick off with haggis, neeps and tatties but follow on with boeuf bourguignonne from the specials board or veal steak piazziola. By reversing the styles you could begin with garlic mushrooms on tagliatelle or seafood cannelloni and go on to a locally-sourced meat such as roast rack of lamb, fillet steak with black pudding or a venison steak, served in red wine and red berry sauce. Starters are all under a fiver, mains between £10 and £15.

Some of the bar snacks and light meals, again featuring local produce, are offered in small and large portions, so potted Berwick crab and crayfish and avocado are both £6/£9, haggis £5/£8 and salmon and prawn fishcake £5/£7. Pub favourites such as bangers and mash, cod and chips and a pie of the day are also available.

★ ❀ S V ♿ P ⚡ 👪 C

RESTON

Red Lion

Main street, TD14 5JP

- ▶ Off A1 10 miles N of Berwick
- Mon-Fri 5.30-11pm; Sat & Sun 12-11pm
- Tue-Fri 6-9pm; Sat & Sun 12-2pm, 6-9pm
- T (01890) 761266
- E general@a1redlionreston.co.uk
- W www.a1redlionreston.co.uk
- Beer range varies
- Freshly-cooked menu offering plenty of choice
- Village pub and restaurant built in 1781

The chef at the Red Lion is the landlord's son, preparing to order an interesting range of fish, meat and vegetarian dishes using fresh produce, which have earned much praise from diners – one said 'better than anything I had in London'.

Typical starters include fresh vegetable soup of the day, haggis and black pudding with whisky sauce, smoked salmon and strawberries in a dill dressing, deep-fried Camembert with cranberry jelly and filo pastry baskets filled with mussels, priced from £3-£4.75. Main dishes might be crispy pheasant and pigeon breasts with apple and Calvados sauce, oven-roasted lamb shanks with redcurrant and mint sauce, roast chicken with fresh apricot and onion sauce, pork fillet stuffed with black pudding on cranberry sauce, or fresh Scottish salmon supreme slowly roasted with bacon and red wine.

Vegetarian choices deserve a special mention – roast leeks, mushrooms, peppers and chestnuts finished with red pepper coulis and almonds, butternut squash stuffed with spinach and Brie, sprinkled with sesame seeds and roasted, or mushroom and chestnut strudel served with sage butter. Main courses, all served with fresh seasonal vegetables and potatoes, range from around £9-£12.50.

★ 🏰 Q ❀ V 🍺 ♿ 🍎 P 👪 C

ST MARY'S LOCH
Tibbie Shiels Inn
TD7 5LH

▶ On bank of the loch on A708 Moffat-Selkirk
Mon-Sat 11am-11pm; Sun 12.30-11pm
Daily 12.30-8pm
T (01750) 42231
F (01750) 42302
E info@tibbieshiels.com
W www.tibbieshielsinn.com
Belhaven 80/-; Broughton Greenmantle IPA
Traditional simple bar food
Spectacular loch setting with literary connections and possible ghost

Simple dishes at low prices and a hint that you are entering (or leaving) Scotland start with home-made chicken liver and port pâté with oatcakes, £2.50, or home-made soup with crusty bread at £2.25. Main courses on the set menu include Yarrow trout poached or fried and served with chips, salad or veg, fried haddock, the well-loved Hole Mole Chilli with rice, salad and garlic bread, rib eye steak, ploughmans of pâté or cheese, home-baked ham with salad or lamb cutlets with tomato and mint jelly, and beef burgers, prices from £3.75 to £7.95 for the steak. The vegetarian selection is cashew nut loaf with tomato and herb salad, mushroom and hazelnut crumble or vegetable strudel, all £4.75. Desserts include traditional Scottish clootie dumpling (a sort of boiled fruitcake) home made and served with cream, as well as fruit pie, spotted dick, treacle sponge and the usual Death by Chocolate. In addition, daily specials are on the board.

★ Q S V P C

SWINTON
☆ Wheatsheaf
Main Street, TD11 3JJ

▶ Off A6112 between Duns and Coldstream
Daily 11am-3pm, 6-11.30pm
Daily 12-2pm, 6-9pm
T (01890) 860257
F (01890) 860688
E reception@wheatsheaf-swinton.co.uk
W www.wheatsheaf-swinton.co.uk
Caledonian Deuchars IPA; guest
Gastropub specialising in local seafood and game
Cosy, comfortable country inn, full of character, warmed by log fires; at peak meal times customers just wanting a drink may be turned away

A member of the Scottish Beef Club, the Wheatsheaf guarantees the quality of the produce it serves; all its beef is fully traceable. Other local produce coming from the wonderful Scottish borders 'larder' includes the famous rack of lamb, venison and wild mushrooms. Local seafood is a speciality of the house and the specials board usually features scallops, langoustine and fillet of halibut in addition to the fresh crab and pan-fried salmon that feature on the lunch and dinner menus. Vegetarians are well catered for; if nothing takes your fancy you can discuss other options with the staff.

Exciting starters include smoked haddock Scotch egg with curried mango mayo, sautéed Paris mushrooms and bacon in filo pastry case with Tobermory cheddar glaze and Eyemouth crab, pak choi and shitake mushroom spring roll on a sweet chilli sauce. At dinner time you can refresh your palate with a passion fruit sorbet, £2.95, before going on to Gressingham duck breast on parsnip mash with plum and port sauce or peppered fillet of wild venison on creamed celeriac with juniper and redcurrant sauce for around £16. Desserts around a fiver include sticky ginger and pear pud with hot fudge sauce or apple streusel tart, both served with ice cream.

Q V P C

TWEEDSMUIR
Crook Inn
ML12 6QN

- ▶ Just north of Tweedsmuir on A701
- ☼ Daily 9am-11pm
- 🍴 Daily 12-2.30pm, 5.30-8.30pm
- T (01899) 880272
- F (01899) 880294
- E thecrookinn@btinternet.com
- W www.crookinn.co.uk
- 🍺 Broughton ales
- ☺ Traditional Scottish with local specialities
- ◉ Historic inn with listed 17th-century bar on old coaching route

Landlady Susan Bell is the chef making an early start with a full Scottish breakfast for her B&B guests (eight en-suite rooms). The snack menu is available all day with bar food at lunchtimes and dining room menu, all freshly prepared to order, in the evening. Using fresh local produce as far as possible, specialities include Crook Pillows – cheese, mushroom and leek parcels, Borders shepherds pie and haggis layered with neeps and tatties served with whisky sauce. Susan uses only Scottish meat, and all her haddock comes from Arbroath.

The main menu includes starters such as beer-battered beetroot, risotto of sun-dried tomato, basil and Parmesan, or terrine with plum chutney and oatcakes priced from £3.25-£3.95. Main dishes include the popular 20oz gammon steak with fried egg or pineapple, Gressingham duck served with soy and honey on herby mash with buttered cabbage, and strips of chicken fillet in beer batter with sweet and sour sauce, priced £7.95-£11.95. Fine Scottish steaks range from sirloin at £11.95 to a 20oz T-bone at £16.50. A good selection of veggie dishes includes vegetarian cheese salad, pasta in mushroom sauce, those Crook Pillows and Crook's own vegetarian haggis. The listed early 17th-century Willie Wastle's Bar started out as the inn's kitchen and still has the original flagstone floor.

★ 🏰 Q ❀ 🛏 S V 🅿 ⚟ 👪 C

CALLANDER
Claymore Bar
Waverley Hotel, 88-94 Main Street, FK17 8BD

- ▶ 15 miles NW of Stirling, via the A84
- ☼ Daily 11am-midnight (1am Fri & Sat)
- 🍴 Mon-Fri 12-3pm, 6-8.30pm; Sat & Sun 12-8.30pm
- T (01877) 330245
- F (01877) 331120
- E enquiries@thewaverleycallander.com
- W www.thewaverleycallander.com
- 🍺 Beer range varies
- ☺ Wholesome, home-made Scottish fare with some original dishes
- ◉ Family-run hotel and bar that is gaining a good reputation for its food and ale

Not only does the Claymore offer beers from just about every Scottish micro-brewery (and quite a few English ones), it also stages two week-long beer festivals. The bar also offers a fine menu of home cooked dishes, including some of its own invention such as the black pudding stack, served on a bed of hot roasted vegetable sauce, and the haggis pakora (spiced haggis coated in oatmeal and deep fried, served with garlic mayo, green salad and coleslaw), both on the starters list for under a fiver. Other appetisers include smoked scotch salmon cornets filled with cream cheese, smoked haddock fish cake and one of a long list of home-made soups.

All kinds of interesting special dishes might follow, perhaps collops of beef in cask ale, creamed kidneys and wild rice, pork medallions in real cider, venison and port stroganoff (wild Perthshire venison slowly braised with cherries and port) or possibly its own version of chilli – Trossachs Fiery Beef. Pasta, fish and a vegetarian dish of the day are always available. Main courses are mostly £6.50-£9, but a classic Highland fillet steak flamed in Scotch whisky will set you back £15. For afters, why not try the home-made clootie dumpling or Ma Scott's millennium pudding, apple sponge flavoured with cinnamon and whisky?

🛏 S V 🍺 ♿ ♣ 🍎 ⚟ 👪 C

DOLLAR
Castle Campbell Hotel
11 Bridge Street, FK14 7DE

- On A91next to bridge with clock tower
- Mon-Fri 12-11.30pm (1am Fri); Sat 12-midnight; Sun 12.30-11pm
- Mon-Sat 12-2pm, 5.30-9pm; Sun 12-3pm, 5-9pm
- T (01259) 742519
- F (01259) 743742
- E bookings@castle-campbell.co.uk
- W www.castle-campbell.co.uk
- Harviestoun Bitter & Twisted; guest
- Well prepared pub food using quality Scottish ingredients
- Warm and welcoming hotel situated on Dollar Burn at the foot of the Ochil Hills

A hotel offering some good Scottish staples, with sandwiches from smoked salmon to cold roast beef and ploughman's with Isle of Mull Cheddar or Dunsyre Blue among the lunchtime snacks. Main meals include starters of fresh soup, Scottish mussels with thyme and chilli, five bean, tuna and red onion salad, vegetable terrine with oatcakes and chutney, vegetable and goats' cheese tart or warm black pudding and apple salad, £2.55-£4.70.

Main courses are smoked haddock pancake with cheese, haddock fillet in batter, roast salmon with hollandaise, smoked salmon with scrambled eggs, haggis, neeps and tatties, steak pie topped with proper shortcrust pastry, char-grilled lamb chops and chicken breast topped with Cheddar, smoked bacon and roast tomato. For vegetarians there is mushroom stroganoff or lasagne verdi. Main course prices range from £7-£9.50. At night the menu is augmented by Aberdeen Angus steaks – 8oz or 12oz sirloin or fillet with béarnaise or Arran mustard sauce, £15-£24. Desserts at lunchtime and evening are ginger and golden syrup sponge with custard, apple and sultana oat crumble with ice cream, baked cheesecake, chocolate fudge cake with ice cream or sticky toffee pudding, all £3.75.

V P C

STIRLING
Birds & Bees
Easter Cornton Road, Causewayhead, FK9 5PB

- Near the Wallace monument in Causewayhead
- Daily 11am-1am
- Mon-Fri 12-2.30pm, 5-9.30pm; Sat & Sun 12.30-10pm
- T 01786 473663
- W www.thebirdsandthebees-stirling.com
- Caledonian Deuchars IPA, 80/-; guests
- Superb Scottish and international dishes
- A cosy, farmsteading conversion with quirky features; courtyard beer garden contains petanque

An eclectic menu of both Scottish and international cuisine highlights prime Scottish beef – ranging from 6oz 'minute' to 8oz sirloin or fillet, £9.50-£14.50, with a variety of sauces including Rob Roy made with malt whisky, spring onions and cream. Starters include home-made soup, crisp coated haggis medallions with malt whisky and mustard mayo, Dublin Bay mussels steamed with lemongrass, coriander and cream, herb coated Brie bites with smoked bacon and thyme mayo or home-made chicken pakoras, £2.95-£4.95.

Main courses include traditional pub dishes such as steak and onion pie, ploughman's platter of Scottish cheeses and pickles, beef burgers with choice of cheese, pepper sauce, chilli or coleslaw, or deep-fried haddock, prices £6.50-£7.50. You will also find spicy chorizo pasta with red wine and mushrooms, poached salmon with caper and herb butter sauce, fresh king prawns with spring onion, ginger and oyster sauce, or pasta carbonara. In the international section the choice is Mexican enchilada, chicken satay, beef fillet in black bean sauce with basmati rice, chicken breast in crisp batter with sweet orange sauce and rice, Mexican enchiladas or beef Nentara – fillet in tomato and coriander sauce. Desserts include caramel apple pie, chocolate and brandy pot or banana fritter.

★ S V P C

GATEHOUSE OF FLEET

☆ Masonic Arms

10 Ann Street, DG7 2HU

- ▶ Turning next to Gatehouse clock tower
- ☼ Daily summer 11.30am-11.30pm; winter 11.30am-2.30pm, 5.30-11.30pm
- Daily 12-2pm, 6-9pm
- T (01557) 814335
- E info@themasonic-arms.co-uk
- W www.themasonic-arms.co.uk
- Beer range varies
- Gastropub with bar, brasserie and restaurant, using Scottish produce
- Situated in a pretty town close to the coast, with a contemporary restaurant and attractive Mediterranean conservatory

Seasonal local produce is intrinsic to chef and patron Chris Walker's cooking. His menus focus on fresh ingredients sourced from suppliers from the surrounding area: fresh fish, langoustines and lobsters from Galloway Smokehouse, Loch Arthur cheeses, venison and grass fed beef from local farmer Bryce Taylor and ice creams from Cream O' Galloway round the corner.

Starters might be home-made soup with home-made bread, haggis and tattie scone tower, wild duck, pheasant and foie gras terrine, or home-made Thai chicken wontons, £3.10 to £4.95. 'Pub grub and posh nosh' includes fresh haddock in beer batter with fries, tartare sauce and mushy peas, king scallops also in beer batter on buttered fettucine with sweet chilli sauce, Galloway scampi, venison and marmalade bangers on bubble and squeak with red wine jus, Scottish salmon with broad bean and smoked bacon potato cakes, smoked haddock lasagne with saffron cream, and filo parcels of Galloway lamb with port and redcurrant sauce; prices range from £8.95-£13.25. Fine rib eye, sirloin and fillet grass fed beef steaks are £11.95-£16.95, and for vegetarians there is a choice of red pepper, courgette and thyme risotto or mushroom, cranberry and Brie wellington. The house beer Masonic Boom is brewed by Sulwath.

Q ✿ S V C

HAUGH OF URR

Laurie Arms

11-13 Main Street, DG7 3YA

- ▶ On B794, 1 mile S of A75 and 14 miles W of Dumfries
- ☼ Daily 11.45am-2.30pm (3 Sun), 5.30 (6 Sun)-11pm (midnight Sat)
- Mon-Sat 11.45am-1.45pm, 5.30-8.45pm; Sun 11.45am-2pm, 6-9pm
- T (01556) 660246
- Beer range varies
- Home-cooked food based on local produce; char grilled steaks a speciality
- Award-winning pub on the main street of a quiet village in the Urr Valley

This welcoming rural pub is renowned locally both for its variety of ales and the quality of its food, particularly the char grilled steaks. These come in a good variety from plain fillet, sirloin or T-bone, or steak Diane, peppered fillet or the Laurie special (thinly sliced fillet cooked slowly in garlic butter, red wine and fresh cream), £12.50-£14.95. Other house specialities are mulled venison steaks baked in the oven with baby onions and cranberry sauce, £7.25, or Laurie beef, £6.50, marinated overnight in real ale, herbs and onions then slowly oven cooked.

A good range of starters, mostly under £4, includes Stilton and bacon fritters served with a spicy tomato dip, breaded lobster tails with tartare sauce or local haggis topped with a creamy onion sauce. The famous Scottish dish can also be ordered as a main course served traditionally with 'neeps and tatties', or you can have Highland chicken – a fillet filled with haggis and whisky sauce. There is a reasonable choice of fish, such as Galloway salmon with creamy parsley sauce or deep fried plaice or haddock. Home-made desserts include sherry trifle, apple pie, pavlova or banoffee pie. At lunchtime there is also a good choice of sandwiches, toasties and jacket spuds with various fillings – including haggis!

★ Q ✿ S V P

MOFFAT
Black Bull Hotel & Railway Bar
Churchgate, DG10 9ES

▶ Take Moffat road from M74/A74 jct 15, hotel is on right on entering town
☼ Daily 11am-11pm
🍴 Daily 12-9pm
T (01683) 220206
F (01683) 220483
E hotel@blackbullmoffat.co.uk
W www.blackbullmoffat.co.uk
🍺 Caledonian Deuchars IPA; McEwan's 80/-; Theakston Best Bitter; guests
☺ Good, wholesome food with a real Scottish flavour
◙ Historic inn full of character; visit the Railway Bar, replete with railway memorabilia, across the courtyard

Many hostelries in Scotland claim a connection with the Scottish bard; it is said that Robert Burns wrote his famous 'epigram to a scrimpit nature' at the Black Bull. You can dine in the Burns Room or in the Claverhouse Restaurant, which has its own history – the inn was used in the 1680s as the HQ for Graham of Claverhouse and his dragoons before being sent by the English King to put down religious rebels on the border.

The food here has a definite Scottish emphasis; you can start with 'sporran' of black pudding – deep fried in Scotch ale batter and smothered in a creamy whisky mustard sauce, £3.75, or 'kilted' smoked salmon – prawns with cream cheese wrapped in smoked Solway salmon, £4.75. Haggis, served with 'bashed tatties and champit neeps' and Kippford mussels are offered as a starter or main course. The menu does have a list of 'dishes from around the world' but they are not as enticing as the Moffat ram pie (shepherd's pie made with Annandale lamb), Black Bull hotpot, Eskdale venison sausage with red wine and onion gravy, deep-fried fillet of Scottish breaded haddock, all £6.95, or indeed the house speciality, Black Bull sizzlers – steaks served on a hot cast iron platter with accompaniments.

S V C

THORNHILL
Buccleuch & Queensberry Hotel
112 Drumlanrig Street, DG3 5LU

▶ Thornhill is on the A76, approx 10 miles N of Dumfries
☼ Daily 11am-1am
🍴 Daily 12-2.30pm, 5.30-9.30pm
T (01848) 330215
E Naomi@bucchleuchhotel.co.uk
W www.buccleuchhotel.co.uk
🍺 Caledonian 80/-; guests
☺ Freshly prepared meals from premium Scottish produce
◙ Built in 1851 as a coaching inn, the hotel stands at the market cross in a picturesque conservation village; the bar has a log fire

Situated close to Drumlanrig Castle (home of the Duke of Buccleuch, and worth a visit) and the River Nith, famed for its salmon fishing, the hotel caters for tourists, anglers and visitors keen on outdoor pursuits. The food here comes in hearty portions and is carefully prepared from fresh, seasonal, mostly local ingredients. The beef comes from the renowned Buccleuch Estate and all breads, pastries and sweets are freshly baked on the premises.

To begin your meal you could choose from ham haugh terrine with red onion chutney and brioche bread, haggis rissoles with swede and whisky sauce, prawn and shallot timbale with rocket salad and basil oil or maybe baked parmesan crusted goats' cheese with cucumber and crème fraîche, all under £5. Favourite main courses on the menu include beef, beer and mushroom pie, prime roast topside of beef or the award-winning haggis with 'neeps and tatties' (mashed turnips and potatoes). But before you choose it is worth consulting the specials board – there may be pan-fried duck breast with black pudding, seafood pancake or poached fillet of Scottish salmon. Or you could have something from the char grill – fillet or sirloin steak or lamb cutlets all served with peppered onions and fat cut chips. Prices range from £13-£14.25.

★ Q S V P C

ANSTRUTHER
Dreel Tavern

16 High Street West, KY10 3DL

- Town centre
- Daily 11am-midnight
- Daily 12-2pm, 5.30-9pm
- T (01333) 310727
- Caledonian Deuchars IPA; Greene King Old Speckled Hen; guest
- Traditional pub food with good seafood dishes
- Former old-stone coaching inn dating back to the 16th-century; exposed beams and an open fire

This pub has a magnificent philosophy: 'our menu is a guideline – if we have the ingredients we'll create whatever you desire'. And, with fresh, seasonal produce delivered to the pub on a daily basis, meals can vary every day. The local butcher supplies meat that has been properly hung for 21 days, which is then slow cooked for the most tender pies and casseroles. You could start your meal with deep-fried Camembert with cranberry coulis, marinated herring with brown bread, king prawns in filo pastry and sweet chilli dip, potato skins with a choice of dips or home-made soup or pâté, £2-£4.50.

There are main courses to cater for all tastes including mouth-watering home-made pies – steak, or steak, mushroom and Guinness, or smoked fish – all topped with puff pastry. Or Burgundy lamb braised in a rich wine sauce with seasonal veg, char-grilled sirloin or gammon steak, and chicken dishes such as pan-fried Cajun chicken or breast stuffed with Stilton, crushed walnuts and apples then wrapped in bacon and roasted with garlic butter. For fish lovers haddock fillets can be poached or fried in the pub's own recipe batter, and poached salmon is served with either a cheese and prawn or lemon and parsley sauce. There is always a vegetarian dish of the day; main courses are £7-£12.50.

★ S V C

ABERNETHY
Crees Inn

Main Street, PH2 9LA

- Take A912 (jct 9) turn off M90, village is 7 miles S of Perth
- Daily 11am-2.30pm, 5.30-11.30pm
- Daily 12-2pm, 6-8.45pm
- T (01738) 850714
- E creesinn@creesinn.co.uk
- W www.creesinn.co.uk
- Beer range varies
- Traditional home-cooked Scottish dishes
- This listed building, formerly a farmhouse, has been sympathetically renovated as a homely pub with a small restaurant

The Crees is situated at the centre of the picturesque conservation village of Abernethy in the shadow of one of only two remaining Pictish watchtowers in Scotland. Abernethy was once the southern Pictish capital of Scotland and, like the inn, has been the subject of sympathetic renovation. The busy restaurant serves freshly cooked produce on a Scottish theme at reasonable prices. Starters, £3.50 or less, might include haggis fritters (haggis, neeps and tatties with a splash of Drambuie), mushroom ravioli with Stilton sauce, prawn filo parcels with lemon and dill dressing, spinach and feta goujons with garlic mayo dip or Prawn Breton, in a creamy grain mustard mayonnaise.

To follow there is a good choice of fish, such as battered haddock with tartare sauce, breaded wholetail scampi and poached Scottish salmon fillet with sun dried tomato and basil butter. The spicy and fruity lamb casserole sounds very tempting – diced gigot in cumin and coriander sauce, served with apricots and rice – while another spicy offering is the breast of chicken salad with mango and curry mayonnaise, topped with diced apple. For more traditional tastes there is, of course, a steak and ale pie, plus chicken breast in creamy mustard and bacon sauce, and a vegetarian dish of the day chalked up on the blackboard. Main courses are all under £8.

★ Q S V P C

BRIDGE OF CALLY
Bridge of Cally Hotel
PH10 7JJ

- ▶ On A93, 6 miles N of Blairgowrie
- Mon-Thu 11-11pm; Fri & Sat 11-12.30am; Sun 12.30-11pm
- Daily 12-9.30pm
- T (01250) 886231
- F (01250) 886793
- E enquiries@bridgeofcalyhotel.com
- W www.bridgeofcallyhotel.com
- Beer range varies
- ☺ Good freshly-cooked produce including local game, meat and seasonal vegetables
- Quiet, family run inn by the River Ardle, set in one and a half acres of private moorland

An ideal base for an outdoor pursuits holiday, the hotel is near the Glen Shee ski slopes and has a new rod and gun room. The estate provides much of the game served here and vegetables are grown in the walled garden. A full bistro menu and daily specials are served in the bar, conservatory or dining room, lunchtime and evening. Starters, under £4, include smoked haddock omelette or warm salad of estate shot pigeon with pancetta, black pudding and oyster mushrooms. Mains, £6.75-£10.95, might be navarin of lamb or fresh haddock in beer batter. Snacks are served during the afternoon.

The £25 restaurant menu includes three courses plus coffee and petit fours. To start there might be soup of the day, seared scallops with parsnip purée and white truffle oil, chicken liver parfait and toasted brioche or smoked salmon. Main courses are fillet of Angus beef with potato rösti, wild mushrooms and Madeira jus, loin of lamb with black pudding, mash and ratatouille, selection of market fish and thyme-scented potatoes slices with langoustine ravioli and shellfish sauce or spaghetti with cherry tomatoes, garlic and rocket with pesto sauce and Parmesan. Desserts include apple bavarois and granny smith sorbet, coffee crème brûlée or cheese and oatcakes.

Q S V P C

BROUGHTY FERRY
Fisherman's Tavern
10-16 Fort Street, DD5 2AD

- ▶ Next to the RNLI station
- Daily 11am-1am
- Daily 11.30am-2.30pm (3.30pm Sat & Sun)
- T (01382) 775941
- F (01382) 477466
- E bookings@fishermans-tavern-hotel.co.uk
- W www.fishermans-tavern-hotel.co.uk
- Beer range varies
- ☺ Specialises in seafood and Scottish dishes
- Set in a terrace of colourful 17th-century buildings; originally opened by a whelk fisherman, it is now a small hotel with secluded walled garden

The Fisherman's is the only Scottish pub to appear for 30 consecutive years in CAMRA's Good Beer Guide, and is a former Scottish and British CAMRA Pub of the Year. Only lunchtime meals (and breakfast for guests) are served here, but you can dine at night in the pub's sister establishment, the Royal Arch in the main shopping centre. For fresh fish, consult the daily blackboard of special dishes. For a snack lunch there is a good selection of baguettes, ciabattas and rolls, or baked potatoes with some unusual fillings such as Brie with Parma ham, coronation chicken or scrambled egg with smoked salmon.

Main courses (apart from steaks) are all under £8 and some are available as smaller portions for children. Choose from seafood crêpe topped with Parmesan, home-made smokie pie with potatoes and cheese, smoked haddock kedgeree, steak and St Andrews ale pie, chicken curry, pan fried lamb's liver with bacon and onions or a selection of soufflé omelettes. There is also a good choice of seasonal salads at £7.50. A special business lunch is offered – soup of the day plus a choice of five main courses or a main course with dessert. Heart-warming puds include sticky toffee, chocolate fudge cake and caramel apple betty.

★ Q S V (Broughty Ferry) C

BROUGHTY FERRY
Royal Arch Bar
285 Brook Street, DD5 2DS

- Three streets in from seafront
- Mon-Sat 11am-midnight; Sun 12.30pm-midnight
- Sun-Thu 11.30am (12.30 Sun)-2.30pm, 5-8pm; Fri & Sat 11.30am-7.30pm
- T (01382) 779741
- W www.royal-arch.co.uk
- Caledonian Deuchars IPA; guests
- Traditional pub menu plus daily specials
- Community local in busy shopping area near seafront; wood carved gantry and bar, art deco style lounge

A varied menu offers staple pub grub plus chef's specials, using meat from a nearby butcher and fresh fish from a local fish merchant. Seafood is popular with customers: the seafood platter of smoked mackerel, Arbroath smokie, prawns, mussels, crab salad and scampi is a favourite at £6.95. House specials include beef highlander – that's steak in a creamy tomato sauce with brandy and paprika, beef goulash, chicken fricassee with a creamy sherry sauce, beef fajitas and chicken tikka masala, all priced £6-£6.75.

Traditional dishes include both steak pie and steak and Guinness pie, liver cooked with sausages and bacon in onion gravy, sweet and sour chicken, prawn curry and chilli con carne, £5.75-£6.50, while the dearest dish is grilled sirloin steak at £9.95. There is a fair vegetarian choice – macaroni cheese, mushroom and nut fettuccine, mushroom stroganoff and vegetarian omelettes, £5.50-£6.25. Starters include home-made soup, mozzarella fingers with hot chillies in batter plus salsa dip, and there is a selection of light meals and snacks – stuffed potato skins, toasted BLT sandwich, all sorts of burgers, and paninis with fillings from chicken curry to parma ham with Brie. Desserts include caramel apple granny and bread and butter pud. The Royal Arch is in the Eat Scotland scheme. Children are allowed on Sunday only.

★ S V (Broughty Ferry) C

DUNKELD
Taybank
Tay Terrace, PH8 0AQ

- Just off A9, in the village
- Daily 11am-11pm (midnight Fri & Sat)
- 11am-8.45pm 'most days'
- T (01350) 727340
- F (01350) 727940
- E admin@thetaybank.com
- W www.thetaybank.com
- Inveralmond Ossian's Ale
- Varied pub menu, stovies are a speciality
- Full of character, with a garden on the bank of the River Tay; also known as 'Scotland's musical meeting place'

The Taybank is beloved of traditional Scottish and Irish music fans; so much so that the bar is equipped with a range of musical instruments (including a piano) for visitors who do not bring their own, and live events are staged regularly in the small music room. The pub is also definitely worth visiting for the food. Stovies – stoved potatoes, a popular Scottish one-pot dish based on potatoes and onions – are a house speciality here at any time of day, priced around £4.50. You can choose from the Highlander (the original stovie of potato, onion and corned beef), Tribute (with haggis and onion gravy), Butterstone (strips of chicken and bacon with carrots and onions and a hint of tarragon), Beinn a' Chally (local Perthshire lamb with onions and carrots and a hint of mint), Taybank (beef and horseradish) or the Tay Valley (a vegetarian option incorporating broccoli and Stilton cheese). The menu also offers a good choice of pasta dishes, all under £6.50, including several vegetarian recipes, home-made burgers and pub favourites such as lasagne, scampi and steak and ale pie. Warm baguettes with interesting fillings, sandwiches and toasties are also available.

★ S V P C

MEIKLEOUR
Meikleour Hotel
PH2 6EB

- Off A93 between Perth and Blairgowrie
- Mon-Fri 11am-3pm, 6-11pm (midnight Fri); Sat 11am-midnight; Sun 11am-11pm
- Daily 12.15 (12.30 Sun)-2.30pm, 6.30-9pm
- T (01250) 883206
- F (01250) 883406
- E visitus@meikleourhotel.co.uk
- W www.meikleourhotel.co.uk
- Beer range varies
- Modern Scottish cuisine based on fresh ingredients
- Refurbished coaching inn with a stone flagged bar, comfortable lounge and attractive restaurant, popular with walkers and anglers

You will see the turn off the main road to Meikleour because of its famous landmark: the Meikleour beech hedge at 100 feet high and a third of a mile long was planted in 1745 and is recognised by the Guinness Book of Records as the tallest hedge in the world. All the food served here is prepared in the hotel's kitchens, where they make their own sausages, terrines, jams and marmalade. They have their own herd of cows providing top quality beef and they air cure their own salmon; the Lure of Meikleour beer made especially by Inveralmond is named after the fishing fly used by anglers on the Tay and Spey to catch the fish.

The hotel has developed a reputation for devising its own recipes, such as a giant Yorkshire pudding filled with beef and horseradish stew, marinated salmon and pigeon and exotic dishes made with wild boar, ostrich and even kangaroo. Other popular items on the menu are haddock fried in ale and spring water batter, Parmesan crusted seabass and lamb shanks. If you do not want a full meal you can enjoy a hearty snack in the bar; a children's menu is served in both the bar and dining room.

★ Q S V C

PERTH
Greyfriars
15 South Street, PH2 8PG

- In the city centre
- Mon-Sat 11am-11pm (11.45pm Fri & Sat); Sun 3-11pm
- Mon-Sat 11.45am-2.30pm, Fri & Sat 7.30pm set dinner
- T (01738) 633036
- E thegreyfriar@blueyonder.co.uk
- Caledonian Deuchars IPA; Taylor Landlord; guests
- Good snacks plus a mix of traditional and contemporary lunch dishes
- Vibrant and friendly, one of the smallest lounge bars in the city centre; meals can also be taken in a small upstairs room

Handy for the Victorian theatre, art gallery and museum, the Greyfriars offers good value lunches. Everything is produced on the premises, apart from 'chips, haggis and burgers'. It is renowned for its soups: cullen skink, cream of spinach, minestrone, asparagus, beef broth and cockie leekie. Indeed soup is always the first course on the menu at the gourmet dinner served on Friday and Saturday evenings, £19.95 for five courses, booking essential. On the bar menu, soups are just £2.25. Other popular lunchtime dishes are the omelettes – mushroom, cheese, ham or pepper and onion – served with chips and salad for £4.75, or for £3.25 you can opt for the 'Express lunch' of soup and a sandwich.

The lunch menus change seasonally as all ingredients are purchased locally. In summer there are various salads, while in winter steak, mushroom and tipple ale pie or hot beef or bean chilli go down better. You will usually find Scottish dishes such as haggis, neeps and champit tatties with whisky gravy, £5.95, fresh haddock in batter, and mince and tatties. Puddings are a mere £2.50: bread and butter pudding with cinnamon custard, chocolate profiteroles or rhubarb pie and custard, for example.

★ Q S V

PITLOCHRY
Moulin Inn
Kirkmichael Road, PH16 5EH

- ▶ On A924, half a mile from Pitlochry
- ☼ Daily 12-11pm
- Daily 12-9.30pm
- T (01796) 472196
- F (01796) 474098
- E enquiries@moulinhotel.co.uk
- W www.moulinhotel.co.uk
- Moulin Light, Braveheart, Ale of Atholl, Old Remedial
- ☺ Traditional, home-made Scottish dishes
- Dating from 1695, the inn is the oldest part of the Moulin Hotel which has its own brewery situated in a former coach house

This lovely old inn makes an ideal base for walkers, standing on an ancient crossroads near Pitlochry – the 'gateway to the Highlands'. Real ale fans will want to try the delightful beers from its own brewery. And if you also want to try Scottish fare this is the place to come too. The menu lists such dishes as the Sporran O'plenty – a 6oz minute steak stuffed with haggis, Venison Braveheart –strips of local venison pan fried with mushrooms and their own Braveheart beer and Scotman's Bunnet – a batter pudding filled with highland meat and vegetable stew.

Some of the dishes such as Angus steak and game casserole McDuff need no explanation but I couldn't even guess 'vrackie grostel'; in fact it is sauté potatoes with smoked bacon, lightly herbed and topped with a fried egg. I've had something similar in Stockholm, so maybe the name has Viking roots. Main courses range from £6.50 for haggis, neeps and tatties to £12 for the steak. Vegetarian options include sautéed mushroom pancakes, stuffed peppers and vegetarian chilli, all around £7. You may not manage a starter and pudding so you will have to decide between, say, the Skye mussels or smoked meat platter, both £5.75, and the home-made apple pie or sticky whisky fudge cake.

★ ❀ S V ♿ (Pitlochry)
P C

WESTER BALGEDIE
☆ Balgedie Toll Tavern
KY13 9HE

- ▶ From Milnathort or Kinross follow signs for Kinneswood and Scotlandwell
- ☼ Mon-Thu 11am-11pm; Fri & Sat 11am-12.30am; Sun 12.30pm-11pm
- Mon-Sat 12-3pm, 5-9pm; Sun 12.30-9pm
- T (01592) 840212
- Harviestoun Bitter & Twisted; guest
- ☺ Extensive menu and daily specials, all freshly cooked to order
- The oldest part of this former toll house dates from circa 1534; traditional country pub replete with exposed beams and old settles

In the days when travellers had to pay tolls they were forced to break their journey here; anyone passing through today would also be well advised to stop off for a meal as the tavern enjoys a good reputation locally for its food. The extensive menu caters for all tastes and pockets: starters are £2.40-£5.25, mains £6-£15 and desserts around £4. Vegetarians have plenty of choice and other special dietary requirements, particularly wheat/gluten free dishes, can be catered for on request.

The specials board lists a good selection of local seafood and game. The house specialities are Balgedie smokie, served as a starter or main course – local fillet of smoked haddock, lightly poached in cream and topped with Scottish cheddar gratin –and loin of venison and haggis en croute – encased in golden pastry and served with redcurrant, rosemary and wine sauce, dauphinoise potatoes and fresh veg. The menu majors on traditional pub favourites – steak pie, deep fried east coast haddock, local bangers and mash – but also features more upmarket dishes such as roast loin of pork stuffed with tomato, ham, salami and basil with apple arran mustard sauce. Puddings are all home made, so leave room for cherry and almond tart, sticky toffee pud or Balgedie banoffee pie.

★ Q ❀ S V ♿ P C

ABERDEEN
The Office at the Atholl Hotel
54 Kings Gate, AB15 4YN

- ▶ 1.5 miles from city centre
- ☼ Mon-Sat 11am-2.30pm, 5-11pm (11.30pm Fri & Sat); Sun 12-11pm
- Ⓨ Mon-Sat 12-2.15pm, 6 (5.30 Fri & Sat)-9.30pm; Sun 12-8.30pm
- T (01224) 323505
- F (01224) 321555
- E info@atholl-aberdeen.co.uk
- W www.atholl-aberdeen.com
- Courage Directors, Timothy Taylor Landlord
- ☺ Scottish with some European influences
- Comfortable lounge bar, no background music or TV

A hotel bar serving plenty of traditional Scottish dishes – among the favourites are a huge fresh local haddock in crisp light batter and oatmeal skirlie accompanying roast Buchan chicken or minced beef. Using local produce and suppliers as far as possible, the delicious steaks are Aberdeen Angus, lamb cutlets from Highland lamb. Main courses start at £6.95 for pork sausages with mash and onion gravy rising to £11.45 for pheasant breast set on haggis with a Drambuie cream sauce. Other dishes include steak and ale pie, smoked haddock risotto topped with a poached egg, steamed rock turbot on a prawn and basil sauce, roast chump of lamb on a carrot and coriander purée and pork with glazed apples on a prune and sage sauce.

The lunchtime snack menu offers a good selection of baked potatoes, wraps or warm ciabatta with fillings including honey roast gammon, home-roasted beef with horseradish or feta with black olives and capers. Tempting home-made desserts include baked lemon tart, profiteroles filled with strawberry cream, apple and cinnamon crumble and – most popular - sticky toffee pudding. They are very proud of their Scottish cheeses including Strathdon Blue, Caboc, Gruth Dhu, Galic Stone and smoked Cheddar, a platter served with fruit chutney at a very reasonable £4.50.

Q S V P C

ALVES
Crooked Inn
14 Burghead Road, IV30 BUU

- ▶ On A96, edge of village, between Elgin and Forres
- ☼ Mon-Sat 12-2pm, 5.30-11pm; Sun 12-11pm
- Ⓨ Mon-Sat 12-2pm, 5.30-9pm; Sun 12.30-8pm
- T (01343) 850646
- Beer range varies
- ☺ Simple bar menu plus fresh, seasonal restaurant menu
- Traditional country pub with low ceilings, real fires and bags of character

'I will never receive a Michelin star because my policy is to make a little bit of money from a lot of people…' says landlord Kevin Edwards who won several CAMRA awards at his previous pub in East Lancs and has now introduced real ale to the Crooked Inn. Four chefs produce a keenly priced bar menu and monthly changing restaurant menu using as much local produce as possible. Beef is bred locally and matured at the nearby abattoir, fowl and game come from up the road, and in season most vegetables are locally grown.

In the bar, choose from steak sizzlers, steak and ale pie, big Yorkies with fillings such as mince and mashed tatties, Aberdeen Angus burger and an unusual choice of sandwiches, plus home-made soup for an extra £1. Restaurant dishes might be breast of woodpigeon on haggis croute, cullen skink and black pudding dumplings among the starters, then haddock in beer batter, seafood ragout, Moray chicken on award winning haggis and 'bashed neeps' with wild garlic and cream, Highland venison collops on black pudding and skirlie potato cakes, char-grilled loin of hill fed lamb and superb steaks. Vegetarian choices could be ratatouille and mushroom lasagne or broccoli filo baskets. There are pasta and salad alternatives.

★ Q S V P C

CATTERLINE

☆ Creel Inn

AB39 2UL

- On coast off A92, 5 miles S of Stonehaven
- Mon-Sat 12-3pm, 6-11pm (midnight Sat); Sunday 12-11pm
- Mon-Sat 12-2pm, 6-9.30pm; Sun 12-9pm
- T (01569) 750254
- E info@thecreelinn.co.uk
- W www.thecreelinn.co.uk
- Beer range varies
- Caledonian cuisine with seafood specialities
- Country inn on a cliff top with sea views

A pub where you can truly marry food to ale, for there is an extensive international beer list as well as British draught. Lambic and fruit beers, Trappist and Abbey beers, beers from Belgium, Germany and even Montreal, not forgetting Scottish micros such as Houston Peter's Well and Orkney Dark Island, can all be found here – some beers are used in cooking. Lobster and crab are caught in Catterline Bay below the pub, served in both the lounge bar and restaurant.

The seasonal menu is changed every quarter, using fresh produce with meat delivered daily from the butcher in Stonehaven and fish from Aberdeen fish market. Typical starters might be house speciality crab soup, smoked haddock and pea risotto cake, or chicken liver, haggis and malt whisky pâté – and the Creel take on garlic bread is a whole roasted garlic bulb with pan-fried olive oil bread and salsa! Fish choices include trio of seared fish with spring onion mash, Italian oven baked crab, monkfish brochette or freshly battered Gourdon haddock, prices from £8.50 to £13.95 unless you want to splash out £40 on a gargantuan seafood platter for two. Meat dishes feature wild venison pot roasted in Trappist ale with juniper, beef wrapped round haggis braised in Orkney Stout, chicken supreme and fine steaks. Fresh veggie dishes are on the specials board, and desserts include 'unique' sticky apple and carrot pudding, old fashioned rice pud or cheese plate.

V C

GLENKINDIE

Glenkindie Arms Hotel

AB33 8SX

- On A97, at edge of village
- Mon-Fri 12-2.30pm, 5-11pm; Sat & Sun 12-midnight
- Daily 12-2pm, 5-9pm
- T (01975) 641288
- F (01975) 641319
- E eddie@falk303.freeserve.co.uk
- W www.glenkindiearms.co.uk
- Beer range varies
- Showcases fresh fish and local game
- 400-year-old drovers' inn overlooking River Don, countryside and mountains

The landlady is the chef at a pub that bravely encompasses all tastes from the traditional to exotic, and does so using plenty of fresh produce. On the traditional Scottish side look for cullen skink (smoked haddock and potato soup), venison broth, haggis and neeps in whisky sauce, or chestnut and Stilton pâté among starters, mainly under £4. Still trad, main courses feature venison sausages with mash, steak and ale pie and local game (as available) including pheasant casserole and venison McDuff, the meat cooked in red wine with mushrooms and cranberry jelly. Game also gets the spicy treatment in dishes such as venison marinated in lemon, chilli and coriander.

On the fish front you will find unusual dishes such as monkfish in tandoori batter, John Dory with sweet ginger, and smoked haddock with creamy mustard sauce on pasta as well as char-grilled sardines with tomato sauce, haddock mornay or traditional fresh haddock in batter, prices £7-10. 'Hot and spicy' includes Thai chicken with prawns in coconut cream, lemon chicken in tempura batter and Ghandi's revenge – hot stir-fried beef. Irresistible home made desserts number tangy Key lime pie, and Scottish cranachan mixing fresh raspberries, toasted oatmeal, whisky and cream.

S V C

KINGSWELLS

Four Mile House

Old Skene Road, AB15 8QA

- 4 miles W of Aberdeen off A944
- Mon-Wed 11am-11pm; Thu-Sat 11am-midnight; Sun 11am-11pm
- Mon-Sat 12-2pm, 5.30-9.30pm; Sun 12.30-8.30pm
- T (01224) 740318
- F (01224) 749886
- E shspink@hotmail.com
- Beer range varies
- Cosmopolitan choice, different menus served lunch and evening
- Mixture of old and modern, games room, public and lounge bars, restaurant

Two different but quite extensive menus are served lunchtime and evening at the Four Mile House carvery and restaurant. At lunchtime try the combo of home-made soup and cracked black pepper baguette filled with roast beef and fried onions or humous and roast vegetables at a bargain £4.95. Main dishes at lunchtime range from chef's curry of the day at £5.80 to tortilla basket filled with hot chilli, chicken and bacon lasagne, Cumberland sausage on wholegrain mustard mash, North Sea haddock mornay to rib eye steak in a floury bap at £6.85.

In the evening some of these choices are repeated, but in addition you'll find fresh haddock in batter, grilled seabass fillets topped with toasted sesame seeds, Black Isle chicken stuffed with black pudding then wrapped in bacon, pork fillet stuffed with apricots and wrapped in bacon on a mango cream sauce, sweet chilli beef in a light tempura batter, grilled scallops with lemon butter topped with deep fried leeks served on potato rosti, and king prawns with bamboo shoots, water chestnuts and bean sprouts in a sweet chilli sauce – prices from around £8-£11.75. Vegetarian choices include mushroom stroganoff, vegetable fajitas, oriental noodles with baby corn, peppers, roasted cashews and chilli or mushroom and asparagus baskets.

❀ S V 🍺 ♿ P ✂ 👪 C

OLDMELDRUM

Redgarth Hotel

Kirk Brae, AB51 0DJ

- Off A947, towards golf course
- Daily 11am-3pm, 5-11.30pm
- Daily 12-2pm, 5-9pm (9.30pm Sat & Sun)
- T (01651) 872353
- E info@redgarth.com
- W www.redgarth.com
- Beer range varies
- Varied menu with all food locally sourced
- Traditional inn with panoramic views over eastern Grampian mountains

Fish from Aberdeen market, meat from the nearby butcher and vegetables from the local greengrocer are served on a menu that changes fortnightly. Meals can be accompanied by beers from all over the UK, but especially Scottish micros including Kelburn, Cairngorm, Skye and Atlas. Among the starters you could find melon and pineapple in port, oriental beef pancake, mushroom pâté en croute, or soups such as tomato with orange and rosemary. There is always a catch of the day as well as deep-fried haddock often in beer batter. Other main courses could be pork fillet pan-fried with Parma ham and sage finished with port, mixed game pie with shortcrust pastry, roast lamb with all the trimmings, chicken Maryland, steak and ale pie and vegetarian choices such as vegetable samosa pie with coriander dressing or spinach and four cheese cannelloni. Mains all include vegetables and chips or baked potato and are priced £8-£9. Salads include home-cooked gammon, tuna and peach or chicken, apple and cider with melted Camembert dressing; grills go from sausage, bacon and egg to Aberdeen Angus fillet steak at £14.95. Desserts could be sherry trifle or apple cake with brandy butterscotch sauce. Sandwiches and snacks are served in the bar and the standard children's menu offers burger, fish fingers or chicken nuggets.

Q ❀ 🛏 S V ♿ P ✂ 👪 C

STONEHAVEN

Marine Hotel

9-10 Shorehead, AB39 2JY

- Overlooking harbour
- Mon-Sat 11am-1am; Sun 11am-midnight
- Daily 11am-2.15pm, 5-9.15pm
- T (01569) 762155
- E philipduncan@fsbdial.co.uk
- Taylor Landlord; guests
- Menus based on fresh, local produce with plenty of seafood
- Picturesque, harbourside pub with wood-panelled bar plus lounge with huge fire; former Scottish CAMRA Pub of the Year

A pub that serves five real ales, the ever-changing guest list mainly from Scottish regional and micro breweries. A plain bar menu offers traditional pub dishes such as sausage and mash, steak pies, haggis, neeps and tatties, chicken fillets, a pasta dish such as penne with fresh tomato and basil sauce, spicy bean burgers, sandwiches and toasties, meals around £4.95-£6.95.

The main dining menu provides the local seafood the Marine is renowned for, such as fresh grilled mackerel with gooseberry purée, pan fried scallops with bacon and garlic in season, sea bass, monkfish, lobster served plain or thermidor, smoked salmon salad and dressed local crab. Meat dishes include game in winter such as roast pheasant or venison steak with red wine sauce, as well as roast chump of lamb with garlic mash, chicken Rob Roy – fillet stuffed with haggis – pork schnitzel and a range of Scottish steaks, rump, sirloin or fillet. All main dishes are accompanied by fresh vegetables or chips, prices starting at £7.95 and rising to around £15 for fillet steak. Scottish soup cullen skink of smoked haddock and potatoes is among the starters, also Scotch broth and prawn whisky Mac with a whisky and ginger dressing. Home-made desserts could be bread and butter pud, crème brulee or apple pie.

★ S V C

APPLECROSS

Applecross Inn

Shore Street, IV54 8LR

- On unclassified road off A896, OS711445
- Daily 11am-11.30pm
- Daily 12-9pm
- T (01520) 744262
- F (01520) 744400
- E applecrossinn@globalnet.co.uk
- W www.applecross.uk.com
- Isle of Skye ales
- Shellfish is a speciality on a menu of mainly local produce
- Traditional black and white inn in spectacular setting on the Applecross Peninsula reached by the highest single-track road in Britain

Landlady Judith Fish is part of the family that has run this inn since 1989. An appropriate name at a pub where seafood is the speciality – fish and shellfish from Applecross Bay include prawns, crab, squat lobster, scallops and oysters. Other local produce embraces venison from Applecross Estate, pork from a nearby butcher who makes his own sausages, lamb and beef from local crofters, salads and herbs from Toscaig Herbs, cheese from West Highland Dairy, ales from Isle of Skye Brewery and over 50 malt whiskies.

Favourite dishes from the menu are starters such as smoked haddock chowder, half a pint of prawns, half a dozen oysters (at an amazing £5.95), locally-smoked salmon and haggis flamed in Drambuie. Popular main dishes include king scallops with garlic, lemon and crispy bacon on rice, whole Applecross Bay prawns in garlic and lemon, huge fresh haddock with chips and peas, Diabaig pork sausage incorporating local herbs on mash with a rich onion gravy, home-made beef, spinach and mozzarella lasagne, priced £7.95-£12.95. Puddings, all home made and all £3.25, could be Scottish dessert cranachan with raspberries, oats, cream and whisky or sticky toffee pudding and ice cream.

S V C

AVIEMORE

Old Bridge Inn

23 Dalfaber Road, PH22 1PU

- 100 yards from jct with Cairngorm ski road, B970
- Mon-Sat 11am-11pm; Sun 12.30-11pm
- Daily 12-2pm, 6-9pm
- T (01479) 811137
- E Nigel@oldbridgeinn.co.uk
- W www.oldbridgeinn.co.uk
- Beer range varies
- Scottish and European using local produce, fish and game
- Traditional Highland inn with ospreys circling overhead, popular in both summer and winter for the skiing season

Catering is growing in size and reputation at this popular and busy pub, originally a cottage but now much extended, including a fairly new self-catering bunkhouse for up to 40 guests. A daily specials menu features the best of locally-sourced ingredients, whether fish, beef, game or vegetables, while the two guest beers normally include one from Cairngorm brewery.

On the char-grill menu you might find main dishes such as chicken breast marinated in yoghurt, lime and coriander, Strathspey salmon with lemon and parsley butter, trio of lamb chops with redcurrant jelly, half pound Highland venison steak marinated in red wine and juniper berries, 10oz Aberdeen Angus rib eye steak or 8oz sirloin, all accompanied by fresh vegetables or crisp salad, prices from £8.75-£12.75. Seasonal menus vary but include a hearty soup or broth, starters such as spicy sweet potato, tzatziki dip, pork and oregano rillette or deep fried calamari, £2.60 to £5.50. Main courses could be haunch of hare with red wine and apricots, monkfish marinated in ginger and soy sauce on lime rice or roast pepper terrine with garlic bread, £9-£14. During the ski season there is a Highland gathering with food and drink every Tuesday night at £17.50 per head, with a piper to start the evening.

★ Q S V (Aviemore) C

CAWDOR
☆ Cawdor Tavern
IV12 5XP

- ▶ Signposted on B9090 off A96 Inverness-Nairn
- ☼ Mon-Sat 11am-11pm (midnight Fri & Sat); Sun 12.30-11pm; winter closed 3-5pm Mon-Fri
- 🍴 Mon-Sat 12-2pm, 5.30-9pm; Sun 12.30-3pm
- T (01667) 404777
- E cawdortavern@btopenworld.com
- 🍺 Cairngorm Stag, Trade Winds, seasonal
- ☺ Modern Scottish using fresh, local produce
- ◉ Traditional Highlands pub with oak panelling and log fires

Featuring local produce as much as possible, especially fresh fish and seafood from Mallaig, the Cawdor's menu is entirely made from 'raw materials' down to home-baked bread including regular favourite, soda bread, and home-made ice cream. Chef Stuart Urquhart smokes meats such as venison and duck for superb starters, and uses herbs from the pub garden.

Apart from daily specials, the lunchtime menu offers salt cod and chive fritter, roast pepper, basil and Parmesan risotto cake and mini seafood platter of prawns, smoked Mallaig mackerel, marinated herring and poached salmon as starters from £2.95-£5.75. Mains include chicken Culloden (chicken fillets on haggis with Drambuie and mushroom sauce), Scotch beef casseroled with local ale in a large Yorkshire pudding, fresh Mallaig haddock in batter or mushroom and spring onion risotto, £7.95-£8.95. Light bites include chestnut mushrooms with leeks, Stilton and pear in puff pastry and the chef's platter of smoked meats.

Evening main courses include loin of lamb on black pudding mousseline, Morayshire pork medallions on parsnip mash with mustard and heather honey sauce, duet of salmon and sea bass on Parmesan gnocchi and roast Mediterranean vegetable stack.

★ Q S V C

DRUMNADROCHIT
Benleva Hotel
IV63 6UH

- ▶ Just off A82 Inverness-Fort William, well signposted
- ☼ Daily 12-midnight (1am Fri)
- 🍴 Daily 12-3pm, 5.30-9.30pm (winter 6-8pm)
- T (01456) 450080
- E enquiry@benleva.co.uk
- W www.benleva.co.uk
- 🍺 Beer range varies
- ☺ Local produce, freshly prepared, focusing on Highland foods
- ◉ 400-year-old former manse, now a popular village hotel handy for hunting the Loch Ness monster. Highlands CAMRA Pub of the Year 2003 and 2004

Head chef and joint owner of the Benleva, James Beaton, dishes up freshly-prepared meals using locally-supplied produce as far as possible. In winter the menu is shorter when demand is less, because James would rather stick to fresh food than resort to the freezer, but in summer he gets a chance to stretch his wings. 'The emphasis is on real ale and real food because we believe they go hand in hand,' says Beaton.

Local meat is a speciality – Scotch beef, venison and lamb in particular; also, locally sourced seafood such as scallops, langoustines, crab, monkfish and salmon. He also serves Stornoway black pudding for breakfast and on the evening menu, and makes a mean steak and ale pie, using rump steak simmered in a darker beer such as Isle of Skye Black Cuillin. A sample selection from the menu includes Islay king scallops with bacon and Parmesan crust, pan-fried loin of lamb with lemon, thyme and pak choi, roast Lochaber venison with bramble jus and pomme Lyonnaise, grilled Minch cod with roast pepper and tomato sauce and wild mushroom pasta with smoked cheese sauce, sweet pea and onion salad, prices from £8.95-£12.50.

Q S V C

FORTROSE
☆ Anderson
Union Street, IV10 8TD

- From A9, follow signs to Fortrose
- Mon-Sat 11.30am-11.30pm; Sun 12.30-11pm
- Mon-Sat 11.30am-2pm, 5-9pm; Sun 12.30-9pm (shorter hours in winter)
- T (01381) 620236
- E info@theanderson.co.uk
- W www.theanderson.co.uk
- Beer range varies
- Global cuisine, with menu changing daily
- Rustic bar plus lounge bar and restaurant in nine-bedroom hotel owned by international beer writer/broadcaster Jim Anderson

Jim Anderson's passion for the hop finds expression in a single handpump serving ales from independents – and a stonking list of over 60 Belgian beers with tasting notes. This inspirational selection is perfectly partnered by the cooking of his wife Anne, a New Orleans trained chef who, having never visited the UK before, was unburdened with preconceived notions about what pub cuisine should or shouldn't be. So she does her own thing, a romp through the nations from Britain to Thailand, Lebanon, France, Greece, US, Switzerland, China and beyond, using fresh, seasonal produce, and putting some of it in a Memphis-style smoker.

The menu changes daily, but expect Aberdeen beef and lamb, West Coast scallops, East coast lobster and crab, game from venison to wild boar, and Anne's famous home-made Black Isle burger topped with haggis and bacon, £6.50 with chips. Always on the menu are Brussels salad, warm goats' cheese with roast beetroot and her famous 10oz trimmed Scotch sirloin steak. Sample specials: gravadlax Français, Lebanese falafel salad or baked oysters, £2.50-£5. Mains might be lemon sole, Lancashire hotpot, vegetable tempura or chicken Verona, £7-£12.50.

★ S V C

GAIRLOCH
Old Inn
IV21 2BD

- Opposite harbour
- 11am-1am (midnight Fri & Sat); Sun 12.30-11.30pm
- Summer 12-10pm; winter 12-2pm, 5-8.30pm
- T (01445) 712006
- E enquiries@theoldinn.net
- W www.theoldinn.net
- Beer range varies
- Tempting seafood and Highland game
- 17th-century Highland coaching inn on busy harbour at the foot of Flowerdale Glen, with pottery and walkers' lodge in the grounds

The Old Inn is renowned for its food and recipes by its chefs often appear in cookery books and newspapers, including a favourite, hare in Red Cuillin Ale with saffron, which appears in this guide. Food is served in the restaurant, bistro, lounge and bar, using fish straight from the boats all filleted in the pub kitchen, and game from local estates such as venison, hare, partridge and pheasant, while rare breed pork is used to make sausages. Ice cream, cakes, bread, pasta and pizzas are also home made.

A sample menu might offer the Old Inn Seafood Kettle – a selection from langoustines, mussels, squat lobsters, scallops, skate, monkfish and squid in a seafood broth – cold shellfish platter of crab, squat lobster and langoustine tails, ceviche of sea fresh scallops marinated in lime and coriander, lamb tagine of champ steak with couscous and apricot and chickpea sauce, wild venison steaks with mash, confit of garlic and braised red cabbage on port and blue cheese sauce, steamed turbot on Greek salad with prawn stuffed courgette and red pesto dressing or, for vegetarians, caramelised chicory bake with pine nuts and parsnip fritters. Up to eight real ales are served in summer, three in winter, with beers from local breweries such as An Teallach, Isle of Skye and Orkney.

S V C

GLENSHIEL

Kintail Lodge Hotel

IV40 8HL

- On A87 to Skye, 6 miles S of Dornie
- Mon-Fri 12-3pm, 6-11pm; Sat 11.30am-11pm; Sun 12-10.30pm
- Mon-Fri 12-2.30pm, 6-9.30pm; Sat & Sun 12.30-9.30pm
- T (01599) 511275
- E kintaillodgehotel@btinternet.com
- W www.kintaillodgehotel.co.uk
- Isle of Skye Red Cuillin, Black Cuillin; guests
- Plain, modern Scottish with occasional twist; fresh seafood
- Traditional pub with accommodation in popular touring area; locals meet here for a 'crack'; occasional live music

On the edge of Loch Duich, the Kintail benefits from plentiful seafood. Fishing boats bring the chefs scallops, langoustines and mussels straight from the sea; catches of white fish delivered several times a week are cooked simply so as not to detract from their freshness. Organic lamb comes from nearby Glenelg, beef from Aberdeen, cheese from Achmore.

The most requested dishes are mussels with pesto and cream, venison sausages with mash and onion gravy, fresh haddock in beer batter, Cockburns haggis with clapshot and chicken breast stuffed with skirlie served with curly kale, cider and thyme, prices from £4.50-£8.95. Hand-dived scallops with sweet chilli sauce, haunch of venison and rib of Aberdeen beef are dearer, £13.50-£16.50. Also featured on the bar menu are smoked haddock and leek tart, seafood risotto with parmesan crisp, coq a leekie pie with chips and fresh vegetables and lamb shank braised with root vegetables. Home-made desserts, all £4.25, are pot au chocolat with raspberry coulis and shortbread, crème brûlée, sticky toffee pudding or baked apple, rhubarb and ginger crumble. At lunchtime there are home-made soups and terrines, filled savoury tarts and baguettes.

S V P C

PLOCKTON

☆ Plockton Inn

Innes Street, IV52 8TW

- 50 yards from sea front
- Mon-Sat 11am-midnight; Sun 12.30-11pm
- Daily 12-2.30pm, 6-9pm (longer in summer)
- T (01599) 544222
- E stay@plocktoninn.co.uk
- W www.plocktoninn.co.uk
- Beer range varies
- Local produce, seafood a speciality
- Family-run inn near sea front in beautiful village on west Highland coast

Splendid locally-caught fish and shellfish take pride of place at the Plockton, named Scotland's Seafood Pub of the Year 2004, where the owners create good food from local produce. They serve Plockton langoustines, queenie scallops from Loch Carron, king scallops caught by island divers, with the majority of fresh fish arriving from Mallaig. Cheese comes from West Highland Dairies in Achmore and they also supply the superb yoghurt and crème fraiche used in desserts and sauces. A butcher in Kyle brings the venison, beef, lamb, guinea fowl, pheasant and chicken; in summer herbs and lettuce come across the water from Skye. Their own home-smoked fish and shellfish and home-cured gravadlax are on the lavish seafood platter, a snip at £13.95.

Starters include fresh oysters in a glass of bloody Mary, haggis, neeps and tatties with home pickled beetroot or fish soup, £3-£4, followed by baked sea bass, skate wing with black butter or the seafood platter. Main meat dishes could be walnut and ginger stuffed pork or a Scottish sirloin steak, or ratatouille pasta topped with Cullin cheese for vegetarians. Yummy desserts include lemon and ginger crunch pie or Cranachan ice cream; the cheeseboard boasts Highland Blue, soft Cullin, smoked cheddar from Lochaber or creamy Highland Brie.

S V (Plockton) P C

WATERNISH
Stein Inn

Isle of Skye, IV55 8GA

- N of Dunvegan on B886, less than 5 miles from Fairy Bridge
- Summer 11am-midnight; winter 4-11pm
- Mon-Sat 12-4pm, 6-9.30pm; Sun 12.30-4pm, 6-9pm
- T (01470) 592362
- E angus.teresa@steininn.co.uk
- W www.steininn.co.uk
- Caledonian Deuchars IPA; Isle of Skye Red Cuillin, Black Cuillin; guests
- Daily specials, local fish and set menu plus fabulous breakfast menu
- Traditional Highland hostelry on a sea loch with fine views to Rubha Maol; moorings for seafarers

Let's face it, when you get to the Isle of Skye, you're there for the night – and a breakfast like this clinches it. How about organic oatmeal porridge followed by bacon, venison sausages, black pudding, potato scones, mushrooms, tomatoes, free-range eggs any way you like, peat smoked kippers, a selection of cheeses, smoked salmon or ham, brown and white toast, coffee, Earl Grey tea or hot chocolate?

At main meal times, seafood landed at the nearby jetty could include Loch Dunvegan langoustines or smaller prawns, both served with salad at £13.50 and £9.50 respectively. There is also darne of salmon in mustard sauce and fresh cod with parsley butter. Other main courses are gammon steak with a fried egg, Irish stew, Scottish steak braised in Skye ale, aubergine stuffed with onion and tomato, all served with fresh vegetables, side salad and choice of potatoes at £6-£9.40. Starters might include Highland lentil broth or pea and ham soup with locally-made chunky bread at £2.30, breaded goats' cheese or Thai fish cakes, both £3.95. Salads are topside of Highland beef, honey roast ham, tuna or quiche lorraine, all but the beef under £6. For desserts choose from home-made raspberry pavlova with cream or sticky toffee pudding with toffee sauce, while Mull of Kintyre Cheddar and Scottish Brie are on the cheese board.

Q S V P C

EDINBURGH
Cambridge

20 Young Street, EH2 4JB

- ▶ In city centre, just off Charlotte Square
- ☼ Mon-Sat 11am-11pm (midnight Thu, 1am Fri & Sat); Sun 1pm-11pm
- 🍴 Daily 12-9pm
- T (0131) 226 2120
- E info@thecambridgebar.co.uk
- W www.thecambridgebar.co.uk
- Caledonian Deuchars IPA; guest
- ☺ Gourmet burgers
- Stylish, recently refurbished New Town bar in heart of town centre

Eat your heart out McDonald's – this is the ultimate burger bar. Fast food it is certainly not – all the food here is cooked to order while you relax in surroundings that are a far cry from the average burger joint. In fact you can even reserve a table here. Everything is home made, including all the relishes, and the sourdough sesame buns are baked daily. The burgers themselves are 7oz of finest Scotch beef, starting with the Classic, £4.95, simply char grilled and served with salad, mayo and relish. There follows a long list of variations, many of them also available as vegetarian bean burgers. As well as the usual accompaniments such as blue cheese or chilli there are some more whacky combos such as the Aussie, £6.95, which incorporates beetroot, fried egg, pineapple and cheddar. For dieters there is the low-carb option, served without a bun but with extra salad. If you don't fancy a burger at all you can have the Portabella – a whole portabella mushroom filled with sun dried tomatoes, mozzarella, char-grilled peppers and rocket. For afters there are waffles or ice cream. Takeaway orders are possible.

V ♿ C

EDINBURGH
Guildford Arms

1-5 West Register Street, EH2 2AA

- ▶ E end of Princes Street
- ☼ Daily 11am-11pm (midnight Fri & Sat)
- 🍴 Daily 12-2.30pm, 6-9.30pm
- T (0131) 556 4312
- E manager@guildfordarms.com
- W www.guildfordarms.com
- Caledonian Deuchars IPA; Harviestoun Bitter and Twisted; Orkney Dark Island
- ☺ Modern eclectic with Scottish touches
- City centre pub with ornate plasterwork

Ten real ales, including four guests, make a diverse accompaniment to diverse food which includes Scottish treats such as Shetland mussels in a choice of sauces – garlic and cream, chilli and coconut or shallots, bacon and white wine, £5.25 for a small portion, £7.95 for large, organic Scottish salmon with chilli lemon butter, carrot and coriander mash at £8.75, or 8oz Aberdeen Angus steak at £10.95. Starters also include fresh soup of the day, grilled goats' cheese with tomato and caramelised onion, crispy lamb's liver on garlic toast with bacon and rosemary, calamari with sweet chilli, lime, garlic or grilled asparagus wrapped in parma ham with tomato, basil and Parmesan, prices £2.95-£4.95.

Main meals might be pub dishes such as beef or vegetable chilli with rice, steak and ale pie, freshly breaded haddock with a lemon and caper mayonnaise, fries and salad, or Crombies' famous sausages – flavours of the day on the blackboard – served with mash, prices a reasonable £6.25-£7.25. In addition there are salads such as warm chicken with pancetta and mustard or honey dressing, and veggie choices such as pepper stuffed with curried rice and mild coconut sauce with stir-fried vegetables, or wild mushroom risotto. Specials and desserts of the day are listed on the blackboard. From the restaurant there is a view of the bar's magnificent Jacobean ceiling.

★ V ⇌ (Edinburgh Waverley) **C**

EDINBURGH
☆ Halfway House

Fleshmarket Close, 24 High Street, EH1 1BX

- ▶ 50 metres from Old Town exit Waverley Station, up steps towards Cockburn St
- ☼ Sun-Thu 11am-11pm; Fri & Sat 11am-1pm
- Throughout opening hours
- T (0131) 225 7101
- F (01890) 817186
- E allantoninn@supanet.com
- Beer range varies
- ☺ Traditional Scottish
- Friendly and welcoming genuine free house with a small, cosy bar

This may be the Halfway House, but there are no half measures with the food. Look for hearty soups made using only fresh vegetables – in winter thick ham and lentil or game broth and in summer more cosmopolitan flavours such as tomato and red pepper – and, available all year, cullen skink of smoked haddock, leek and potato. All soups are priced at £2.50-£3 including roll and butter. Fittingly for a pub in Fleshmarket Close, in the cold season it features rich casseroles such as game stew made with Berwickshire venison, pheasant, hare, pigeon or rabbit simmered in ale or red wine at only £5-£6 a portion. Summer dishes are lighter, maybe chicken and leek in cream sauce, or sausage and mash with onion gravy, both under £5. All year round you can try traditional Scottish tastes such as haggis, neeps and tatties at just £3.20, or stovies (a mixture of potatoes, meat and onions) served in the authentic manner with oatcakes. Puddings are made on an 'occasional basis' but are worth waiting for – bread and butter marmalade pudding, apple and blackberry crumble and other traditional favourites, at £2.50. Also available at all times, coffee, tea, herbal and fruit teas and hot chocolate.

Q ❀ **S V** ⇌ (Edinburgh Waverley) 👪

EDINBURGH
☆ Johnsburn House

64 Johnsburn Road, Balerno, EH14 7BB

- ▶ Off A70, enter Balerno at first roundabout
- ☼ Mon 6pm-1am; Tue-Fri 12-2.30pm, 6pm-1am; Sat & Sun 12-1am
- Throughout opening hours
- T (0131) 449 3847
- E johns1760@aol.com
- Caledonian Deuchars IPA; Marston's Pedigree; guests
- ☺ Gastropub serving fresh Scottish produce
- Britain's 'most awarded' pub in a listed baronial mansion with beer garden

Since 1989, when Johnsburn House chef and proprietor Martin Mitchell was named Scotland and Northern Ireland Pub Caterer of the Year, the pub has won over 100 accolades. To eat here is to go on a glorious gastronomic journey, and a real ale one, too, for Martin has served over 1, 500 different beers in the past 15 years. He is a passionate foodie, a member of the Master Chefs of Great Britain, who strives to use local produce and create highly original slants on traditional dishes. The menu changes daily depending on what is good and in season, but a typical day might include starters such as Leith trout thermidor, local pheasant, pigeon and black pudding potato salad or red pepper and lentil soup with tarragon cream.

Main dishes romp from pub grub such as home-made cheeseburger and chips or bangers and mash with onion gravy through fresh haddock and Mongolian spicy beef to seafood risotto, Pentland snipe breast with black pudding, venison pie or stuffed loin of venison, Thai sweet chilli crayfish and noodles or a superb Aberdeen Angus fillet steak, perfectly cooked. Vegetarians have at least five choices, such as courgette, apple and Brie crepe or vegetable korma with Thai style rice. Main courses average £7-9; desserts, £4, are irresistible, local cheeses impressive. A four-course menu (advance booking) is £27.50.

★ 🏰 **Q** ❀ **S V** ♿ ⇌ (Curriehill) ♣ Ⓟ ⚡ 👪 **C**

EDINBURGH
Old Dock Bar
3-5 Dock Place, EH6 6LU

- ▶ Just off Commercial Street close to The Shore waterside in Leith
- ☼ Mon-Thu 12-11pm; Fri & Sat 12pm-1am; Sun 12.30-11pm
- 🍴 Daily 12-10pm
- T (0131) 555 4474
- Atlas Latitude; Taylor Landlord; guests
- ☺ Enterprising seasonal menu all produced on the premises with a delicious brunch at weekends
- Rustic interior with horseshoe bar and bistro-style restaurant

A delightful full breakfast menu on Saturdays and Sundays includes the usual sausage, bacon and black pudding with eggs or a veggie version, but also eggs Benedict – scrambled eggs with smoked salmon and French toast with maple syrup. All produce is bought locally and prepared to order, including the extremely popular Dock burger of fresh minced steak with its special blend of herbs and spices cooked rare, medium or well done. The seasonal menu includes home-made soup such as tomato, rice and vegetable, mushroom or Stilton and broccoli at £2.60 with a bread basket. There are typical pub dishes such as steak and real ale pie, pub curry, quiches, fresh haddock in real ale batter ('more like a whale – portions are huge here'), gammon with fresh pineapple and eggs, chicken and vegetable pie, home-made vegetarian lasagne with a crusty cheese topping, prices from around £5.95 up to £9.95 for surf 'n' turf of steak and prawns. You might also find grilled tuna with citrus sauce, a French-style lamb stew with a rich tomato sauce, Italian chicken wrapped in parma ham on linguine. Starters include fresh mussels cooked with wine and cream, tempura vegetables, strips of crispy chicken in home-made batter with a dip or bacon, or spinach and avocado salad.

★ S V ♣ P C

EDINBURGH
Starbank Inn
64 Laverockbank Road, Newhaven, EH5 3BZ

- ▶ Overlooking River Forth between Leith and Granton
- ☼ Mon-Wed 11am-11pm; Thur-Sat 11am-midnight; Sun 12.30pm-11pm
- 🍴 Mon-Fri 12-2.30pm, 6-9pm; Sat & Sun 12.30pm-9pm
- T (0131) 552 4141
- Belhaven Sandy Hunters, 80/-; Caledonian Deuchars IPA; Taylor Landlord; guests
- ☺ Traditional home cooking
- Bright, airy ale house with bar and conservatory overlooking the River Forth; live music twice monthly

Plain home-cooked fare at plain prices is freshly prepared by the two cooks at the Starbank, beginning with home-made soup such as Scotch broth or vegetable with crusty bread at just £1.50, chicken liver pâté, marinated rollmop herrings or prawn salad. To follow there is roast leg of lamb with all the trimmings for £6, steak and ale pie, breast of chicken with redcurrant gravy, home-cooked gammon with salad, minute steak with pepper sauce, a vegetarian dish of the day and fish including haddock mornay, smoked haddock topped with a poached egg, poached salmon with lemon butter and a seafood salad as well as a traditional ploughman's – no main course costs more than £6.50. Cold desserts are served with cream or ice cream, or choose cheese and biscuits at £3.50. As well as eight real ales including four changing guests, served from handpumps on the bar, you can get a pot of tea or choice of coffees – filter, cappuccino, espresso and latte. Food is served in the bar and a no-smoking conservatory. Live music is performed one Saturday evening and one Sunday afternoon per month.

Q V C

GIFFORD
Goblin Ha' Hotel
Main Street, EH41 4QH

- 5 miles S of Haddington
- Mon-Thu 11am-11pm; Sat & Sun 11am-midnight
- Mon-Thu 12-2pm, 6-9pm; Fri-Sun 12-3pm, 6-9.30pm
- T (01620) 810244
- E (01620) 810718
- W www.goblinha.com
- Caledonian Deuchars IPA; Hop Back Summer Lightning; Taylor Landlord; guests
- Mix of gastro and traditional
- Village inn with traditional public bar and more modern lounge, conservatory and beer garden

Prepared by joint cooks Mike Gulliver and Barry Hynds, dishes are made on the premises using 90 per cent fresh produce. Choose from exciting starters such as smoked haddock and bacon tartlet, chicken liver pâté with red onion marmalade, roast vine tomato with black pudding and chilli jam, smoked salmon and lemongrass fishcakes with rocket mayonnaise, deep fried Brie with ginger relish for vegetarians or the day's home-made soup. Then move on to a traditional comfort dish such as roast sirloin with Yorkshire pudding, poacher's venison pie with wild mushrooms, steak and ale pie and beer battered haddock. Or something slightly glitzier such as duck breast with roast pear and ginger jus or grilled salmon thermidor with mustard mash, roast vine tomato and poached egg. There are also home-made Goblin burgers, chilli served with nachos, and scampi. The choice is limited for vegetarians – just home-made leek and ricotta cannelloni with tomato sauce among the main dishes. Desserts include sticky toffee pudding with caramel sauce, hazelnut and raspberry meringue, pineapple brandy basket or toffee and apple pie. Starters range from £3-£5, mains £6.25 to £14.50 – vegetables £2.50 extra; all desserts are £4.50.

S V C

GULLANE
Old Clubhouse
East Links Road, EH31 2AF

- W end of village, off main road
- Sun-Wed 11am-11pm; Thu-Sat 11am-midnight
- Daily 12-9.30pm
- T (01620) 842008
- F (01620) 842044
- E info@oldclubhouse.com
- W www.oldclubhouse.com
- Caledonian Deuchars IPA; Taylor Landlord; guests
- Eclectic menu
- Converted golf club in Tudor style building; view to Lammermuir Hills

A team of five chefs presides over an extensive menu that ranges from burgers to their renowned Scottish steaks – sirloin, rib-eye, fillet and T-bone – but specialises in local produce and fresh fish, offering several traditional Scottish dishes. Dishes are freshly prepared with a high proportion of daily specials using seasonal ingredients. A sample menu includes starters such as fresh Orkney mussels, home-made liver pâté, nachos for two, Scottish smoked salmon and local haggis (also served as a main course).

To follow, you could find fresh fried haddock, marinated tuna, grilled rainbow trout or whole grilled fresh fish of the day. As well as steaks, from the barbecue expect Scottish lamb chops, harissa lamb kebabs and char-grilled pork spare ribs. There are salads warm – hot smoked duck and char-grilled vegetables with goats' cheese – and cold from prawn to roast beef. Several pasta choices include arrabiatta with bacon, tomatoes and chilli, and tortellini with cream and mushrooms. Main courses are priced from around £6-£15.75 for a 14oz T-bone. Death by chocolate is hanging on in there on the dessert list along with rum and raisin steamed pudding, carrot cake, peach melba and banana split. Children's portions are available.

Q S V C

LASSWADE

Laird & Dog Hotel

5 High Street, EH18 1NA

▶ Just SE of Edinburgh, on A768, near river bridge

☼ Mon-Thu 11am-midnight; Fri & Sat 11am-1am; Sun 12.30-11.30pm

🍴 Daily 12-9pm

T (0131) 663 9219

W www.lairdanddog.btinternet.co.uk

🍺 Beer range varies

☺ Home-made food ranging from traditional Scottish to more exotic dishes

◉ An olde worlde pub with new conservatory and 11 bedrooms, catering for music fans, pool players, drinkers and diners

Food is served every day except Christmas Day and New Year's Day. The bar menu comprises fresh haddock from a local supplier cooked in batter with chips, steak pie with puff pastry topping, braised lamb shanks, spicy beef, grilled gammon and chicken chasseur, around £6-£7 including vegetables (generally three or four) sourced locally. High quality meat delivered daily includes sirloin and fillet steaks, game, lamb and beef for the home-made burgers; the 'haggis tower' is popular all year round. On the fish side, as well as fresh haddock, you often find salmon, trout, smoked haddock, crevettes, seabass, plaice and cod.

Sample dishes from the evening à la carte menu include starters such as home-made soup, flat cap mushrooms, melon, cucumber and cherry tomato salad, continental meats with asparagus or local haggis and black pudding in batter with Drambuie sauce, £2.50-£4.50. Among the main course are chicken Islay flamed with malt whisky, rack of lamb with heather honey and lavender, pheasant breast filled with haggis and parma ham, chicken stuffed with ham and leek on orange, Cointreau and mustard sauce or salmon blackened with rock salt and brown sugar, served with angel hair pasta and red wine essence, £8.25-£9.95.

Q S V P C

LINLITHGOW

Four Marys

65-67 High Street, EH49 7ED

☼ Mon-Thu 12-11pm;Fri & Sat 12-midnight; Sun 12.30-11pm

🍴 Daily 12-3pm, 5-9pm

T (01506) 842171

F (01506) 844410

🍺 Belhaven 80/-, St Andrew's Ale; Caledonian Deuchars IPA; guests

☺ Good quality traditional home-cooked meals

◉ Built around 1500 as a dwelling house, it was named after Mary Queen of Scots' four ladies-in-waiting

A meaty menu, with a feature made of steaks and burgers. Char-grilled steaks include gammon, rib eye, sirloin, fillet, or surf 'n' turf of sirloin with tiger prawns and scampi, all served with onion rings, tomato, mushrooms, salad and chips or potatoes, £6.95-£14.95. The burger section has the clansman (plain beef), chieftain (with Scottish cheddar and bacon), chicken fillet, Texan chicken and veggie burger, prices £5.25-£6.95 with chips and salad, or you can build your own burger by adding various toppings. More traditional old favourites include home-made steak pie, lamb's liver with bacon and onion gravy, chicken stuffed with haggis with whisky sauce, hand-made smoked haggis fish cakes with cheese sauce and fresh vegetables, haggis, neeps and tatties or fresh haddock fillet cooked in the pub's special beer batter, prices £6-£6.50. Starters range from home-made Scottish soup cullen skink of smoked haddock to chilli nachos, and there are various pasta dishes including vegetarian. The set menu also provides the Four Marys curry of the day, beef stroganoff, a proper chilli con carne or Cajun butterfly chicken. In addition there are daily changing specials boards plus desserts, and a Sunday roast at £6.75. The pub hosts beer festivals in May and October.

★ S V ≠ (Linlithgow) C

NORTH BERWICK

Ship

7-9 Quality Street, EH39 4HJ

- Centre of village
- Sun-Wed 11am-11pm; Thu-Sat 11am-midnight (1am Fri)
- Daily 12-3pm (4pm Sat & Sun)
- T (01620) 890676
- Atlas Nimbus; Caledonian Deuchars IPA; guests
- Locally caught fresh fish and traditional pub dishes
- Nautically themed coastal pub: pine floorboards, mahogany counter, dado tile work and maritime tableaux

Some of the fish is caught by the landlady's husband, a local fisherman, and includes bowls of fresh mussels at the weekend and fresh haddock deep fried in crumbs and langoustines. Mackerel is simply baked whole with herbs, head and tail left on, and snapped up as soon as it comes out of the oven. From Monday to Friday a daily changing lunch costs £6.95 for two courses, £7.95 for three including lovely home-made soups such as pumpkin, green pea, lentil, sweet potato, tomato and basil or French onion or other starters such as haggis and black pudding stack or tuna, prawn and egg mayonnaise.

Main dishes could be fresh salmon in a cheese and wholegrain mustard sauce, lemon pepper marinated chicken breast, sweet pepper and sherry chicken, red pepper and goats' cheese cannelloni, a hot steak sandwich or haggis, neeps and tatties either as a main course or starter with oatcakes. Desserts include deep-fried banana with chocolate sauce, syrup sponge or sticky toffee pudding. On the set menu, main meals include Scottish rib eye steak at £7.95, home-made steak pie, burgers of beef or Cajun chicken and smoked haddock fish cakes, served with chips and salad or potatoes and fresh vegetables, prices around £5.95-£6.95.

S V ♿ ⇌ (North Berwick) **C**

A recipe to gladden the heart of any vegetarian comes from Chris Walker of the Masonic Arms in the picturesque Scottish coastal resort Gatehouse of Fleet.

OPEN LASAGNE OF WILD MUSHROOMS AND ASPARAGUS WITH BASIL OIL

(Serves 4)

100g (4oz) mixed wild mushrooms
50g (2oz) butter
1 onion, finely chopped
2 cloves garlic, finely chopped
150ml (¼ pint) white wine
300ml (½ pint) double cream
1 tbsp fresh chopped parsley
16 fresh, briefly steamed asparagus spears
12 sheets fresh lasagne
Parmesan
Salt and black pepper

Basil oil

6 basil leaves
6 sprigs flat parsley
1-2 tbsps olive oil
2 tsps caster sugar

Sauté the wild mushrooms in the butter with the onions and garlic, then add the wine, reduce, and stir in the cream, parsley, seasoning and asparagus. Cook the lasagne sheets in plenty of boiling, salted water. Spoon a quarter of the mushroom mix into the bottom of a deep, buttered, rectangular pasta dish. Cover with a cooked lasagne sheet. Continue layering to create a three-layer lasagne, ending with mushroom mix and the last asparagus spears. Sprinkle with Parmesan and finish in a hot oven (220C/425F/gas mark 7) for around 15 minutes, until bubbling.

Serve with basil oil made by combining basil leaves and parsley in a blender. Slowly add olive oil, lemon juice and caster sugar.

BANGOR

☆ Esplanade

12 Ballyholme Esplanade, BT20 5LZ

- ▶ On the coast; from town centre follow Groomsport road
- ☼ Daily 11.30am-11pm
- (food) Mon-Sat 12-2.15pm, 5-9pm; Sun 1-7pm
- T (028) 9127 0954
- E welcome@esplanadebars.com
- W www.esplanadebars.com
- (beer) Beer range varies
- ☺ Good, traditional Irish and European dishes
- ◙ Overlooking Ballyholme Bay, the Esplanade has a lounge and sports bar on the ground floor, a first floor restaurant and a garden

The Esplanade is one of just a few free houses remaining in Bangor, serving a range of traditional cask ales. The lounge and restaurant offer spectacular views over the bay – on a clear day you may be able to glimpse the far shores of Scotland. Situated on the coast, it offers good fish and seafood specialities such as monkfish in bacon and cream sauce, moules marinière, scampi mornay and roll mop herrings. Most of the meat and other ingredients are sourced in Northern Ireland – though game and tropical fruits are imported.

The standard menu is made up of pub favourites to allow the cooks to make the best use of the daily specials board with seasonal produce. For starters you could find pan-seared scallops and Clontakilty black pudding with confit of garlic, £6.75, smoked bacon and leek tart with asparagus and walnut oil, £6.25, or wild mushroom and asparagus risotto with parmesan, £5.50. Main courses include fillet of beef with foie gras, jus of forest mushrooms and olive oil mash, herb roasted rack of lamb with rich red wine gravy or pan-seared seabass with char-grilled veg and asparagus butter, £13-£16. Home-made desserts are mostly around £5.50: poached peach melba, freshly baked chocolate tart or a trio of caramel desserts with ice cream, or you could finish with Irish cheeses and grapes.

Q ❀ S V ≠ (Bangor) C

BELFAST

Botanic Inn

23-27 Malone Road, BT9 6RU

- ▶ A short walk from Queen's University
- ☼ Mon-Sat 11.30am-1am; Sun 12pm-12am
- (food) Daily 12-8pm
- T (028) 9050 9740
- E info@thebotanicinn.com
- W www.thebotanicinn.com
- (beer) Whitewater Belfast Ale
- ☺ Good value pub grub and a Sunday carvery
- ◙ Lively, community local serving the business community during the day and students at night; disco upstairs Wed-Sat evenings

This large, busy pub is popular with students and sports fans and offers excellent value for money meals, particularly the Sunday carvery, £5.45 for two courses. It can feed up to 100 people at a time, seated throughout its three bar areas. For a snack there are chunky sandwiches, £2.50, home-made soup, £2.25, or soup and sandwich combo, £4.45, or you could have a dish of traditional Irish lamb stew for £4.25. The main menu offers chicken dishes such as tempura (goujons in sesame seed batter with sweet chilli coulis), Cajun pitta pocket (spicy Cajun chicken sautéed with green leeks in a hot pitta pocket), Mexican fajitas with wok-fried chicken, peppers, mushrooms and onions tossed in fajita spices and served in a tortilla, or roast chicken breast with sticky barbecue sauce. Other choices are chilli beef pitta, Gaelic minute steak (with whiskey, mushroom and onion sauce), peppered beef in a creamy sauce of mushrooms, onions and black peppercorns, steak and Guinness pie and a couple of veggie options. Most main courses are around a fiver. The Sunday carvery, served until 5pm, offers lamb, sirloin, gammon or chicken breast with a choice of pudding, probably sticky toffee with vanilla ice cream or citrus tart with lemon sorbet.

S V C

BELFAST
John Hewitt Bar & Restaurant
51 Donegall Street, BT1 2FH

▶ City centre, near St Anne's Cathedral
☼ Mon-Sat 11.30am-1am;
Sun varies, according to live gigs
🍴 Mon-Sat 12-3pm
T (028) 9023 3678
F (028) 9096 1110
E info@thejohnhewitt.com
W www.thejohnhewitt.com
Hilden Ale; guests
☺ Mix of traditional and modern Asian cuisine on a weekly changing menu
◙ Typical city bar with wooden floor, marble counter and high ceilings

The John Hewitt is a restaurant during the day and a bar by night, with live music every evening. Full meals are served every lunchtime (except Sunday) and a lighter menu is available on Friday and Saturday afternoons until 6pm. The reasonably priced menu changes every week on a Tuesday, although the home-made soup is different every day and there are two daily specials. The menu is fairly limited but typically includes a soup and two dishes each of fish, meat and vegetarian; all the food is freshly prepared on the premises.

One week's menu might be soup of the day, roast plum tomato, spinach and goats' cheese tart with garlic potatoes and salad, steak, onion and Hilden ale pie with champ and buttered veg, grilled fillet of salmon with spinach mash and balsamic syrup, garlic roasted pork loin with hot and sour veg and coriander rice, crispy fried marinated chicken baguette with sweet chilli mayo, vegetable and chick pea fritter with cumin scented potatoes, and fried fillet of cod with olive oil mash, chilli spiked tomato and red onion salsa. Main courses are around £6. For dessert there is a choice of warm apple pie, chocolate and orange cheesecake, both £2.95, a selection of ice cream or Irish and continental cheeses with biscuits. Children are allowed until 4pm.

★ V ♿ P **C**

BELFAST
McHugh's Bar and Restaurant
29-31 Queen's Square, BT1 3FG

▶ Follow High Street from city centre
☼ Daily 12pm-1am
🍴 Daily 12-10.30pm
T (028) 9050 9999
F (028) 9050 9998
E info@mchughsbar.com
W www.mchughsbar.com
Whitewater Belfast Ale; guest
☺ Award-winning classical dishes with a twist
◙ Dating from 1711 it claims to be the oldest building in Belfast; the basement bar hosts live music

Although part of the same stable as the Botanic Inn and with a similar capacity, McHugh's caters for a different clientele, partly because it has a separate restaurant and partly because of its emphasis on traditional Irish dishes, albeit with a modern approach. It aims to promote recipes and ingredients from all over Northern Ireland with specialities such as Portavogie seafood chowder served with wheaten bread, char-grilled rib eye steak with Bushmills Gaelic sauce and home-cut chips, Dundrum Bay mussels in saffron cream with crispy Irish bacon and toasted soda bread and, for afters, warm home-made Barnbrack bread and butter pudding with caramelised apples and whiskey ice cream.

McHugh's motto is 'don't served anything you wouldn't eat yourself', and it maintains a strong belief in healthy products, so its home-made terrines, pâtés, breads and desserts incorporate well-balanced ingredients without sacrificing flavour. The menus are seasonal; in summer you could start with a duo of Irish salmon and asparagus terrine for £5.50, followed by grilled Irish goats' cheese salad with poached apple and ginger scented honey for £7.95, or a warm salad of duck confit with watercress and orange £9.50. It offers the same Sunday carvery deal as the Botanic (or two adults and two children can eat for £15).

★ Q ❀ S V ♿ (Central) **C**

HILLSBOROUGH

☆ Hillside

21 Main Street, BT26 6AE

- ▶ Off M1 to Hillsborough, centre of town
- ☼ 12-11.30pm (1am Fri & Sat); Sun 12-11pm
- Throughout opening hours
- T (02892) 682765
- E hillside@carmichaelgroup.co.uk
- W www.carmichaelgroup.co.uk
- Beer range varies
- ☺ Choice of menus offering fine local produce in a wide range of dishes
- Popular pub in historic Georgian village, food served in rustic bar, informal refectory and upstairs à la carte restaurant

Award-winning executive chef Albert Neely and his team create exciting dining using fresh local produce on a choice of menus. In the evening starters could include home-made soup with fresh baked roll, Parma ham, pineapple and peach salad, garlic slice with Spanish sausage and mixed beans or spiced chicken and red onion wrap, £2.95-£5.25. Main dishes might be scampi in light ale batter, stir-fried oriental duck wrapped in a tortilla, cod wrapped in Parma on mash, Indian beef, chicken or combo curry with basmati rice, cured salmon fillet on creamed spinach and Buffalo mozzarella, or Cajun chicken salad, £8.95-£11.50. Veggie choices might be Greek salad with melon in oregano vinaigrette, or spinach, nut, mushroom and smoked cheese lasagne; side orders range from champ to criss cross fries.

There is a set three-course meal at £24.95 with starters such as smoked haddock, asparagus and fried egg ravioli, sea trout or duck confit, followed by mains from beef fillet and quail duo with parsnip mash, broccoli and almond gratin, chicken stuffed with red pepper and crab mousse, to sirloin steak with honey and mustard or mixed vegetable tart in smoked garlic and red pepper dressing. There are desserts or local cheese – and don't forget the malt whiskeys.

★ Q S V C

SAINTFIELD

White Horse

49-55 Main Street, BT24 7AB

- ▶ 10 miles S of Belfast city centre
- ☼ Mon-Sat 11.30am-11pm; Sun 12-10pm
- Mon-Sat 12-2.30pm, 5-8.45pm
- T (028) 9751 1143
- Beer range varies
- ☺ Restaurant and bistro menus featuring local produce
- Cosy, friendly 18th-century pub with wood-burning fire; the bistro is on the ground floor, restaurant in the basement

Since renovation work on this Whitewater Brewery pub was completed to make it more spacious, it has been rewarded with the title of Northern Ireland CAMRA Pub of the Year 2005. It stages an annual beer festival with up to 20 beers to try. Set over two floors, the pub serves meals in the bistro on the ground floor or in the Oast House restaurant downstairs. Some of the starters are also available as main course portions, such as the prawn and bacon salad, Caesar salad (with or without Cajun chicken) and the steamed mussels. Other starters are mushrooms stuffed with cheese, breadcrumbed and deep fried, served with pesto and garlic mayo, deep-fried Brie with oriental plum and sweet and sour veg or chicken liver pâté served with redcurrant compote and toasted bruschetta.

The main courses cater for all tastes – you could have sticky ginger chicken (deep fried with ginger sauce and crunchy veg), char-grilled seabass with stir-fried Asian greens, baked gammon on a bed of colcannon with chive and parsley sauce, a char-grilled rib eye steak sandwich, home-made tagliatelle with chorizo, bacon and roast pepper, finished with cream and topped with pesto and cheese or a vegetarian dish such as filo tart filled with creamed leeks and roasted peppers. Expect to pay between £11 and £20 for two courses.

Q S V C

CHANNEL ISLES

CASTEL
Fleur du Jardin
Kings Mills, Guernsey, GY5 7JT

- Daily 11.30am-11.45pm
- Daily 12-2pm, 6-9.30pm
- T (01481) 257996
- E info@fleurdujardin.guernsey.net
- W www.fleurdujardin.guernsey.net
- Draught Bass; guest
- Gastropub offering a wide selection including local shellfish
- Country pub with garden, open fires, small cosy bar, larger bar and restaurant

The Fleur menu blossoms from an exciting bar menu into a longer evening menu with tempting specials that change daily. Using local fish and produce, bar meals feature starters such as Guernsey scallops a l'orange with grilled black pudding, melon and papaya with ginger and mint syrup or dill and chilli cured salmon with local crab and crème fraîche, £2.75-£6.25. Main courses include steak, kidney and real ale pudding with thyme roast root vegetables, Kashmiri lamb curry, scampi in batter – the oldest house special – with home made tartare sauce, roast monkfish wrapped in prosciutto, corn fed chicken breast filled with crab, and traditional Fleur fish 'n' chips with mushy peas. Prices range from £8.95-£10.75. A wide veggie choice starts at £5.95 with a three-egg garden herb omelette, as well as linguine tossed with porcini, cherry tomatoes and spinach.

Typical specials might be a game terrine starter at £3.50 followed by confit duck leg with parsnip mash and orange sauce, roast seabass wrapped in Bayonne ham, Cajun spiced salmon on a pesto mash, seafood panache in dry white wine and dill cream, or whole grilled lemon sole with capers and prawn, £11.95-£13.95. In the evening there are rib eye and fillet steaks, too, while desserts include home made ice cream, lemon soufflé with hazelnut brittle and cheeses with home made chutney.

★ Q S V P C

ST BRELADE
Old Smugglers Inn
Ouaisne Bay, Jersey, JE3 8AW

- Daily 11am-11.30pm
- Daily 12-2pm, 6-9pm
- T (01534) 741510
- Draught Bass; guests
- Extensive menu supplemented by daily specials and children's meals
- Historic pub on several levels with low beams and open fires; it hosts mini beer festivals several times a year

The Smugglers has been voted CAMRA Jersey Pub of the Year four times since the Millennium and it is described in the 2006 Good Beer Guide as 'the jewel in the crown of the Jersey real ale scene' for its variety of guest beers. The food menu, too, offers an extensive choice, with everything from filled baguettes (lunchtime only), salads, hot baked spuds served with salad and flame-grilled burgers to a full three-course meal. For a snack or salad you can expect to pay between £4 and £7.50.

On the main menu starters, £5.40 or under, include southern fried mushrooms with garlic mayo, warm goats' cheese on salad leaves with mango and pineapple salsa, crispy duck confit on spicy avocado, Thai crab cakes and sweet chilli dip and Yankee fried potato skins with garlic mayo and barbecue sauce. To follow there are steaks, from £9.25, and other grills, prime steak and Guinness pie, curries, home-made vegetable lasagne or roasts such as breast of Aylesbury duck or half a roast chicken. The 'Smugs fish box' offers a good selection, too: Ouaisne catch fish bake, seafood ragout in cream and white wine sauce with rice, cod or haddock in home-made beer batter or pan-fried tuna steak, from £6.75-£8.95. For daily specials, consult the blackboards.

★ Q V P C

ST HELIER
Lamplighter
9 Mulcaster Street, Jersey, JE2 3NJ

- Near Liberation Square, by the bus station
- Daily 10am (Sun 11am)-11pm
- Daily 12-2.15pm (3pm Sat, 4pm Sun)
- T (01534) 723119
- Draught Bass; Courage Directors; Ringwood BB, Fortyniner; John Smith's Bitter; Theakston Mild; Wadworth 6X; Wells Bombardier; guests
- Traditional pub meals plus local seafood and a range of curries
- Stalwart of local real ale scene; gas lamps retained in recent facelift

Tempting specials and authentic curries light up the Lamplighter, with typical daily specials including fresh locally-caught mackerel with Dijon mustard coating, Jersey Royal potatoes and fresh garden peas, whole seabass roasted with fennel served with dauphinoise potatoes, and possibly fresh local lobster or chancre crab salad. The fish is at market prices, but other specials are an eminently reasonable £6.50-£6.95, such as grilled Jersey pork chops with sage and apple compote, braised lamb shank in Shiraz and shallot gravy, or pork hock in sage and apple jus with creamy mash. On Sundays a choice of three traditional roasts each costs £5.95.

'Eastern delights' include chicken, beef, king prawn or mushroom korma, tikka masala, balti, rogan josh or Thai green curries, all £5.75 with rice and naan bread (£1.50 extra for king prawns), and Oriental sizzlers at £6.50: chicken or beef in Shanghai blackbean sauce with red chillies and ginger, Vietnamese sweet chilli sauce or Japanese teriyaki and ginger.

The set menu offers plenty of snacks from jacket potatoes to hot or cold sandwiches and wraps, home-made cottage pie, southern fried chicken, home-made pie of the day with mash, deep-fried cod in batter with chips and mushy peas or goats' cheese and red onion tart with salad. Children are allowed until 9pm.

V ♿ ♣ C

ST HELIER
Original Wine Bar
86 Bath Street, Jersey, JE2 4SU

- Mon-Sat 11am-11pm; Sun 3-11pm
- Mon-Sat 12-3pm plus bar tapas 11am-9.30pm
- T (01534) 871119
- E donald@goodbars.co.uk
- Courage Directors; Ringwood BB; Tipsy Toad Jimmy's Bitter; guests
- Gastro style eats and tapas on a weekly changing menu
- Winner of many CAMRA awards; plays background jazz

Chef Cho enjoys the reputation of being one of the best on a foodie island, his menus so innovative that staff as well as customers look forward to what's new. The market on the doorstep provides meat, fruit and vegetables while the bar grows its own herbs. Speciality food and drink days are very popular and have included Polish, Australian, St Patrick's, St Andrew's and St George's.

A tapas fridge was recently imported from Spain so the bar can now offer authentic tapas as well as a lunchtime menu. The main menu features home-made soup, sandwiches from soft roes with smoked salmon to pork sausages and onion served with Kettle chips at £3.75, light bites such as field mushroom with chicken mousse and garlic breadcrumbs, Merguez sausages with tzatziki and tabbouleh, black pudding potato cake with poached egg or pork and chicken liver pâté with prunes, all £4.95.

Hot sarnies, wraps and burgers, all with salad and fries, include steak and onions on ciabatta, shredded duck with spring onions and hoi sin or grilled goats' cheese with tomato and aubergine tartine. Specials could be grilled rib eye steak, venison sausages with polenta and red wine gravy, or asparagus, new potato and goats' cheese frittata with pesto noodles, priced from £6-£9.75. Children are allowed until 9pm during the week, 7pm Fri & Sat.

★ V ♿ ♣ C

ISLE OF MAN

DALBY
Ballacallin
IM5 3BT

- Follow A27 coast road S from Peel
- Daily 6-11pm (later at weekends)
- Daily 6-9pm
- T (01624) 841100
- F (01624) 845055
- E info@ballacallin.com
- W www.ballacallin.com
- Bushy's Castletown Bitter; Okells Bitter; guests
- Homely British/Manx cooking
- Old Manx farmhouse, now a country lodge style hotel occupying a commanding position on the scenic west coast

A good base for exploring the western side of the island, the hotel is surrounded by walking and cycling country with good fishing and bird watching facilities. Only open in the evenings, the hotel offers a home-cooked supper menu that features fresh fish and seafood. Its specialities include small, sweet baked Manx queenies (queen scallops) in cheese sauce, local (Peel) kippers, monkfish, seafood pie and whole seabass stuffed with herbs and baked. Starters are all either seafood or vegetarian options: freshly-made soup with home-baked bread, potted Manx kipper pâté, locally smoked salmon with honey and sunflower bread. The chestnut, stout and Stilton pâté and goats' cheese tart are particularly popular appetisers. All the meat is sourced locally; dishes include steak, Guinness and mushroom pie, braised Manx lamb shank, char-grilled pork loin steak, Radcliffe butcher's pork and leek sausages and chicken jalfrezi. Vegetarian main courses are aubergine parmigiana and penne pasta with black olives, feta and fresh basil. Puddings are all home made – favourites are caramelised bread and butter pudding, spiced pears in red wine, sticky toffee pud and chocolate medley, or you can finish your meal with locally made ice cream or cheeses. Children are welcome when dining only.

Q V P C

GREEBA
Hawthorn Inn
Main Road, IM4 3LF

- 6 miles from Douglas on the road to Peel
- Daily 12-11pm
- Daily 12-9pm (8pm Sundays)
- T (01624) 801268
- Okells Bitter; guest
- A wide variety of home-made dishes to suit all tastes on an all-day menu
- Family run, food oriented country inn

At the Hawthorn you can start with a simple bowl of olives and bread or home-made chicken liver pâté flavoured with brandy served with red onion marmalade, followed by a diverse choice of meals freshly cooked all day. A selection of daily specials could include local queenie scallops cooked with bacon, garlic and cream, Irish stew, home-made fish cakes, smoked haddock topped with a poached egg, lamb's liver with onions or steak and kidney pie.

The set menu features cod in home-made light lager batter or oven baked and served with citrus parsley cream, Manx lamb chops, steak braised with onions, mushrooms and Manx Okells Bitter, Cumberland sausage with mixed beans, mash and gravy, Creole cod with stir-fried vegetables and salsa, Caribbean chicken with pineapple fritter, fish and prawn pie with shortcrust topping, home-made Indian style meat curry with naan and fragrant rice, braised lamb shank with vegetable cassoulet on mash, or grilled loin of pork topped with Mozzarella and apples in cider sauce. Prices are mainly £7.25-£9.75, rising to £15.25 for a daunting mixed grill of rump steak, gammon, lamb and pork chops, two sausages, onion rings, white pudding, mushrooms, tomato, fried egg, peas and chips. There are several veggie choices, and all puds are home made – bread and butter, sticky toffee, rhubarb crumble, chocolate sponge, banana split...

★ Q V P C

PORT ERIN

Falcon's Nest Hotel

Station Road, IM9 6AF

- On A5 (the promenade) at village centre, 14 miles S of Douglas
- Daily 11am-1pm
- Daily 12-9pm
- T (01624) 834077
- f (01624) 835370
- E falconsnest@enterprise.net
- W www.falconsnesthotel.co.uk
- Bushy's Bitter; Okells Bitter; guests
- Wide range of home-produced meals and a popular Sunday carvery
- Victorian coaching inn overlooking a sandy beach with beautiful bay views; large restaurant and attractive lounge with stained glass

This independent hotel has been run by the same family for more than 20 years and enjoys a well-deserved reputation for the quality of its food. As far as possible, local suppliers are used for meat, fish and vegetables, and while certain items – king prawns for example – are bought in frozen, the majority of produce is fresh. House specialities are fish and chips using callig – a local white fish that they believe is more tasty than cod – and small scallops, known as queenies, that are caught around the coast here and served in white wine sauce. Home-made Manx kipper pâté is also served as a starter.

The Sunday carvery, three courses for £13.50, is rightly popular, when customers can choose from five meats, accompanied by up to eight fresh vegetables. The main menu always offers a roast of the day, alongside steaks, fish dishes and other specials such as pan-fried duck breast with plum sauce, grilled halibut with cream sauce, warm chicken and bacon salad, and pork chop with cider sauce. Prices start at around £6 for honey roast ham, egg and chips, up to £10.50 for a fillet steak. For a lighter meal at lunchtime there is a choice of 'melts' – tuna, ham or cheese, sandwiches, baguettes, jacket spuds or burgers, all under a fiver.

★ S V (Port Erin) P C

PORT ST MARY
Albert Hotel
Athol Street, IM9 5DS

- ▶ Opposite the harbour, by the bus terminal
- Mon-Sat 11am-midnight (1am Fri & Sat); Sun 12-midnight
- Daily 12-2pm, 6-9pm
- T (01624) 832118
- E omega@manx.net
- Bushy's Old Bushy Tail; Okells Bitter; guests
- Traditional pub food at lunchtime; à la carte evening menu
- Free house overlooking the inner harbour with a bustling public bar, cosy lounge with a nautical theme and small restaurant

Straightforward, home-cooked meals and bar snacks are available at lunchtime: gammon steak, cod in beer batter, curry of the day, steak, ale and mushroom pie, and vegetarian options such as spicy bean and coriander chilli or roasted vegetable lasagne, all for around £7-£8. In the evening, Rupert's restaurant (named after the chef, Rupert Ward), offers a more interesting menu, alongside the list of 'old favourites' served at lunchtime. For starters there might be king prawns in lime, chilli and coriander butter, crab claws sautéed in garlic butter, prawn cocktail with basil mayonnaise (or Marie Rose sauce for the traditionalists), simple toasted goats' cheese on rustic bread or home-made soup, £3.25-£5.95. After that you could choose between braised lamb shank with root veg and chive mash, chicken with mushroom and tarragon cream sauce and wild rice, a sizzling platter of roasted vegetables with herbs and Parmesan shavings or Rupert's hearty mixed grill. There is also king prawns in spiced Cajun batter with various dips, a list of fish choices on the specials board, and steaks £9.50-£14.95. All the main courses come with a trio of fresh vegetables and chips or new potatoes. Desserts are chalked up daily, mostly priced at £3.50.

★ S V P C

SULBY
☆ Sulby Glen Hotel
Main Road, IM7 2HR

- ▶ On Sulby Straight section of TT course
- Daily noon to midnight
- Daily 12-2.30pm, 6-around 8.30pm
- T (01624) 897240
- W www.sulbyglenhotel.net
- Bushy's Bitter, seasonal; guests
- Traditional and innovative dishes using Manx produce and fresh seafood
- Village centre hotel and former local CAMRA pub of the Year, with photos of TT riders through the ages

Chef Geoff Betts has 25 years' experience in restaurants and country inns, devising his own recipes and combining the traditional with the inventive. Here he uses only local produce including all meat and seafood to create his specialities – king scallops, lobster and seabass alongside Manx broth, Irish stew, home-made chicken liver pâté and Manx queenie scallops.

The bar menu offers home-made burgers and three rasher back bacon baps at around £2, starters such as stock pot soup, and bar meals including traditional roast of the day with roast spuds and Yorkshire pudding, steak and ale pie, his 'very special' home-made curry, freshly battered cod with fries and mushy peas, or a prime steak sandwich with fries, all around £6. Veggie dishes are outstanding – carrot and coriander goujons with spicy dip, bean, celery and coriander chilli, and cannelloni filled with goats' cheese in a creamy spinach sauce, from £3.95-£8. In the bistro start with Manx kipper pâté laced with Manx spirit, home-made soup or Donegal mussels, then enjoy duck breast with orange sauce, local pork loin with honey and chilli glaze, lamb tagine, roast rack of Manx lamb with seasoned mash, and special veggie dishes of risotto with wild mushrooms or vegetable Wellington, £8.50-£12.75, superb steaks from a Ramsey butcher and the day's fresh fish board.

Q S V P C